Planet Cat

Planet Cat

A Cat-alog

SANDRA CHORON, HARRY CHORON, AND ARDEN MOORE

Houghton Mifflin Company   Boston New York 2007

Library of Congress Cataloging-in-Publication Data

Choron, Sandra.
Planet cat : a cat-alog / Sandra Choron, Harry Choron, and Arden Moore.
p. cm.
Includes index.
ISBN-13: 978-0-618-81259-2
ISBN-10: 0-618-81259-8
1. Cats. 2. Cats — Miscellanea.
I. Choron, Harry. II. Moore, Arden.
III. Title.
SF442.C496 2007
636.8—dc22   2007009414

Book design by Lisa Diercks
Typeset in DIN, Chalet, New Bold, and French Script

Printed in the United States of America
MP 10 9 8 7 6 5 4 3 2 1

For Elvis, the King

—Sandra and Harry Choron

And for Little Guy (aka Dude),

who nearly made it to 20 years. This feline friend taught me the joys of sharing and the benefits of afternoon naps.

—Arden Moore

Contents

PART 3: Cat Anatomy and Behavior ⌁ 175

Acknowledgments

Cats may be loners at heart, but their human counterparts are pack-oriented: supportive, thoughtful, always, it seems, willing to jump in and help. In working with the many websites, publishers, and veterinary professionals who contributed to this volume, we found ourselves truly humbled by the generosity of those whose souls have been soothed by cats. While contributions are credited throughout the book, we offer additional thanks to these honorary cat people:

Ilene Phillips, who helped with many of the lists here and who should just write her own book;

Amy Seefeldt and Holly Price, whose ideas and expertise were invaluable;

John Tebbel, who will be surprised to see his name here but whose help with logistics and sundries was very much appreciated;

Dave Marsh, for always pointing us in the right direction.

William O'Reilly, DVM, is our medical expert in residence, and we thank him for ensuring that Planet Cat is a safe place for all. We learned so much from him about the kind of caring and love our animals deserve.

For general help with research and materials, we thank Simon Glover of Orange Multimedia Operations in Leeds; Mick at rulingcatsanddogs.com; and ever-helpful cat wrangler Dusty Rainbolt of the Cat Fanciers' Association.

It's difficult to think of a proper way to thank Susan Canavan, who is always perfectly in tune with what we are trying to accomplish and always finds ways to help us do it better. In sharing our view of "the planets," she is as much a collaborator as she is an editor. We thank the able, good-humored Will Vincent for assistance throughout, and the hard work of manuscript editor Susanna Brougham.

Lisa Diercks's book design brings as much to this book as any portion of the text. We are so grateful to her for her clever ideas, her thoughtful contributions, and for knowing just how to communicate the spirit of this book.

Humor writer Dan Greenberg once said, "Cats are dangerous companions for writers because cat watching is a near-perfect method of writing avoidance." We agree with the sentiment but nevertheless thank our cats for their loving, furry friendship and for inspiring us to write a book that will hopefully improve the lives of cats everywhere.

Illustration Credits

Please note that unless otherwise indicated, the images in this book belong to the authors' private collection and/or are in the public domain. Best efforts have been made to contact the rights holders in all cases.

Photo of Maneki Neko cat, page 20, courtesy of Bob Walker

Felix Martin guitar, page 38, photo courtesy of C. F. Martin and Co.

British inn signs, pages 48–49, and cat postage stamps, pages 52–53, courtesy of Patrick Roberts

Poezenboot cats, page 56, courtesy Judith Gobets, Poezenboot

Mighty Morris, the cat, page 99. Morris is a registered trademark of Del Monte Corporation. All rights reserved.

Garfield, page 105, courtesy of Jim Davis / Kim Campbell

Photo of Bengal kittens, page 117, courtesy of Holly Webber

Bill Clinton with Socks, page 122, courtesy of William J. Clinton Presidential Library

Circus cat with bird, page 142, courtesy of Ringling Bros. Barnum & Bailey

The Algonquin Cat, page 144, courtesy of Elizabeth McCrocklin, Algonquin Hotel

Cat paintings, page 152, courtesy of Eve Riser-Roberts

Dewey the Library Cat, page 156, courtesy of Vicki Myron, Spencer Public Library, Spencer, Iowa

Dancing cats, pages 164–165, from *Dancing with Cats,* copyright © 1999 by Origination Trust. Used with permission of Chronicle Books LLC, San Francisco. Visit ChronicleBooks.com.

Cat drawing, page 167, courtesy of Ralph Steadman. All rights reserved.

White and brown cat, page 175, courtesy of the Norich family

Cat breed photos, pages 181–189, 191, 194, 195, 285, courtesy of Helmi Flick. All rights reserved.

Drawings of cat faces, page 210; diagram of how cats fall, page 216; cat brain drawing, page 218; and drawings of cat tail positions, page 221 by Casey Choron. All rights reserved.

Photo of cat on top of door, page 223, courtesy of Phyllis Geller

Photo of cat painting, page 225, by Weems S. Hutto, courtesy of Dusty Rainbolt

Bob Walker photographing a cat, page 378, courtesy of Bob Walker

Cat headstone, page 389: The Art Archive / Jarrold Publishing

All cartoons courtesy of Randy Glasbergen

We are grateful to the Kobal Collection for use of the following photographs:

Fish and cat painting, page 7: The Art Archive / Victoria and Albert Museum London / Eileen Tweedy

Catland magazine cover, page 11: The Art Archive / Michael O'Mara Books

Rhubarb, page 88: The Kobal Collection / Paramount

The Incredible Shrinking Man, page 88: The Kobal Collection / Universal

The Three Lives of Thomasina, page 89: The Kobal Collection / Walt Disney

Cat's Eye, page 90: The Kobal Collection / Famous Films / MGM/UA

Austin Powers: The Spy Who Shagged Me, page 93: The Kobal Collection / New Line / Wright, K.

The Godfather, page 94: The Kobal Collection / Paramount

Breakfast at Tiffany's, page 95: The Kobal Collection / Paramount

Incredible Journey poster, page 133: The Kobal Collection / Cangary / Walt Disney

Book covers:

Braun, Lilian, *The Cat Who Said Cheese* (New York, Jove), 1997

Braun, Lilian, *The Cat Who Sniffed Glue* (New York: Jove), 1989

Brown, Rita Mae, *Sneaky Pie's Cookbook for Mystery Lovers* (New York: Bantam), 1999

Crumb, Robert, *The Life and Death of Fritz the Cat* (New York: Fantagraphics), 1993

Datlow, Ellen, *Twists of the Tale* (New York: Dell), 1996

Dr. Seuss, *The Cat in the Hat,* reprint edition (New York: Random House), 1997. From *The Cat in the Hat* by Dr. Seuss, TM and copyright © by Dr. Seuss Enterprises, L.P. 1957, renewed 1985. Used by permission of Random House Children's Books, a division of Random House, Inc.

Eliot, T. S., *Old Possums's Book of Practical Cats* (New York: Harcourt Brace), 1939

Fireman, Judy (ed.), *Cat Catalog* (New York: Crown), 1983

Gallico, Paul, *The Abandoned,* reprint edition (New York: International Polygonics), 1995

Hale, Rachael, *101 Cataclysms* (New York: Bulfinch), 2004

Kipling, Rudyard, *The Cat That Walked by Himself* (Wiltshire, U.K.: Child's Play International), 1990

Little, Denise (ed.), *A Constellation of Cats* (New York: DAW), 2001

Schaeffer, Susan Fromberg, *The Autobiography of Foudini M. Cat* (New York, Random House), 1999

Silvester, Hans, *Cats in the Sun* (San Francisco: Chronicle), 2005

Simon, Clea, *The Feline Mystique: On the Mysterious Connection Between Women and Cats* (New York: St. Martin's Press), 2002

Smolan, Rick, and Cohen, David Eliot, *Cats 24/7* (San Francisco: Chronicle), 2005

Van Vechten, Carl, *The Tiger in the House* (New York: Dorset Press), 1920

Contributors

We are grateful to the following contributors for their material, time, expertise, and enthusiasm:

Clea Simon for "Clea Simon on the Feline-Feminine Connection"

Sarah Hartwell for "Cats in Nursery Rhymes," "When It's Time to Let Go: 12 Questions to Ask Yourself," and "7 Good Reasons to Euthanize"

Patrick Roberts for "Cats on British Inn Signs" and "Cats Who Went Postal: Feline Philately"

Jane Teresa Anderson for "15 Cat Dreams and What They Mean"

Glenda Moore for "35 Famous Cat Lovers," "76 Cat Idioms," and "The Cats Are Not Pampered!"

Bill and Cathy Brown of MillCreekBengals.com for "45 Cartoon Cats"

Kim Campbell and Jim Davis for "The World According to Garfield"

Elizabeth McCrocklin of the Algonquin Hotel for "The Algonquin Cat"

Eve Riser-Roberts for "3 Great Artistic Imposters"

Vikki Myron, of the Spencer Public Library in Spencer, Iowa, for "Dewey's Guide for Library Cats"

Holly Webber for "Cat Show Know-How," "19 Steps for Cat-Proofing Your Home," "Kitty Accoutrements: What You'll Need"

Dumb Friends League and Linda Houlihan for "The 5 Developmental Stages of Kittens"

Karen Lee Stevens of *Catnip* for "How and Why Cats Purr"

Cats International and Betsy Lipscomb for "The Fountain of Youth Has Whiskers," "Welcome Home, Furry Baby!," "When Purrs Become Bites," "The New Cat on The Block: And Then There Were Two," and "How to Choose Your Second Cat"

Linda Frano for "Astrology for Cats"

Dr. Marty Becker for "I'm in the Mood for Love: Feline Mating Rituals," "Birthing Rituals," and "How Cats Groom Themselves"

Dr. Alice Moon-Fanelli and Dr. Arnold Plotnick for "Cattitudes: How Cats Think" and Dr. Moon-Fanelli and Dr. John Wright for "10 Things Humans Do That Drive Cats Crazy"

Amy Shojai for "Top 10 Cat Behavior Issues"

Iams Pet Company for "24 Things Cats Do for Us"

Veterinary Pet Insurance Co. and Brian Ianessa for "The 60 Most Common Cat Names"

"The Naming of Cats" from *Old Possum's Book of Practical Cats*, copyright © 1939 by T. S. Eliot and renewed in 1967 by Esme Valerie Eliot, reprinted by permission of Harcourt, Inc.

The Humane Society of the United States for "The Top 10 Essentials of Cat Care," "17 Tips for Preparing Your Cat for the New Baby," "Please Fence Me In," "7 Ways to Help the Fearful Cat," "How to 'Summerize' Your Cat," "How Much Will Kitty Cost?," "8 Reasons Not to Buy a Kitten from a Pet Store"

Julia Wilson, of Cat-World.com for "The 9 Most Common Mistakes Made by Cat Owners"

DogBreedInfo.com and Sharon Maguire for "29 Dogs Who Hate Cats"

Dr. Ronald Hines for "5 Reasons to Declaw a Cat," "Caring for Kitty's Teeth," "8 Reasons Why Your Cat Bites — and What You Can Do," and "Special Care for Your Aging Cat"

Thecatgroup.org and Sue Edwards for "6 Things You Should Know About Pregnancy and Toxoplasmosis"

Myhealthycat.com and Debra Garcia for "Microchipping Your Cat"

Arnold Plotnick for "Curious About Catnip?"

Anne Moss for "Bathing Your Cat: Survival Tips" and "The 5 Top-Selling Cat Toys"

Bud Herron for "Cat Bathing as a Martial Art"

PAWS Animal Shelter of Norwalk, Connecticut, and Alexis Heydt-Long for "12 Tips for Solving Litter-Box Problems"

Dan Christian for "7 Winter Cat-Care Tips"

Dr. Debra Eldridge for "How to Give Your Cat Medications"

Havahart.com and Annette Minich for "How to Trap a Feral Cat"

The American Red Cross for "Cats and Disaster: Be Prepared"

Jean Craighead George for "How to Talk Cat"

Bob Walker for "11 Helpful Hints for Photographing Your Cat"

Introduction

The first cat book in prose was published in Paris in 1727. It was called *Les Chats,* and for the rest of his life the author, François-Augustin Paradis de Moncrif, was unmercifully ridiculed for believing that a subject as trivial as cats was worthy of an entire volume. He was greeted everywhere by "catcalls," and when he was elected to the Académie française, cats were released during his inaugural address.

So we thank Monsieur Moncrif for paving the way for *Planet Cat,* but we wonder how he managed to limit his treatment of the subject to only one volume!

Try to write about cats and you'll find yourself so far afield of veterinary studies that it's hard to believe you're still on Planet Cat. For intrinsic to any investigation of the cat is an understanding of history, anthropology, biology, literature, art, and even physics. My cat seemed to sense my wonder at this discovery. Typically, as I worked on the book, he would purr at me as I typed, incessantly demanding my attention. When I would finally take a break and look into eyes that appear to be every color of green there is, he seemed to say, "Remember that you are not just writing about cats. You are writing about thousands of years of history and a cultural journey that no other animal has taken. You are writing about an animal who has only recently emerged from the wild, whose tradition reflects the adoration, the hatred, and the fear — sometimes simultaneously — of humans who so often did not understand us. We have been deified and we have been vilified, and we have enjoyed or suffered every status in between. "When you write about cats," Elvis seemed to say, "you write about the world."

We kept his message in mind when marking out the territory this book would cover. Thus Part 1, "The Culture of Cats," explores the history and tradition of the cat but also points to the ways in which the cat infuses almost every aspect of our existence — our music and our literature, our language, our favorite advertising images, our belief systems, and our folklore. In looking at "Top Cats" in Part 2, we meet the felines whom we have elevated to stardom, ranging from household names such as Morris, Garfield, and the Cheshire Cat to some of the less-well-known cat stars, who nonetheless tell us much about who we are: the hero cats of the World Trade Center; the literary cats who serve as muses for writers or haunt our libraries; and the amazing felines who have come to our aid in times of war. In

Part 3, "Cat Anatomy and Behavior," we examine the cat, with all its marvels and quirks of physiology and personality; and in Part 4, "Tender Loving Care and Training," we offer cat-care basics, with an emphasis on how we as humans interact with felines: how to understand them better, how to interpret their special language, when to play with them, and when not to. That is, throughout this book, we have tried to go beyond the basics to fully explore Planet Cat, the space we share with our beloved felines.

We are taught that the greatest difference between cats and dogs is the fact that cats are loners, whereas dogs are pack animals. Why is it, then, that cat-friendly households tend to house multiple cats, but dog-friendly homes usually have only one dog in residence? Do cats hold secrets that they still have not revealed to us? (How does one account, for instance, for the "loner" cats who have adopted birds, mice, and even puppies?) Or is it just that with all their eccentricities and unpredictability, and for the love they provide and the chance they give us to see ourselves in them, we just can't get enough of them?

Planet Cat suggests some answers.

— s. c.

Planet Cat

Part One

"Some people own cats and go on to lead normal lives."
— SOURCE UNKNOWN

Learn about the history of cats and you are likely to learn something about yourself. In the beginning, we idolized cats with monuments and rituals. Then we demonized them. Then our industries fell victim to plagues of rodents, and we rediscovered them for their marvelous mousing talents. We brought them back into favor, this time endowing them with power to prophesy and cure disease. We interpreted their movements to predict the weather and both good and bad fortune. We learned about ourselves by interpreting the dreams we had about them. They aided us in times of war, and they have helped sailors both aboard ship and on shore.

They have done what no other animal has done, for throughout it all, no matter the level or the nature of the relationship between human and feline, cats have maintained their independence. They didn't kill mice because we told them to, and in the loving relationships we form with them, there is a good chance that we humans are getting the better part of the bargain.

These days, we are back to idolizing them, this time by pasting their images

all around us—in museums, books, and films, on our advertising signs, our greeting cards, and even the stamps we use to mail them.

They infuse our literature, the art we create, the music we make, and every other form of creative endeavor. If nothing else, their journey—and this chapter—proves that what goes around, comes around.

CATS: A TIMELINE

8000 B.C. Date of the first evidence that the cat has been domesticated— their bones are found on the island of Cyprus.

3500 B.C. Authorities generally agree that by this date, the African wildcat has been domesticated in Egypt. Like the synergistic relationship that occurred when a human being and a dog acknowledged their mutual need for shelter and protection, cats proved useful to Egyptian farmers by countering the threat posed by rats and vermin, which attacked their fields and grain supplies. The cats were attracted by food that was left out for just that purpose. Those cats that performed best were rewarded with more food and with house privileges. Such practices, along with what we assume are certain genetic changes, produced the common housecat.

It wasn't long before cat and human forged their own special relationship. Cats were admired for their grace and beauty and loved for the companionship they provided. Cats were welcomed into homes and hearts, loved and pampered for the same reasons we hold them in such high esteem today.

3000 B.C. Approximate date of the earliest known portrait of Bastet, the Egyptian goddess commonly depicted as having the body of a woman and the head of a cat. By this time, the Egyptians deify cats. The apparent feline ability to see in the dark fascinates members of a culture that fears darkness; the people believe cats can protect them from its power.

950 B.C. The catlike Bastet becomes the primary Egyptian goddess, and worship of the cat is at its peak. It is estimated that some 700,000 people annually make the pilgrimage to Bubastis, on the east coast of the Nile Delta, to honor Bastet. These "spiritual" celebrations actually take the form of ecstatic fertility rites, meant to increase the number of crops, animals, and humans alike.

Cats were thought to embody Bastet, whose responsibilities included sexuality and fertility, protection of the dead, and the making of rain. So insistent were the Egyptians that the cat had power to heal the sick that killing a cat was punishable by death. The passing of a family cat sent the bereaved into a period of mourning marked by public breast-beating, long, sad funeral processions, elaborate mummification procedures, and even the shaving off of family members' eyebrows.

> "I have an Egyptian Cat. He leaves a pyramid in every room."
> — RODNEY DANGERFIELD

500 B.C. A military legend dating to this period shows the high status of cats in ancient Egypt. According to the story, the Egyptians thought they had warded off the invading Persians when, after just one battle, the Persians retreated for eight days. The Egyptians thought they had the upper hand and felt ready to resume fighting once the Persians reappeared, but they weren't prepared for the ultimate surprise tactic. The Persians returned with the most powerful weapon of all — cats! The savvy Persians knew that the Egyptians revered this animal and would never risk killing one, so on the battlefield they released hundreds of cats, and each soldier carried yet another kitty under his arm — the best shield of all. Not a single blow was exchanged; the Persians triumphed.

Also by this time, the domestic cat is established in China. Initially, only emperors were permitted to own a cat. Later, the nobility and priests, and then commoners, were allowed to own them as well. A great number of these domestic cats interbred with the smaller local wild cats and created some of the breeds we know today.

300 B.C. It is believed that by this time, cats have arrived in India, brought by Phoenician traders. Two Indian epics from this time, the Mahabharata and the Ramayana, contain references to cats.

100 B.C. Although Egyptians outlawed the exportation of their precious cats, Phoenician traders and smugglers manage to sneak them out. By this date, cats are being exported all over Europe, the Mediterranean, and Asia, where they are welcomed as ratters, admired for their beauty, and generally thought to bring good luck. Now that they have become so common, they fall from grace with Egyptians and begin to lose their deified status. They now freely roam China and Southeast Asia, Japan, southern Russia, and northern Europe. They reach Norway via mercenaries from Byzantium (now Istanbul) and Latvia some 400 years later.

A.D. 500 Cats may have fallen from the high status of deity, but their practical uses are still appreciated. Europe is invaded by barbarians at this time, and they bring with them rats and the plague. Cats to the rescue!

A.D. 600 Buddhist monks introduce the cat in Japan around this time. But not until the 13-year-old emperor Ichijo raises a litter of kittens at the Imperial Palace in Tokyo, c. A.D. 1000, will cats achieve high status there.

A.D. 936 The prince of Wales, Hywel Dda, now known as Howel the Good, made feline history by introducing laws to protect domestic cats. The Dimetian Code of Wales, instituted in the year 900, had accorded a monetary value to the cat (and stated that in order to establish a lawful hamlet one had to have nine buildings, a plow, a kiln, a churn, a bull, a cock, one herdsman — and a cat). Now Howel, believing that the cat, for all its services, deserves respect, lays down precise laws and statutes, including the worth of a cat based on its age.

A.D. 1000 In Japan royal cats are considered sacred. The emperor's cats are served the finest foods and even receive clothing to wear. The popularity of the cat grows throughout Japan within both royal and common society.

continued on page 8

How to Mummify a Cat in 8 Easy Steps

Ancient Egyptians believed that in order for an individual to go on to a successful afterlife — to be immortal and join Osiris, the god of rebirth — the body had to be mummified or embalmed. They believed that unless Osiris could recognize the body, it would not live forever in the afterlife. Egyptians adored their cats and went to great lengths to ensure their place in Paradise. The process of feline mummification consisted of eight steps:

1. The skull was cracked open, and the cat's brain was removed through its nose using hooked bronze rods.

2. The internal organs were then removed and replaced with fake organs.

3. The body was washed with natron, a salty liquid, perfumed with frankincense, and then dried.

4. The body was stuffed with sand or other packing material.

5. The cat was placed in a sitting position.

6. The cat was then wrapped tightly in linen.

7. Faces were then painted on the wrappings with black ink.

8. Finally, the body was left to dry, allowing natural dehydration to help preserve the body.

A History of Cats in Ancient Art

Whether regarded as demonic, cute and adorable, or worthy of worship, the cat has inspired strong feelings among people at different times and places. These attitudes are evidenced in art that portrays cats. Presented here is information about the depiction of cats in art during various eras.

The Egyptian goddess Bastet, with sistrum and sacred cats.

Ancient Egypt

Because ancient Egyptians adored and deified their cats, or *mious,* as they called them, they glorified them in art. By 1000 B.C., Bastet, the daughter of the sun god, Ra, and the goddess of fire, cats, pregnant women, music, dance, home, and family, was portrayed as a woman with the head of a cat. Cats decked out in jewels and precious stones could be found in paintings, jewelry, and sculptures of this period. Later in Egyptian history statues of cats were created as shrines and as funeral decorations. Statues of cats, often cast in bronze, were adorned with gold or silver earrings; the eyes were fashioned from crystal or other precious stones. Cat art was also visible in everyday life. Common citizens owned images of the cat in the form of bracelets, amulets, rings, and painted pots. Though these were not especially valuable objects, the Egyptians treasured all cat-related art.

Ancient Rome

The Roman citizens loved incorporating the natural world into their homes. Images of cats collected by ordinary Romans showed the cat as a part of the family. Domestic scenes often depicted cats interacting with a family or with other animals.

Persia

The Muslims of Persia looked favorably upon the cat because the prophet Muhammad had one as a pet. While images of cats in Persian art are very rare, they have been found on small figurines and paintings. Bottles and boxes in the shape of cats have also been uncovered.

India and the Far East

The cat in India was regarded as a symbol of wealth and status. Cats in paintings have an exalted appearance. In Thailand, paintings of cats demonstrate the brilliant colors of their coats and a variety of feline poses. The cat did not appear in Chinese art until c. A.D. 1000, but as in India, it was presented with dignity and affection and embued with high status. The Chinese emperor Hsuan Tsung, who reigned 1426–1435, painted kittens and cats frolicking in his garden.

Europe in the Early Middle Ages

Cats were depicted in the Lindisfarne Gospels (c. A.D. 700) and in the Irish Book of Kells (c. A.D. 800); it was considered appropriate to adorn holy writ with the feline image, among other animal forms. But in the later Middle Ages (from about 1100) cats were portrayed with disfavor. In fact, cats were rarely the subject of art because of their supposed association with witchcraft. Even after cats reappeared in art after the fifteenth century, they were still vilified. In *The Last Supper,* a painting by Italian artist Domenico Ghirlandaio, a cat sits at the feet of Judas, Jesus' betrayer. Hieronymus Bosch, fantasy artist supreme, depicted cats as demonic in his painting *The Temptations of St. Anthony*. During the next two centuries cats were usually depicted as lazy, gluttonous, and evil.

An Indian painting in the Kalighat style, which flourished in the bazaars of nineteenth-century Calcutta. The style became popular in the early twentieth century, when Kalighat paintings were no longer being produced, and it enjoyed a new wave of popularity at the turn of the twenty-first century.

1484 The glory days of the cat come to an end in Europe. In the Church's fight against paganism, a reign of terror against cats ensues. Pope Innocent VIII denounces the cat and anyone who would befriend one. Once associated with deities, the cat is now perceived as the embodiment of Satan. Hundreds of thousands of cats are tortured and killed — crucified, burned alive, or thrown from the tops of towers. So vehement is this campaign that Christians are encouraged to inflict as much pain as possible on the wretched cat before it is finally allowed to die. However, a fringe of the population, particularly in Rome, Scotland, and Denmark, continues to perceive the cat as the patron saint of the hearth. Those who persecute the cat will live to regret it.

When the writer Petrarch died in 1370, his son-in-law had his cat put to death and mummified. It can be viewed today in a glass case in Petrarch's preserved study in the Vaucluse valley in southern France.

1500s Returning Crusaders couldn't have known about the Asiatic black rats that hid in dark places on their ships. The vermin carry the bubonic plague, ushering in one of the most terrifying periods in human history, when three out of every four people — 25 million in all — lose their lives. With cats out of the way for the most part, thanks to good Christians everywhere, rats help themselves to Europe — to its farms, its streets, and even its children. Those who still harbor cats fare better than others. All in all, those who survive this brutal attack on humanity owe their life to the cat. While it would take centuries for the cat to regain its former status, the Christian inquisition against cats comes to a halt.

1602 A law is passed in Japan declaring all cats free. It forces civilians to release all adult cats so that they can protect the silk industry, which is seriously threatened by rodents.

King Henry I (1068–1135) was tough on kitty-krime. He declared that the punishment for killing a cat was a fine of 60 bushels of corn.

1620 At least one cat is known to arrive at Plymouth Rock on the *Mayflower.*

c. 1700 Sir Isaac Newton invents the cat flap, a small door that allows cats to come and go as they please, for his own kitty, Spithead.

1736 The Catholic Church officially abolishes all witchcraft laws, and a hellish period for cats finally comes to an end. Eventually church leaders will become fans of the feline. In the nineteenth century, Micetto, Pope Leo XII's cat, will be born in the Vatican; Pope Pius IX will often sit with his cat on his knee while giving an audience.

1749 Colonists in the New World are forced to send for hundreds of cats from Europe in order to stem the tide of an infestation of black rats. But the supply is scarce.

1758 Carolus Linnaeus creates the method of zoological classification used today. He dubs the domestic cat *Felis catus,* and despite all the differences among them, considers all felines as members of the same species.

1860 Competitive cat racing makes a brief appearance in Belgium, where races are held annually. The *Pictorial Times* of June 16, 1860, explains this phenomenon:

"Cat-racing is a sport which stands high in popular favor. In one of the suburbs of Liège it is an affair of annual observance during carnival time. . . . The cats are tied up in sacks, and as soon as the clock strikes the solemn hour of midnight, the sacks are unfastened, the cats let loose, and the race begins. The winner is the cat which first reaches home, and the prize awarded to its owner is sometimes a ham, sometimes a silver spoon. On the occasion of the last competition the prize was won by a blind cat."

1866 Henry Bergh takes a lesson from Britain's earl of Harrowby, who founded the Royal Society for the Prevention of Cruelty to Animals (RSPCA) in London. Bergh founds its American counterpart. With a full-time staff of just three, the ASPCA sets out to protect animals everywhere by demanding new legislation and raising public consciousness. By the time of Bergh's death in 1888, ASPCA centers have sprung up throughout the country, and 37 states have adopted animal cruelty laws.

This new awareness of animals as companionable creatures — as well as Queen Victoria's passion for cats — impacts the Victorian era, and household pets, cats in particular, are sentimentalized. Cats are typically depicted snuggling by the fire, romping with children, or nuzzling one another. Pampered, adored, and admired, cats symbolize hearth, home, and happiness.

1871 The first cat show is organized by Harrison Weir and is held at the Crystal Palace in London. Weir, the first president of the English National Cat Club,

> "To err is human, to purr is feline."
> **— ROBERT BYRNE**

who organized the show, said, "I wish everyone to see how beautiful a well-cared-for cat is, how docile, gentle, and — may I use the term? — cossetty. Why should not the cat that sits purring in front of us before the fire be the object of interest, and be selected for its color, markings, and form? Now come with me . . . and see the first Cat Show."

1872 In *The Expression of Emotions,* Charles Darwin examines the emotions of cats and writes that a cat's body posture, gait, and manner of movement express its moods. Darwin observes that affectionate cats rub against their masters or mistresses, contented cats tend to roll around on the floor, and a happy cat frequently chases its tail. In comparing dogs to cats, Darwin determines that smiling is far less frequent in cats than it is in dogs, perhaps because "their more subtle and subdued humor seldom necessitates laughter."

1886 As Emily Wain lays dying, she receives comfort only from gazing at Peter, her beloved cat. Her grieving husband, Louis, begins drawing pictures of Peter to amuse Emily. When she dies, Wain's artistic career is launched, and he becomes one of the most famous cat artists of all time. His first illustration of anthropomorphized cats, *A Kittens' Christmas Party,* is published in the *Illustrated London News.* Many of the 150 cats in the drawing resemble Peter. H. G. Wells would later say of Wain that "He invented a cat style, a cat society, a whole cat world. English cats that do not look and live like Louis Wain cats are ashamed of themselves." Wain's cat illustrations show the animals walking upright and engaged in the activities of Victorian men: fishing, going to the opera, playing cards, and smoking. Over the course of his career, Wain illustrated close to 100 children's books, and his work was featured in magazines and newspapers. He was known to take his sketchbook to public places and draw people going about their business — as cats. Eventually, Wain became so obsessed with the study of cats that he was declared insane and committed to an asylum. The entire British nation mourned his death in 1939. His delightful cats still charm us today.

A postcard from 1903.

1888 Outside the Egyptian town of Beni Hasan, a tomb containing the mummified bodies of 80,000 cats and kittens dating back to 1000–2000 B.C. is uncovered. Yet despite their significance to ancient history, most of the cats were destroyed by the farmer who discovered them; he ground them into fertilizer. Some remains did survive and were examined by scientists; some are on display today at the British Museum.

William Martin Conway, the only Egyptologist to visit Beni Hasan after the tomb was uncovered, wrote, "The plundering of the cemetery was a sight to see, but one had to stand well windward. The village children came . . . and provided themselves with the most attractive mummies they could find. These they took down to the riverbank to sell for the smallest coin to passing travelers. The path became strewn with mummy cloth and bits of cats' skulls and bones and fur in horrid positions, and the wind blew the fragments about and carried the stink afar."

1895 J. T. Hyde holds the first American cat show at Madison Square Garden in New York City. For the first time, cat fanciers from distant parts have a chance to meet and compare notes, breeds, medical information, and experiences. Club-sponsored cat shows are born.

1900s Louis Pasteur's work has awakened the world to an understanding of hygiene, and animals that were once welcomed at the dinner table are now banished to the barn; white gloves were required for handling a potentially disease-carrying dog. Cats, on the other hand, are upheld as models of cleanliness, and they hold their heads higher now. Having left their paw prints on art, literature, and history, cats once again come into general favor.

Cover of *Catland* magazine (1903), illustrated by Louis Wain.

1910 The Governing Council of the Cat Fancy (GCCF) is formed to settle the many disputes arising from the popularity of breeding and showing cats. Even today, the council is among the most prestigious of organizations dedicated to felines. In addition to acting as a disciplinary council, it also governs the rules of cat shows, issues pedigrees, and establishes the standards for judging each breed.

1916 Archy and Mehitabel, the subjects of poems written by humorist Donald "Don" Marquis, make their debut. Archy is a cockroach with a penchant for writing; Mehitabel is his alley cat companion, who claims to have been Cleopatra in

11 Legendary Cats

1. Bastet, or Ubasti, or Bast
Although her duties have changed over the course of time, the Egyptian goddess has been known as the guardian of cats, women, children, love, fertility, birth, music, and dance. She has been dated to at least the Second Dynasty (c. 2890–2686 B.C.) and is often depicted as a young woman with the head of a domestic cat, sometimes holding a musical instrument known as a sistrum.

2. Butter Cat
From Scandinavia, a protector and provider. It was believed that cats were "bringers of gifts," such as butter and milk; thus the name.

3. Cait Sith
Scottish folklore tells of a black fairy cat, believed to be a transformed witch.

In his seventeenth-century work *Natural History*, the Italian naturalist Aldrovandus listed the curly-legged cat as a freak of nature. The cat never existed.

4. Ccoa
An evil cat demon originating in Peru and greatly feared by the Quechua people. He controlled rain and lightning, with which he could destroy crops and human life.

5. Golden Flower
In Japan, orange cats, rather than black ones, had all the power. Believed to be supernatural, these cats had the purported ability to transform themselves into beautiful women.

6. The Scottish Grimalkin
This cat was said to be a wraith that took the form of a human by day and a fierce panther by night. Grimalkins were associated with witchcraft and thought to be just as devilish as their mistresses. The name comes from its gray color and the archaic word *malkin*, meaning "cat."

7. Matagot
In the south of France especially, it was believed that the Matagot was a magical greedy cat that could bring great wealth. To access its powers, you had to lure the cat with a chicken, take it home, and feed it the first mouthful of every meal you ate. In Britain, a version of the Matagot is known as Chat d'argent, a black cat who was able to serve nine masters at once.

8. Patripatan
Of Indian origin, Patripatan was sent to heaven to pick a flower but got sidetracked and didn't return home for 300 years, during which time his prince and his people had ceased to age. When Patripatan returned, the country was endowed with beauty and serenity.

9. Ra
In ancient Egypt it was believed that each night the great sun god, Ra, took the form of a cat as he went off on his nightly battle against the serpent Apopis. The sun rose every morning because Ra won all the battles.

10. Sinh
According to Burmese legend, Sinh was the founding father of the Birman breed, which is the sacred cat of Burma. Sinh belonged to the high priest Mun-Ha. When the old man died, Sinh placed his paws on the priest's body and thereby absorbed his soul. As he did so, his paws turned white.

Winged cat, from an engraved French pistol made by Henri Le Page, 1837.

11. Yule Cat
In Iceland, a frightening tradition teaches children the importance of preparing autumn wool before the onset of winter. In the fall, children are given gifts of new clothing. Those who don't receive them — either because they didn't participate in gathering wool or because they did not merit such gifts — risk the wrath of the Yule Cat, a giant feline with glaring eyes and sharp whiskers. The only way to avoid being eaten by the Yule Cat on Christmas Eve is to stand at the window wearing a new garment, even if it's just a new pair of socks.

a previous life. Their rowdy adventures suggest that Mehitabel might be the forerunner of the ever-horny Fritz the Cat. Collections of the stories have been published in various volumes, and the first one, *archy and mehitabel* (Archy wrote only in lowercase type, as he was unable to hit the shift key), published in 1927, is still in print.

1919 A feline hero named Master Tom debuts in a Paramount Pictures short film called *Feline Follies,* directed by animator and cartoonist Otto Messmer. Master Tom reappears in the film *The Musical Mews,* released the same year. Paramount Pictures producer John King decides the cat should be renamed, and Felix the Cat makes his onscreen debut a few years later in *The Adventures of Felix.*

1920s The Sabcat symbol, a wild black cat with its back arched and fangs bared, is designed by Ralph Chaplin, a member of the Industrial Workers of the World (IWW, also known as the Wobblies). Sabcat (*sab* as in *sabotage*) becomes a widely used symbol for anarchism and radical unionizing, inspiring "wildcat" strikes. The name Black Cat has since been used by many anarchist cooperatives and collectives.

1930s Canned cat food is first introduced to the marketplace.

1933 Chessie the cat is first used to advertise the Chesapeake and Ohio Railway. "Sleep like a Kitten and Wake Up Fresh as a Daisy in Air-Conditioned Comfort" is the tag line in the *Fortune* magazine advertisement. The railroad develops a complete advertising campaign based on Chessie's image, placing it on timetables, calendars, clothing, and children's books. (See page 145 for more about Chessie.)

1940s The animated cat-and-mouse team Tom and Jerry star in a series of very successful short cartoon films created, directed, and written by Joseph Barbera and William Hanna. Each film continues the plot line in which Tom, the cat, tries to catch Jerry, the mouse. The series was produced by MGM until its animation studio closed in 1958, but the program was outsourced to a European company and continued to be popular. In the 1970s Tom and Jerry made the leap to TV, and today they still appear in various programs produced by Hanna-Barbera Studios.

"I love my cats because I love my home, and little by little they become its visible soul."
— JEAN COCTEAU

The Sabcat logo, a symbol for anarchism and radical unionizing.

1940 Catwoman first appears as a character called "The Cat" in the comic *Batman #1*. She is Batman's nemesis and later becomes one of his many love interests. Her alter ego is Selina Kyle.

> "The clever cat eats cheese and breathes down rat holes with baited breath."
> — **W. C. FIELDS**

1945 Gene Deitch's character The Cat first appears in comic strips and panels in the jazz collectors' magazine *The Record Changer*. Deitch, father of underground cartoonist Kim Deitch (*Waldo, Hollywoodland*), infuses the character with his own passion for jazz music. Deitch later explains that The Cat was inspired by early recordings of Louis Armstrong, in which jazz musicians and listeners are referred to as "cats."

1945 Famed animator Fritz Freleng creates the black-and-white cat who speaks with a lisp, later known as Sylvester. In 1947 the cat is teamed with a canary named Tweetie Pie and together they strike cartoon gold in their first film, *Tweetie Pie*, which wins an Academy Award for Best Cartoon Short Subject. Tweetie Pie's famous line, "I tawt I taw a puddy tat," enters American pop culture. Sylvester is known as Thomas in the film and doesn't get the name Sylvester until 1948's *Scaredy Cat*, directed by Chuck Jones. Sylvester is voiced by the legendary Mel Blanc. His trademark is a lispy delivery of the now-famous phrase "Thufferin' thuccotash!"

1946 Cats Protection, a charity, adopts and promotes the idea of spaying female cats (tomcats were routinely neutered, along with other farm animals), who until this time often produce as many as 200 kittens in a lifetime. Birth control for cats has arrived, and it becomes an important aspect of public welfare.

1947 Kitty litter is invented by a woman who visits her local sawmill, only to find that no sawdust is available that day. The proprietor, instead, offers her some dried clay normally used for cleaning up grease spills. The clay works, and the cats seem to love it.

1949 Simon, the cat on board the British warship HMS *Amethyst*, receives the Dickin Medal for services performed during the Yangtze incident: surviving injuries from a cannon shell, raising ship morale, and killing off a rat infestation. Named for Maria Dickin, founder of the U.K. veterinary charity PDSA (People's

Dispensary for Sick Animals), the award goes to animals displaying conspicuous gallantry and devotion to duty while serving with civil emergency or armed forces. Homing pigeons received the bulk of Dickin Medals awarded during World War II.

1953 The Governing Council of the Cat Fancy (GCCF) holds its first cat show, "Crufts for the Cat Fancy." Known as the Coronation Cat Show, it is attended by 388 cats.

1961 Top Cat is the star of a popular Hanna-Barbera prime-time animated TV series of the same name, aired on the ABC network for a year. The hero, Top Cat, AKA T.C., is the leader of a gang of New York City street cats. In a recurring plot device, the beat policeman, Officer Dibble, attempts to evict the feline gang from their home.

1965 The first issue of *Cat Fancy* is published. The magazine is a complete guide to caring for and understanding the cat and includes a centerfold poster of a comely feline in each issue.

1968 The original Morris the Cat is discovered in a Chicago animal shelter by professional animal handler Bob Martwick, who adopts the ginger tabby and pitches him as the celebrity spokes-cat of 9Lives cat food. Morris stars in countless television and print ads as the finicky cat who loves 9Lives cat food, voiced by John Erwin. In 1973, Morris was featured in a film role in *Shamus* alongside Burt Reynolds and Dyan Cannon. *Time* magazine named him "the

18 Concepts That the Cat Symbolizes

Throughout the Great Depression, many a hobo ("a man who travels and is willing to work") roamed the country. Hoboes had their own culture and even their own language: They drew symbols on fence posts and such to alert other hoboes to the demeanor of the family who owned them. Five circles meant that work could be found, and "18" meant I-8, or "I ate." But the symbol that hoboes sought most was that of the cat — it meant that a kindhearted woman lived there and that a hobo might be provided with a hot meal and a place to sleep.

HE'S A MASON ON THE SQUARE

A vintage postcard attests to the fine, upstanding character of the cat.

All cultures use symbols to express the underlying structure of their social systems and to identify cultural characteristics. In art and literature, the peripatetic cat has represented these qualities and ideas:

Craftiness	Love	Satan
Divination	Magic	The sun
Evil	The moon	Vampires
The female gender	Mystery	The Virgin Mary
Fertility	The occult	The weather
Liberty	Psychic ability	Witches

feline Burt Reynolds" in 1983. He coauthored three books, the most recent published in 1986. Morris appeared on talk shows and morning TV shows. In 1991 he was the host of a prime-time television special, *Salute to America's Pets.* Morris launched a presidential campaign in both 1988 and 1992. The current Morris lives in L.A. with his handler, Rose Ordile. The original Morris passed away in 1975.

1972 Ralston Purina launches Meow Mix cat food with the now-famous Singing Cat commercial created by advertising agency Della Femina, Travisano & Partners. An orange tabby cat sings "Meow, meow, meow . . ." to illustrate the tag line "Tastes so good, cats ask for it by name."

> ## "How we behave toward cats here below determines our status in heaven."
> — **ROBERT A. HEINLEIN**

1973 California governor Ronald Reagan signs a bill into state law making it possible to send a person to prison for kicking and injuring another person's cat.

1975 B. Kliban's first book, *Cat,* is published. Born in 1935, he had been a cartoonist for *Playboy* magazine since 1962. An editor at *Playboy* saw some of his cat doodles and asked Kliban for permission to show the drawings to an agent. This resulted in a publishing deal for *Cat.* The book is the first of several, and merchandise based on Kliban's cat cartoons range from magnets to beach towels.

1976 Hello Kitty is copyrighted as a trademark by the Japanese company Sanrio. The character Hello Kitty is an anthropomorphized white cat without a mouth; she wears a bow on her left ear. She originally appeared on small novelty items such as purses for young girls. There are now over 22,000 products sporting the Hello Kitty logo, and their worldwide sales form half of Sanrio's annual revenue. Other spinoffs include video games, cartoons, a Hello Kitty credit card imprint, and a couture Hello Kitty Diamond Watch designed by Kimora Lee Simmons.

1978 Garfield the cat debuts in a comic strip by Jim Davis. As of 2006, *Garfield* holds the Guinness World Record as the most widely syndicated comic strip in the world. The strip has also spun off a television series, TV specials, and two feature films. (For more about Garfield, see page 105.)

1985 The Maine Coon Cat becomes the official state cat of Maine.

1988 Massachusetts state law makes the tabby the official state cat.

2001 The state of Maryland adds a law to the books to name the calico cat as the state cat.

CC the cat, the world's first cloned animal, is born at the College of Veterinary Medicine at Texas A&M University. She is part brown tabby and part white domestic shorthair. Her genetic donor was a calico domestic shorthair, and her surrogate mother was a tabby. She was the only one of 87 embryos to survive a research project known as "Operation CopyCat" — hence her name. She lives now in the home of Dr. Duane Kramer, one of the scientists on the project.

2003 The Oxygen cable network premieres *Meow TV,* a half-hour program produced by Meow Mix cat food. The series features scenes designed to amuse cats, such as footage of birds, mice, etc., as well as advice for cat owners.

2006 Reality television shows throw characters together in a challenging situation and environment and then lets viewers see what happens. Following the models of *Big Brother* and *Survivor, Meow Mix House,* a ten-week TV series sponsored by the cat food company of the same name, features ten cats attempting to live together in a swank New York City apartment. Each week the cats, chosen from shelters in ten cities, compete in contests designed to weed out the less proficient felines, week by week. But instead of leaving empty-handed, as contestants do on most reality TV shows, each voted-out cat wins a loving home and a year's supply of Meow Mix cereal. On the final episode, August 18, the last one standing, a cat named Cisco, was promoted to vice president of research and development at the Meow Mix company, a job that entails taste-testing future Meow Mix concoctions. A cat named Elise was the viewers-choice winner.

"Cats, as a class, have never completely got over the snootiness caused by the fact that in Ancient Egypt they were worshipped as gods. This makes them prone to set themselves up as critics and censors of the frail and erring human beings whose lot they share."
— P. G. WODEHOUSE

Cats in Ancient Cultures

In the first century A.D., the Egyptian Copts, one of the first Christian sects, believed they would be judged by cats after death. (The Egyptian god Osiris, the Lord of the Dead, was often depicted as a cat.)

The Egyptian sun god, Ra, was said to turn himself into a cat each night in order to fight the evil serpent Apopis. A solar eclipse signified Ra's defeat. Meanwhile, in ancient Greece, the goddess Artemis turned herself into a cat and hid in the moon to avoid the dragon-headed monster Typhon.

The cat is the only domesticated animal not mentioned in the Old Testament, although the Talmud includes a cat-related spell for gaining the power to see demons: "Find and burn the placenta of the first litter of a black cat (which must have been from its mother's first litter), then beat it to a powder and rub it into the eyes."

A portion of the Jewish Talmud written around A.D. 500 describes the admirable qualities of the cat and urges people to acquire them in order to keep their houses clean.

In Hungary it was believed that a cat would automatically turn into a witch between the ages of 7 and 12 unless an incision in the shape of a crucifix was made in the skin at birth.

In A.D. 962, the Cat's Parade in Ypres, France, featured cats being thrown from a belfry. This was done because the animals were associated with witches. (Today the parade can be freely enjoyed by cat lovers because only toy cats are thrown, just for fun.)

During the second century A.D., the philosopher Plutarch wrote that the Egyptian cat will always give birth to one kitten in her first littler, two in her second, and so on until she reached seven, at which point she will have given birth to 28 kittens — the exact number of days on the lunar calendar. Generally, Egyptians believed that the life cycle of the cat was related to the cycle of life.

The Babylonian gods of silver, gold, and wood were commonly depicted with cats on their shoulders. These cats possessed various powers, including an extraordinary ability to hunt, night vision, and the ability to dwell between the living and the dead.

As the Greek goddess of magic, Hecate used cats to conjure up the spirits of the dead, and she employed a woman who had been turned into a cat, Galenthias, to raid tombs.

Romans embraced the cat and deified it, much as the Egyptians had, so it is no surprise that the cat turns up in Roman mythology. The goddess Diana (based on the Greek Artemis) turned herself into a cat when the need for fast escape arose. This Roman goddess of liberty is often depicted with a cup, a broken scepter, and a cat, the most independent of domestic animals, at her feet.

Li Shou was a cat worshiped by the ancient Chinese. It was believed that she could speak but chose to pass this gift on to humans. She was also considered a vital fertility goddess, responsible for guarding crops and bringing rain. Ancient Chinese farmers held orgiastic festivals in her honor at every harvest.

In both China and Japan, the cat was believed to be a mischievous character who stole precious objects and produced rolling balls of fire at will. The cat sometimes grew a forked tail, thereby turning itself into a demon. But the most pervasive belief concerning the cat in the Orient had to do with reincarnation. Deceased loved ones were often believed to return as cats, and so cats generally came to represent the embodiment of former souls. In Japan, the "Kimono Cat" — one born with a special black mark on its back — was believed to contain the spirit of one of the owner's ancestors.

According to an Italian folktale, the devil himself sent one hundred mice to torment Saint Francis in his cell in Assisi. They nibbled on his fingers and toes, ate all his food, and kept him awake at night. So God sent him Felix, who surprised the mice by exterminating all but two.

A Celtic legend of the fourth century recounts the tale of Jesus' birth. Mary could not get her baby to sleep, so she called on all the animals to help her. None could, until a gray tabby kitten climbed into the manger and curled up beside the infant, at which point the child fell asleep. It is said that the Madonna rewarded the cat by promising that all tabby kittens would wear the letter *M* on their foreheads thereafter.

Celts believed black cats to be reincarnated beings who could foretell future events.

Although American Indian mythology seems to have ignored the domestic cat, the wild cat's hunting skills were much admired, and

it is believed that Tirawa, "the one above," appointed the wild cat, together with the bear and the wolf, to guard the evening star.

Sephardic Jews believe that Lilith, Adam's first wife, who was banished from the Garden of Eden, took the form of a giant cat named El Broosha, and that this demonic cat sucked the blood of newborns.

In the original canons of Buddhism, cats were excluded from a list of protected animals because upon Buddha's death, when all the animals wept, only the cat and the snake remained dry-eyed. Nevertheless, Buddhist faith in Southeast Asia held that those souls most spiritually enlightened at the time of death would next take the body of a cat, and it was not until that cat died that the soul could enter Paradise.

The Nordic goddess Freya often traveled in a chariot drawn by a team of cats, who symbolized Freya's qualities of fecundity and ferocity.

The Finnish people believed that a cat-drawn sleigh comes to take the soul away at death, a process immortalized in the epic poem *The Kalevala*.

In the Germanic myth of Thor and the Midgard Serpent, the serpent, who seeks to destroy the earth, is transformed into a cat.

Orthodox Hinduism states that every household must feed and house a cat.

In Thailand as recently as 1920, and going back to ancient times, a cat was included in the king's coronation ceremony. It was believed that through the cat's eyes, the late king would be able to witness the festivities.

According to Sanskrit writings, cats are the original yoga experts, having invented hatha yoga by demonstrating a complete range of stretching and movement for an Indian boy who was frustrated in his attempt to learn karma yoga, the most advanced spiritual form of the practice.

The Druids believed that black cats were human beings who were being punished for their evil deeds.

Among the Peruvian Quechua tribe, a mythological cat demon named Ccoa was believed to destroy crops with hail and lightning when she was displeased.

In Japan, mythological creatures known as Golden Flowers, or Kinkwaneko, were greatly feared. These red cats could transform themselves into beautiful women. In either form, they could not be trusted.

Cat-worshiping sects with ancient roots still exist today in Thailand, China, Burma, and India.

Maneki Neko, the "Beckoning Cat"

Japanese merchants often keep some kind of lucky charm at the front or back of their shop, in the hope that it will bring in lots of customers and that a thriving business will result. The Maneki Neko, the Japanese name for their "beckoning cat," is one of the most common lucky charms in Japan. Maneki Neko, usually in the form of a ceramic figurine with its paw raised and bent, is frequently found in shop windows, positioned as if beckoning customers to enter. Its origins probably lie in the legend of the temple of Go-To-Ku-Ji. One day the resident cat was washing its face as a band of samurai rode by. Seeing the little cat with its paw to its ear, the warriors interpreted it as a welcoming gesture and rode into the temple peacefully.

Here are some interesting historical facts about Japan's favorite feline.

It is commonly believed that the Maneki Neko became popular in the latter half of the Edo Period (1603–1867), although it is rarely mentioned by name in documents of the era. However, by the Meiji Period (1868–1912), images of this cat begin to appear with great regularity in publications, and its statue is found in business establishments.

During the cultural isolation of the Edo Period, an indigenous "amusement" culture (a sex industry) grew side by side with the expanding merchant class. In the "Yuukaku" zones, the Maneki Neko cat was used to beckon to potential clients, and the tradition soon spread to restaurants and other businesses. Poster images of the Yuukaku zones show women beckoning with a gesture just like that of the Maneki Neko cat.

There are two different kinds of Maneki Neko: ne raises its left paw, and the other raises its right paw. The left paw invites customers into a shop, while the right one invites good fortune. In present-day Japan, the increasing number of Maneki Nekos with the right paw up reflects a desire for wealth. The height of the paw also has a meaning: the higher the paw, the greater the fortune and the greater number of customers being invited.

The Maneki Neko exported abroad beckons by showing the back of its paw, while the Maneki Neko made for domestic Japanese use beckons by showing its palm.

The color of the Maneki Neko is of great significance. The tri-colored cat is the most popular, and the tri-colored male is considered especially lucky for sailors. Genetic studies indicate that the chances of a tri-color gene expressed in real male cats are very small. This rarity makes them all the more valuable as a lucky charm. The white version is the second most popular Maneki Neko, symbolizing purity. The black Maneki Neko is a talisman against evil; it has gained popularity among women to ward off stalkers. The red cat exorcises evil spirits and illness; the gold one invites money; and the pink one attracts love.

Maneki Neko and Friends.

How the Church of England Would Deal with the Statement "The Cat Sat on the Mat" If It Appeared in the Bible

The liberal theologians would point out that such a passage did not of course mean that the cat literally sat on the mat. Also, cat and mat had different meanings in those days from today, and anyway, the text should be interpreted according to the customs and practices of the period.

This would lead to an immediate backlash from the evangelicals. They would make it an essential condition of faith that a real physical, living cat, being a domestic pet of the species *Domesticus,* and having a whiskered head, a furry body, four legs, and a tail, did physically place its whole body on a floor covering, designed for that purpose, and which is on the floor but not of the floor. The expression "on the floor but not of the floor" would be explained in a leaflet.

Meanwhile, the Catholics would have developed the Feast of the Sedentation of the Blessed Cat. This would teach that the cat was white, and majestically reclined on a mat of gold thread before its assumption to the Great Cat Basket of Heaven. This is commemorated by singing the "Magnificat" and "Felix namque," lighting three candles, and ringing a bell five times.

This would cause a schism with the Orthodox Church, which believes tradition requires Holy Cats Days (as it is colloquially known) to be marked by lighting SIX candles and ringing the bell FOUR times. This would partly be resolved by the Cuckoo Land Declaration recognizing the traditional validity of each.

Eventually the House of Bishops would issue a statement on the Doctrine of the Feline Sedentation. It would explain that, traditionally, the text describes a domestic feline quadruped superjacent to an unattached covering on a fundamental surface. For determining its salvific and eschatological significations, we follow the heuristic analytical principles adopted in dealing with the Canine Fenestration Question (How much is that doggie in the window?) and the Affirmative Musaceous Paradox (Yes, we have no bananas). And so on, for another 210 pages.

The General Synod would then commend this report as helpful resource material for clergy to explain to the man in the pew the difficult doctrine of "the cat sat on the mat."

—AUTHOR UNKNOWN

 **4 Cat Saints**

1. **Saint Gertrude** is known as the patron saint of cats.

2. **Saint Agatha** is also known as Saint Gato ("cat").

3. **Saint Yves**, the patron saint of lawyers, is often accompanied by a cat and is sometimes even represented as one.

4. **Saint Francis of Assisi** was largely responsible for influencing thirteenth-century artists to portray cats sympathetically rather than as entities of evil.

Cats and Witchcraft

The idea of the cat as the witch's familiar has its origins in Britain. There, witches were thought to have various animal servants who helped them carry out their wicked deeds. The cat seems to have won the popularity contest as the witch's most likely collaborator. Thus, when so-called witches were persecuted throughout Europe, their cats were murdered as well. (Odd that Christians resorted to pagan rituals in order to eradicate pagan spirits.) In 1566, during the reign of Elizabeth I, three women, Elizabeth Francis, Agnes Waterhouse, and her daughter Joan, were accused of communicating with the devil via their cat, who was named Satan. Witch trials had been held as early as the fifteenth century, but this one is credited as spawning the witch craze that would rage throughout Europe well into the eighteenth century. Somehow, cats managed to escape the witch hysteria in North America, perhaps because they performed so spectacularly as ratters and simply couldn't be spared.

Here are some highlights and lowlights of the witch's best friend.

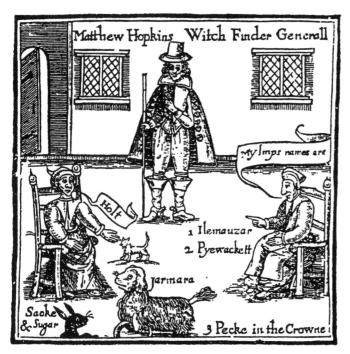

Detail of a 1647 woodcut showing two seated witches as they name their familiars, including a cat called Pyewacket.

In the fourteenth century, under threat of torture, members of the Order of Knights Templar admitted that they worshiped the devil, who appeared to them in the form of a black cat.

In 1427, a woman claimed to have murdered 30 children by sucking their blood. She confessed to Bernardino of Siena that she had anointed herself, and although appearing unchanged to others, believed she had turned herself into a cat. She was burned as a witch.

In the sixteenth century, during one of the very first English witch trials, Elizabeth Francis of Hatfield Peverel admitted that her grandmother had counseled her to renounce God and his word and to give of her blood to Satan, who came to her in the likeness of a white spotted cat. She was taught to feed it, to keep it in a basket, and to call it by the name of Satan.

Some Protestant reformers believed that the pope could turn himself into a black cat in order to confuse honest Christians. *The Book of Martyrs,* written by John Foxe in 1563, showed a cat dressed as a Roman Catholic priest.

In 1579, an accused witch on trial in Windsor, England, admitted that she fed a demon — in the form of a cat — each day with a diet of bread, milk, and her own blood.

In some witchcraft trials, cats were described as sacrificial victims used in the casting of spells. In 1590, John Fian and his alleged coven were accused of trying to drown Queen Anne and her husband, King James, on their ocean voyage to Denmark. It was said that they christened a cat, tied it to a chopped-up human body, and threw the bundle into the ocean, all the while reciting incantations.

According to a German account, a woman judged to be a witch was sentenced to be burned at the stake. She was not a compliant penitent, however; she defied the judge and mocked the executioner and the priest with blasphemies. When the wood was set alight, her body was enveloped with smoke, and the priest knelt in prayer. Suddenly, with a wild screech, a black cat leaped out of the flames. The witch, disappearing among the startled crowds, escaped.

A seventeenth-century woodcut. Although cats were victimized during savage witch-hunts, it was not the cat that was feared but rather the fiend that supposedly occupied its body. Not that it mattered to the cat.

In 1607 Shakespeare finished writing *Macbeth,* Galileo showed that the path of a projectile is parabolic, and a committee of 54 translators was halfway through its translation of scripture that would result in the King James Bible. It was also the year that a cleric named Edward Topsel published his remarkable 1,100-page work called *The History of Four-footed Beasts and Serpents Describing at Large Their True and Lively Figure, Their Several names, Conditions, Kinds, Virtues . . .* (the original title goes on and on). In it we learn that "the familiars of Witches do most ordinarily appear in the shape of Cats, which is an argument that this beast is dangerous to soul and body."

In 1618, a woman named Joan Flower confessed to a plot to kill the earl of Rutland's children, using magic and the assistance of a black cat named Rutterkin. The following year, Ellen Green reportedly caused her cat, Puss, to bewitch and kill a shopkeeper. Just around the same time, Frances Moore admitted that she would feed her cat, Tissy, blood from her finger before she sent him out on his deadly duties.

In 1618, Margaret and Philippa Flower were burned to death at Lincoln, England, for the alleged crime of witchcraft. With their mother, Joan Flower, they had been confidential servants of the earl and countess of Rutland, at Belvoir Castle.

In 1699, in Mora, Sweden, 300 children were accused of using demon cats to help them steal food from the local villagers. Fifteen children were put to death, and 36 of them were whipped in front of the church every Sunday morning for a year.

In the seventeenth century, Isobel Gowdie revealed the formula by which she turned herself into a cat and back into a woman again. To change into a cat, she would say the following three times:

I shall goe intill ane catt,
With sorrow, and sych, and a blak shott;
And I sall goe in the Divellis nam,
Ay will I com hom againe.

To change back into her human form, she would say the following three times:

Catt, catt, God send thee a blak shott.
I am in a cattis liknes just now,
Bot I sal be in a womanis liknes ewin now.
Catt, catt, God send thee a blak shott

In 1718, A British man named William Montgomery reported that every night hundreds of cats gathered outside his house and spoke in human language. One night, he killed two of them and learned the next morning that two old women in the neighborhood had been found in their beds, mysteriously dead.

In France, a popular legend told of a knight who traveled to the town of Metz while an epidemic of St. Vitus's Dance raged throughout the village, causing victims to twitch and jump. In the evening, an enormous black cat appeared before the knight. He drew his sword, scaring off the cat, at which point everyone in the village was magically cured.

Members of a Bengali tribe believed that some women have the power to change their souls into black cats and that such cats are easily recognized by their distinct way of mewing.

The Black Cat

Sleek and mysterious, the black cat has held a special place in feline history. While bearing the brunt of anti-cat sentiment, black cats have been the object of contradictory superstitions and lore and the source of awe, fear, and laughter among admirers and detractors alike. Here are some highlights in the illustrious history of the black cat.

A wooden black cat named Kaspar sometimes joins dinner parties at the Savoy Hotel in London. The staff provides the cat to round out parties numbering 13 people, thus avoiding bad luck.

During the period when cats were persecuted by the Christian church, all cats were considered wicked, but the black cat was singled out as especially associated with the devil, who was believed to borrow the coat of the black cat when he ventured out nightly to pursue his victims. Thus, whereas cats of all colors were being destroyed, black cats were the first of "Satan's felines" to go. Such cats had to be all black; any sign of white indicated a possibility that the cat was not a true disciple of the devil.

In Britain and Japan, it is considered good luck when a black cat crosses a person's path, the rea-

Until the twentieth century, the image of the black cat rarely appeared in American art, as many folk artists believed that creating the figure of the witch's cat would summon the cat itself.

THE BEST PRESENT I COULD SEND YOU...
SOME **GOOD LUCK!**

son being that the bad luck the cat carries has passed the person by. By contrast, in North America and some European countries, the presence of a black cat is considered bad luck, since by tradition the creature contains an evil spirit. In Russia, there is still a popular belief that if a black cat crosses a person's path, that person should either choose a different direction in order to avoid the cat's path or cross its path while holding a button in the fingers.

The black cat's ability to remain unseen in dark places and at night made it easy to associate this cat with witches. It was believed that witches could change into cats nine times within a lifetime, which seems related to the belief that cats have nine lives.

Since the 1880s, the color black has been associated with anarchism. The black cat, in an alert, fighting stance, was later adopted as a symbol of anarchism and the labor union movement. More specifically, the black cat is associated with anarcho-syndicalism, a branch of anarchism that focuses on workers' rights. Wildcat strikes are, of course, common in labor history.

So special are black cats that folklore includes many superstitions focused on this cat alone. Here are just a few:

- A strange black cat on your porch brings prosperity.
- A black cat crossing your path brings bad luck.
- A black cat seen from behind is a bad omen.
- To get a black cat to help you find buried treasure, find an intersection where five roads meet, turn the cat loose, and follow it wherever it goes.
- A black cat crossing one's path by moonlight means death in an epidemic.
- It's bad luck to pass a black cat after 9 P.M.
- If a black cat walks toward you, it brings good luck; if it walks away from you, it takes luck with him.
- If a black cat lies on the bed of a sick man, the man will die.

40 Cat Superstitions

It's no wonder that so much lore surrounds the cat. In ancient Egypt, cats were constantly watched and tended by priests, who assigned a particular meaning to each of the cat's movements, such as the twitch of whiskers, a yawn, or a stretch. Human imagination — and our penchant for including cats in every aspect of our lives — helped create this folklore. Here are even more of the hundreds of superstitions that exist concerning the cat, derived from many different cultures.

A cat left alone with an infant will suck the very breath out of the baby.

If a cat jumps over a dead body, the corpse will become a vampire unless the cat is killed.

A cat buried in a field will ensure a bountiful crop.

Buddhist tradition holds that a light-colored cat ensures that the home will be filled with silver; a dark-colored cat promises gold.

Rub a cat's paw with butter and it will never leave home.

It's bad luck to see a white cat at night.

It's good luck to see a white cat on a road.

A sneezing cat means good luck for all who hear it.

If a cat leaves a home in which a person is sick and cannot be coaxed back, the person will die.

Kittens born in the month of May bring snakes to the house.

If you wake up in the morning and see cats playing, the rest of the day will be wasted.

To meet a cat at midnight is to meet Satan himself.

A cat who is brought into a new home through a window will never leave.

If you see a one-eyed cat, spit on your thumb, stamp it in the palm of your hand, and make a wish. The wish will come true.

It is bad luck to cross a stream while carrying a cat.

Killing a cat brings 17 years of bad luck.

If a cat sneezes near a bride-to-be on the morning of her wedding, she will have a happy life.

A cat lurking in a coal mine is bad luck.

If a cat washes its face and paws in the front parlor of a home, company is on the way.

A cat washing itself on a doorstep means clergy will soon visit.

If you find a white hair on a black cat, you will have good luck.

If a girl receives a proposal of marriage and does not know whether to accept, she is to place three hairs from a cat's tail into an envelope and place it under her doorstep. In the morning, the hairs will have formed a *Y* or an *N,* and she will know how to answer her suitor.

A cat sneezing three times means the family will catch a cold.

A sneezing cat is a sign of future wealth.

If a cat washes its face in front of several people, the first person it looks at will be the next to wed.

A cat placed in the empty cradle of a newlywed couple will grant their wish for children.

If a farmer kills a cat, his cattle will die.

If you drown a cat, you, too, will drown.

If a girl steps on a cat's tail, she won't find a husband for a year.

If someone in the house is dying, a cat will refuse to remain there.

If a cat enters a room where a dead body lies in state, the next person to touch the cat will go blind (consequently, any cat that entered such a room was killed).

If a funeral procession encounters a black cat, another member of the family will soon die.

A cat sitting on a tombstone means that the person buried there was possessed by the devil.

If two cats are seen fighting near a new grave, the devil and an angel are fighting for the soul of the person buried there.

It is dangerous to discuss private matters in the presence of a cat: a witch may be listening!

Cats' bodies become inhabited by the devil during thunderstorms.

Marking a cat with a cross will prevent it from turning into a witch.

A cat of three colors will protect you from fires and fevers.

Ceramic cats have been used by farmers and city dwellers alike to ward off evil and bad fortune. Such cats can still be seen today perched on French rooftops.

If you use money to pay for a cat, the cat will never be a good mouser.

 ## Curiosity Killed the Cat

The proverb "Curiosity killed the cat" became popular throughout Europe and North America in the early twentieth century, when it was used to instruct children against nosiness and eavesdropping. But the phrase first occurred back in the sixteenth century, when British playwright Ben Jonson used it in his 1598 play, *Every Man in His Humour:* "Care [meaning "worry"] kills a cat." Shakespeare used the phrase in his 1599 play *Much Ado About Nothing:* "What! courage, man! What though care killed a cat, thou hast mettle enough in thee to kill care." The point was that too much worry would lead to an early grave. Over time, the word "care" was changed to "curiosity." By 1909, O. Henry wrote, in his short story "Schools and Schools," "Curiosity can do more things than kill a cat; and if emotions, well recognized as feminine, are inimical to feline life, then jealousy would soon leave the whole world catless." It wasn't until 1920 that the actual phrasing "Curiosity killed a cat" was used, by Eugene O'Neill in his play *Diff'rent*, along with its now-famous addendum: "But satisfaction brought it back."

3 Theories on How the Cat Was Created

Which holds water? We don't really care; we're grateful that cats are among us.

 The Very First Cats

According to Hebrew folklore, Noah was afraid that the mice aboard the ark would eat all the food, so he prayed to God for help and was given the lion, from whose sneeze emerged the cat. In an Islamic version of this story, Noah passed his hand over the head of the lioness three times, causing her to sneeze — and out came the cat!

In a version of the legend from Arabia, Noah's children worried about being attacked by the lions on board. Noah prayed, and the lions were afflicted with a very bad cold, rendering them harmless. But now another dangerous creature appeared: the hungry mouse. Noah turned to God once again and this time was rewarded with the cat.

According to another Arabian legend, the lion aboard the ark was seduced by a monkey, and the result of their union was the cat.

In a medieval legend, the devil created the cat by mistake when he was trying to copy God and create a human being, but failed. Instead he produced a small, pathetic animal with no coat to keep it warm. Saint Peter felt sorry for the cat and gave it a fur coat.

Theory 1

It is reported that the following part of the book of Genesis was discovered among the Dead Sea scrolls. If authentic, it would shed light on the question "Where do pets come from?"

Adam, lonely in the Garden of Eden, one day complained to the Lord about the need for a companion. "No problem!" said God. "I will create a companion for you that will be with you forever and who will be a reflection of my love for you. Regardless of how selfish and childish and unlovable you may be, this new companion will accept you as you are and will love you as I do.

And God created a new animal to be a companion for Adam. And it was a good animal. And God was pleased. He said, "Because I have created this new animal to be a reflection of my love for you, his name will be a reflection of my own name, and you will call him DOG."

And the new animal was pleased to be with Adam, and he wagged his tail.

After a while, it came to pass that Adam's guardian angel came to the Lord and said, "Lord, Adam has become filled with pride. He struts and preens like a peacock and he believes he is worthy of adoration. Dog has indeed taught him that he is loved, but no one has taught him humility."

"No problem!" said the Lord. "I will create for him a companion who will be with him forever and who will see him as he is, who will remind him of his limitations, so he will know that he is not always worthy of adoration."

And God created Cat to be a companion to Adam. And Cat would not obey Adam.

And when Adam gazed into Cat's eyes, he was reminded that he was not the supreme being. And Adam learned humility.

And God was pleased. And Adam was greatly improved.

And Cat did not care one way or the other.

Theory 2

On the first day of creation, God created the cat.

On the second day, God created man to serve the cat.

On the third day, God created all the animals of the earth to serve as potential food for the cat.

On the fourth day, God created honest toil so that man could labor for the good of the cat.

On the fifth day, God created the sparkle ball so that the cat might or might not play with it.

On the sixth day, God created veterinary science to keep the cat healthy and the man broke.

On the seventh day, God tried to rest; but He had to scoop the litter box.

Theory 3

When God made the world, He chose to put animals in it, and decided to give each one a gift of its choice. "What will you have?" God asked the cat.

The cat shrugged modestly. "Oh, whatever scraps you have left over. I don't mind."

"But I'm God. I have everything left over," He said.

"Then I'll have a little bit of everything, please," replied the cat.

And God gave a great shout of laughter at the cleverness of this small animal and gave the cat everything she asked for, adding grace and elegance and, only for her, a gentle purr that would always attract humans and assure her a warm and comfortable home.

But He took away her false modesty.

Cats and Sailors

A small, single-masted boat is known as a catboat, and its rigging is a cat rig. The beam used for carrying an anchor is called a cathead. Hanging the anchor on the cathead is known as catting the anchor. A short rope or iron cramp is called a cat-harpin. Is it any wonder that when sailors invented their own folklore, that cats figured prominently? Here are a few of their superstitions.

On a calm day when no wind fills the sails, sailors lock a cat in a cupboard to bring about a breeze.

Loudly mewing cats foretell a difficult voyage.

A playful cat means a good voyage with gusty winds. (A frisky cat is sometimes referred to as having "a gale of wind in its tail.")

If a cat licks its fur against the grain, a hailstorm is coming.

A cat thrown overboard will bring about the worst possible storm.

Back at home, sailors' wives kept black cats in the house to ensure safety for their husbands.

A cat running ahead of a sailor walking toward the pier brings good luck, but the same cat crossing the sailor's path means bad luck.

An Alfred Mainzer postcard from Switzerland, c. 1930.

Clea Simon on the Feline-Feminine Connection

Clea Simon is the author of *The Feline Mystique: On the Mysterious Connection Between Women and Cats*, which examines the mythology of cats and women and studies some of the famous examples of women and their cats. She is also the author of the Theda Krakow mysteries: *Mew Is for Murder*, *Cattery Row*, and *Cries and Whiskers*. Find out more about this amazing cat lady at *www.cleasimon.com*.

> "I am indebted to the species of the cat for a particular kind of honorable deceit, for a great control over myself, for characteristic aversion to brutal sounds, and for the need to keep silent for long periods of time."
>
> — COLETTE

The single gal who loves only her cats, the crazy old lady who lives in a house lined with fur: What is it with women and cats? In *The Feline Mystique: On the Mysterious Connection Between Women and Cats*, I got to trace this mystical partnership through the ages, from the earliest goddess worship, through witch-hunts, and into contemporary pop culture. Yes, they are all connected. Sound far-fetched? Well, back in prehistoric days, women controlled the mysteries, the big ones of birth and death. Cats, too, seemed to understand these life passages. Partly, because they gave birth apparently easily and to multiple offspring. And partly, probably, because their fabulous night vision and agile leaps made them appear able to defy death, darkness, and everything scary. So from 6000 B.C. on, cats were seen as goddesses and goddesses as cats, from Scandinavia's Freya to Egypt's Bastet. That power turned on us in the tenth century, when some establishment men — who clearly feared us — declared powerful women (and their pets) to be witches. Cats, as well as women, were burned at the stake. Today, remnants of both remain in our consciousness. Catwoman, for example, has power, grace, and strength. But she's a bad girl, not a heroine. And too many of us cat-loving females are derided as "crazy cat ladies" or man haters. Does that get your back up? It should. Cat love, like any pet love, simply expands our souls and makes us more generous, graceful, and connected to all life. So reconnect with your kitty, ladies! Reclaim the goddess within.

> "My husband said it was him or the cat . . . I miss him sometimes."
>
> — SOURCE UNKNOWN

12 Cat Cures (and 1 Health Warning)

Want to lower your blood pressure? Pick up a cat. As early as the Middle Ages, people were aware of the healing powers of cats. Even then, cats were prescribed for patients believed to be going insane. Here are other cat cures (and one health warning), however misguided, that have grown up through the ages. Please don't try these at home!

Stroking the tail of a black cat will cure a sty on the eyelid.

Gout can be treated by rubbing the afflicted area with the fat of a cat.

Another cure for gout, from the generally misinformed cleric Edward Topsel (see "Cats and Witchcraft," page 22), involves burning the head of a black cat and blowing the ashes into the eye three times a day. This was also supposed to cure blindness.

Drinking the broth of a boiled black cat will cure tuberculosis.

Serious injuries can be treated by applying a poultice made from a whole cat boiled in oil.

Tuberculosis? No problem! Try eating gravy made from a stewed black cat.

Warts can be treated by rubbing a cat's tail over them. Or kill a cat and bury it in a black stocking.

You can relieve a toothache by pressing dried cat skin on your face over the inflicted area.

To cure back and leg disabilities, apply grease made from a wild cat.

Treat gallstones by ingesting a powder made from the dried liver of a cat.

Cure a fever by wearing a pouch that contains the dung of a female cat and the claw of an owl.

To cure a sick person, throw water in which the patient has been washed over a cat and then drive the cat out of the house.

If you kick a cat, you will develop rheumatism in that leg.

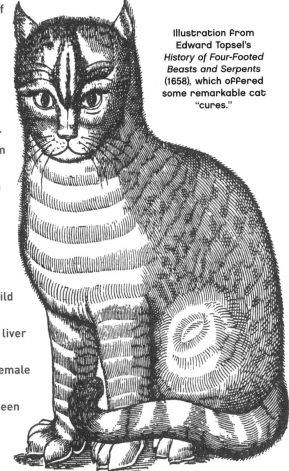

Illustration from Edward Topsel's *History of Four-Footed Beasts and Serpents* (1658), which offered some remarkable cat "cures."

41 Cat Proverbs

A cat is a lion in a jungle of small bushes. (Hindu)

The cat has nine lives: three for playing, three for straying, and three for staying. (English)

The rat stops still when the eyes of the cat shine. (Origin unknown)

Old cats mean young mice. (Italian)

Wherever the mice laugh at the cat, there you will find a hole. (Origin unknown)

A cat bitten once by a snake dreads even rope. (Arabian)

A cat goes to a monastery, but she still remains a cat. (Congolese)

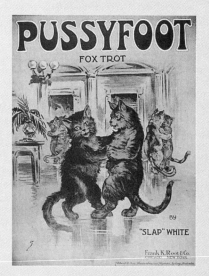

In 1915, this song was released as both "Pussyfoot Fox Trot" and "Pussyfoot Prance."

A cat is mighty dignified until the dog comes by. (Origin unknown)

A cat may look at a king. (English)

A cat will teach her young ones all the tricks, except how to jump backward. (Dutch)

A cat with a straw tail keeps away from fire. (English)

A house without either a cat or a dog is the house of a scoundrel. (Portuguese)

After dark all cats are leopards. (Zuni)

All cats are bad in May. (French)

An old cat will not learn how to dance. (Moroccan)

Beware of people who dislike cats. (Irish)

Books and cats and fair-haired little girls make the best furnishings for a room. (French)

Cats don't catch mice to please God. (Afghan)

Cats, flies, and women are ever at their toilets. (French)

Curiosity killed the cat. Satisfaction brought it back! (English)

Handsome cats and fat dung heaps are the sign of a good farmer. (French)

Happy is the home with at least one cat. (Italian)

Happy owner, happy cat. Indifferent owner, reclusive cat. (Chinese)

I gave an order to a cat, and the cat gave it to its tail. (Chinese)

If stretching were wealth, the cat would be rich. (African)

If you play with a cat, you must not mind her scratch. (Yiddish)

In a cat's eyes, all things belong to cats. (English)

One should not send a cat to deliver cream. (Yiddish)

The cat's a saint when there are no mice about. (Japanese)

The cat is nature's Beauty. (French)

The cat was created when the lion sneezed. (Arabian)

The cat who frightens the mice away is as good as the cat who eats them. (German)

The dog for the man, the cat for the woman. (English)

Those who dislike cats will be carried to the cemetery in the rain. (Dutch)

To live long, eat like a cat, drink like a dog. (German)

When the cat's away, the mice will play. (western Europe)

When the mouse laughs at the cat, there's a hole nearby. (Nigerian)

When rats infest the palace, a lame cat is better than the swiftest horse. (Chinese)

Who cares well for cats will marry as happily as he or she could ever wish. (French)

You will always be lucky if you know how to make friends with strange cats. (colonial American)

You come with a cat and call it a rabbit. (Cameroonian)

Cats and the Weather

The ancients were so dependent on their crops for survival that it didn't take long for them to assign to the cat the power to control the weather and therefore people's lives and livelihoods. Or perhaps these beliefs sprung from the cat's association with witches and the ability to bring about disasters, such as violent storms. In Java, cats are bathed in pools to bring on rain, and similar rituals still exist in Sumatra. Whatever their origins, here are a few feline forecasts that have remained popular.

A cat sleeping with four paws tucked under itself means cold weather is on the way.

If a cat washes behind its ears, it will soon rain.*

When the pupil of a cat's eye broadens, it will rain.

Cats running around wildly mean winds are on the way.

Cats clawing a carpet and curtains signify bad weather ahead.

A cat sitting with its back to the fire indicates that a cold snap is imminent.

A cat sneezing once means rain.

Washing a cat will bring rain. (Even today, the Korat, a native cat of Thailand, is sometimes ceremoniously sprinkled with water to ensure enough rain for the crops.)

A cat scratching itself against the leg of a table means the weather will soon change.

If the tail of a sleeping calico cat is turned to the north or east, a storm is approaching. If it is turned toward the south or west, fair weather is ahead.

* DR. B. L. MOSLEY, A PATHOLOGIST AT THE UNIVERSITY OF MISSOURI, THEORIZED THAT PRIOR TO AN ELECTRICAL STORM, WHEN THE AIR IS CHARGED WITH STATIC ELECTRICITY, DRY CAT FUR ATTRACTED DUST PARTICLES, CAUSING THE CAT TO COMMENCE GROOMING ITSELF.

Against the times of snow or hail,
Or boist'rous windy storms;
She frisks about and wags her tail
And many tricks performs.
— FROM A POETICAL DESCRIPTION OF BEASTS, PUBLISHED IN THE EIGHTEENTH CENTURY

A white cat in Baltimore, Maryland, named Napoleon had the habit of lying prone with his front paws extended and his head tucked down on the ground between them when he sensed oncoming rain — and he was right as rain every time. In 1930, during a drought, Napoleon assumed the position despite a dry national weather forecast. Ms. Shields, his owner, called the newspapers, but they ignored her — until it soon began to rain "cats and dogs." For the next six years, Napoleon the Weather Prophet's forecasts were published in the paper.

8 Cat Games

Black Cat Fortune-Telling Game

Cat-a-Mouse

Cat's Cradle

Kilkenny Cats

Little Kittens

Pin the Tail on the Cat

Puss in the Corner

Tip-Cat

Cat's Cradle

2 Possible Origins of "Cat's Cradle"

1. In medieval Europe, people believed a "cat's cradle" could increase a young married couple's fertility. A month after the wedding, a fertility rite was performed, whereby a cat was secured in a cradle, carried into the newlyweds' house, and rocked back and forth. This procedure ensured that a pregnancy would soon follow. The game played with string creates what looks loosely like a cradle, and over time it came to be called "cat's cradle."

2. In a solar rite performed in countries with hot climates, a cradle was built to lure a cat and give it a cozy place to stay. Since the cat was associated with the sun, its presence would give humans respite from the heat. In cold countries, the opposite effect was desired; the ritual was designed to delay the sun's waning.

11 Urban Cat Legends

We can just about guarantee that none of these stories are true. Rather, these widespread tales are intended to comment on typical attributes of the cat: its curiosity, its mischievous nature, and its way of charming us into providing it with special care. Nevertheless, our neighbor's friend's uncle *swears* that these are all true! (Note: The bonsai kitten website is a total hoax, no matter what anyone tells you.)

1. A woman offers to tend a neighbor's house while the neighbor goes on vacation. The woman is horrified to discover, after a few days, that her own dog has killed the neighbor's cat. The neighbor is frantic. She cleans up the cat, who is matted in mud, and places it on the sofa to make it look as though the cat died in his sleep. When the neighbor returns home, she becomes hysterical. It seems that poor Jaylo had died before she went away, and the cat had been buried in the backyard. Now some cruel prankster has dug up the cat and placed him on the poor woman's sofa! In some versions of this tale, the woman dies of a heart attack, believing that the cat has returned from the grave.

2. A woman throwing a dinner party suspects that the chicken she cooked might be a little "off," so she feeds some to the cat to see what its reaction might be. The cat seems fine, so the woman serves dinner. But as she gets up to serve dessert, she finds her cat in the kitchen, throwing up. The woman confesses to the guests and suggests they all go to the hospital immediately to have their stomach pumped. Without a thought for her own well-being, she takes the cat to the vet — who diagnoses a hairball!

3. The kids arrive home from school to see that their mom has baked their favorite — a blueberry pie. But there's a note next to it explaining that the pie is for

company and they are not to touch it. Their appetites get the better of them, and soon they have polished off the whole thing. Hearing their mother at the front door, they quickly grab the cat and smear its face with the remains of the pie to make it look like the culprit. When the mother comes in and sees what the cat has done, she boots the poor creature right out of the house — straight under a passing truck.

4. A woman walking through a parking lot on a particularly hot day notices a cat lying face-down in the backseat of a car. Horrified at what is happening to the poor creature, she calls the police, who break into the car, only to discover a plush stuffed cat.

5. A man needs to take his cat on a long plane trip, and knowing that Fluffy can be a difficult traveler, he goes to the vet and asks for a sedative for the cat. The junior vet prescribes a morphine tablet to be taken just before take-off. The man gives his cat the pill, at which point its behavior becomes maniacal — screaming, clawing, and scratching its way through the entire trip. In the meantime, the junior vet discovers his mistake; morphine, it turns out, doesn't sedate cats, but rather excites them. So he is ready for a dressing-down when the man comes to report on his trip. "It was awful," he says. "The cat and the passengers were all total wrecks by the time we landed." Just as the young vet is about to confess all, the man continues, "But I'm grateful to you — just think how much worse it would have been if you hadn't provided that pill!"

6. There are many versions of the legend of the woman who is in the habit of popping her Persian into an open oven for a few minutes after he's been out in the rain. Unfortunately, when this woman is given a microwave as a gift, she fails to read the instructions — with disastrous consequences.

7. In another techno-tale, a man who feels guilty about leaving his cat home all day while he's out at work buys one of the popular cat videos that kitties are supposed to enjoy on their own. But arriving home after one day, the man smells a terrible odor of burning fur. The cat, while watching frolicking squirrels on the screen, just had to get to them, and when he tried climbing into the back of the TV set, he was electrocuted. (In some versions of this story, the whole house goes up in smoke, and it's the insurance adjuster who finally solves the mystery.)

8. Then there's the highly questionable legend of a woman who buys a cell phone that is so small, her cat swallows it. It's not until she hears muffled ringing that she realizes what has happened. In most versions of this story, the vet is able to extract the phone.

9. A family moves into their dream home only to discover that they may be living in something resembling the house in *The Amityville Horror.* Strange noises emanate from the walls, and they hear wailing and screaming at night. They finally decide to vacate the place, but just as they are packing up the last of their belongings, the previous homeowners call and ask, "Have you seen our Siamese cat?" Apparently, he had become lost among the boxes as they were leaving and managed to find his way between floorboards when no one was around.

10. Two women in a parking lot at a shopping mall discover a dead kitty. They decide that once they have finished shopping, they will take it home for a proper burial. So they wrap it in plastic and place it in a shopping bag in the backseat of their car. Fearing the odor of the dead animal, they leave their car window open. Later, in view of their car, as they are having lunch, they see a woman lurking near their car. This woman reaches in and swipes the shopping bag. Coincidentally, this woman then takes a seat near them to have her own lunch. Finally, the woman peers inside the bag to view her booty, only to faint at the sight of a dead cat. As the paramedics take her away, the women hand over the shopping bag, saying, "Don't forget her bag — she wouldn't want to lose this!"

11. A woman was shocked to discover that her cat was expecting kittens. The cat had not been spayed, but given that she was an indoor cat and had no contact with other felines, the development was odd at best. What was even odder was the "kitten" that emerged. It was larger than any kitten the family had ever seen; it had a short tail and extended back legs. In fact, the vet reported, the cat had mated with the family's pet rabbit, and the result was a "cabbit." An entire body of legend has grown up around this anomaly. For the record: cats and rabbits bear no degree of genetic compatibility and therefore cannot mate.

The Literary Cat

Title page of an early text on natural history, *Aristotelis Naturalis*, 1546.

1570 A satire on the Roman Catholic Church is published, in the tradition of *Reynard the Fox*. Titled *Beware the Cat,* it was written by William Baldwin. Cats are disparaged in the book, reflecting public contempt toward them. This is one of the earliest known texts to focus on cats, though felines will eventually find their way into every kind of literature imaginable.

1605 A British play tells the story of Dick Whittington and the good-luck-bearing cat that accompanied him to London as he sought his fortune. It becomes a mainstay

An eighteenth-century woodcut tells the story of Dick Whittington and his cat. The tale is based on the real story of Richard Whittington, who lived in London from the late 1350s until 1423. In the most popular version, Dick Whittington goes to London with his cat to make his fortune. Meeting with little success, he is tempted to return home, but he hears a message of hope in the ringing of the city's church bells. With new resolve, he embarks on a series of adventures in which his cat's talents bring him success. Eventually he becomes prosperous and is appointed the mayor of London three times. (The real Richard Whittington served as mayor for four terms.)

of children's literature. Versions of the story appear in Persian, Scandinavian, and Italian folklore; the tale is still popular today. (See page 48 for more about Dick Whittington's cat.)

1697 The character Puss in Boots makes his literary debut in a children's story by Charles Perrault (see page 41). Some 150 years later, the story becomes a mainstay of Christmas tradition.

1727 François-Augustin Paradis de Moncrif, a poet and dramatist, publishes a passionate defense of cats entitled *Les Chats,* now recognized as the first of all great cat books. Moncrif is ridiculed for his effort, which inspires cruel satires.

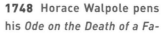

Illustration from Moncrif's *Les Chats,* the earliest of all cat books, published in 1727.

1748 Horace Walpole pens his *Ode on the Death of a Favourite Cat Drowned in a Tub of Gold Fishes* after his tortoiseshell cat drowns in a goldfish bowl.

1760 An anonymously published novel titled *The Life and Adventures of a Cat* contains a hero named Tom. The character is so popular that the term *tomcat* comes to refer to a male domestic cat, previously known as a ram or a boar.

1806 Edward Lear publishes "The Owl and the Pussy-Cat." (See page 47 to read the poem.)

1843 Edgar Allan Poe's "The Black Cat" is published in the *Saturday Evening Post.* The short story tells of a man who becomes possessed by the spirit of a malevolent black cat and commits murder.

1856 Lady Cust publishes the first book on cat care. It is 31 pages long and is considered presumptuous.

1865 The Cheshire Cat grins from the pages of Lewis Carroll's *Alice's Adventures in Wonderland* and becomes one of the most popular characters in this enduring classic. This particular cat is mocking and menacing. Carroll must have had complaints about it; by the time he publishes *Through the Looking-Glass* in 1871, the cat Dinah and her kittens, Snowdrop and Kitty, are sweet and lovable. Carroll, in the meantime, proves himself a cat fancier of the highest order. He commonly allows strays into his home; he once said he provided "rat-tail jelly and buttered mice" for their breakfast.

1874 Whereas Lady Cust's book was only 31 pages long, *Cats,* by William Gordon Stables, goes on for more than 500 pages. This pioneering volume covers cat care and cat breeds and includes cat stories and anecdotes.

An illustration from the 1988 translation of Théophile Gautier's *Ménagerie intime* (originally published in 1871), in which he paid tribute to his black cat, Eponine.

1885 Herman D. Umbstaetter begins publishing a magazine called *The Black Cat;* it spotlights short stories by amateur writers. Each cover features a cat dressed for a particular role — the cat as artist, the cat as minstrel, the cat as court jester, and so on. Created by the publisher's wife, Nellie Littlehale Umbstaetter, the images become popular as framed prints, and the cat illustrations become an important part of the 20,000-copies-a-month success of the magazine. The *New York Herald* calls the publication "the cat that captured the country." *The Black Cat* ceased publication in 1923 after helping to launch the careers of a number of famous writers, including Jack London and Octavius Roy Cohen.

1886 *A Kittens' Christmas Party* is published in the *Illustrated London News,* the first of Louis Wain's illustrations of anthropomorphized cats, and many of the 150 cats in the drawing resemble his own cat, Peter.

1901 Susan Patterson publishes a cat book with a humane theme, which suggests better treatment for felines. *Pussy Meow* does for cats what *Black Beauty* did for horses.

Cover of the September 1896 issue of *The Black Cat.* The cover of each issue featured a cat dressed in a different costume.

1902 Rudyard Kipling elucidates upon "The Cat That Walked by Himself" in the *Just So Stories for Little Children.* The story states that "three proper Men out of five will always throw things at a Cat whenever they meet him, and all proper Dogs will chase

Felix, the father of the cartoon cats, made his first "talkie" appearance in the 1920s.

The legacy of Joe Oriolo, who created Felix the Cat, has been carried on by his son, Don, who wrote and produced *Felix the Cat, the Movie* (1987) and *The Twisted Tales of Felix the Cat* (1996). He's also a talented musician and an avid Martin guitar enthusiast. His story inspired the Limited Edition "FeLiX" Little Martin guitar, lovingly adorned with Felix's image, which first appeared in 2004.

him up a tree . . . he is the Cat that walks by himself, and all places are alike to him."

1909 Beatrix Potter's *The Tale of Ginger and Pickles* is published. Ginger the cat runs a village shop along with Pickles the terrier.

1920 *The Tiger in the House,* by journalist (later photographer and novelist) Carl Van Vechten, is published. This fascinating early study of cat behavior and beliefs contains chapters on cats and the occult, folklore, law, theater, music, and art. The writer is inspired by his cat, Feathers, to whom the book is dedicated.

1928 Wanda Wag's beloved children's story, *Millions of Cats,* is published and goes on to sell over a million copies. Today, it is still one of the most popular cat books for children.

1933 Saha, French novelist Colette's cat, is the focus of her novel *La Chatte.* The book tells of a relationship shared by a man, a woman, and a cat. By the time of her death at age 81, Colette had published more than 50 novels and dozens of short stories. She is known as France's patron saint of cats.

1934 Popular and pioneering science fiction–fantasy writer Andre Norton publishes her first book, *The Prince Commands.* At the time of her death in 2005 she had published over 100 novels and anthologies in which cats play very important roles.

1938 Orlando (The Marmalade Cat) first makes an appearance as the hero of British author Kathleen Hale's series of children's books, which will eventually grow to 18 in number. Orlando later features in a BBC radio series, and a ballet based on his life is performed in 1951 at the Festival of Britain.

1939 T. S. Eliot publishes *Old Possum's Book of Practical Cats,* a collection of charming and surprisingly accessible poetry. The book is widely popular, introducing Macavity the Mystery Cat, Skimbleshanks the Railway Cat, and Bustopher Jones, the Cat About Town. In 1982, these unforgettable characters made their Broadway debut in the musical *Cats,* the longest-running Broadway musical ever, which continued for 18 years before finally closing in 2000.

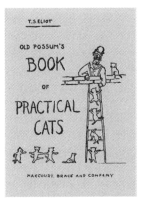

T. S. Eliot's *Old Possum's Book of Practical Cats,* a collection of whimsical poems, was first published in 1939, with a cover illustration by the author. The book is famous for having inspired the Broadway musical *Cats.*

1945 Snowbell is the housecat of the Little family in E. B. White's classic book *Stuart Little.*

1950 *The Abandoned,* by Paul Gallico, tells the story of a boy named Peter who is hit by a car and recovers, only to find that he has become a cat. Another cat named Jen-

nie shows him the ropes; the book is about their adventures together. In Britain, this book is published under the title *Jennie.*

1955 Carbonel the cat is the star of a three-part series by British children's author Barbara Sleigh. The protagonist, Rosemary, finds that the cat she has purchased in a market is actually the King of the Cats, and she helps him to return to his rightful throne, with the help of witchcraft. *Carbonel: The King of the Cats* is followed by *The Kingdom of Carbonel* and then by *Carbonel and Calidor.*

1957 *The Cat in the Hat,* by Dr. Seuss, is published. The book came about when Theodor Seuss Geisel (AKA Dr. Seuss) was approached to write and illustrate a primer teaching 225 vocabulary words to children. It has become one of the most beloved and successful children's books of all time, spawning sequels, board games, and movies.

1957 Paul Gallico's novel *Thomasina: The Cat Who Thought She Was God* is about a cat who believes herself to be an Egyptian cat goddess. In 1964 it is released as a Disney film called *The Three Lives of Thomasina.*

1958 The novella *Breakfast at Tiffany's,* by Truman Capote, is published. Lead character Holly Golightly (later portrayed on film by Audrey Hepburn) has a cat she calls "Cat" because she doesn't feel that she should name him, since they don't really belong to each other. One major scene in the book has Holly taking the cat to an unfamiliar neighborhood and leaving him there, then going back to try to find him.

1961 Sheila Burnford's book *The Incredible Journey* features the Siamese cat Tao as one of three animals who travel across the Canadian wilderness together to find their masters. The other two are a Labrador retriever and a bull terrier. Tao's role is critical — he catches birds for the three of them to eat on the trip.

1962 J.R.R. Tolkien's poem "The Cat" is published in the collection *The Adventures of Tom Bombadil.* The verse tells of "the fat cat on the mat," who, though he is napping on a rug in his owners' home, is close kin to the lion "with huge ruthless tooth in gory jaw" and "kept as a pet, he does not forget." (See page 21 for a spoof on various doctrinal interpretations of the statement "The cat sat on the mat.")

1963 *Undercover Cat,* by Gordon and Mildred Gordon, is published. Darn Cat, AKA D.C., solves a bank robbery, and the story is partially told through his eyes. The book spawns a few sequels and inspires a Disney movie, *That Darn Cat!,* starring Hayley Mills.

1965 The first issue of *Cat Fancy* is published. The magazine is a complete guide to caring for and understanding the cat and includes a centerfold poster in each issue.

1966 A series of murder mysteries by Lilian Jackson Braun is launched with *The Cat Who Could Read Backwards.* As of 2005, 28 books, still in print, star the reporter James Qwilleran and his two Siamese cats, Koko and Yum Yum. The cats help Qwilleran solve local murder cases in his native state of Michigan. Each title starts with the phrase *The Cat Who . . .* (See page 163 for a list of mysteries by Lilian Jackson Braun.)

1967 The first English translation of Mikhail Bulgakov's satirical Russian novel *The Master and Margarita* is published. One of its more memorable characters is Behemoth, a six-foot-tall demonic black cat.

1975 B. Kliban's first book, *Cat,* is published. (See timeline, page 16).

1989 *Felidae,* by German/Turkish writer Akif Pirinçci, is the first of a series of cat crime novels and becomes an international bestseller.

1990 Sneaky Pie Brown makes his literary debut with *Wish You Were Here,* which he "co-writes" with author Rita Mae Brown, whose *Rubyfruit Jungle* has already become a classic. Brown's feline companion, muse, and "coauthor" of her Mrs. Murphy murder mystery series is her tiger cat, who assists in the solving of crimes. The series premiered in 1990 and is going strong, as of this writing, with the publication of its newest book, *Puss 'n Cahoots,* in 2007.

1992 Carole Nelson Douglas kicks off her Midnight Louie series with *Catnap.* As of 2006 there are 19 novels in the series. Midnight Louie is a 19-pound black tomcat private investigator who prowls the streets of Vegas, solving crimes.

2004 *Harry Potter and the Prisoner of Azkaban,* the third in the Harry Potter series, features Crookshanks, Hermione Granger's pet cat. Crookshanks is distinguished by his smashed-in-looking face and bandy legs. He is actually a cross between a cat and a kneazle, which is a highly intelligent, magical catlike creature. Author J. K. Rowling, herself not a cat admirer, based the character on a large ginger-colored cat that she used to see in a London park during her lunch hour.

2007 *Planet Cat* hits the shelves!

Over the years, many cat lovers have asked me: "Dave, how come you never write about cats? Is it because you don't LIKE cats? Is it because cats are vicious, unprincipled household parasites that will stroll up to the person who has fed them for seventeen years and, without provocation, claw this person's shin flesh into lasagna? Is it because they are lazy, ungrateful, hairball-spewing . . . HEY! These aren't cat-lover quotations! You're making these quotations up!" OK, so I do not harbor a great fondness for cats. But I intend to change my ways, because I sincerely, in my heart, want to cash in on the wave of Cat Mania that is sweeping the nation.

— **DAVE BARRY**

Puss in Boots

The story "Puss in Boots" is a European fairy tale collected and rewritten by Charles Perrault in 1697. While other versions of the story have been gathered and told, Perrault's is considered the definitive one. An abbreviated version of the story as written by Perrault goes as follows:

A miller, who was dying, divided his property between his three sons, but left his youngest son with nothing but the granary cat. The boy was very disappointed and even considered eating the animal out of desperation. The cat, aware of what was about to befall him, bargained with the boy and promised that if he gave him a bag and a pair of boots, he would make the boy wealthy. Puss devised a plan.

Puss in Boots, an excellent hunter, captured a number of rabbits, partridges, and other wild game and presented them to the king as presents from his master the "Marquis de Carabas."

Puss learned that the king and his daughter would soon be traveling. He convinced the miller's son to bathe in a river while the royal party would be passing by. Puss stole the young boy's clothes and ran to the road calling for help for his master, the Marquis de Carabas, who he claimed was drowning. The king's men rescued the naked boy and wrapped him in royal robes.

Puss then sped ahead, reaching the land of a powerful ogre. Puss convinced the workers in the ogre's fields to tell the king, who would be passing by shortly, that the land belonged to the Marquis. Puss then convinced the ogre, who was proud of his shape-changing abilities, to turn himself into a mouse. Puss then quickly pounced on and ate him.

When the king finally arrived on the ogre's lands, the Puss welcomed him in his master's name. The king was impressed by the lad and eventually gave him his daughter's hand in marriage, thus securing the boy's future.

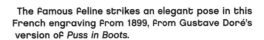

The famous feline strikes an elegant pose in this French engraving from 1899, from Gustave Doré's version of *Puss in Boots*.

Hamlet's Cat's Soliloquy

by Willy Shakespaw

To go outside, and there perchance to stay
Or to remain within: that is the question:
Whether 'tis better for a cat to suffer
The cuffs and buffets of inclement weather
That Nature rains on those who roam abroad,
Or take a nap upon a scrap of carpet,
And so by dozing melt the solid hours
That clog the clock's bright gears with sullen time
And stall the dinner bell.
To sit, to stare Outdoors, and by a stare to seem to
    state
A wish to venture forth without delay,
Then when the portal's opened up, to stand
As if transfixed by doubt.
To prowl; to sleep;
To choose not knowing when we may once more
Our readmittance gain: aye, there's the hairball;
For if a paw were shaped to turn a knob,
Or work a lock or slip a window-catch,
And going out and coming in were made
As simple as the breaking of a bowl,
What cat would bear the household's petty plagues,
The cook's well-practiced kicks, the butler's broom,
The infant's careless pokes, the tickled ears,
The trampled tail, and all the daily shocks
That fur is heir to, when, of his own free will,
He might his exodus or entrance make
With a mere mitten?
Who would spaniels fear,
Or strays trespassing from a neighbor's yard,
But that the dread of our unheeded cries
And scratches at a barricaded door
No claw can open up, dispels our nerve
And makes us rather bear our humans' faults
Than run away to unguessed miseries?
Thus caution doth make housecats of us all;
And thus the bristling hair of resolution
Is softened up with the pale brush of thought,
And since our choices hinge on weighty things,
We pause upon the threshold of decision.

Shakespeare on Cats

Every reference that William Shakespeare made about cats was negative. There's the rub.

"I would endure anything before but a cat."
   —All's Well That Ends Well

"For this description of thine honesty? A pox upon him for me, he's more and more a cat."
   —All's Well That Ends Well

"I could endure any thing before but a cat, and now he's a cat to me."
   —All's Well That Ends Well

"Here is a purr of fortune's, sir, or of fortune's cat . . ."
   —All's Well That Ends Well

" . . . civet is of a baser birth than tar, the very uncleanly flux of a cat."
   —As You Like It

"The mouse ne'er shunn'd the cat as they did budge From rascals worse than they."
   —Coriolanus

"A man may fish with the worm that hath eat of a king, and cat of the fish that hath fed of that worm."
   —Hamlet

"Let Hercules himself do what he may, The cat will mew and dog will have his day."
   —Hamlet

"I am as vigilant as a cat to steal cream."
   —Henry IV, Part I

"Playing the mouse in absence of the cat, To tear and havoc more than she can eat."
   —Henry V

'Sblood, I am as melancholy as a gib cat or a lugged bear."
   —Henry IV, Part I

"Thou owest the worm no silk, the beast no hide, the sheep no wool, the cat no perfume."
   —King Lear

"Thrice the brinded cat hath mew'd."
— *Macbeth*

"Why he cannot abide a gaping pig;
Why he, a harmless necessary cat . . ."
— *The Merchant of Venice*

"I could play Ercles rarely, or a part to tear a cat in, to make all split."
— *A Midsummer Night's Dream*

"Hang me in a bottle like a cat."
— *Much Ado About Nothing*

"What though care killed a cat, thou hast mettle enough in thee to kill care."
— *Much Ado About Nothing*

"The cat, with eyne of burning coal, Now crouches fore the mouse's hole."
— *Pericles, Prince of Tyre*

"Yet, foul night-waking cat, he doth but dally,
While in his hold-fast foot the weak mouse panteth . . ."
— *The Rape of Lucrece*

"'Tis torture, and not mercy: heaven is here, Where Juliet lives; and every cat and dog And little mouse, every unworthy thing . . ."
— *Romeo and Juliet*

"But will you woo this wild-cat?"
— *The Taming of the Shrew*

"They'll take suggestion as a cat laps milk;
They'll tell the clock to any business that
We say befits the hour."
— *The Tempest*

Come on your ways; open your mouth; here is that which will give language to you, cat . . ."
— *The Tempest*

" . . . my sister crying, our maid howling, our cat wringing her hands."
— *The Two Gentlemen of Verona*

The Cat's Tale
by Geoffrey Chaucer's Cat

Geoffrey Chaucer (1328–1400) loved cats for their beauty and the sleekness of their fur, qualities that he manages to mention in many of his tales, including "The Miller's Tale," "Wife of Bath," and "The Manciple's Tale," in which he offers advice as to how to care for a cat; he stresses the need for a comfortable bed of silk. Comfy and cozy, it's no surprise that Chaucer's cat had time to take up the pen.

A Cat there was, a gentil tailless Manx
Our Hoste hadde seen astray on Thames banks
And taken home to ridden him of rats,
At whiche she preved to been the beste of cats.
He longed to bringe on pilgrimage his pette,
But Puss bigan to fussen and to frette
When that she sawgh the leathern hond-luggage
In whiche she was yschlept on viage;
She thinketh that no Canterbury mous
Be worth an expeditioun from hir hous,
And so she took hir leave of us apace
And crept into a secret hiding-place,
And when the folk the pavement gan to pounde,
This Pussie-Cat was nowhere to be founde,
And she was leften in the hostelrye
To keepen all the rodentes compaignye;
And that is how this Cat withouten tail
Became as wel a Cat withouten tale.

Cats in Nursery Rhymes

Nursery rhymes have a fascinating history dating back centuries. They entertain us, lulling us into a state of innocent pleasure, and their simplicity has been useful in teaching language skills, sounds, and even story structure. But there's a serious tradition to them as well: their characters have been assigned political and social motivations, and simple plots have been interpreted as hidden political agendas. For an in-depth, highly entertaining article on the interpretations of nursery rhymes, visit messybeast.com, managed by Sarah Hartwell, author of this list. Here's a sampling of what you'll find.

The Cat and the Pudding String

Sing, sing, what shall I sing?
The cat's run away with the pudding string.
Do, do, what shall I do?
The cat's run away with the pudding, too.

In this day of convenience foods and microwave or canned puddings, it is easy to forget how steamed or boiled puddings used to be made. In many cases, a ball of pudding dough went into a muslin square that was tied shut. The result was a spherical pudding. The trailing string would have been irresistible to a playful cat. A cat that dragged the pudding string away might well have found the pudding still attached, much to the cook's dismay! Other versions have the cat biting the pudding string in two.

The Cat and the Fiddle

Hey diddle diddle, the cat and the fiddle,
The cow jumped over the moon.
The little dog laughed to see such fun
And the dish ran away with the spoon!

Several meanings have become attached to this rhyme, one of several about cats and

An ancient sistrum, with a figure of a sacred cat.

fiddles. It may be a nonsense rhyme based on a corruption of *catus fideles,* "faithful cat," or it may be a list of household animals and implements commonly owned by a poor household. A more elaborate idea claims it refers to a fiddle-shaped Egyptian instrument called a sistrum and to the cat, once worshiped in ancient Egypt. Many depictions of Bastet, an Egyptian cat-goddess, show her holding a sistrum. The cow and moon would represent the Egyptian goddess Hathor, with the sun-disk between her horns. Other variations of the nursery rhyme are suggestive of witchcraft. One obviously misguided suggestion claims the rhyme is a coded poem about England's first Queen Elizabeth, who "fiddled" with her courtiers as though they were mice. The theory is interesting but holds little water: the nursery rhyme wasn't written until 200 years after Elizabeth's reign!

The Cat and the Tree

Diddle-ti diddle-ti dumpty.
The cat's stuck up the plum tree.
Here's a crown to fetch her down,
Diddle-ti diddle-ti dumpty.
Feedum, fiddledum fee,
The cat's got into the tree.

Pussy, come down,
Or I'll crack your crown,
And toss you into the sea.

Cats are very good at climbing trees but less good at getting down again. Their claws provide ample grip when climbing upward, but they face the wrong direction when descending; hence, many cats climb backward down trees. While most versions of this rhyme involve a reward or a bet of a half-crown (a coin) to get the cat down, the second version threatens the cat with a knock on the head, followed by drowning. One suggestion is that the verse alludes to Charles II's escape from the Roundheads in 1651, when he hid in an oak tree following the Battle of Worcester. Kings are often associated with that grandest of cats — the lion — and the verse contains a reference to "crack your crown" and perhaps forcing the captured king into exile overseas.

Saint Ives

As I was going to Saint Ives,
I met a man with seven wives;
Every wife had seven sacks;
Every sack had seven cats;
Every cat had seven kits.
Kits, cats, sacks, and wives,
How many were there going to Saint Ives?

This is a traditional riddle as well as a nursery rhyme. The accepted answer is that only one person was going to Saint Ives (a place in Cornwall) — the person asking the question. The party comprising man, wives, cats, and kittens were departing Saint Ives and hence met the verse's narrator. Some might argue, however, that all parties were traveling toward Saint Ives, and the lone traveler overtook the more heavily encumbered party, in which case the multiplication table and some simple addition will provide the answer.

> ## "If animals could speak the dog would be a blundering outspoken fellow, but the cat would have the rare grace of never saying a word too much."
> **— MARK TWAIN**

Uncertain Toys

Oh kittens, in our hours of ease,
Uncertain toys and full of fleas,
When pain and anguish hang o'er men,
We turn you into sausage then.

This grim rhyme gives a less cozy view of our relationship with cats. When life is easy, the kittens are treated as living toys, but in times of crisis they may become food. During wars and sieges, pet keeping was a luxury that most people could not afford due to food shortages. Pets, strays, and wild cats and dogs ended up in cooking pots when more conventional food sources had been exhausted. During World War II, British cities harbored many stray and abandoned cats, some of which ended up in pies in the guise of "roof rabbit."

8 Aesop's Fables About Cats

Cats have much to teach us, and Aesop, a freed slave who went on to become a well-known writer, knew this back in the sixth century B.C., when he used them — along with an array of other animals — to make his moral points. Even today, these tales are told to children everywhere as basic lessons in humanity.

1. "The Cat and the Cock"

A cat caught a crowing cock early one morning and wondered whether or not to eat him. He accused the cock of disturbing people and not permitting them to sleep. The cock apologized and defended himself by saying that he did this so that people would wake up in time for their work. The cat thought about this for a moment and replied, "Although you have apologized, I must still have dinner," and ate him anyway, proving that *we are not always rewarded in accordance with our performance.*

2. "The Cat and the Birds"

A cat, hearing that the birds in an aviary were sick, dressed himself up as a physician, and, taking a bag of doctor's instruments along, paid them a visit. He knocked at the door and asked the birds how they were feeling and suggested that he could give them medicine to cure them. The birds replied, "We are all very well, and shall continue to be so, if you will only be good enough to go away, and leave us as we are." *Beware of cats bearing gifts!*

3. "The Cat and the Mice"

A certain house was overrun with mice. A cat, discovering this, made her way into the house and began to catch and eat the mice one by one. Fearing for their lives, the mice kept themselves hidden in their holes. The cat decided to lure them out by pretending to be dead. One of the mice peeped out and, seeing the cat, said, "Even though *you* will turn into a meal, we will not come near you." *He who is once deceived is doubly cautious.*

4. "The Eagle, the Cat, and the Wild Sow"

An eagle made her nest at the top of an oak tree; a cat found a convenient hole in the middle of the trunk and moved in; and a wild sow, with her young, took shelter in a hollow at its foot. The cat, annoyed by this arrangement, convinced the eagle that the sow would try to fell the tree in order to eat the eagle's young. She then convinced the sow that the eagle was waiting to pounce on her and her piglets. Fearing each other, the eagle and the sow never dared leave the tree, and both died of hunger, along with their young. The result was that the cat and her kittens now had plenty of food, *having played both ends against the middle.*

5. "The Cat and Venus," or "The Cat-maiden"

A cat fell in love with a handsome young man and begged Venus to change her into the form of a woman. Venus agreed and transformed her into a beautiful maiden. The young man saw her, fell in love, and took her home as his bride. Venus was curious to learn if the cat had changed her habits now that she was a woman, so she placed a mouse in the center of the room. The maiden, forgetting her present state, pounced on the mouse. Venus was so disappointed that she turned the maiden back into a cat. *Nature exceeds nurture; a leopard can't change its spots.*

6. "The Fox and the Cat"

A fox was boasting to a cat of his clever ways of escaping his enemies. "I have a whole bag of tricks," he said, "which contains a hundred ways of escaping my enemies." "I have only one," said the cat, "but I can generally manage with that." Just then they heard the cry of a pack of hounds coming toward them. The cat immediately scampered up a tree and hid herself in the branches. "This is my plan," said the cat. "What are you going to do?" The fox thought first of one way to escape, and then another. While the fox continued to deliberate upon his options, the hounds came nearer and nearer; the fox was then shot by the huntsmen. *Better one safe way than a hundred on which you cannot rely.*

7. "Belling the Cat"
Long ago, mice had a general council to consider what they could do to outwit their common enemy, the cat. While the elder mice were debating this problem, a young mouse got up and suggested that if they were able to place a bell around the cat's neck, they would always be able to hear it coming. This proposal met with great applause, until an old mouse got up and said, "That is all very well, but who is going to bell the cat?" The mice looked at one another, and nobody spoke. "It is easy to propose impossible remedies." *Easier said than done.*

8. "The Cat and the King"
A cat was gazing at a king. "Well," said the monarch, "how do you like me?" "Although you are handsome I would much prefer to see the King of the Mice." The king was so pleased with the wit of the reply that he gave the cat permission to scratch his prime minister's eyes out. *A clever wit can be all one needs to earn a fortune.*

A drawing by Edward Lear.

The Owl and the Pussy-Cat
by Edward Lear

Edward Lear (1812–1888), artist, illustrator, and writer, was devoted to Foss, his tabby cat, who was the subject of many of his drawings, some of which were published in *The Heraldic Blazon of Foss the Cat*. When Lear decided to move to San Remo, Italy, he instructed his architect to design a replica of his old home in England so that Foss would suffer only minimal distress after the relocation. Lear's drawings of his striped tabby cat are well known, especially those that accompany his famous rhyme "The Owl and the Pussy-Cat." When Foss died, he was buried in Lear's Italian garden; Lear died only two months later. Here is his timeless ode to cats.

The Owl and the Pussy-cat went to
    sea
In a beautiful pea-green boat
They took some honey, and plenty of
    money,
Wrapped up in a five-pound note.
The Owl looked up to the stars above,
And sang to a small guitar,
"O lovely Pussy! O Pussy, my love,
What a beautiful Pussy you are,
You are,
You are!
What a beautiful Pussy you are!"

Pussy said to the Owl, "You elegant
    fowl!
How charmingly sweet you sing!
O let us be married! Too long we have
    tarried:

But what shall we do for a ring?"
They sailed away for a year and a
    day,
To the land where the Bong-tree
    grows,
And there in a wood a Piggy-wig
    stood
With a ring at the end of his nose,
His nose,
His nose,
With a ring at the end of his nose.

"Dear Pig, are you willing to sell for
    one shilling
Your ring?" Said the Piggy, "I will."
So they took it away and were
    married next day
By the Turkey who lives on the hill.
They dined on mince, and slices of
    quince,
Which they ate with a runcible spoon;
And hand in hand, on the edge of the
    sand,
They danced by the light of the moon,
The moon,
The moon,
They danced by the light of the moon.

Cats on British Inn Signs

THE CAT WITH NO TAIL

Take a ride through almost any part of the United Kingdom and you're likely to come across at least one "cat" pub. But there'll be more to the sign than just the name of an establishment. Cats on inn and pub signs enjoy a rich tradition, and we're grateful to Patrick Roberts for preserving this fascinating chapter in cat culture and for supplying the information here as well as the accompanying illustrations. Visit purr-n-fur.org.uk/fun/pubsign/sign-index.html for more information, including the exact origins of many of the names mentioned here.

The FAT CAT FREE HOUSE

In 1393 Richard II decreed that innkeepers must by law exhibit a sign, and since most people at the time could not read (or write), the signs were pictorial. Many were, and still are, derived from coats of arms or the armorial badges and devices of noble families; others were connected to the monarchy or its alliances; and another group had religious origins. Then, of course, there were animals — and that's where cats come in! Numerous heraldic signs included lions and leopards; but most inn-sign painters had never seen these animals.

THE CAT & FIDDLE

Thus, many an artist resorted to rendering the domestic cat, with which they were much more familiar.

Of the 50,000-plus pubs in the U.K., approximately 80 of them sport signs featuring the cat.

The most common of these cat names by far is the Cat and Fiddle, of which there are around a dozen, ranging from Bodmin in Cornwall to Macclesfield in Cheshire and Norwich in East Anglia. Some of the inn signs interpret the nursery rhyme, but others do not. The origin of the name is probably not

THE CAT'S BACK A R.E.M. L™ FREEHOUSE

the rhyme but is thought to come from the name of an English knight whom the French (in one of our numerous wars with them) named "Caton le Fidèle." A minion who had fought with Caton returned from the wars to live near Buxton and named his house after the knight — but it became corrupted to the present name.

Puss in Boots graces four pubs, with some nice signs; while other well-known felines include the Cheshire Cat (two); the Owl and the Pussycat, with five examples and again some good representations; and Dick Whittington's (probably fictitious) cat, which appears on the signs of four pubs with different names. There is a Cat's Whiskers with a nice sign in Childwall, Liverpool.

Cheshire Cat

Seven or eight pubs are called simply the Cat, or variations on that, such as the Cat Tavern; there are several Black Cats, several Fat Cats (not including the chain of "café bars" with that name), a couple of Old Cats, and three Red Cats. In Essex there is one inn called just the Cats; the thinking, apparently, is that cats are good lickers, and inside the pub there are good liquors! Less familiar names are the Brass Cat (two), the Cat i' th' Well, and the Cat and Bagpipes (both in Yorkshire); while there are also a couple of Romping Cats, a Mad Cat (Cambridgeshire), a Rampant Cat (Berkshire), and no fewer than three Squinting Cats. There is a Cat with no Tail in — guess where? — the Isle of Man, naturally!

What the connection is between the Cat and Custard Pot, or between the Cat and Lantern, we have no idea. The Cat and Wheel in Bristol, it's said, is a corruption of *catherine wheel*, while we all know the link between the Cat and Canary. Appropriately, it is located at Canary Wharf in Docklands; another London cat is the Cat's Back in Wandsworth, in the southeast of the city.

THE OWL & THE PUSSYCAT

FREEHOUSE

Not all the "cat pubs" have pictorial signs, unfortunately; three that haven't are the intriguingly named Kilkenny Cat, in Llanelli — the only "cat pub" in the whole of Wales — the Charlton Cat in Wiltshire, and the Cat and Cabbage in Rotherham. However, there are stories behind all these names, and you can find them on my website. In Scotland pictorial signs as a whole are less common, too, and so the second Cat's Whiskers, in Elgin, does not have one. The Devonshire Cat in Sheffield just has cats depicted on the windows.

Conversely, cats are sometimes to be found on signs for pubs that aren't named after them. Good examples are the Live and Let Live in Derbyshire and the Star at Beeston, Nottingham. There's also the Catcracker, which is a piece of equipment used in oil refineries shown on the sign of a pub at Stanford-le-Hope, Essex — but they've added a cat figure above it for good measure!

THE SQUINTING CAT

The Owl and the Pussycat

"If a cat spoke, it would say things like, 'Hey, I don't see the problem here.'"
— ROY BLOUNT JR.

2 Theories on the Origin of the Kilkenny Cats

"To fight like a Kilkenny cat" means to engage in a fierce battle that can never be won. The idiom comes from this anonymous limerick:

There were once two cats of Kilkenny.
Each thought there was one cat too many;
So they fought and they fit,
And they scratched and they bit,
Till, excepting their nails
And the tips of their tails,
Instead of two cats, there weren't any.

There are two schools of thought as to the origin of the poem:

1. During the rebellion of Ireland, Kilkenny was garrisoned by a troop of Hessian soldiers who amused themselves in the barracks by the cruel sport of tying two cats together by their tails and throwing them across a clothesline to fight, betting on the outcome. Their officers resolved to stop the cruel practice but had to catch the soldiers in the act. A soldier holding two cats spotted an officer approaching and cut off the cats' tails with a sword. The cats escaped, leaving only their tails behind. When the officer asked what was the meaning of the two bleeding tails, he was told that the two fighting cats had devoured each other and only their tails remained.

2. A more plausible explanation relates to a war of attrition between two Irish towns. During the seventeenth century, the municipalities of Kilkenny and Irishtown contested their boundaries and rights so hotly that that they mutually impoverished each other, leaving little else than "two tails" behind.

The Amusing Game of Kilkenny Cats was manufactured by Parker Brothers from 1890 to 1898.

6 Cat Museums

Mike the Cat was the resident feline at the British Museum in London for 20 years, until 1929. During his career he became so well loved that even during World War I, when the museum was closed, Mike was cared for. The famous Egyptologist Wallis Budge wrote that Mike "preferred sole to whiting and whiting to haddock and sardines to herring; for cod he had no use whatsoever." We assume that all of the following museums have cats in residence, as well they should, since their entire collections are devoted to our timeless love affair with cats.

1. The Kattenkabinet (Cat Cabinet; the Cat Museum)

> Herengracht, 497 1017 BT
> The Netherlands
> Kattenkabinet.nl

This museum has a collection of objets d'art wholly dedicated to the cat, including a wonderful gallery containing a number of Picasso's odes to the cat. The collection is intended as a comprehensive portrayal of the cat in art and culture throughout history. It was founded in commemoration of a frisky red tom, John Pierpont Morgan, the lifelong companion and buddy of the museum's founder, Bob Meijer. Included in the collection are Picasso's 1942 etching "Le Chat," as well as the works of Dutch oil painter Henriette Ronner-Knip, Dutch artist Sal Meijer, and the Swiss graphic poster artist Théophile Steinlen.

2. The Cat Museum

> Petra Jaya
> Kuching (Malaysia's "Cat City")

The Cat Museum has been part of a recent effort to revitalize the tourism industry. The actual floor area of the Cat Museum is just over 1,000 square meters. The four main galleries have more than 2,000 cat artifacts and memorabilia from all over the world. It is the intention of the museum to serve as a meeting place and a seminar and international conference center for cat lovers around the world.

3. The Ramsbottom Cat Museum

> 51–53 Bridge Street
> Ramsbottom, Bury, England

Also known as Kipper's Cats, the museum opened in 1989 as the small private collection of ornamental cat objects belonging to Sylvia Taylor, the museum owner, who also operated a pet shop on the lower floors of the building. Within three years the collection grew to over 1,000 feline items, including jewelry, pictures, and plates. The museum was named after Kipper, the owner's cat, who lived in the pet shop for his entire life. This was the first cat museum founded in England.

4. The Cat Museum in Harrow on the Hill

> 219 High St, Harrow on the Hill
> Middlesex, England

A beautiful collection of about 250 items ranging from cat paintings to a cat matchbox container is curated by Kathleen Mann, the proprietor of this small museum. The collection was started in the 1980 and now contains cat art in pottery, needlework, ivory, leather, and metals. Entry is by appointment only.

5. The Moscow Cat Museum

> Rublyovskoe shosse, 109, bld. 1
> Moscow, Russia
> Moscowcatmuseum.com

Founded in 1993, this museum contains more than 1,500 pieces of cat-related art, including paintings, graphics, ceramics, batiks, tapestries, costumes, and dolls, as well as books, toys, and postcards. The museum also holds cat shows, auctions, cat film festivals, and cat-song-writing contests. Fluffy the Siberian resident cat welcomes all museum guests. Entry is by appointment only.

6. The Cats' Museum

> 18 Zuvininku St.
> Siauliai, Lithuania
> Siauliai.sav.lt

This museum boasts about 10,000 items from countries throughout the world. Included are miniatures of cats created from porcelain, glass, amber, marble, and crystal. Artistic photographs, stained-glass windows, postage stamps, cards, and books have also been lovingly preserved. Lamps, chair seats, and even the museum's banisters are adorned with cat patterns. The collection also includes more than 4,000 poems about cats.

Cats Who Went Postal: Feline Philately

Patrick Roberts has spent more than ten years pursuing cat stamps and related philatelic material. His website, purr-n-fur.org.uk, is something of an encyclopedia of the subject. We're grateful to him for supplying this list of feline philately highlights as well as the accompanying illustrations.

Prior to World War II, only one domestic cat appeared on a stamp; it came from Spain and was part of a 1930 set featuring famous aviators. It showed Lindbergh's *Spirit of Saint Louis;* in one corner, Lindy's black kitten, Patsy, is seen wistfully watching the plane fly by. Apparently Lindbergh had planned to take her on his epic transatlantic flight but thought better of it at the last minute. This is a perfect example of how background history can add to the interest of a collection.

No more cats appeared until 1952, when a stamp from the Netherlands showed a toddler playing with a kitten as part of a child-welfare set. Thereafter there was the occasional cat tucked away in the corner of a painting or a depiction of a fairy tale — cameo appearances, you could call them — but it was 1964 before a whole set of stamps devoted just to cats was issued. It came from Poland, and I still find it one of the most attractive cat sets, despite the hundreds of others that have followed.

From the mid-1960s on, cats started to appear more often on stamps, and many issues from the 1970s and 1980s include them. In the 1990s there was practically an "explosion" of cats on stamps — that is, stamps devoted to cat portraits, rather than "incidental" cats — from a wide range of countries.

Many stamps depicting cats utilize cat art, paintings being the most common.

"Black Cat," by Shunso Hisida, is a fine example of modern Japanese art. Fairy tales and children's stories are another rich source, as they often include cats. By far the best-known is Charles Perrault's "Puss in Boots," who has been given quite a number of stamp outings. But I have come across a number of other tales from diverse lands as a result of finding cats on their stamps; one such is the magnificent example of "Cat and Mice" from Mongolia.

A fair number of Christmas issues have included cats; in fact, the second U.S. stamp with a cat was the 1982 Christ-

mas issue, with a puppy in the snow (yes, we have to put up with accompanying dogs sometimes!). The first American stamp with a cat marked the 1972 centenary of the mail-order business, with a little black cat on a store counter. An amusing printing error on some examples has a shift of black ink, making it look as though the cat has two tails!

Most of the well-known cartoon cats are to be found on stamps — including Garfield, Tom (of Tom and Jerry), Pinocchio's Figaro, Disney's Black Pete, the AristoCats, and various others from foreign countries. There are also plenty of examples of children's paintings with cats; some of these are very good, while others are themselves more like cartoons. And of course many stamps were issued on behalf of animal welfare, such as the U.S. "spay or neuter" ones of 2002.

Thought I'd spin my little yarn.

"If cats could talk, they wouldn't."
— NAN PORTER

A Brief History of Cat Shows

1. The very first cat show on record took place at the **St. Giles Fair** in Winchester, England, in 1598. It took the form of a sideshow at which prizes were awarded for best ratter and best mouser.

2. The first modern-day cat show was held on July 13, 1871, at the **Crystal Palace** in Sydenham, London. Harrison Weir, the well-known author, artist, and cat enthusiast, instituted and produced the show. A total of about 160 felines were exhibited. Journalists who wrote about the show were so put off by the appearance 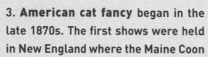 of the Siamese that they called it "a nightmare kind of a cat."

3. **American cat fancy** began in the late 1870s. The first shows were held in New England where the Maine Coon cat was quite the rage. Maine Coon owners had already been keeping pedigree records prior to this.

4. In 1887 Harrison Weir established the **National Cat Club (NCC)** and was elected its first president. Weir wrote the first breed standard descriptions. The NCC was the first organization to keep official records of ancestry. The first cat shows under the auspices of an official organization began with the NCC.

5. In 1888 a rival club called **The Cat Club (TCC)** was established. The TCC has its own studbook and registry. If you wanted to show your cat, you were forced to choose between the NCC and the TCC. You could not show your cat in both.

6. In 1895, an Englishman named James Hyde organized and ran the first formal cat show in America. It was held in **Madison Square Garden** in New York City. A Maine Coon reigned supreme at this show.

7. In 1899, two cat clubs arose in Chicago, Illinois. The **Chicago Cat Club** was founded but was soon eclipsed by the Beresford Club. The **Beresford Club** held its first show in 1900 and published the first studbook and registry in the United States. The function of the Beresford Club was eventually taken over by the **American Cat Association (ACA)**.

8. In 1906 a faction of ACA members with differing ideas and goals broke away from the association and formed a new group called the **Cat Fancier's Organization (CFO)**.

9. In 1910 officers of the NCC met with representatives of the 16 other clubs, and the **Governing Council of the Cat Fancy (GCCF)** was founded. The council was now responsible for maintaining a single cat registry and regulating all shows.

10. In 1953 the **Coronation Cat Show** was held at the Royal Horticultural Society's New Hall in Westminster. Three hundred eighty-eight cats were exhibited at that British show.

11. During America's Great Depression and World War II, interest in cat fancy was set aside but resurfaced in 1954 when the **National Cat Fanciers Association (NCFA)** was established. Over subsequent years other associations were founded, including the **American Cat Fanciers Association (ACFA)**, which would eventually become **The International Cat Association (TICA)**.

The First Cat Show

The first official cat show in Great Britain took place at the Crystal Palace in London on July 13, 1871. The following is an excerpt from the book *Our Cats and All About Them,* by Harrison Weir, first president of the English National Cat Club.

Many years ago, when thinking of the large number of cats kept in London alone, I conceived the idea that it would be well to hold "Cat Shows," so that the different breeds, colors, markings, etc., might be more carefully attended to, and the domestic cat, sitting in front of the fire, would then possess a beauty and an attractiveness to its owner unobserved and unknown because uncultivated heretofore. Prepossessed with this view of the subject, I called on my friend Mr. Wilkinson, the then manager of the Crystal Palace. With his usual businesslike clear-headedness, he saw it was "a thing to be done." In a few days I presented my scheme in full working order: the schedule of prizes, the price of entry, the number of classes, and the points by which they would be judged, the number of prizes in each class, their amount, the different varieties of color, form, size, and sex for which they were to be given; I also made a drawing of the head of a cat to be printed in black on yellow paper for a posting bill. Mr. F. Wilson, the Company's naturalist and show manager, then took the matter in charge, worked hard, got a goodly number of cats together, among which was my blue tabby, "The Old Lady," then about fourteen years old, yet the best in the show of its color and never surpassed, though lately possibly equaled.

My brother, John Jenner Weir, the Rev. J. Macdona, and myself acted as judges, and the result was a success far beyond our most sanguine expectations, so much so that I having made it a labor of love of the feline race, and acting "without fee, gratuity, or reward," the Crystal Palace Company generously presented me with a large silver tankard in token of their high approval of my exertions on behalf of "the Company," and Cats. Now that a Cat Club is formed, shows are more numerous, and the entries increasing, there is every reason to expect a permanent benefit in every way to one of the most intelligent of animals.

Cat Haikus, Part 3

We're almost equals.
I purr to show I love you.
Want to smell my butt?

The food in my bowl
Is old, and more to the point
Contains no tuna.

Seeking solitude,
I am locked in the closet.
For once I need you.

Tiny can, dumped in
Plastic bowl. Presentation,
One star; service: none.

Am I in your way?
You seem to have it backwards:
This pillow's taken.

The dog wags his tail,
Seeking approval. See mine?
Different message.

My brain: walnut-sized.
Yours: largest among primates.
Yet, who leaves for work?

My affection is
conditional. Don't stand up;
It's your lap I love.

Cats can't steal the breath
Of children. But if my tail's
Pulled again, I'll learn.

So you call this thing
Your "cat carrier." I call
These my "blades of death."

Toy mice, dancing yarn,
Meowing sounds. I'm convinced:
You're an idiot.

The Story of Poezenboot

Poezenboot ("The Cat Boat"), the only floating animal sanctuary in the Netherlands, is a refuge for stray and abandoned cats, which, thanks to its unique location on a houseboat in Amsterdam's picturesque canal belt, has become a world-famous tourist attraction.

Since 1966, the Cat Boat has evolved into a modern and professional sanctuary providing tender loving care to countless cats. It all began when Henriette va Weelde found a feline family sheltering under a tree opposite her house on Amsterdam's Herengracht canal. Henriette took them in, and before long, another stray soon joined them, then another and another. Henriette quickly became known as "the cat lady," and she was awarded with strays and unwanted cats from all over Amsterdam. Eventually they filled her home — then her garden and her roof terrace. Soon there would be no space left. But the cats kept coming. What could she do with them all? The solution was right outside Henriette's front door.

In 1968, Henriette acquired the first vessel, an old Dutch sailing barge. The interior was stripped and converted into feline-friendly accommodations. Soon the first residents moved

Feeding time on the Poezenboot.

in, and before long, the barge wasn't just bursting with cats but with loving volunteers as well.

By 1971, a second boat was purchased. Popularity soared, and in 1979, the original barge was retired and replaced with a type of Dutch houseboat known as an "ark."

Nobody back in 1966 could have dreamed that one mother cat and her kittens would begin what was now the world's most famous cat sanctuary. June 3, 1987, marked the creation of Stichting de Poezenboot — the Cat Boat Foundation, which depends on the kindness of cat lovers everywhere to keep its cats housed in an environment that meets high standards for an animal sanctuary. If you're unable to visit Poezenboot on your next trip to Amsterdam, go to www.poezenboot.nl for the next best thing. Donations are gratefully accepted.

The Poezenboot at its current home in Amsterdam.

The Musical Cat

From the sixteenth to the eighteenth century, barbaric amusements known as cat organs were popular. A cat was confined in a narrow box from which its tail protruded. The tail was then tied to the keys of an organ. When a key was pressed, the tail would be pulled, and the poor cat would yowl. Sadly, audiences found the desperate cries amusing.

"A Catch on the Midnight Cats," from 1690, is typical of a spate of songs from this period that compare tomcats to their human counterparts, reflecting on their pursuit of love.

Composer Domenico Scarlatti (1658–1757) wrote of how his cat, Pulcinella, would walk up and down the keys of his harpsichord: "Sometimes he would pause longer on one note, listening closely until the vibration ceased." The sounds inspired Scarlatti to write *The Cat's Fugue*, which recalls Pulcinella's meowing tones.

In 1758, Georges Bisset (not to be confused with Bizet) produced *A Cat's Opera*, and a number of cats participated. The composer trained them to perform in choirs that meowed and caterwauled on cue. (We prefer not to think about the nature of the cue.)

In 1816, on the opening night of Gioacchino Rossini's *The Barber of Seville*, at a particularly emotional moment a cat wandered onstage, provoking gales of laughter from the audience.

The two females heard meowing their way up and down the scales in Rossini's "Duetto Buffo dei due Gatti" ("Comic Duo for Two Cats," c. 1860) are probably the best-known classical cats.

Jenny Lind (1849–1887), despondent over her lack of success, spent hours sitting near a window singing to her cat, and she was finally discovered while doing so.

Tchaikovsky's *The Sleeping Beauty* is probably the most famous ballet to honor the cat. It premiered in 1890 and features the characters Puss in Boots and the White Cat dancing with feline moves as the orchestra provides music that "meows and spits."

One of the most popular cat songs of all time, "The Cat Came Back," was first published in 1893 and over time evolved into versions fit for various occasions. The first verse inevitably speaks of the demise of the human race or some other calamity:

The atom bomb fell just the other day.
The H-bomb fell in the very same way.
Russia went, England went, and then the U.S.A.,
The human race was finished without a chance to pray.

Then the rousing refrain lifts the song to its humorous height:

The cat came back, couldn't stay no longer,
Yes, the cat came back the very next day.
The cat came back, thought he was a goner,
But the cat came back for it wouldn't stay away.

Cats figure prominently in jazz, not only in that the culture went so far as to adopt the word "cat" to mean "man," but the genre has produced many songs inspired by the movement of the cat. Zez Confrey's "Kitten on the Keys," from 1921, is one of the best-known classics.

The role of cats is played by woodwinds in Prokofiev's *Peter and the Wolf*, which was written in just two weeks in 1936.

Andrew Lloyd Webber has the distinction of writing the longest-running Broadway musical to date, *Cats*, which premiered in 1981. It is based on T. S. Eliot's 1939 classic, *Old Possum's Book of Practical Cats*. (See "The Major Cats of *Cats*," page 106.)

A concert at Alice Tully Hall in New York City featured a full orchestra, two singers, and six soloists — all cats. They "sang" their little hearts out in the hopes of winning

4 Musical Instruments **That Sound Like Cats**

Cats haven't just influenced music; they even inspired some musical instruments.

1. **Javanese saron**: This bronze chime makes meowing sounds.

2. **Musical saw**: An ordinary saw can be played by bending the blade at varying tensions and sounding it with a violin bow. Its screeching "music" sounds just like yowls from a cat.

3. **Samisen**: This three-string Japanese type of guitar was popular among street performers and geishas.

The infamous "cat organ," which relied on the cries of tormented cats to produce "music."

4. **Sistrum**: This ancient Egyptian percussion instrument consists of a thin metal frame with rods or loops that jingle when shaken. The goddess Bastet is often depicted holding a sistrum.

The catgut formerly used as strings in tennis rackets and musical instruments does not come from cats. Catgut actually comes from the intestines of sheep, hogs, and horses.

the Ralston Purina Company's "Magical Musical Meow-Off." An orange part-Persian named Pumpkin won the $25,000 first prize and got to appear in a cat food commercial, and a cat named Spike won $5,000 for being runner-up. Ralston Purina also donated 20 tons of Meow Mix to homeless cats. The program was attended almost entirely by specially invited children, and the music consisted of a 45-minute cantata entitled "The Meow That Saved the Kingdom," which told of a cat kingdom under a spell that could be broken only by the most musical of meows.

The high point of Edward "Zez" Confrey's career was the fast-paced "Kitten on the Keys," published in 1921. The lyrics that were added in 1922 proclaimed, "Anybody listenin' can't help whistlin' 'Kitten on the Keys.'"

9 Popular Songs About Cats

Most songs with the word *cat* in the title are not about cats at all. These, however, were written with real cats in mind.

1. "I Tawt I Taw a Puddy Tat," 1950
The song, written by Alan Livingston, Billy May, and Warren Foster, is about the cartoon cat and canary duo Sylvester and Tweety. It was performed by the legendary cartoon voiceover artist Mel Blanc.

2. "The Siamese Cat Song," 1955
This song, recorded by Peggy Lee for the Walt Disney film *Lady and the Tramp* in 1955, is about the adventures of two cats, Si and Am, who state they are Siamese "if you please" or "if you don't please." Written by Peggy Lee with Sonny Burke, it has been covered by artists as diverse as Bobby McFerrin, Freddie and the Dreamers, and Mitch Miller.

3. "Tom Cat," 1963
This song about a cat who loved to strut around town was The Rooftop Singers' follow-up to their 1963 number-one hit "Walk Right In." In this ditty, when Ringtail "Tom" goes out, "all the others cats in the neighborhood they begin to shout."

4. "Walking My Cat Named Dog," 1966
Norma Tanega had a hit record with this song. She actually had a cat named Dog that she used to love taking for walks around the neighborhood.

5. "The Cat in the Window," 1967
Both Petula Clark and the Turtles recorded this song, in which the singer sympathizes with a cat watching a bird: "He'd love to fly out the window . . . and so would I."

6. "The Cat Came Back," 1976
The Muppets recorded this classic song about a kitty that refuses to get lost, no matter how far it is taken from home. "But the cat came back, she wouldn't stay away, she was sitting on the porch the very next day."

7. "Stray Cat Strut," 1981
This song by rockabilly band Stray Cats is about a feline gigolo, "a ladies' cat" who likes to strut his stuff.

8. "Smelly Cat," 1995
This hilarious song was performed by Phoebe Buffay, the character portrayed by Lisa Kudrow on the TV show *Friends.* The song was one of the mainstays of her act at the Central Perk coffee shop.

9. "Brownie the Cat," 2001
This song, recorded by the Japanese rock band Brilliant Green, is a lighthearted ode to cats: "You took me inside your dream to a moon of cheese and cream."

"Whether they be the musician cats in my band or the real cats of the world, they all got style."

— RAY CHARLES

84 Songs About Cats

"Alaska Cats" — Garrison Keillor and Frederica von Stade (1991)

"The Alley Cat" — Bent Fabric (instrumental) (1962)

"Alley Katz" — Hall & Oates (1978)

"Bear Cat" — Rufus Thomas (1953)

"Big Electric Cat" — Adrian Belew (1982)

"Black Cat" — Janet Jackson (1989)

"Black Cat Blues" — John Lee Hooker (1948)

"Black Cat Blues" — Memphis Minnie (1930s)

"Black Cat Bone" — Roy Rogers (1989)

"Black Cat Moan" — Beck, Bogert & Appice (1973)

"Black Cat Shuffle" — Al DiMeola (1981)

"Can Your Pussy Do the Dog?" — The Cramps (1986)

"The Cat" — Jimmy Smith (1962)

"The Cat Came Back" — trad. children's song (1893)

"Cat Fever" — Little Feat (1972)

"Cat Food" — King Crimson (1970)

"Cat in the Hat" — Little Benny and the Masters (1987)

"The Cat in the Window (The Bird in the Sky)" — Petula Clark (1967)

"Cat Man" — Gene Vincent (1957)

"Catmelody" — Pete Townshend and Ronnie Lane (1977)

"Cat People (Putting Out Fire)" — David Bowie (1982)

"Cat Scratch Fever" — Ted Nugent (1977)

"Cat's in the Cradle" — Harry Chapin (1974)

"Cat's in the Cupboard" — Pete Townshend (1980)

"Cat's in the Well" — Bob Dylan (1990)

"The Cat Song" — Laura Nyro (1976)

"Cats Under the Stars" — Jerry Garcia (1978)

"Catwalk" — Art of Noise (1989)

"China Cat Sunflower" — Grateful Dead (1969)

"Cleopatra's Cat" — Spin Doctors (1994)

A vintage postcard from the Alfred Mainzer Company.

"Cool Cat" — Queen (1982)

"Cool for Cats" — Squeeze (1979)

"Crosseyed Cat" — Muddy Waters (1977)

"Curiosity Killed the Cat" — Curiosity Killed the Cat (1987)

"Dead Cat" — Shellyan Orphan (1991)

"Dead Cat Alley" — Dirty White Boy (1990)

"Dead Cat on the Line" — Lucky Peterson (1989)

"Everybody Wants to Be a Cat" — Phil Harris (1996)

"Fat Cat" — Bootsy Collins (1980)

"Fat Cat Keeps Getting Fatter" — Squirrel Nut Zippers (1998)

"Feline" — Bobby McFerrin (1982)

"Hell Cat" — Scorpions (1976)

"Honky Cat" — Elton John (1972)

"How to Skin a Cat" — Hüsker Dü (1985)

"I Am a Cat" — Shonen Knife (1993)

"I Tawt I Taw a Puddy Tat" — Mel Blanc (1950)

"I've Lost That Lovin' Feline" — Third Eye Foundation (2000)

"Kitten on the Keys" — Claude Bolling (1966)

"Kitty Cat Song" — Lee Dorsey (1966)

"Leave My Kitten Alone" — Little Willie John (1959)

"Litter Box" — Meat Puppets (1982)

"Maltese Cat Blues" — Blind Lemon Jefferson (1928)

"Mean-Eyed Cat" — Johnny Cash (1950s)

"My Cat Fell in the Well (Well! Well! Well!)" — Manhattan Transfer (1984)

"My Cat's Name Is Maceo" — Jane's Addiction (1997)

"Nashville Cats" — Lovin' Spoonful (1967)

"Nyot Nyow! (The Pussycat Song)" — Jo Stafford and Gordon Macrae (1948)

"Pads, Paws, and Claws" — Elvis Costello (1989)

"Pattin' That Cat" — Bill Hinckley with Judy Larson (1994)

"Phenomenal Cat" — The Kinks (1968)

"Pink-Eyed Pussycat" — Billy Haley and the Comets (1970)

"Pink Pussycat" — Devo (1979)

"Pussy Cat Blues" — Big Bill Broonzy (1930s)

"Pussycat Meow" — Dee-Lite (1992)

"Pussycat Moan" — Katie Webster (1990)

"Put Your Cat Clothes On" — Carl Perkins (1957)

"The Siamese Cat Song" — Peggy Lee (1955)

"Stray Cat Blues" — Rolling Stones (1968)

"Stray Cat Strut" — Stray Cats (1981)

"Sweetest Kittens (Have the Sharpest Claws)" — Meatmen (1986)

"Thanks to the Cat House" — Johnny Paycheck (1979)

"That Cat Is High" — Manhattan Transfer (1975)

"This Black Cat Has 9 Lives" — Louis Armstrong (1970)

"Three Cool Cats" — The Coasters (1959)

"Tom Cat" — Rooftop Singers (1963)

"Tom Cat Blues" — Jelly Roll Morton (1923)

"Two Old Cats Like Us" — Ray Charles (1984)

"Walking My Cat Named Dog" — Norma Tanega (1966)

"What's New Pussycat?" — Tom Jones (1967)

"Wholly Cats" — Charlie Christian (1939)

"Wild as a Wildcat" — Charlie Walker (1965)

"Wild Cats of Kilkenny" — The Pogues (1985)

"Year of the Cat" — Al Stewart (1976)

"Yellow Cat" — John Denver (1969)

Bands and Artists with Cat Names

Black Cats

Black Cat Bones

Catatonia

A Cat Born in an Oven Isn't a Cake

Cat Butt

Cat Mother and the All-Night News Boys

Cat Power

Cat Rapes Dog

Cat Stevens

Curiosity Killed the Cat

Faster Pussycat

Harry Pussy

Hepcat

Jason's Cat Died

Josie and the Pussy Cats

Lip Smacking Kitten Lunch

Nervous Christians and the Lions

Octapussy

Oedipussy

Power of Pussy

Procol Harum*

Pussycat

Pussycat Dolls

Pussy Crush

Pussy Galore

Stray Cats

* THE NAME OF A SIAMESE CAT BELONGING TO A FRIEND OF THE BAND, KEITH REID.

5 CDs Just for Cats

There's been a recent spate of CDs specifically created and engineered to keep kitties calm and happy. Those listed here are available at amazon.com, except as noted.

1. *Songs of the Cat*, 2005
This album, featuring Garrison Keillor, German opera superstar Frederica von Stade, and noted conductor Philip Brunelle, contains sixteen songs honoring our feline friends. Titles include "My Grandmother's Cat," "Cat O Cat Come Home," "Cats May Safely Sleep," and, "Cat, You Better Come Home."

2. *Irish Drinking Songs for Cat Lovers*, 2005
Recorded by Marc Gunn & The Dubliners' Tabby Cats, this collection of parodies includes "A Cat Named Rover," "When Kitty Eyes Are Smiling," "Lord of the Pounce," and "The Demented Cat Game," a parody of the "Patriot Game." If you love cats and Celts alike — and who doesn't? — this is the record for you.

3. *Cat-A-Tonic*, 2003
Dedicated to creating original music inspired by the relationship between animals and their people, this is the cat edition of a line of CDs released by Laurel Canyon Animal Company. You don't need four paws to enjoy "Felinicity," "Cat Thinks He's a Dog," and "It's All About Me-ow."

The sound of the note E of the fourth octave on a piano can stimulate some cats into sexual activity. The same sound can affect some kittens that have not yet reached puberty: they'll defecate.

4. *Meowy Christmas*, by the Jingle Cats, 1994
Cheese Puff, Max, Sprocket, Binky, Clara, Cueball, Graymer, Twizzler, Petunia — and the occasional dog — meow and bark and let their animal nature sing 20 (count 'em, 20!) holiday favorites. You'll be awestruck, dumbstruck, and struck yet again hearing these felines "sing" and, ah, scat their way through the usual roundup of holiday music, relying on a beat box and different arrangements, including a folkish, harmonica-driven version of a hymn by Handel.

5. *Pet Melodies*, 2004
This CD contains classical music, nature sounds, and biorhythms to relieve stress, promote mental stimulation, and reduce separation anxiety.

Cats hear three times better than dogs do. In households where the volume is cranked up — especially on metallic rock music — it is little wonder that cats will flee the scene in search of a quieter place in the house. Animal behaviorists report that cats tend to like rhythmic music played at low or moderate volume.

35 Famous Cat Lovers

What have you done for a cat lately? These famous ailurophiles have all contributed to the welfare of cats in one way or another, by influencing public attitudes toward them, by preserving their heritage, and, most simply, by loving them. We're grateful to Glenda Moore for her help in assembling this list.

1. Cleveland Amory (1917–1998) This author devoted his life to promoting animal rights. He was best known for his books about his cat Polar Bear, whom he rescued from New York streets on Christmas Eve, 1977. Amory cofounded the Humane Society of the United States and established the Fund for Animals. He was also the president of NEAVS (New England Anti Vivisection Society) from 1987 to 1998.

2. Pope Benedict XVI (b. 1927) The present head of the Roman Catholic Church and sovereign of Vatican City has a black-and-white domestic shorthair named Chico. Chico continues to live at the pope's home in Tübingen, Germany (due to a recent change in policy, pets are not allowed in the Vatican). Cardinal Roger Mahony, archbishop of Los Angeles, who was in Rome for the pope's installation, says, "The street talk that the pope loves cats is incorrect. The pope *adores* cats."

3. William S. Burroughs (1914–1997) The author lived with several cats, who became significant in his personal mythology and were watched over by friends and protégés. He wrote *Naked Lunch* and *The Cat Inside*, among many other books.

4. Amy Carter (b. 1967) The daughter of former U.S. president Jimmy Carter has owned several cats, including a Siamese cat with the peculiar name Misty Malarky Ying Yang, who lived with her in the White House.

5. Raymond Chandler (1888–1959) The author of the Philip Marlowe private-eye novels talked to his black Persian, Taki, as though she were human and called her his secretary because she sat on his manuscripts as he tried to revise them. He stated, "A cat never behaves as if you were the only bright spot in an otherwise clouded existence . . . this is another way of saying that a cat is not a sentimentalist, which does not mean that it has no affection."

6. Sir Winston Churchill (1874–1965) The legendary British politician and prime minister during World War II owned several cats. Churchill's marmalade cat, Jock, slept with him, shared his dining table, and attended numerous wartime Cabinet meetings. If Jock was late for a meal, Churchill would send servants to find him, waiting to eat until the cat was present. Jock was said to be present when his master died. Churchill had another cat, Nelson, named after the famous British admiral Lord Nelson.

His other cats were named Margate and Tango (AKA Mr. Cat).

7. Jean Maurice Eugène Clément Cocteau (1889–1963) The French poet, novelist, dramatist, designer, boxing manager, and filmmaker is perhaps best known for his 1946 film *Beauty and the Beast.* His famous quotes include: "I love cats because I enjoy my home; and little by little, they become its visible soul" and "A meow massages the heart." He dedicated *Drôle de ménage* to his cat Karoun, whom he described as "the king of cats."

8. James Dean (1931–1955) During the filming of *Giant,* Elizabeth Taylor presented Dean with a Siamese kitten, whom he named Marcus. Dean fed it only a special diet that Taylor had developed for all of her cats. We can't recommend this unbalanced regimen, but the recipe was as follows:

> 1 teaspoon white Karo syrup
> 1 large can evaporated milk
> 1 egg yolk
> Equal parts boiled or distilled water
> *Combine and chill.*

9. Charles Dickens (1812–1870) Dickens was the author of works such as *Oliver Twist, Nicholas Nick-*

leby, *David Copperfield,* and *A Christmas Carol.* Dickens's cat, Willamena, produced a litter of kittens in his study. Dickens was determined not to keep the kittens, but he fell in love with one female kitten who was known as Master's Cat. She kept him company in his study as he wrote, and when she wanted his attention, she was known to snuff out his reading candle.

10. **Alexandre Dumas (1802–1870)** The author of *The Three Musketeers* and *The Count of Monte Cristo,* Dumas owned a cat called Mysouff I. This cat was known for his extrasensory perception of time. Mysouff was in the habit of accompanying his master on his way to a certain spot each morning on Dumas's way to work and meeting him at that same spot when Dumas returned home in the evening. Oddly, when Dumas came home late from work, Mysouff would skip his afternoon stroll. Dumas had two other cats, Mysouff II and Le Docteur. Mysouff II was black and white and Dumas's favorite, even though it once ate all his exotic birds.

11. **El Dahar Beybars (thirteenth century)** The great Muslim warrior El Dahar Beybars, sultan of Egypt and Syria in the thirteenth century, is said to have bequeathed a vast garden, which he named Gheyt al Quottah ("The Cat's Orchard"), for the protection of stray cats. The orchard eventually fell into ruin, but the tradition of feeding strays remained strong in the area for centuries thereafter.

12. **T. S. Eliot (1888–1965)** The Nobel Prize–winning British poet and playwright was a cat lover and wrote an entire book of poems about this animal. His *Old Possum's Book of Practical Cats* was set to music by Andrew Lloyd Webber and became the long-running musical on Broadway, *Cats.* His own cats included Noilly Prat, Pattipaws, Pushdragon, Tantomile, and Wiscus.

13. **Robert Goulet (b. 1933)** A recording artist and star of stage, screen, and television, Goulet has loved cats since childhood. When he toured the country as King Arthur in Lerner and Loewe's musical *Camelot,* he took along two of his cats, Vincent and Wart. The cat count in Goulet's Las Vegas home has been known to reach as many as seven.

14. **Rutherford B. Hayes (1822–1893)** U.S. president from 1877 to 1881, Hayes received as a gift the first Siamese cat ever brought to the United States. He named his cat Siam.

15. **Ernest Hemingway (1899–1961)** Hemingway, whose classic works of literature include *For Whom the Bell Tolls, The Sun Also Rises,* and *The Old Man and the Sea,* shared his Key West home with more than 30 cats. Hemingway once said, "A cat has absolute emotional honesty; human beings, for one reason or another, may hide their feelings, but a cat does not." (See page 112 for more about Hemingway's cats and their descendants.)

16. **Victor Hugo (1802–1885)** Hugo is considered one of the greatest authors in the history of French literature, one notable book being *Les Misérables.* He wrote fondly in his diary about his cats Mouche and Gavroche, the latter eventually renamed Chanoine ("the canon," a member of the clergy) because he was so indolent.

17. **Dr. Samuel Johnson (1709–1784)** The great English man of letters had a generous heart, a kind spirit, and a pet cat named Hodge to whom he fed oysters and other extravagant treats. Johnson would go to town himself to buy oysters for his beloved cat, who was immortalized in John Boswell's *Life of Johnson* (1799) and also the subject of a bronze statue that stands outside Number 17 Gough Square in London, where Hodge lived with his owner.

18. **Robert E. Lee (1807–1870)** The Civil War Confederate general had several cats that he referred to often in letters to his family: "I am very solitary and my only company is my dog and cats. Spec [a dog] has become so jealous now that he will hardly let me look at the cats." He chose cats to share his tent at Camp Cooper, Texas, partly for mousing and partly for company.

19. Pope Leo XII (1760–1829) Head of the Roman Catholic Church and sovereign of Vatican City, Pope Leo owned a grayish red cat with black stripes called Micette, who was born in the Vatican and lived with the pope. Reportedly, the pope occasionally gave audiences with the cat hidden on his lap, under his robes. Similarly, an earlier religious figure, Saint Gregory the Great (540–604), possessed no worldly goods except a cat, which he held and stroked while meditating.

20. Marilyn Monroe (1926–1962) The often lonely star had at least one friend in Hollywood, a Persian cat named Mitsou. Monroe found that it wasn't easy being a famous cat-mom. She confessed, referring to the time she had to call a vet, "They think I'm kidding when I say, 'This is Marilyn Monroe. My cat's having kittens.' They think I'm some kind of nut and hang up."

21. Muhammad, prophet (570–632) The founder of the Muslim faith loved cats. The story is told that one day when he was being called to pray, he noticed his cat, Muezza, sleeping on the folds of his sleeve. Rather than disturb the sleeping cat, Muhammad cut off the sleeve of his robe. They say that cats are often seen near the place where the prophet was laid to rest.

22. Sir Isaac Newton (1643–1727) The famed scientist and philosopher invented the cat flap (a small door), most likely so he wouldn't be disturbed by his cats' comings and goings.

23. Florence Nightingale (1820–1910) This famed nurse and humanitarian had a large Persian named Bismarck. She owned more than 60 cats over the course of her lifetime and named each one after a famous person. Her brood included Disraeli, Gladstone, and Bismarck.

24. Francesco Petrarch (1304–1374) The Italian scholar, poet, and humanist was said to have been even more devoted to his cat than to the memory of his great love, Laura. When the poet died, his cat was put to death and mummified.

25. Edgar Allan Poe (1809–1849) The famed author used cats as symbols of the sinister in several of his stories, although he himself owned and loved cats. He used his tortoiseshell cat Catarina as the inspiration for his story "The Black Cat." This feline sometimes sat on the author's shoulder as he wrote. In winter 1846, Catarina would curl up on the bed with Poe's wife, who was dying of tuberculosis, and provide warmth.

26. Saint Ives (1253–1303) The patron saint of lawyers believed that his cat brought him inner peace and serenity. In portraits, he is often seen standing near cats, and in some he is actually depicted as a cat.

In 1982, a well-known veterinarian named Louis Camuti reported the case of an elderly widow who wanted her cat to be buried with her. So when he passed on, she had the body placed in a casket and sent to a pet cemetery where it would lie until her own death. In the meantime, she discovered that her plan violated state health laws; it was not permissible to have the cat placed in her coffin. The woman would not be deterred, however. She asked Dr. Camuti to cremate the cat, whose ashes she then sewed into the hem of her wedding dress, the gown in which she planned to be buried.

27. Albert Schweitzer (1875–1965) The German theologian, musician, philosopher, and physician prized his cats. He rescued a kitten after he heard her plaintive "meow" beneath the floor of a building under construction. Named Sizi, she sat on his desk as he wrote, often falling asleep on his left arm — at such times Dr. Schweitzer, who was left-handed, wrote prescriptions with his right hand. This went on for 23 years. Another cat, Piccolo, slept on papers stacked on Dr. Schweitzer's desk; if someone needed the papers, they were required to wait till the cat awoke. Schweitzer once said, "There are two means of refuge from the miseries of life: music and cats."

28. Sir Walter Scott (1771–1832) The poet and author whose works include *Rob Roy* and *Ivanhoe* was devoted to cats, and a portrait of him by John Watson Gordon shows him at work at his desk with his tabby, Hinx, lying close by. This tomcat was known to terrorize Scott's dogs. Scott wrote, "Cats are a mysterious kind of folk. There is more passing in their minds than we are aware of."

29. Théophile Steinlen (1859–1923) The Swiss artist loved cats, and his Paris home was known as "Cats' Corner." In addition to paintings and drawings, he also did a small amount of sculpture, most notably figures of cats, which are also seen in many of his paintings.

30. Harriet Beecher Stowe (1811–1896) The author of *Uncle Tom's Cabin* had a large Maltese cat called Calvin; her husband was also named Calvin. Calvin (the cat) arrived on Harriet's doorstep one day, moved in, and took over the household. Stowe enjoyed his company, and Calvin (the cat) often sat on her shoulder as she wrote.

31. Mark Twain (Samuel Clemens) (1835–1910) The American humorist, author, and lecturer kept 11 cats at his farm in Connecticut. He wrote, "I simply can't resist a cat, particularly a purring one. They are the cleanest, cunningest, and most intelligent things I know, outside of the girl you love, of course." He also quipped, "If you hold a cat by the tail you learn things you cannot learn any other way" and "The cat, having sat upon a hot stove lid, will not sit upon a hot stove lid again. But he won't sit upon a cold stove lid, either."

32. Queen Victoria (1819–1901) Given the long widowhood of the Queen Empress, it's no surprise that she was extremely fond of cats. Her 64-year reign saw an explosion in the popularity of cats. Books and stories about them appeared frequently, and in typical Victorian style, they were sentimentalized, usually depicted in sweet, playful poses.

33. H. G. Wells (1866–1946) The English journalist and author of *The Time Machine* (1895) and *War of the Worlds* (1989) was devoted to his cat, Mr. Peter Wells, who was known to get up and ostentatiously make for the door if one of Wells's guests spoke too long or too loudly.

34. William Wordsworth (1770–1850) This poet wrote the poems "The Kitten and Falling Leaves" and "Loving and Liking," both of which concern felines.

35. John Barrymore (1882–1942) The actor became an avid and eccentric animal collector in his senior years. He owned numerous birds and dogs, a monkey, a mouse deer, and dozens of Siamese cats.

---

from ' Loving and Liking '

Long may you love your pensioner mouse,
Though one of a tribe that torment the house:
Nor dislike for her cruel sport the cat,
Deadly foe both of mouse and rat;
Remember she follows the law of her kind,
And Instinct is neither wayward nor blind.
Then think of her beautiful gliding form,
Her tread that would scarcely crush a worm,
And her soothing song by the winter fire,
Soft as the dying throb of the lyre.

— William Wordsworth

2 Theories as to Why There Is No Chinese Year of the Cat

The Chinese zodiac has 12 signs. Each of the 12 earthly branches came to be designated by an animal sign: rat, ox, tiger, rabbit, dragon, snake, horse, sheep, monkey, rooster, dog, and boar. How did the cat lose out? Here are two possible theories.

Theory 1

A Chinese folktale holds that centuries ago, Buddha called all animals together to designate each of them a year. When the cat heard this proclamation, he let his friend the rat know about it and the two planned to arrive together. But the rat neglected to wake the napping cat in time for the journey, and the cat never made it to the ceremony. Chinese legend cites this as the source of the cat's animosity toward the rat. A variation of this theory suggests that the rat lied about the date of this meeting and tricked the cat into arriving on the wrong day.

> "The problem with cats is that they get the same exact look whether they see a moth or an axe murderer."
> — PAULA POUNDSTONE

The Chinese symbol for the cat.

Theory 2

When the animals appeared before Buddha, they were given a challenge. Each was to cross a river, and the order in which they arrived on the opposite shore would determine the year that each of them would be assigned. The cat, being afraid of water, did not know how it would get across. An ox was also fearful of making the cross because of its poor eyesight. The rat suggested that the cat jump onto the ox's back and guide him across. The rat then sneaked up behind the unsuspecting cat and pushed him into the water. The cat finished so far behind that he was never given a position on the Chinese calendar, and he's hated the rat ever since.

9 Cat Hoarders

Cat hoarding, as animal-control professionals refer to it, is a strange psychological phenomenon that primarily besets single, post-middle-age women. Hoarders begin with the idea of giving a home to a stray and soon become overwhelmed by the number of cats they have accumulated. Unable to care for them all, hoarders often lose sight of the unhealthful environment they have created. The hoarder sees her cats as members of her family, and she is deeply connected to them emotionally. Here are the stories of some of the most notorious hoarders.

1. In July 2005, **487** cats were seized at the Virginia home of 82-year-old Ruth Knueven. Law enforcement officials reported that **120** cats had been discovered there four years before, but Ms. Knueven just kept on collecting more.

2. In April 2003, Boston officials discovered **60** feline cadavers in the Beacon Hill apartment of Heidi Erickson. At the time of the investigation, Ms. Erickson, who claimed to be a part-time breeder of Persians, lived with **5** cats and a Great Dane, all malnourished. The Boston Housing Court barred her from ever owning another cat. It was later discovered that Ms. Erickson had rented a second apartment in a neighboring city, where she accumulated an additional **52** sick and malnourished cats.

3. In 2006, police in Omaha, Nebraska, were on the trail of a suspect when they were overpowered by the odor emanating from a home nearby. When they investigated, they found **270** cats in the house. **Fifty-eight** had died and were stored in a freezer. Ironically, the woman who owned the home was licensed to operate a cattery. She was eventually charged with animal cruelty.

4. In 2002, in Cooper City, Florida, a woman was charged with 92 counts of animal neglect when police entered her home after neighbors complained of a horrendous odor. Police discovered **32** kittens and **36** cats in her freezer. The woman, who once worked as an animal control officer,

The homeowner had a refrigerator magnet that said it all: "Cats are like potato chips — it's hard to have just one."

had **24** living cats. Neighbors described her as a kind woman and well-intentioned, but unfortunately she made it a habit of taking in any kind of stray, including a 12-foot python.

5. In 2001, almost **400** dead cats were found in a freezer in the Piedmont, California, home of a married couple who provided only one litter box for a huge brood of living cats, all of which had upper-respiratory infections and suffered from leukemia. Only **6** could be saved. Surprisingly, psychological tests were conducted on the couple, and they were declared competent.

6. In 2001, in East Orange, New Jersey, **200** dead cats were discovered in garbage bags in the backyard of a woman who owned and operated one of the few no-kill shelters in the New York metropolitan area. The shelter was called Kitty Kind.

7. On May 23, 2001, Marilyn Barletta, a wealthy San Francisco woman who bought a Petaluma home exclusively to house her cats, was arrested after city animal services officials discov-

ered more than **170** cats living there in squalid conditions. Ms. Barletta *did* furnish the cats with ample feeding dishes, toys, and scratching posts, but she visited the cats only once a day. None of the cats had been spayed or neutered, and the population in the house soon spiraled out of control. It took officials over two days to round up all the cats.

8. At least **62** cats were removed from the Matteson, Illinois, home of an unnamed man. Cat food, litter, and waste covered every square inch of the home, and the animals had burrowed into the walls and ceiling.

A bone yard of decayed cats covered the lawn behind the property. The homeowner had a refrigerator magnet that said it all: "Cats are like potato chips — it's hard to have just one."

9. In 2005, a woman from Omaha, Nebraska, appeared on *Oprah* and talked about her bizarre attachment to her cats, who numbered an astounding **81**. She began hoarding cats ten years earlier while she was a single mother, and cats helped her fill a void in her life. She admitted that the cats — and her six dogs — were taking over her life.

10 Signs That You Are Turning into a "Cat Lady"

1. Realizing that it's a hopeless cause, people at work have stopped offering you lint brushes.

2. The framed photos in your house depict only the four-legged members of your family.

3. There are litter boxes in every room of your house.

4. You have been known to suffer through six hours of boring infomercials rather than disturb the cat sleeping on the remote.

5. Your opinion of your friends is influenced by how well your cats like them.

6. You introduce your cats by name to the pizza delivery guy.

7. On your last census questionnaire, you lied about how many cats you really own.

8. You buy clothing and furniture in the exact shade of your cat's coat.

9. You're starting to wonder what the chicken feast with bacon bits really tastes like.

10. You wouldn't even *dream* of requesting a *doggie* bag.

14 Famous Cat Haters

They're ailurophobics — people who suffer from an irrational fear of cats. Genghis Khan, Alexander the Great, Julius Caesar, Benito Mussolini, and Adolf Hitler were all ailurophobic, not because, as some have guessed, their dreams of dominating the world were challenged by the aloofness of cats, who cannot be controlled; more likely, they experienced traumatic experiences involving cats when they were small children, as is the case with most ailurophobics. The cure for ailurophobia involves familiarization exercises that work gradually to reduce the intensity of the phobia until the victim can overcome it entirely. For more information on overcoming this and other phobias, visit healthkc.net/articles/fear/Are_You_Afraid.php.

1. **Alexander the Great (356–323 B.C.)** He is said to have swooned at the sight of a cat.

2. **Johannes Brahms (1833–1897)** The composer took great delight at shooting neighborhood cats with a bow and arrow as he sat at the window of his Vienna home.

3. **Napoleon Bonaparte (1769–1821)** Napoleon was once found sweating with fear and lunging about wildly with his sword, which he aimed at the tapestry-covered walls. The source of his fear was a small kitten. Once Fluffy was removed from the room, the emperor was able to get back to the business of leading a country at war.

4. **Noah Webster (1758–1843)** He once described the cat as a "deceitful animal and when enraged, extremely spiteful."

5. **Dwight D. Eisenhower (1890–1969)** This former U.S. president hated cats so much that he gave his staff orders to shoot any seen on the grounds of his home.

6. **Henri III of France (1551–1589)** Henri was as bold as a lion when persecuting the Protestant minority in France, but the presence of a cat turned him into a chicken. He would faint if a cat came near him. He was responsible for the death of 30,000 cats during his reign.

7. **Georges Louis Leclerc de Buffon (1707–1788)** The French naturalist claimed that cats possess "an innate malice and perverse disposition which increases as they grow up."

8. **Wu-Chao, Empress of China (625–705)** A lady-in-waiting condemned to death by Wu-Chao put a curse on the empress. She swore that the ruler would become a rat in the afterlife and the lady-in-waiting would become a cat and hunt the empress down. For the rest of her life Wu-Chao feared cats.

9. **Pope Gregory IX (1143–1241)** It was during Gregory's rule that Christians began persecuting cats. The destruction of so-called "diabolical" cats was carried out on a massive scale for five centuries. During this time millions of cats were tortured and burned. These sadistic practices were continued under the auspices of Pope Innocent VII, Pope Innocent III, and a monarch as well, Elizabeth I of England.

10. **William Shakespeare (1564–1616)** The bard's references to cats were always negative in nature. (See "Shakespeare on Cats," page 42.)

11. **King Louis XIV of France (1638–1715)** When the monarch was only 10 years old, he ordered hundreds of cats to be burned alive and literally danced around the flames as the cats were screaming.

> ## "A cat can look at a king, but a dictator can seldom bear that look."
> — PROVERB

12. Isadora Duncan (1878–1927)
The famous dancer/choreographer lived next door to a cat sanctuary. The cats that invaded her property were sometimes hunted, captured, and hanged.

13. Rockwell Sayre (1885–1930)
The Chicago banker was known as the worst cat hater of them all. He felt that cats were "filthy and useless," and his goal in life was to see to it that cats throughout the world were destroyed. In the early 1920s he began offering rewards to cat killers in the hope of ridding the world of cats by 1925. The plan didn't work, so he extended the campaign by ten years but died before the term was up.

14. Ivan the Terrible (1530–1584)
Terrible even as a child, this Russian ruler was known to throw cats and other animals out of high windows in the palace, simply to amuse himself.

16 Definitions of the Word <u>Cat</u>

1. A small carnivorous mammal (*Felis catus* or *F. domesticus*) domesticated since early times as a catcher of rats and mice and as a pet and existing in several distinctive breeds and varieties.

2. Any of various other carnivorous mammals of the family Felidae, which includes the lion, tiger, leopard, and lynx.

3. The fur of a domestic cat.

4. A woman who is regarded as spiteful.

5. A person, especially a man.

6. A player or devotee of jazz music.

7. A strong tackle used to hoist an anchor to the cathead of a ship.

8. A low movable defensive structure used in medieval warfare as a means of approaching fortifications.

9. The tapered peg used in the game of tipcat.

10. A seagoing ship with a narrow stern.

11. A double tripod that rests on three of its legs, usually as a stand near or over an open fireplace.

12. Part of the first coat of plaster going between strips of wood that form a lattice.

13. The heraldic representation of a European wildcat or a domestic cat.

14. To flog with a cat-o-nine-tails.

15. To vomit.

16. To search for a sexual mate.

21 Weird Laws About Cats

1. In Sterling, Colorado, it is unlawful to allow a cat to run loose at night without wearing a taillight.

2. In Cresskill, New Jersey, cats must wear three bells on their collar to warn birds of their whereabouts.

3. In Barber, North Carolina, cats and dogs are not allowed to fight.

4. In Zion, Illinois, it is illegal for anyone to give lighted cigars to cats, dogs, or other domestic pets.

5. In Ventura County, California, cats and dogs are not allowed to mate unless owners obtain a breeding permit from the county courthouse.

6. In Tennessee, it is illegal to use a lasso to catch a fish — take heed, all you cowboy cats!

7. In French Lick Springs, Indiana, officials once passed a law requiring all black cats to wear bells on Friday the 13th.

8. In Baltimore, Maryland, it is illegal to take a lion to the movies. (Guess you will have to rent *The Lion King* for your big tabby!)

9. In Korea, the eating of stray cats is illegal.

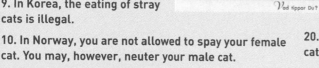

Vad tippar Du?

10. In Norway, you are not allowed to spay your female cat. You may, however, neuter your male cat.

11. In Reed City, Michigan, it is against the law to own both a cat and a bird.

12. In Natchez, Mississippi, cats may not drink beer.

13. In California, the law specifies prison penalties for kicking or injuring another person's cat. The bill was signed by Governor Ronald Reagan in 1973.

14. Cats can only be taken on to the street on leads in Lorinc, Hungary. Officials say the measure will protect the public from the "dangerous menace of free-range cats."

15. Joint custody of a family pet, including cats, is not allowed when a couple divorces in Madison, Wisconsin. The feline is legally awarded to whichever party happens to possess it at the time of the initial separation.

16. Cats in International Falls, Minnesota, are not allowed to chase dogs up telephone poles.

17. Cats are not allowed to sleep in bakeries in Duluth, Minnesota.

18. California bans cats from mating publicly within 1,500 feet of a tavern, school, or place of worship.

19. Cats may not yowl after 9 P.M. in Columbus, Georgia.

20. In Topeka, Kansas, you may not own more than five cats at a time.

21. In Shorewood, Wisconsin, however, no more than two cats can be owned by the same family.

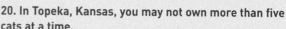

When a cat named Mousam received a notice ordering him to appear for jury duty, his owners complained. The Board of Elections rescinded the order, not because he was a cat but because he couldn't speak English.

76 Cat Idioms

You've heard the phrase "Cat got your tongue?" but did you know that this expression originated in the Middle East hundreds of years ago? Glenda Moore of www.xmission.com has researched not only cat idioms but in many cases their meanings and origins as well. Find out more about this expression as well as 75 others in Glenda's list below:

1. **A bag of cats**: A bad-tempered person.

2. **A cat in gloves catches no mice**: Sometimes you can't accomplish a goal by being careful and polite — an idiom attributed to Ben Franklin in *Poor Richard's Almanack*.

3. **Alley cat**: A stray or homeless cat. The "alley" portion probably refers to prostitutes, who at one point in time literally carried mattresses around with them. The "cat" probably alludes to the mating habits of female cats.

4. **Another breed of cat**: Something different from anything else.

5. **As much chance as a wax cat in hell**: No chance at all.

6. **As nervous as a cat in a room full of rocking chairs**: Description of someone with frayed nerves. It alludes to the fact that cats don't like having their tails tromped on.

7. **Busier than a one-eyed cat watching two mouse holes**: Very busy, almost to the point of frenzy.

8. **Busier than a three-legged cat in a dry sand box**: Very busy, almost to the point of panic.

9. **Cat-and-dog**: Resembling or having the character of the proverbial antagonism between cat and dog.

10. **Cat around**: To live an aimless, immoral life. (See also *alley cat, tomcat*.)

11. **Cat-eyed or having cat eyes**: Able to see in the dark. Coined in recognition of a cat's ability to see in conditions of very low lighting.

12. **Cat got your tongue?**: Why aren't you talking? The phrase probably comes from a custom of the Middle East dating from hundreds of years ago. Then, it was common to punish a liar by ripping out the tongue. The severed body part was fed to the king's pet cats.

13. **Cat ice**: Thin, dangerous ice; ice that would not even support a cat.

14. **Cat-in-hell chance**: No likelihood of success. It originally referred to the hopelessness of fighting with inadequate weapons. (The complete expression is "No more chance than a cat in hell without claws.")

15. **Cat's melody**: Harsh noises or cries.

16. **Cat's meow**: Something considered outstanding. Coined by American cartoonist Thomas A. Dorgan (1877–1929), whose work appeared in many American newspapers. (See also *cat's pajamas, cat's whiskers*.)

17. **Cat's pajamas**: Something considered outstanding. The be-all and end-all!

Sheet music cover from 1922.

18. **Cat's paw**: To be labeled a "cat's paw" means someone has taken advantage of you. The phrase has its origins in an old folktale in which a clever monkey tricks a cat into reaching into a fireplace to pull out some roasting chestnuts. The monkey gets the chestnuts, but the cat gets burned.

19. **Cat's whisker**: Before diodes were invented, people made a kind of diode by touching a long thin wire against a germanium crystal. This was enough

to rectify a radio signal to the point where it could drive a single earpiece. The radio was a "crystal set" and the long wire was the "cat's whisker," which resembles a cat's whiskers.

20. Cat's whiskers: Something considered really special. Also coined by American cartoonist Thomas A. Dorgan.

21. Catty remarks: Derogatory comments made by a woman, usually about another woman.

22. Clowder of cats: A group of cats. *Clowder* is the ancient word for "clutter."

23. Conceited as a barber's cat: Very conceited.

24. Cool cat: Someone who keeps up with the latest trends. The term originated in the Roaring '20s, and its meaning hasn't changed. Means the same as *hep cat*.

25. Copycat: A person who copies others. Probably a reference to the way kittens learn by copying their mother's actions.

26. Couldn't cuss a cat without getting fur in your mouth: Refers to tight, cramped spaces.

27. Curiosity killed the cat: A warning to be cautious when investigating something. The original saying was "Care kills a cat," dating from the sixteenth century. This version was a warning that worry is bad for health and can lead to an early grave; it points to the cautious, careful behavior of the cat. Over time, the word *care* evolved into *curiosity*, and thus the meaning of the expression changed. It now alludes to a cat's desire to explore and discover.

28. Dead cat bounce: An automatic recovery in a financial market. Refers to the lore that a cat "bounces back" from death many times.

29. Dead cat on the line: Something suspicious or "fishy" going on. The phrase refers to fishing for catfish. The fishing lines are checked every day, so if there's a dead catfish on the line, there's something wrong. An alternative definition provided by *Science* magazine in the early 1980s has nothing to do with fishing, however. An article about colloquialisms dates the term to the mid-1970s or even earlier, when many folks had party lines for telephone service. If someone was listening in, you would hear a click. The way one speaker would alert another to keep the conversation off confidential subjects was to say, "There's a dead cat on the line."

30. Dog my cats: An expression of astonishment, similar to "Well, what do you know!" Possibly coined by O. Henry (1862–1910) in his short story "Memoirs of a Yellow Dog."

31. Dust kitten: A clump of dust or lint; also known as a "dust bunny."

32. Enough to make a cat laugh: Something that is ridiculously silly. Cats don't laugh.

33. Fat cat: A wealthy and privileged person. Cats that are well-fed and cared for are seldom skinny; hence, a person living the good life is a fat cat.

The Sound of Purring in 10 Different Languages

1. Danish: *pierr*
2. Dutch: *prrr*
3. Finnish: *hrr*
4. French: *ronron*
5. German: *srr*
6. Hungarian: *doromb*
7. Italian: *purr*
8. Japanese: *goro goro*
9. Russian: *mrrr*
10. Spanish: *rrr*

34. **Fight like cats and dogs**: To quarrel viciously.

35. **Fight like Kilkenny cats**: To fight until both parties are destroyed. Lore has it that in the ancient town of Kilkenny, on the River Nore in southeast Ireland, bored soldiers would tie two cats together for sport until they killed each other. (See the related limerick on page 50.)

36. **Glamour puss**: A glamorous woman. Probably derived from the ancient word *buss,* which means "face," especially referring to the lips. Over time, the word began to be pronounced as "puss," associating it with the cat and referring to the sleek feline pose.

37. **Grinning like a Cheshire cat**: Displaying a mysterious grin. From Lewis Carroll's novel *Alice's Adventures in Wonderland.*

38. **Having kittens**: A state of rage, having a fit, going ballistic, losing your temper. In medieval times it was believed that if a pregnant woman was in pain, she might have been cursed by a witch. In such a case, instead of a baby, she would be carrying kittens, whose claws were causing the pain. A woman believing she was going to give birth to a litter of kittens would understandably become hysterical, and thus the phrase came into use.

39. **Hellcat**: A bad-tempered woman. Refers to the hissing and spitting of an angry feline.

40. **Hep cat**: See *cool cat.*

41. **High as the hair on a cat's back**: Very expensive.

42. **Honest as the cat when the meat's out of reach**: Will not steal if likely to be caught.

43. **Keep no more cats than will catch mice**: Don't surround yourself with people who will be dependent on you.

44. **Let sleeping cats lie**: Leave things as they are. From a French proverb.

45. **Like a cat on a hot tin roof**: Excited, nervous, behaving as a cat literally would on a hot tin roof. The phrase originated from the title of Tennessee Williams's play *Cat on a Hot Tin Roof.* The movie adaptation starred Elizabeth Taylor, who played Maggie "The Cat" Pollitt.

46. **Like a cat on hot bricks**: Having frayed nerves; jumpy. A similar expression is "Nimble as a cat on a hot bake-stone" (a large stone on which bread was baked), meaning able to get away quickly.

47. **Like herding cats**: An effort that will likely be futile or at least very difficult to accomplish.

48. **Looking like a cat that swallowed a canary**: Displaying a self-satisfied grin.

49. **Look what the cat dragged in**: A slightly derogatory comment on someone's arrival. An obvious reference to the cat's tendency to bring home its prey, tattered and torn.

50. **Make the fur fly**: Start a fight; a reference to how a cat and dog fight.

51. **Morals of an alley cat and scruples of a snake**: Having no morals at all.

"Cats are like Baptists. You know they raise hell, but you can never catch them at it."
— JAMES PATTERSON

52. **Playing cat and mouse**: Playing a game of strategy and stealth, or acting in a cruel or teasing way.

53. **Pussyfooting around**: To tread or move warily or stealthily or to refrain from committing oneself. Refers to the careful movements of a hunting cat.

54. **Put the cat among the pigeons**: A British saying, meaning to cause an enormous fight or flap, usually by revealing a controversial fact or secret. When Britain governed India, a popular pastime was to put a wild cat in a pen with pigeons — bets were then taken to see how many birds the cat would bring down with one swipe of its paw.

55. **Raining cats and dogs**: Raining very hard. There are two possible origins. According to one, the dog, an attendant of the storm king Odin, was a symbol of wind. Cats came to symbolize pouring rain, and dogs, strong gusts of wind. A very heavy storm, therefore, indicated that both cats and dogs were involved. Another explanation is that the phrase came about in early-seventeenth-century London, when during heavy downpours of rain, many of the stray and feral cats and dogs that roamed the streets were drowned, and their bodies could be seen floating in the torrents.

56. **Rub someone's fur the wrong way**: To irritate or upset someone. Refers to the annoyance a cat displays if its fur is stroked backward.

57. **Scaredy-cat/Fraidy cat**: A person who won't act on a dare or who is afraid to try something new. The phrase was coined in recognition of a cat's trait of not standing up against a dog many times its size.

58. **See which way the cat jumps**: Wait and see what happens. A cruel sport in the olden days was to place a cat in a tree as a target; the "sportsman" would wait to see which way the cat jumped before pulling the trigger.

59. **Sitting in the catbird seat**: Being in an advantageous position or having control. The phrase was coined by sports announcer Red Barber and reported in James Thurber's novel *The Catbird Seat,* in which the phrase is defined as "sitting pretty, like a batter with three balls and no strikes on him."

60. **Smelling a rat**: Thinking there is something hidden or concealed. The allusion, according to *Brewer's Dictionary of Phrase and Fable,* is to a cat smelling a rat.

61. **Sourpuss**: Someone who is cranky. Probably derived from the ancient word *buss,* which means "face," especially in reference to the lips. Over time, the word began to be pronounced as "puss," associating it with the cat.

62. **Sweeten the kitty**: Increase the amount or offer a better deal. In the game of faro, the "tiger" referred to the bank of the house. Gamblers called the tiger a kitty, and thus "kitty" became the name for the payout in various card games. Sweetening or fattening the kitty, then, means increasing the pot or improving the deal.

63. **Tabby**: The silks created by weavers in Baghdad, Iraq, were inspired by the varied colors and markings of cat coats. These fabrics were called tabby by European traders. The term now refers to cats having a striped or variegated coat.

64. **The cat may look at a king**: An insolent remark of insubordination, meaning, "I am as good as you."

65. **The cat's out of the bag**: A secret that has been revealed. In medieval England, piglets were sold in the open marketplace. The seller usually kept the pig in a bag, so it would be easier for the buyer to take it home. But shady sellers often tried to trick their buyers by putting a cat in the bag instead of a pig. If a shrewd shopper looked in the bag, then the cat was literally out of the bag. (Incidentally, the bag was also called a "poke," which is likely where the phrase "a pig in a poke" originated.)

66. **There's more than one way to skin a cat**: There is more than one way to accomplish a task. The reference is to preparing a catfish (named as such because of its long whiskers), which must be skinned before eating because the skin is so tough. There are various methods of accomplishing the task.

67. **There's not enough room to swing a cat**: The room is very cramped and crowded. In olden days, sailors were punished by being whipped with a cat-o'-nine-tails. Below deck, there wasn't enough room to lash the whip, so the punishment was given on deck, where there was "enough room to swing the cat."

68. To bell a cat: To do the impossible. From Aesop's fable "The Belling of the Cat."

69. To get one's back up: Showing anger or annoyance. The allusion is to a cat, which gets its back up when threatened.

70. To live a cat-and-dog life: To always be arguing. The phrase was coined by Thomas Carlyle in his book *Frederick the Great:* "There will be jealousies, and a cat-and-dog life over yonder worse than ever."

71. Tomcat: A male who enjoys the favors of many women. The expression comes from a book written in the mid-1700s in England called *The Life and Adventures of a Cat.* The "hero" of the book, a male cat who enjoyed the favors of many female cats, was named Tom.

72. Under the cat's foot: To live under the cat's foot is to allow someone to control you.

73. Walk like a cat on eggs: Tread very lightly.

74. Walk the cat back: To attempt to understand the true nature of a situation by reconstructing events chronologically from the present to the past. The earliest reference to the phrase appeared in a *New York Times* article by Robert A. Bennett, on February 19, 1984.

75. Weak as a cat: Very weak; ineffective.

76. When the cat's away, the mice will play: Without supervision, people misbehave.

 # Cats by Any Other Name

Albanian: macë

Apache: gídí

Arabic: kitte *or* qitah

Armenian: gatz

Basque: catua

Breton: kaz

Bulgarian: kotka

Catalan: gat

Cherokee: Wesa

Chinese: miu *or* mau

Cornish: kat

Cree: bushi

Croatian: macka

Czechoslovakian: koāka *or* kocka

Danish: kat

Dutch: kat *or* poes

Egyptian: mau *or* mait

Eskimo: Pussi

Esperanto: kat/o

Estonian: kiisu

Ethiopian: dMt

Farsi: Gorbe

Filipino: cat

Finnish: kissa

French: chat

Gaelic: pishyakan *or* cait

Gaulish: cattos

German: Katti, Katze, *or* Ket

Greek: catta *or* kata

Gypsy: Muca

Hawaiian: popoki

Hebrew: Cha'tool

Hindi: billi

Hungarian: macska *or* cica

Icelandic: köttur

Indonesian: kucing

Italian: gatto

Japanese: neko

Korean: ko-yang-i

Latin: cattus *or* felis

Lithuanian: katinas

Malay: kucing

Maltese: qattus

Mayan: miss

Navajo: moasi

Norwegian: katt

Polish: kot *or* gatto

Portuguese: gato

Pusa: cat

Rumanian: pisica

Russian: koshka *or* kots

Sign Language: two pulls at an imaginary whisker

Slovak: macka

Spanish: gato

Swahili: paka

Swedish: katt

Thai: meo

Turkish: kedi

Ukrainian: kotuk

Vietnamese: meo

Welsh: kath

Yiddish: chatul *or* gattus

Zulu: ikati

15 Cat Dreams and What They Mean

Dreaming of a cat is generally regarded as an unfortunate omen, indicating treachery as well as a run of bad luck. Yet folklore also holds that dreaming of a white cat signifies good luck. Good luck? Bad luck? Which is right? Thankfully, neither.

According to Jane Teresa Anderson, author of *Dream Alchemy* as well as four other books, dreams are not about luck or predicting the future. Dreams help you to understand yourself and the way your mind works, and armed with this powerful information, you can create enough good luck of your own to fill a lifetime. Visit Jane online at dream.net.au for a wealth of information on dreams and dreaming, as well as professional consultation services.

This list contains clues to the meaning of your cat dreams. Remember that all your dreams are really about *you* and that all dream interpretations depend on the unique psyche of the dreamer.

If you dream of a hungry wildcat attacking you, ask yourself why your own wildcatlike instincts are not being fulfilled.

If you dream of a witch's black cat leading you on a journey, ask yourself where, in your life, you may be taking a negative or manipulating attitude.

If you dream of a witch's white cat leading you on a journey, ask yourself how you can better tune in to your inner, instinctive, healing, positive energies.

If you dream of a long-departed pet cat, ask yourself why this is a good time in your life to think back to the days when that cat was alive and well, and what you can learn by comparing those days to today.

If you dream of a talking cat, remind yourself that any voice in a dream is voicing your own attitudes and beliefs, including those unconscious ones you didn't know you had. If the cat is criticizing you, for example, your dream suggests you may be too critical about yourself, and that this may be blocking your progress in life.

Dreams love puns and clichés. If you're familiar with the saying "Cat got your tongue?" and you dream of a cat eating a tongue, perhaps you haven't been speaking up for yourself!

See the tail of a cat disappearing around a door frame in your dream? Ask yourself where you're seeing the "tail end" of something in your life. How you felt about this in the dream is a clue to your true feelings about this ending.

When you come eye-to-eye with a cat — or anyone — in your dreams, you're coming face to face with yourself. The strong emotions you feel in the dream are the strong emotions you're reconnecting to within yourself.

If your dream cat is licking its paws, ask yourself what a cat is thinking when it does this. What is the attitude of a paw-licking cat? The attitude you see is *your* attitude reflected back to you in your dream. Know yourself!

Did your dream cat have kittens? What new things, projects, ideas, or attitudes are you giving birth to in

"If happiness is a warm dog, is sadness a cold cat?"
— SIRIA GAMEZ, 12, MIAMI, FLORIDA

your life? Or is this a dream cliché about the cat having kittens, meaning you are shocked, worried, or surprised?

Did you find a poor, bedraggled cat in your dreams and wake up intensely sad or crying? Chances are you have met your own grief and sadness in your dream, sometimes from long ago. Do you need to let go? Is healing in order?

Have you lost your pet cat in a dream? First, decide what your pet cat means to you: companionship, feline power, perhaps. Or you might associate your pet with what was happening when it came into your life. Your dream suggests you are losing touch with this.

Many people see cats as sexy in a feminine, feline way. Your dream cat, especially if it is slinky and powerful, may reveal your own feminine, feline sexuality. Have you shut it out? How does this energy express itself in your life?

Have you dreamed of cats fighting? Any fight in a dream suggests an inner or outer conflict.

Does a black cat cross your path in a dream? Here's where folklore and dreams overlap, because your dreams reflect what *you* believe. If you're familiar with folklore that holds that a black cat is lucky or unlucky, then your dream is about how you feel about luck.

20 Cat Words

1. **catbird seat**: a position of great prominence.

2. **cat burglar**: a nimble, silent, sneaky thief.

3. **catcall**: in the theater, a way of expressing disapproval or contempt, based on the catlike hissing noises that discontented audiences often made.

4. **caterwaul**: to cry, as cats do during rutting time.

5. **cat-eyed**: able to see in the dark.

6. **catfight**: an intensely personal dispute or argument.

7. **catfish**: a fish that has long tactile barbels resembling a cat's whiskers.

8. **cat fit**: a conniption.

9. **catfoot**: to move in the stealthy manner of a cat.

10. **catgut**: what tennis racket and violin strings are supposedly made of. The word derives from the German word *Kitgut*, meaning "a small fiddle." Catgut strings are actually made from the intestines of a sheep or goat.

11. **catkins**: the fluffy flower bracts of willow and birch trees, which look like small cats' tails. (Other plant names refer to cats also, such as pussywillow and cattail.)

12. **catlap**: a weak drink fit only for a cat to lap.

13. **catnap**: a short period of sleep, referring to the cat's ability to sleep frequently and lightly.

14. **cat's-eyes**: precious or semiprecious gems that have a changing luster; also road markers that reflect car lights.

15. **cat skin**: the skin and fur of a cat used for clothing.

16. **cattail**: a plant.

17. **cattery**: a place for the breeding, care, and raising of cats.

18. **catty**: given to malicious gossip.

19. **catwalk**: a narrow walkway, referring to a cat's ability to balance on very narrow surfaces.

20. **catwort**: catnip.

Wacky Cats on the 'Net

You might not want to get caught watching these at work.

1. **Action Cats, www.poetv.com/video.php?vid=3484**
A "fake commercial" from *Saturday Night Live*, in which kids can dress up their cats as action heroes (batteries and cats sold separately)!

Some cats look like dictators; others just act like them.

2. **Bonsai Kitten, www.flurl.com/item/bonsai_kitten_u_147056/**
A kitten crawls inside a glass jar and then crawls back out. It's a hoax, but it sure is wild to watch.

3. **Catcam, Catcam.com**
A Webcam, set up in the home of Erik Max Fran-cis, is pointed toward the floor of his kitchen, and beyond into his foyer. Cats can often be seen milling around — the kitchen is where the food and water dish are. The images are updated every five minutes.

4. **Cats Being Awesome, www.poetv.com/video.php?vid=3337**
A fun clip-fest of cats doing crazy things, such as jumping up into the air, boxing with a dog, leaping into an aquarium and right back out, and playing with small children and babies.

5. **Cats in a Punk Rock Band, www.eyeenvision.com/litterbox/hissofdeath.html**
The all-cat death-metal band Litterbox performs its hit song "Hiss of Death."

6. **Cats in Sinks, catsinsinks.com**
It's about cats, in sinks. What is Cats in Sinks? It's obvious. It's about cats. And kittens. Who like sinks. And basins.

7. **Catsize Entertainment, www.catsizeentertainment.com/funnyCatsGallery.php**
Flying cats, cats in cute clothing, cats napping in weird places — all very funny.

8. **Cats That Look Like Hitler, www.catsthatlooklikehitler.com**
Do you wake up in a cold sweat every night, wondering if your cat is going to up and invade Poland? Does he keep raising his right paw

while making a noise that sounds suspiciously like "Sieg Miaow"? If so, your cat has company.

9. Cats in the News, Blogs.orlandosentinel.com/features_lifestyle_animal/cats/index.html

This blog on the *Orlando Sentinel*'s website often carries offbeat stories of cats who make headlines throughout the United States and around the world.

10. Crazy Cat Photos, home.arcor.de/ragnara/catsown.jpg

These funny faces range from the creepy to the lovable. Great captions.

11. Cats on the Go, Catsinparis.com

Dalli and Sammy from Houston, Texas, are world travelers. You can keep track of their travels to Paris, Hong Kong, Scotland, and Bermuda. Dalli is the one with the dots, and Sammy, his little sister, is a Siamese. Hope you enjoy the photo!

12. Cranky Cats, Mycathatesyou.com

Welcome to My Cat Hates You dot-com! Started in 2000, the site proudly presents you with the largest collection of sour-faced, indignant felines on the Internet.

13. Cutie Cats, www.killsometime.com/Video/video.asp?ID=514

More crazy clips, such as a cat playing piano, trying to stop a record on the turntable, picking up a cat food can in its mouth, trying to stop a CD from going into the CD changer, and other zany antics.

"A Nigerian prince wants to send me 10 million dead mice!"

14. The Days of Their Lives, Yourdailymedia.com/media/1149162261/Funny_Cats_Compilation

Here are some very funny video clips of cats being cats.

15. Dharmacat, Dharmathecat.com

You'll find cartoons that blend humor and spirituality — on the rocky path to nirvana with a Buddhist cat, a novice monk, and a mouse hell-bent on cheese. Dharma the Cat offers Eastern philosophy, Buddhist ideas, spiritual development, personal stories, articles, and anecdotes about coping with life, and lots of humor — of the thoughtful kind!

16. Follow the Cat, ferryhalim.com/orisinal/g3/cats.htm

You'll find a truly delightful online "follow the leader" cat game with a wonderful soundtrack at this site. Touch the cats with your mouse to make them sit or walk, but remember, all the cats have to follow the actions of the leader cat. If the leader sits, you have to make the other cats sit. If the leader walks, make the other cats walk. Score points and extra game time along the way.

17. Graymalkin's Anatomy, Altervistas.com /sites/weird/653
Feline medical curiosities and anomalies are to be found on this site, if you have the stomach for this sort of thing. You'll see green cats and pink cats as well as two-headed kittens.

"I love cats. I even think we have one at home." — EDWARD L. BURLINGAME

18. Insanely Funny Cat Video, http://www .extremelysharp.com/direct/catvideo.html
Cats encountering themselves in mirrors, leaping at chandeliers, and romping in the bath. Very entertaining.

19. Home Alone, www.funny-games.biz /videos/547-dontletyourcatsalone.html
This is what happens when your cats know you're away. This is actually a PETA commercial for spaying cats.

20. The Infinite Cat Project, www.infinite cat.com
This is amazing: Here are cats regarding cats regarding cats in an electronic milieu. It starts with a photo of a cat, and the next photo is of a cat looking at a monitor with that cat's photo on it, and the next photo is of another cat looking at a monitor with a photo of the previous cat

who is looking at the first cat's photo on a monitor . . . and on into infinity. Very clever.

21. Kitten vs. Powerbook, www.poetv.com /video.php?vid=3767
A kitten is completely mystified by the changes on a PowerBook screen that occur every time its paw hits a key on the keyboard.

22. Kitties at Play, www.yourdailymedia .com/media/1149162261/Funny_Cats _Compilation
Great clips of cats exhibiting normal cat behavior that just happens to be side-splitting.

23. Live Nude Cats, www.livenudecats.com
A sex site the whole family can enjoy, although you must be 18 months or older to enter. These send-ups of tabloid covers imply racy stories about cats.

24. Meankitty Gallery, www.meankitty.com /index.html
This site has a great gallery of cat photos and bios of kitties with a mean streak. E-cards and T-shirts are also available.

25. Shopcats, shopcat.com
A website dedicated to cats who work in stores, hotels, libraries, etc. Sorted by state! Literally hours of fun.

26. Silly Cats, www.amazingcatcollection .com/index.php?page=1
This site sports a new amazing cat photo every day. Cats and kittens in all kinds of rapturous and silly poses, cats with dogs, and even cats in hats. A great collection.

27. Stuff on My Cat, stuffonmycat.com/index.php?startpos=90

This site makes the Internet seem like a vacation in the Twilight Zone, and we mean that in the best way possible. The site's motto is STUFF + CATS = AWESOME. A cat wearing a coffee filter on its head, a cat draped with the Canadian flag, a cat wearing sunglasses appearing to talk on a cell phone. Well worth a visit!

28. Talking cats, Wimp.com/cats

Hear cats talk! Really!

29. Talking Cats, Part 2, www.youtube.com/watch?v=vRvf1WgYl5k

Extremely clever cats trying to imitate their owners' speech.

30. Trippy Cats, www.metacafe.com/watch/154227/trippy_cats/

Cats sliding, slipping, tripping, romancing a Ken doll.

31. Viking Kittens, users.wolfcrews.com/toys/vikings/

You'll cry with laughter when you see these animated kitties in Viking regalia sailing the sea to the tune of Led Zeppelin's "Immigrant Song." Crank this one up!

32. Virtual Kitty, www.virtualkitty.com

If allergies prevail, you don't have to go without. Here you can adopt a kitty to your own specs and enjoy daily cat-kisses without ever having to change a litter box.

33. Whacky Cat, www.abum.com/show/16858/whacky_cat.html

What has to be one of the most vocal cats in the world delivers an entire speech. Of course, no one can understand a word.

"I stole your cat's identity over the Internet. I'm here to scratch your furniture and lick the butter."

34. Xtreme Cats, ebaumsworld.com/videos/ultimate-cat-fighting.html

The "extreme sports" model is applied to this film of two cat champions who fight each other before a huge crowd. Very clever.

35. Rock 'n' Roll Cats, b3ta.hnldesign.nl/rsc/

These record-store cats, boppin' along to their favorite tunes, are absolutely mesmerizing.

Part Two

Top Cats

"Cats can be very funny, and of showing they're glad to peed in our shoes."

They have changed history, they have outsmarted our enemies on the battlefield, they have sold us billions of dollars of everything from shaving cream to cars, and they have graced the silver screen with performances so funny they made us laugh until we cried. Here are the cats who have distinguished themselves above and beyond all others. Some have garnered awards, some have won our wholesale interest and adoration, and some have disappeared into the jungle of history, unnamed and unsung except for the gifts they left behind.

In paying homage to top cats, it would be impossible to separate the real cats from their legendary counterparts, and so you'll find them both here. The Cheshire Cat and the Cat in the Hat, after all, have contributed at least as much to our culture as the mighty Morris and the cat who saved the day when the building of the Coulee Dam came to a standstill. And although we try to cover as many of them as space will allow — the heroes, the record holders, the film stars, the unforgettable literary characters, and the working cats who continually amaze us with their abilities — we must confess that these represent only a small number of the talented and brave felines with whom we are lucky enough to share the planet.

have the oddest ways see you. Rudimac always

— W. H. AUDEN

29 Movies About Cats

In 1894, the 30-second movie *Boxing Cats* showed two kitties in boxing gear in a miniature ring. They didn't really fight much, and such short movies were soon replaced by full-length features. What's notable is the filmmaker — none other than Thomas Alva Edison, who was responsible for developing the phonograph, the telephone, and modern motion picture technology. Thus Edison gets credit for the thousands of films that his inventions made possible, including these, about cats.

1. ***The Case of the Black Cat*** **(1936)** A grade B movie based on Erle Stanley Gardner's story "The Case of the Caretaker's Cat," this mystery involved three murders, a hectic treasure hunt, and a screeching gray — not black — cat.

2. ***Rhubarb*** **(1951)** A still-popular story about a stray cat who is adopted by an eccentric millionaire who soon dies. Rhubarb inherits the estate, lock, stock, and ball club. As the new owner of the Brooklyn Loons, Rhubarb becomes the focus of a kitty-heist. Look carefully for a glimpse of young Leonard Nimoy as a ballplayer. Based on the novel by H. Allen Smith.

3. ***The Incredible Shrinking Man*** **(1957)** The cat in this movie is the real villain, terrorizing the poor little title character. Special effects and a giant paw were used to add to the thrills.

4. ***Bell, Book, and Candle*** **(1958)** Gillian, a beautiful modern-day witch, falls for a handsome neighbor who is engaged to another. With the help of her familiar, a cat named Pyewacket, she enchants him and he soon falls in love with her instead. She eventually lifts the spell, only to discover that his love is real.

5. ***The Shadow of the Cat*** **(1961)** A determined black cat seeks revenge for her owner's

Cat at bat, from *Rhubarb*.

From *The Incredible Shrinking Man*.

murder. "Stare into these eyes if you dare," challenged the original movie poster.

6. *One Day, a Cat* (Czech) (1963) Hailed as one of the best anthropological studies on human behavior, this fantastic fable features a cat who is capable of seeing human beings for what they really are. With glasses off, the cat exposes the real feelings and the mostly self-ish personalities of people: red for those in love, purple for the hypocrites, yellow for the unfaithful, and gray for the dishonest. A beautiful fable about human behavior; a great moral lesson that avoids being trite.

7. *The Three Lives of Thomasina* (1964) Based on Paul Gallico's book *Thomasina, The Cat Who Thought She Was God*, the story is about a widower veterinarian (played by Patrick McGoohan) in rural Scotland and his daughter, Mary, who dotes on her pet cat. Relations between father and daughter have been strained since the death of her mother. Thomasina is hurt, and the vet decides she must be put to sleep. Mary and her friends stage a funeral for the cat, and they are chanced upon by a woods-woman healer, Lori MacGregor, whom the townspeople believe to be a witch. The children scatter in fear, and Lori finds that the cat still has a heartbeat and nurses it back to health. Meanwhile, Thomasina believes herself to be descended from the cat goddesses of Egypt. Lori ends up bringing Mary and her father closer together and everyone lives happily ever after. It is, after all, a Disney movie.

8. *Eye of the Cat* (1969) The hairdresser of a wealthy widow searches out a derelict and takes him home. He is the nephew of the rich Aunt Danny, and unless this favorite nephew returns to claim his inheritance, his aunt's money will all go to a cat shelter. The pair plan to kill Aunt Danny and split the money. But when the nephew enters the mansion, Aunt Danny's dozens of cats paralyze him with fear.

9. *The AristoCats* (1970) Disney thrills again with this animated film, which takes place in Paris in 1910. Duchess, the beloved, pampered housecat of a retired opera star, Adelaide, finds herself stranded in the countryside with her three kittens, the victims of a plot by their owner's butler to cheat them out of the money left to them at Adelaide's death. They must find their way back to their home with the help of a tomcat, Thomas O'Malley, and other animal accomplices, while evading the butler and foiling his murderous plan.

10. *Le Chat* (1971) A dazzling performance by film legend Simone Signoret. A husband and wife have grown bored after 25 years of marriage. Once a passionate lover, the husband now shows affection only to a stray cat, which drives Signoret's character to wild, can't-stop-watching distraction. The tag line for the film at its release sums it up: "A love-hate relationship so strong it destroyed everything — the man, the woman — even the cat."

11. *Fritz the Cat* (1972) X-rated and animated, based on R. Crumb's 1960s comic book about a college-student cat who is crass but cool. This one, along with *The Nine Lives of Fritz the Cat* (1974), is a cult classic still available today on DVD.

12. *Harry and Tonto* (1974) In the style of *Travels with Charley*, Art Carney plays an old codger who takes a cross-country trip with his aging orange cat, Tonto, as a companion. The cat, on a leash, steals the film, which is wonderful in its own right.

13. *The Night of a Thousand Cats* (AKA *Blood Feast*) (1974) The theater lobby posters exclaimed: "Alone, only a harmless pet . . . One thousand strong, they become a man-eating machine! When The Cats Are Hungry . . . Run For Your Lives!" This Mexican horror film, re-

From *The Three Lives of Thomasina.*

leased in Mexico in 1972, tells of the lustful and bloody appetites of a millionaire playboy and his ferocious accomplices.

14. *I Am a Cat* (1975) Adapted from the masterpiece novel by Natsume Soseki, this is a comic portrait of a Tokyo teacher in about 1900 who details his illnesses and disappointments. He studies the local cat population with great interest and learns from feline Blackie an object lesson in perseverance. The teacher's cat is on the soundtrack, musing on existentialism —before falling down drunk.

15. *The Cat from Outer Space* (1978) A UFO is stranded on earth and impounded by the U.S. government. Its pilot, a space cat with the ability to communicate with humans, eludes the authorities. He enlists help to reclaim and repair his ship to get back home.

16. *The Black Cat* (1981) Edgar Allan Poe's spine tingler of the same name inspired this thriller about a psychic professor who must summon the dead and direct their wayward spirits into his black cat, who then becomes his instrument for revenge. The versions of this film that appeared in 1934 and 1941 bore a closer resemblance to Poe's original story.

Young Drew Barrymore with her costar, from Stephen King's Cat's Eye.

17. *Stephen King's Cat's Eye* (1985) In this trilogy by Stephen King, a supernatural stray wanders from tale to tale, figuring most prominently in the story called *The General,* in which a character played by the young Drew Barrymore befriends the cat despite the evil that seems to surround it. Check out the feline antics in the credits sequence, in which the cat passes through three of his nine lives.

18. *The Adventures of Milo and Otis* (1989) Milo, a kitten, and Otis, a Pug, are pals with a penchant for mischief. When they fall into a raging river, they set in motion an unanticipated —but delightful —adventure. The story is emotional, and the panoramic scenery is breathtaking. While some of the animal stunt scenes boggle the mind, filmmaker Masanori Hata has assured the public that no animals were harmed in the course of making the film.

19. *Pet Sematary* (1989) This "pet sematary" isn't an ordinary cemetery but rather a portal from the land of the dead. When Church, the beloved family cat, meets up with an eighteen-wheeler, the father takes the cat's corpse to the not-so-hallowed ground, where the fun begins. And hey, if it works for a cat . . .

20. *Romeo and Juliet* (1990) An all-cat version of *Romeo and Juliet*? Yep. The cast consisted of one hundred cats and only one human —John Hurt —in the role of an old Venetian bag lady. The movie is artistically filmed using slow-motion effects and clever editing, which create an illusion of interaction among the characters. Unfortunately, it's almost impossible to find copies of this film, and its interest is limited mainly to Shakespeare enthusiasts, although we can't imagine why.

21. *Strays* (1991) When the Jarretts move into a deserted country home, they contract a strange case of cat-scratch fever. It seems Mrs. Jarrett has been feeding the neighborhood's feral cats. But it's not Fancy Feast they're after — it's blood!

22. *The Cat* (1992) A black cat with mystical powers and more than nine lives wreaks havoc on a small city; is it preordained or just coincidence?

23. *Sleepwalkers* (1992) A mother-and-son team of vampires come to town seeking a virgin on which to feed. One sexually curious ingénue falls for the new boy in school — only to learn that he's a life-sucking Sleepwalker who can mutate at will from nice guy to savage. It's the town's cats who face off with the monsters in their midst.

24. *Homeward Bound: The Incredible Journey* (1993) In this version of 1963's *Incredible Journey*, Shadow, a Golden Retriever, and Chance, an American Bulldog, travel with Sassy the cat on a journey across the country. Trainers employed numerous tricks — and plenty of patience — to help the animals achieve their memorable performances.

25. *That Darn Cat!* (1965, 1997) Hey, this could happen! When a bank teller is kidnapped during a robbery, she manages to slip her watch around a stray cat's neck, hoping that the enterprising feline will lead rescuers to her location. The cat finds his way to Hayley Mills, who sets out to rescue all. The remake starred Christina Ricci.

26. *Cats — The Musical* (1998) Based on a book of poems by T. S. Eliot, *Old Possum's Book of Practical Cats,* the Broadway smash hit produced a litter of 26 foreign versions of the play and was seen by some 50 million patrons. Deuteronomy, Mistoffelees, and Grizabella do their best to reproduce the stage extravaganza in the made-for-DVD film, produced by Andrew Lloyd Webber in 1998, but it cannot capture the magic of the stage version.

27. *Cats and Dogs* (2001) In the first Great War of the Pets, cats and dogs slug it out to see who will control the universe. The four-legged stars of this film are helped along the way by animation techniques, but at the heart of it all, they needed dogs and cats to do the job. The feline stars of the film are Mr. Tinkles, a white Persian on a power trip; Calico, a brown classic tabby Exotic Shorthair; Russian Blue, actually played by a British shorthair kitten; and a team of Devon Rexes as the Ninja cats.

28. *Take Care of My Cat* (2002) Five young Korean women who were best friends in high school find their paths diverging as they step into the adult world. A lost cat, Tee Tee, enters their lives, passing from one owner to the next as circumstances pull lives and friends apart while bringing others together.

29. *The Cat in the Hat* (2003) Home alone, nothing to do, it's raining outside. Sounds like a boring day? It is, until Mike Myers, as Dr. Seuss's irascible Cat in the Hat, shows up and introduces a couple of kids to their imagination. It's all fun and games until the kids find out just how difficult it can be to get rid of a cat.

5 Movies About Cat People

1. *Cat People* (1942, 1982)

2. *The Curse of the Cat People* (1944)

3. *Cat-Women of the Moon* (1954)

4. *Teenage Catgirls in Heat* (1997)

5. *Catwoman* (2004)

The Fat on the Cat in the Hat

 *The Cat in the Hat* is one of the most cherished of all children's books. Written in 1957 by the beloved writer and illustrator Theodor Seuss Geisel (1904–1991), well known as Dr. Seuss, it tells the story of two children who find themselves home alone with a rakish, hat-wearing feline who is the "poster cat" for bad behavior. Here are some interesting facts about this enchanting book.

 In May 1954, *Life* magazine published a report on illiteracy among schoolchildren, suggesting that children were having trouble learning to read because their books were boring. This problem led to a joint venture between Houghton Mifflin and Random House, who jointly challenged Seuss to write an entertaining children's book utilizing only 250 words. Nine months later, using only 223 words, Dr. Seuss successfully completed *The Cat in the Hat,* which went on to achieve legendary success.

 At the time of his death on September 24, 1991, Dr. Seuss had written and illustrated 44 children's books. Over 200 million copies had found their way into homes and hearts around the world.

 *The Cat in the Hat* has been popular since its publication, and a logo featuring the Cat himself adorns all Dr. Seuss publications and animated films produced since the appearance of *The Cat in the Hat.*

 Literary critics occasionally write spoof essays about the book, having fun with issues such as the absence of the mother and the psychological or symbolic characterizations of Cat, Things, and Fish. These critics have, with tongue in cheek, suggested that the relationship between the brother and sister is incestuous, that the cat represents Satan, and that the fish symbolizes Jesus.

 In 1997, an account of the O. J. Simpson murder case written in verse and titled *The Cat Not in the Hat,* by Dr. Juice, was ruled to infringe on the copyright held by Dr. Seuss's widow, Audrey Geisel, and could not therefore be published. The court ruled that the parody defense could be applied only if there was a clear and direct commentary on the original work and that *The Cat Not in the Hat* did not accomplish this; it merely used the original book as a framework for describing the Simpson trial.

 *The Cat in the Hat* has been translated into 27 languages including Spanish (*El Gato en el Sombrero*), Latin (*Cattus Petasatus*), Yiddish (*Di Kats Der Payats*), Hebrew (*Chatul Ta-a'a-lool*), and Klingon (*mlv tuQbogh vIghro''e'*).

 The sequel, *The Cat in the Hat Comes Back,* was published in 1958.

Cats Go to the Movies

The first feline movie star was a gray alley cat named Pepper who wandered onto a Charlie Chaplin set in 1920 and wound up appearing in many of his delightful comedies. The cat disappeared shortly after his favorite costar, a Great Dane named Teddy, died. But Pepper left behind paw prints in which other cat stars would follow.

And follow they did, finding their way into almost every type of film imaginable, possibly because their presence tells us so much about the characters with whom they interact and the grace they lend to the screen. Or maybe it's because the director is a cat lover and just couldn't bear to be away from his cat for so many hours a day. Cats have even created their own traditions: Blofeld's unnamed cat from the James Bond movies inspired Dr. Evil's Mr. Bigglesworth in the Austin Powers films. Here are 82 of the most memorable cats to represent Hollywood's fabulous feline history.

1. **Alpha**: Lead cat in *Cat-Women of the Moon* (1953)

2. **Amber**: One of the two Abyssinians who play the title character in *The Cat from Outer Space* (1978)

3. **Angus**: From *Jinxed* (1982)

4. **Ayatollah**: The black-and-white shorthair who lives with the title character in *Diva* (1981)

5. **Babe**: From *Enemy of the State* (1998)

6. **Beeswax**: From *Her Alibi* (1989)

7. **Berlioz and Marre**: From *The AristoCats* (1970)

8. **Bettleheim**: The cat in *Doctor Dolittle* (1998), voiced by Chad Einbinder

9. **Binks**: The boy-turned-cat due to the magic worked by three witches in *Hocus Pocus* (1993)

10. **Blackjack**: From *Stand Up Confidential* (1987)

11. **Bob**: The cat in *One Fine Day* (1996)

12. **Bobby Seale**: The cat who dies at the beginning of *P.S. Your Cat Is Dead* (2003)

13. **Burbank**: Danny Glover's pet in *Lethal Weapon* (1987)

14. **Cassandra**: A cat who wears magical eyeglasses through which he sees the true nature of deceptive people, in the Czechoslovakian film *Az Prijde Kocour (That Cat)* (1963)

15. **Cat**: Holly Golightly's "poor slob without a name" in *Breakfast at Tiffany's* (1961), played by a cat named Putney

16. **The Cat**: Played by Mike Myers in the film adaptation of Dr. Seuss's *The Cat in the* Hat (2003)

17. **Catzilla**: Brought in to catch the pesky mice in *Mouse Hunt* (1997)

18. **Chuck**: Actually played by a cat named Felix in *Heart Condition* (1990)

Mini-Me and Mini-Cat stole the show. From *Austin Powers: The Spy Who Shagged Me.*

Our favorite mob cat was actually a stray that Marlon Brando found just before shooting the first scene of *The Godfather*. The cat purred so loudly during filming that it drowned out the voices of the other players, whose lines had to be redubbed.

19. **Church**: The cat who returns from the dead in Stephen King's *Pet Sematary* (1989)

20. **Clovis**: A shorthair tabby from the film *Sleepwalkers* (1992)

21. **Coco**: The white Persian in *Jungle 2 Jungle* (1997)

22. **Cosmic Creepers**: An ugly black cat in *Bedknobs and Broomsticks* (1971)

23. **Dandiol**: From *The Fly* (1986)

24. **Danny**: From *Cats Don't Dance* (1997)

25. **D.C. (code name: Informant X-14)**: The Siamese cat in *That Darn Cat!* (1965, remade in 1997), Disney's adaptation of the book *Undercover Cat,* by Gordon and Mildred Gordon

26. **Duchess**: The nasty housecat in *Babe* (1995)

27. **Edmond**: From *Rock-a-Doodle* (1991)

28. **Elmyra**: The calico cat that belongs to the schoolteacher in *Children of the Corn II: The Final Sacrifice* (1993)

29. **Fellini**: From *Breaking Away* (1979)

30. **Felix**: The star of *Felix the Cat* (1960)

31. **Felix and Chuck**: From *Heart Condition* (1990)

32. **Figaro**: From *Pinocchio* (1984)

33. **Fritz**: The star of *Fritz the Cat* (1972)

34. **General**: The cat who saves the life of the character played by Drew Barrymore in *Stephen King's Cat's Eye* (1985)

35. **General Sterling Price**: The cat that belongs to Rooster Cogburn (played by John Wayne) in *True Grit* (1969)

36. **Gris-gris**: The missing cat in *When the Cat's Away* (1996)

37. **Heathcliff**: From *Touch and Go* (1955)

38. **Hobbie**: From *Birdy* (1984)

39. **Humphrey**: From *British Office* (1999)

40. **Jackson**: Mrs. Hotchkin's cat in the spooky film *The Crawling Hand* (1963)

41. **Jake and Rumple**: The two extraterrestrial cats who have a close encounter of the purred kind in *The Cat from Outer Space* (1978)

42. **Jarvis**: From *The Man with Two Brains* (1983)

43. **Jaune-Tom**: From *Gay Purr-ee* (1962)

44. **Jones**: The orange cat who is the only survivor, along with the character played by Sigourney Weaver, in *Alien* (1979)

45. **Kitty**: Tommy's kitten in the ridiculously funny *The Pod People* (1983)

46. **Kitty Kitty**: Kathleen Turner's ill-fated cat in *The War of the Roses* (1989), played by a cat named Tyler

47. **Lambda**: One of the cats in *Cat-Women of the Moon* (1953)

48. **Lucifer**: The cat in *Cinderella* (1950)

49. **Lucy-Belle**: Sandy Duncan's fluffy white cat in *The Cat from Outer Space* (1978)

50. **Madcat**: From *The Amazing Adventures of Inspector Gadget* (1986)

51. **Mathilda**: From *The Stars Fell on Henrietta* (1995)

52. **Midnight**: An Egyptian Mau seen in the film *Catwoman* (2004)

53. **Milo**: The clever cat in *The Adventures of Milo and Otis* (1986)

54. **Miss Kitty**: Catwoman's pet in *Batman Returns* (1992)

55. **Mr. Bigglesworth**: Dr. Evil's pet who is rendered bald by the freezing process in *Austin Powers, International Man of Mystery* (1997)

56. **Mr. Jinx**: Robert De Niro's beloved Himalayan from *Meet the Parents* (2000) and its sequel, *Meet the Fockers* (2004), in which Mr. Jinx tries to flush a dog down a toilet

57. **Mr. Tinkles**: The power-hungry Persian from *Cats and Dogs* (2001)

58. **Muffy**: In *Mars Attacks* (1996)

59. **Nathan**: The gray striped cat in *Doppelganger: The Evil Within* (1992)

60. **Neutron**: From *This Island Earth* (1954)

61. **Oliver**: From *Oliver and Company* (1988)

62. **Orion**: The ginger-and-white cat who has "the galaxy" around his neck in *Men in Black* (1997)

63. **Pepper**: The ginger cat in over a dozen silent films of the early twentieth century, including *Back to the Kitchen, Never Too Old,* and *The Dentist* (1919 for all three)

64. **P.J.**: From *Pajama Game* (1957)

65. **Princess Kitty**: Played Ernest Hemingway's cat Princess in the Key West segment of the early 1990s PBS miniseries on the life of the writer

66. **Princess Leah Lucky Buttons**: From *Go* (1999)

67. **Puss**: From *Puss in Boots* (1986)

68. **Pyewacket**: The Siamese cat and witch's familiar in the romantic-comedy film *Bell, Book, and Candle* (1958)

69. **Rhubarb**: A cat who inherits an entire professional baseball team from its owner, in *Rhubarb* (1951), in a Patsy Award–winning performance (The Patsy Award is the equivalent of the Oscar for animals.)

70. **Rufus**: From *The Re-Animator* (1985)

71. **Sassy**: The Himalayan who crossed the country with two dogs in *Homeward Bound: The Incredible Journey* (1962, 1993)

72. **Si** and **Am**: From *Lady and the Tramp* (1955)

73. **Spot**: Data's orange short-hair tabby seen in *Star Trek: Generations* and *Star Trek: Nemesis.* (The original Spot seen in *Star Trek: The Next Generation* was a Somali.)

74. **Sylvester**: From *A Streetcar Named Sylvester* (1953)

75. **Tao**: A Siamese cat in *The Incredible Journey* (1963), based on the novel of the same title

Audrey Hepburn with Orangey, from *Breakfast at Tiffany's.*

76. **T.C.**: From *Top Cat* (1960)

77. **Tee Tee**: The cat who passes through the lives of five different women in the Korean film *Take Care of My Cat* (2002)

78. **Thomasina**: The orange tabby cat who dies and returns, reuniting a family, in *Thomasina: The Cat Who Thought She Was God* (1957), remade by Disney as *The Three Lives of Thomasina* (1964)

79. **Tigger**: From *The Many Adventures of Winnie the Pooh* (1997)

80. **Tonto**: Art Carney's orange tabby in *Harry and Tonto* (1974)

81. **Whitey**: Eve's cat in *Stage Door* (1937)

82. **Zeta**: One of the cats in *Cat-Women of the Moon* (1953)

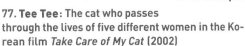

"If I die before my cat, I want a little of my ashes put in his food so I can live inside him." — **DREW BARRYMORE**

The Infamous Fritz the Cat

Fritz the cat, created by Robert Crumb, AKA R. Crumb, became a star of the underground comics movement during the 1960s.

Robert Crumb created Fritz with the help of his brother Charles. They began their collaboration as youngsters and based the character on a housecat named Fred. As Fred took on human characteristics, such as walking on his hind legs and wearing clothing, he was renamed Fritz. Fritz first appeared in the January 1965 issue of the magazine *Help!* The story was called "Fritz Comes On Strong." In it, Fritz brings a young (cat) girl home and picks fleas off her in a rather explicit scene. The publisher agreed to print the comic, though he was sure he would be arrested because of the images and racy language.

The animated film *Fritz the Cat,* directed and animated by Ralph Bakshi, has the dubious distinction of being the first X-rated feature-length cartoon seen in theaters. As a psychedelic soundtrack plays, cats and other animals behave like porn stars.

Set in the 1960s, the film is a satire of college life. Fritz "attends" (he doesn't actually go to any classes) New York University, where he majors in sex, drugs, and whatever. Along the way, Fritz connects with radical hippies, causes a shooting, meets a biker rabbit, and encounters activists with a penchant for making bombs.

Crumb was unhappy with the film and tried to prevent its release. He later told reporters that the film was an embarrassment to him.

The film was released in 1972, after the heyday of the hippie movement. It may have been intended as an homage to the 1960s but came across as a mockery.

The movie grossed $25 million in the United States and over $90 million worldwide.

Crumb was so displeased with the movie that he decided to kill off the main character in a comic strip to prevent the production of more films. But Fritz's death on paper did not have that effect. A sequel released in 1974, titled *The Nine Lives of Fritz the Cat,* involved neither Crumb nor Bakshi and bombed at the box office.

A first edition of R. Crumb's book *Fritz the Cat* (first printing, October 1969) is valued at approximately $150.

8 Hollywood Cats

In June 2003 the cable channel Oxygen launched the premier of the TV show *Meow TV*, with video segments for feline viewers. With segments such as "Squirrel Alert," a 15-second spot of intense squirrel watching, and "Cat Yoga," *Meow TV* made a bold statement about the way we feel about our cats. For decades cats have been some of the biggest stars in movies, television, and print. Of course, mane man Morris refuses to share a page with any other cat. (See page 99 for more about Morris.) Here are just a few of our favorite Hollywood mousers.

1. **Mimsey** Born in 1968, Mimsey, otherwise known as the *Mary Tyler Moore* cat, was used in a parody of the old Metro-Goldwyn-Mayer film studio's roaring lion. Looking for a mascot of their own, the MTM folks were inspired by newborn kittens belonging to the son of one of the company's film editors. They set up a camera crew in hopes of catching a toothy snarl as the kittens played, but not one kitten made a peep or a growl. Only when a kitten yawned did the camera capture an appropriate shot. Mimsey went on to open other programs produced by MTM productions before she passed away in 1988. Here are the highlights of her career.

The Bob Newhart Show Mimsey the kitten meows normally, as on *The MTM Show.*
The Duck Factory As the logo forms, an off-screen voice states, "And now, here's the cat!" Instead of meowing, Mimsey says, "Quack!"
The Galloping Gourmet Mimsey wears a chef's hat.
Hill Street Blues Mimsey sports a police officer's hat.
Newhart Mimsey lip-syncs "Meow" (to the voice of Bob Newhart). In the last episode, Mimsey lip-syncs Darryl and Darryl, yelling "QUIET!!!"
Remington Steele Mimsey sports a Sherlock Holmes deerstalker cap and meerschaum pipe. As she begins to meow, the pipe falls out of her mouth and rests in front of the word "Productions."
St. Elsewhere Mimsey wears a surgical mask and smock. In the final episode, Mimsey is shown under the credits, hooked up to life support. As the show's credits reach their conclusion, Mimsey flatlines.
The Steve Allen Show Mimsey lip-syncs "Schmock!" (voice of Steve Allen).
The White Shadow Mimsey, with black splotches, dribbles a basketball off both M's in the MTM logo.
WKRP in Cincinnati On the original series, Mimsey meows normally. On the new series, *The New WKRP in Cincinnati,* Mimsey lip-syncs Les Nessman saying "Ooooooh!"
Xuxa Mimsey lip-syncs Xuxa saying "Ciao!"

2. **Orangey** If you remember Audrey Hepburn standing in the rain holding Cat at the end of *Breakfast at Tiffany's,* you're already familiar with an animal icon who appeared in a dozen movies in the 1960s. But beneath the façade of a cute, cuddly kitty lay the heart of an alley cat — a mean one. Once called "the world's meanest cat" by a movie executive, Orangey was often violent with his costars, scratching and spitting after a scene was complete. The consummate professional during the shooting of a scene, he displayed star quality, often work-

---

3 Cat People

1. Before **Elvis Presley** became "the King," he was known as "the Hillbilly Cat."

2. **Cat Stevens**'s real name is Steven Dimitri Georgiou.

3. **Elizabeth Taylor** played the title role as Maggie "The Cat" Pollitt in Tennessee Williams's *Cat on a Hot Tin Roof.*

6 Actors Who Played Catwoman

1. **Lee Merriweather** was the first actress to play Catwoman on the 1966–1968 TV hit series *Batman*.

2. **Julie Newmar** was the second actress to portray Catwoman on the TV screen.

3. **Ertha Kitt** replaced Newmar as the new Catwoman for the final season.

4. **Michelle Pfeiffer** portrayed a lusty Catwoman in the 1992 film *Batman Returns*.

5. **Julia Rose**, a Zambian actress, portrayed Catwoman in a 2003 made-for-TV movie, *Return to the Batcave: The Misadventures of Adam and Burt*.

6. **Halle Berry** portrayed Catwoman in a 2004 film totally unrelated to the Batman story line.

ing for interminable hours. But once the scene wrapped, Orangey would often flee, shutting down production until he could be found again. Trainer Frank Inn was known to place guard dogs at the studio's entrance doors to prevent Orangey from escaping.

3. **Pepper** In the 1930s, when the Keystone Kops were at the height of their popularity, it seemed everyone was trying to get into the action. One day a slender black cat crawled though a floorboard and sauntered onto the set. So captivating was the cat, director Mack Sennett worked him into the next scene and declared, "Henceforth you shall be known as Pepper, and I predict a long and brilliant career for another member of the Sennett realm." And so it was. Pepper went on to star with Charlie Chaplin, Fatty Arbuckle, and the Keystone Kops. She also worked with a Great Dane named Teddy, with whom she formed a strong bond. When Teddy died, Pepper went into mourning, refusing to work. Several other dogs were intro-

duced to her, but she refused them, and one day she simply disappeared.

4. **Salem** Starring as Sabrina's sidekick in the popular show *Sabrina the Teenage Witch,* the character Salem, a sleek, black shorthair, wasn't everything he appeared to be; more than half of his scenes actually featured a mechanical cat. Nonetheless, Salem is a bona fide prime-time feline star. Working alongside Melissa Joan Hart and Soleil Moon Frye, Salem method acts the typical cat — self-centered, loving, and loyal.

5 and 6. **Sassy I** and **Sassy II** With the American Humane Society on the set of the 1993 production of *Homeward Bound,* Sassy II, the Himalayan with a taste for adventure, was closely monitored. But in the 1963 production of *The Incredible Journey,* Sassy I used up most of her nine lives being chased by dogs and tossed into moving streams. The audience sees poor Sassy II thrown into the water, tossed down a waterfall, chased by wild animals, and forced to cross narrow passages, but there is no need to worry about the cat's well-being — Sassy had two stunt doubles, a robot and a stuffed toy.

7. **Snowbell** As Stuart Little's cat in the 1999 movie, one will get you four — Persians, that is. Snowbell was actually played by the doubles Ruffy and Tuffy for stunts, Rocky did the running sequences, and Lucky Prince stood in for close-ups. More complicated sequences, such as airborne cat-launches, utilized a toy cat.

8. **Syn Cat** In 1965, show biz's favorite cat seemed to be the orange tabby. Then a Siamese named Syn Cat stepped into the limelight, debuting in a movie called *That Darn Cat!* Not one to loll in a sunny window, Syn Cat was at the heart of a botched bank robbery, an FBI investigation, and international intrigue. This movie launched Syn Cat into superstardom. Unlike other star cats, Syn Cat was reportedly down-to-earth, easy to deal with, and able to perform all his own stunts.

Mighty Morris

Beginning in 1968, Morris the Cat was 9Lives cat food's spokes-cat and "the world's most finicky cat." As a kitten he was called Lucky and showed amazing powers of concentration. Rescued from the Humane Society in Hinsdale, Illinois, by animal trainer Bob Martwick, Morris found himself just one year later as the 9Lives cat-food star. Dubbed "the Clark Gable of Cats," he had his own staff and private chauffeur. Here are the highlights of his amazing career.

🐾 When the not-yet-named Morris passed several tests of concentration, Martwick paid five dollars for him.

🐾 After costarring with Burt Reynolds and Dyan Cannon in the hit movie *Shamus,* Morris was awarded the Patsy Award in 1973 (the animal equivalent of the Oscar) for Outstanding Performance.

🐾 Morris's voice was that of John Irwin, of the Leo Burdett Advertising Agency, who also booked the wildly successful ad campaigns, making Morris the most recognized cat in America.

🐾 As honorary director of StarKist Foods, Inc., then the parent company of 9Lives, Morris held veto power over cat-food brands.

🐾 Morris "authored" three books promoting responsible pet ownership, pet health, and pet adoptions: *The Morris Approach, The Morris Method,* and *The Morris Prescription.*

🐾 Morris graced the covers of *Cat Fancy*'s 30th anniversary issue in 1995, and in 1996 he appeared on the cover of Ilene Hochberg's satiric book *Good Mousekeeping.*

🐾 Morris visited the White House and signed a bill with his paw.

🐾 In 1974, a book about his life was published: *Morris: An Intimate Biography,* by Mary Daniels.

🐾 Over the years several cats have portrayed Morris while the original Morris mellowed into retirement at Bob Martwick's house; he passed away in 1975. The current Morris lives in Los Angeles with his handler, Rose Ordile.

Morris®

"The cat who doesn't act finicky loses control of his humans."
— MORRIS

45 Cartoon Cats

1. **The AristoCats**. The Walt Disney movie *AristoCats* was released in 1970. Duchess, voiced by Eva Gabor, is an elegant cat from Paris who is kidnapped. She meets O'Malley, voiced by Phil Harris, who helps her return to Paris.

2. **Arlene** is Garfield's girlfriend in the famous comic strip. She first appeared on December 17, 1980. Arlene and Garfield argue incessantly, but they're perfect together in their love-hate relationship: Garfield loves himself, and Arlene hates that.

3. **Azrael** appeared in the 1980s TV cartoon *The Smurfs*. Azrael wanted the Smurfs as a snack. The cartoon was about tiny blue people called Smurfs who lived in the woods. Their leader was Papa Smurf, and they normally were at odds with Azrael and his master, the villain Gargamel.

4. **Bagpuss**, Emily's much-loved saggy old cloth cat, was the star of a television cartoon in England during the 1980s. This classic British stop-motion animation features Bagpuss, Madeline the Ragdoll, Gabriel the Toad, Professor Yaffle, and the mice of the mouse-organ.

5. **Beans** was the chubby cat who made his debut in 1935 alongside Porky Pig. He starred in seven Warner Brothers cartoons.

6. **Bill the Cat** was a character from the Berkeley Breathed Comic Strip "Bloom County." The story was set in the late 1970s and became an instant hit.

7. **Binka** is a very large furry cat who is one-quarter Persian prince and three-quarters greedy. He appears in a preschool children's program on the BBC called *Binka*.

8. Cats are known to be aloof, but "cattitude" reaches new heights in *Get Fuzzy*, the biting, hilarious comic strip from cartoonist Darby Conley. The strip revolves around an ad executive named Rob Wilco and his family, including **Bucky**, a one-fanged Siamese cat who clearly wears the pants in this eccentric household. *Get Fuzzy* is the most downloaded and e-mailed comic strip from United Feature Syndicate since *Dilbert*.

9. **Carlyle**, of the comic strip *Kit 'n' Carlyle*, is the quintessential kitten. Anyone who knows and loves cats recognizes him as the real thing. He is mischievous and lovable all at once, exhibiting classic feline behavior. Carlyle was created by Larry Wright in 1980.

10. **Catbert** is Dilbert's cat in the television series *Dilbert 1999*.

11. **CatDog** was a half-cat, half-dog character in the animated cartoon on the Nickelodeon TV network from 1998 to 1999. The feline half was voiced by Jim Cummings.

12. **The Cat in the Hat** is probably the most well known cartoon cat, one of the memorable lead characters created by Dr. Seuss in his many children's books. The story tells of a cat that speaks in rhymes and entertains a brother and a sister for the afternoon.

After turning the house upside-down, he magically cleans the house before Mom returns home.

13. **Cat R. Waul** is the villain from *An American Tale: Fievel Goes West* (Universal, 1991 Animation). He is voiced by John Cleese.

14. **The Chattanooga Cats** were a feline hillbilly rock-and-roll band created by Hanna-Barbera in 1969. It consisted of Cheesie, Scoots, Groove, Country, Kitty Jo, and a large shaggy dog named Teenie Tim.

15. **Courageous Cat** was created by Bob Kane; Batman is another brainchild of his. Courageous Cat had a sidekick named Minute Mouse and was based in the Bat Cave — oops, the Cat Cave — and received his orders from the Police Chief of Empire City, who happened to be a dog. The crime-fighting duo traveled around in the Catmobile and carried a multipurpose Catgun. Bob McFadden supplied the voices for both lead characters.

16. **Custard** is Strawberry Shortcake's pet in the cartoon series *Strawberry Shortcake*.

17. **Felix the Cat** was one of the first great stars of the animated cartoon, the braincat of Otto Messmer, who invented the character in 1919. The wide-eyed, grinning black cat, originally called Tom, was an immediate hit and went on to perform his antics in several movies and comic strips. At the height of his fame, Felix the Cat was

as popular as Mickey Mouse, who eventually eclipsed him.

18. **Figaro** is Geppetto's kitten in Disney's 1940 film *Pinocchio.* Here, he is a sweet black cat with a white stripe. In subsequent film appearances (*Cleo and the Goldfish,* 1943; *Pluto's Sweater,* 1949) Figaro takes on a much more mischievous purrsona. Clarence Nash, best known as the voice of Donald Duck, was the voice of Figaro.

19. **Garfield** is the striped, bulgy-eyed comic-strip cat known for his obnoxious comments, hefty appetite, and lazy lifestyle. He often plays nasty tricks on his owner, Jon, and Odie, the family dog. Garfield was created by Jim Davis and made his first appearance in 1978. Since then Garfield has appeared in newspapers and television.

20. **Heathcliff**, the mischievous orange cat, got his cartoon start in 1973 in the funny pages, about five years before Garfield. The comic strip was created by George Gatley, and the soon-familiar image of Heathcliff appeared on an array of merchandise, a series of paperbacks, and a cartoon series. In 1985 he had his silver-screen debut in the animated film *Healthcliff: The Movie.* When he's not overturning trash cans and generally causing havoc, Heathcliff spends his time battling a bulldog called Spike.

21. **Hello Kitty** is an animated cat created by the Japanese company Sanrio. Also known as Kitty-Chan, she first appeared in 1975 on a plastic coin purse and now graces thousands of items. She is one of the most merchandised cats ever.

22. **Hobbes** was featured in the syndicated comic strip *Calvin and Hobbes,* by Bill Watterson, who named the character after a seventeenth-century philosopher with a dim view of human nature. (For more about Calvin and Hobbes, see page 151.)

23. *King Leonardo,* later named *The King and Odie,* premiered on NBC in 1960. It was the second color cartoon series on the network's Saturday morning lineup, replacing the first run of *Ruff and Reddy.* **King Leonardo** was the lion ruler of the mythical kingdom of Bongo-Congo, but his ever-faithful companion Odie Cologne, a skunk, was the real brains behind the throne.

24. **Korky** the cat, a male black cat, is a character in the British comic strip *The Dandy.* Korky, first introduced to the public in 1937, underwent numerous changes in appearance during his 65-year history (that's 455 years, in cat years). Korky and his adventures were retired in January 2005 but were brought out of retirement within the year.

25. **Lucifer** was Cinderella's cat, who was always trying to catch her friends — who happened to be mice.

26. **Mr. Jinks** the cat was the constant, playful menace of the mice Pixie and Dixie in Hanna-Barbera's hit TV cartoon show *The Huckleberry Hound Show.* Mr. Jinks may have "hated meeces to pieces," but he loved his Raisin Bran cereal, made by the show's sponsor, Kellogg's. The series was a low-budget remake of the old *Tom and Jerry* cartoons, with the addition of an extra mouse.

Kit-Cat never starred in a movie, but the familiar image of the Kit-Cat Klock has been gracing homes all over the world since the mid-1930s, when this feline cheered a Depression-weary nation with his persistent smile. In the 1970s, Kit-Kat became the darling of kitsch, and the company that makes Kit-Kats has been enjoying success ever since. These days, the clocks come in various colors and styles (we love the one with the football helmet), and the image now appears in cartoons, in books, and on clothing. Take a stroll down Nostalgia Lane at kit-cat.com, and don't forget Kit-Cat's creed:

Put a smile on everyone's face;
Love in everyone's heart;
Energy in everyone's body;
And be a positive force in everyone's life!

5 Cats Who Appeared on **The Simpsons**

What do four Snowballs and a Coltrane have in common? They are the cats of the Simpsons.

1. **Snowball**, AKA Snowball I, was the Simpsons' first snowy white cat. She was, according to a poem by Lisa Simpson, run over by a Chrysler. It was later discovered that she was actually run over by Clovis Quimby, Mayor Quimby's drunken brother. Snowball appeared on the show even after she died, in scenes in which characters were having near-death visions.

2. **Snowball II** was the Simpsons' second cat, named after Snowball I despite the fact that, unlike Snowball I, she had black fur. Snowball II met a tragic end when she was killed, hit by Dr. Hibbert's Mercedes-Benz.

3. **Snowball III** also met with a tragic end when she drowned, trying to catch a fish, while Lisa was preparing cat food in the kitchen.

4. **Coltrane**, the Simpsons' fourth cat, was named after legendary jazz saxophonist John Coltrane. It died when it jumped out the window after hearing the squealing sound of Lisa's saxophone.

5. **Snowball IV**, AKA Snowball II, was renamed by Lisa in order to save money by not having to buy her a new cat dish.

---

27. **Nermal**, who appears in the *Garfield* comic strip, is the self-proclaimed "World's Cutest Kitten" and has been annoying Garfield since 1979. He taunts Garfield about his looks and age, and in turn Garfield mails him to Abu Dhabi every chance he gets. Of course, Nermal inevitably finds his way home every time.

28. **Oil Can Harry** was the feline arch villain of the cartoon character Mighty Mouse. With his cry of "Here I come to save the day!" Mighty Mouse would rescue his girlfriend, Pearl Pureheart, from the clutches of Oil Can Harry. He first appeared in Terrytoons in 1955 (an earlier character of the same name was not a cat).

29. **Penelope Pussycat** was an attractive female cat who inadvertently had a white stripe painted down her back and tail. Pepé Le Pew mistook her as a skunk and chose her as his mate and true love. She has been trying to get rid of him, and his scent, since their first meeting in 1949 as *Looney Tunes* cartoon characters.

30. The cartoon character known as the **Pink Panther**, created by Friz Freleng, first appeared in 1964 in the opening credits of the comedy *The Pink Panther*, which actually referred to a diamond that had a flaw in the shape of a pink panther. The character went on to star in a number of cartoon series during 1976–1978, including *The New Pink Panther Show, The Pink Panther Laff and a Half Hour*, and *Think Pink Panther*.

31. **Scratchy** is the cat in the TV show *Itchy & Scratchy* (Itchy is the mouse). Matt Groening created them as the cartoon-show-within-the-cartoon-show of *The Simpsons*. Violent clashes between the two antagonists result in the death of Scratchy. Not for cat lovers.

32. **Sebastian** is Alexandra's pet in the cartoon *Josie and the Pussycats*. As it turns out, Sebastian is the reincarnation of Alex and Alexandra Cabot's deceased uncle, who was prosecuted over 300 years ago for consorting with witches. Alexandra quickly finds that she can cast spells when stroking Sebastian's back. He gets Josie and the gang out of all sorts of trouble by picking locks with his claws, stealing keys, or, in true cat fashion, digging his claws into the bad guys' heads.

33. A cat named **Sergeant Tibs** helps rescue the Dalmatian puppies from the evil Cruella De Vil in Disney's *101 Dalmatians*.

34. **Si** and **Am** are the two mean Siamese cats from the Disney animated movie *Lady and the Tramp*.

35. **Snagglepuss** originally appeared in 1959 as a minor character on some episodes of Hanna-Barbera's television cartoon shows. He had such great appeal that he was given his own segment of *The Yogi Bear Show* when it premiered in 1961. Snagglepuss's favorite sayings are "Exit, stage left" and "Heavens to Murgatroid." The voice was provided by Daws Butler.

36. **Snowball** was the original family cat in the television cartoon sitcom *The Simpsons.* (See page 102 for more about Snowball.)

37. **Sonja**, from the Heathcliff comics, was the girlfriend of Riff Raff, the leader of the Catillac Cats, who lived in a junkyard guarded by an incompetent guard dog named Leroy. Sonja lived in a music store with a dog named Bush.

38. **Stimpy** was the cat who teamed with a Chihuahua named Ren in Nickolodeon's *Ren and Stimpy.* The show was shameless in its gross (and funny!) nature but sometimes dealt with serious issues such as cruelty to animals.

39. **Sylvester** tried millions of tricks, but never managed to catch Tweety Pie, the canary, and always wound up the fool. Sylvester was created by Friz Freleng in 1945 for the cartoon *Life with Feathers*, where he first uttered those immortal words, "Thufferin' thuccotash!" Legendary voiceover artist Mel Blanc gave Sylvester his voice.

40. **Thomas Cat** is the famous feline half of the popular cat-and-mouse team of Tom and Jerry. The characters were created by Hanna-Barbera for MGM and debuted in the animated cartoon *Puss Gets the Boot,* in which Tom was originally called Jasper. Chuck Jones created new cartoon adventures for *The Tom and Jerry Show* in 1965. Tom is a fiendish opportunist, always anxious to ingratiate himself with the powers that be, whether housekeeper, dog, or even, on occasion, mouse. Tom routinely got chopped, sliced, diced, run over by lawnmowers, or blown up, but still kept on truckin'.

41. **Tiger** is the mouse Fievel's companion in the animated film *An American Tale: Fievel Goes West,* released by Universal in 1991. He's a large and extremely furry orange cat voiced by Dom DeLuise. Since Tiger is a vegetarian, he doesn't eat Fievel on sight and is one of the two "nice" cats in the movie. He is silly, fat, and seemingly inflatable.

42. The cat character **Tigger** was created by the writer A. A. Milne. He is one of Winnie the Pooh's friends and first appeared in 1928 in *The House at Pooh Corner.* Tigger is known for his famous phrase "Ta ta for now." He is featured in several Disney films, and his voice was provided by Paul Winchell.

43. **Tony the Tiger** was introduced to the world by Kellogg's in 1952 as the spokes-tiger for Kellogg's Sugar Frosted Flakes. In 1953, Tony was featured in a four-color spread in the August issue of *Life* magazine. His son, who was originally called "Boy," became Tony Jr., appearing along with his dad. Thurl Ravenscroft provided the sole voice-over for Tony and his trademark growl, "They're grrrreat!"

44. *Top Cat* was a Hanna-Barbera cartoon that first aired in 1961. **Top Cat** lived in a Manhattan garbage can on Madison Avenue near the 13th police precinct. He devised clever get-rich schemes while keeping a lookout for the local cop, Officer Dibble. The Top Cat character was inspired by Sergeant Bilko from the military comedy *You'll Never Get Rich.* Top Cat, "T.C." to his friends and his pals Benny, Brain, Choo Coo, Spook, and Fancy Fancy, dressed in a purple vest and flat hat. His voice was provided by Arnold Stang.

45. **Waldo Kitty** appeared in thirteen episodes of NBC's *The Secret Lives of Waldo Kitty* in 1975. Based on James Thurber's *The Secret Life of Walter Mitty,* Waldo was constantly imagining himself as a hero: supercat Catman, jungle hero Catzan, and the benevolent Robin Cat.

"Fans think they want to see more than the ten or twenty seconds of Itchy and Scratchy that we put on the show, but my feeling is, less is more. Once you've skinned and flayed a cat, ripped his head off, made him drink acid, and tied his tongue to the moon, there really isn't that much to say."

— **MATT GROENING**

17 TV Kitties

1. Boo-boo Kitty,[1] *Laverne and Shirley*

2. Bonkers, *All My Children*

3. Fluffy, *The Brady Bunch*

4. Henrietta Pussycat, *Mr. Rogers' Neighborhood*

5. Kit, *Charmed*

6. Lucky, *Alf*

7. Marmalade and Rusty, *The Beverly Hillbillies*

8. Minerva, *Our Miss Brooks*

9. Miss Kitty Fantastico, *Buffy the Vampire Slayer*

10. Myrtle, *The X-Files*

11. Pequita,[2] *Seinfeld*

12. Salem, *Sabrina the Teenage Witch*

13. Salty and Tiki, *Caroline in the City*

14. Smelly Cat,[3] *Friends*

15. Spot,[4] *Star Trek: The Next Generation*

16. Tiddles,[5] *Are You Being Served?*

17. Toonces,[6] *Saturday Night Live*

1 SHIRLEY'S STUFFED CAT.

2 ANTONIO THE BUSBOY'S CAT, WHO RAN AWAY WHEN GEORGE CAME OVER TO APOLOGIZE FOR GETTING HIM FIRED.

3 PHOEBE WROTE A SONG FOR HIM.

4 DATA'S CAT.

5 MRS. SLOCOMBE'S "PUSSY," A LARGELY UNSEEN CHARACTER AND THE SOURCE OF MUCH INNUENDO, APPEARED ONLY ONCE, WHEN MRS. SLOCOMBE BROUGHT IT TO THE STORE, BUT ONLY ITS TAIL WAS VISIBLE THROUGH THE CAT CARRIER.

6 THE SILVER TABBY WAS THE PET OF LYLE (STEVE MARTIN ORIGINALLY, THEN DANA CARVEY) AND BRENDA CLARK (VICTORIA JACKSON). HE WAS ALLOWED TO DRIVE THE FAMILY CAR, WHICH HE OFTEN DID—OFF CLIFFS, MOSTLY. TOONCES, PORTRAYED BY A REAL CAT AND A PUPPET, APPEARED ON FIVE EPISODES FROM 1989 TO 1993 AND IN OVER 250 TV COMMERCIALS.

9 Cats Who Have Won Acting Awards

When a horse was accidentally killed during the filming of *Jesse James*, the American Humane Association instituted the Patsys — awards to honor animal performers. Francis the Mule received the first Patsy in 1951, and since then contenders have included dogs, cats, pigs, and even goats. These are the feline frontrunners who have been honored with Patsys.

1. **Orangey** (1952). For his role as the title character of *Rhubarb*

2. **Pyewacket** (1959). For his role in *Bell, Book, and Candle*

3. **Orangey** (1962). For his portrayal of "Cat" in *Breakfast at Tiffany's*

4. **Syn Cat** (1966). For his performance in *That Darn Cat!*

5. **Morris** (1973). For his work in the 9Lives cat food commercials

6. **Midnight** (1974). For his TV appearances on *Mannix*

7. **Tonto** (1976). For his role as one of the stars of *Harry and Tonto*

8. **17*** (1977). For his appearance in the cult fave *Dr. Shrinker*

9. **Amber** (1978). For her role in *The Cat from Outer Space*

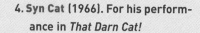

The World According to Garfield

People relate to Garfield because Garfield is *them*. "He's a human in a cat suit," creator Jim Davis likes to say. Garfield loves TV and hates Mondays. He'd rather pig out than work out; his passion for food and sleep is matched only by his aversion to diet and exercise (he prefers lay-downs to sit-ups). He'd like mornings better if they started later. Drinking coffee "strong enough to sit up and bark" is the only way to start the day. What could be more human?

The real-life success story of this fictional feline began with mastermind cartoonist Jim Davis. *Garfield* was introduced to the world in just 41 newspapers in 1978 but quickly became the fastest-growing and most widely syndicated comic strip ever. Today, the strip appears in over 2,570 newspapers and is read daily by 263 million people around the world. A popular animated TV show, *Garfield & Friends,* which appeared on CBS from 1988 to 1995, is currently in worldwide syndication. Garfield also enjoys a thriving licensing program, whereby nearly 400 manufacturers crank out his image daily, on everything from Christmas ornaments and stationery to underwear and golf-club covers. Garfield's vast empire includes 111 countries, a popular website (www.garfield.com), and an online catalog, Garfield Stuff (www.garfieldstuff.com). Over 130 million Garfield books have been sold worldwide.

Twentieth Century Fox immortalized the fat cat in two feature films, *Garfield: The Movie* (2004) and *Garfield: A Tail of Two Kitties* (2006), and he is a staple of the Macy's Thanksgiving Day Parade in New York City.

Here is some of the wit and wisdom of Garfield:

"The meek shall inherit squat."

"A little ego goes nowhere."

"Start each day with a smile (and get it over with)."

"All work and no play is out of the question."

"Show me a good mouser, and I'll show you a cat with bad breath."

"Give me coffee and no one gets hurt."

"Life is a constant battle between diet and dessert."

"The best things in life are edible."

"I'm not overweight. I'm undertall."

"I'm a creature of habit . . . all the bad ones."

"Anything worth doing is worth overdoing."

"Remember to stop and eat the flowers along the way."

"Every time I think I've hit bottom, somebody throws me a shovel."

"Some call it laziness. I call it deep thought."

"One good thing about lethargy. You don't have to work at it."

Midnight was a bizarre violin-playing cat who said only the word "Niiiiice" on Smilin' Ed's Buster Brown Gang radio show in the 1940s and 1950s. When the show went to TV in the 1950s as Andy's Gang, Midnight followed, as cats often do.

The Major Cats of <u>Cats</u>

Andrew Lloyd Webber's musical *Cats* has proved to be one of the most popular musicals of all time. The show, based on the felines in *Old Possum's Book of Practical Cats* and other poems by T. S. Eliot, has been translated into over 20 languages and has played in about 250 cities throughout the world. The show premiered in 1981 at the New London Theatre in London's West End and proceeded to break attendance records both in England and on Broadway. The story centers on a tribe of cats known as the Jellicles, whose members gather each year at the Jellicle Ball, during which time Old Deuteronomy, the tribe's leader, chooses a member worthy enough to ascend to Heaviside Layer, or cat heaven, if you will. The cats each perform a song or dance number and are then judged by Old Deuteronomy.

Admetus, a young cat, who in many productions also doubles as Macavity. Omitted from some productions.

Alonzo, a black-and-white tom in most productions; in the United States and the first German productions, he is depicted as black and gold. Often considered the "second-hand-man" to Munkustrap.

Asparagus (nicknamed Gus), the theater cat. In the filmed version, Gus and Asparagus are two separate characters; on stage the same actor usually plays them both.

Bill Bailey, a young black, white, and brown male. Sometimes interchangeable with the character of Tumblebrutus. Omitted from some productions.

Bombalurina, a saucy red female, often believed to be the leader of the female "queen" cats. She is close friends with Demeter.

Bustopher Jones, a fat "25 pounder," dresses in a snappy tuxedo and spats. Respected by all as the upper-class "St James Street Cat."

Carbucketty, the "knockabout cat." Sometimes interchangeable with the character of Pouncival. Omitted from some productions.

Cassandra, a brown-and-cream female, with a braided tail and rolled wig. Unique and somewhat mysterious.

Coricopat, male twin to Tantomile. Both of them are intuitive or even psychic. Omitted from some productions.

Demeter, a very skittish cat, possibly due to a bad relationship with Macavity in her past. She is close friends with Bombalurina.

Electra, an orange-and-black tabby kitten who seems to be friends with Etcetera as well as a fan of Rum Tum Tugger.

Etcetera, a happy, energetic kitten who is a big fan of Rum Tum Tugger. Omitted from some productions.

Exotica, a female character who appears only in the filmed version. A role created especially for actress Femi Taylor.

George, a young male kitten, omitted from most productions.

Ghengis or **Gilbert**, the leader of the crew of Siamese cats who lead to Growltiger's demise. Usually played by the actor who portrays Mungojerrie, Tumblebrutus, or Coricopat.

Grizabella, the former Glamour Cat who has lost her sparkle and now wants only to be accepted. Ultimately, she is the one chosen to ascend to the Heaviside Layer and be reborn.

Growltiger, a theatrical character Gus recalls playing in his youth, who appears in Gus's memory of the production of "Growltiger's Last Stand." In some productions he is portrayed as a vicious pirate; in others he's more of a parody of a pirate. Does not appear in productions that omit "Growltiger's Last Stand."

Jellylorum, named after one of T. S. Eliot's cats. A female who watches out for the kittens, along with Jennyanydots. She has a close relationship with Gus.

Jemima, who can be cast interchangeably with Sillabub. Jemima appears in most international productions. Sillabub was a name created for the American productions. However, Japanese casts include both Sillabub and Jemima as different characters.

Jennyanydots, the old Gumbie cat. She rules the mice by day and the cockroaches by night.

Lady Griddlebone, a fluffy white cat and Growltiger's lover in "Growltiger's Last Stand," where she sings "The Ballad of Billy McCaw" or the mock Italian aria "In una tepida notte" (depending on the production) with Growltiger. Almost always played by the actress playing Jellylorum. Does not appear in productions that omit "Growltiger's Last Stand."

Macavity, the show's only real villain. He is actually a literary allusion to the Sherlock Holmes character Professor Moriarty. He executes the kidnapping of Old Deuteronomy in the second act and also attempts to abduct Demeter.

The Magical Mr. Mistoffelees, a young tom who has magical powers including the ability to create flash explosions (or bolt lightning, in the filmed version, thanks to computer technology). His signature dance move is "The Conjuring Turn," which is approximately twenty-five spins on one foot. In most productions, Mistoffelees has an alter ego named Quaxo, who appears as a general chorus cat throughout the show and is dressed slightly differently.

Mungojerrie, half of a pair of notorious "cat-burglars," Mungojerrie and Rumpelteazer. Usually plays Ghengis/Gilbert.

Munkustrap, a black-and-silver tom who is leader and protector of the Jellicle tribe. He also narrates "The Awefull Battle of the Pekes and the Pollicles." Considered the storyteller of the tribe.

Old Deuteronomy, the lovable patriarch of the Jellicle tribe.

Plato, sometimes used interchangeably with George or Admetus. He does a pas de deux with Victoria during the Jellicle Ball. Omitted from some productions.

Pouncival, a playful tom kitten.

Rumpleteazer, the female half of a pair of notorious "cat-burglars," Mungojerrie and Rumpleteazer. Her name can also be spelled "Rumpelteazer," the spelling originally used by T. S. Eliot; this is the spelling used by most productions.

T. S. Eliot's Cats
George Pushdragon
Jellylorum
Mirza Murad Alibeg
Noilly Prat
Pattipaws or Pettipaws
Wiscus
Tantomile

Rumpus Cat, the great spiky-haired brave cat with glowing red eyes, as mentioned in "The Awefull Battle of the Pekes and the Pollicles," seen as a heroic figure among the Jellicles. Does not appear in productions that omit the song "The Awefull Battle of the Pekes and the Pollicles." Usually played by Alonzo or Admetus.

Rum Tum Tugger, the ladies' tom. His temperament ranges from clownish to serious, though he is always flirtatious, a sort of feline equivalent of Mick Jagger, noticeable for his wild mane.

Sillabub, the Broadway version's Jemima, although the Japanese version contains both characters.

Skimbleshanks, the railway cat. An active orange tabby cat who lives on the trains and acts as an unofficial chaperone.

Tantomile, the "Witch's Cat," female twin of Coricopat. Both of them are perceived as intuitive or even psychic.

Tumblebrutus, U.S. counterpart of Bill Bailey.

Victor, a young male. Sometimes known as part of the "Cats chorus." Omitted from some productions.

Victoria, a white kitten extremely gifted in dancing. The official Jellicle Ball begins with her solo dance.

Cats of Famous People

Florence Nightingale owned more than 60 cats in her lifetime and often complained of mysterious "stains" on her paperwork.

Historical Figures

Daniel Boone	Bluegrass
King Charles I	Luck
Chinese emperor Chu Hou-Tsung	Shuang-mei (meaning "Frost Eyebrows")
Winston Churchill	Cat, Nelson, Jock
John Kenneth Galbraith	Ahmedabad, nicknamed "Ahmed" then renamed Gujarat, when Islamic officials took offense at the original name while Galbraith was U.S. ambassador to India. (See page 119 for more about this cat.)
Charles de Gaulle	Gris (meaning "gray")
Peggy Guggenheim	Gypsy
Emperor Ichijo of Japan	Myobu No Omoto (meaning "Lady-in-Waiting")
Pope Leo XII	Micette *or* Micetto
Charles Lindbergh	Patsy
Muhammad	Muezza
Florence Nightingale	Bismarck, Disraeli, and Gladstone, all large Persians, as well as many others
Nostradamus	Grimalkin
Albert Schweitzer	Sizi
Sir Walter Scott	Hinse
3rd Earl of Southampton	Trixie, who allegedly stayed with him for two years in the Tower of London
Queen Victoria	White Heather, a white Persian
Horace Walpole	Selima, a tortoiseshell; drowned in a goldfish bowl, inspiring Thomas Gray's poem "Ode on the Death of a Favourite Cat Drowned in a Tub of Goldfishes" (1748)

Media Figures

Muhammad Ali	Icarus
Ian Anderson (leader of Jethro Tull)	Rupi, who inspired the title song of Anderson's 2004 solo album *Rupi's Dance*
Joan Baez	Carlangas
Warren Beatty	Cake
Robert Bigelow (real estate mogul)	Mortgage, Writeoff, and Taxes
George Burns	Willie, so named "Because when you told the cat what to do, it was always a question of will he or won't he"
Wilt Chamberlain	Zip and Zap
Walter Cronkite	Dancer
Billy Crystal	Mittens

James Dean	Marcus, a Siamese; gift from Elizabeth Taylor
Cameron Diaz	Little Man
Kirsten Dunst	Tasmania, or Taz
Elvira, Mistress of the Dark, AKA Cassandra Peters	Hecate and Renfeld Dracu
Michael Feinstein	Bing Clawsby
Roberta Flack	Caruso
Leeza Gibbons	Alex
Matt Groening	Frosty
Peggy Guggenheim	Romeo
Whitney Houston	Marilyn Miste
Cyndi Lauper	Weasel
John Lennon	Elvis
Jay Leno	Cheeser
Ann-Margret	Big Red
Pamela Mason	Flower-Face, a Siamese discussed in Mason's book *The Cats in Our Lives* (1949)
Freddie Mercury	Delilah, Tom, Jerry, Oscar, Tiffany, Goliath, Miko, Romeo, and Lily; paid tribute to Delilah, a male tortoiseshell, on the Queen album *Innuendo*
Charles Mingus	Nightlife
Marilyn Monroe	Mitsou, a white Persian
Martin Mull	Alice
Graham Nash	Frogurt
Aaron Neville	Tiger
Kim Novak	Pyewacket; starred with Novak in *Bell, Book, and Candle*
Gary Oldman	Soymilk
Yoko Ono	Charo, Sascha, and Misha
Jane Pauley	Meatball
Bernadette Peters	Murphy
Regis Philbin	Sara, Sascha
Trent Reznor	Fuckchop
Molly Ringwald	Tigerlily
Gloria Steinem	Magritte
Martha Stewart	Teeny, Weeny, Mozart, Beethoven, Verdi, Vivaldi, Berlioz, and Bartok
Julia Sweeney	Rita, a black cat
Elizabeth Taylor	Jeepers Creepers

E=MICE²

Einstein's cat.

"The cat does not offer services. The cat offers itself. Of course he wants care and shelter. You don't buy love for nothing. Like all pure creatures, cats are practical."

— **WILLIAM S. BURROUGHS**

A vintage postcard from 1912.

Mark Twain's drawing of the cats he adored. We're glad he stuck to writing.

Alex Trebek	Linger Dinger
Robert Wagner	Dweezil, gift from Dweezil Zappa
Vanna White	Ashley, Rhett Butler

Artists

George Booth	Amberson/Ambrosia; called Ambrosia, until Booth found the cat was male; Tata, named James Taylor until Booth found the cat was female
R. Crumb	Fred, inspiration for the infamous Fritz
Paul Klee	Bimbo, a white longhaired cat, and Fritzi, a mackerel tabby, depicted in Marina Algerghini's *Il Gatto Cosmico* (1993)
Jean-Claude Suarès	Maurice, named for Suarès's wife's lover, who was "not allowed on the bed either"
Andy Warhol	Hester, Sam
Benjamin West	Grimalkin

Writers

Kingsley Amis	Sarah Snow, a white longhaired, green-eyed cat
Cleveland Amory	Polar Bear
Matthew Arnold	Atossa, a three-legged cat
Jorge Luis Borges	Beppo
Emily Brontë	Tiger, who played at Brontë's feet while she wrote *Wuthering Heights*
Samuel Butler	Purdoe
Lord Byron	Beppo, one of five cats who traveled with him
Raymond Chandler	Taki, a black female Persian
Jean Cocteau	Karoun, Drôle
Charles Dickens	William, renamed Williamina when she had kittens, which she moved into Dickens's study; Master's Cat, the only one of Williamina's kittens that Dickens kept, would snuff his reading candle to get attention.
Alexandre Dumas	Le Docteur, Mysouff I, and Mysouff II
F. Scott Fitzgerald	Chopin
Peter Gethers	Norton, a Scottish Fold tabby memorialized in the novels *The Cat Who Went to Paris*, *A Cat Abroad*, and *The Cat Who'll Live Forever*
Thomas Hardy	Cobby, a Blue Persian given to Hardy late in life; vanished when Hardy died in 1928
Thomas Hood	Scratchaway
Victor Hugo	Chanoine (originally called Gavroche) and Mouche
Dr. Samuel Johnson	Hodge; also Lilly, a white kitling
Michael Joseph	Minna Minna Mowbray, the focus of an entire chapter in *Cat's Company* (1946)

Edward Lear	Foss
Alice Liddell	Dinah, the feline friend of the real-life inspiration for Alice of *Alice's Adventures in Wonderland*
Christopher Morley	Taffy, the thieving cat commemorated in Morley's 1929 poem "In Honor of Taffy Topaz"
Iris Murdoch	General Butchkin
Edgar Allan Poe	Catarina
Gabriele Rossetti	Zoë, a black-and-white female cat
George Sand (Amantine-Lucile-Aurore Dupin)	Minou, who ate her breakfast from Sand's own bowl
Dorothy L. Sayers	Timothy, a white cat mentioned in two poems by Sayers: "For Timothy" and "War Cat"
Liz Smith	Mr. Sotto Voce
Robert Southey	Bona Marietta, Virgil, Hurlyburlybuss, and Lord Nelson, who, over the years, ascended in rank from baron, to viscount, to earl, for "services performed against the Rats"
Harriet Beecher Stowe	Calvin, a Maltese stray
Mark Twain	Apollinaris, Beelzebub, Blatherskite, Buffalo Bill, Sin, Sour Mash, Tammany, Zoroaster, etc. — too many to name!
Kurt Vonnegut	Claude
H. G. Wells	Mr. Peter Wells
Tennessee Williams	Topaz
Christopher Wren	Henrietta, devoted to the *New York Times* foreign correspondent and made famous by the book *The Cat Who Covered the World*

Edward Lear's striped tomcat, Foss, was immortalized by the author. The end of the cat's tail was cut off by a superstitious servant who believed that this would stop the animal from straying.

"I never shall forget the indulgence with which he treated Hodge, his cat: for whom he himself used to go out and buy oysters, lest the servants having that trouble should take a dislike to the poor creature. I am, unluckily, one of those who have an antipathy to a cat, so that I am uneasy when in the room with one; and I own, I frequently suffered a good deal from the presence of this same Hodge. I recollect him one day scrambling up Dr. Johnson's breast, apparently with much satisfaction, while my friend smiling and half-whistling, rubbed down his back, and pulled him by the tail; and when I observed he was a fine cat, saying, 'Why yes, Sir, but I have had cats whom I liked better than this'; and then as if perceiving Hodge to be out of countenance, adding, 'but he is a very fine cat, a very fine cat indeed.'

This reminds me of the ludicrous account which he gave Mr. Langton, of the despicable state of a young Gentleman of good family. 'Sir, when I heard of him last, he was running about town shooting cats.' And then in a sort of kindly reverie, he bethought himself of his own favorite cat, and said, 'But Hodge shan't be shot; no, no, Hodge shall not be shot.'"

—JAMES BOSWELL, LIFE OF JOHNSON

Hemingway's Cats

Hemingway acquired his first cat from a ship's captain in Key West, Florida, where he made his home for a number of years. This cat, which may have been a Maine Coon, had extra toes on its paws (known as a polydactyl, Latin for "many digits"). Today, approximately 60 cats, half of them polydactyl, live in the Ernest Hemingway Museum and Home in Key West, protected by the terms of his will. At least some are descendants of Hemingway's first cat, and they have the sort of fanciful names that the author liked to give his cats. Hemingway and his wife, Mary, were devoted to their cats and believed that cats had souls and that they would eventually see them again in heaven. Here are the names of some of Hemingway's cats:

Ambrose. Called the "kitchen cat," Ambrose was a black-and-white Cuban cat who was known for being somewhat neurotic.

Bates. This cat was named after Bob Bates, a Red Cross captain who was a close friend of Hemingway while he was in Italy.

Big Boy Peterson. Ernest adopted him after finding him on his doorstep. Big Boy, a loving and trustworthy cat, ate and slept with Hemingway every night. Some believe that Big Boy was the last creature to see Hemingway alive.

Blindie. This is the name of two blind Cuban kittens who had been inbred.

Boise. This cat was named after the navy cruiser *Boise* and was one of Ernest's favorites. Boise slept with the author and was even fed from his plate. Boise was immortalized in Hemingway's novel *Islands in the Stream.* Hemingway devoted 35 pages of the book to Boise.

Catherine Tiger. Catherine was one of the cats that Hemingway grew up with in Illinois. She was named after Catherine the Great because of her strong-willed personality.

Cristobal. Cristobal became Hemingway's main squeeze after Boise, Willy, Princessa, and Friendless passed on. Cristobal was extremely playful and loved people. He often hung out with Hemingway while he was writing.

Ecstasy. Also known as Smelly, Ecstasy loved to stalk birds. He was gentle and affectionate and would sniff at anything he was investigating.

Fatso. Also included in *Islands in the Stream,* this fat cat was the son of Boise and Princessa. Unfortunately, Fatso developed the nasty habit of killing other cats and had to be destroyed.

F. Puss. This large, affectionate Persian cat was Hemingway's son John's babysitter and would not allow anyone to come near the boy. Hemingway wrote about F. Puss in his novel *A Moveable Feast.*

Feather Kcat. Feather was adopted by Ernest and his wife, Hadley, when they lived in Canada, and this cat kept Hadley company during a pregnancy.

Feather Kitty. This Cuban cat had gray and white stripes and was considered quite ornery but also deemed an excellent mother to Izzy the Cat and Cristobal.

Friendless. Hemingway and Friendless became drinking buddies. Friendless would be allowed a small amount of whiskey in his milk. He was sired by Boise and had a reputation for being very cheerful.

Friendless Brother, AKA Bro. When she was born, everyone thought she was a male until they realized their mistake. This quiet Cuban cat loved her master. She also makes an appearance in *Islands in the Stream.*

Furhouse. This boy cat was sired by Princessa and Boise and became a catnip junky.

Good Will. This beautiful tiger angora cat was a gift that Hemingway received. Will was quite the acrobat, loved performing in front of his master, and enjoyed having his picture taken.

Izzy the Cat, AKA The Queen. Izzy, short for Isabella, was named after Queen Isabella of Spain. She was a fearsome cat with an adventurous spirit. She was accidentally killed after she tried eating the family dog's food.

Littlest Kitty. A gorgeous Cuban black cat that Hemingway adored and wrote about in *Islands in the Stream.*

Manx. Although not a Manx at birth, he got his name because of an accident that resulted in the loss of his tail. Manx was a childhood pet of Hemingway's.

Miss Kitty. Part wild tiger cat, Miss Kitty was found living in a barn on the property of a Hemingway summer rental in Idaho. She was eventually adopted by a family friend.

Mooky. Hemingway befriended and was impressed by Mooky, who survived a battle with a badger.

Pelusa. Pelusa was a gift to Hemingway's secretary in Cuba. Hemingway's staff cared for Pelusa after the secretary left Cuba.

Pony. This little kitten was diagnosed with and eventually died of distemper.

Princessa. Although the Hemingways originally named her Tester, the household staff renamed this elegant cat Princessa. She became the mother of all the cats at Finca Vigia, Hemingway's home in Cuba. She is also written about in *Islands in the Stream*.

Shopsky. The Hemingways originally named him Shakespeare but later felt the name was too cumbersome for a little kitten. They renamed him Barbershop but eventually shortened that to Shopsky. Shopsky had to be put down after he began killing other cats.

Sir Winston Churchill. Winston didn't much care for milk or cream but loved eating food that had been marinated in alcohol.

Sister Kitty. She was left on the Hemingways' doorstep at their summer retreat in Idaho. Sister was a nasty little critter but was adored just the same.

Spendy. Shopsky and Ecstasy's brother, Spendy shadowed Mary Hemingway wherever she went and was known for her continuous purring.

Stranger. This fragile little kitten was a descendant of Princessa.

Taskforce. This fur ball adored catnip and is also mentioned in *Islands in the Stream*.

Thruster. This cat was the daughter of Boise, with whom she later mated. Unfortunately, the resulting litter produced two blind cats.

Uncle Wolfer, AKA Stoopy. Another son of Princessa and Boise, this long-haired cat was not adventurous and didn't even like catnip. However, Stoopy did like performing tricks for Hemingway's amusement.

Willy. Mary Hemingway described Willy as a "banker type" who did not think of himself as a cat, but loved catnip just the same. Willy loved people but disliked other cats. This cuddly creature adored the Hemingways and was adored in return. When Willy died, he was buried in a special area reserved for the Hemingways' favorite cats.

> "He started to climb again and at the top he fell and lay for some time with the mast across his shoulder. He tried to get up. But it was too difficult and he sat there with the mast on his shoulder and looked at the road. A cat passed on the far side going about its business and the old man watched it. Then he just watched the road."
>
> — **THE OLD MAN AND THE SEA**

In 2006 the descendants of Ernest Hemingway's polydactyl cats who roam the grounds of the Hemingway Home in Key West, Florida, wandered into a bit of a legal problem when the U.S. Department of Agriculture targeted the Hemingway home as an "exhibitor" of cats, which would require that its officials obtain a USDA Animal Welfare License. Officials of the home disputed the position.

Richelieu's Cats

Cardinal Richelieu, Armand Jean du Plessis (1585–1642), French clergyman, nobleman, statesman, and Louis XIII's chief minister, kept dozens of cats, even building a cattery at Versailles for his wards and leaving money to maintain the cats after his death. These are just some of the many cats he owned.

Cardinal Richelieu and his famous collection of cats. Taken from *Les Animaux Historiques*, 1861.

Félimare, striped like a tiger; one of many cats Richelieu had when he died

Gazette, described by Richelieu as "indiscreet"

Lucifer, jet black

Ludovic le Cruel, savage rat-killer

Ludoviska, a Polish cat

Mimi-Paillon, Angora

Mounard le Fougueux, a "quarrelsome, capricious, and worldly" cat who was among the many cats Richelieu owned when he died in 1642

Perruque, who, as a kitten, fell at Richelieu's feet from the wig (*perruque,* in French) of an academic named Racan

Pyrame, so named because he and Thisbé slept together with paws intertwined, like the mythological lovers

Racan, named for the academic Racan

Rubis sur l'Ongle, especially fond of milk

Serpolet, fond of sunning himself in a window

Soumise, Richelieu's favorite

Thisbé, named, with Pyrame, after the mythological lovers

Anne Frank's Cats

Anne Frank, a 13-year-old Jewish girl, and her family went into hiding in 1942 to escape persecution by the Nazis. They shared a small warehouse attic in Amsterdam. The story was immortalized with the publication, in 1947, of *The Diary of Anne Frank.* Although the girl was killed at Bergen-Belsen, Germany, in 1945, her story became a classic chapter in the literature of World War II, largely for its realistic depiction in marvelous detail of twenty-five months in hiding. Although the family was isolated from the rest of the world, three of the cats listed here did manage to find their way into the Franks' home, and each brought with it the pleasures that only a cat can provide.

1. **Moortje** was a beloved black cat whom Anne left with neighbors before she went into hiding with her family. In her book *Anne Frank Remembered*, Miep Gies says the family had owned a different cat also named Moortje when Anne was only 8 or 9 years old. Gies describes the Franks as "cat people" and admired a charcoal drawing of a mother cat and her two kittens displayed in their home. Many years later, Otto Frank made a present of this charcoal drawing to Gies, herself a cat lover.

2. **Boche** was an aggressive warehouse cat who was occupying the attic when the Franks arrived, named after a derogatory slang word for "German."

3. **Mouschi** was a stray young male cat brought into the Secret Annex by Peter van Pels.

4. **Moffie**, a warehouse cat, also male, was described by Miep Gies as a "big, fat black-and-white tomcat with a slightly battered face." According to Gies: "A *Moffen* was a biscuit in the shape of a fat little pig . . . our cat was known to steal food from other houses in the neighborhood, just as the Germans were doing with our food."

5. **Tommy**, a cat who constantly battled Boche, ran away before Anne began her diary.

Colette's Cats

Sidonie-Gabrielle Colette's (1873–1954) most famous work is probably *Gigi*, but she was also known as an enthusiastic aurophile who often wrote about cats in her books. "The only risk you ever run in befriending a cat is enriching yourself," she was known to say. In *La Chatte*, published in English in 1936 as *The Cat*, the main character, Alain, must choose between a beautiful Russian Blue and his young bride, who tries to kill the cat. She also wrote "Dialogue des Bêtes," a conversation between a cat and a dog.

These are only a few of the cats that Colette kept.

Ba-tu Belle Aude	Kro	Muscat
Chatte Grise	La Bergère	Musette
Domino	La Chatte	One and Only
Fanfare	La Chatte Dernière	Petiteu
Fossette	La Noire	Pinichette
Franchette	La Touteu	Poucette
Jeune Bleue	Mini-mini	Saha
Kapok	Minionne	Toune
Kiki-la-Doucette	Moune	Zwerg

24 Record-Holding Cats

1. **First Cat to Have a Name** Bouhaki, traditionally the first cat known to have been given a name, appears in Egyptian carvings dating back as far as the Eleventh Dynasty (1950 B.C.). It has a fat body and a curled tail.

2. **Fattest Cat** Himmey, a neutered male tabby, weighed 46 pounds and 15.5 ounces (21 kilos and 300 grams) when he died of respiratory failure. He had a 15-inch neck, a 33-inch waist, and was 38 inches long. He is listed in *The Guinness Book of World Records.*

3. **Longest Cat** A large white cat from Scotland named Snowbie, measuring 40.8 inches long from tip of nose to tip of tail, held the official title until 2002, when Verismo Leonetti Reserve Red (his friends call him Leo), a Maine Coon measuring 48 inches, snatched it away. Leo's paws fit snugly in a child's size 2 shoe.

4. **Smallest Cat** Mr. Peebles, of Pekin, Illinois, has been verified by Guinness as record-holder for the smallest cat. He is only 6.1 inches tall and 19.2 inches long. He is full size and fully grown, suffering from a birth defect that restricts his weight, which is only three pounds.

5. **Smartest Cat** Hema Chandras, a performer in New Delhi, India, claims that Cuty Boy, a purebred Persian, is the smartest cat alive; he has been featured on cat websites and in periodicals worldwide. He can allegedly say no and yes in response to questions; he answers by rocking his head back and forth and by kissing his owner, who claims that this cat can do math and has been tested by teachers. He is reputed to understand eight languages, including Gujarati, Arabic, French, and English.

6. **The Oldest Cats** Two deceased cats, both of whom lived for 34 years, hold the record as the oldest cats — a female tabby named Ma died in 1957; Granpa, who belonged to Jake Perry of Austin, Texas, and ate bacon and eggs with broccoli and coffee every morning for breakfast, died in 1998. Second place goes to Spike, an orange tabby from Dorset, England, who survived a Rottweiler attack at the age of 19 and then lived to the ripe old age of 31. As of this writing, Guinness recognizes Katallena Lady of Victoria, born on March 11, 1977, as the oldest cat alive. Another contender, the 2002 Guinness record holder, Bluebell, owned by Lea Yergler, of St. Maries, Idaho, was 24 at the time. (See also item 11 on this list.)

7. **The Most Expensive Cat Wedding** Their owners shelled out the equivalent of almost $17,000 to celebrate the marriage of Phet and Ploy, two rare "diamond-eyed" cats (possessing a rare type of glaucoma and believed to be symbols of God) who exchanged meows in Thailand in 1996. Phet arrived in a Rolls-Royce, and Ploy, by helicopter. A parrot acted as best man and an iguana as the maid of honor. With more than 500 guests in attendance, the couple raked in over $60,000 in gifts.

8. **Best Climber** On September 6, 1950, a 4-month-old kitten belonging to Josephine Aufdenblatten of Geneva, Switzerland, followed a group of climbers to the top of the 14,691-foot Matterhorn in the Alps. Once at the summit, he shared a meal with astounded fellow climbers and afterward became famous as the Matterhorn Cat.

9. **Most Kittens in a Lifetime** Proving once and for all the need for spaying and neutering, a tabby named Dusty gave birth to 420 kittens over the course of her lifetime.

10. **Best Mouser** The greatest number of mice known to be killed by one cat is 28,899. Towser, a tortoiseshell

"Everything I know I learned from my cat: When you're hungry, eat. When you're tired, nap in a sunbeam. When you go to the vet's, pee on your owner." —GARY SMITH

tabby in charge of rodent control at the Glenturret Distillery in Scotland until she died at the age of 21 in 1987, achieved this record. Her average was four mice a day.

11. Oldest Feline Mother Kitty, owned by George Johnstone of England, produced two kittens at age 30 in May 1987. She died just short of her 32nd birthday, having given birth to a known total of 218 kittens.

12. Largest Litter The largest litter was produced by a Burmese-Siamese mother who gave birth to 19 kittens at one time on August 7, 1970; 4 of them were stillborn.

13. Most Unusual Cat A domestic cat was born in the United States in 1975 with 5 legs, 6 paws, and 30 toes.

14. Most Toes An orange tabby named Jake from Deep River, New York, was confirmed to have seven toes on each foot. The previous record-holder was another orange tabby named Mickey, who had 27 toes, all told.

15. Longest Fall Andy, who belonged to Florida senator Ken Myer in the 1970s, fell 16 floors from a balcony and holds the record for the longest nonfatal fall in feline history.

16. Longest Trip Home on Foot A Persian cat walked 1,488 miles over a period of 13 months to find her owners.

17. Longest Trip Home via Air Guinness named Hamlet the world's most traveled cat. He got stuck in a Canadian airplane, where he remained for a period of seven weeks, inadvertently traveling some 360,000 miles.

18. Most Cats Owned A farmer in Texas kept 1,400 cats, some feral, on his farm. However, Jack Wright of Kingston, Ontario, is the *Guinness Book* record-holder for the owner of the most cats at one time, 689, all of which were domestic. "You can visualize a hundred cats. Beyond that, you can't. Two hundred, five hundred, it all looks the same," Wright said in an interview.

19. Most Frequent-Flyer Miles In 2002, Babi and Kuukie, owned by Elayne Rifkin of White Plains, New York, became the first cats to earn frequent-flyer miles after making three trips from New York to Israel.

20. Longest Survival During a Disaster Eighty days after an earthquake in Taiwan in 1999 that killed 2,400 people, a cat was discovered in a collapsed building in Taichung. She made a full recovery.

Bengal kittens.

21. Most Finicky Cat A cat called Schimmy refuses to eat anything but Chinese takeout food. His owner, who eats Chinese food five days a week, started giving Schimmy a small bowl of leftover shrimp or chicken chow mein each night, and Schimmy now refuses to eat anything else. A veterinarian reported, "It is strange but not at all harmful to him."

22. Most Chutzpah Boris, a cat, almost managed to order 450 cans of his favorite food on an Internet shopping site while his owner wasn't looking. His owner had ordered six cans. Apparently Boris didn't think that was enough, so he hit the keyboard, increasing the quantity.

23. Most Expensive Cat In February 1998, an F2 Bengal cat named Cato made the Guinness World Records as the most expensive cat ever purchased, bought for $41,435.00. A worthy runner-up is a California Spangled cat bought for $24,000 in January 1987. The cat had appeared in the 1986 Neiman Marcus catalog.

24. Largest Collection of Cat Memorabilia Since 1979, Florence Groff of France has amassed a record-breaking collection of 11,717 cat-related items. Among the collection are 2,118 different cat figurines (48 of which are fridge magnets), 86 decorative plates, 60 pieces of crystal, 140 metallic boxes, 9 lamps, 36 stuffed toys, 41 painted eggs, and 2,666 pussy postcards.

7 Cats Who Changed History

1. Sir Henry Wyatt, born in Yorkshire in about 1460, was imprisoned in the Tower of London by Richard III, who perceived him as a threat. There, in a cold, narrow tower, Sir Henry suffered torture on the rack and was forced to swallow vinegar and mustard, among other torments. Only in his twenties, starving and broken in spirit, Sir Henry prayed for death. One day, a cat found her way into the dun-

Charmian, Cleoptra's cat, is said to have inspired the shape and style of Cleopatra's makeup and facial decorations, which in turn have influenced makeup styles that are still popular today. We can't help but wonder how different the world would be had she kept a raccoon instead of a cat.

geon, and the two became friends. Sir Henry showered her with love, and one day, with the kind of awareness that only a cat can have, it seems, she brought him a pigeon (which was cooked for him by the one friendly guard). Thereafter, it was the cat who kept him alive; she became known as "**Sir Henry's caterer**" until 1485, when he was released, upon Henry Tudor's ascension to the throne.

In the Church of St. Mary the Virgin and All Saints in Maidstone, Kent, above the choir stalls,

Radioactive Cats In 1996, a pregnant cat managed to find her way through the security gate at the San Onofre power plant. The kittens she had there were named Alpa, Beta, Gamma, and Neutron when it was discovered that they had become slightly radioactive. They weren't in any danger, and seven months after they were removed from the plant, they were pronounced radiation-free.

near the altar, is a large stone memorial bearing this inscription: "To the memory of Sir Henry Wiat, of Alington Casle, Knight banneret, descended of that ancient family, who was imprisoned and tortured in the Tower, in the reign of King Richard the third, kept in the dungeon, where fed and preserved by a cat . . ."

2. While constructing the Grand Coulee Dam in the state of Washington, engineers were at a loss when faced with the problem of threading a cable through a pipeline until an **anonymous stray cat** saved the day. Harnessed to the cable, this little hero crawled through the pipeline maze to successfully finish the job.

3. **Félix** became the first of only two cats to be sent into space. The French government purchased this Paris street cat from a dealer, and, along with 13 other cats, Félix underwent intensive training for spaceflight. His fairly arduous tasks involved a compression chamber and a centrifuge. On his big day Félix blasted off in a special capsule on top of a French Véronique AG1 rocket, from the Colomb Bacar rocket base at Hammaguir in the Algerian Sahara desert. He did not go into orbit, but traveled some 130 miles into space, where the capsule separated from the rocket and then descended by parachute. Throughout the flight, electrodes implanted in Félix's brain transmitted neurological impulses back to Earth, and this lucky kitty survived the flight. Some 30 years after his historic voyage, Félix was commemorated on several postage stamps from former French colonies.

4. **CC**, short for **CopyCat** or **Carbon Copy**, is the first cloned pet. She is part brown tabby and part white domestic shorthair, was born on December 22, 2001, under the direction of Dr. Mark Westhusin and Dr. Taeyoung Shin at the College of Veterinary

Medicine at Texas A&M University. She is the only one of 87 cloned embryos that survived. Today CC lives in the household of Duane Kraemer, one of the team members of the cloning operation.

5. **Little Nicky**, born on October 20, 2004, is the first cat cloned commercially. The cat was cloned from a deceased family pet owned by a woman in Texas (name withheld) who paid $50,000 for the procedure. She claims that the new Little Nicky is very similar in personality to the original 17-year-old. The cloning was denounced by the Humane Society and other animal activists who felt that the money could have helped save millions of pets who are destroyed each year.

6. In about 1880, Serbian inventor, physicist, and mechanical and electrical engineer Nikola Tesla discovered that sparks were generated when he stroked his cat, **Macak**. The curious event led him to focus his studies on electricity, and he went on to discover the rotating magnetic field, the basis of most alternating-current machinery; he also developed the Tesla coil, an induction coil widely used in radio technology.

7. **Ahmed**, a Siamese cat belonging to John Kenneth Galbraith, U.S. ambassador to India in 1963, was the cause of an international furor when Abbas Ali of the Islamic Democratic Group of Pakistan pointed out that Ahmed is one of the forms of the name Muhammad; therefore, the cat's name was a deliberate insult to Muslims everywhere. Ali demanded that the National Assembly put aside its schedule to deal with the matter. The government deemed the problem "much more serious than American arms aid to India." A U.S. spokesman pointed out that the cat was not actually named Ahmed but rather Ahmedabad, after the capital city of the state of Gujarat, where the cat had been presented to Galbraith's children as a gift. The children, having learned diplomacy from the best, renamed the cat Gujarat.

Schrödinger's cat is not a living cat but rather a famous illustration of the principle in quantum theory of superposition, proposed by Erwin Schrödinger in 1935. In his experiment, a cat is placed in a steel chamber, along with a device containing a vial of hydrocyanic acid. There is, in the chamber, a very small amount of a radioactive substance. If even a single atom of the substance decays during the test period, a relay mechanism will trip a hammer, which will, in turn, break the vial and kill the cat. The observer cannot know whether or not an atom of the substance has decayed, and consequently, cannot know whether the vial has been broken, the hydrocyanic acid released, and the cat killed. Since we cannot know, the cat is both dead and alive according to quantum law, in a superposition of states. It is only when we open the box and learn the condition of the cat that the superposition is lost, and the cat becomes one or the other (dead or alive). This situation is sometimes called **quantum indeterminacy** or **the observer's paradox:** the observation or measurement itself affects an outcome, so that it can never be known what the outcome would have been if it were not observed. In other words, if a tree falls in the forest . . .

6 War Cats

Sadly, military history contains some gruesome stories of cats used to sniff out deadly chemicals (their death would alert soldiers to the presence of gases) and carry flaming weapons under buildings. During the Middle Ages, besieging armies even managed to put the *cat* in *catapult*, so to speak. And in America, during the eighteenth century, a particularly sadistic torture device involved dangling a fearful cat by its tail and then pulling it back and forth across a victim's back. On a cozier note, Siamese warriors trained cats to sit on their shoulders and warn them if the enemy approached. Here are a few of the more dignified military uses of the feline's talents.

1. Father Ross took pity on the poor little stray cat that kept returning to London's St. Augustine and St. Faith's Church on Watling Street, no matter how many times she had been put out. Finally, little **Faith**, as he called her, settled in, catching mice, growing sleek and plump, and attending church services, sitting in the pulpit at Ross's feet while he preached.

Faith's Tribute

Our dear little church cat of St. Augustine and St. Faith. The bravest cat in the world.

On Monday, September 9, 1940, she endured horrors and perils beyond the power of words to tell.

Shielding her kitten in a sort of recess in the house (a spot she selected three days before the tragedy occurred), she sat the whole frightful night of bombing and fire, guarding her little kitten.

The roofs and masonry exploded. The whole house blazed. Four floors fell through in front of her. Fire and water and ruin all round her.

Yet she stayed calm and steadfast and waited for help. We rescued her in the early morning while the place was still burning, and by the mercy of Almighty God, she and her kitten were not only saved, but unhurt. God be praised and thanked for His goodness and mercy to our dear little pet.

In August 1940 Faith gave birth to a tiny kitten, and the congregation celebrated the new arrival, named **Panda**, for his coloring. One day in September, Faith was observed bringing her kitten down to the empty basement of the church, and no one knew why. She returned for her evening meal, then disappeared again. When Father Ross investigated, he found Faith curled up in a cold, dark corner, cuddled up with Panda. He took them both to a warmer place upstairs, but Faith persistently kept returning to her hideaway. Some ladies in the church suggested that Faith was trying to protect her kitten from some perceived danger, and she should be allowed to act on her instinct.

Shortly thereafter, a series of heavy air raids struck the city. A massive amount of property was destroyed and more than 400 people died. Although Father Ross was elsewhere at the time, his worst fears were realized. The church had been hit badly, and it was plain to see that there were no survivors — except two: Faith and her Panda, buried but alive under the rubble. Faith's story spread, and some five years later, she was awarded the PDSA Dickin Medal, usually reserved for military animals, at a ceremony attended by the archbishop of Canterbury. News of her death, in 1948, spread to four continents, and her memorial service took place in a packed church.

2. **Mourka**, the hero-cat of Stalingrad, carried messages about enemy gun emplacements from a group of Russian scouts to a house across the street.

7 Really Fat Cats

Sadly for these cats, Guinness no longer recognizes the fattest cat, lest zealous owners overfeed their pets just to get the award.

1. Iggy, a **50-pounder** from St. Joseph, Missouri, stands 14 inches tall and has a 33-inch waist. Joyce Kirk, his owner, reports that he's perfectly healthy and quite active, although he can't groom himself, so Kirk brushes his coat every day. He eats 30 pounds of food each week.

2. Kailee, a tabby who tips the scales at **40 pounds**, eats 20 pounds of food each week and often steals food from his brother, who weighs a mere 14 pounds. Named after former Minnesota Vikings linebacker Kailee Wong, he is the same weight as an average 4-year-old human.

3. Katy, a Siamese living in Russia, weighs a little over **50 pounds**. She has a 26-inch waist and her whiskers are almost 6 inches long.

4. In 1992, Morris, a **36-pounder** owned by Fred and Jeannie Scott of Ottawa, Kansas, took the *National Examiner*'s prize for fattest cat.

5. Sam, a tabby, weighs in at **45 pounds** and is perfectly healthy. At birth, he could fit inside a coffee mug. Owned by real estate agent Paul Webster, he is a celebrity in his hometown of Smyrna, Georgia.

6. In 1991, the winner of the *National Enquirer*'s fattest cat contest was Spike, a **37-pound, 13.5-ounce** tabby owned by Gary Kirkpatrick of Madrid, Iowa.

7. Thomas, a 10-year-old moggie (a British nickname for a housecat or mongrel cat), claims to be Britain's fattest cat at **28 pounds**. Thomas scarfs down four huge meals a day. Owner Gladys Jarvis said, "I've tried him on a diet, but he's having none of it."

"You should wear stripes. Spots make your hips look big."

3. A cat nicknamed **Bomber** helped his fellow Britons during World War II. Bomber could distinguish between sounds made by the aircraft of the RAF (the Royal Air Force) and those made by German planes. Bomber thus became a great early-warning device as well as a companion to his human friends.

4. Wing commander Guy Gibson of the RAF was often accompanied on his dangerous missions during World War II by his cat, **Windy**, a swimming, flying cat who put in more hours than many pilots.

5. During World War II, cats were employed to hunt for vermin in food stores, and their talents were rewarded with a powdered milk ration. The United States later launched a **Cats for Europe** campaign and shipped thousands of cats to feline-poor France for similar purposes.

6. A family in Pennsylvania shipped their **black cat** to Europe during World War II in hopes that he would cross Hitler's path.

First Felines:
White House Cats

Bill Clinton is actually allergic to cats. What a guy!

These are the cats that have prowled the White House and the presidents they voted for.

Martin Van Buren (1837–1841) owned a pair of tiger cubs for a short time.

Tad Lincoln, the son of Abraham Lincoln (1861–1865), owned a cat named **Tabby**.

Rutherford B. Hayes (1877–1881) had two Siamese cats named **Siam** and **Miss Pussy**. He also had a cat named **Piccolomini**.

William McKinley (1897–1901) had two Angoras named **Valeriano Weyler** and **Enrique DeLome**.

Teddy Roosevelt (1901–1909) owned two cats, **Tom Quartz** and **Slippers**, a gray-blue polydactyl.

Woodrow Wilson (1913–1921) had a cat named **Puffins**.

Calvin Coolidge (1923–1929) adopted a stray cat that he named **Tiger**, who turned out to be a one-cat wrecking crew.

Caroline Kennedy, the daughter of John F. Kennedy (1961–1963), owned a cat named **Tom Kitten**. He was the first cat to live in the White House after Teddy Roosevelt's Slippers. (Puffins and Tiger had lived at the private residences of their presidential owners.) Tom Kitten died in 1962.

Susan Ford, the daughter of Gerald Ford (1974–1977), owned a Siamese cat named **Shan**.

Amy Carter, the daughter of Jimmy Carter (1977–1981), owned various cats, including a Siamese cat named **Misty Malarky Ying Yang**.

The most famous presidential cat of all was **Socks**. Bill Clinton (1993–2001) loved his cat and forbade photographers to touch her.

George W. Bush (2001–2008) had a cat named **India** who was named after Rubén Sierra, AKA El Indio, of the Texas Rangers baseball team.

5 Famous Ship's Cats

1. Able Seaman Simon
Mascot of the HMS *Amethyst,* Able Seaman Simon was wounded in 1949 during the Yangtse Incident at Nanjing. He won the Dickin Medal for animal bravery for having sustained injuries, for staving off a rat infestation, and for raising morale.

2. Freddy
Freddy, shipwrecked with a cargo of pianos on the SS *Hawksdale* while en route to Australia, was heroically rescued by an apprentice sailor.

3. Oscar
The crew of the HMS *Cossack* rescued Oscar from the famous German battleship *Bismarck* when British forces sank it in 1941; they made the cat their own. When, six months later, the *Cossack* was sunk by a German submarine, crew members of the HMS *Royal Ark* discovered Oscar happily afloat on a piece of driftwood. Oddly, the *Royal Ark* was sunk only three weeks later, leading some to theorize that Oscar secretly remained loyal to the Third Reich.

4. Trim
Matthew Flinders mapped the coast of Australia in 1802 aboard the ship *Tryall,* accompanied by his remarkable black-and-white cat, Trim, who had been born aboard the HMS *Reliance* on a voyage from the Cape of Good Hope to Botany Bay. When Flinders was accused of spying and imprisoned by the French in Mauritius on his return voyage to England, Trim shared his captivity until his unexplained disappearance, which Flinders attributed to his being stolen and eaten by hungry slaves. In 1996 a bronze statue of Trim by sculptor John Cornwell was erected on a window ledge of the Mitchell Library in Sydney, directly behind a statue of his owner. The popularity of the statue has since led to the development of a range of Trim merchandise.

5. Wunpound Cat
So named because he was found at the pound and bought for one pound, this Royal Navy cat served from 1966 to 1974 aboard the HMS *Hecate,* traveling more than 250,000 miles during his military career. He was retired when the Royal Navy passed anti-cat regulations for health purposes.

"In [the cat's] flawless grace and superior self-sufficiency I have seen a symbol of the perfect beauty and bland impersonality of the universe itself, objectively considered, and in its air of silent mystery there resides for me all the wonder and fascination of the unknown."

— H. P. LOVECRAFT

21 Hero-i-cats

While cats don't have the resources that enable dogs to perform great acts of heroism, some feisty felines have managed to do the seemingly impossible. Even during wartime, cats have been known to carry messages, poisons, and even listening devices around their necks in canisters, all in loyalty to their homeland. In studying hundreds of examples of hero cats, we were stunned by the number who had saved their families from fires, inclement weather, and threatening wildlife. Thus, each story here is representative of scores more. These kitties deserve extra treats.

1. In 1976, in the Friuli district of northeastern Italy, people noticed that their cats were running about madly, scratching at doors to get out of the house and disappearing once outside. The odd behavior began in the early evening. Later that night, a major earthquake hit the area. The same thing happened in 1975 in Haicheng, China. Seismologists evacuated the city 24 hours before a major earthquake hit. They later reported that it was the cats' behavior, not their scientific equipment, that led to the evacuation. In Messina, Italy, a similar event took place when a merchant noticed his cats in an agitated state — scratching and tearing at the ground — just before an earthquake.

In the 1980s, the U.S. Geological Service operated Earthquake Watch, in which some 1,700 volunteers along the West Coast charted the behavior of their animals daily, reporting any aberrations that might indicate an oncoming earthquake.

> Many female cats have been known to carry their kittens outside just before an earthquake, and it is not known exactly how a cat can sense such things. One theory ascribes the behavior to ESP; another suggests that cats are more sensitive to the earth's vibrations than are even the most sophisticated instruments available.

2. **Ringo**, a tabby from Bowling Green, Ohio, received the coveted Stillman Award for heroism in 1998. His owners, Carol and Ray Steiner, couldn't understand why they both began suffering the same strange symptoms of high blood pressure, memory loss, nausea, and headaches. One day, their golden tabby displayed the most bizarre behavior they had ever seen. He seemed to go crazy, slamming himself into the back door until Carol finally let him out. Ringo made a beeline for the gas meter out in the yard and immediately began digging. (Cats do not normally dig!) Carol was shocked when, moments later, peering into the hole that Ringo made, she discovered a natural-gas leak. She immediately contacted the gas company, and a representative told her that the leak might have caused a dangerous explosion, and the constant seeping of gas into the house could eventually have killed the family. "We probably would have gone to sleep one night and never woken up if it wasn't for Ringo's incredible intelligence," said a very grateful Ray Steiner.

3. **Fred**, a tabby who found fame as the "Undercover Kitten," was a rescued stray when he was enlisted by New York law enforcers in a sting operation. Fred's job was to pose as a patient to help police nab a man pretending to be a veterinarian. The mission was successful, and Fred was honored at a press conference, where he sported a tiny badge on his collar. Fred received a Law Enforcement Appreciation Award and was honored at "Broadway Barks," the New York theater district's adopt-a-thon benefit annually hosted by Mary Tyler Moore and Bernadette Peters. Sadly, in 2006, Fred wandered into traffic and was run over by a car. The district attorney's office stated that Fred had been "preparing for a new career in education," with a "significant role" in classroom programs that teach children how to care for animals.

4. In Sheffield, England, cat owner Michael Edmonds suffers from complex epilepsy and could find no way of anticipating a seizure before it occurred — until **Tee Cee** came into his life. The cat is able to predict attacks and notifies his owner by sitting very close to him and staring at him intently. Indeed, reports Edmonds, the cat is right every time.

5. In Dora, Alabama, Teresa Harper stood by helplessly as Lacy Jane, her poodle, was attacked by an enraged pit bull. Luckily, **Sparky** was close by. Harper's cat suddenly sprang from 12 feet away and landed on the dog's head, which she proceeded to gouge, raking her claws over its muzzle. Lacy Jane and Sparky both suffered extensive wounds but, happily, survived.

6. **Duke**, of Kansas City, gave his life for his family. One night, alert to a fire in the house, he awoke two family members by meowing furiously. Once 9-year-old Jessica and 14-year-old Felicia were out of the house, Duke stayed back, waiting for the parents to reach safety. Rescue workers saved the rest of the family, but sadly, Duke lost his way and died in the fire.

7. Walt Hutching was mugged on his way home from work and suffered a head wound. But he was able to get home, where he immediately passed out on the kitchen floor. **Mi-Kitten** to the rescue! Seeing his human in distress, he sat upon the man's chest and proceeded to scream until neighbors finally came to investigate. At the hospital, Hutching was told that he would surely have died if Mi-Kitten had not acted.

8. Frances Martin has a sign in front of her house that reads Beware — Guard Cat on Duty. She has good reason. Years before, in the middle of the night, she awoke to an intruder looming over her as she slept. Even before she could make a sound, her normally shy, mouse-colored cat, named **Mouse**, screamed and sprang, attaching herself to the intruder's face. He ran from the house, with Mouse holding on for dear life. Although the man got away, he was easily identified later by the damage to his face.

9. In Quebec, Kimberly Kotar was in her garden when, suddenly, she was confronted by a snake. Only inches away, hissing and shaking its tail, the viper was ready to strike.

Kotar's cat, **Sosa**, immediately interceded, lashing out at the snake, which was later identified as an Eastern Cottonmouth, a highly poisonous snake that is not native to Quebec. Had Kimberly been bitten, the wound might have been fatal because there is no ready supply of serum in the province. Sosa sustained extensive injuries but survived after being hospitalized for three days.

10. Debra Blume was losing patience with her cat, **Casper**, who insistently clawed at her legs as she washed the supper dishes. She turned around to boot the cat out of the house, but Casper ran off — into the baby's room. Blue followed, and to her horror, there little Shannon Blume lay in her crib, choking on mucus. Blume is certain that Casper saved her little girl's life.

11. **Samantha**, a gray cat living in San Diego, fell into the habit of greeting a little girl in the neighborhood each day as she came home from school. One day, when the girl didn't appear as usual, Samantha alerted her owner, who went to investigate and learned that the child, Jennifer, had been abducted. Police units sprang into action, and when Samantha's owner, Charlie Jones, a retired cop, heard that Jennifer and her kidnapper had been spotted close by, he headed that way in his car, with Samantha riding shotgun. At the scene, police feared for the little girl's life as the kidnapper held a gun to her head and ordered the officers to back off. Just as the criminal was about to drag Jennifer off, Samantha sprang from behind, sinking her teeth into the kidnapper's neck. He dropped the gun, and police moved in.

12. Ten-year-old Maria lay in her bed in Mexico, in a coma after a bicycle accident. Although there was nothing medical personnel could do for her, they admitted that anything might awaken her. After many months, Maria's mother had not given up hope. She kept the window open in the little girl's room — she had always like fresh air. One day, her mother was perplexed to find a stray cat licking Maria's thumb. She was about to remove the cat when she saw what she believed was a miracle: as the cat licked the girl's thumb, Maria's hand began to move. Now the cat, named **Miguel**, was invited to stay, and she slept each night at Maria's side. Eight days after Miguel's arrival, Maria woke up and spoke for the first time in seven months.

3 British VICs

For the past century, the British government has employed an army of up to 100 cats as civil servants to keep government office buildings rodent-free. Here are some other Brit cats with admirable distinctions.

1. **Humphrey** Employed as a mouser at 10 Downing Street from October 1989 until November 1997, Humphrey arrived as a 1-year-old stray and served under Margaret Thatcher, John Major, and Tony Blair. At a cost of about £100 a year (paid for from the Cabinet Office's budget), most of which went toward food, Humphrey was said to be of considerably better value than the Cabinet's professional pest controller, who charged £4,000 a year and is reported to have never caught a mouse. By the time of his retirement, Humphrey had risen to the position of Chief Mouser to the Cabinet Office. He died in 2006; Tony Blair announced the cat's death to the nation.

2. **Queenie** At Christmastime 1998, a stray tortoiseshell cat turned up at Sandringham just as the royal family were arriving for the holidays. The cat stayed at Sandringham until January and was nicknamed Queenie. The queen's staff looked after the kitty until she could be placed in a local shelter.

3. **Wilberforce** This cat lived at 10 Downing Street from 1973 to 1987 and served under four British prime ministers, including Edward Heath, Harold Wilson, Jim Callaghan, and Margaret Thatcher. His chief function was to catch mice. According to Bernard Ingham, the former press secretary to Margaret Thatcher, Wilberforce was a normal cat for whom Thatcher once bought "a tin of sardines in a Moscow supermarket." Wilberforce the cat also inspired Wilberforce the band, which is named after him. He retired on April 3, 1987, and died in 1988.

13. **Stuart** saved the day when burglars tried to break into the home of his owner, Sandra Price, in Congleton, England. Sandra had been decorating her bedroom and was asleep downstairs, having left the bedroom window open to clear the paint fumes. Stuart woke Sandra in the middle of the night by uncharacteristically jumping on her and meowing loudly. Sandra immediately realized that someone had been trying to break into the house. Luckily, the person was unable to enter — or was frightened off by Stuart's meowing. In the morning, footprints on the windowsill confirmed the prowler's presence.

14. In New York City, when his owners were held naked at gunpoint by a robber, a cat named **Booboo Kitty** wandered in. The robber picked up the cat, who hissed and scratched him, causing the robber to drop him. The cat ran to another room, and the robber, his thieving pride wounded, chased him, giving one of the victims a chance to escape and call the police.

15. When an officer entered a Columbus, Ohio, home in response to a 911 call, he was perplexed to find an orange-and-tan-striped cat lying by a telephone on the living room floor. The cat's owner, Gary Rosheisen, lay on the floor near his bed, having fallen out of his wheelchair. Rosheisen said his cat, **Tommy**, must have hit the right buttons to call 911. Rosheisen said he couldn't get up because of pain from osteoporosis and poor balance caused by a series of mini-strokes. He also wasn't wearing his medical-alert necklace. The man had gotten Tommy three years earlier to help lower his blood pressure. He tried to train him to call 911 but could not be sure that the cat would come through in an emergency. He is no longer a doubting Tommy.

16. A cat saved the life of a newborn baby abandoned on the doorstep of a house in Berlin, Germany, in the middle of the night. The kitty meowed loudly until someone woke up to see why the cat was making so much noise. The person was shocked to discover the baby lying in a basket in below-zero temperatures. "The cat is a hero," police spokesman Uwe Beier said. "Its loud meowing got the attention of the homeowner and saved the baby from suffering life-threatening hypothermia."

17. Holly Lenz of Laguna Niguel, California, froze in fear.

She had entered her son's nursery to investigate a strange hissing sound and discovered a deadly rattlesnake. **Lucy**, the family cat, had prevented the serpent from attacking little Adam as he napped. Lucy stood by loyally, fending off the serpent. Holly was able to dial 911 while Lucy stood watch, and the snake was removed before the child awoke.

18. When Sucile, a woman living in South Dakota, named her cat **Lucky**, she had no idea how fitting the mane would prove. It seemed that Lucky could predict the weather. "If it was a couple of hours before a storm or a tornado was coming, she would run up my wall. I finally realized that she was warning me in advance of every storm," reported Sucile.

One day, Sucile looked out the window and couldn't believe her eyes. A lightning bolt had created a dangerous phenomenon known as ball lightning, and now the deadly charge was coming straight at her. All of a sudden, Lucky and the new kitten they had just acquired positioned themselves to create a barrier between Sucile and the danger. "The cats just lit up," reported Sucile. "Their entire bodies glowed." Firemen could not believe that the cats had saved Sucile or even survived themselves, having lost their hair and suffered severe burns. On the advice of her vet, Sucile rewarded the cats by putting them out of their misery. The cats would never again suffer on her behalf.

19. Florence had just about lost patience. The stray cat she called **Billy** kept stealing into the house despite the fact that she put him out every single time. Even with the doors closed, Billy managed to squeeze through a hole in a window screen. Florence finally covered the hole with a cardboard barrier. That would be that — but not for long. She was soon awakened from a nap by Billy, who had pushed past the barrier, pounced on her chest, and was now yowling uncontrollably. Once she fully awoke, Billy jumped

down and started toward the kitchen. Florence followed, only to find her 4-year-old son, Franklin, choking on a chunk of cookie that had lodged in his throat. Florence was able to successfully perform the Heimlich maneuver, but it was Billy who saved his life.

20. **Rusik**, Russia's only sniffer cat, successfully located smugglers of sturgeon, who operated an elaborate $2 bil-

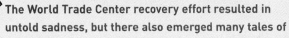

World Trade Center Cats

The World Trade Center recovery effort resulted in untold sadness, but there also emerged many tales of bravery and survival. These include some very resourceful cats.

Precious was never partial to dogs, but the resourceful feline didn't mind being found by this one. It was, after all, a search-and-rescue dog, and the cat had been abandoned for 18 days after the September 11 attack on the World Trade Center in New York City. Suffering from burns, dehydration, eye injuries, and smoke inhalation, she somehow managed to find her way to the roof of the building in which she was trapped, where she proceeded to cry for help. Precious's story had a happy ending during that sad period, and she was named Cat of the Year at the 2001 Westminster Cat Show.

Beneath the decimated area where the World Trade Center once stood, life was found in a forgotten basement. Rescuers discovered a blast survivor curled up in a carton of napkins. When the box was retrieved, even more survivors were found inside — three kittens. They were given appropriate names. Mom was christened **Hope**, and the babies were called **Freedom**, **Amber**, and **Flag**.

lion black-market caviar industry in that country. In 2003 Rusik led authorities to Stavropol, the site of major smuggling operations, and arrests were made. But a week later, criminals struck back: Rusik was run over by a mafia-owned car.

21. Wise beyond his months, **Shadow**, a six-month-old kitten, saved Harry Dostie's life by pouncing on his head to alert him to the fact that the sleep apnea device was burning and sending noxious fumes into his breathing tube.

9 Lives and Still Counting: 18 Stories of Survival

Given that they survived the persecution of the Middle Ages and their reputation for living nine lives, it should be no wonder that cats are resilient. Yet these stories of cats who managed to endure prolonged periods of hunger, thirst, and severe discomfort seem to defy science. Here are just a few of the hundreds of similar stories that affirm for cat lovers what they have always known: sometimes it takes more than nine lives.

1. A stray black cat who wandered into a freight company was immediately adopted by the men who worked there, and they fed her daily. One day, after shipping a car to Australia, the men noticed that the cat was gone. When the car was delivered some 50 days later, the woman who had ordered it discovered the stowaway — a very thin but nevertheless live black cat. She adopted her and named her after the car in which she had arrived, **Mercedes**.

2. When Sergeant Guy Jones was transferred from Guam to San Francisco, he had his two Siamese cats shipped off to his new location. But only one cat arrived; the other, **Sherry**, seemed to have disappeared in transit. Jones and his wife grieved for the cat, but only for 32 days, after which Sherry was discovered in the hold of the giant Pan Am jet on which she had been shipped. Sherry had traveled some 225,000 miles and touched down in 12 countries before finally coming home.

3. While builders took a lunch break one day, **Timmy**, a tomcat, stole into the building site and fell asleep in a hole in an unfinished wall. Unaware of this visitor, the workers returned and bricked up the wall. It wasn't until 24 days later that one of the men heard Timmy's plaintive cries. It took the police and the fire department to break through the wall. When they did, there was Timmy, apparently no worse for the wear.

4. British workers opened a sealed crate from Malaysia and couldn't believe their eyes as a kitten stared back at them. It had survived for over a month by licking condensation off the crate's walls. The tortoiseshell was tired and thin but instantly greeted workers with a friendly meow. Workers plucked the female kitten from the crate and called the RSPCA. The kitten had crawled into the crate at the port of Penang and was sealed inside, then loaded onto a ship. She then endured a voyage to Southampton and a truck trip to Salisbury without food or light. The eight-week-old was named **Flowerpot**.

5. Thousands of plant lovers travel to the Chelsea Flower Show in England each year, but none would risk their life to do so. Nevertheless, four-month-old kittens **Smokey** and **Dotty** did just that when they hitched a ride from their plant-nursery home in Hampshire to the show on the undercarriage of a trailer truck. For 60 miles they perched on a ledge only two feet from the ground, staying put even when the vehicle stopped at traffic lights. Ninety minutes later the lorry finally came to a halt at the showground, and the terrified cats were discovered. The cats' owner, Rosy Hardy, had been exhibiting at the Flower Show for ten years.

6. In March 1999, a tabby cat wandered into an electricity substation and received an 11,000-volt electric shock. A Yorkshire Electricity engineer spotted him and managed to carry him clear of a 132,000-volt live terminal. The cat was given the nickname **Sparky**. He was left with burned paws, singed fur and whiskers, and paralyzed ears and a front leg. Sparky was very lucky to be alive, however, as an electric shock of that magnitude would more than likely kill a human being. Sparky was reunited with his owner, Tricia Watts of Hull, U.K., after his photo appeared in a newspaper.

7. In March 1999, **Talbot**, a 6-month-old stray cat, wandered into the Peugeot plant at Ryton, U.K., and went to

sleep in the car body shell of a Peugeot 206 on the assembly line. The shell went into the paint-baking oven, heated to a temperature of 145 degrees Fahrenheit, with the cat still asleep inside. The workers noticed him half an hour later when the shell emerged. Workers used a hose to cool the cat down. Fortunately, he survived, although his paw pads were completely burned off and his fur was singed.

8. Workers at a storage facility in Roy, Utah, were perplexed one day in 1993 to hear strange sounds emanating from a chest of drawers that they had been storing for a military family. Opening a drawer, they found what they described as "a bag of bones." It was, of course, the family's cat, who had disappeared during the move to Utah. Apparently, the cat survived for two weeks without food or water.

9. Estelle Littmann, of Montgomery, Alabama, had heard all sorts of horror stories about the dangers of women traveling alone, so when a strange man pulled up in a brown van near hers and tried to get her attention as she drove to work one day, she ignored him. When he started gesturing and waving, she became alarmed and took off. But she couldn't seem to lose him, and now Estelle became terrified. She finally pulled into a housing development, and a guard came running toward her, asking her if she knew there was a cat perched on the roof of her car. Sure enough, clinging to the luggage rack for dear life was her cat, **Ronald**. Littmann reports that it took almost three days for poor Ronald to "thaw" after his hell ride but that he did eventually recover.

10. On the day that workmen were repairing a patio floor, **Marty** was engaged in his favorite pastime — chasing mice into holes. But when the concrete and stones had been replaced, Marty was gone. The family assumed he was on one of his familiar extended outings. But nine days later, when there was still no sign of him, they assumed the worst. Two days after that, they were shocked to find Marty on their doorstep, covered with dirt and mud, his claws worn away from scratching his way to freedom from beneath the patio floor. Marty apparently survived by eating the pockets of mice he uncovered as he burrowed his way home.

11. While driving along a highway on a cold wintry night, Roberta Johnson saw an astonishing sight: a block of ice lying on the road, with a cat frozen inside. Even more astonishing was the "meow" she heard coming from inside the block. Roberta was able to rescue and adopt the cat, whom she named **Car Cat**. It was later surmised that the cat had become frozen in a block of ice that had formed around a car's wheel arch, where she had fallen asleep; the block had then become dislodged, falling to the road, where Roberta found her.

12. In 2001, a cat named **Gurbe**, who lived in the Netherlands, survived 90 minutes of being tossed around inside a clothes dryer set at 70 degrees centigrade. She was discovered when her owner, Metha de Bruin, opened the dryer and spotted cat hair in the filter and blood on the laundry. The cat required medical care but survived the ordeal.

13. Ten-week-old **Fizzy** traveled 2,000 miles in a sealed crate shipped from Tel Aviv, Israel, to Peterborough, England. Fizzy stayed alive by licking up condensation.

14. **Bessie** drank rainwater for seven weeks while trapped in a chimney in Shoreham, Kent, U.K. Sarah Philip, her owner, had given up hope of finding her beloved cat until, almost two months after his disappearance, he became so thin from lack of food that he fell right into her fireplace. Luckily, it was a warm October evening.

15. Laura Delfonso had a bizarre thought after her cat went missing: what if he had climbed into one of the vending machines she had just sold to a man in Baton Rouge, Louisiana? After all, the cat had disappeared just when the machines had been carted off the week before, and she had looked everywhere. She called the buyer, Martin Napier, and asked him to check the ma-

What Goes Up . . .

Most of the time it comes down. But not always.

🐾 In Gulfport, Mississippi, during Hurricane Georges in 1998, a cat was blown onto the roof of a shop, then fell 60 feet into an oak tree — and stayed there! In an interview in May 2001, Ron Roland, **Big Boy**'s caretaker, said Big Boy had never left the tree — he ate and slept among the branches, climbing from limb to limb for exercise.

🐾 In Argentina in the late 1940s, a female cat named **Mincha** found herself up a 40-foot tree and was so comfortable there that she made it her home for the next six years. She gave birth to three litters up there, thanks to relentless admirers, and was fed by locals, who attached her food to long poles.

chines. He poked at them, listened to them, and reasoned that a cat could not possibly fit through any of the openings. He was shocked, then, when, 37 days later, he opened the machines in order to stock them and discovered little **Smokey**, alive but too weak to stand. Happily, she made a full recovery and never left her owner's side again.

16. When Rhea Mayfield and her daughter were moving their coffee table to the basement of their apartment building, they left the apartment door open, and they figured that **Kelly**, their tabby, made off then. They couldn't have guessed that she had fallen asleep inside a compartment of the table and would spend the next 46 days trapped inside until the building superintendent investigated some strange noises. Kelly, a plump cat who had weighed in at 17 pounds be-

fore her ordeal, was now down to 5. The veterinarian theorized that Kelly was probably saved by the cold temperature in the storeroom, which no doubt slowed her metabolism.

17. Neglected and abused like so many cats abandoned in New York City, **Scarlett** found a home in an old building and it was there that she gave birth. When the building caught fire, it was thought to be completely uninhabited, but then firefighter David Gianelli saw a cat emerge from the building, holding a kitten by the scruff of his neck. He went to grab her, but she was too quick. Once she dropped her kitten, Scarlett disappeared back inside the burning building. Time and again she returned inside until she had saved each of her brood. Gianelli immediately arranged for treatment of Scarlett and her kittens, and the heartwarming story of rescue and devotion was documented in the 1997 book *Scarlett Saves Her Family: The Heartwarming True Story of a Homeless Mother Cat Who Rescued Her Kittens from a Raging Fire,* by Jean Martin and Jean-Charles Suares.

18. Barbara Jarmin watched helplessly as a family of foxes tormented a stray cat, and she knew the story could not have a happy ending. She finally lured the frightened cat to safety, only to learn that he had been blinded as a result of deliberate cruelty. She was determined to put the poor thing out of his misery when the vet offered to remove the cat's eye for free if Barbara promised to care for him. She named him **Arnie** for Arnold Schwarzenegger's strength and he lived a contented life, using his ears and whiskers to navigate his surroundings. Arnie was honored with the Best Turn-Around Award at the Cats Protection Rescue Cat of the Year Ceremony in 2003.

Strange Bedfellows

Cats are generally lone, aloof creatures with little care for others around them. Guess again. Jayne Pupek, author of the novel *Tomato Girl* (Algonquin, 2008), shares her Maidens, Virginia, home with 2 monkeys, 5 parrots, 8 rats, 3 poodles, 1 mutt, 2 mice, 2 hamsters, 8 guinea pigs, 1 rabbit, 1 iguana, 1 bearded dragon, 1 tortoise . . . and yes, even a cat! Of course, we begged her for a photo, and here was her wise reply: "I've had friends who've lost small animals to cats, so I keep the kitty at bay when other animals are out and about, and I don't have photos of her with any of the animals."

Here are some cats who prove that inside those tiny furry bodies, big hearts beat.

Huan, a cat in Thailand, reputed to be an excellent mouser, shocked her owners by falling in love with a baby mouse she found in a closet. Huan adopted the mouse and raised it as her own. Huan's family named the mouse Jerry, and the unlikely pair even drank milk from the same bowl.

In 1997, **Fluffy**, of Argos Corner, Delaware, made international news when she took on the care of five babies in addition to the seven she already had. Most astounding, the five babies were squirrels whose mother had died.

A cat named **Mouse** added an orphaned Chihuahua puppy to her litter of four kittens. One night, stuck outside the house after her owners went to bed, Mouse demonstrated her extraordinary maternal instincts by climbing onto the roof and entering the house through the chimney, à la Santa.

T.K. is the feline companion of Tondayelo, an orangutan at Zoo World in Panama City Beach, Florida. Depressed after losing her mate a few years ago, Tonda had lost interest in most everything until an orange tabby came along and installed herself as Tonda's constant companion. Tonda couldn't be more delighted.

In recent years in Porto Alegre, Brazil, a cat named **Chiquita** adopted an injured bird and raised it as if it were her own. They ate from the same plate, and the bird, named Pitico, even started to eat meat.

Two of the most famous residents of the Wildlife Images Rehabilitation and Education Center in Oregon were best friends **Cat**, an orange tabby, and her buddy, Gritz, a 600-pound grizzly bear. They bonded over lunch one day in 1995 when Gritz did the unthinkable, at least for a bear: he offered to share his food with Cat. They became inseparable; at night Cat slept curled up under Gritz's chin.

15 Incredible Journeys

There are two types of homing journeys made by cats. The first type occurs after a cat has been taken from its home. As the following list proves, there are numerous documented cases of cats who found their way home over great distances. How do they do it? The scientific explanation has much to do with the cat's sensitivity to the earth's magnetic forces. The second type of homing instinct is more difficult to explain: A cat's owners have moved and left the cat behind. Now the cat must negotiate its way through unfamiliar territory to find its new home. Consider the comments of the late Nikko Tinbergen, a leading animal ethologist and Nobel Prize winner, who said of extrasensory perception: "If one applies the term to perception by processes not yet known to us, extrasensory perception among living creatures may well apply widely." Whatever the explanation, even more astounding than the fact that cats *can* do it is the fact that they are motivated to do it at all. Could it be love?

1. It is impossible to know how little **Lapis** made it from Boulder, Colorado, where her owner discovered her missing, to the Yukon, 3,000 miles away, in just a matter of weeks. Chances are, she hopped a ride with a long-distance trucker. What's just as remarkable is the fact that her hunting skills kept her alive in an area teeming with coyotes, wolves, and bears. Happily, a young girl discovered the cat and the phone number that had been embedded in her collar, and so Lapis was able to make the return trip home in relative style.

2. The cat who traveled the longest distance must be **Tom**, owned by the Smiths of St. Petersburg, Florida, who simply wouldn't stand for being left behind when his family moved 2,500 miles away to San Gabriel, California. It took him two years and six months to make the trip.

3. **Sugar** didn't like traveling, so when her owners, the Woodses, planned to move 1,500 miles away to Oklahoma, they left Sugar behind in the care of neighbors who had agreed to adopt her. They were sorry to hear, two months later, that Sugar had run away. Fourteen months after that, a cat who looked just like Sugar suddenly sprang through a window onto Mrs. Woods's shoulder. The woman was dubious; could this possibly be the same cat? Sugar had an unmistakable deformity in her left hip; the vet confirmed the good news.

4. **Church**, a 10-year-old cat living with the Goldbergs in

A classified ad in the <u>Albuquerque Journal</u>, dated February 1, 1991: "Lost since March 1983, tortoiseshell female cat, reward."

Eatontown, New Jersey, was given away to a family 60 miles to the north, in Kearny. It only took him seven hours to make it back to Eatontown, minus some whiskers and with a marked limp. The Goldbergs know better than to try to get rid of this particular cat ever again.

5. In September 2001, Charmin Sampson and her son, Jason, were sad to return home from their vacation at Wisconsin Dells to Hibbing, Minnesota, without **Skittles**, their cat, who had disappeared. In February, 140 days after he'd gone missing in Wisconsin, Skittles turned up at home, having navigated his way across two states and 350 miles.

6. Madeline Martinet just couldn't afford to feed her beloved cat, **Gribouille**, so she gave him to the nice man across the street, Jean-Paul Marquart; after all, she could still see him each day. She hadn't counted on Marquart's decision, made a month after she gave him the cat, to move 600 miles away to Germany. Gribouille didn't like it much either. A Frenchman to the end, he turned up on Martinet's doorstep two years later, starving and nearly blind. Could it really be him? He would have negotiated superhighways, forests, mountains, and freezing temperatures to make the trip. Martinet didn't doubt it for a minute. Her cat was home at last.

7. Georgette and Jean-Louis Assemat couldn't change their little girl's medical condition: after a fall from a four-story window, she was unable to speak, partially blind, and paralyzed on her left side. At least the little cat they brought home for her seemed to lift her spirits. Soon Aurélie and her cat, **Scrooge**, were inseparable. So when Scrooge disappeared into the countryside while the family vacationed,

THREE AGAINST THE WILDERNESS!

They face an unknown world of adventure with instinct their only guide to home

WALT DISNEY presents
The Incredible Journey

Based on Sheila Burnford's international best-selling novel that all the world has taken to its heart!

BODGER the Bull Terrier · TAO the Siamese Cat · LUATH the Labrador Retriever ·· EMILE GENEST · SANDRA SCOTT · JOHN DRAINIE
TECHNICOLOR®

it broke their hearts to return home without him. Aurélie cried all the way, a 600-mile journey. Over the next months, the little girl's condition deteriorated so badly that the Assemats feared for her life. She was unable to eat or sleep, and she spent most of the day sobbing. Then, a miracle: Georgette opened the door one morning to find — to her utter amazement — Scrooge, bedraggled, injured, but present nonetheless. Then, another miracle: Aurélie spoke for the first time since her accident. "Scrooge! It's my Scrooge! He's come home," she exclaimed, to everyone's astonishment. Over the next few months, Aurélie did what doctors had assumed was impossible. With therapy, she resumed her natural speech and even learned to walk with crutches. "My love guided Scrooge home," she explained to her mother.

8. **Misele** was so devoted to her owner, an 82-year-old man named Alfonse Mondry, that she couldn't bear to be left behind when the man was taken to the hospital in Sarrebourg, France, some nine miles away. So she was allowed to stay when she was discovered later that night in the hospital, happily purring in the lap of the old man. How she managed to cross highways and bridges, no less find her way to a place to which she had never been, remains a mystery.

9. It took him a year (he must have stopped to rest along the way), but **Smokey**, a cat who lived in Tulsa, Oklahoma, traveled 417 miles to his owners' new home in Memphis, Tennessee, in 1952.

10. **Li-Ping** traveled 1,586 miles, from Sandusky, Ohio, to Orlando, Florida, in 1955 to find her owner, Vivian Allgood, who had given her up before moving away. The trek lasted a month.

11. In 1949, it took **Rusty** 83 days to walk from Boston to Chicago to find his owners after he wandered off during a vacation and the family was forced to return home without him.

12. Jonathan and Katie were distraught when the flight crew opened the baggage hold after their trip from Qatar to the U.K., only to find that their cat, **Ozzy**, was missing. Assuming he had somehow gotten out during a stopover, they resigned themselves to their loss. Just ten days — and some 63,000 miles later — Ozzy turned up in a storage compartment of the plane and was returned to his grateful owners.

13. An 8-month-old kitten named **Lilo** hitched a ride inside a set of box springs that were being shipped from Hawaii to Kansas, a month-long journey, in 2002. Lilo survived the trip without any injuries.

14. A British kitten survived a 300-mile journey made while it was stuck under the hood of a car. The driver of the car heard the 10-week-old gray tabby meowing after he had driven from York to Carlisle and back again, via Manchester.

15. A kitten had the drive of her life when a nap in the warmth of a car engine landed her 400 miles from home. The 6-month-old black-and-white cat, **Megan**, was found curled up next to the engine of the Peugeot 406 by its new owner. Apart from being slightly shocked, the kitten did not seem harmed by the journey.

According to the *Daily Mail*, since January 2007 a white cat has been a regular passenger on the bus route from Walsall to Wolverhampton in England's West Midlands. The cat hops on the bus three times a week at the same stop and then jumps off farther down the road, near a fish-and-chips shop. Nicknamed Macavity, after T. S. Eliot's mischievous character, the cat has been described as "the perfect passenger, really: he sits quietly, minds his own business, and then gets off."

7 Very Wealthy Cats

Many people love cats. From time to time, newspapers print stories about some elderly widow who died and left her entire estate to her cat. Cats read these stories, too, and are always plotting to get named as beneficiaries in their owners' wills. Did you ever wonder where your cat goes when it wanders off for several hours? It meets with other cats in estate-planning seminars. We just thought you should know.

"I desire my sister, Marie Bluteau, and my niece, Madame Calonge, to look to my cats. If both cats should survive me, thirty sous a week must be laid out upon them, in order that they may live well. They are to be served daily, in a clean and proper manner, with two meals of meat soup, the same as we eat ourselves, but it is to be given to them separately in two soup plates. The bread is not to be cut up into the soup, but must be broken into squares the size of a nut, otherwise they will refuse to eat it. A ration of meat, finely minced, is to be added to it; the whole is then to be mildly seasoned, put into a clean pan, covered close, and carefully simmered before it is dished up. If only one cat should survive, half the sum mentioned will suffice."

— From the will of Madame Dupuis, a famous French harpist of the seventeenth century

1. David Harper, a somewhat reclusive cat owner, died in March 2005 at the age of 79, leaving an estate worth $1.1 million to his beloved tabby, **Red**. The United Church of Canada was appointed administrator of the funds, in accordance with Harper's will, and is responsible for the 3-year-old cat's care, feeding, and veterinarian bills for the rest of its life.

2. In 1969, **Joseph**, a striped tomcat, inherited over $1 million when his owner, Ms. Agatha Higgins, passed away. Joseph remained at the Higgins mansion until his death. After Joseph passed on, the rest of the fortune was divided among Higgins's family members.

3. Margaret Layne, who lived in a small suburb of London, left her entire fortune to her cat, **Tinker**. Tinker inherited an estimated $900,000, and Layne left detailed instructions regarding specific treats to which Tinker had grown accustomed. The house was not to be sold until Tinker's death.

4. In the 1960s Dr. William Grier left his cats, **Brownie** and **Hellcat**, $415,000 in his will. The cats died two years later, and the remaining funds went to George Washington University in Washington, D.C.

5. Ben Rea, a British recluse who died in 1988, left $15 million to his cat, **Blackie**, and various cat charities — but not one farthing to his relatives.

6. In 1999 two cats became landlords in Queens, New York, when their owners, two elderly sisters who died within months of each other, bequeathed to them their two-story, 1,400-square-foot home. A woman who lived

In 1996, a businessman from Thailand spent £18,000 for the marriage of his male diamond-eyed pet cat, Phet, to a female diamond-eyed cat named Ploy. Five hundred guests attended the wedding, after which the cats were given a dowry of over £23,000.

in the apartment building was appointed executor, and all was well until the executor decided to move all of her cats — including the many strays she had been bringing into her apartment — to the country. She was willing to leave the two landlord cats behind, according to the terms of the will, which required that they remain at the Queens residence, but the place was overrun with cats, and no one was quite sure which two were the cats in question. In the end, the woman was allowed to move all her cats, selling the property for just under $1 million.

7. Woodbury Rand left $40,000 to his cat, **Buster**, cutting off his relatives without a penny due to their "cruelty to my cat." Buster died in 1945, intestate.

"One of the oldest human needs is having someone to wonder where you are when you don't come home at night."

— MARGARET MEAD, ON CATS

Koko's Cats

Koko is the name of the captive gorilla housed at Stanford University who was trained by Dr. Francine Patterson and other scientists to communicate by using more than 1,000 signs based on American Sign Language. In 1984, just around the time of her twelfth birthday, Koko asked her trainer for a cat. She chose a kitten from an abandoned litter and actually named it herself — All-Ball. Koko is one of the few nonhumans known to keep pets of a different species (Toto was another gorilla known to have cared for a cat). When All-Ball escaped her cage and was run over by a car, Koko found a way to communicate the words *sad* and *cry*, and it is said that she wept for more than two days. Happily, All-Ball was replaced with not one but two kittens. All-Ball was featured in the 1987 book *Koko's Kitten,* by Dr. Patterson.

1. All-Ball
2. Lipstick
3. Shirley

12 Cat Burglars

Animal behaviorists call it "misdirected predation," an urbanized response to the hunting instinct, and it is almost impossible to stop.

1. A pair of mischievous cats had their owner, Elaine Floodgate, in a flap after boosting the neighborhood crime rate in a London suburb. **Major Benjie** and **Georgie** were caught red-handed following mysterious cat burglaries next door to their home. Oriental tabby Major Benjie started the crime wave by sneaking through the neighbor's cat flap and returning with a cuddly toy. Days later, the bold cat came home with more loot. Georgie then sneaked next door and made a beeline for an expensive watch left lying on a bench. The cats were caught after the neighbor mentioned that things were disappearing. The criminal conspirators have been banished from their neighbor's house.

2. **Dandelion**, age 3, first started "collecting" when he was a year old and in two years has stolen more than 700 items, according to his British owner, Sara Peacock. "I own a cat burglar. He goes into people's homes and steals things," Miss Peacock said. "It's an anxiety thing. He wants to please me by bringing me home presents." The Oriental bi-color cat steals at least one thing a day and has a fetish for socks. "His specialty is socks. He'll bring home one and go back to get the other. We have lots of pairs, but it's really embarrassing, as it's not just one a day . . . but five or six!" To complicate matters, Dandelion has expanded his collection to shoes, clothes, toys, purses, gloves, underwear, rags, pincushions, sun hats, jewelry, and more. Unable to locate the owners of the stolen loot, Peacock took to hanging things on a tree in front of her house. "I hear people walking past, saying, 'Hey, that's mine!'"

3. The mystery of the disappearing slippers has been solved—with **Jenkins** the Siamese cat fingered as the culprit. The pet, owned by Barbara Davies of the U.K., was seen by a neighbor struggling over a wall with a furry purple slipper nearly as big as himself. To Barbara's amazement, he dragged the slipper home and struggled through the cat flap. A few days later Jenkins repeated the performance with the matching slipper. Feeling sure that the owner of the slippers would be missing their warmth in the winter cold, Barbara telephoned neighbors, but no one had lost a pair of purple furry slippers. Finally, after posting signs throughout the village, the puzzled owner of the missing items was found and reunited with his stolen property.

4. Residents of the Dunedin suburb of Mornington, New Zealand, were being terrorized by a second-generation thief, apparently born into a life of crime. **Podge**, whose mother used to steal rugby socks, spent the better part of two and a half years taking shoes from porches. He lost part of his tail during one late-night raid — his owner, Aileen Smith, suspected it was caught in a door as he tried to get away — but he continued to steal shoes by the pair. After a quiet period of some weeks, Podge stole four more pairs of shoes and was finally caught. Animal behaviorist and associate professor at Massey University Kevin Stafford said that Podge had most likely learned his craft from his mother, Kizzi, who continues to steal slippers and stuffed toys from neighbors.

5. It's a caper of epic proportions. Residents in the Willowbridge subdivision in northwest Harris County in the U.K. are dealing with a real criminal with an unreal identity. **Sammy** the cat has been stealing from his neighbors for years: hats, slippers, workout pants, gold towels, shoes, and much more. Janet Vaught, his owner, said things just started showing up several years ago. "First it was the balls, then the sandals, then it was the shoes." Neighbors Kim and Morgan Hurst were disbelieving until they rummaged through stolen items and

found seven things that had vanished from their home, six houses down the street. The items included a floor rug that Sammy was able to drag over a six-foot fence.

6. A mischievous moggie could be behind the disappearance of up to 50 cuddly toys from a cemetery. Police were called after toys started to go missing from graves in Durham Road, Stockton, in Teesside, U.K. Initially, owner Samantha Wilks thought the items had come from neighboring homes, but after reading a newspaper report about vandals targeting babies' graves, she became suspicious. "There's nothing I can do to stop him," said Wilks. "I don't know why he does it."

7. A New Zealand family was under siege. Each weekend, something would go missing off their clothesline. Not just anything, but rather their best woolens. The saga began with the disappearance of Rosemary's black merino V-neck sweater. Then it was the navy Fair Isle, followed by daughter Georgia's Wellington Girls jersey. The list went on — socks, trousers, more socks. The only member of the family not to have anything nicked was Casey the cat. The Alexander-Neilsons began counting the number of items they hung out to dry, then counting them again when they brought the wash in. "We were becoming really paranoid," said Rosemary. "We started hanging out stuff we didn't care about, just to try and catch whoever it was. But that was never taken; it was just the good-quality stuff."

The family was getting worked up. "You just start wondering what sort of person would be doing this. You want to protect your family," said Neville Alexander-Neilson. He padlocked the front gate. The police were called. Finally, a video camera was set up, and **two cat burglars** were caught red-pawed. The cats' owners were tracked down and the clothes repossessed. Once the Alexander-

Neilsons stopped laughing, they heaved huge sighs of relief, knowing they weren't dealing with a crazed criminal. "I really just wanted to put a face to it. Once I knew it was a cat, it was totally over," said Neville, happy to have the affair behind him.

8. In Pelham, New York, Jeanine Goche has posted a sign in front of her house that says, "Our cat is a glove snatcher. Please take these if yours." **Willy**, who loves gloves, specializes in gardening gloves. On any given day, passersby will see rows of gloves strung up, waiting for their rightful owners. "This all started about the time people began working in their gardens, I guess March or April. Willy would just show up with a glove, or we'd see them on the front steps," said Goche. "A lot of these looked brand new; some of them are really nice." She doesn't know how far afield Willy goes to find gloves, but she has learned that it takes him two trips to bring home a matched pair.

9. Sue Boyd lets her cat, **Midnight**, bask in his booty for a few moments before bagging it up for the neighbors to reclaim in her Simi Valley, California, neighborhood. Night after night, the four-legged street pirate plunders garages, sheds, backyards, and patios for his loot, which he proudly carries home to his distressed owners, Sue and Richard Boyd. Midnight has an affinity for shoes, hats, shirts, and panties, all of which he easily drags through the quiet streets to his house, as late-night witnesses to his pilfering attest. On occasion, he has surprised his owners with some interesting acquisitions. Once Midnight brought home a Christmas gift. "It was wrapped and everything. He's like a little klepto cat," said Boyd, who swears Midnight is an otherwise loving kitty. Each day, his owners leave a bag with the purloined goods hanging from their mailbox, so neighbors

can reclaim missing items. Deena Case-Pall, a Camarillo-based psychologist who specializes in animal behavior, suggests that Midnight's career was triggered by the family's acquisition of a Doberman pinscher.

10. When night falls in Manurewa, New Zealand, **Holly** starts on her quest, prowling through suburban streets to prey on trusting residents. Holly stockpiles her loot at the back door of her home, but if she's disturbed on her journey, she simply drops her goods in the street. This petite and friendly female doesn't look like the stealing type, but she has a shoe fetish rivaled by few others, often going the extra mile for a matching pair. Kay McKillion, who lives in the same neighborhood, thought she was being targeted by thieves when the seventh pair of shoes disappeared from her home, and she called the police to complain. "Every time someone walked past my house, I would go out and see if they were wearing my shoes," she says. The mystery was solved when a neighbor told her about Holly and she was directed to the house nearby, where boxes of shoes lay waiting to be claimed.

11. **Tommy** the tomcat has a big problem — he can't keep his paws off other people's property. For three years Tommy has been slipping out through his cat flap and returning with his booty, including designer clothes, shoes, socks, trousers, a bag full of coins, a hat, and even a golf umbrella. Owner Ali Daffin, of the U.K., said, "It was funny at first. He was so proud of himself, with socks . . . and the odd slipper. But the haul just got more and more adventurous, with matching pairs of expensive sneakers. He would bring the left one home one morning and then two days later I would get the right. He hollers at the bottom of the stairs until I come down to inspect it all." Proud Tommy just loves showing off his haul.

12. "**Tisiphone** is a Munchkin, and breeders always emphasize the fact that these cats are like magpies, always stealing small shiny things. I disregarded this as a fancy," reported Corine Jenkins of the U.K. "After all, a lot of cats will make off with small things as toys and then disregard them. However, when Tisiphone entered my household, I noticed that certain things were disappearing, most noticeably pens and pencils. One minute you would have a jar full of pens, next you're searching the house for something to write with." One day Jenkins followed Tisiphone as she crept by, with a pen in her mouth. The owner saw Tisiphone push the pen under a bookcase. When, later, she moved the bookcase, she found over 30 pens, a couple of pencils, key holders, a necklace, socks, cat toys, and various other items. "We now also suspect her of stealing my husband's wedding ring, but unfortunately since I took back all of the items she had so carefully stashed, she must have found a new hiding place for her hoard," said Jenkins. The woman is still searching for the ring.

"By associating with the cat, one only risks becoming richer." — COLETTE

4 Really Bad Cats

1. Five-year-old **Lewis** is best known in his Connecticut neighborhood as the Terrorist of Sunset Circle for his violent attacks on several neighbors and an Avon lady. Lewis has caused so much damage that a judge was finally forced to slap him with a restraining order. With six toes on each foot, each with a long claw, violence comes easily to Lewis. One victim reported: "I was walking along the sidewalk when he sprang at me. I never saw it coming, but that's how it often is. He comes at you from behind, springs, and wraps himself around your legs, biting and scratching." As of this writing, the Avon lady has filed a lawsuit against Lewis's owner in Superior Court.

2. A mother cat in London didn't like it one bit when her owner sold the house and left her behind. To vent her anger, she kept the new owner hostage by hissing and snarling loudly for three hours until fire rescuers finally were able to separate the frightened woman from the furious feline.

3. **Jack**, of West Milford, New Jersey, made felines everywhere proud in June 2006 when a bear invaded his backyard territory. When the bear first came into the yard, Jack went after him and scared him up a tree. After 15 minutes the bear finally gathered up enough courage to climb back down, only to be chased up another tree by Jack, minutes later. Finally, worried for the safety of their 15-pound pussy, Jack's owners called him back into the house and the bear escaped.

4. Amy Dowell, of Ohio, reports that her boyfriend showed up one night madder than a wet cat. Here's why: **Blackjack** did not like riding in cars, but Mike was forced to bring him along on an errand. To offset Blackjack's anxiety, Mike put the cat in a travel carrier, but an hour into the trip, the cat relieved himself in it. While Mike got out of the car to clean the carrier, Blackjack hit the automatic door locks, leaving Mike outside in pouring rain. It took two hours and a call to roadside assistance to get back in the car.

"Women and cats will do as they please, and men and dogs should relax and get used to the idea."
— ROBERT A. HEINLEIN

13 Working Cats

The butcher, the baker, and even the candlestick maker have called on the talents of cats. Cats have guarded priceless art works, they have sold us everything from batteries to baby food, and they have acted as companions for lonely soldiers. During the 1930s, when British health officials banned the transportation of food on commercial airlines, cats were used to sniff out violations. In the famous portrait by George Stubbs of his beloved stallion, the Godolphin Arabian, the horse's devoted companion, a tabby, is included. (When the horse died, the cat refused to leave the carcass until it was buried; he then skulked off and was soon found dead.) Here are some blue-collar cats who have distinguished themselves on the job.

1. **Baker** and **Taylor**, the official mascots of the largest book distributor in the world, resided at the Douglas County Library in Minden, Nevada, when they weren't acting in their official capacity. Baker and Taylor were just as spoiled as could be, receiving all kinds of attention from their adoring fans. They constantly sought out human company, to the delight of the library patrons, and they had a fan club, run by a second-grade teacher at the Jefferson Elementary School in Guhannan, Ohio. The cats received numerous letters and gifts and even had a song written about them.

2. **Beerbohm**, named for Herbert Beerbohm Tree, the famous actor-manager at Her Majesty's Theatre, where he was born in the 1970s, was the resident mouser at the Globe Theatre (now the Gielgud Theatre) in London's West End for 20 years. The large tabby was London's longest-serving theatre cat and often upstaged the actors when he would wander on stage during a performance. He passed away in 1995.

3. **Donut** is the only patrol guard at Lockheed's Shipyard in Harbor Island, Seattle. He wears his badge (I.D. #52½) around his neck. He resides in the company's payroll booth and has never missed a day of work. He has his own locker, marked with his name, where he keeps his toys and his flea powder.

4. **Fang** is another cat with his own picture I.D. He's head mouser at the Grand Prairie Police Station in Texas. The feline was transferred there from the local animal shelter after rats were found feasting on evidence. He is described as the "biggest, baddest cat there is."

5. **Feedback** was appropriately named. Mice droppings were bad enough, but when a few of the critters shut down the radio station by chewing through wires early in the 1980s, the manager of radio station WJCO in Jackson, Michigan, brought in the heavy artillery in the form of a cat, who was adopted from the local humane society. Feedback easily rounded up every mouse in sight and soon became a host, greeting visitors in the lobby where he worked. He was even known to wander into the studio and add his own special comments to the broadcast, and he received gifts and cards from as far away as Arizona, California, and New Jersey.

6. **Inga** was the weather crew cat who lived at the Mount Washington Observatory in New Hampshire until 1993, when he was succeeded by another cat, named **Nin**.

"Your job would be to keep my chair warm when I'm out and rub up against my feet when I slip off my shoes. You seem qualified, but we'd prefer a college graduate."

In the late nineteenth century, a breeder in Pittsburgh, Pennsylvania, developed a breed he called "refrigerator cats," who could control rodent populations in cold-storage warehouses. Their heavily furred coats, thick Persian-like tails, and tufted ears helped them adapt to cold temperatures.

7. **Mike**, a popular black cat whose fans were many, reigned at the gate of the British Museum for 20 years, from 1909 to 1929. Although his predecessor, **Black Jack**, had been much admired by staff and patrons alike, he was granted an early retirement after spending a night in a room of bound newspapers and turning them into confetti! When Mike died, a 165-page obituary was published, and poems were written in his memory.

8. **Night Watchman**, at Webster's Feed Store on Pine Island, New York, just showed up for work one day in the 1970s and stayed for about 18 years, after which he died quietly in his sleep. Night Watchman was known as an excellent mouser but was also officially appointed office manager. It is said that no one passed a bad check while he was at the helm.

9. **Sam** is the quintessential collegiate cat and enjoys free run of New Hall at Cambridge University, where he can be found sunbathing on the walkways or curled up in the most comfortable chair of any college office. Everyone, from the porters to the housekeepers, makes sure that he is well fed, and each new year, entering students soon join the fun of pampering the sometimes finicky feline. Only during the springtime, when ducklings are hatching in Fountain Court, are his movements restricted.

10. **Smudge** was a feline celebrity in Glasgow, where he was employed by the People's Palace Museum to deal with a rodent problem in 1979. Smudge became a fixture of the museum, which sold Smudge merchandise, including ceramic replicas designed by a noted potter. In the 1980s, he became a member of the General, Municipal and Boilermakers Trade Union, after another union refused him admission as a blue-collar worker. Smudge participated in many of the museum's advertising campaigns. He died in 2000 after a long illness.

11. **Sumo** was a rather large ginger-and-white tomcat who patrolled the 35 acres surrounding Hever Castle, where Henry VIII courted Anne Boleyn. Sumo became so fat from all the treats that visitors bestowed on him that the waterfowl around the castle learned to completely ignore him.

12. **Tiddles**, formerly a stray cat, worked for many years in the ladies' room at the London Railway station in Paddington. The tabby was known as a peeping tom, squeezing under stall doors from time to time in order to become better acquainted with travelers. He weighed in at 25 pounds, no doubt a result of his diet of steak, lamb, and cod, and received fan mail from all over the world.

13. The five nuns at the Byzantine convent of **St. Nicholas of the Cats** in Cyprus are outnumbered by the 200 cats that reside there as well. The feline community here actually dates back to the fourth century, when a disastrous drought resulted in an infestation of snakes. Serpent-killing cats were imported from Egypt and taken to St. Nicholas, located in an area appropriately named Cape Gata, "Cape Cat." The convent has been destroyed and rebuilt many times over the centuries, always with a cat population in attendance.

Is Your Cat Tax-Deductible?

In the 1980s, a deaf man claimed that his cat alerted him to danger and thereby functioned as a hearing aid, which made the cost of the cat's care tax-deductible. The IRS allowed the deduction but stated that the decision applied to this taxpayer only and that future claims would be examined individually.

Circus Cats

When Phineas Barnum proudly announced that he had a genuine cherry-colored cat, the fascinated public lined up to buy tickets. But after paying their money, they were sorely disappointed to find themselves staring at an ordinary black cat. Barnum refused to refund their money — after all, he pointed out, some cherries are indeed black.

The introduction of wild animals to the circus dates from about 1819, when the French trainer Henri Martin, performing in Nuremburg, Germany, entered a cage with a tiger. Big cats went on to become the highlight of just about every circus on earth, but some small cats have distinguished themselves under the big top as well. Here are a few:

The Moscow Cats Theatre is actually the only entertainment of its kind in the world. Performances feature nonstop action by a troop of talented felines performing original and astounding acrobatic feats. Created almost 30 years ago by renowned circus performer Yuri Kuklachev, the Moscow Cats Theatre has grown into one of the most popular weekend outings for Moscow kids and adults, selling out every performance. Kuklachev decided to start working with cats after finding an abandoned kitten in a park. A juggler, flying gymnast, illusionist, and clown, he kept on training cats, disproving a widespread belief that cats cannot be tamed. "The cats are the stars of this show — they walk tightropes, balance balls on their noses, do paw-stands, jump from great heights, and unerringly negotiate complex mazes," says Kuklachev. "We glorify them and that's why we provide a traveling entourage, including a vet, kitty caretakers, and personal stylists, to tend to the needs of our feline superstars." The show has toured extensively and has been embraced by the media and fans alike. With appearances on *Good Morning America, Good Day New York, CBS Early Show, Inside Edition,* and *The Montel Williams Show,* the Russian cats are the talk of the town. To learn more, visit the circus online at moscowcatstheatre.com.

One of the funniest aspects of the Ringling Brothers Barnum & Bailey Circus is its cadre of circus cats. We know that dogs can do tricks, and canines are part of the performance, but the trained cats stun the audience as they push pigeons

around in little wheelbarrows, among other tricks. Most cats are not talented in this way and would more likely view their feathered friends as a nice snack. The cats are trained by Madame Svetlana Shamsheeva, a former Russian zookeeper. Visit Ringling.com for their tour schedule.

Dominique "the Catman" LeFort, renowned entertainer and cat trainer, performs regularly at Sunset Celebration at the Hilton Pier in Key West, Florida. The act is more comedy than performance, but, with the help of his trained housecats, Oscar and Cossette, Sara, Chopin, George, and Mandarine, the Catman's show is a marvel to watch. Often outfitted in theatrical lion-tamer garb, the shaggy-coiffed blond Dominique is more than half the show himself. Mixing mime, dance postures, and French-accented demands to his enthralled audience and feline acrobats, he comes off as Maurice Chevalier playing Marcel Marceau playing Gunther Gebel-Williams. The shows are hilarious and popular with audiences of all ages. To find out more, visit CatManKeyWest.com.

8 Psychic Cats

While he was a graduate student at UCLA, Dr. Franklin Ruehl, today a science writer and nuclear physicist, acquired a cat named Simba, who typically rushed toward the phone seconds before it rang. Oddly, Simba could demonstrate this behavior only when Dr. Ruehl was in the room. Was he especially sensitive to the vibrational frequency of incoming calls to that telephone, or was there a special connection between the cat and his owner? Although Ruehl performed numerous similar experiments, no scientifically sound conclusions were ever drawn. Owners of cats with special abilities, however, need no such proof.

1. During World War II, residents in London reported agitated cat behavior before sirens went off warning of bombs.

2. Honoré de Balzac, the French novelist, owned a cat who came to meet him on his way home from work each day. When Balzac occasionally changed his plans and didn't come home, his cat stayed home.

3. In *A Cat Is Watching*, Roger Caras tells of a stray cat who showed up on his family's property whenever their daughter, Pamela, came home from college, some two 200 miles away. She never appeared there at any other time.

4. French author Claude Farrère awoke one night to find Kare Kedi, his cat, howling and staring at the wall. But all seemed quiet, and Farrère went back to bed. The next morning he learned that his neighbor had been murdered at the time that Kare Kedi had had her outburst.

5. A cat named Charley gave birth to kittens in the middle of an office and insisted on keeping her kittens right there, despite the inconvenience to those who were forced to literally work around her. But when the kittens were just a week old, Charley was found frantically moving her kittens to a sheltered spot — just before a rock came crashing through the window, landing just where the kittens had been nestling.

6. The owner of a Persian left her cat in the care of a neighbor while she went on an extended vacation. The cat adjusted well to his new surroundings until about a month into his visit, when he suddenly became visibly depressed, refusing to eat, rejecting tenderness, and finally curling up in a corner, howling mournfully. It was just then that the neighbor received a phone call saying that the cat's owner was dead.

7. Toto lived near Mount Vesuvius in Italy. In 1944, it was reported that he roused his sleeping owner by scratching his cheek over and over again. The man's wife sensed Toto was trying to communicate to the couple and insisted that they pack some belongings and leave their home. An hour later, a volcano erupted, completely engulfing their home and killing 30 people.

8. In 1975, in Haicheng, China, a swarm of cats running about madly in the town convinced savvy seismologists to evacuate the city 24 hours before a major earthquake struck.

Animal Planet's world-famous pet psychic Sonya Fitzpatrick contends that cats and other companion animals communicate with pictures and feelings, which they send telepathically to each other and to certain humans. In her book **Cat Talk: The Secrets of Communicating with Your Cat**, she shares ways in which people can tap into what cats are thinking and offers a step-by-step guide to learning cat talk. For another fun read on how to better grasp the paranormal powers of cats, check out the book **Test Your Cat's Psychic Powers**, by Missy Camp Dizick.

The Algonquin Cat

The first Algonquin cat wandered into the New York hotel in the 1930s, so the story goes. Legendary manager Frank Case adopted the cat, or the cat adopted the hotel, depending on whose story you believe. The cat, a ragtag stray, was given the name Hamlet to fit in with the hotel's elegant reputation. Since then, a cat has become a permanent fixture in the lobby. Males are named Hamlet; females are Matilda.

Currently Matilda, a beautiful Birman, reigns at the hotel. She prefers sleeping behind the computers at the front desk or else on the baggage trolley. She's 11 years old and throws birthday parties to benefit local animal shelters and encourage pet adoptions. Matilda, of course, sets the tone of the party. A few years ago, she celebrated an event by jumping into the cake.

Matilda has been named Cat of the Year at the prestigious Westchester Cat Show, an honor bestowed in November. She's a working cat, answering e-mail, giving out business cards, appearing in books (such as *The Algonquin Cat*), and generally charming guests. She receives hundreds of e-mails each year from guests all over the world. (You can reach her at algonquin cat@algonquinhotel.com.) And she answers each one individually, with her classic signature:

Have a PURRfect day

^..^
→←

Matilda

ABOVE: **Matilda, the current reigning Algonquin cat.**
RIGHT: **The signature of Hamlet, an Algonquin cat of the past.**

11 Advertising Cats

Since the dawn of advertising, cats have sold us everything from thread and cigarettes to breakfast cereal and condoms. Typical feline qualities are used to make products attractive to consumers: satisfaction (the image of a cat purring away an afternoon); safety and protection (a mama cat protecting her little ones); home and well-being (a kitten curled around a pair of bedroom slippers); durability (their nine lives); and delicacy (poise and light-footed agility).

As effective spokespurrsons, cat images have become synonymous with certain products, Eveready Batteries and My Sin perfume among them. Possibly because kitties are so careful with their young, they are popular images for moving van and insurance companies alike. After years of promoting cigarettes and cigars, cats finally posed for the American Lung Association's 1983 poster featuring three irresistible felines, who simply stated, "We Don't Want You to Smoke."

Of course, no one made more money for his owners than Morris (see page 99), but here are a few contenders.

1. Arthur
Between 1966 and 1975, Arthur won hearts throughout Great Britain when, in commercials for Spillers cat food, he would scoop food out of a tin with his paw. Arthur became a merchandising empire unto himself, as fans snatched up T-shirts, towels, and other "I ♥ Arthur" accessories.

But Arthur's story took a sinister turn when his guardian reclaimed him and sued Spillers, claiming that the company had had Arthur's teeth pulled in order to encourage his famous scooping gesture. The courts ruled in Spillers's favor but the company lost out in the end, as Arthur and his guardian found political asylum in the Russian embassy.

In 1987, Arthur II, a shelter cat, took over the job of selling Spillers cat food, demonstrating his "odd" ability to scoop food with his paw, just as the original Arthur had. Arthur II retired after nine years to make way for a younger successor.

2. Biscuit
In the 1970s, when Poppin' Fresh, the ticklish Pillsbury dough boy, turned five, his creator, Leo Burnett, gave him a cat named Biscuit (along with a wife named Poppie; a son, Popper; a baby daughter, Bun Bun; GrandPopper and GranMommer, the grandparents; a dog, Flapjack; and a bachelor uncle, Rollie). The clan never made it into the commericals or the movies, but replicas sold briskly in Sears stores for a while.

3. Chessie
Beginning in 1933, the Chesapeake and Ohio Railway used a cute kitten to speak for the comfort they offered passengers. "Sleep like a kitten on the C&O," boasted their advertising. Derived from an etching by Viennese artist Guido Gruenwald (the company paid five dollars to use the image), Chessie first appeared in the September 1933 issue of *Fortune* magazine. The ads were so successful that the railroad developed a campaign around Chessie, including print advertising, calendars, clothing, jewelry, pocket knives,

Chessie charmed the country with her famous promise, "Sleep like a kitten." The Chesapeake and Ohio Railway featured her in a host of ads.

An early ad featuring Crinkle, the Kellogg's kitty.

playing cards, and tote bags. During World War II, "America's Sleepheart" promoted war bonds and the war effort. When in 1972 the C&O merged with the Baltimore and Ohio Railroad and the Western Maryland Railway, the newly formed company was named the Chessie System. That company later merged with other railroads to become the CSX Corporation. Though the Chessie logo was eventually phased out, the cat is still the mascot of the CSX Corporation, and some railway cars, yet to be repainted, still bear her image. Chessie's story was told in an out-of-print children's book and more recently in Thomas Dixon's *Chessie the Railroad Kitten* (1996).

4. Crinkle
Before Tony the Tiger, there was Crinkle, a gray cat who appeared on boxes of Kellogg's Toasted Corn Flakes cereal around 1914, along with the slogan "For Kiddies Not Kitties."

5. Glitter
A silver tabby British shorthair is the spokes-cat for Whiskas cat food. Glitter is a fat, happy cat who takes 29-minute naps between photo shoots.

6. Kitty
In 1972, Kellogg's used a 10-inch-tall green frog in a baseball cap named Dig 'Em to promote Sugar Smacks (sold today under the politically correct name Honey Smacks). The character helped spike sales dramatically, and he kept hopping until 1986. One of Dig 'Em's favorite activities was chasing a cat named Kitty, who was always trying to steal his Smacks. Of course, Dig 'Em always won, while Kitty usually got knocked senseless.

7. Nacho
In 1995, Taco Bell introduced two mascots: Nacho and Dog. Nacho was a crazy cat who learned everything he needed to know by watching TV and was obsessed with Mexican food. Dog, a dog, was refined and well-read. The two were dropped in mid-1997, but the taco-touting kitty still appears in many in-store promotions. It's hard to compete with that crazy Chihuahua!

8. Peake
Chessie, the Chesapeake and Ohio mascot, became so popular with the public that her creators decided to give her two kittens in 1935. There was an immediate public outcry questioning the identity of the father of the kittens. Lest Chessie gain a reputation for catting around, Peake was introduced.

9. SH III
The original Fancy Feast cat, known as SH III, was trained alongside an understudy appropriately named Maybe. He got his chance when SH III, whose real name was Shithead, passed away in 1997 at the age of 20. SH III appeared in the Steve Martin movie *The Jerk,* and it was Maybe who modeled for the *Scrooge* movie poster. Both were warmly greeted at many personal appearances.

10. Snowy
The white spokes-cat for the Utica and Mohawk Cotton Mills in the 1930s and 1940s was created by Harry Frees, whose stories and unique animal photography appeared in magazines of the time, including *Woman's World* and *Child Life.* The first five pages of a 28-page booklet titled "Restful Sleep," created for U&I, followed Snowy as she purchased new

sheets, washed and ironed them, and finally demonstrated the proper way to make a bed.

11. Tommy
In 1883, the Great Atlantic and Pacific Tea Company distributed advertising cards to each of its 135 stores. The sign featured one cat trying to fondle another with the caption "Don't, Tommy, don't." While the meaning here escapes us, A&P stores did go on to become a supermarket empire.

Logo of the Cooper Underwear Company, popular prior to 1911.

7 Cigar Brands Named After Cats

1. **Two Toms**

2. **Cats**

3. **Old Tom**

4. **Pussy**

5. **Tabby**

6. **Me-Ow**

7. **White Cat**

25 Cat-Fancying Artists, Illustrators, and Cartoonists

It's impossible to imagine that any artist who ever owned a cat never bothered to paint it. The complex feline markings and poses can challenge even the greatest masters; a sleek, lean coat looks different when the cat sits, and the slightest movement can change the model's musculature. Here are just a few of the many painters who immortalized their cats in timeless works of art.

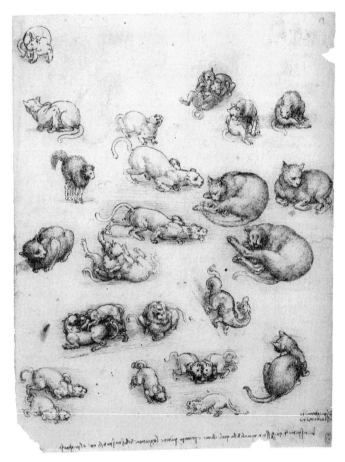

Study of cat movements and positions by Leonardo da Vinci.

1. **Leonardo da Vinci (1452–1519)** After a long period of absence from art, due to the cat haters of the Middle Ages, the cat reappeared as a subject during the Renaissance (1400–1600). In 1517 Italian scientist and artist Leonardo da Vinci began sketching the cat as a study of anatomy and movement. He sketched a total of 20 cats in various poses and activities. His famous saying "The smallest feline is a masterpiece" attests to his artistic interest in the cat.

2. **Albrecht Dürer (1471–1528)** Dürer's engraving *Adam and Eve*, created in 1504, depicts the Garden of Eden. The idyllic scene includes a mouse and a cat lying side by side.

3. **Jan Steen (1626–1679)** Dutch artist Jan Steen's 1666 painting *The Family Concert* shows a family making music in their home. In the foreground we see a cat feeding at its bowl, with a dog approaching. Steen's *The Cat's Dancing Lesson* portrays a cat being held upright atop the kitchen table while one child plays a flute as two laughing children stand by.

4. **William Hogarth (1697–1764)** William Hogarth, renowned artist and commentator on social evils of the eighteenth century, did a series of engravings called *The Four Stages of Cruelty*. In a scene showing cruelty to various animals, people tie two cats together while betting on which cat will survive the fight to the death. In Hogarth's series of engravings called *Harlot's Progress*, a cat is shown ready to mate, and in his portrait *The Graham Children* a cat appears as an antagonist, hungrily eyeing a caged bird.

5. Jean-Baptiste-Simeon Chardin (1699–1779) Chardin's *Still Life with Cat and Fish*, painted in 1728, is an interesting study of cat behavior. The loose brush strokes capture the cat's movement and the texture of its fur. In the still life *The Ray*, Chardin again delicately depicts the cat's coat as the kitty focuses on a filleted fish.

6. Goya (Francisco Jose de Goya y Lucientes, 1746–1828) Goya felt that animals typified human weaknesses in all its forms. In his painting *The Cat Fight*, Goya portrays combative cats frozen in time. Goya did a series of works in 1794 and 1795 called the "witchcraft paintings," based on witchcraft mythology, in which the cat and other animals symbolize the misfortune that affects men's dreams.

7. Hokusai Katsushika (1760–1849) With his sketches, woodblock prints, notebooks, storybooks, and illustrated poetry, Katsushika proved himself one of Japan's finest artists. In his famous painting *Cat and Butterfly*, he presents a cat as the central figure of the painting, a practice unheard of in the West. Katsushika, who began drawing at the age of 6, greatly influenced Western artists and designers with his sense of style and simplicity. Like many others in Japan society, Katsushika saw the cat as symbolic of sex and desire.

8. Gustave Courbet (1819–1877) Among French artists, Gustave Courbet's most noted painting is *Woman with a Cat*, executed in 1864. Courbet championed the realist movement during the mid-1800s. The painting reveals the sensuous relationship between cat and woman. His depiction of the cat has erotic overtones typical of many of his paintings.

9. Henrietta Ronner-Knip (1821–1909) Dutch-born artist Ronner-Knip is well known for her cat paintings, which can be seen at the Rijksmuseum in Amsterdam. By 1870 she began painting cats and kittens exclusively. Her paintings, such as *Contentment*, *On Top of the World*, and *Pretty Kitten*, capture the beauty, elegance, and sweet nature of her beloved felines, whom she endowed with almost human characteristics.

10. Pierre-Auguste Renoir (1841–1919) French impressionist Renoir's cat paintings, *A Boy with a Cat* and *Girl and Cat*, both capture the intense relationship between human and feline. In each image the cat is caressed by its human companion. Renoir, known for his beautiful nudes, also painted *Sleeping Girl with Cat*, which is both colorful and sensuous.

11. Théophile Steinlen (1859–1923) A master of art nouveau, Steinlen did thousands of drawings of cats. He adored felines and drew them as if he felt their sensations himself, imagining what it was like to be a sleeping or dancing cat. In doing so, Steinlen felt he was expressing what he felt were the cat's deepest secrets. Steinlen is noted for his posters featuring a black tomcat with a tattered tail.

12. Louis Wain (1860–1939) Wain, an English artist, is most famous for his cat drawings. His fascination with cats began while he was a young man. By 1900 he was a household name in Eng-

Two of Théophile Steinlen's many beloved cats.

land because of the popularity of the "Louis Wain Cat," with its mischievous countenance. (See page 10 for more about Wain.)

13. George Herriman (1880–1944) American cartoonist Herriman was the creator of the classic comic strip *Krazy Kat*, the most popular cartoon strip during World War I. It was so highly regarded that each panel of the strip was appreciated as an individual piece of art on its own merits. Most of the stories had to do with Krazy Kat's unrequited love for Ignatz, a mouse. Originally drawn in black and white, *Krazy Kat* became a color strip in 1935. Herriman's use of color was often surreal, with skies of purple or green, while hills and valleys could appear polkadotted or striped. *Krazy Kat* was especially popular with jazz musicians and writers who admired Herriman's illustration style and use of patois language. James Joyce and E. E. Cummings were fans of the strip, and William Randolph Hearst produced several animated films featuring Krazy Kat in the early twentieth century.

"I want to create a cat like the real cats I see crossing the streets, not like those you see in houses. They have nothing in common. The cat of the streets has bristling fur. It runs like a fiend, and if it looks at you, you think it is going to jump in your face."
— **PABLO PICASSO**

14. Pablo Picasso (1881–1973) Picasso is arguably the most prolific and important artist of the twentieth century, and he used the cat as the subject of numerous works. *Wounded Bird and Cat,* painted in 1938, is perhaps his most famous cat painting and an early work from his cubist period. The painting was a political statement: the cat symbolized the cruelty of the laws of nature. In what is called Picasso's "circus period" he employed the cat as a symbol of affection.

15. Marc Chagall (1887–1985) Russian-born artist Chagall had a lifelong love of animals, often including them

Ancient Egyptian artists never portrayed cats in a sleeping position but rather upright, reflecting the respect they had for the cat's wisdom.

in his drawings and paintings. In *Paris Through the Window,* created in 1913, a cat is perched on a windowsill in a dreamlike state, somewhere between fantasy and reality. In 1926, he painted *The Cat Transformed into a Woman,* in which a cat has been changed into a woman by its adoring master.

16. Theodor Geisel (Dr. Seuss, 1904–1991) Known for the rhyming children's books that appeal to people of all ages, Theodor Geisel, or Dr. Seuss, was born in Springfield, Massachusetts, in 1904. With the release of *The Cat in the Hat* in 1957, Dr. Seuss achieved acclaim as a children's book author and illustrator. He followed that book, about a fictional, fiendish cat, with *The Cat in the Hat Comes Back* in 1958. By the time of his death in 1991, he had written and illustrated 44 children's books, which have been translated into more than 15 languages and sold more than 200 million copies.

17. Chuck Jones (1912–2002) In 1943 Jones created the character Claude Cat, a very nervous and good-for-nothing character who tries to defend his territory against Hubie and Bertie, a pair of manipulative mice. In 1950 Claude reappears in the film *The HypoChondri-Cat,* in which the mice

convince Claude that he is dead. Claude again leaves his paw prints on 1951's *Cheese Chasers* and again in *Mouse Warming* in 1952. Jones also created the *Cat Portfolio,* a series of ten cat illustrations.

18. Saul Steinberg (1914–1999) Steinberg, illustrator for *The New Yorker* magazine, was responsible for much of the magazine's cover and interior art. His cover illustration for the March 20, 1954, issue shows a family of cats portrayed in simple but highly evocative black-and-white line drawings. In his 1966 *Still Life with Cat,* Steinberg gives his cat a deadpan human-like profile resembling his own visage. *The New Yorker Book of Cat Cartoons,* published in 1997, contains several of Steinberg's cat pieces.

19. George Booth (b. 1926) Booth is another artist at *The New Yorker* magazine who created many cartoons with neurotic cats as central figures. In 1983 Booth's first book, *Think Good Thoughts About a Pussycat,* was published. *The Essential George Booth* is a collection of cartoons, published in 1998, in which hundreds of cats are doing all kinds of wacky things. Booth created a character called Ambrosia (based on his own real cat of the same name) whom he later renamed Amberson after discovering that she was a he. His work is included in *The New Yorker Book of Cat Cartoons.*

20. B. Kliban (1935–1990) Kliban is perhaps the originator of a family of outrageous cartoon cats. His first book, *Cat,* sometimes referred to as "the mother of all cat books," is based on a character by that name. (For more about Kliban, see page 16.)

21. Buck Jones (b. 1944) Mixing humor with artistic skill, this Iowa illustrator and cartoonist has been making people chuckle for more than 20 years with illustrations that have appeared in a variety of magazines, comic strips, and advertising campaigns. His work has appeared in *Cat Fancy, Dog Fancy, Puppies USA, Mad,* and the Simple Solution dog book series by Bowtie Books.

22. Jim Davis (b. 1945) Davis, who created the character Garfield in 1978, grew up surrounded by cats. *Garfield* has become one the most popular comic strips ever. The character Garfield was named after James Garfield Davis, Davis's grandfather, who had been named after President Garfield. The animated cartoon series *Garfield and Friends* aired on TV from 1988 to 1994. The comic strip made its debut in 41 newspapers in 1978 and today appears in more than 2,600 daily newspapers and is read by more than 263 million feline fans. Fast feline fact: Garfield ranks as the most widely syndicated comic strip in the world, according to *The Guinness Book of World Records* as of 2006. And yes, Garfield has gone to Hollywood, with two successful movies. As for Davis? He prefers being behind the scenes and letting his creation hog the spotlight.

23. Art Spiegelman (b. 1949) In Spiegelman's famous graphic novel *Maus,* the artist presents the tragic events of World War II by pitting natural enemies against each other. Jews are represented as mice and the Nazis as cats. The Nazis find nothing whatsoever wrong with exterminating all the mice. The work is both moving and unforgettable.

24. Bill Watterson (b. 1958) Bill Watterson designed grocery ads for four years for the *Cincinnati Post* prior to working on the comic strip that made him famous: *Calvin and Hobbes.* The strip depicted the relationship between a 6-year-old boy named Calvin and his tiger, Hobbes. Watterson got the inspiration for Hobbes from his own cat, Sprite, an intelligent, friendly, good-natured gray tabby who had perfected his own sneak-up-and-pounce technique. Syndicated in 1985, the comic strip appeared in more than 2,400 newspapers until its last installment, on December 31, 1995. Watterson received the National Cartoonist Society's Humor Comic Strip Award in 1988 and the society's Reuben Award in 1986, the youngest person ever to receive that honor. In 2005, the three-volume, 1,440-page, 23-pound *The Complete Calvin and Hobbes* was published.

25. Darby Conley (b. 1970) Conley is the originator of the popular comic strip *Get Fuzzy,* which features Satchel Pooch and Bucky Katt. Bucky, always in a state of hostility, with his ears in a permanently flattened position, has complete reign of the household. Conley, whose drawings are replete with detail, spends 100 hours preparing each week's strip.

Judas, the biblical betrayer, is often portrayed with a sinister-looking cat at his side.

In the mid-1800s, Japanese artist Kuniyoshi published Cats for the Fifty-three Stations of Tokaido Road, an artistic study of cats and kittens shown in naturalistic poses, including sleeping, romping, bathing, hunting, and crouching.

3 Great Artistic Imposters
The Art of Eve Riser-Roberts

Eve Riser-Roberts was a scientist for 20 years before returning to her first love, art. Studying in London and Wales and participating in numerous art workshops conducted by acclaimed artists, she created paintings and drawings currently in art collections in England, Germany, and the United States. Prints of some of her irresistible paintings are available on her website, thecatgallery.com, along with a range of unusual cat gifts.

LEFT: Henri Matisse left his still life arrangement, which included fish in bowl, to get a cup of coffee. He got back just in time to catch his cat, who had stepped into the scene with ulterior motives. The cat, of course, denied it all.

ABOVE: One day Vincent van Gogh took a break from painting a still life of sunflowers. While he was gone, his cat hopped onto the forbidden table and started chewing the flowers. In the portrait he painted next, the cat is shown with only one ear.

LEFT: Paul Gauguin was seen painting three young Tahitian girls as they enjoyed passing the time in the shade of a large tree. They were oblivious to the white dog that watched Gauguin's cat as it almost invisibly stalked a chicken through the tall grass.

8 Really Expensive Cats

In 2002, the Skinner Gallery in Boston, Massachusetts, held the first art auction exclusively dedicated to cat art. Over 450 items, including paintings, illustrations, and objets d'art, were put on the auction block. Listed here are a number of the pricier pieces, as well as other auction art from galleries across the United States.

1. The Skinner Gallery put *Studio Kittens,* a lovely painting by Dutch artist Henriette Ronner-Knip, up for auction. The painting, measuring a mere 8½ by 6¾ inches, had an estimated value of $25,000 but did not sell.

2. Carl Kahler's painting *My Wife's Lovers* portrays a cadre of at least 30 cats. Skinner had valued this painting, measuring 70 by 101 inches, at $450,000 to $750,000. Unfortunately the painting did not sell.

3. Julius Adams's painting *The Straw Hat* depicts a group of six cats playing with a hat in a pastoral setting. The painting, measuring 23½ by 34 inches, was appraised at $50,000.

4. In 2002, Sotheby's, in New York City, placed a Veracruz polychrome jaguar, c. A.D. 550–950, up for auction. This striking work measures 24 inches in height and shows a jaguar wearing a thick collar with a pendant and crouching on its haunches in a ferocious stance. It had an estimate of $50,000 to $70,000 but failed to sell despite the fact that it is a stunning work.

5. In 2005, The Treadway-Toomey Galleries' Twentieth-Century Art and Design Auction sold an unusual Clément Massier plate, which featured an etched design of a mother cat holding her kitten by the scruff of its neck. The piece, covered in a red iridescent glaze, was signed by the French ceramist. Measuring only 8 inches wide, this plate sold for $1,920 ($400 more than its estimated value).

6. Cincinnati Art Galleries auctioned a Rookwood Pottery vase measuring just 6¼ inches in height, with an estimated value of approximately $6,000. This vase, called the "Cat' Meow," was decorated in 1902 by artist Edward Timothy Hurley. The vase is marked with the Rookwood symbol, the date, and Hurley's incised signature. The vase sold for $12,075, twice its estimated value.

7. According to Findartinfo.com, a database with art auction results around the world, three paintings by famed artist Louis Wain fetched a hefty price when auctioned in 2005. *All Eyes on the Beetle,* an oil-on-canvas piece depicting cats examining a beetle and measuring 14 by 27 inches, sold for $29,427. Wain's *Din-Din Please,* which portrays cats waiting for their supper and measures only 8.1 by 13 inches, is a watercolor and pen-and-ink drawing. It sold for $12,874. *A Tea Party on the Lawn,* showing cats frolicking, is a watercolor measuring only 8.7 by 11.2 inches. It sold for $13,794.

8. Hello Kitty, the globally popular Japanese icon of cuteness, made its foray into the currency market with gold and silver euro coins. The most expensive one-ounce gold coin is priced at $1,400.

"Time spent with cats is never wasted." — COLETTE

Library Cats

Bookums, the cat who formerly resided in the Windsor Locks Library in Windsor Locks, Connecticut, found fame posthumously in a documentary called *Puss in Books: Adventures of the Library Cat,* in 2006. The film was named Best Documentary at the United States 8mm Film and Video Festival and has been screened around the world. Bookums is only seen once, but his appearance is crucial in the film, which blends humor with the issue of whether the majority or the minority should prevail when patrons object to cats in libraries. We can't help but wonder if the naysayers would prefer that mice be allowed to feast on precious volumes. Nevertheless, those with allergies argue that libraries are for them, too.

Given their role as muse to some of the greatest writers in the world — not to mention their talent for dealing with pests — it's no wonder that cats have always been comfortable around books. Thousands of them reside in libraries throughout the world. Here are samples representing each of the United States except Delaware, Wyoming, and South Dakota, whose libraries, to the best of our knowledge, remain hypoallergenic.

Alabama	Tigger	b. 1998	Smiths Station Intermediate School Library, Smiths Station
Alaska	John	1965–1985	Sand Lake Elementary School, Sand Lake
Arizona	Elsie	b. 2002	Huachuca City Library, Huachuca City
Arkansas	Big Footsie	b. 2001	Arkansas School for the Blind Library, Little Rock
California	Brigid	b. 1990s	Saint Mark's Episcopal Church Library, Berkeley
Colorado	Judge Kitty	b. 1995	Fairplay Library, Fairplay
Connecticut	Bob	b. 2004	Hall Memorial Library, Ellington
Florida	Chewie	b. 2002	Lady Lake Public Library, Lady Lake
Georgia	Eudora	b. 2003	Cave Spring Public Library, Cave Spring
Hawaii	Junior	b. 1990s	Kihei Public Library, Kihei
Idaho	Archie	b. 1991	Payette Public Library, Payette
Illinois	Max	b. 2002	Paxton Carnegie Library, Paxton
Indiana	Miss Peabody	b. 1998	North Manchester Public Library, Manchester
Iowa	Oliver	b. 2005	Richland Park Public Library, Richland
Kansas	Tiger	b. 1996	Stanton County Library, Johnson City
Kentucky	Smokey Dickens	b. 1996	Bowling Green Public Library, Bowling Green
Louisiana	Davey Crockett	b. 1999	Lakeshore Branch Library, Metairie
Maine	Poppy Seed	b. 2003	Abbott Memorial Library, Dexter
Maryland	Jesse	1966–1977	Anne Arundel County Library, Annapolis
Massachusetts	Leo Katz	b. 1992	Brockton Public Library, Brockton
Michigan	404	b. 1995	Internet Public Library, Ann Arbor
Minnesota	Browser	b. 2002	Pine River Public Library, Pine River
Mississippi	Miss Gussie	b. 1996	Evans Memorial Library, Aberdeen

Missouri	Emerson Booker	b. 2000	Gentry County Library, Stanberry
Montana	Maizie	b. 1994	Paul M. Adams Memorial Library, Rocky Mountain College, Billings
Nebraska	TLC*	b. 1999	Broken Bow Public Library, Broken Bow
Nevada	Dewey	b. 1995	Elko County Library, Elko
New Hampshire	Louie	b. 2004	Freedom Public Library, Freedom
New Jersey	Chrissie	b. 2000	New Jersey Library Association, Trenton
New Mexico	Maui	b. 2001	Manzano Day School Library, Albuquerque
New York	Bookend	b. 1997	Jervis Public Library, Rome
North Carolina	Salem	b. 2000	Haywood County Library, Waynesville
North Dakota	Cleo Boom Boom Marie	1987–1990	Fargo Public Library, Fargo
Ohio	Ms. Kitty	b. 1988	Lane Public Library, Oxford
Oklahoma	Dewey	b. 2006	Ada Public Library, Ada
Oregon	Libby	b. 1999	Cresswell High School Library, Cresswell
Pennsylvania	Whispurr	b. 2000	Bradford Public Library, Bradford
Rhode Island	Barcode	1993–1998	Island Free Library, Block Island
South Carolina	Bobby Radar	b. 1999	Horger Library, South Carolina State Hospital, Columbia
Tennessee	Nimrod Porker	b. 2002	Maury County Archives, Columbia
Texas	Monty	b. 1992	Montgomery Elementary School, Farmers Branch
Utah	Libby	1993–1995	College of Eastern Utah Library, Price
Vermont	Pages	1996–1999	Brandon Public Library, Brandon
Virginia	Purrl Readmore	b. 2004	Wythe-Grayson Regional Library, Independence
Washington	Cloud	b. 1996	Timberland Regional Library, Amanda Park
West Virginia	Ms. Dewey	b. 1998	Fairview Public Library, Fairview
Wisconsin	Minerva	b. 2004	Hayward Carnegie Library, Hayward

Dewey's Guide for Library Cats

Dewey Readmore Books was the resident cat at Spencer Public Library in Spencer, Iowa. He was placed in the book return one cold January night in 1988, and when the staff found him the next morning, they decided to adopt him. After the library's board of trustees and the city council approved, the kitten was neutered and given the proper vaccinations. A contest was held to pick a name, and Dewey Readmore Books was officially added to the staff. The staff cared for Dewey and donated their soda pop cans to raise funds to feed the kitty. Patrons and friends from as far away as New York have donated money for Dewey's care. Dr. Jim Esterly, a local veterinarian, gave Dewey a "city employee discount" on services when Dewey needed medical attention.

Dewey has generated lots of publicity for the library. He's appeared in newspapers and magazines and on TV. He is also the video star of *Puss in Books,* a documentary about library cats. Sadly, Dewey passed away in 2006. But

"Never forget, nor let humans forget, that you own the joint!"
— DEWEY

he made a very special contribution to this book by preparing his own official job description, with the help of Vikki Myron, the library's director.

1. If you are feeling particularly lonely and want more attention from the staff, sit on whatever papers, project, or computer they happen to be working on — but do so with your back to the person, and act aloof, so as not to appear too needy. Also, continually rub against the leg of the staff person who is wearing dark brown, blue, or black clothes, for maximum effect.

Dewey the library cat.

2. No matter how long the patron plans on staying at the library, climb into the person's briefcase or book bag for a long, comfortable sleep. Enjoy it — and give the person a guilt-inducing pout when he or she tries to extricate you, in order to leave.

3. Never miss an opportunity to climb on ladders. It does not matter which human is on the ladder. It only matters that you get to the top and stay there.

4. Wait until 10 minutes before closing time to get up from your nap. Just as the staff is getting ready to turn out the lights and lock the door, do all your cutest tricks in an effort to get them to stay and play with you. (This doesn't work as often as one would like.)

5. Your humans must realize that all boxes that enter the library are yours. It doesn't matter how large, how small, or how full the box is, it is yours! If you cannot fit your entire body into the box, then use whatever part of your body fits, to assume ownership for naptime. (I have used one or two paws, my head, or even just my tail to gain entry, and each works equally well for a truly restful sleep.)

6. No matter the group, timing, or subject matter, if a meeting is scheduled in the meeting room, you have an obligation to attend. If a closed door prevents your entry, cry pitifully until someone lets you in or opens the door to use the restroom or get a drink of water. After you gain entry, greet each attendee. Don't let anyone ignore you. If there is a film or slide show, climb on a table close to the screen, settle in, and watch. As the credits roll, feign extreme boredom and leave the room.

57 Literary Cats

1. **Aineko**, a talking robot cat in the Accelerando series of science-fiction short stories (and novel) by Charles Stross

2. **Aslan**, the lion in *The Lion, the Witch, and the Wardrobe* and other Narnia stories by C. S. Lewis

3. **Bagheera**, the panther in Rudyard Kipling's *The Jungle Book* and *The Second Jungle Book*

4. **Behemoth** (or **Begemot**), the huge, trolley-riding, satanic black cat in Mikhail Bulgakov's *The Master and Margarita*

5. **The Black Cat**, in Edgar Allan Poe's short story of the same name, a study of the psychology of guilt

6. **Blackmalkin, Greymalkin,** and **Nibbins,** witches' cats in *The Midnight Folk*, by John Masefield

7. **Bloomberg**, the Glass family's large tomcat in *Franny & Zooey*, by J. D. Salinger

8. **Brobdingnagian**, a gigantic domestic cat "three times larger than an ox," in *Gulliver's Travels*, by Jonathan Swift

9. **Broccoli**, from *The Broccoli Tapes*, by Jan Slepian

10. **Carbonel, King of the Cats**, in Barbara Sleigh's Carbonel trilogy

11. **Catasauqua**, a female manx in *Letters from the Earth*, by Mark Twain, invented as a bedtime story for the author's daughters

12. *The Cat in the Hat*, by Dr. Seuss

13. The **cat with the fiddle who played hey-diddle-diddle**, in J.R.R. Tolkien's *The Man in the Moon Stayed Up Too Late*

14. **The Cheshire Cat**, in Lewis Carroll's *Alice's Adventures in Wonderland*

15. **Chester**, the cat in *Bunnicula* and its sequels, by James Howe

16. **Church**, the cat who comes back to life in Stephen King's *Pet Sematary*

17. **Clarence**, a pacifist library-dwelling cat who sleeps on the photocopier in *Clarence the Copy Cat*, by Patricia Lakin

18. **C'mell**, a humanoid cat, one of the animal-derived "underpeople" in stories by Cordwainer Smith

19. **Crookshanks**, Hermione Granger's cat in the Harry Potter novels

20. **Damn Cat**, hero of the Gordons' *Undercover Cat*, who returns from a nightly prowl with a kidnapped woman's bracelet around his neck . . . But where has he been? Later adapted as the Disney film *That Darn Cat!*

21. **Dinah**, Alice's pet cat, featured in Lewis Carroll's *Alice's Adventures in Wonderland* and *Through the Looking-Glass*

22. **Dragon**, the farmer's cat in Robert C. O'Brien's *Mrs. Frisby and the Rats of NIMH*

23. **Edgewood Dirk**, the "prism cat" in the Landover novels by Terry Brooks

24. **Eureka**, Dorothy's cat in *Dorothy and the Wizard in Oz*, by L. Frank Baum; also known as the Pink Kitten

25. **Francis** the feline detective, in the novels *Felidae* and *Felidae on the Road*, by Akif Pirinçci

26. **Fritti Tailchaser**, along with companions Eatbugs and Pouncequick and a host of both supporting feline characters and mythical felines, in the Tad Williams novel *Tailchaser's Song*

27. **Gareth**, a black cat with a white ankh on his chest who travels through time with his human companion, Jason, in *Time Cat*, by Lloyd Alexander

28. **Ginger**, the yellow tomcat who kept shop with Pickles the dog in Beatrix Potter's *Ginger and Pickles*

29. **Gingivere**, Tsarmina's brother in Brian Jacques's Redwall book *Mossflower,* who helped the woodlanders free Mossflower from Tsarmina

30. **Good Fortune**, the cat who goes to heaven in the award-winning story of the same name, by Elizabeth Coatsworth

31. **Graymalkin**, the first witch's familiar in act 1, scene 1, of William Shakespeare's *Macbeth*

32. **Gummitch** the superkitten, in Fritz Leiber's *Spacetime for Springers*

33. **Joe Grey, Dulcie,** and **Kit**, cats able to speak to humans and solve murder mysteries in books by Shirley Rousseau Murphy

34. **Kitty**, the family mouser in Laura Ingalls Wilder's Little House books

35. **Koko** and **Yum Yum**, James Qwilleran's two Siamese cats in the *The Cat Who . . .* mystery novels by Lilian Jackson Braun

36. **Lionel**, the title character who cajoles his wizard companion into making him human in *The Cat Who Wished to Be a Man,* by Lloyd Alexander

37. **Lipshen**, the grand high witch's cat in Roald Dahl's *The Witches*

38. **Little Cats A through Z**, from Dr. Seuss's *The Cat in the Hat Comes Back*

39. **Minnaloushe**, from William Butler Yeats's poem "The Cat and the Moon"

40. **Mogget**, a magical entity in the form of a cat, in the fantasy novels *Sabriel, Lirael,* and *Abhorsen,* by Garth Nix

41. **Mrs. Murphy**, a cat who helps her human, Mary Minor "Harry" Haristeen, solve mysteries, in a series of novels by Rita Mae Brown (Her cat, Sneaky Pie Brown, is credited as coauthor.)

42. **Mr. Underfoot**, in Robert A. Heinlein's *Friday*

43. **Petronius Arbiter**, a cat who is convinced that even in winter, a door leading outside will take him into summer, in Robert A. Heinlein's *The Door into Summer*

44. **Picky-Picky**, a calico cat who sometimes appears in Beverly Cleary's Ramona books

45. **Pixel**, in Robert A. Heinlein's novel *To Sail Beyond the Sunset,* and appearing briefly in other Heinlein stories. (Despite the name of the book and one character's unique ability to cause an interdimensional cat door to appear in any surface, the novel *The Cat Who Walks Through Walls* is not about Pixel.)

46. **Professor McGonagall**, who can shapeshift into a tabby cat in the Harry Potter books

"It is a very inconvenient habit of kittens (Alice had once made the remark) that whatever you say to them, they always purr."
— **LEWIS CARROLL**

The Cheshire Cat

It's been said that Lewis Carroll intended the Cheshire Cat to be Wonderland's god; he does, after all, accompany Alice on her journey, acting as something of a guide. The cat with the unforgettable smile (he would disappear gradually until only his grin remained) was omniscient and omnipresent, could become invisible, and could instantly "teleport" and change size. Carroll apparently found inspiration for the Cheshire Cat in a carving in a church where his father had been rector. The cat is named after Carroll's home county, Cheshire.

The grinning Cheshire Cat, from Lewis Carroll's *Alice's Adventures in Wonderland* (1865).

"What sort of people live about here?"

"In that direction," the Cat said, waving its right paw round, "lives a Hatter: and in that direction," waving the other paw, "lives a March Hare. Visit either you like: they're both mad."

"But I don't want to go among mad people," Alice remarked.

"Oh, you can't help that," said the Cat: "we're all mad here. I'm mad. You're mad."

"How do you know I'm mad?" said Alice.

"You must be," said the Cat, "or you wouldn't have come here."

—From *Alice's Adventures in Wonderland*, by Lewis Carroll

---

47. **Sinbad**, a kitten rescued by the Walker children off the Dutch coast in the Swallows and Amazons novel *We Didn't Mean to Go to Sea*, by Arthur Ransome

48. **Slinky Malinki**, a cat featured in a series of books by Lynley Dodd

49. **Solembum**, a werecat from the Inheritance Trilogy books by Christopher Paolini

50. **Tabby**, the cat belonging to Mildred in *The Worst Witch*, by Jill Murphy

51. **Tao**, the Siamese cat from Sheila Burnford's novel *The Incredible Journey*

52. **Tib**, the farmyard tabby who helps locate the missing dogs in *101 Dalmations*, by Dodie Smith

53. **Tigerishka**, from Fritz Leiber's novel *The Wanderer*

54. **Tigger** in *Winnie the Pooh*

55. **Tom Kitten**, a curious but disobedient young cat in the children's stories "The Tale of Tom Kitten" and "The Roly Poly Pudding" by Beatrix Potter; also Tom's mother, Mrs. Tabitha Twitchit, and his siblings Moppet and Mittens.

56. **Tug**, the cat given by Ged to Alder to protect him from nightmares, in *The Other Wind*, by Ursula Le Guin

57. **Zapaquilda**, the feline heroine who is abducted on her wedding day in Lope de Vega's epic poem "The Battle of the Cats," a satire on the literary form

11 Cat Fiction Anthologies

1. Collins, Barbara, and Collins, Max Allen, *Too Many Tomcats and Other Feline Tales of Suspense* **(2000)** This small collection of 11 unusual short stories of mystery and suspense with cat themes features characters who lean toward the eccentric and plots that tend toward the bizarre.

2. Datlow, Ellen, *Twists of the Tale* **(1996)** Most of

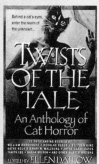

the stories here comment on the variety of relationships between cats and humans — especially those humans who are obsessed, alienated, or neglected. The 24 authors include Nicholas Royle, Kathe Koja, and Barry Malzberg; Joyce Carol Oates; Stephen King; and William S. Burroughs.

3. Elliot, Charles, *The Greatest Cat Stories Ever Told: 30 Incredible Tales by Mark Twain, Rudyard Kipling, Dorothy L. Sayers, and Many Others* **(2004)** Fascinating, frustrating, frolicsome, or frosty, this treasury is filled with 30 tales of memorable felines in a testament to the amazing variety of kitty personalities

4. Gorman, Edward, *Kittens, Cats, and Crime* **(2003)** This follow-up to *Felonious Felines* (also edited by Ed Gorman) showcases 11 original stories by a variety of authors including Kristine Kathryn Rush, P. N. Elrod, and Edward D. Hoch.

5. Greenberg, Martin H., *Cat Crimes* **(1993)** These 15 original stories by some of the best mystery writers feature a bevy of baffling crimes set in exotic vacation spots — and all featuring a four-footed friend. In "Midnight Sun," a telltale clue in a cat's luscious fur exposes a killer; in "The Envelopes, Please," a screenwriter is saved by a fondness for felines. Greenberg has edited many similar cat collections, and the stories he chooses are always amusing, intelligent, and clever.

6. Little, Denise, *A Constellation of Cats* **(2001)** Fantasy's finest tale-spinners present a brand-new collec-

tion of four-legged fiction that will catapult our favorite felines into space, time, and the many realms of the fantastic.

7. Murphy, Shirley Rousseau (editor), *Christmas Cats* **(2005)** Cat lovers will be happy to find this eclectic collection (some original stories, some previously published) under the Christmas tree. Murphy, the author of a popular mystery series featuring a feline crime-solver (see page 162), presents 19 short stories, essays, and poems that commemorate cats at Christmastime. Amy D. Shojai leads off with a lighthearted memoir of how her husband came to adjust to his wife's feisty Siamese kitten just in time for the holiday. Far more sobering is a recollection by Renie Burghardt: During World War II her 19-year-old mother died shortly after giving birth to her. She writes of Paprika, the cat who consoled her when she and her grandparents sought safety in war-torn rural Hungary.

8. Necker, Claire, *Supernatural Cats: An Anthology* **(1972)** Talking cats, psychic cats, ghostly cats, and reincarnated cats — these are just some of the fantastic felines highlighted in this sci-fi compilation. The settings range from ancient Japan to the (not-so-distant?) future when cats travel in space.

9. Norton, Andre, and Greenberg, Martin H., *Catfantastic: Nine Lives and Fifteen Tales* **(1989; 2004)** This assortment of original science fiction stories should cast a spell on all those with cat friends. Some tales are

> The first mention of a cat in European literature was written by an eighth-century Irish scholar who wrote a poem about his cat, Pangur Bán, the first verse of which reads:
>
> I and Pangur Bán, my cat,
> 'Tis a like task we are at.
> Hunting mice is his delight,
> Hunting words I sit all night.

set in the distant future and unknown worlds; others take place on earth, but in a different dimension.

10. O'Mara, Lesley, *Best Cat Stories* (1992) A literary feast for cat lovers, here are the finest of cats stories from James Herriot, P. G. Wodehouse, Damon Runyon, Doris Lessing, Patricia Highsmith, and others. With an introduction by Doris Lessing.

11. Shrader, Esther (editor), *Twisted Cat Tales* (2006) Thirty-seven chilling and disturbing stories from horror to fantasy, dark humor, and science fiction. Some are told by observers, some by cats, and still others by the objects of the cats' attention — for good or evil. Editor Schrader spans the globe, gathering unique stories from Australia, Canada, India, Israel, the United Kingdom, and the United States. From the flying felines in the opening story to the lonely lion in the final tale, these cats will get their claws into you.

Mysteries for Cat Lovers

1. Adamson, Lydia, the Alice Nestleton Mystery Series Alice Nestleton, a beautiful off-Broadway star who pays her bills by cat-sitting between stage roles, has a special talent for detection. She's as crafty as Miss Marple, as ingenious as Hercule Poirot, and as cunning as a cat.

2. Allen, Garrison, *Baseball Cat* (1998, the Big Mike Series When the owner of the Coyotes baseball team is bludgeoned to death, Penelope Warren, along with feline detective Big Mike, is plunged into a world of management disputes, marital problems, and money issues, where a wealth of suspects is waiting for their chance at bat. Some titles feature cats: *A Cat on a Beach Blanket* (1998), *A Cat with No Clue* (2001).

3. Babson, Maria, *The Cat Next Door* (2003) Arriving in England after spending some time in New York, Margot is shocked to discover that her cousin Chloe is in prison, awaiting trial for murdering her twin sister, Claudia. As the trial approaches, Margot soon discovers, with a little help from the family cat, that Chloe might be innocent, when another murder occurs. Also: *Please Do Feed the Cat* (2004).

4. Barnes, Linda, *A Trouble of Fools* (2004) T.C. is notified that he has won $20,000 in a sweepstakes. All he has to do to collect the money is to appear with his wife. Trouble is, T.C. is a cat. Six-foot-one redhead Carlotta Carlyle, a former Boston cop and sometime Boston cabbie who is now an independent P.I., is on the job.

5. Block, Lawrence, Bernie Rhodenbarr Mystery Series In a mystery series with a sense of humor, Bernie Rhodenbarr is a burglar trying to go straight. He now owns a bookstore in New York City complete with a cat named Raffles. Bernie's world is full of humor, wit, and crime, and when things get tough, the tough start stealing — again. The titles include *The Burglar Who Thought He Was Bogart* (1996) and *The Burglar in the Rye* (2002).

6. **Brown, Rita Mae, Mrs. Murphy Mystery Series** Curiosity just might be the death of the cat and her human companion in this series set in Crozet, Virginia, and featuring the town's postmistress, Mary Minor Haristeen (Harry), and her wonderfully intelligent gray tiger cat, Mrs. Murphy. Titles include *Murder, She Meowed* (1997) and *Cat on the Scent* (2000).

7. **Campbell, R. Wright, *The Cat's Meow* (1990)** Chicago sleuth Jimmy Flannery investigates some strange occurrences over at St. Patrick's Church, including a dead cat's ghostly wails, signs of satanic services, and the discovery of Father Mulrooney's lifeless body.

8. **Davis, Philip J., *Thomas Gray, Philosopher Cat* (1990)** Thomas Gray, a female cat of metaphysical inclinations, and the eccentric Lucas Fysst, historian of science, Anglican priest, and fellow of Pembroke College, Cambridge, unravel their first mystery in this novella. Their adventures continue in *Thomas Gray in Copenhagen: In Which the Philosopher Cat Meets the Ghost of Hans Christian Andersen* (1995).

9. **Dawson, Janet, the Jeri Howard Mystery Series** Set in Oakland, California, this series features feisty private investigator Jeri Howard and her cat, Abigail. The first book in the series, *Kindred Crimes,* won the St. Martin's Press–Private Eye Writers of America Contest for Best First Private-Eye Novel. Titles include *Where the Bodies Are Buried* (1999) and *A Killing at the Track* (2000).

10. **Douglas, Carole Nelson, the Midnight Louie Mystery Series** Set in Las Vegas, this series features Midnight Louie, a tousle-eared black tomcat who's a combination of Nathan Detroit and Sam Spade, and his human companion, Temple Barr, a public relations expert whose fondness for high-heeled shoes is matched only by her aptitude for getting into trouble. Titles include *Cat on a Blue Monday* (1994) and *Cat in an Indigo Mood* (1999).

11. **Friedman, Kinky, the Kinky Friedman Mystery Series** Set in New York's Greenwich Village, Kinky is a detective with a strong relationship with his cat, a remarkable animal who gets into trouble for smoking cigars in public places, looks askance at most of the human race, and exhibits a penchant for inventive language. Titles include *God Bless John Wayne* (1996) and *Road Kill* (1998).

12. **Gardner, Erle Stanley, *The Case of the Caretaker's Cat* (1985)** A caretaker's missing cat becomes the clue to double-dealings over the million-dollar estate of a deceased tycoon, bringing expert lawyer Perry Mason to the scene.

13. **Guiver, Patricia, *Delilah Doolittle and the Careless Coyote* (1998)** Delilah Doolittle, a transplanted Brit living in Southern California, is a pet detective. When the beloved Abyssinian of Mavis Byrde disappears right before her next-door neighbor is murdered, Delilah must rely on her own devices to get to the bottom of both cases.

14. **Hahn, Harriet, the Harriet Hahn Mystery Series** Hahn's "purrsonified" cat character, James, is a multi-talented cat-about-town who spends his days directing musicals, recovering stolen artifacts, and embarking on various ventures in London. He lives there with his American gentleman and stars in *James, the Connoisseur Cat* (1992) and *James, Fabulous Feline: Further Adventures of a Connoisseur Cat* (1993), among others.

15. **Kaplow, Robert, *The Cat Who Killed Lilian Jackson Braun: A Parody* (2003)** A send-up of Braun's Cat Who mysteries. Braun is found beheaded in the men's room of a gay bar in Manhattan. The police are baffled. It is up to Braun's friend James Q. and his two Siamese cats to solve the ghastly murder.

16. **King, Gabriel, *The Golden Cat* (1999)** Tag the cat and his companions have vanquished the evil human known as the Alchemist, and the Queen of Cats has delivered three beautiful golden kittens. When two of the kittens disappear, Tag must find them and restore the magic before all is lost.

17. **Marshall, Evan, the Jane Stuart and Winky Mystery Series** Set in New York City and New Jersey, this series features the well-read detective duo of Jane Stuart, a widowed literary agent, and her tortoiseshell cat, Winky. Titles include *Hanging Hannah* (2001) and *Itching Ivy* (2002).

18. **Matthews, Alex, the Cassidy McCabe Mystery Series** Set in Chicago, this series features psychotherapist Cassidy McCabe, a bright and sassy heroine who has a penchant for trouble and a weakness for her cat, Starshine. Titles include *Secret Shadow* (1998) and *Cat's Claw* (2001).

19. **Murphy, Shirley Rousseau, the Joe Grey Mystery**

Series Joe Grey is a P.I. with a twist —
he's a cat. After witnessing a murder, a
startled Joe realizes he has the ability
to understand human speech ("Who
would have guessed they had so little
to say?") and the ability to speak, which
is useful for scaring dogs. Titles include
Cat on the Edge (1996) and *Cat Spitting
Mad* (2001).

20. Richardson, Bill, *Waiting for Gertrude: A Graveyard Gothic* (2001) A
quirky novel featuring mystery, intrigue,
and famous people finding themselves
reincarnated as stray cats. Their known
eccentricities remain: Alice B. Toklas
pines for the return of her beloved Gertrude Stein, Jim Morrison is a swagger-
ing sexy tomcat, Oscar Wilde falls in love
with Morrison, Isadora Duncan still
dances in the moonlight with ribbons,
Colette still exudes desire, Maria Callas
is still quite the diva, Sarah Bernhardt
remains the consummate actress, and
Proust becomes a reclusive private eye.

21. Simon, Clea, *Mew Is for Murder*
(2005) When Theda Krakow, a freelance
writer, goes to interview the crazy cat
lady at her home in Cambridge, Massachusetts, she discovers the woman
dead and her many cats circling her
body in distress. Was her death an accident or was it murder?

22. Smith, Nick, *The Kitty Killer Cult*
(2004) In the style of Raymond Chandler, this is hard-boiled detective fiction set in the city of Nub, where cats
are king. Tiger Straight, P.I., is past his
prime, homeless, and unemployed, until
Connie Hant shows up. The P.I. is back,
pawing the mean streets of Nub that he
knows so well. His mission is to catch
the killers of Connie's brothers.

29 Mysteries by Lilian Jackson Braun

Even though Lilian Jackson Braun claims that her cats have
never done anything extraordinary, her fictional cats Koko
and Yum Yum solve crimes and delight fans in book after
book, and they've been doing it for more than 40 years.

Braun says the reason for her success is
that "people are simply tired of all the
blood. I write what is called the classic
mystery." She says that while "not all mystery fans may like cats, all cat-fanciers
seem to like mysteries. That makes for a large audience,
since 26 percent of all American households own 53.9 million cats between them." Here are the delightful titles of
her 29 novels. We hope she writes at least 29 more!

The Cat Who . . .

1. . . . *Could Read Backwards* (1966)
2. . . . *Ate Danish Modern* (1967)
3. . . . *Turned On and Off* (1968)
4. . . . *Saw Red* (1986)
5. . . . *Played Brahms* (1987)
6. . . . *Played Post Office* (1987)
7. . . . *Knew Shakespeare* (1988)
8. . . . *Sniffed Glue* (1988)
9. . . . *Went Underground* (1989)
10. . . . *Talked to Ghosts* (1990)
11. . . . *Lived High* (1990)
12. . . . *Knew a Cardinal* (1991)
13. . . . *Moved a Mountain* (1992)
14. . . . *Wasn't There* (1992)
15. . . . *Went into the Closet* (1993)
16. . . . *Came to Breakfast* (1994)
17. . . . *Blew the Whistle* (1995)
18. . . . *Said Cheese* (1996)
19. . . . *Tailed a Thief* (1997)
20. . . . *Sang for the Birds* (1998)
21. . . . *Saw Stars* (1999)
22. . . . *Robbed a Bank* (2000)
23. . . . *Smelled a Rat* (2001)
24. . . . *Went up the Creek* (2002)
25. . . . *Brought Down the House* (2003)
26. . . . *Talked Turkey* (2004)
27. . . . *Went Bananas* (2005)
28. . . . *Dropped a Bombshell* (2006)
29. . . . *Had 60 Whiskers* (2007)

"They were a pair of elegant Siamese whose seal-brown
points were in striking contrast to their pale fawn
bodies. The male, Kao K'o Kung, answered to the name
of Koko; he was long, lithe, and muscular, and his fathom-
less blue eyes brimmed with intelligence. His female companion, Yum Yum, was small and delicate, with violet-blue
eyes that could be large and heart-melting when she
wanted to sit on a lap, yet that dainty creature could
utter a piercing shriek when dinner was behind schedule."
— From **The Cat Who Said Cheese**

15 Nonfiction Books That Explore the World of Cats

All of these books examine cats from odd angles. None purport to be comprehensive; instead, each takes an original approach to its subject, with emphasis on the ways in which cats fit into our society.

1. **Anderson, Allen and Linda,** *Angel Cats* **(2004)** A feline friend helps a man get his "purr" back. A cat comforts a young girl during the Holocaust. A mother-daughter cat team comes to the rescue of a woman with a heart ailment. These and the other moving accounts address the spiritual connection between cat people and their cats. The meditations that follow each short chapter are especially thoughtful.

2. **Amory, Cleveland,** *The Best Cat Ever* **(1993)** Picking up where *The Cat Who Came for Christmas* and *The Cat and the Curmudgeon* left off, this book continues the story of the cat named Polar Bear and his grumpy, lovable owner.

3. **Burroughs, William S.,** *The Cat Inside* **(2002)** Burroughs is best known for the satire *Naked Lunch.* Here he writes with unexpected tenderness and intensity about the enduring, mysterious relationship between cats and humans.

4. **Caras, Roger A.,** *A Cat Is Watching: A Look at the Way Cats See Us* **(1989)** Filled with charming stories about the felines in the author's own life, the book helps readers see wild and domestic cats for the remarkable creatures they are.

5. **Caras, Roger A.,** *The Cats of Thistle Hill: A Mostly Peaceable Kingdom* **(1994)** Caras introduces readers to his feline companions and to the dogs, horses, cows, and even the llama with whom he shares a "mostly peaceable kingdom."

6. **Dohanyos, Franklin,** *The Cats of Our Lives: Funny and Heartwarming Reminiscences of Feline Companions* **(2000)** Memorable stories about people and their favorite felines are gathered here. Some of the contributors are well known, some are not, but all have in common a story to tell about a special cat who changed their life.

7. **Fireman, Judy (editor),** *Cat Catalog: The Ultimate Cat Book* **(1976)** More than 100 original essays and 250 pho-

tographs and line drawings explore all aspects of the cat. The book is a classic in its category, sadly out of print, but still available from used-book sellers. Experts from all fields have contributed essays in the areas of history and legend, anatomy and behavior, care and training, and loads of entertaining miscellany.

8. Geyer, Georgie Anne, *When Cats Reigned like Kings: On the Trail of the Sacred Cats* (2004) Geyer's curiosity about her own cats inspired her to study the history of the human-feline relationship, especially cats' exalted status among ancients as royal or sacred beings. The result will delight and amaze cat lovers.

9. Herriot, James, *James Herriot's Cat Stories* (1994) Between these covers, teller and tales finally meet in a warm and joyful new collection that will bring delight to the hearts of readers the world over. Here are Buster, the kitten who arrived on Christmas; Alfred, the cat at the sweet shop; little Emily, who lived with the gentleman tramp; and Olly and Ginny, the kittens who charmed readers when they first appeared at the Herriots' house in the worldwide bestseller *Every Living Thing*. Each story is told with that magical blend of gentle wit and human compassion that marks every word from James Herriot's pen.

10. Jordan, William, *A Cat Named Darwin: How a Stray Cat Changed a Man into a Human Being* (2002) An uncommon look at the human need to bond with animals is offered by the author of *Divorce Among the Gulls,* a reformed biologist whose life is changed forever by a big orange tomcat.

11. Lessing, Doris Mae, *Particularly Cats — and Rufus* (1991) Originally published in 1967 as *Particularly Cats,* this book is a series of interconnected vignettes about the felines who have slinked, bullied, and charmed their way into Lessing's life. Rufus's story was added to the collection in 1991 when he joined the Lessing household.

12. Malkin, Nina, *An Unlikely Cat Lady: Feral Adventures in the Backyard Jungle* (2007) The sassy voice of the Brooklyn, New York, magazine journalist perfectly portrays the plight of the reluctant ailurophile. Although Malkin already owned two cats, it wasn't until she started feeding, bonding with, and, of course, naming the feral cats who wandered into her backyard that she became known as the neighborhood's "crazy cat lady." Useful information on cat care is scattered throughout. *Publishers Weekly* predicted that this book might even convert a few dog lovers.

13. Morris, Willie, *My Cat, Spit McGee* (1999) Morris had always thought of himself as a dog man. When he fell in love with a woman who loved cats, they were presented with quite a dilemma. The turning point came when Morris saved Spit's life.

14. Muncaster, Alice L., and Yanow, Ellen, *The Cat Made Me Buy It* (1984) Fluffy and scruffy, playful, and most of all, convincing, here are the four-footed sales cats that have sold us shoes, chocolate, soap, cigars, and sewing supplies. Magazine ads and trade cards are reproduced in full color, and the text provides an entertaining history of early-twentieth-century advertising.

15. Piercy, Marge, *Sleeping with Cats: A Memoir* (2002) Throughout this memoir, Piercy pays tribute to the one loving constant in her life that offered her comfort and meaning, her beloved pet cats. Piercy also shares her perspective on life and explores her development as a woman and writer.

Can a cat be a graceful dance partner? According to Burton Silver and Heather Busch, the answer is yes. Find out more about feline fancy footwork in *Dancing with Cats* (1999).

17 Photo Books for Cat Lovers

1. Anderson, Karen, *Just Cats* **(1999)** Part of Anderson's *Just* series, *Just Cats* is an intimate portrait of the some-times moody and always mysterious *Felis catus.* The book explores the extraordinary lives of these popular animals in thoughtful prose and over 200 color photographs. Mousers, alleys cats, and pampered purebreds are all treated with dignity. The final chapter featuring kittens is a great way to top off this wonderful book.

2. Chittock, Lorraine, *Cats of Cairo — Egypt's Enduring Legacy* **(2001)** The street cats of Cairo are honored today much as they were in ancient Egypt. Chittock spent seven years there, photographing the cat population, and has cap-tured incredibly beautiful scenes shared by the feline and human residents of the city, accompanied by Islamic quo-tations and poetry. The introduction was written by Anne-marie Schimmel, a renowned scholar of Islam and an avid cat lover.

3. Dratfield, Jim, and Coughlin, Paul, *The Quotable Fe-line* **(2000)** This charming collection of photos matches 45 cats in various interesting poses with either a humorous quotation or a poem. The photos, presented in lush sepia tones, capture beautiful cats of all ages and sizes, living in the human world. The quotations are drawn from the writ-ings of Ernest Hemingway, Tennessee Williams, Joyce Carol Oates, and Chekhov, to name a few.

4. Edgar, Jim, *Bad Cat: 244 Not-So-Pretty Kitties and Cats Gone Bad* **(2004)** Not since Kliban has there been a cat book this edgy. In this sequel to *Bad Dog,* Edgar's cats are brooding, deranged, or antisocial, plus they have really bad cat-itude and borderline personality problems. Each full-color photo has an accompanying quotation, together with the name, breed, and age of the featured cat. Readers have described this book as flat-out hilarious.

5. Farber, Jules, *Classic Cats by Great Photographers* **(2005)** Art collector and journalist Jules Farber has as-sembled this collection of photos featuring the work of famed photographers such as Felix Nadar, Jacques-Henri Lartigue, and Man Ray. Contemporary photographers Robert Capa, Willy Ronis, and Edward Steichen are also represented in this volume.

6. Gray, Rhonda, *Cats at Work* **(1991)** Cats have been earning their living since ancient times, from the banks of the Nile to medieval Europe. Gray presents 85 full-color, on-the-job portraits of New York's most industrious cats, giving name, age, breed, place of business, and comments from owners. We see cats patrolling for rodents, shop cats rearranging window displays, and pet cats comforting their human companions in this beautiful volume.

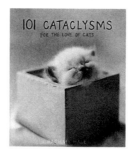

7. Hale, Rachael, *101 Cata-clysms: For the Love of Cats* **(2004)** Here is a tribute to the world's most popular pet — and it is cheeky, sassy, playful, and charming. *101 Cataclysms* show-cases award-winning portraitist Rachael Hale's special rapport with animals and her ability to capture the essence of her sub-jects. Among the featured cats are the sassy Persian ball of fluff named Puffy and the ever-playful British Shorthair named Yabba Dabba Doo.

8. Hale, Rachel, *Smitten* **(2006)** If you look up the word *cute* in the dictionary, it just might say "See *Smitten,* by Rachel Hale." The award-winning photographer with a shelf of books to her name features kittens as they frolic, sleep, and explore. They are amusing, adorable, and in-structive: never underestimate the power of a good nap.

9. Manferto De Fabianis, Valeria, *Cats* **(2005)** Cats take on an almost three-dimensional form to present moments "stolen" by expert photographers from the everyday lives of cats. Sinuous and agile, playful, intelligent, and pitiless, cats of all stripes come alive in these splendid color pho-tographs. Accompanied by the writings of leading zoolo-gists and journalists, these images remind us that our cuddly companions have not lost all the instincts of their cousins in the wild, namely, lions, tigers, and leopards. The book's "cube format" makes this one a perfect gift.

10. **Otani, Shin,** *The Cats of Venice* (1998) Famous for its beautiful waterways, Venice is also renowned for its slinky, stoical, but adorable cats. Otani presents 80 color images, which offer a cat's-eye view of the city. We see an assortment of mostly tabby cats asleep in shop windows, relaxing on park benches, basking on bridges, peering from the windowsills of *palazzi,* playing with dogs and pigeons, and roaming the cobbled streets in this charming little book.

11. **Shaff, Valerie, and Blount, Roy, Jr.,** *I Am the Cat, Don't Forget That: Feline Expressions* (2004) Shaff's gorgeous photography more than does justice to the true nature of the cat, while Roy Blount Jr.'s companion verse seems to capture each cat's thoughts, gestures, and body language. On every page is the story of a cat, accompanied by a photo. The combined result is a touching and often hilarious take on the minds and hearts of felines.

12. **Silvester, Hans,** *The Complete Cats in the Sun* (2000) The felines from *Cats in the Sun, Asleep in the Sun,* and *The Mediterranean Cat* come together in one volume to capture the warmth and free-spirited magic of the Greek Isles. Silvester, whose cat photos are considered some of the finest, spent eight years studying and photographing the cats who roam the 22 islands of Greece. He shows us cats leaping from one fishing boat to another, prowling rooftops, and lazing in the Mediterranean sun.

13. **Smolan, Rick, and Cohen, David Eliot,** *Cats 24/7* (2005) From the creators of the best-selling *America 24/7* comes a heartwarming new book celebrating cats. Culled from thousands of images taken all across the country by professional and amateur photographers, the abundance of photos (more than 500) and

Illustration by Ralph Steadman, 1976.

You can still find copies of the sadly out-of-print **The Illustrated Cat,** by Jean-Claude Suares and Seymour Chwast. With excellent commentary throughout, the book includes myriad styles of drawings and paintings, with artwork by Andrew Wyeth, Pablo Picasso, James Thurber, Edward Lear, John Lennon, Ralph Steadman, and Ronald Searle, among others, and a charming cover painting by Paul Davis.

For a truly personalized copy of this book, visit **cats24-7.com.** Upload a photo, and order a new version of the book cover featuring your very own cat. The service is also available for other volumes in the 24/7 series.

accompanying captions tell a story of the intimate connections we share with our feline friends, be they purebreds, alley cats, fat cats, or just cool cats.

14. Suares, Jean-Claude, *Fat Cats* **(1997)** A cat weighing in at 43 pounds is just one of the fabulous portly felines included in this volume of beautiful black-and-white images of fat cats.

15. Walker, Bob, *The Cats' House* **(1996)** This is a colorful tribute to the author's nine felines. Walker, along with his wife, Frances Mooney, put together a 110-foot series of catwalks, stairs, and mouse holes throughout their home. This house, which has been painted with over 40 bright colors, gives the cats an enjoyable space to play in to their hearts' content.

16. Walker, Bob, *Cats into Everything* **(1999)** This follow-up to *The Cats' House* records the activities of the resident cats who this time around are photographed at night. A camera was set up over Walker's bed and captures his cats' nocturnal activities as well as their daytime antics.

17. Yaginuma, Yoshiyuki, *Zen Cats* **(2001)** Yaginuma's more than 60 irresistible portraits of felines, in the serene solitude of ancient temples and gardens, capture the essence of Zen and cats. Fascinated by these animals, Yaginuma regularly visits temples and other places where they reside, as they wait to greet him and his camera. Commentary provided by Jana Martin discusses the role of the cat in myth, folklore, and Zen writings.

7 Cats Who Wrote Books

1. Sneaky Pie Brown has collaborated with her human, author Rita Mae Brown, on over 13 Mrs. Murphy mysteries and *Sneaky Pie's Cookbook for Mystery Lovers.* Sneaky Pie was discovered by Rita Mae Brown at her local SPCA.

2. Paul Gallico's cat offers explicit instructions for finding, captivating, and taking over a human family in *The Silent Miaow* (1964).

3. In *Diary of a Cat: True Confessions and Lifelong Observations of a Well-Adjusted House Cat* (1995), Leigh W. Rutledge's cat offers a year's worth of revelations, such as what a cat is thinking when it stares for hours at a speck on the wall, how it feels about a new kitten in the house, why sleeping in a warm sunny spot is such a vital activity, and what can happen to an unattended Thanksgiving turkey. Along the way readers will meet a delightful cast of characters whose lives are touched by their cats.

4. Leigh W. Rutledge also helped out when **Mrs. Moore,** a feline dowager of 31, reflected on her days as a stowaway kitten in 1899 aboard the *Estella Gomez,* which cruised the straits of Florida in search of priceless Spanish limes, in *The Lighthouse, the Cat, and the Sea* (1999).

5. In *The Autobiography of Foudini M. Cat,* written with the help of Susan Fromberg Schaeffer in 1997, **Foudini** tells of his perilous tale, beginning with a frail but valiant mother who left in search of food and never returned. Foudini is taken to a frightening room with cages and men in white coats. Facing death, the homeless cat is adopted by a woman he later calls Warm.

6. In *Space Cat* (1952), by Doug Cushman, a delightful children's classic, a small kitten named **Flyball** smuggles himself onto a test flight to the moon. He is discovered and given his very own pressure suit. Once on the moon, he discovers aliens and becomes a hero. Flyball tells the whole tale — with the help of Todd Ruthven — from his own original point of view.

7. *Mrs. Chippy's Last Expedition* is the entertaining story of Ernest Shackleton's cat's journey to Antarctica. **Mrs. Chippy** tells her story in journal form and delights cat lovers with a keen view of the adventure as only a cat would see things. Caroline Alexander does an excellent job of capturing the intelligence and demeanor of cats: "The dogs were barking like mad . . . I suspect they are bewildered much of the time by what goes on around them." Entertaining for both cat lovers and as an adjunct to any book on the true Shackleton adventure.

41 Kid Lit Cats

1. **Broccoli**, from *The Broccoli Tapes*, by Jan Slepian

2. **Carbonel, King of the Cats**, in Barbara Sleigh's Carbonel trilogy

3. *The Cat in the Hat*, by Dr. Seuss

4. **"The Cat That Walked by Himself,"** in Rudyard Kipling's *Just So Stories*.

5. **The cat with the fiddle who played hey-diddle-diddle** in J.R.R. Tolkien's *The Man in the Moon Stayed Up Too Late*

6. **The Cheshire Cat**, in Lewis Carroll's *Alice's Adventures in Wonderland*

7. **Chester the cat**, in *Bunnicula* and its sequels, by James Howe

8. **Clarence**, a pacifist library-dwelling cat who sleeps on the photocopier in *Clarence the Copy Cat*, by Patricia Lakin

9. **Dinah**, Alice's pet cat, featured in Lewis Carroll's books *Alice's Adventures in Wonderland* and *Through the Looking-Glass*

10. **Dragon**, the farmer's cat in Robert C. O'Brien's *Mrs. Frisby and the Rats of NIMH*

11. **Eureka**, Dorothy's cat in L. Frank Baum's *Dorothy and the Wizard in Oz*; also known as the Pink Kitten

12. **Ginger**, the yellow tomcat who kept shop with Pickles the dog in Beatrix Potter's *The Tale of Ginger and Pickles*

13. **The Glass Cat**, a cat made of glass in Baum's *The Patchwork Girl of Oz*

14. **Gobbolino**, in *the Witch's Cat*, by Ursula Moray Williams. Her other books with eponymous feline protagonists include *Jeffy, the Burglar's Cat* and *The Nine Lives of Island Mackenzie*.

15. **Good Fortune**, the cat who goes to heaven in the award-winning story of the same name, by Elizabeth Coatsworth

16. **Graybar**, the black, mouse-hating stray cat in the book *Ragweed*, by Avi and Brian Floca, part of the Poppy Books series

17. **Grimalkin**, cat that adopted Sham and Agba in *King of the Wind*, by Marguerite Henry

18. **Itty**, in Hugh Lofting's *Doctor Dolittle's Return*

19. **Jennie**, the tabby who teaches a boy how to act like a cat, in Paul Gallico's book *The Abandoned*

20. **Jenny Linsky**, a small black cat, and her brothers, **Checkers** and **Edward**, along with her cat friends **Pickles**, **Florio**, and **Macaroni**, from Esther Averill's children's books

21. **Joe Grey**, **Dulcie**, and **Kit**, able to speak to humans and solve murder mysteries in books by Shirley Rousseau Murphy

22. **Kitty**, the Ingalls family mouser in Laura Ingalls Wilder's Little House books

23. **Lipshen**, the grand high witch's cat in Roald Dahl's *The Witches*

24. **Little Cats A through Z**, from Dr. Seuss's *The Cat in the Hat Comes Back*

25. **Mog,** who starred in the Meg and Mog series of children's books by Jan Pienkowski

26. **Mottyl,** the cat in *Not Wanted on the Voyage,* by Timothy Findlay

27. **Mowzer,** the singing cat from Antonia Barber's book *The Mousehole Cat*

28. **Orlando (The Marmalade Cat),** the eponymous hero of a series of illustrated books by Kathleen Hale

29. **Pussy-Cat,** the Owl's fiancée in Edward Lear's poem "The Owl and the Pussy-Cat"

30. **Ribby,** the cat who serves Duchess the dog a traumatizing pie in Beatrix Potter's *The Pie and the Patty Pan*

31. *The Shy Little Kitten* of the book written by Cathleen Schurr and illustrated by Gustaf Tenggren

32. **Silversides,** the white, mouse-hating cat in the book *Ragweed,* by Avi and Brian Floca, part of the Poppy Books series

33. **Simpkin,** in Beatrix Potter's *The Tailor of Gloucester*

34. **Sinbad,** a kitten rescued by the Walker children off the Dutch coast in the Swallows and Amazons novel *We Didn't Mean to Go to Sea,* by Arthur Ransome

35. **Spiegel,** from *Spiegel the Cat,* by Gottfried Keller

36. **Tabby,** Mildred's cat in *The Worst Witch,* by Jill Murphy

37. **Tao,** the Siamese cat from Sheila Burnford's novel *The Incredible Journey*

38. **Tom Kitten,** a curious but disobedient young cat in the stories *The Tale of Tom Kitten* and *The Roly Poly Pudding,* by Beatrix Potter; also Tom's mother, **Mrs. Tabitha Twitchit,** and his siblings, **Moppet** and **Mittens**

39. **Tug,** the cat given by Ged to Alder to protect him from nightmares, in *The Other Wind,* by Ursula K. Le Guin

40. **The yellow tom** on the ship *Pound of Candles,* who helped Little Pig Robinson escape becoming dinner and who was engaged to a "snowy owl of Lapland," in Beatrix Potter's *The Tale of Little Pig Robinson*

41. **Zoom,** in Tim Wynne-Jones's series of books, including *Zoom at Sea*

> "He will kill mice, and he will be kind to babies when he is in the house, just as long as they do not pull his tail too hard. But when he has done that, and between times, and when the moon gets up and night comes, he is the Cat that walks by himself, and all places are alike to him. Then he goes out to the Wet Wild Woods or up the Wet Wild Trees or on the Wet Wild Roofs, waving his wild tail and walking by his wild lone."
>
> — From **"The Cat That Walked by Himself,"** by Rudyard Kipling

"God has created the cat to give man the pleasure of caressing the tiger." — THÉOPHILE GAUTIER

The 7 Major Cat Shows

1. The American Association of Cat Enthusiasts, Inc., founded in 1993, strives to provide shows that are both fair and fun. During the show year, which extends from November 1 to October 31, affiliated clubs hold 10–12 sanctioned shows. The AACE recognizes 47 breeds in the Championship and Alter classes and offers a Household Pet class. Since its inception the AACE has registered over 20,000 cats and 1,500 catteries and has 50 member clubs. To learn more, visit aaceinc.org.

2. Founded in 1955, the **American Cat Fanciers Association (ACFA)** has grown to be one of the world's largest cat organizations. The ACFA was the first to introduce the "multiple-ring" championship show and the first to require prospective judges to successfully complete written exams prior to licensing. Because the ACFA's scoring system is not a "total point" system, exhibitors don't have to incur the expense of campaigning a cat every weekend to be in competition. To find out more about the ACFA, visit acfacats.com.

3. The International Cat Association (TICA) is the world's largest genetic registry of purebred and household pet cats and one of the world's largest sanctioning bodies for cat shows. Its shows promote both pedigreed and nonpedigreed cats in a professional manner that is both enjoyable and educational for exhibitors, judges, and the general public. Countries included in the 2007 schedule of shows include Argentina, Austria, Belgium, Brazil, Canada, England, Hungary, Japan, Switzerland, and the United States. To learn more about TICA shows, visit tica.org.

4. The Canadian Cat Association was founded in 1960. Since that time CCA has maintained a registry of purebred cats of such quality that their records are accepted by all associations throughout the world. The CCA's registry lists over 190,000 individual cats. To learn more, visit cca-afc.com.

5. The Cat Fanciers' Association (CFA), a nonprofit organization founded in 1906, is the world's largest registry of pedigreed cats. It has over 500 member clubs and sanctions cat shows around the world. The CFA holds approximately 400 shows around the globe each year. Its shows are judged by individuals who meet high qualification criteria and have completed a rigorous training program, which well qualifies them to evaluate each show cat based on CFA breed standards. To learn more, visit cfa.org.

6. The Supreme Cat Show is the official show of the Governing Council of the Cat Fancy (GCCF). The GCCF licenses about 135 championship, sanction, and exemption shows each year, which are staged by affiliated clubs throughout the United Kingdom. The "Supreme" is unique in that it is run by the GCCF itself. To learn more, visit Supremecatshow.org.

7. The Fédération Internationale Féline (FIFe) is a federation of cat registries. There are currently 39 member organizations in 37 countries. Membership spans Europe, South America, and Asia. The organization was founded by Madame Marguerite Ravel in 1949 in Paris, France. At their first General Assembly in Ghent, Belgium, the federation was officially founded. The original name was Fédération Internationale Féline d'Europe (FIFE). The goal of the federation is to promote the health and well-being of cats.

Cat Show Know-How

Cool Show Cats Seek Kids

To keep cat shows going — and growing — you need to instill interest among youngsters. That's why many cat show registries offer Junior Showmanship programs. These programs teach cat-loving kids what they need to know in order to compete in cat shows, including sportsmanship, basic cat care, breed standard tutoring, and presentation advice. To learn more, contact the Cat Fanciers' Association at www.cfainc.org/shows/jr-show manship.html.

How the Cat Show Works

1. The pedigreed cats in competition are grouped as kittens (cats 4 to 8 months old), alters (spayed or neutered cats), or championship (cats that are used in breeding programs).

2. The judge presides over a ring, examines the cats, and must choose which of them are the best examples of their breed standard.

3. Each ring has a clerk who announces which cats should come to be judged. Order is determined by the number each cat is given when entering the show.

4. Cats are carried to the ring by their owners after the clerk announces that it is time to be judged.

5. For example, if the kittens are scheduled to be judged, the judge handles all the kittens and chooses the best for each breed represented.

6. The judge, after handling all the kittens in the competition, will choose the Top 10 Kittens, which receive ribbons at a Final, back at the ring.

7. The judge follows the same procedure for the alters and championship cats. Each judge will handle all the cats at the show.

8. Household pet cats (HHP) entered in the show also make up a show group.

9. You can show a household cat if it is at least 4 months old. The cat cannot be declawed, and it must be neutered or spayed if it is older than 8 months.

10. The judge handles all the household pets and chooses the Top 10. Ribbons are awarded after calling the cats back to the ring for a Final.

11. Many shows have Best of the Best awards, given at the end of the show to the top winning kitten, alter, championship cat, and household pet.

The 7 Main Cat Show Divisions

Your feline does not have to be dubbed "best in show" in order to feel like a winner. A cat can earn ribbons and accolades through the various rounds of competition and in various categories.

The type and number of classes vary by the breed registry sponsoring the cat show. This is how the Cat Fanciers' Association, the world's largest cat-breed registry, divides up the cat competition:

1. **Kitten** — Pedigreed kittens of ages 4 to 8 months are eligible for this class. They can be unaltered or altered.

2. **Championship** — This class is for only altered, pedigreed cats beyond 8 months of age.

3. **Premiership** — Altered, pedigreed cats beyond age 8 months vie for honors in this class.

4. **Provisional** — This class features breeds that have not yet achieved championship status by the CFA.

5. **Miscellaneous** — Breeds not yet accepted for provisional status, but accepted for registration and showing by the CFA compete in this class.

6. **Veteran Class** — Think of this as the class for senior felines. Any male or female pedigreed, altered or unaltered, must be at least 7 years old to vie for top cat honors in this class.

7. **Household Pet** — Calling all feline mutts! This class

VALERIE MAASS

features all random-bred or non-pedigreed cats, which are judged for their physical attributes and must not be declawed. Contenders must be at least 4 months of age, and any feline older than 8 months of age must be neutered or spayed.

What the Judges Look For

Think Champ has what it takes to reign as a champ? Before you consider stepping into the cat show ring, be prepared to devote a lot of time, energy, and money to this demanding — and rewarding — pastime.

1. Your cat's coat must be faultlessly clean and in peak condition. This means more than a good brushing, as nutrition, heredity, and the environment factor in the condition of a cat's coat.

2. Judges look for an even temperament. A cat is expected to be calm when being examined by a judge.

3. Feline competitors must sport clear eyes and shining coats and be at an ideal weight.

4. Most important, cats are expected to be as close to the "standard" of their breed as possible. The CFA defines the breed standard as follows: "The standard does not describe a living cat. It is an artistic ideal that is never completely attained in one specimen. We merely try to approach the ideal, always aware that perfection lies beyond our grasp. This is what keeps us inspired, much as an artist is inspired."

5. Good luck!

Part Three

Cat Anatomy and Behavior

"When dogs leap on your bed, with you. When cats leap they adore your bed."

What a masterpiece of physical wonders is the cat. More intelligent than all other animals, barring the ape and the chimpanzee, cats outrank us (and dogs) in hearing (they can hear tones one and a half octaves higher than those that humans can hear), eyesight (their field of vision is about 185 degrees, and although they cannot see in the dark, they come darned close), and even bone count (245 to our 206). Yet study them as we will, they remain mystifying and draw us into a quest to understand why they do the things they do. What goes on in their adorable little heads as they sleep and dream? How did they get their reputation for being so finicky? Why are they always seemingly drawn to the one person in the room who is indifferent to cats? And why, oh why are they *always* on the wrong side of the door?

This chapter explores the anatomy and day-to-day behavior of cats as well as some of their less well known talents: They paint, they dance, they possess astounding homing and survival instincts that allow them to seemingly defy the laws of physics. In the end, we can only conclude that for all we know about cats, they will, forever, continue to harbor their wonderful secrets.

it's because they adore being on to your bed, it's because

— ALISHA EVERETT

18 Cat Commandments

If you've ever tried giving your cat a tablet, you know how difficult it can be. Nor did the cat take particularly well to those that Moses handed down.

Thou shalt not jump onto the keyboard when thy human is at the computer.

Thou shalt not pull the phone cord out of the back of the modem.

Thou shalt not unroll all the toilet paper off the roll.

Thou shalt not sit in front of the television or computer monitor, as thou art not transparent.

Thou shalt not projectile-vomit from the top of the refrigerator.

Thou shalt not walk in on a dinner party and commence licking thy butt.

Thou shalt not lie down with thy butt in thy human's face.

Thou shalt not leap from great heights onto thy human's lap.

Thou shalt not climb onto the garbage can with the hinged lid, as thou wilt fall in and trap thyself.

Thou shalt not reset thy human's alarm clock by walking on it.

Fast as thou art, thou canst not run through closed doors.

Thou shalt not jump onto the toilet seat just as thy human is sitting down.

Thou shalt not jump onto thy sleeping human's bladder at 4 A.M.

Thou shalt realize that the house is not a prison from which to escape at any opportunity.

Thou shalt not trip thy human even if said human walkest too slow.

Thou shalt not push open the bathroom door when there are guests in the house.

Thou shalt remember that thou art a carnivore and that houseplants are not meat.

Thou shalt show remorse when being scolded.

26 Feline Laws of Physics

1. **Law of Cat Inertia** A cat at rest will tend to remain at rest, unless acted upon by some outside force — such as the opening of cat food or a nearby scurrying mouse.

2. **Law of Cat Motion** A cat will move in a straight line, unless there is a really good reason to change direction.

3. **Law of Cat Magnetism** All blue blazers and black sweaters attract cat hair in direct proportion to the darkness of the fabric.

4. **Law of Cat Thermodynamics** Heat flows from a warmer to a cooler body, except in the case of a cat, in which case all heat flows to the cat.

5. **Law of Cat Stretching** A cat will stretch to a distance proportional to the length of the nap just taken.

6. **Law of Cat Sleeping** All cats must sleep with people whenever possible, in a position as uncomfortable for the people involved, and as comfortable as possible for the cat.

7. **Law of Cat Elongation** A cat can make its body long enough to reach just about any countertop that has anything remotely interesting on it.

8. **Law of Cat Obstruction** A cat must lie on the floor in such a position to obstruct the maximum amount of human foot traffic.

9. **Law of Cat Acceleration** A cat will accelerate at a constant rate, until it gets good and ready to stop.

10. **Law of Dinner Table Attendance** Cats must attend all meals when anything good is served.

11. **Law of Rug Configuration** No rug may remain in its naturally flat state for very long.

12. **Law of Obedience Resistance** A cat's resistance varies in proportion to a human's desire for it to do something.

13. **First Law of Energy Conservation** Cats know that energy can be neither created nor destroyed, and they will, therefore, use as little energy as possible.

14. **Second Law of Energy Conservation** Cats also know that energy can be stored only by a lot of napping.

15. **Law of Refrigerator Observation** If a cat watches a refrigerator long enough, someone will come along and take out something good to eat.

16. **Law of Electric Blanket Attraction** Turn on an electric blanket and a cat will jump into bed at the speed of light.

17. **Law of Random Comfort Seeking** A cat will always seek, and usually take over, the most comfortable spot in any given room.

18. **Law of Bag/Box Occupancy** All bags and boxes in a given room must contain a cat within the earliest possible nanosecond.

19. **Law of Cat Embarrassment** A cat's irritation rises in direct proportion to its embarrassment times the amount of human laughter.

20. **Law of Milk Consumption** A cat will drink its weight in milk, squared, just to show you it can.

21. **Law of Furniture Replacement** A cat's desire to scratch furniture is directly proportional to the cost of the furniture.

22. **Law of Cat Landing** A cat will always land in the softest place possible — often the midsection of an unsuspecting, reclining human.

23. **Law of Fluid Displacement** A cat immersed in milk will displace its own volume, minus the amount of milk consumed.

24. **Law of Cat Disinterest** A cat's interest level will vary in inverse proportion to the amount of effort a human expends in trying to interest it.

25. **Law of Pill Rejection** Any pill given to a cat has the potential energy to reach escape velocity.

26. **Law of Cat Composition** A cat is composed of Matter + Anti-Matter + It Doesn't Matter.

The Physiology of the Cat

A cat's brain is more like that of a human than that of a dog.

An adult domestic cat is about 8 to 10 inches tall.

The length from the tip of the nose to the base of the tail averages 18 to 20 inches.

The tail measures about 10 to 15 inches long.

Males usually weigh from 10 to 15 pounds, while females usually weigh from 6 to 10 pounds.

The head is large in comparison with the rest of the cat's body.

The ear contains a total of 32 muscles. The ears are large, and they taper to rounded or pointed tips and stand erect in almost all breeds.

A cat's hearing is more acute than that of a human or a dog.

Pure white cats that have blue eyes are very often deaf.

The size and position of the cat's eyes are such that they permit as much light as possible to enter. This provides the cat with a wide field of vision, which is essential for hunting and nocturnal prowling.

The cat's skeleton contains 245 bones. Human skeletons, although larger, have only 206. These extra skeletal bones provide the cat with extra flexibility.

Cats do not have a collarbone. This allows them to fit through any opening the size of their head.

About 10 percent of a cat's bones are in its tail, which helps a cat maintain balance.

The cat's respiratory rate is 20–40 breaths per minute.

A cat's normal body temperature is 102 degrees F.

A cat's normal pulse rate is 195 beats per minute, on average.

The domestic cat is the only species able to hold its tail vertically while walking.

The position in which a cat holds its tail will reveal what is on its mind. (See page 221.)

A cat cannot see in total darkness, but it can see better in dim light than can most other kinds of animals. In fact, a cat's vision is six times better than a human's at night.

Cats have the largest eyes of any mammal in relation to body size.

Studies have revealed that cats can see the colors blue and green, but the jury is still out on the color red.

A cat's whiskers serve as delicate sense organs of touch. Four rows of stiff whiskers grow on the upper lip on each side of the nose. The cat has a total of 24 whiskers.

When cats and foxes walk, their back feet land exactly in the footprints left by their forefeet.

Only three animals — the cat, the giraffe, and the camel — walk naturally by moving the two right feet, then the two left feet. Dogs and horses alternate left and right, front and back.

🐈 A cat uses its whiskers for measuring distances.

🐈 Cats have a special scent organ located in the roof of the mouth, called the Jacobson's organ. It analyzes odors. This accounts for why you sometimes see your cat "sneer" when it encounters a strong smell.

🐈 A human has from 5 million to 10 million olfactory cells. The cat has approximately 70 million.

🐈 A cat's teeth serve primarily as weapons as well as for tearing food. The animal has 30 permanent teeth. Kittens have baby or deciduous teeth, which are replaced by adult teeth at 7 months of age.

🐈 Although a cat's jaws are short, they are extremely strong. Cats tear and crush their food, they do not chew it. The jaw can move only up and down, not side to side.

🐈 A cat's tongue is rough. All cats use the tongue as a grooming tool to clean and comb the fur, but they also use it to strip flesh off the bones of prey.

🐈 The cat uses the barbs on the back of its tongue to scoop up liquids so it can drink.

🐈 All cats, whether wild or domestic, purr. No one knows the actual mechanism that makes purring happen. The cat's purr has a frequency identical to that of an idling diesel engine, about 26 cycles per second.

🐈 The legs appear short when compared with the length of the body, but they are powerful.

🐈 Cats walk on their toes.

🐈 The domestic cat can sprint at about 30 miles per hour.

🐈 The sharp angles of the knee and "heel" of the hind legs contribute power to sudden sprints, climbing, and jumping.

🐈 The claws of the cat are retractable and come out when the cat fights, hunts, or climbs. The claws are also used to mark territory; they leave a visible mark on scratched objects.

🐈 Most cats have five toes in the forepaws and four in the hind paws.

🐈 The original coat of the domestic cat was brown-gray. This coloration allowed the cat to disguise itself when needed. All other fur colors are the result of genetic changes.

🐈 Cat urine glows under a black light.

Cats can recognize the sound of their owner's footsteps from several hundred feet away. They can also discern the sound of their owner's car approaching, distinguishing it from others on the street.

The 10 Most Popular Breeds in the United States

In order of popularity:

1. Persian

History: This breed likely originated from longhaired cats from Persia (now Iran), Burma (now Myanmar), China, and Russia. However, Egyptian hieroglyphics dating back to 1684 B.C. depict Persians. These crossbred cats were transported to Europe about 300 years ago.

Bragging Rights: Step aside, felines. Persians can boast that they are the most popular breed in North America. Persians were already wowing cat admirers at the first modern cat show in 1871, at London's Crystal Palace.

The Persian Look: With their trademark long, flowing coats, cherubic faces, and expressive round eyes, this longhaired breed can prove irresistible. Persians sport heavy-boned legs, wide, stocky bodies, and itty-bitty round-tipped ears.

The Name Game: This breed was called Longhair rather than Persian until the early 1960s in the United States. The cats are still referred to as Longhairs in Great Britain.

Bring out the Brush: This breed's high-maintenance coat requires daily attention to prevent tangles and mats from forming. It has the longest and thickest fur of all domestic cats. The hairs of the topcoat can be up to five inches long.

The Persian Attitude: Don't expect this breed to amaze you with athletics. Persians prefer to commandeer laps, rejoice in quiet homes, and expect set routines. They love to love and display a gentle nature. No surprises, please — especially noisy houseguests or unruly children. Once seeing these rude intruders, your Persian is apt to exit.

Kittens of the most popular cat breed, the Persian.

Hollywood Persians: Tobey Maguire provided the voice of Mr. Tinkles in the movie *Cats & Dogs* (2001), which featured more than 20 live cat stars. Ernst Stavro Blofeld, James Bond's archenemy and head of the evil terrorist organization SPECTRE, usually appears on screen with a white Persian in his lap. Two Persian red cats by the name of Crackerjack and Pumpkin played the role of Hermione's cat, Crookshanks, in the film *Harry Potter and the Prisoner of Azkaban.*

Health Alert: Persians are at risk for PKD (polycystic kidney disease), an inherited renal disease that causes kidneys to enlarge, function improperly, and fail. This condition shows up from ages 3 to 10.

The Point Behind Points

A colorpoint in a pedigreed cat, such as a blue-point Persian, refers to accent colors on a cat's mask, ears, legs, and tail. Points come in a rainbow of colors, including seal, chocolate, and lilac.

Officially Recognized: Persians were first recognized as a breed by the Cat Fanciers' Association in 1909. They are judged in sevel color divisions in competition.

Record Setters: A Persian named Bluebell had a 14-kitten litter in December 1974 in South Africa. All the kittens were born alive. The usual number is four to six kittens. The smallest domestic cat on record was a male blue-point Himalayan-Persian cat named Tinker Toy, who was just over two inches tall and seven inches long. The purported smartest cat in the world is a Persian from New Delhi, India, who can allegedly respond to questions and add numbers. A Persian cat can claim the longest trip home made on foot by a feline.

2. Maine Coon

Origin Tale: This all-American cat originated in the great state of Maine and is America's only indigenous breed of domestic cat.

A Sail of a Tale: Some contend that Maine Coons got their start as a result of a botched plan to rescue Marie Antoinette. It is said that Captain Nathaniel Cloud attempted to free the imprisoned Marie Antoinette during the French Revolution and took her household possessions, including six Persian or Angora cats, onto his ship, the *Sally*, for safekeeping. But when it came time to sneak the queen out of her prison cell, she refused to leave without her son. Captain Cloud's ship sailed to the New World with the cats, who landed in Wiscasset, Maine. The assumption is that these royal cats roamed freely and passed the longhair gene to some of the local cats.

AKA: "Gentle Giants," "Feline Greeters of the World," "Shags"

Size Matters: The Maine Coon stands head and shoulders above most breeds. Males weigh in at 13 to 18 pounds.

The Maine Coon Look: This breed's shaggy, weatherproof coat and ear and toe tufts provide protection from harsh New England winters. The coat is surprisingly easy to maintain, requiring only weekly combing to remain mat free. The square-shaped head is broad, and the eyes are big, expressive, and wide set.

The Maine Coon Attitude: This breed put the *m* in *mellow* and has a well-deserved reputation for getting along with other cats, dogs, and people of all ages. This cat is super-sweet, smart, and easygoing. A Maine Coon displays affection by butting the head against its lucky human friend and emitting chirps and trills.

Maine Coon Antics: Keep tabs on the water bowl. This breed is known to act like a raccoon and take a drink by scooping water with its front paws. Maine Coons apparently like to dunk favorite toys in water bowls. They also use their paws to pick up food.

Plenty of Patience: In the early 1900s, the Maine Coon came to be snubbed at cat shows in favor of imported longhair breeds,

A clowder of Maine Coon cats.

even though its hardy genes were used to bolster the Persian breeds. Finally, the Maine Coon prevailed, earning championship status by the CFA in the 1950s. They have since become one of the darling breeds of the show world.

Health Alert: Due to its large size, the Maine Coon represents one of the few cat breeds that can develop hip dysplasia, a condition common in large-breed dogs.

Cat Show No-No: A Maine Coon can sport a variety of coat colors, but the tail must be kink-free to make a cat a contender at cat shows.

Cat Bytes: This breed is four to five times the size of the Singapura, the smallest breed of feline. The longest whisker on record belonged to a Maine Coon cat named Missi. The whiskers measured 7.5 inches. Leo, a Maine Coon cat residing in Chicago, Illinois, holds the record as the longest cat, measuring 48 inches from nose to tail.

3. Exotic

Born by Design: The Exotic originated thanks to careful planning and partnering among American Shorthair breeders. They mated their cats with Persians to produce the Exotic, a shorthaired cat with a Persian-like face.

The Name Game: The originally proposed name for this new breed was to be Sterling, due to its beautiful silver color, but the name Exotic was finally accepted.

AKA: "The lazy man's Persian," the Exotic Shorthair

The Exotic Look: Bred to mimic the Persian in every way, but with an easier-to-maintain coat, the Exotic has thick, plush, tangle-free fur. Exotics have the flat face of the Persian and the typical soft, squeaky Persian voice. Exotics look like a cross between a Persian and a teddy bear.

The Exotic Attitude: This breed is a good pick for those who want a quiet, calm, easygoing cat. If these cats want your attention, they will be sweet about it, not demanding. Exotics keep their kittenlike qualities throughout their lives. They are very playful and make great companions.

Exotic kittens, also known as the "lazy man's Persian."

Grooming Bonus: This breed's coat does not tangle and mat and requires far less combing that a Persian coat. They are a great choice for people who love Persians but don't want to take the time to groom one.

Color Me Exotic: Originally silver in color, the most popular colors among the Exotic cats now are black, tortoiseshell, red tabby, brown tabby, and, recently, bi-color.

Boys Versus Girls: Breeders report that females may act a bit aloof, and males tend to be more affectionate.

Officially Recognized: In 1967 the CFA gave formal recognition to the Exotic Shorthair as a breed.

4. Siamese

Royal Roots: A true feline aristocrat, the Siamese came from Thailand where it was known as the "Siam." Centuries ago the royal family of Siam bestowed these cats as gifts to visiting dignitaries. The cats were treasured, as they belonged only to royalty. Mere commoners could only ogle these cats through art and literature.

Going Global: The breed began showing up in other parts of the world in the late 1800s. Siamese started wowing

So many Siamese!

judges at cat shows in Great Britain during the late nineteenth century and was considered a rare breed in the United States until after World War II. The first known Siamese to reach American shores was a gift to First Lady Lucy Webb Hayes from the American consul in Bangkok. Today, the Siamese ranks among the top three breeds in terms of registration in the United States.

Popular Siamese Folklore: A popular legend has it that the Siamese originated from a love match between an ape and a lioness on Noah's ark.

The Siamese Look: Let's start with those deep blue, almond-shaped eyes and then move on to the sleek, slender, muscular body and chiseled features of the triangle-shaped head, with its large, pointed ears. These features bear little resemblance to the original Siamese of ancient Siam, however. Back then, this breed sported a stocky body, crossed eyes, and kinked tails — traits that would disqualify them from any cat show today. Siamese kittens are born white because of the heat inside the mother's uterus, a condition particular to Siamese. The color points of Siamese cats are heat related, so the cooler the environment, the darker the points.

The Siamese Attitude: If this breed took an IQ test, it would put most other felines to shame. We're talking supersmart plus well adapted to communicating through voice and body language. This feline is no wallflower. The Siamese actively seeks interaction and can convey its wants in sounds ranging from delicate mews to loud, raspy calls.

Strange but True: The distinctive tone of the Siamese voice mimics the sound of a human baby.

Hollywood Connection: A Siamese named Syn was featured in the 1965 Disney flick *That Darn Cat!* and became the first cat to win a Patsy Award (see page 104). A seal-point Siamese named Pyewacket was the second cat to win a Patsy Award, for his role opposite Kim Novak in the 1958 movie *Bell, Book, and Candle.* The Disney classic film *Lady and the Tramp* features "The Siamese Cat Song."

Officially Recognized: The Siamese was accepted by the CFA in stages, based on color. The blue-point Siamese first gained recognition in 1934. Next came the chocolate point in 1946, followed by the lilac point in 1955. Other colors, including red points, tortie points, and lynx points, are accepted in some cat associations but not others.

How the Siamese Got Crossed Eyes: A monk in a Buddhist temple, whose job it was to stand guard over a precious golden goblet, wandered off and left two cats to take over the task. After a while, one of the cats, wondering where the monk had gone, went to search for him. This left only one cat to guard the goblet. After dutifully staring at the golden cup for a very long time, the eyes of the cat became crossed.

Cat Bytes: In 1964, two Siamese cats living in the Dutch embassy in Moscow detected bugging equipment inside the walls. Their constant meowing and clawing led to the discovery of microphones placed there by the Russian government.

Katy, a Siamese living in Russia, is purported to weigh over 50 pounds. She has a 26-inch waist and 6-inch-long whiskers.

5. Abyssinian

Bragging Rights: Hailed as one of the oldest known cat breeds and ranked as one of the top five most popular today, the Abyssinian still sports the jungle look of *Felis lybica*, the African wildcat ancestor of all domestic cats.

Origin: Historians believe that the ancient Egyptians bred these cats, based on images of cats in Egyptian paintings and sculptures. In fact, mummified cats in Egyptian tombs discovered by modern archaeologists do resemble today's Abyssinian. But the Aby competes with the Egyptian Mau for top honors as the most direct descendant of ancient Egyptian cats.

Historic Cat Fight: According to legend, the emperor of Abyssinia (a former name of Ethiopia) in the 1860s was quite smitten with Queen Victoria, who did not share the sentiment. Disappointed, he began arresting British citizens living in his country. Dumb move. The queen ordered her troops to invade, and the emperor ended up shooting himself in the head with a gun that — ironically — had been a gift from her. It is believed that when that battle ended in 1868, a British solder brought home a kitten named Zula — considered the grand dame of all modern Abys.

America-Bound: The first Abys arrived on North American soil in the early 1900s from Great Britain, but the breed

Abyssinians, one of the oldest cat breeds.

didn't grow in popularity until the 1930s. It was first listed as a distinct breed in 1882.

AKA: The "Bunny Cat," "Child of the Gods"

The Aby Look: The long, muscular torso, arched neck, large ears, and almond-shaped eyes make this cat physically appealing. The Abyssinian coat comes in ruddy, red, blue, and fawn and feels soft, like bunny fur.

Grooming Tip: Their thick, dense shorthaired coats require very little brushing. These cats rarely need to be bathed.

The Aby Attitude: Their intelligence, people-seeking nature, and ability to master tricks make them popular among cat lovers. They are friendly, fearless, affectionate, gentle, and playful.

Household Hints: Because of the Aby's active — and athletic — nature, it is wise to keep valued breakables inside cabinets, behind glass doors. Do not leave them on open shelves to be pawed by an Aby.

Historic Aby: The oldest example of the modern Abyssinian cat is believed to be Patrie, a taxidermy specimen from the 1830s on display at the Leiden Zoological Museum in the Netherlands.

Movie Trivia: Abyssinian cats Amber and Rumpler played the part of Jake, the stranded alien cat in the 1978 movie *The Cat from Outer Space.* Actor Ronnie Schell provided the voice of Jake.

6. Ragdoll

Origin Info: This breed originated in the 1960s in Riverside, California, when a longhaired female named Josephine, with Siamese markings, was purposely bred to a male carrying Siamese markings. The results were kittens born with nonmatting coats and easygoing personalities. The breed was named the Ragdoll because many of these cats go completely limp when picked up.

Many Ragdoll cats go completely limp when picked up, thus the name.

AKA: Female Ragdolls are referred to as "daughters of Josephine."

Ragdoll Urban Legend: Talk about the call of the wild — as in wild tales. Rumors have swirled about the origin of this popular breed. One tale tells that the Ragdoll was created by extraterrestrials. Another story centers on a white Persian-like cat who was struck by a car while pregnant, thus causing the kittens to mutate into the Ragdoll; according to a third, kittens' traits and personalities were genetically altered by the use of human genes. These legends don't hold up under the scrutiny of science, however.

Big Breed: A male Ragdoll can tip the scale at up to 20 pounds, but they are anything but feline bullies. Females can weigh up to 15 pounds. *The Guinness Book of World Records* lists the Ragdoll as the largest feline breed.

Taking Its Sweet Time: Ragdolls take up to four years to fully mature.

The Ragdoll Look: This breed sports a light-colored longhaired coat, with Siamese-like points and big, blue eyes. The body is big, muscular, and well boned. The wedge-shaped head sports a well-developed chin and wide-set ears.

The Ragdoll Attitude: This feline is known for its docile and loving nature and is arguably the gentlest, most well mannered, and most easygoing of all the cat breeds. Ragdolls tend to behave politely around children and seniors. They enjoy quietly greeting houseguests and hanging out on the floor. This is not a cat that will want to perch on a top shelf.

Ragdoll Antics: They are fascinated by water and have been known to leap into full bathtubs or sit on the edge of the tub while their people bathe. In addition, they can be too trusting, so please, keep them as indoor cats for their own safety.

Grooming Advice: This low-shedding breed sports a satin-soft coat that does not mat.

Health Alert: The Ragdoll is prone to hypertrophic cardiomyopathy (HCM), which is why responsible breeders have ultrasound screening performed on their litters. It appears that some bloodlines carry this heart disease.

Officially Recognized: Identified as one of the fastest-growing breeds in the International Cat Association — second only to the Bengal — the Ragdoll waited for many years to be accepted by the CFA. Ragdolls have championship status in all associations except for the CFA, which allows the bi-colors to be shown in the miscellaneous class and lets the colorpoint and mitted patterns be registered but not shown.

7. Birman

Birthplace: This breed's history begins in Burma, but it came to the United States in 1959 via France and England. There are two theories as to how this came about. The first involves a pregnant Birman who was secretly shipped to France around 1919. The second cites two temple cats in Indochina given as a gift to two French citizens.

Birman Legend: Some contend that the Birman first served as a feline companion for Kittah priests. When bandits invaded the Khmer Temple in Burma to steal a golden statue in the image of the blue-eyed goddess Tsun-Kyan-Kse, Mun-Ha, the high priest, was injured during the confrontation. As he lay dying, his loyal Birman, Sinh, was said to come to his side and gently rest his paws on his chest, offering him companionship in his final moments. The priest died and his cat was transformed. Sinh's fur turned golden like the goddess and his eyes took on her eye color as well. His paws turned pure white, symbolizing the feline's devotion to his dying priest.

AKA: The Sacred Cat of Burma

Birman Clout: It is said that when a Birman cat dies, the soul of a priest guides the feline to heaven.

The Birman Look: Sporting a large, long stocky frame, the Birman has long, silky hair with a mat-free texture and round, deep blue eyes. In ideal examples, the white feet are symmetrical. The "gloves" on the front feet, if perfect, line up horizontally, and those on the back feet, called "laces," end in a point up the back of the leg.

The Birman Attitude: The Birman seeks human company and displays a sweet, quiet, yet active personality. This quiet cat has a soft, sweet voice. It is definitely a one-person cat, who promises to be gentle and playful. However,

The Birman, also known as the Sacred Cat of Burma.

this kitty will never be considered an Einstein among felines. Birmans have been described as "puppy dogs in cat bodies."

Birman Preferences: Please do not make this cat the only critter in your home. This breed likes being part of a multi-species pack, even if that means sharing your attention with a d-o-g.

Grooming Tips: This cat's silky hair is virtually mat-free.

Birman Bragging Rights: It's amazing that this breed ranks as the third most popular feline breed in the United States, considering that only a pair of Birmans was believed to survive World War II in Europe. Birman admirers rallied and created a program to reestablish the breed. They succeeded in achieving five generations of pure breeding in order to fully accredit the Birman for championship competition.

Officially Recognized: Birmans were recognized by England in 1966 and by the CFA in 1967. Birmans are a patient bunch. It took five years from their initial acceptance into championship competition in the CFA for the first Birman to earn the title of grand champion. Take a well-deserved bow, Griswold's Romar of Bybee.

8. American Shorthair

Birthplace: As the name implies, this breed is all-American.

Origin Tale: It is believed that ancestors of the American Shorthair arrived in North America with early European settlers; some may have hitched a ride on the *Mayflower* in 1602. They were brought to hunt rats on ships bound for the New World. The breed was originally called the Domestic Shorthair.

Pioneer Cats: Westward-bound pioneers brought these cats to the frontier. During the California Gold Rush of 1849, cats were purchased for the handsome sum of $50 each to keep down the critter population.

The American Shorthair Look: This medium-to-large-size cat features a full-cheeked face, ears slightly rounded at the tips, bright and alert-looking eyes, strong jaws, a solid and broad torso, and a medium-long tail. Its dense coat helps it weather the cold and protects it from superficial skin injuries.

Color Me American Shorthair: This breed comes in more than 80 different colors and patterns, ranging from brown-patched to silver tabby.

American Shorthair Attitude: Blessed with robust health, longevity, smart looks, friendliness, and a quiet disposition, this breed is understandably popular. It is not uncommon for American Shorthairs to live for 20 years. They are great with kids and dogs and are superb hunters.

The all-American American Shorthair.

American Shorthair Asset: This breed's strong, powerful jaws make it one of most feared felines among mice and other rodents.

Kitty Ka-Ching: According to CFA records, a brown tabby American Shorthair was offered for sale for $2,500 at the Second Annual Cat Show at Madison Square Garden in 1896.

Bragging Rights: The American Shorthair ranks as one of

the ten most popular breeds. In the show ring, this one stands out as a real contender. The American Shorthair has claimed two titles as CFA Cat of the Year and one title as CFA Kitten of the Year. American Shorthairs are often selected as Best Cat in Show at various events.

Officially Recognized: This breed enjoys a very long and honored history. It is one of the first five breeds registered by the CFA — way back in 1906.

9. Oriental

Birthplace: This breed owes its origin to Baroness Von Ullman of the Roofspringer Cattery in England. In 1950, she crossed a seal-point Siamese with a Russian Blue and several generations later produced the Oriental — a new breed with a Siamese body but in a rich solid chestnut color.

The Name Game: In 1973, Vicki and Peter Markstein of Petmark Cattery in New York organized a meeting of breeders who agreed to categorize all the colors as a single breed and switched the name from Foreign to Oriental Shorthair. The Oriental Shorthair International Club was created in 1976.

AKA: The Oriental is also called Oriental Shorthair and a "Foreign Type."

The Feline Color Palette: The Oriental was purposely created as a way to explore all possible colors and patterns. This cat comes in more than 300 colors and patterns.

The Oriental Look: This breed features a triangle-shaped head, almond-shaped eyes that slant upward, a sleek, long body, and a whippy tail. It has a Siamese body type, but it is color that sets the Oriental apart. Orientals come in virtually every coat color and pattern. Solid colors include chestnut, lavender, blue, white, red, and cream.

What do you get when you cross a Siamese with a Russian Blue? The exquisite Oriental.

The Oriental Attitude: Personality-wise, the Oriental is a total extrovert who makes no apologies for being rowdy and active. This cat has no qualms about pestering the people it adores. An Oriental will help you brush your teeth and lace your sneakers and will be waiting at the door when you come home.

Survival Tip: Due to this breed's Velcro-like desire to bond and its talkative nature, consider getting a second Oriental so that the feline pals can share their outgoing nature.

Skip the Bath: This breed's easy-maintenance coat rarely needs a bath or much grooming. Oriental Shorthairs need little more than regular stroking to keep their coats in good

"The phrase 'domestic cat' is an oxymoron." — GEORGE F. WILL

41 CFA-Recognized Cat Breeds

Unlike other organizations or societies, the Cat Fanciers' Association recognizes only the following 41 breeds in their shows.

1. Abyssinian
2. American Bobtail
3. American Curl
4. American Shorthair
5. American Wirehair
6. Balinese
7. Birman
8. Bombay
9. British Shorthair
10. Burmese
11. Chartreux
12. Colorpoint Shorthair
13. Cornish Rex
14. Devon Rex
15. Egyptian Mau
16. European Burmese
17. Exotic
18. Havana Brown
19. Japanese Bobtail
20. Javanese
21. Korat
22. Laperm (provisional)
23. Maine Coon
24. Manx
25. Norwegian Forest Cat
26. Ocicat
27. Oriental
28. Persian (includes the Himalayan)
29. Ragamuffin (included as miscellaneous)
30. Ragdoll
31. Russian Blue
32. Scottish Fold
33. Selkirk Rex
34. Siamese
35. Siberian
36. Singapura
37. Somali
38. Sphynx
39. Tonkinese
40. Turkish Angora
41. Turkish Van

condition, but you can brush the coat occasionally with a rubber cat brush for better results.

Popularity Contest: Despite being a relative newcomer, the Oriental has quickly become one of the most popular breeds.

Officially Recognized: The CFA granted championship status to this breed in 1977 and recognized the bi-color Oriental Shorthair in 1985.

Cat Show No-No: The eye color for this breed can be green, blue, or even odd (one blue and one green), but any hint of being crossed-eye disqualifies an Oriental from cat-show honors.

10. Sphynx

Bald Beginnings: Cat experts report that a domestic cat gave birth to a hairless kitten in Toronto, Canada, in 1966. It was discovered to be a natural mutation.

AKA: "Love Mooch" and "Canadian Hairless"

The Sphynx Look: Proud to be the one and only hairless feline breed, the Sphynx does look like an alien. What it lacks in hair, it makes up for with a strong medium-sized frame, well-developed muscles, beckoning big eyes, and a friendly expression. What draws the most stares, however, is the potbelly, the wrinkles, and the batlike ears. The skin feels like heated chamois to the touch. And because of the lack of an insulating coat common to other breeds, these cats actually perspire in order to regulate body temperature.

Special Grooming: No need for a brush or comb for this breed. However, daily sponging is recommended because the skin produces natural oils that can leave spots where they sit or lie — perhaps on your prized sofa.

The Sphynx Attitude: This cat seeks the spotlight and

"There are no ordinary cats."
— COLETTE

The Sphynx is the one and only hairless feline breed.

revels in playful mischief. When it's time to nap, a Sphynx turns into a heat-seeking missile to find a toasty place, usually under the covers. Some of them love to swim and play in water.

Hollywood Connection: In the popular Austin Powers movies, Mr. Bigglesworth was played by two Sphynx cats, Ted Nude-gent and Mel Gibskin. Mr. Bigglesworth was Dr. Evil's adored cat.

Healthy Boast: This breed is regarded as very robust, with few health or genetic problems. Despite the lack of hair, these cats are not hypoallergenic. In fact, people who are highly allergic to cats can be extremely uncomfortable around the Sphynx.

Officially Recognized: The Sphynx was accepted into the miscellaneous class by the CFA in 1998.

Cat Show Routine: At cat shows, it is common to spot breeders of Sphynx cats toting their feline contenders in polar-fleece bags, to keep them warm.

 24 Definitions of a Cat

1. A diagram and pattern of subtle air
2. A four-footed allergen
3. An animal who never cries over spilled milk
4. Nobody's fool
5. The only real self-cleaning appliance in the house
6. A furry keyboard cover
7. An alarm clock
8. An ego with fur
9. A lap warmer
10. A companion in grace, beauty, mystery, and curiosity
11. Murphy's way of saying "Nice furniture!"
12. A natural paper-shredder
13. A way for the rest of us to learn tolerance
14. A control freak
15. An expert on the art of the nap
16. A puzzle for which there is no solution
17. Ruler of the world
18. Sneaky, evil, and cruel
19. An absolute individual, with its own ideas about everything, including the humans it owns
20. The ultimate narcissist
21. A connoisseur of comfort
22. A well into which we throw our emotions
23. A migratory organism with a tropism for where it's not wanted
24. Purrfect

19 Differences Between Cats and Dogs

1. The cats belong to the family of felines. Dogs, on the other hand, are canines.

2. Dogs hunt in packs. Cats hunt alone.

3. While both are members of the class *Mammalia* and the order *Carnivora,* the cat can't survive unless it eats meat of some kind. A dog is an omnivore and will eat just about anything. Cats need numerous nutrients and chemicals that can be acquired only from animal-derived tissues.

4. Although a dog's reflexes are fast, a cat's reflexes are much faster.

5. Dogs are pack animals, and since your pet dog considers you a member of its pack, it needs and expects lots of affection and attention. Cats are loners and don't require quite as much affection.

6. Dogs are attached to their people more so than their surroundings. If you take a dog with you somewhere unfamiliar, it will adjust. Cats are very territorial, and faced with a change of scenery they will become anxious and fearful.

7. A dog can bark, howl, or whine. The cat, on the other hand, will meow and purr around humans — but when a cat is around another cat, it's an entirely different story.

8. Dogs are very aware of their status and rank in the human household. Cats couldn't care less.

9. How high dogs hold their tail expresses their rank. If one dog meets another dog and one holds its tail up, it has the higher status. When a cat holds its tail up, it means it is happy,

10. Cats are nocturnal, meaning they are active at night. Dogs, however, are day animals.

11. Dogs are somewhat smarter than cats in learning responses to verbal command. A dog can be trained to sit in a matter of five minutes. By contrast, it would take at least five weeks to teach a cat to sit — if you're lucky.

12. Unlike those of a dog, a cat's claws are retractable. The cat is born with sharp claws, but they are kept inside until they are needed. Thus they do not become dull from walking, as a dog's claws do.

13. A cat's tongue has little barbs, or hooks, that are used to get every last bit of meat off a bone. Therefore a cat can simply lick a bone and the meat will come off. The dog does not have such barbs on its tongue; a dog uses its tongue to sweat.

14. Dogs require housetraining; cats use the litter box instinctively.

15. Generally, a dog can learn from punishment; not so the cat.

16. Cats are agile jumpers and climbers, far superior to dogs, who can at best leap onto the sofa or the dining room table. Feline muscles and skeletal build enable cats to scale and soar quickly and easily, abilities that help them escape predators and hunt prey.

17. Dogs can be aggressive when it comes to defending themselves from a threat. Cats avoid harmful situations by climbing or running away; they have a more highly developed fight-or-flight response.

18. Cats are ambush hunters; they sneak up on their prey and pounce on it, using their sharp claws to grip it. Most dogs, on the other hand, are adapted to run for long distances to chase their prey.

19. Dogs trap their prey with their snout; cats use their claws.

"Let's say, heaven forbid, that you died alone in the company of your pet. A dog would normally wait, in this situation, until it is very hungry—often a couple of days—before feeding on its beloved owner. A hungry cat will decide that you'll do as a protein source before your body is even cold. . . . As one forensics expert put it: 'On those lazy afternoons when your cat is lying there on the sofa watching you with half-closed eyes, it's likely thinking about lunch and checking to see if your chest is still moving up and down.'"

—FROM <u>CATS DON'T ALWAYS LAND ON THEIR FEET</u>, BY ERWIN BARRETT AND JACK MINGO

22 Cat Myths Debunked

A great deal of misinformation has been spread about the cat, its behavior, and its intelligence. Unfortunately, these errors of fact can sometimes endanger our little friends. Here are a number of myths, debunked.

1. Cats should be kept away from pregnant women. Most physicians are concerned about the parasite called *Toxoplasmosis gondi,* which can be transmitted by a cat, but in fact very rarely is. Most adults have already been exposed to the virus and have acquired immunity. A simple blood test can determine whether or not the expectant mother needs to worry. (See "8 Tips for Avoiding Toxoplasmosis," page 289.)

2. Cats are loners. The truth is, cats really don't like being left alone. In fact, feral cats often form colonies for the sole purpose of companionship. So, if you have a busy lifestyle that requires a great deal of time away from home, it's best to have two cats, to keep each other company.

Cats are not loners! The Burmese is known as the "Velcro cat" for its penchant for shadowing its favorite people.

3. Cats can see in the dark. Although a cat's night vision has been proven to be 10 times better than that of a human, a feline is not able to see in complete darkness. Cats do not rely on night vision alone when sensing movement or objects in the dark; their whiskers and sense of smell help, too.

4. Cats must drink milk. Aside from the fact that milk has little or no nutritional value for cats, most felines are actually lactose intolerant, and milk may cause diarrhea. But cats do love the taste of milk, so it's all right to spoil them from time to time. Your little guy will, however, be much better off with fresh, cool water.

5. Cats have nine lives. We only wish.

6. Cats that hunt do so because they are not well fed. The hunting instinct is very strong in felines. Whether they are well fed or not has no effect on this innate drive.

7. Cats purr only when they are happy. Although cats *do* purr when happy and contented, they also purr when they have been injured, while giving birth, and sometimes when they need attention. In fact, cats tend to purr when they are feeling any strong emotion. The cat's purr is the equivalent of a human smile, which can express happiness but also nervousness or uncertainty.

8. Cat fur causes allergies. The primary cause of allergic reactions to cats is the allergens found in the cat's sebaceous glands, located in its skin. An example is the allergenic glycoprotein called Fel D1 (short for *Felis domesticus*), which is also secreted via saliva in lesser quantities. When cats lick themselves, they spread this rather sticky protein, which adheres to dust particles, home furnishings, clothing, and the cat's fur, no matter whether it's long, short, straight, curly, or absent. Since all cats have sebaceous glands, all cat breeds can potentially cause allergic reactions. Allergens are also found in the feces, serum, urine, mucus, dander, and hair roots of the cat.

9. Cats will get fat and lazy if they are neutered or spayed. Much is accomplished by spaying or neutering your cat. You can prevent it from contributing to the pet overpopulation problem, and if your cat is a male, you will reduce its likelihood of developing testicular cancer and injuries associated with fighting. Female cats benefit by spaying in that they have a smaller chance of getting breast cancer. This basic surgery will also minimize the possibility that your cat will wander off and get injured or lost. A desexed cat might lose weight searching for a mate, but a neutered cat will not gain weight.

10. Cats always land on their feet. Do cats always land on their feet? It depends. If the cat falls a very short distance from the ground, it doesn't have enough time to right itself. On the other hand, a cat will be seriously injured and quite possibly killed if it falls from a great height. (See "How Cats Fall," page 216.)

11. Cats cannot be harmed by declawing. According to some cat welfare advocates, when a cat is declawed, not only are its nails removed, but so is the last bone of the cat's claw. This is extremely painful to the cat, and many cats never get over the trauma. Declawed cats often end up in shelters because of the resulting changes in behavior. And, because cats walk on their toes, walking becomes not only difficult but painful as well. If your cat likes to scratch at your furniture, get a scratching post or nail caps. Don't even consider declawing as an option.

12. Calico or tortoiseshell cats are always female. This is not completely true, but males of these patternings are extremely rare. Only about one in three thousand calicoes is male. Besides, you couldn't have calicoes if there weren't any males, could you?

You can play in the water with your Turkish Van.

13. Cats hate water. Most cats hate water, but not all do. Turkish Vans are known to be fond of water and enjoy swimming. Bengals, too, have been known to appreciate water play.

14. Siamese cats are mean. The film *The Lady and the Tramp* is partially responsible for the bad rap that Siamese cats have gotten. Si and Am, the cats of this film, are characterized as exceedingly cruel. The fact that the Siamese is one of the most popular cat breeds in the world should dispel that myth.

15. Cats cannot get rabies. Most warm-blooded mammals, including cats, bats, skunks, and ferrets, can carry rabies. Take your cat to the vet regularly for a rabies vaccination.

16. A cat's sense of balance is in its whiskers. The cat's righting reflex has nothing to do with its whiskers. Cats use their whiskers as "feelers," to judge distance, and to help guide them in darkness, but not to maintain their balance.

17. **Cats will intentionally interfere with you when you're on the telephone.** Your cat has no idea what a phone is. But when it hears you talking, it thinks you are speaking to it. The cat is not demonstrating jealousy when you are on the phone, just affection.

18. **Cats get depressed when reprimanded.** Occasionally it becomes necessary to reprimand a cat. But does the cat actually sulk? The cat does not feel degraded when scolded. When it retreats, it is merely surrendering to the top cat in the family.

19. **Cats are finicky eaters.** Most experts maintain that a cat will eat anything, provided it is a meat derivative, and that cats don't especially care for carbohydrates. If your cat is acting finicky, it may want to be fed at a different time of day or may prefer smaller but more frequent meals.

20. **Cats hate being walked.** Some cats actually enjoy being led on a harness. Try it! It's great exercise for an overweight cat, and it's a good way to bond, too.

21. **Tomcats regularly kill kittens.** This myth isn't completely false. Both male and female cats are very attentive to their offspring. However, a male who is in a state of arousal will sometimes grab a female kitten by the scruff of the neck and accidentally kill it while trying to mate with an unwilling female.

22. **Cats can suffocate babies.** This myth is based on two false notions. The first is that a cat can smell milk on a baby's breath and suck the breath right out of the infant, and the second is that a cat can suffocate a baby by sitting on the baby's chest. Both of these ideas are utterly false. A cat cannot suck a baby's breath, and babies are too resilient to be crushed by a cat.

Polydactyl Cats

Cats normally have five toes on their front paws, but some American polydactyl cats have as many as seven. These cats are believed to have arrived on American shores during the colonial period. Polydactyl cats can be found in any breed, but American polydactyl cats are bred specifically for their extra toes.

The most famous American polydactyl cats were those Ernest Hemingway wrote about, and as a result this type of cat is sometimes known as the "Hemingway cat" or "Mitten cat." At the present time, there are at least 30 polydactyl cats living at the Ernest Hemingway Museum and Home, in Key West, Florida, and thus have been protected in Hemingway's will. (See "Hemingway's Cats," page 112.)

Polydactyl cats seem to have a more relaxed and mellow personality than other cats and are reputed to be affectionate and patient with children. These cats are quite hardy and can survive even in snowy weather. Their extra toes afford them greater traction.

Some American polydactyls have bobtails; these cats have shorter bodies than those with long tails.

The hind legs of an American polydactyl are noticeably longer than the front legs.

One of the extra toes looks like a thumb, and for this reason American polydactyl cats are also known as "cats with thumbs."

Polydactyls sometimes have a three-toed foot attached to the four-toed foot.

According to the CFA breed standards, a polydactyl would be disqualified at any cat show.

It is believed that 40 percent of Maine Coon cats, one of the oldest breeds in North America, have extra toes.

The Life Expectancy of Cats

The average life expectancy of a domestic cat has a lot to do with whether or not it is part of the "in crowd." By that, we don't mean that "cool" cats live longer than geeky ones. We're referring to how much time a cat spends indoors versus the big, bad, dangerous outside world.

Longevity is heavily influenced by risk factors. Outdoor-only cats, on average, tend to live for fewer years than their indoor counterparts do, according to The Humane Society of the United States. That's because they risk the dangers of Mother Nature's climate, coyotes, dogs and other predators, cars, environmental hazards such as pesticides, and lack of a steady food supply.

Indoor-only cats live, on average, from 12 to 18 years. That's because these cats tend to receive regular veterinary care to protect them against diseases, enjoy free meals provided by caring owners, and can find plenty of cozy spots to catnap without fear of being stalked by a coyote.

Learn more about why the indoor life is the best — and safest — choice for your feline friend by visiting the Indoor Cat Initiative website sponsored by Ohio State University's School of Veterinary Medicine at www.indoorcat.org.

A British cat named Puss bears the distinction of being the oldest cat on record. The feline Methuselah passed away in 1939 at the astonishing age of 36 — an astounding 162 in human years!

How Old Is Your Cat?

Unlike dogs, cats don't go gray in the muzzle when they reach their senior years. But figuring out a cat's age — in human years — can be done. First, however, you need to let go of the popular myth that "one cat's year equals seven human years." That's just not the case.

Veterinary experts report that a 1-year-old cat is roughly equal to a 15-year-old person. A 2-year-old cat is similar to a 24-year-old person. Cats reach senior status by the age of 7 and their golden years at 12. Here's an age comparison chart on cats from ages 1 to 21:

Age of Cat	Comparable Human Age	Age of Cat	Comparable Human Age
1	15	12	64
2	24	13	68
3	28	14	72
4	32	15	76
5	36	16	80
6	40	17	84
7	44	18	88
8	48	19	92
9	52	20	96
10	56	21	100
11	60		

The Anatomy of a Cat

More than the other carnivores, cats have evolved to eat flesh almost exclusively. Therefore they have also become the most highly adapted for hunting and devouring prey. Here are some amazing facts about the anatomy of this wonderful creature.

Basic Structure Cats have a uniform structure. Unlike the dog, whose breeding has produced many different body types, most cats have an almost identical physical structure. The exceptions are the Manx and the Japanese Bobtail.

Brain The cat's brain is more like a human's than a dog's. The cat is considered one of the most highly intelligent animals, along with the ape and the chimpanzee.

Skull The jaw is the most significant feature of a cat's skull.

Ears With a remarkably acute sense of hearing, a cat can hear tones 1.5 octaves higher than people can. Because 27 muscles control each ear, a cat can turn its head quickly to determine the source of a sound. Ear position also expresses feeling. Upright ears mean a cat is content; flat ones mean it is angry. If the ears point forward, the kitty is extremely happy or excited.

Eyes In relation to body size, cats have the largest eyes of any mammal. A cat's field of vision is about 185 degrees. Cats do not have eyelashes.

Whiskers Cats have 24 whiskers, in 4 rows on each side. Whiskerlike hairs are also located throughout a cat's fur. Cheek and eyebrow whiskers are coarse and wiry, each with a root replete with nerve endings. They help the cat sense differences in air pressure so it can judge distances and assess whether it can fit through a small opening.

Nose A domestic cat's sense of smell is about 14 times stronger than a human's. Cats have twice as many smell-sensitive nasal cells than we do; they pick up scents we are not aware of. During nocturnal hunts the cat relies primarily on its nose to locate prey.

Teeth Cats have 30 teeth (12 incisors, 10 premolars, 4 canines, and 4 molars). Kittens have baby teeth, which are replaced by permanent ones at about 7 months. The teeth are designed to puncture and tear the flesh of prey.

Mouth Cats have a special scent organ, called the Jacobson's organ, located in the roof of the mouth. It analyzes smells—and is the reason cats seem to grimace when they encounter a strong odor. Cats also smell through their nose.

Tongue When drinking, the cat uses its barbed tongue to scoop up liquid and move it back down the throat.

Skeleton The skeleton of the cat has 245 bones. Because the cat has no collarbone, it can squeeze into narrow passages and climb and walk atop narrow fences.

Spine The cat's spine is extremely flexible because of the loose connection of the vertebrae. This enables the cat to rest comfortably in a number of poses as well as to stretch, jump, climb, and position its head to clean almost any part of its body.

Muscles A cat's muscles are powerful and quite large in proportion to the rest of its body.

Coat The cat's three-layered coat protects it from both heat and cold. A cat sheds much of its coat for summer, a process triggered by the lengthening of daylight hours. The outer coat (the guard hairs) keeps the cat dry and warm. The middle layer (the awn hairs) and the innermost and softest layer (the down hairs) help regulate temperature.

Tail The cat is the only animal that can walk with its tail upright. Its tail contains 10 percent of its bones, and its main function is to help cats with balance, especially while running and jumping. It is also a barometer of the cat's emotional state.

Feet The cat is equipped with soft pads on the bottom of the feet, giving it an advantage as a silent, effective hunter.

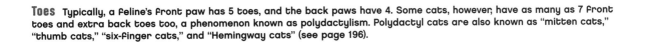

Toes Typically, a feline's front paw has 5 toes, and the back paws have 4. Some cats, however, have as many as 7 front toes and extra back toes too, a phenomenon known as polydactylism. Polydactyl cats are also known as "mitten cats," "thumb cats," "six-finger cats," and "Hemingway cats" (see page 196).

Claws Sharp, curved, retractable claws are a cat's first line of defense. Each forepaw has an extra claw called the dewclaw, which is used to trip running prey. Made from the same protein as human fingernails, claws grow in layers; the outer one is shed every 4–6 weeks. Cats scratch to maintain their claws, to mark territory, and simply to enjoy the sensation.

Astrology for Cats

Ever wonder why Floozy just doesn't behave like all the other Persians on the block or why Elvis actually comes when he's called? It could be that his sun sign is showing. Linda Frano, an astrologer for over 30 years and a member of the American Federation of Astrologers and the International Society of Astrological Professionals, offers this guide to your cat's special astrological profile. Knowing what you can or can't expect from your cat will hopefully contribute to a more loving and understanding relationship. Visit Angelsastrology.com to have your cat's complete chart interpreted.

Aries: March 21 to April 20. Your Aries feline might be quite the surprise at first—at least until you let him know who's boss. Fierce and quick, he strikes unnoticed and proves it with his continual gifts left for your viewing pleasure. Red/orange colored, Aries cats are very playful, sometimes displaying way too much energy. Give him lots of room and greens to munch on. It will put out some of that fire.

Taurus: April 21 to May 21. These gorgeous cats love the outdoors and can often be found in the garden among the flowerbeds. A Taurus cat is quite happy to lounge around all day, until its insatiable appetite must seek a mouse treat. Short and stocky, this cat can be quite a meowful and must watch its diet, for its laid-back attitude doesn't exactly burn butt. It doesn't matter, though, because despite its gluttonous ways, a Taurus cat is beautiful and will adore you just as you are.

Gemini: May 22 to June 21. Get ready for the playmate of the century. Quick and feisty, Gemini cats always hit the mark. They are great at aerial catches, so be sure to keep those bird feeders high. These cats are always on the prowl and extremely sensitive to sounds. Frequently found sleeping or lounging in high places, they are thin and agile and enjoy frequent small meals. Although they can easily entertain themselves, they prefer companionship, feline or otherwise.

Cancer: June 22 to July 23. These cats are very possessive of their owners, whom they will follow everywhere. They often hang around the kitchen; their love of seafood is notorious, and attempting fishing is not below them, whether from pond or aquarium. They are finicky eaters but love sweets, so watch their weight. Keep a source of water nearby for drinking, and never raise your voice around them, for they are oh so sensitive to all emotions and will retreat if threatened. They are generally expressive and intuitive.

Leo: July 24 to August 23. Here is the true feline displayed in all its glory. Leo is the head honcho, the king or the queen of the house. The Leo cat is the boss, and that's all there is to it. Just show this cat how much you worship it, keep it groomed and pampered, and it will provide you with love like no other. Leos rule the heart and will surely win yours. They are often noted for their beautiful coat.

Virgo: August 24 to September 23. They are athletic, agile, and quick, with every move well balanced. Be sure they always have a toy to care for and amuse themselves with. They are often finicky and enjoy frequent small meals of little delicacies. They love frequent playtimes and appreciate a good window for bird watching. They'll love you even more if you stick to healthful foods, including greens and catnip.

Libra: September 24 to October 23. This cat just wants everyone to get along and is more than willing to give up a tasty morsel to some other houseguest to ensure that all goes well. They are very social and love to be at your side. Because their ruling planet is Venus, they are usually very attractive. They love to be kept in beautiful and peaceful surroundings.

Scorpio: October 24 to November 22. Not merely possessive, these cats *own* you. They might even try to mark you and your clothing, so be sure to put your things away carefully. They also like to take special items to a secret stash site. Psychic, sensitive, and curious, they can get themselves into trouble while investigating unknown territories such as walls and heating ducts.

They can be cautious around strangers and will usually hide until they are sure all is well.

Sagittarius: November 23 to December 21. The Sagittarian cat is the hippest of all. It's the one that will show the whole tribe the way. This cat is often the leader and loves outdoor adventures. It can be fiery in nature but not necessarily impulsive. These cats relate well to other pets, if those pets make it possible, and they love to communicate. Think of that sly and cool Sylvester the Cat. Must have been a Sagittarius.

Capricorn: December 22 to January 20. Cappy Cats don't like to share, so don't even think about taking their comfy belongings from them, and make sure their companions are on the submissive side. They are earthy, and subtly beautiful, calm, and comfortable with who they are. Capricorn cats exude assuredness.

Aquarius: January 21 to February 19. These electric, magnetic kitties will do anything for attention. You're bound to have a lot of fun with these cats. They often act as the ringleader of many other animals. They crave companionship and lots of playtime. Wired for sound, they love to talk and will benefit from socializing. They can develop their own group of furry friends, whom they'll consider family.

Pisces: February 20 to March 20. This cat needs to feel loved and adored by you. Frequent petting is required. Keep it close to your heart, and it will reward you with endless devotion. This cat will miss you terribly when you're not at home. Keep the catfish coming, and you'll keep this feline happy and content. But keep the noise and stress to a minimum, for this cat feels intense emotions and will retreat if feeling stressed.

18 Politically Correct Explanations of Cat Behavior

The cat does not barf hairballs; he is a floor/rug redecorator.

The cat does not break things; she helps gravity do its job.

The cat does not fear dogs; they are merely sprint practice tools.

The cat does not gobble; she eats with alacrity.

The cat does not scratch; he is a furniture/rug/skin ventilator.

The cat does not yowl; he is singing off key.

The cat is not a "shedding machine"; she is a hair relocation stylist.

The cat is not a "treat-seeking missile"; she enjoys the proximity of food.

The cat is not a bed hog; he is a mattress appreciator.

The cat is not a chatterbox; she is advising me on what to do next.

The cat is not a dope addict; she is catnip appreciative.

The cat is not a lap fungus; he is bed selective.

The cat is not a pest; she is attention deprived.

The cat is not a ruthless hunter; she is a wildlife control expert.

The cat is not evil; she is badness enhanced.

The cat is not fat; he is mass enhanced.

The cat is not lazy; he is motivationally challenged.

The cat is not underfoot; she is shepherding me to the next destination, the food dish.

The 6 Nutritional Needs of Cats

Cats are classified as obligate carnivores — big meat eaters, that is — but some felines won't turn down an occasional non-meat selection, such as grass, green beans, or yogurt.

A cat's digestive system contains a fairly short, small intestine and a small stomach. This design is best suited for a diet that is concentrated, highly digestible, and low in residue.

Among carnivores, cats rank among the most specialized meat eaters. They possess special biochemical mechanisms that allow them to benefit from eating a diet high in protein and fat and low in carbohydrates. Like all mammals, cats require the following six nutritional needs in order to thrive:

1. **Water** — Cats need clean, fresh water daily. Seventy percent of the feline body is composed of water, which also helps flush out toxins and keep a cat hydrated.

2. **Protein** — Cats need to consume more than twice the amount of protein (pound for pound) that a dog or person does. Top protein picks are meat, poultry, fish, and dairy products. Protein consists of amino acids, a body's building blocks.

3. **Fats** — People fret about how much fat they eat, but felines need a fairly high percentage of fat from animal sources. The reason is that these sources contain essential fatty acids required to absorb and transport certain vitamins inside a cat's body.

4. **Minerals** — Specifically, cats benefit by eating foods that contain certain minerals. Topping the list are calcium, chloride, iron, magnesium, phosphorus, potassium, and zinc.

5. **Vitamins** — Like people, cats need two types of vitamins: water-soluble (vitamins B and C) and fat-soluble (such as vitamins A, D, E, and K).

6. **Energy** — This need comes in the form of carbohydrates (sugars and starches). Cats possess special enzymes capable of breaking down and converting sugars and starches into nutrients that their bodies can use.

The average canned or dry cat meal is the nutritional equivalent of eating five mice.

Why isn't mouse-flavored cat food available? It's because the test subjects (cats, naturally!) turned up their noses at the formula!

I'm in the Mood for Love: Feline Mating Rituals

To get the lowdown on the feline facts of life, we appreciate these insights offered by Marty Becker, DVM, a veterinarian, best-selling author, popular veterinary correspondent for ABC's *Good Morning America,* and host of PBS's *The Pet Doctor with Marty Becker.*

1. **Calling all tomcats!** When a queen needs to attract a male cat from a distance, she puts up the olfactory equivalent of billboard advertising. The female cat has scents called pheromones in her urine that indicate to suitors her fertility and location.

2. **What's all this yowling about?** About 20 percent of queens have a preheat, during which they make shrill, discordant caterwauling noises, rub up against anything and everything, roll, tread in place, or claw themselves forward on the carpet while dragging slightly elevated hindquarters. Cat owners often mistake these antics for an indication of extreme pain. However, this feline break-dance is simply a way to attract a partner.

3. **Looking for many suitors.** Many people view female cats as sexually promiscuous creatures. One of the reasons for this notion is that when female cats are in heat, they call out to let males know about it. They also mate frequently and often with different males that have fought with each other to win mating rights.

4. **Who's your daddy?** A litter can be sired by more than one feline daddy. In fact, studies show that cats who copulate only once get pregnant only 50 percent of the time. Unlike human females, cats do not ovulate (release their eggs) until after several matings have taken place. This is because cats (in evolutionary terms) are solitary hunting creatures. Females seek to mate frequently with more than one male before releasing their eggs, to heighten the chance of fertilization and maintaining genetic variety in the feline gene pool.

5. **Details on the actual act.** During copulation, the queen will scream and attempt to break free by turning and rolling, or striking at the tom with her claws. In what looks like a judo move, the tom grasps her by the neck with his teeth to prevent her from biting him. The stalking courtship may take hours, but mating lasts from one to four minutes. Actual penetration and ejaculation take only a few seconds. There are barbs on the male cat's penis, and these are structured in a way that makes penetration easy but withdrawal painful for the female cat. It is actually the withdrawal process that stimulates the female.

6. **Forget about pillow talk.** After sex, the tom runs off and the queen has what is called an "after reaction," meaning that she'll roll or thrash around like a fish out of water and clean herself. This reaction may last up to 10 minutes. The queen is typically ready to mate again in as little as 5 minutes or up to 30 minutes, and may allow up to 30 matings in a heat cycle with multiple toms.

7. **Only when I'm good and ready.** Intact adult males can also be ready to perform, but the queen ovulates only when in season. In nature, females come into season during the winter solstice, as daylight and temperatures increase, giving birth 60 to 65 days later when food is most abundant. In controlled cat colonies, with 14 hours of light, 10 hours of darkness, and constant temperatures, female cats will breed year-round.

8. **Being fertile for forever.** A female is able to bear young as early as 7 months of age and remains fertile until about age 9 years. Unless spayed, she will enter heat cycles multiple times during the breeding season, typically from January or February to October or November. By comparison, a male cat's fertility time period can start as young as 6 months and last 14 years or more if he is not neutered.

9. **Uniquely feline.** Unlike other companion animals, female cats in season, or heat, are induced to release eggs from the ovary by the physical act of mating. This is called reflex ovulation and is nature's way of making sure that sperm and egg are most likely to meet. This is also why queens stay in heat (estrus) for 2 to 19 days.

3 Ways to Tell If Your Cat Is Pregnant

You can informally try to tell whether your cat is expecting kittens. Within 18 to 20 days of conception, a pregnant cat's nipples will turn pink and enlarge. Another sign of pregnancy (and far trickier to detect) is the presence of what feels like a string of pearls in her abdomen.

For more conclusive tests, book an appointment with your veterinarian, who can perform the following tests to confirm feline pregnancy:

1. An ultrasound can be performed on a cat as early as 22 days into the pregnancy. A veterinarian can detect the heart rate of the fetuses starting from day 26.

2. A blood test can verify a pregnancy, providing the cat is at least 30 days into her pregnancy.

3. A radiograph can identify the number of kittens in the litter by day 45. At this point, the kittens will have mineralized their skeletons and be visible on an x-ray.

Birthing Rituals

When the birth date nears, the mother-to-be tends to seek out a secluded "birthing den" — a private place. In the wild, females pick places where they can remain quiet, undetected by would-be predators. In your home, offer her a quiet location with soft bedding.

During pregnancy, cats tend to be low maintenance. Serve your cat a good-quality commercial diet high in calories that meets the growth needs for her soon-to-be-born kittens. Expect her to develop a huge appetite. Most queens consume three times their normal portions after delivery and while nursing the newborns.

Up to a day before delivery, many females exhibit restlessness. They pace, pant, cry, self-groom, and nest — all signals that labor has started. The cat's body temperature will also drop. She will seek out her quiet place to roost and start to purr.

During the second stage of labor, hard contractions begin, followed by the birth of the kittens. They tend to arrive within 30 minutes to an hour of one another, with the entire litter appearing within six hours.

In the third stage, the placenta passes. The mother quickly devours it, along with the kittens' urine and feces. This instinctive action can be traced to cats in the wild, who learned to destroy any evidence of a new family so that roaming predators would not attack.

The proud new mother may experience vaginal discharge that is black or reddish in color for up to three weeks postpartum. This is normal. However, if her discharge is bloody or con-

1. Flea anemia is ranked as one of the top causes of death in neonatal kittens. Provide protection during pregnancy and lactation by applying a veterinarian-approved flea topical medicine such as Revolution.

2. Keep your female cat up-to-date on her vaccinations, but do not vaccinate her during her pregnancy. Fetuses and newborns are vulnerable to live viruses used in modified live-virus vaccinations, especially feline distemper.

tains pus, contact your veterinarian. The cat may have developed a uterine infection.

What about the proud papa? Most times, the daddy has pulled a disappearing act during the entire pregnancy and birthing ritual. In natural colonies, toms sometimes kill newborn kittens, and females cooperate to protect the litter, even when a kitten is not their own.

"No matter how much cats fight, there always seems to be plenty of kittens."
— ABRAHAM LINCOLN

The 5 Developmental Stages of Kittens

Well-socialized cats are more likely to have well-socialized kittens. Kittens learn from their mother's calm or fearful attitude toward people. Although feeding time is an important time to establish a bond, it's also vital to include petting, talking, and playing in order to build a kitten's "people skills." Kittens are usually weaned at six or seven weeks but may continue to suckle for comfort as their mother gradually draws away from them. Orphaned kittens, or those weaned too soon, are more likely to exhibit inappropriate suckling behaviors later in life. Ideally, kittens should stay with their littermates (or other role-model cats) for at least 12 weeks.

Kittens orphaned or separated from their mother and/or littermates too early often fail to develop appropriate "social skills," such as learning how to send and receive signals, what an "inhibited bite" means, how far to go in play-wrestling, and so forth. Play is important for kittens because it increases their physical coordination, social skills, and learning. By interacting with their mother and littermates, kittens learn "how to be a cat" and explore the ranking process (determining "who's in charge").

Kittens that are handled 15 to 40 minutes a day during the first seven weeks are likely to develop larger brains. They're more exploratory and playful and are better learners. Skills not acquired during the first eight weeks may be lost forever. While these stages are important and fairly consistent, a cat's mind remains receptive to new experiences and lessons well beyond kittenhood. Most cats are still kittens, in mind and body, through the first two years.

The following information, generously provided by dumbfriendsleague.com, outlines the kitten's stages of development.

1. Neonatal Stage (birth to 2 weeks) The newborn kitten is blind, deaf, and weak, and it can crawl only a few inches at a time. Its only desire is for food and warmth. When Mom leaves the nest, it will cry, sounding like a tiny trumpet. At this stage the newborn kitten is learning to orient itself toward sound. By the second week its eyes are beginning to open, and the competition for rank and territory among littermates begins. Separation from the mother and littermates at this point can lead to poor learning skills and aggression toward people and other pets, including other cats.

2. Socialization Stage (2 to 7 weeks) By the third week, the sense of smell is well developed, and the kitten can see well enough to find its mother. By the fourth week, smell is fully mature and hearing is well developed. The kitty starts to interact with its littermates. At this age the kitten can walk fairly well, and its teeth are beginning to erupt. By the fifth week, sight is fully mature, the kitten can right itself, run, place its feet precisely, avoid obstacles, stalk and pounce, and "catch prey" with its eyes. The kitten begins self-grooming and grooming its brothers and sisters. And, by the sixth and seventh weeks, it begins to develop adult sleeping patterns, motor abilities, and social interaction.

3. Active Stage (7 to 14 weeks) The kitten become very active at this age. Its social and object play help develop its physical coordination and social skills. Most of its learning is accomplished by observing its mother. Social play includes belly-ups, hugging, ambushing, and licking. Object play includes scooping, tossing, pawing, mouthing, and holding. Social/object play includes tail chasing, pouncing, leaping, and dancing.

4. Ranking Period (3 to 6 months) The kitten is now influenced by its littermates and members of other species. It now is able to discern and observe ranking (dominant and submissive status) within the household, including among humans.

5. Adolescence (6 to 18 months) The kitten is now experimenting with its sense of dominance and often will challenge humans. If the kitten is not spayed or neutered at this age, sexual behavior will begin.

How and Why Cats Purr

Someone once said, "A cat's purr is the sound of mystery and enigma."

Profound words, indeed. The velvety vibrations of the cat's purr have long intrigued scientists and cat lovers alike. Although it was once commonly believed that cats and kittens purr only when happy, new research shows that cats purr for other reasons as well. And a cat's purr may also have the potential to heal a variety of ailments.

Here are nine facts and theories on purring:

Of all the sounds cats make — including meowing, hissing, growling, chirping, and grunting — the purr has piqued the most curiosity among both feline fans and the veterinary medical community.

The exact mechanism cats use to purr remains one of life's big mysteries. But experts are sure of three things: Air moves through the lungs, causing the diaphragm to vibrate and produce purring; purring emanates from vibrations in the chest and abdominal regions; and purring is produced by blood passing through the vena cava, a large vessel located in the thoracic and abdominal cavity.

Cats are quite talented. They can purr while both inhaling and exhaling. People can't do that. Don't believe it? Try making a purring sound while inhaling.

Purr vibrations occur so quickly that they cannot be caught on high-tech imaging equipment such as ultrasound or MRI.

Cats that are under anesthesia or unconscious for some other reason do not purr.

Cats purr when they're happy, sick, or even in the process of dying. Why pain, sickness, and death would cause a cat to purr as if purely happy is a bit of a paradox — and a mystery.

Frightened felines may purr to communicate submissiveness to other cats to avoid a confrontation or a fight.

A female cat will purr when she is giving birth and whenever she is caring for her kittens. Her newborn kittens will purr in response.

Nursing kittens have the ability to purr and nurse at the same time.

Cats and Scents

If you plan to go nose-to-nose with your cat, you both will lose. Here's why:

1. People have about 5 million odor-sensitive cells. That pales in comparison to a cat's endowment of about 200 million odor-sensitive cells.

2. Cats also rely on scent glands located in their paws, head, and base of the tail to transmit information to the other cats. When cats rub on objects with their faces and bodies, they are leaving an olfactory message to other cats. This is the feline equivalent of a business card for other cats to sniff and interpret.

3. Cats pick up the scent of pheromones (chemicals produced by a female cat to signal her readiness to breed) and other subtle smells through the vomeronasal organ (VNO), or Jacobson's organ. Cats practically taste the smell in the air using the VNO and by performing what's known as the Flehmen Reaction (FR). Also known as gaping, this reaction occurs when a cat opens its mouth slightly and curls back its lips in a grimace-like expression. The cat draws in air to capture the scent.

Those Wise, Wily Whiskers

Most people assume cats sport whiskers only on their cheekbones and above their eyes. But look closely and you will see that cats also have whiskers on the backs of their front legs and wispy ones under their chin.

Whiskers, which are really extensions of the cat's skin, serve these main purposes:

Whiskers assist cats in identifying objects in their environment that they might not be able to see. These sensitive protrusions are also capable of detecting small movements and changes in air currents. The whiskers can rotate and scan for signs of possible prey. The bundles of nerves in the whiskers supply the brain with lots of data.

Whiskers serve as measuring tools for cats. The width of the whiskers along the sides of the face assess openings, letting the cat know if its body is wide enough to fit through.

Whiskers convey feline moods. When relaxed, a cat's whiskers are held slightly to the side. But when it becomes intrigued or feels threatened, the whiskers automatically tense up and point forward.

Whiskers are technically known as vibrissae. Grab a magnifying glass and take a close look. A cat's whiskers are about twice as thick as the hair on its coat, and the roots of the whiskers are about three times deeper than hair roots. Cats sport from 8 to 12 long whiskers on each side of their upper lip. They lose a few whiskers at a time as part of the normal shedding process, never losing them all at once.

The Fountain of Youth Has Whiskers

Cat lovers have always known that living with a cat is life-enhancing, but now researchers have compiled a mountain of statistics showing that cats can add as many as 10 years to a person's life.

Dr. Horst Becker's astonishing claims come from the most exhaustive study ever undertaken on the relationship between humans and their pets. Seven scientists of the Berlin Longevity Institute worked for 5 years before drawing their conclusions. Becker and his associates studied more than 3,000 cat owners and found that these wonderful animals have an almost instantaneous calming effect. Just moments after a person picks up a cat, his or her blood pressure drops and the heart rate slows. According to Becker, "We didn't zero in on the amazing powers of cats until our figures began to show they acted like a fountain of youth for their owners. Any pet will add a few years to its owner's life, but cats add a whopping average of 10.3 years to people who've had one since childhood."

"Someone had said that the pupil of the cat's eye marks the time: at midnight, noon, sunrise, and sunset, it is like a thread; at four o'clock and ten o'clock morning and evening, it is round like a full moon; while at two o'clock and eight o'clock, morning and evening, it is elliptical like the kernel of a date."
— FROM AN ANCIENT CHINESE TEXT

The Eye of the Cat

Cats' eyes have always fascinated us. When gazing into those deep green liquid pools, we find them both mysterious and alluring. Films and books have made mention of them, as well as countless poems. There are even gemstones named cat's-eyes. Here are some interesting facts about the eye of the cat.

1. It is widely believed that cats can see in the dark, but though the cat's night vision is far, far superior to that of humans, they can't see in total darkness.

2. Because cats evolved as nocturnal hunters, the ability to see well at night was essential to their survival.

3. In darkness, cats' eyes are able to function in approximately one-sixth of the light needed for human vision. Cats are able to do this by increasing the amount of light that passes through their retinas. A reflecting layer called the tapetum provides the cat with this ability. It also makes a cat's eyes shine at night when a bright light is pointed at them.

4. The cat's iris can quickly help it adjust to changes in light. The iris will narrow into a vertical slit when a light is bright, and it will open completely when it is dark.

5. The size of the cat's eye is proportionally larger than those of the human, and the lens and cornea allow the cat to focus more effectively because they are both curved and therefore direct more light into the eye.

6. Cats cannot see directly beneath their nose.

7. Cats are not colorblind, but their ability to see color is not as enhanced as ours. They usually see the world in shades of blue and green.

8. The vision of a cat is typically 20/100, compared to 20/20 human vision. The cat can see faraway objects, but up close, such items may appear fuzzy or blurred. This may explain why cats sniff when greeting friends — the sense of smell provides a more accurate means of identification.

A cat cannot see directly under its nose. This is why the cat cannot seem to find tidbits on the floor.

9. When your cat stares at you for a long time and then starts to slowly blink its eyes, it is sending you kisses. If you want to let it know that you feel the same way, just give it a long stare and then a slow blink.

10. Most white cats with blue eyes are deaf.

11. Those dark lines connecting to a cat's eyes are called mascara lines.

Who can believe that there is no soul behind those luminous eyes?
— THEOPHILE BATES

How to Read a Cat's Ears

Cats use their extraordinary ears to listen for prey, convey emotions, and regulate body temperature.

Cats move their ears to concentrate sound, allowing them to hear better. The wide-ranging ear movement enables the cat to focus each ear independently. Thus cats can listen for sounds from any direction without turning their head.

When it comes to emotions, the feline ears take different poses to express different feelings. Here are the four main types:

1. **Contented** — a cat will relax its whiskers, half-close its eyes, and point its ears slightly forward and slightly outward.

2. **Interested** — a cat will make its ears rigid to better enable the earflap to collect and enhance the sound.

3. **Angry and ready to attack** — a cat will flatten its ears, point them back against its head, and move its whiskers forward.

4. **Scared** — a cat will flatten its ears parallel to the ground.

Finally, a cat's ears regulate its internal body temperature. When the body is too warm, blood vessels in the pinnae, or upright portion of the ears, dilate, and the cat loses body heat. When the body becomes too cold, the blood vessels constrict, and the cat's body heat increases.

Alert

Offensive Threat

Increasing Fear

Fight or Flight

Defensive Threat

Snarl

Coats of Many Colors and Patterns

No two cats are exactly alike — and that includes littermates. Sure, you can easily distinguish a Persian from a Siamese, but if you look closer, you will see marking and color differences within the same cat breed.

But no matter if a particular cat is purebred or what's diplomatically referred to as "random-bred": (AKA a mutt), the coat pattern in the feline world falls into one of five main categories — solid, tabby, bi-color, tri-color/tortoise-shell, or colorpoint.

1. Solid

Cats with uniformly same-color coats used to be rare, but thanks to selective breeding, they are abundant in all parts of the cat-adoring world. They come in basic colors such as black, blue, brown, red, and white, as well as more exotic-sounding hues such as lilac and fawn. This category of cats consistently sports one color right down to the root of each hair, without recognizable stripes, spots, ticking, patches, or shading. Solid-color cats can be found in many breeds. In Great Britain, these cats are often referred to as "self-colored."

Some coat colors are called "dilute"; a recessive-color gene "pales" the original color. That explains why a chocolate-colored cat can give birth to kittens with a lilac-colored coat.

These are the common solid colors and typical breeds that sport them:

Black. Ebony to the roots, this color is found in many breeds, including the Persian, the Oriental Shorthair, and the Bombay.

Blue. Solid-blue breeds including the aptly named Russian Blue, the Korat, and the Chartreux.

Brown. This hue is seen in breeds such as the Havana Brown and the Chantilly Tiffany.

The Russian Blue is possibly the direct descendant of the royal cat of the Russian czars.

Red. Known as red, this color looks more like orange and can be found in many breeds.

White — As white as snow, this color is found in many breeds. The white Persian is particularly striking.

Lilac. This pale pinkish gray shade is found in breeds such as the Oriental Shorthair.

Fawn. This warm pink or buff color is found in many breeds.

Chocolate. This rich medium-brown hue can be spotted in Oriental breeds.

Cream. Described as a light, warm beige color, cream is found in many breeds.

2. Tabby

There is certainly no shortage of tabby cats on the planet! Many breeds, as well as random-bred domestic cats, have tabby coats. The term *tabby* does not refer to a breed of cat, however. Any cat with naturally occurring stripes, dots, and/or swirling coat patterns is a tabby — the term refers to a coat pattern, not a coat color. The word *tabby* comes from the French word *tabis,* a subtly patterned silk. Of the several tabby varieties, these three are generally recognized by cat breeders and fanciers:

Mackerel. This coat pattern features thin vertical stripes that curve on the side of the torso. An *M* pattern is commonly spotted on the forehead. This ranks as the most easily recognized tabby pattern. Many breeds possess it, including the American Shorthair and the Maine Coon.

Classic, or blotched. Cats with this tabby coat pattern also sport an *M* pattern on the forehead, but their body features wider stripes and even bull's-eye swirls. Examples of breeds with this pattern include the American Shorthair and the Maine Coon.

Ticked, or agouti. This tabby coat pattern is distinguished by bands of colors in a salt-and-pepper style. Each hair is decorated with alternating bands of light and dark colors, ending with a dark tip. The classic example of a breed displaying the ticked pattern is the Abyssinian, followed by the Singapura.

3. Bi-color

Next after the solid patterns, bi-color ones are easy to identify because cats with these coats have white fur paired with another color. Bi-color cats often have white patches splashed on their paws, chest, and belly. This coat pattern includes the tuxedo (a black-and-white cat) as well as the Van pattern (a white cat with color on the top of its head and tail). This bi-color pattern can show up in breeds such as the Himalayan and the Turkish Van. For political trivia fans, Socks, the black-and-white cat who roamed the White House during the Clinton administration, exemplifies the tuxedo bi-color coat pattern.

4. Tri-color/Tortoiseshell

Tri-color coat patterns are as easy to identify as one-two-three. The common pattern features white, black, and red colors — or dilute versions (white with cream and blue). White rules as the majority color. Calicos, with their patched patterns of white, black, and red, are common examples of the tri-color coat pattern. By contrast, a pattern featuring more black and red than white is identified as a tortoiseshell, or "tortie." Calicos and torties tend to be female, and when the pattern does appear in males, those males tend to be born sterile.

5. Colorpoint

Cats with this coat pattern are blessed with highlight hues, worthy of the envy of other felines. Their tails, paws, and faces appear darker in color than the rest of the body because these "points" contain more pigment.

In fact, the amount of pigment distributed in the hairs depends on temperature — the cooler the temperature, the more pigment is produced. The skin temperature in the extremities is a few degrees lower than that of the body and therefore attracts more pigmentation.

Points vary in color and shade, ranging from dark brown (seal), to red (flame), to blue and even lilac. Popular breeds with colorpoint patterns include the Siamese and the Himalayan. Common colors include the following:

Seal point. Pale fawn or cream body, with deep seal brown on the points

Blue point. Platinum gray or bluish body, with deeper grayish blue points

Chocolate point. Ivory body, with warm milk-chocolate points

Lilac point. Even milk-white body, with lilac-gray or pinkish points

Fawn point. Ivory-cream body, with warm beige to taupe points

Red point. Warm cream-white body, with deep orange-red points

Cream point. White body, with cream points

Tortie point. Creamy white, with seal and red patches on the points

Lynx point. Light-colored body, with dark tabby stripes on the points

Tortie lynx point. Creamy white or pale fawn body and beige-brown points, with dark brown tabby markings and patches of red

To Sleep, Purrchance to Dream

While we can only guess at the topics cats focus on during dreamtime, scientists confirm that cats do enter a stage of sleep that includes dreaming.

Sleep ranks as the most time-consuming activity in a cat's life, as felines snooze, on average, 17 to 18 hours each day. Just like human sleep, feline sleep falls into two main stages — REM (sleep characterized by rapid eye movement, during which dreams happen) and non-REM (deep sleep). You can tell when a cat enters REM sleep because it is likely to move its whiskers and twitch its legs. If you look closely, you might even detect the subtle movement of the eyes behind closed eyelids. Studies that used electroencephalograms (EEGs) to read brain activity in sleeping cats have indicated that REM sleep occupies about 30 percent of their sleeping time and that their brain-wave patterns during REM are similar to those of humans. During REM sleep, cats have been observed changing their body postures, making pawing movements, twitching their whiskers, flicking their ears, and even vocalizing.

Burton Price's Favorite Joke
Q. Who sleeps with cats?
A. Mrs. Katz

What they dream about remains a mystery. At best guess, animal behaviorists speculate that cats dream about previous experiences, such as dashing away when the mail carrier appeared, cackling at crows perched on a branch, or devouring a plate of tuna.

In non-REM sleep, or deep sleep, the feline body quietly works to repair and regenerate bones and muscles and fortify the immune system to defend against disease. The only movement you can detect during this sleep stage is the rise and fall of the chest as your cat inhales and exhales.

A 15-year-old-cat has probably spent 10 years of its life sleeping.

The Need to Knead

The feline ritual of rhythmically pumping the paws up and down starts at birth. Newborns push their paws around their mother's nipples while they suckle, to hasten the flow of milk. Even after they are weaned, kittens remember the happy feeling of a full belly that came with kneading and nursing. As adults, kneading — jokingly referred to as "making biscuits" — evokes a sense of comfort.

Some cats can go a little overboard, though. Some drool while kneading, and others become so enthusiastic that they drive their sharp claws into human legs. If your cat is turning you into a pincushion, make a habit of keeping those claws trimmed. Cats will also knead in the air — when they are upside-down in a lap being combed, for instance. They knead on a surface when they are happy, too. It is definitely a sign that a cat experiences pleasure, and it shouldn't be discouraged.

How Cats Groom Themselves

Next to sleeping, grooming gobbles up most of a cat's waking hours. Some cats can spend up to 50 percent of their time keeping their coats looking their best.

Marty Becker, DVM, veterinarian, and popular veterinary correspondent for ABC's *Good Morning America*, provides some insights into why and how cats groom themselves:

Have you ever noticed that your cat routinely primps more than a teenager before a big prom date? Why all the fuss about the fur?

Instinctively, cats know that a healthy coat of fur helps keep them hot or cold depending on the season, distributes their unique scent — or cat-cologne, if you will — across their whole body, provides a first line of defense against external parasites, and provides a social bonding opportunity for cats to groom each other. Adult cats spend up to 50 percent of their waking time in some form of grooming activity.

A cat's coat is also a health barometer. Each of the hundreds of thousands of individual hairs is made of keratin (the same thing claws are made of) and are 95 percent protein. When cats feel bad, they stop grooming. That's why one sign of feline malnutrition is dull, lifeless fur.

For a cat, grooming comes as naturally as breathing. And most cats can groom themselves quite handily. However, older cats, overweight cats, arthritic cats, and extravagantly furred breeds such as Persians need some human help.

Cats are very ritualistic in their grooming behavior and can do it on autopilot. Kittens rely on Mom to groom them for the first couple of weeks of life (she'll even lick around their anus to stimulate them to defecate), but by the third week, they start a grooming process

A spokes-cat for Boraxine peddles Maple City Self Washing Soap, first made around 1880. The company was sold in 1908 and is better known today as Procter & Gamble. This brand was easily eclipsed by Ivory.

seared over the millennia into a very pre-dictable front-to-back pattern.

Cats start by licking their lips. Then using this moisture to wet the side of their paw, they take the damp paw and rub it over the side of their face. This process is repeated for both sides of the face. After a good face washing, they lick the following items, in this order: They start with their front legs, shoul-der, and side. Moving down the body they se-quentially hike each rear leg straight up in the air while cleaning their genitals, then the legs themselves. To finish, they lick their tail, starting from the base and moving out to the end that flicks. Yup, it's a tip of the nose to the tip of the tail groom-a-thon.

The end result: a beautiful coat that's ready for the human family members to caress. A caress that can soothe stresses, make you relax, or bring a smile to your face.

Grooming Overload

Cats who groom excessively suffer from a disorder known as psychogenic alopecia. They may not only groom to the point of leaving bald spots on their skin, but also pull hair out. Ruling out a medical reason for the condi-tion, these cats often need anti-obsessive medications containing fluoxetine (such as Prozac). Con-sult your veterinarian if your cat fits this description.

Antigravity: The Feline Butterology Theory

If you drop a buttered piece of bread, it will fall on the floor buttered side down.

If a cat is dropped from a window or other high and towering place, it will land on its feet.

With this in mind, if you attach a buttered piece of bread, but-tered side up, to a cat's back and toss them both out the win-dow, will the cat land on its feet? Or will the butter splat on the ground?

In theory, even if you are too lazy to do the experiment your-self, you should be able to deduce the result. The laws of but-terology demand that the butter hit the ground, and the equally strict laws of feline aerodynamics demand that the cat not land on its furry back. If the combined construct were to land, nature would have no way to resolve this paradox.

Therefore, they simply do not fall. That's right, you clever mortal (well, as clever as a mortal can get), you have discov-ered the secret of antigravity! To expand on this theory, a cat attached to a buttered piece of bread will, when released, quickly move to a height where the forces of cat-twisting and butter repulsion are in equilibrium. This point can be cali-brated as desired by scraping off some of the butter, provid-ing lift, or removing some of the cat's limbs.

Most of the civilized species of the universe already use this principle to propel their spaceships. The loud humming heard by most sighters of UFOs is, in fact, the purring of several hundred tabbies. Larger craft use the Maine Coon breed and a lengthwise loaf of sliced sourdough. The one obvious dan-ger occurs, of course, when the cats manage to eat the bread off their backs. This will cause them to instantly plummet. This, as you all know, happened in Roswell 50 years ago.

Of course, the cats will land on their feet, but this won't do them much good, since right after they make their graceful landing, several tons of red-hot starship and a bunch of be-wildered aliens will crash on top of them.

How Cats Fall

An important factor contributing to a cat's survival is its ability to land on its feet. It is not uncommon to hear of a cat that has fallen from a considerable height and survived. This is one reason why cats are fabled to have nine lives. But keep in mind that a cat can be injured by falling from even a short distance, so always treat your cat gently. Here are some of the mechanisms that enable cats to fall safely. Although this system of balance is present in most mammals, in the cat it is highly refined.

1. A cat's ear contains a vestibular apparatus, a tiny fluid-filled organ that is responsible for balance. This organ is comprised of tiny chambers and tubes lined with sensitive hairs. It is also filled with liquid and tiny floating crystals. When your cat moves, the fluid in its ear shifts, transmitting information about its body position. The vestibular apparatus becomes active as the cat falls, enabling it to know which way is up. Your cat can move itself in midair by simply adjusting its body position.

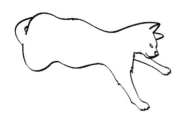

2. The "righting reflex" lets your cat know which way is up and allows its head, in less than a tenth of a second, to rotate to the right-side-up position. The cat then brings its front legs close to its face, ready to protect its head from impact. It twists the upper part of its backbone to align the front half of its body with its head. The cat then bends its hind legs so that all four limbs are ready for landing. Finally, the cat twists the rear half of its body to catch up with the front.

3. Nerves in the spine also contribute to a safe landing by allowing the back end of the body to turn around.

4. Your cat's skeleton also helps it adjust. A cat's backbone moves faster than that of other animals.

5. The tail acts as a counterbalance to prevent overrotation.

6. By arching its back to absorb some of the shock of hitting the ground, the cat usually lands successfully and without injury.

Top 10 Cat Behavior Issues

Amy D. Shojai is an IAABC certified animal behavior consultant and the author of 22 pet-care titles, including *Chicken Soup for the Cat Lover's Soul* and *PETiQuette: Solving Behavior Problems in Your Multipet Household*. Here's her take on cat behavior:

Cats and their caretakers need all the help they can get, and the International Association of Animal Behavior Consultants has stepped up to the plate. Founded in 2003 by Pittsburgh dog trainer Lynn Hoover, the IAABC offers continuing education, resources, and certification to experts in the dog, parrot, horse — and CAT — behavior fields.

Animal behavior consultants can evaluate, manage, and modify a wide range of challenging animal behaviors. They build and strengthen relationships between the human and pet members of a household. And they help minimize the stress of living and interacting with your critter companions.

Animal behavior consultants emphasize preventing behavior problems by teaching owners how to create a proper feline atmosphere and enriching the environment, one that provides pets with what they need to stay emotionally healthy, as well as teaching them how to live in harmony with all members of the household — human and otherwise.

In the best of all possible worlds, our companion animals understand us, we understand them, and all live peaceably together. But when the fur (or feathers) flies, take comfort in knowing help is available. Visit www.iaabc.org for more information and a listing of members and certified consultants to help with your feline's foibles.

Animal behavior consultants often address these top ten behavior concerns, plus many other companion animal issues:

1. Hit-or-miss bathroom behaviors

2. Aggressive behavior toward people or other pets

3. Shy or fearful behaviors

4. Household issues, such as countertop cruising or swinging from the drapes

5. Excessive vocalization, such as loud-mouth kitties yowling for attention

6. Destructive behaviors, including chewing, digging, scratching, and clawing

7. Introductions of new pets or humans to a resident pet

8. Environmental challenges, such as transitioning outdoor cats inside

9. Attachment issues, separation anxiety, and related problems

10. Self-directed behaviors, such as excessive grooming, obsessive tail chasing, or self-barbering of fur

"I hate to bother you, but I've run out of things to knock off the kitchen table."

Cattitudes: How Cats Think

To provide insights into how cats regard the world, we called on Alice Moon-Fanelli, Ph.D., a certified applied animal behaviorist and assistant clinical professor at Cummings School of Veterinary Medicine at Tufts University in North Grafton, Massachusetts, and Arnold Plotnick, DVM, a veterinarian board-certified in internal medicine who operates a cats-only practice in New York City and is the medical editor for *Catnip*, a national newsletter.

1. Cats prefer set routines. They like to wake up at a certain time and eat at a certain time, and they expect you home at a certain time. They quickly learn your daily schedule and adapt accordingly. Cats' penchant for regularity may partially explain why some wake us up a few minutes before our alarm clock chimes. When their inner body clock sounds the signal, it's time to get out of bed and start a new day.

2. Cats abhor confusion and change. That's why some scoot under the bed when your Aunt Dottie pays a surprise overnight visit or when they see packing boxes stacked in your living room.

3. Cats are big into turf. They feel most comfortable inside familiar surroundings. This is how they differ from dogs. Dogs are people oriented. They want to join their favorite people pals and go to strange new places. Cats prefer to stay at home. Your house is their castle.

4. Cats love to sleep. Some Rip Van Felines will snooze up to 18 hours a day. I've yet to meet a cat with insomnia. They have favorite nap spots, typically perched on a high shelf or on a sunny windowsill, tucked inside a dark closet, or snuggled up among stuff that smells like you.

5. Cats put the *c* in *candid*. They never pretend. They never lie. If they don't want to sit on your lap, they will

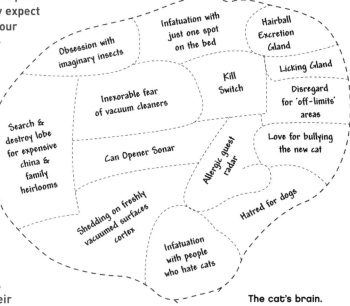

The cat's brain.

make like Houdini to wiggle free. It's nothing personal; they would just rather be elsewhere.

6. But if your cat wants to snuggle up next to you, it will unabashedly march over and sit on top of the Sunday newspaper you're trying to read. Anything for attention.

7. *Finicky* is often the first adjective to come to mind when describing cats around a food bowl. But the fact is, far too many felines are fat; more than 25 percent of all pet cats are overweight. Just like some people, some cats eat out of boredom or to fight stress.

Perhaps one reason why some cats seem fussy about food is that felines possess only 473 taste buds — compared to the 9,000 or so in people.

In addition, the taste buds on the cat's tongue are poorly developed. Felines compensate for a weak sense of taste by relying on their powerful sense of smell. **For cats, it's all about the aroma.**

8. **Cats are generally solitary creatures.** They prefer to introduce themselves to people rather than be approached by strangers. That explains why cats seem to seek out the particular person in the room who (a) hates cats, (b) is afraid of cats, (c) is allergic to cats, or (d) is ambivalent toward cats. Such a person tends to sit still and refrain from addressing the cat or making eye contact. In response, the cat will approach and mark the person by rubbing its cheek or body against the person's leg.

9. **Cats, like people, come to like and dislike certain individuals of their own kind.** Within a multicat household, cats have preferred associates. That explains why, in the same house, Cat A can be best pals with Cat B, but tolerate Cat C, and downright despise Cat D. According to Dr. Moon-Fanelli, physical space matters between cats who share the same home. Generally speaking (there are always exceptions). females and related cats tend to be friends. Unrelated males — especially if not neutered — can be competitive and combative.

31 Body Language Signals and What They Mean

Your cat's body language is its only way of communicating with you, a way of saying, "This is how I feel" or "This is what I need." Observing the kitty closely and learning to understand its body language will enable you to forge an even closer bond than the one you have now. Here are some common body signals and what they are telling you.

1. When the cat arches its back with the fur on end, it wants you to leave it alone. However, if you're dealing with a kitten, you're receiving just the opposite message — "I'm ready to play."

2. When the cat expands its body and tries to look as large as possible, it is feeling threatened and wants the enemy to be frightened.

3. When the cat kneads you with its paws, it is letting you know that it is happy, although experts disagree on the significance of this behavior.

4. When the cat rubs against you with its body or the side of its face, it is marking you as its property and warning other cats to stay away. But if the cat rubs you with its head or nose, it is letting you know that it loves you.

5. The cat stretches out its legs when it is feeling relaxed and confident. But if the hind legs are bent, the cat is feeling timid or confused.

> "To respect the cat is the beginning of the aesthetic sense."
> — ERASMUS DARWIN

6. If your cat exposes its tummy, it is paying you the greatest compliment. The kitty trusts you. Trust is everything to a cat. But don't make the mistake of thinking this is an invitation to be tickled in that sensitive area. In response, the cat will probably take a swipe at you.

7. When its tail is flying high, the cat is feeling great.

8. If the cat twitches its tail, it usually means it is excited.

9. If the tail is tucked in, something is scaring the cat. Flattened ears and dialted pupils express even more fear.

10. When the cat swishes its tail in broad sweeps, it is feeling annoyed.

11. Tiny swishing movements indicate that the cat is feeling excited or curious about something.

12. A quivering tail is the greatest gesture of love the cat can show you. It's letting you know how special you are.

13. If the cat holds its tail stiffly at a right angle to its body, it's saying, "Hi, I missed you."

14. When the cat moves its tail rapidly from side to side, it is telling you to get out of its face.

15. If the tail is held low and fluffed out, the cat is letting you know that it is frightened.

16. If the cat holds its tail in a straight and vertical position, with the tip also straight, it is expressing extreme happiness.

17. When the ears are back and the body is low to the ground, your cat probably has done something wrong and is feeling a little guilty.

18. When the cat blinks or winks at you, it is letting you know that you're a good friend and all is well.

19. When the cat's eyes are wide open, it is feeling curious and happy.

20. If its eyes are half-closed, the cat may be ready to sleep. But if it remains awake with eyes half-closed, it might be a sign that the cat is sick.

21. If the pupils are dilated, the cat may be frightened of something and could possibly get aggressive.

22. Pricked ears generally indicate that a cat is curious about what is going on.

23. When the ears are up and directed toward a new sound, the cat is feeling happy and well.

24. If a cat is frightened, it will flatten the ears against the side of the head; this is a sign of submission. But if the ears are positioned forward, the cat may be ready to attack.

25. When the cat's body position is crouched low to the ground or is advancing at a crawl, watch out! It's about to attack.

26. A quiet clicking noise may mean that the cat has spotted an unsuspecting mouse and is about to enjoy a snack.

27. Purring means that she is content and happy, but it can also mean just the opposite.

28. If a cat hisses, it is letting you know it's really unhappy and you'd better get out of its face.

29. When the cat makes a slight chirping sound, it is just being friendly and saying hi.

30. If the whiskers are fully extended, the cat is feeling either happy or curious.

31. If the whiskers are pulled back close to the face, the cat is either ill or feeling irritated.

Note: Keep in mind that some body language may indicate an illness and suggest a trip to the vet. By learning your kitty's body language, you will be able to discern its state of health.

The 9 Most Common Tail Positions and What They Mean

Hail, hail, to the feline tail; it performs many roles. Physically, the tail acts as a rudder, helping the cat to maintain balance. Communication-wise, the tail acts as a mood barometer by allowing the cat to convey many emotions and messages without uttering a single mew.

1. **Hoisted high.** A confident, contented cat holds its tail high in the air as it roams its turf. A tail that is erect like a flagpole signals a happy mood or a friendly greeting. Cats often send this message as they approach a welcoming person. If the top third of the tail twitches as the cat nears you, this means that he totally adores you.

2. **Question mark.** A tail bent in a question mark shape often signals that the cat is in a playful mood. Get out the toys!

3. **Flying low.** A tail positioned straight down, parallel to the legs, may represent an aggressive mood. Be wary. There are breed exceptions, though. Persians, Exotics, and Scottish Folds normally carry their tail straight down, lower than their backs, when they walk.

4. **Tucked away.** A tail curved beneath the body signals fear or submission. Something is making that cat nervous.

5. **Puffed up.** A pipe cleaner of a tail reflects a severely agitated and frightened cat who is trying to look bigger in order to ward off danger.

6. **Whipping.** A tail that whips rapidly back and forth indicates both fear and aggression. Stay away.

7. **Swishing.** A tail that swishes slowly from side to side usually means the cat is focused on an object. Cats often swish the tail right before they pounce on a toy mouse, for instance. It is part of their predatory positioning.

8. **Twitching.** A tail that twitches just at the tip is a sign of curiosity and excitement.

9. **Cat-to-cat.** A tail wrapped around another cat is equivalent to a person casually putting an arm around a favorite pal. It conveys feline friendship.

Why Do They Do That? 17 Mystifying Behaviors Explained

Ever wonder why your cat licks your face or tries to groom you, why it kneads with its paws, why it pushes its head against you, or why it purrs? Here are some explanations for the most common and often curious cat behaviors.

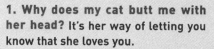

1. Why does my cat butt me with her head? It's her way of letting you know that she loves you.

2. Why does my cat rub up against me? He is actually marking you as his property by leaving his scent on your body.

3. Why do cats use a litter box? This trait is a carryover from the cat's wild ancestry. Cats had to hide their feces in order to prevent predators from picking up their scent.

4. Why does my cat lick my face? Grooming between cats is a sign of affection and caring. When little Petunia licks your face or hair, she is showing you that she cares for you.

5. Why does my cat attack my ankles? He is actually playing a little war game with you. These mock attacks are his way of drawing you in.

6. Why is my cat so curious? Cats are predators and therefore are always on the hunt, whether for food or a new adventure.

7. Why does my cat bring me dead things? Your cat is presenting you with these gross little gifts for one of two reasons. He's either demonstrating his affection by giving you a gift or he thinks you need instruction on how to properly catch a mouse or bird.

8. Why does my cat roll on her back? Exposing the most vulnerable part of her body is her ultimate expression of trust.

9. Why doesn't my cat like catnip? It's a genetic thing. Some cats have the "I love catnip gene" and others do not.

10. Why does my cat love high places? The higher up she is, the better the view she has of her domain.

11. Why do cats hate getting wet? Many cats actually enjoy water but want to experience it in their own way. They don't appreciate humans choosing the time and place for them.

12. Why does my cat interrupt me when I'm on the phone? Your cat can't see the person you're talking to, so you are obviously talking to her.

13. Why does my cat bite me while I'm petting her? Your cat is not biting you out of spite. She loves the petting, but if you linger on a sensitive area of her body, her reflexive response is to nip at you to make you stop.

14. Why does my cat seem to sulk? Unfortunately, cats often are intimidated by our size and react to disciplinary action by retreating.

15. Why do my cat's teeth chatter when he sees a bird? This is most likely a sign of agitation that occurs because he sees a bird but knows that he can't get to it. The sound he produces is a combination of teeth grinding together and lips smacking.

16. Why is my cat always on the wrong side of the door? Cats are highly territorial and mark their turf with their scent. Your cat wants to get to his marked area before the scent wears off.

17. Does my cat think? Cats are considered a highly intelligent species. They are certainly intelligent enough to do whatever is necessary to protect themselves, avoid danger, and obtain food.

Why Cats Paint

It turns out that some Leonardo da Vincis and Monets emerged within the cat crowd as far back as 3000 B.C. in ancient Egypt, where cats were revered. In 1990, Australian archaeologists working at the tomb of Vizir Aperia along the Nile discovered painted scrolls from cats named Etak and Tikk.

Cat painting has become a popular activity in recent years and has led to the creation of Cat Art Societies around the world; a popular book, *Why Cats Paint: A Theory of Feline Aesthetics,* by Heather Busch and Burton Silver (Ten Speed Press, 1994); and a documentary (*Why Cats Paint,* 1999), which spotlights prominent cat artists and their works. As cats deepen their roles as family members, more feline art will likely be created and displayed internationally.

One of the most famous feline art galleries is the Philip Wood Gallery in Berkeley, California, which opened its doors in 1994 and hosted the first international exhibition of paintings and works created by cats. Among the works on display is a limited-edition print of *Beam Me Up* done by world-renowned cat artist Orangello.

To introduce people to the world of cat painting, officials from the Museum of Non-Primate Art (MONPA) have answered the following frequently asked questions regarding feline painters on their website (www.monpa.com):

Do all cats paint?
Only a very small percentage of domestic cats are known to paint. While about 60 percent of domestic cats (USA data) will demarcate their territory with claw marks on trees, furniture, etc., perhaps only 0.001 percent will take paint on their paws and apply it to a surface. However, with the recent growth of interest in feline aesthetics due to the international success of books like *Why Cats Paint* and the formation of Cat Art Societies around the world, it is anticipated that more owners will encourage their cats to paint, and the number of cats actually painting and exhibiting is expected to rise dramatically in the next few years.

Are some breeds more likely to paint than others?
Cats who don't mind getting their paws wet, such as Birmans, are more likely to take to painting than other breeds, but there appears to be no one breed that is more "artistic" than any other.

How do I know if my cat will paint?
The best way of determining whether your cat has artistic ability is to carefully observe it in certain situations. For example, does it sit and contemplate the marks it makes in its litter tray? Are the marks curved or aesthetic in any way? Does it make marks on the wall with the fine litter left on its paws after using the litter tray? Does it scratch in just one place on the furniture, as if constructing an ongoing artwork? Does it take great care in arranging and presenting its prey or parts of prey? Does it like to play and make patterns with its dry cat food? Does it like to watch TV, and can it recognize other animals on the two-dimensional screen? If you show your cat a picture of cat food from a cat food advertisement, will it sniff at it? Does your cat make territorial claw marks on trees? If you make marks in the same places your cat does on trees or furniture, does it show interest? If you can answer all of these 10 questions with a yes, then you may well have a cat that will paint. The fewer the positive responses, the less likely it is. (Count each *yes* as 10 percent. For example, four *yes*'s will give your cat a 40 percent chance of painting.)

How can I encourage my cat to paint?

If you think your cat has artistic ability, there are several things you can do to encourage it to paint. The most effective method is to leave a saucer of nontoxic scented acrylic paint (warmed to room temperature) near its regular toilet areas or by its litter tray, along with a sheet of smooth board that will easily take the paint. Cats commonly mark their territory with scent by leaving their feces in a prominent position or by spraying their urine around so that its unique smell will act as a warning to other cats. Cats will often use their front paws to scrape at earth (or litter) that has been soaked with their urine and then transfer the scented earth to a tree trunk or wall. In this way they can get their scent into a higher position, from where it will carry more effectively. Because the ammonia in the scented acrylics smells a lot like cat pee, cats will mark with it in the same way they do with the earth. Obviously, if you can manage to mix in a little of the cat's own urine with the paints, the cat will be more likely to use them. After a while your cat will come to see that the unique marks it makes in applying the scented paint are just as representative of itself as the scent is. These marks become its signature, and the moment the cat begins to manipulate them in order to refine that signature (and make it more distinguishable from other cats' marks), it is making its first genuine aesthetic gesture.

How can you tell if a cat painting is genuine?

Because of the recent growth in popularity of cat art and the often very large sums of money that are made from their sale, forgeries are inevitable. While most curators of cat art have little trouble in spotting a fake, the only way to ensure that a work is genuine is to make sure it is accompanied by a sequence of verifying photographs, which clearly show the cat actually working on the painting. Video footage is even better. Most genuine works come with the seal of a Museum of Non-Primate Art and a certification number.

Riou, at age 7, tends to destroy his masterpieces shortly upon their completion. Like so many tragic artists before him, he stands in the way of his own success.

How can I tell what my cat's painting is all about?

As we can't actually talk with our cats, it's almost impossible to determine what they are trying to express and whether their work is intended to communicate something to us or other cats, or whether it's simply a self-rewarding activity (SRA), as some biologists believe. Other biologists argue that it is no more than a form of territorial marking behavior. However, mounting evidence suggests that some cats' marks are aesthetically motivated and should be treated as genuine works of non-primate art. Dr. Arthur Mann proved that cats are capable of making crude representational works but for some unknown reason, often render them upside-down — a practice known as Invertism. The most accessible information on what cat painting is all about can be found in *Why Cats Paint*, by author and critic Burton Silver and photographer/curator Heather Busch. This clearly written work analyzes the work of 12 major cat artists and attempts to uncover their possible motivations. As the authors say in the preface, it is their hope that by exploring the marks that cats make, they may stimulate interest in a unique feline way of perceiving the world and perhaps derive valuable insights from it.

If we don't know what a cat painting is about, how can we give it a title?

Almost all cat paintings are given a title, by either their owners or curators. The reason for this is straightforward. "Just as surrounding a painting with an expensive frame and hanging it in a gallery places a value on it, so too, naming a work confirms artistic intent and allows the work to be legitimated and taken seriously. Certainly, by titling a cat's painting, we provide a context within which judgments of aesthetic worth are made. A title such as *Fluff and Kittens* is likely to suggest a different level of worth than *Maternal Arrangements* or *Coital Consequences #4*. Be that as it may, titles provide a clue, a starting point, no matter how arbitrary or contextually based, from which to begin our journey of discovery into the fascinating world of feline creativity. Without them, we run the risk of dismissing cat art as being no more relevant than the mindless territorial daubings of the graffitist." — From *Why Cats Paint*

Who is the legal owner of a cat's painting?

Animals cannot hold copyrights or have moral rights, so the legal owner of the copyright of a cat's painting is the person or persons who supplied the materials the cat used to make the painting. If your cat stays at a boarding cattery that offers a creative program and supplies paints and canvas, then any works the cat completes during its stay will belong to the cattery. If the owners supply the materials, then they will own the works.

Why did a woman in California pay an artist $5,000 to paint her cat to look like a pig? What made a New York stockbroker spend even more than that to have the image of Charlie Chaplin painted on his cat's posterior? Following the international success of **Why Cats Paint**, Burton Silver took the concept one step further with his book, **Why Paint Cats: The**

Cats Who Paint

1. **Mattisa**, who lived in the 1880s, was the first of the modern artistic cats. She was the star of what was billed as the most extraordinary traveling exhibit in the world, offering "compelling sketches occasioned by deft movements of the paw." The show's proprietor, a Mrs. Broadmoore, was actually a man disguised as an upper-class matron. True to the program's promises, audiences were delighted by the resulting "pawtraits." It wasn't until . . .

2. **Lu Lu**, a seal lynx, has collaborated on paintings with Wong Wong, a small Havana Brown. They have produced over a dozen paintings, and their most famous, *Wonglu*, sold at auction for $19,000 in 1993.

3. **Pepper** started his career in 1981, experimenting with moisturizer on a mirror. As he grew more bold, he went on to using cosmetics and finally arrived at acrylics. In 1988 a showing of his work took place, the first ever all-cat art exhibit. Pepper retired in 1999 when his companion, another painter cat named Venus, became crippled with arthritis.

4. **Misty** couldn't seem to limit herself to just canvas, as she was known to extend her artwork to surrounding walls. In 1993, her painting *Interring the Terrier* sold for $21,000. It has been interpreted as depicting a headless dog being stuffed into a red armchair by two frogs and a sardine.

5. **Minnie Monet Manet** was known to swat at her canvases with lightning speed and was so occupied when she worked that she rarely looked at her own canvases until they were complete. In the hope that talent runs in the family, an art lover bought one of her kittens for $20,000.

6. **Charlie** was inadvertently trapped in an unplugged refrigerator for five hours but managed to put his suffering to good use. When he was finally freed, Charlie began painting, showing a special penchant for painting the refrigerator. Authors Busch and Silver suggested that this new pastime helped Charlie overcome the effects of his ordeal by redesigning the place of his trauma.

7. **Bootsie** took up painting to relieve his stress after a single difficult week, in which his family moved, he was neutered, and he he his got tail caught in a heating unit. The new pastime worked; within four years he had five art exhibitions and earned over $75,000. In 1993 he won the Zampa d'Oro (Golden Paw) award at the Esposizione dell'Arte Felino in Milan.

Ethics of Feline Aesthetics. The book shows the cat as canvas instead of artist. The author's conclusions about the impact of painted cats on the future of art will provoke and amuse.

8 Fine Documentaries About Cats

Big cats. Small cats. Musical cats. Felines have forever intrigued and mystified humans. We present a sampling of some documentaries — each distinctive in its quest — that help us better understand cats of all sizes — tame and wild — real and reel.

1. *Cats Without a Home,* **produced by The Humane Society, Silicon Valley (2006)** This 30-minute documentary features homeless cats in Santa Clara County, California. Six individuals who work to reduce unnecessary euthanasia of homeless cats are also profiled. Learn more by visiting www.catswithoutahome.com.

2. *A Cat's World,* **Wall to Wall Television Productions (1997)** This 50-minute documentary, under the supervision of executive producer Jonathan Hewes, is one in a six-part series that also profiles dogs, lions, chimpanzees, elephants, and horses. The feline show explores the "secret world" of felines, who have lived alongside people since the days of ancient Egypt. This show reveals how cats really perceive us and the world around them.

3. *City of the Wild Cats,* **Australian Broadcasting Corporation (2000)** This Australian documentary produced by Hugh Pearson profiles the heritage and story of a wildcat colony living within the ancient ruins of central Rome. It takes an inside look at ferals who behave more like lions than the average household moggie (that's an Australian term for a mongrel housecat).

4. *Private Life of a Cat* **(1947)** This earlier film features superb footage of two domestic cats welcoming a litter of kittens into the world. We see the kittens being born and nurtured by their mother, while an interested and proud dad lends his support; the absence of humans is refreshing. Beautifully filmed by Alexander Hammid and Maya Deren, well-known Czechoslovakian filmmakers who worked between the two world wars. Available with English subtitles. Google this film and watch it on the Internet.

5. *Puss in Books,* **Iron Frog Productions (1998)** This documentary spotlights true literary cats — felines throughout the United States who call a library their home. Most of these felines are cared for by the Library Cat Society, an organization whose mission is "to promote the establishment of a cat or cats in a library setting." This documentary goes behind the scenes — and between the stacks — to tell the story of library cats and the challenges of coping with library patrons who are allergic to — or afraid of — felines. Learn more at ironfrog.com.

6. *The Standard of Perfection: Show Cats,* **Public Broadcasting System (2005)** Recognized for injecting comedy into his series of nature-themed documentaries called Animal Magic, producer Mark Lewis turns his camera lens on the world of show cats. He captures champion cats, human showmanship, pride, some tears, passion, and jubilation as owners claw their way to the cat world's highest honor.

7. *Ten Million Wild Cats,* **Australian Broadcasting Corporation (2002)** According to film producers Gary Steer and Tina Dalton-Hagege, Australia ranks as the only continent completely overrun by feral cats — estimated to exceed 10 million. This documentary explores where these feral cats came from, how they grew so quickly in numbers, and the role they've played in destroying the country's fauna and native animals.

8. *The Truth About Cats, Dogs, and Lawn Chemicals,* **Sanford Lewis and Jody Shapiro (2006)** This documentary demonstrates the frightening connection between lawn-care treatments and serious illnesses among our companion animals. The truth: Lawn chemicals are toxic; they stick to paws and fur when dogs and cats walk on grass, sidewalks, parks, and streets, and are ingested and absorbed through the skin. The film uses humor, reality-TV documentation, and expert interviews to show pet owners how to have beautiful, chemical-free lawns that are safe for animals. To learn more, visit catsdogslawns.org.

17 New Year's Resolutions for Cats

1. I will not flush the toilet while my human is in the shower.

2. I will not puff my entire body to twice its size for no reason after my humans watch a horror movie.

3. I will not slurp fish food from the surface of the aquarium.

4. I will not lean over to drink out of the tub, fall in, and then run screaming into the box of clumping cat litter.

5. I will not use the humans' bathtub to store live mice for late-night snacks.

6. I will not eat large numbers of assorted bugs, then come home and barf them up, so the humans can see that I'm getting plenty of roughage.

7. My human will never let me eat her pet rat, and I am at peace with that.

8. I will not help myself to Q-tips, and if I do, I will not attempt to stuff them down the drain to dispose of them.

9. I will not perch on my human's chest in the middle of the night and stare into her eyes until she wakes up.

10. As fast as I am, I must remember that I cannot run through closed doors.

11. I will remember that I am a walking static generator. My human does not need my help installing her new computer.

12. I will not sit on pizza.

13. I will not knead my male human's groin at 3 A.M. with claws extended. It seems to cause him some discomfort, and he wakes up all grumpy.

14. I will not attempt to stop the human's snoring by sticking my paws into his mouth.

15. I will not run through the house with a condom wrapper in my mouth when my human's grandmother is visiting.

16. I will not teach the parrot to meow in a loud and raucous manner.

17. When the humans play darts, I will not leap into the air and attempt to catch them.

Part Four

Tender Loving Care and Training

"Cats are intended to teach nature has a purpose."

They warm our laps; they lower our blood pressure. They show us how to land on our feet, how to stretch, how to smile. They keep mice on the run, and they can make even the shabbiest couch look chic. Given all they do for us, isn't it only fair that we pay them back in kind?

Your furry baby, while still a tiny kitten, is something to behold. But don't blink or linger on the thought — it will soon grow into a mischievous ball of energy, presenting a host of challenges you might never have anticipated. This chapter will help you answer some of the questions that arise in caring for a cat. What are the consequences of allowing outdoor privileges, and how can you minimize the negative ones? Do other members of your household — including those of the canine persuasion — respect your cat's rights? How do you get a cat out of a tree? What should be done about feral cats?

us that not everything in
— GARRISON KEILLOR

In other words, how do we show our little lions the same regard that they seem to always show us? Knowing the proper techniques for caring for your cats is the best way to tell them "thank you" for all they do.

In this chapter we'll help you choose a new cat well suited to your lifestyle and taste. We spotlight the most popular cat breeds, their special characteristics, and their talents. Are you looking for a pet that will provide company? Consider the Korat, known as the "Good Luck Cat of Thailand," which converses with humans in a variety of sounds. Does your home already include a dog? No problem for the American Shorthair, which gets along with kids and other pets just fine. On the other hand, if you love the idea of a cat with an interesting past, meet the semi-longhaired Siberian, which roamed Russia for centuries before gracing American shores in 1990.

While *Planet Cat* is not intended as a medical reference, we also provide basic information about typical ailments and ways to ensure maximum health for your feline friend. We are grateful to Dr. William O'Reilly, DVM, who advised us about the medical information we provide here and who showed us even more ways to tell our furry friends "I love you."

The Cat's Bill of Rights

These guidelines are shared among cat lovers everywhere.

Humans shall make no law respecting an establishment of boundaries or prohibiting the free exercise therein, or abridging the freedom of access, or the right to peaceful assembly. In other words: *The cat is entitled to GO OUTSIDE anytime it wants.*

A well-carried provisional chamber, being necessary to the fulfillment of a feline's whims, shall not be infringed. *The cat is entitled to EAT anytime it wants.*

The right of the feline to be secure in its domain and left undisturbed shall not be violated. *The cat is entitled to SLEEP anytime it wants.*

Humans shall issue no warrants or decrees or edicts as prescribed to the demarcation of possessions or property that are in direct conflict with right to life, liberty, and the pursuit of feline affirmation. *The cat is entitled to SLEEP anywhere it wants.*

The feline shall be immune to all criminal accusations, indictments, and complaints. The accused shall enjoy the right to a speedy and impartial dismissal of any and all charges provided said feline's compulsory right to obtain any or all witnesses, including character witnesses, are obtained in his favor. *Cats can DO anything they want as long as it's cute.*

Neither serfdom, vassalage, nor involuntary servitude will be tolerated, except by said cats in proprietorship of their humans. *What the cat SAYS, goes.*

No *Canis familiaris* shall, in time of peace or at any other time, be quartered in any dwelling without the consent of the potentate, nor in time of war, but in a manner to be prescribed by sovereign. *NO DOGS in the house without the cat's permission.*

The right of the feline to be protected against unreasonable search and seizure shall not be breached or infringed upon at any time or any place. *DON'T DISTURB the cat when it is sleeping.*

24 Things Cats Do for Us

Warm our laps.

Give us someone to talk to.

Help lower high blood pressure.

Bring the winter air inside, nestled in their coats.

Create a kindred feeling with other "cat people."

Keep mice on the run.

Make us smile.

Inspire poets and playwrights.

Teach us how to land on our feet.

Let us indulge our desires to really spoil someone.

Make our homes warmer.

Remind us that life is mysterious.

Share with us the all-is-well experience of purring.

Instruct us in the luxurious art of stretching.

Show us how to lick our wounds and move on.

Give us cool cartoon characters.

Make even an old worn couch look beautiful.

Open our hearts.

"My therapy is a little different. I don't make your problems disappear, I just teach you how to sleep through them!"

Turn common household objects, such as bottle caps, into toys.

Make us more aware of birds.

Donate their services as alarm clocks.

Display daring acrobatic feats right in front of our eyes.

Contribute to living a longer life.

Make a windowsill more beautiful.

"I'm glad you finally found a stress-management technique that works for you, Bradley."

10 Major Cat Associations and Organizations

For those who love cats and want to learn about individual breeds, there are thousands of cat organizations throughout the country and the world created just to distribute accurate information about cats. Listing them would fill a book. Each of those smaller clubs is governed by larger umbrella organizations that establish goals and policies; they are listed here.

1. Cat Fanciers' Association (CFA)

P.O. Box 1005
Manasquan, NJ 08736
(732) 528-9797
cfainc.org.

The world's largest registry of pedigreed cats is dedicated to the preservation of the pedigreed cat and to enhancing the well-being of all cats. The CFA provides information on cat shows, cat breeds, and cat care; it also showcases top winning cats.

2. Governing Council of the Cat Fancy (GCCF)

5 King's Castle Business Park, The Drove,
Bridgwater
Somerset TA6 4AG
United Kingdom
+ 44 (0) 1278 427575
gccfcats.org

The GCCF is the primary governing body of the cat fancy in the United Kingdom — the feline equivalent of the Kennel Club. The GCCF was established as an independent body in 1910, formed from the three or four cat clubs registering cats at that time. It now has 144 affiliated cat clubs, licenses approximately 135 cat shows, and registers an average of 30,000 pedigreed cats per year. In March 2006, the GCCF was accepted as a member of the World Cat Congress.

3. Co-ordinating Cat Council of Australia (CCC of A)

G.P.O. Box 4317
Sydney NSW 2001
Australia
03 9758 6011
cccofa.asn.au

This national council of all cat-control bodies in Australia was established along the lines of the Australian National Kennel Council. Its goal is to ensure uniform breeding and show rules, thus making it easier for exhibitors to show their cats Australia-wide. It also established policies for the conduct of shows, appointment of judges, registration of cats, definition of classes, and the awarding of championships, to make life easier for the exhibitors and breeders of cats in Australia.

4. American Association of Cat Enthusiasts (AACE)

P.O. Box 213
Pine Brook, NJ 07058
(973) 335-6717
aaceinc.org

The goal of the AACE is to give exhibitors a cat show that is both rewarding and fun and to make sure that ribbons are awarded to the top-quality pets, all in a pleasant, educational atmosphere. They encourage exhibitors to talk to attendees about their breeds, and their goal is to be known as "the friendliest bunch around."

5. American Cat Fanciers Association (ACFA)

P.O. Box 1949
Nixa, MO 65714-1949
(417) 725-1530
acfacats.com

The ACFA's goal is to promote the welfare, education, knowledge, and interest in all domesticated, purebred, and nonpurebred cats, to breeders, owners, exhibitors of cats, and the general public.

6. Fédération Internationale Féline (FIFe)

fifeweb.org for more information on member clubs

This federation represents members in almost 40 countries. Their purpose is to establish uniformity among cat breeds across these countries. This common interest among member organizations has helped create the high standards for which FIFe is internationally known.

7. Canadian Cat Association (CCA)

289 Rutherford Road
S #18, Brampton, ON L6W 3R9
Canada
(905) 459-1481
cca-afc.com

This is Canada's only purebred feline registry with affiliated clubs across Canada. They promote the welfare of all cats in Canada and further the improvement of all breeds by maintaining a registry of purebred cats. To date the CCA has over 190,000 individual cats registered.

8. Cat Fanciers Federation (CFF)

P.O. Box 661
Gratis, OH 45330
(937) 787-9009
cffinc.org

The CFF is a feline purebred cat registry with clubs and judges in the northeastern United States and parts of Canada. The CFF and member clubs put on shows to promote a general interest in cats. These shows raise money to fund programs that educate people on cat care and on the benefits of owning a cat.

9. The International Cat Association (TICA)

P.O. Box 2684
Harlingen, TX 78551
(956) 428-8046
tica.org

TICA is the world's largest genetic registry of purebred and household pet cats, the second-largest registry in North America, and one of the world's largest sanctioning bodies for cat shows. The organization strives to encourage its members to be caring, responsible owners and breeders of cats who work together to promote the preservation of pedigreed cats and domestic cats. The organization's goal is to build the most accurate and comprehensive certified pedigree registry in the world.

10. New Zealand Cat Fancy (NZCF)

Private Bag 6103
Napier, New Zealand
+64 (0) 6 839 7811
nzcatfancy.gen.nz

The NZCF is the primary cat registry and governing body for cat clubs and their members in New Zealand who are interested in the breeding, welfare, and showing of pedigreed and domestic cats. It represents 37 affiliate member clubs, encompassing both specialist and all-breeds clubs throughout New Zealand. The NZCF's goals are "generally to promote, foster, encourage, improve and assist in every way the breeding of cats registered with the Fancy in New Zealand."

The 5 Top Cat Magazines

1. *Cat Fancy*
Arguably the number-one publication on cat care in the United States, this full-color monthly sports the best name recognition in feline-related publications. Each issue includes a cover shot of a specific breed, ten feature stories, plus monthly columns written by top veterinarians and animal behaviorists. In trying to expand its audience to the next generation, *Cat Fancy* recently added a regular column called "Cats for Kids." Each issue also includes a breeder directory and calendar of cat events. To subscribe, contact Bowtie Magazines at www.catchannel.com.

2. *Kittens USA; Cats USA*
These thick annual publications, produced by Bowtie Magazines, are full of oodles of information on everything C-A-T. As their names imply, the first is devoted to addressing the health, nutritional, and behavioral needs of felines during their first year of life, and the second focuses on adult cat issues. To subscribe, contact Bowtie Magazines at www.catchannel.com.

3. *Cat World*
Curious as to how cats live in Europe? This monthly publication based in the United Kingdom features British wit and advice on sharing one's life with a cat. A recent issue profiled the chinchilla cat immortalized in two James Bond films as well as an article on how to survive a relocation with a cat. Regular columns include "Cats on the Couch," breed profiles, and book reviews. To subscribe, visit catworld.co.uk.

4. *Best Friends*
This magazine, published six times a year, designates proceeds from subscriptions to support animals at the Best Friends Animal Sanctuary in Kanab, Utah, and the No More Homeless Pets program. Recent issues spot-

lighted efforts by Best Friends staff and volunteers in caring for animals victimized by natural disasters, including Hurricane Katrina. On the lighter side, a recent feature focused on how two musicians cajoled and relied on "treat bribery" to get 13 cats to vocalize for the *Purrfect Symphony* CD. Stories from past issues are available online in a PDF format. To subscribe, visit best-friends.org.

5. *All Animals*
Published quarterly by The Humane Society of the United States for its members, this magazine profiles cats, dogs, and other creatures, including chimpanzees and whales. The format is inviting, with space for readers to comment, a section of quick takes on news in the animal kingdom, and an expert question-and-answer column. A recent issue offered the top five ways to keep your indoor cat happy. The photos are stunning and expressive. To learn more, visit hsus.org.

3 Great Cat Newsletters

Just as there are dozens of cat breeds, there are hundreds of local and regional newsletters for each. They focus on specific aspects of cats and cat causes. Here are three national newsletters that focus on feline health and behavior.

Alley Cat Action

This quarterly publication is produced by Alley Cat Allies, a national feral-cat resource organization based in Bethesda, Maryland. The entire focus is on advocating humane methods to reduce outdoor cat populations. The publication campaigns for Trap-Neuter-Return (TNR), a management strategy by which stray and feral cats already living outdoors are humanely trapped, evaluated, vaccinated, and sterilized by veterinarians. Those deemed tame are adopted into homes, while those considered too wild are returned to their familiar habitat and cared for by volunteers. Back issues are available online. To learn more, visit www.alleycat.org.

Catnip

Voted the best cat publication in 2004–2005 and 2006 by the Cat Writers Association, *Catnip* is a 24-page monthly published in affiliation with Cummings School of Veterinary Medicine at Tufts University in North Grafton, Massachusetts. As the "Newsletter for Caring Cat Owners," *Catnip* offers four to six features that cover cat issues from allergies to kidney disease to curbing cat spats. In addition, this newsletter conducts independent tests on various feline products and publishes results. Popular columns include "My Cat," written by readers, and "Dear Doctor," featuring answers to cat quandaries from the Tufts advisory board of experts. To subscribe, contact catnipeditor@tufts.edu.

CatWatch

Billed as the "Newsletter for Cat People," this 16-page monthly is published in affiliation with Cornell University's College of Veterinary Medicine at Ithaca, New York. Each ad-free issue offers four to six features on topics ranging from choosing the perfect kitten to understanding advances in anesthesia. In addition, readers are treated to expert advice in a behavior column called "Mind of the Cat," by Ellen Lindell, DVM, and a medical column by James Richards, DVM. To subscribe, contact Belvoir Publications at www.catwatch-newsletter.com.

19 Reasons to Love Cats

1. They're a warm, comforting presence.
2. They're fun to watch.
3. They're beautiful.
4. They're graceful and walk with confidence.
5. They have a mind of their own.
6. They're loyal and loving creatures.
7. They purr.
8. They're affectionate.
9. They know how to relax.
10. They're playful.
11. They're clean.
12. They're courageous.
13. They have dignity.
14. They know how to have a good time.
15. They're never afraid to ask for what they want.
16. They're mysterious.
17. They're inquisitive.
18. Each has its own personality.
19. They're miniature lions.

15 Great Cat-Care Websites

1. **Catsinthebag.org** This valuable site offers great tips for finding lost and missing pets, whether an indoor cat or an outdoor cat. You'll learn how to systematically search and hopefully find little Petunia.

2. **Cats.org.uk** Formed in 1927, Cats Protection (CP) at Cats.org has grown to become the United Kingdom's leading feline welfare charity. Members rescue and find new homes for around 60,000 cats and kittens every year, through their network of 29 adoption centers and 260 volunteer-run branches. The site has enlisted over 5,600 active rescue volunteers.

3. **Cfainc.org** The official website of the Cat Fanciers' Association provides cat enthusiasts with information on breeds, cat shows, junior showmanship, the latest developments in legislative news, and the proper care of cats.

4. **Hsus.org** At the official site of The Humane Society of the United States you'll find hundreds of articles devoted to the care and welfare of our feline friends. The HSUS is the nation's largest and most powerful animal protection organization, working in the United States and abroad.

5. **Kids.cfa.org** This website, offered by the Cat Fanciers' Association, is a great primer for kids who have a budding interest in either owning a cat or the world of cats in general. It offers games such as "match the cats," interactive crossword puzzles, jigsaw puzzles, word jumbles, and coloring pages.

6. **Moggies.co.uk** This site, originating in the United Kingdom, is not much on design but has a wealth of information. Moggies is devoted to the health and well-being

of kittens and cats everywhere. There are lots of great articles and stories posted at this site, as well as information on cat care and adoption services.

7. **Petfinder.com** Enter the breed, sex, and size of the cat you wish to adopt, along with your zip code, and Petfinder.com will locate shelters in your area that have cats and kittens waiting for you to bring them home. Photos and a medical history for each cat are posted on this extensive site, which covers all 50 states.

8. **Petloss.com** This website offers compassion and gentle advice for pet lovers who are grieving the death of a pet or helping a pet that is gravely ill. Here you will find personal support, thoughtful advice, the Monday Pet Loss Candle Ceremony, tribute pages, healing poetry, and much more.

9. **Petplace.com** Nicely designed and high in content, this is perhaps the best of all the feline sites on the Internet. Although not devoted entirely to cats, the cat section is extensive and offers information on adopting or buying a cat, care and behavior, first aid, training and understanding your cat, and a wide variety of other topics.

10. **Pusscats.com** A one-stop shop for cat and kitten information includes cat breed descriptions, cat- and kitten-care tips, cat health and behavior guidelines, and solutions to common cat problems. Browse the picture galleries for cute, funny pictures of cats and kittens, or view images of an assortment of cat breeds.

11. **Scattycats.com** Scatty Cats is an online resource for cat lovers, breeders, and owners. It is devoted to providing valuable information, products, and contacts. Search the cat guide index and dis-

cover a wealth of information on topics ranging from cat anatomy to cats in history.

12. Sniksnak.com/cathealth This site, developed by Pawprints and Purrs, Inc., a nonprofit organization, is highly informative. Their goal is to provide educational services to the public, prevent cruelty to animals, and effect social change in the United States and abroad to ensure that animals are treated with dignity and as loving companions. Their feline index of topics is extensive, and the articles are well written.

13. Veterinarypartner.com This site supports both you and your veterinarian in the care of your companion animals by offering reliable, up-to-date animal health information from the veterinarians and experts of the Veterinary Information Network (VIN), the world's first and largest online veterinary database and community.

14. Xmission.com/~emailbox /index.html This site, online since 1995, celebrates one of the most wonderful creatures in the world: the domestic cat. You'll find entertaining graphics, a huge library of articles, games, great humor, visuals, and much, much more.

15. whiskas.com Select-a-cat is a special program that analyzes the lifestyle information you enter and then recommends the most compatible breed for you and your home.

35 Free Things for Cats

If you're going to pamper your cat, you might as well do it for free. Below is a list of websites that feature cat-friendly products and promotions.

1. **ID tag:** The Humane Society of Canada's Pet Recovery Team wants to help unite families with their lost pets by providing free ID tags. On one side, your cat's name and your contact telephone numbers are printed. The other side has a unique serial number for your cat, and The Humane Society of Canada's toll-free number. The Humane Society will accept calls from anywhere in the world. Go to humanesociety.com, and click on the link "Join the HSC Pet Recovery Team."

2. **Birthday gift:** Join Petmart's Birthday Club and receive a coupon for a free birthday gift for your cat on its birthday. Visit www.complete petmart.com.

3. **Cat food:** Each month, Bil-Jac, makers of dog food and cat food, awards a visitor to the company website with a free bag of dog food or cat food. All you have to do is sign the guestbook at www.BilJac.com.

4. **Cat grass seeds:** Poopsiecat offers a free bag of Natural Oat Grass seeds to satisfy the vegetarian in your cat. Just send them a self-addressed stamped envelope. Details are available at www.poopsie cat.com/sample.html.

5. **Emergency pet sticker:** Alert people that your kitty's inside your home in the event of an emergency by posting a sticker from the ASPCA. Go to aspca.com and click on "In Case of Emergency" to sign up.

6. **Paw points rewards:** If you use Fresh Step kitty litter, you can redeem your points for free cat stuff at freshstep.com.

7. **Cat lovers' e-mail address:** At I-Love-Cats.com you can arrange to express your love for cats in every e-mail that you send. Your new e-mail address will be YourName@I-Love-Cats.com.

8. **Cat lovers' website:** Make your own free cat website at awesome cats.com, complete with guest books, forums, counters, calendars, and other interactive tools.

9. **Cat food recipes:** I-Love-Cats.com has a huge selection of free recipes to create for your feline.

10. **Cat names:** From Abby to Ziegfeld, I-Love-Cats.com has a library of cat names to choose from.

continued on page 242

11. **Low-cost neuter-spay programs:** Lovethatcat.com provides a list of free or low-cost neuter-spay programs in the United States.

12. **Kitty newsletter:** Cozycatfurniture.com provides a free cat newsletter with advice about cat health, behavior, care, and fun. Also, the ASPCA has a free weekly e-mail newsletter that you can sign up for at aspca.com.

13. **Digital calendar:** You and your cat can enjoy a free calendar from friskies.com, with photos of adorable Friskies kitties.

14. **Kitten advice:** Purina will send you free information customized to the age of your kitten at kittenwise.com. Topics range from health and nutrition to kitten grooming. They also send you savings on Purina foods and treats.

15. **Poison-control magnet:** You can sign up to get this handy magnet, complete with the Animal Poison Control Center's toll-free number and Web address. Visit aspca.com, and click on "Poison Control."

16. **Catnip:** Get a free sample of "Purr-furred by the Boss" catnip by sending a self-addressed stamped envelope. Find out more at www.shirleyscatnip.com/free.htm.

17. **Magazine:** Get a free issue of *Cats and Kittens* magazine at www.petpublishing.com/catkit/.

18. **Kitty litter:** Go to the Nature's Earth website and print out a rebate coupon for a free bag of litter at felinepine.com.

19. **Fancy Feast promotions:** Become eligible for special promotions and free offers by visiting fancyfeast.com.

20. **Kitten care kit:** Register for the free Essential Kitten Care Kit, which includes a cat-care booklet, a relaxing CD for your kitten, a coupon for Purina Kitten Chow, a coupon for Tidy Cats brand cat litter, and a "Tell-a-Friend" card to help a friend care for a kitten. Visit https://offers.purina.com/offer.aspx?offer=KCKIT.

21. **Cat journal:** Register at http://www.petparents.com/Association-Registration.asp, and download a free journal in which to keep a personalized record of your cat's medical history and memories.

22. **Cat treats:** Request a free sample of Greenies cat treats at http://smarttreater.com/en/.

23. **Cat food:** At http://www.royalcanin.us/myroyalcanin.html, you can obtain free samples of Royal Health Nutrition products.

24. **Cat-care DVD:** Get a free DVD, *How to Keep Your Pet Healthy*, at hillspet.com.

25. **Planner for providing for your pet's future:** The Humane Society of the United States will provide you with a free kit about making plans for the care of your cat, should your pet outlive you. This gift includes a six-page fact sheet, wallet-size alert cards, emergency decals for windows and doors, and caregiver information forms. Find out more at http://www.hsus.org/pets/pet_care/providing_for_your_pets_future_without_you/.

26. **Cat ring tones:** You and your cat can listen to the soothing sound of a screeching cat on your phone. Down-loads are available at coolfreeringtones.com.

27. **Club membership:** Sign up and receive money-saving offers and a booklet for free at http://www.armhammerpets.com/Register.aspx.

28. **Cat food:** Obtain free Life's Abundance cat food at http://www.premium4pets.com/justforcats.html.

29. **Hartz coupons:** From shampoo to dental chew treats — send away for a free packet of coupons for various products at hartz.com.

30. **Worm medication:** Your cat will be worm free when you go to noworms.com and fill out a simple form.

31. **Virtual kitty:** Download a new virtual friend for you and your cat at meowmix.com. This cat walks, plays, eats, and lives on your desktop.

32. **Vitamins:** At http://countrysidegoldens.homestead.com/nuvet.html, you can send for natural vitamins to support your cat's health.

33. **Health supplements:** Pawmax.com provides a free sample of cat health supplements.

34. **Horoscopes:** Horoscopes are updated weekly for your pet at http://www.veternet.com/horoscopes/horoscopes.html.

35. **Musical postcards:** Pour a cold glass of Guinness, snuggle up with your kitty, and listen to Marc Gunn's Celtic drinking songs for cat lovers. At cat-drinkingsongs.com, you can download one of his free musical postcards to send to your cat-loving friends. And if you like his music, you can buy a CD on the website (and get a few more free gifts).

The 60 Most Common Cat Names

Veterinarians from Veterinary Pet Insurance Company (VPI), the nation's oldest and largest health insurance provider for pets, suggests that new pet owners take time to get to know their new fuzzy family member before deciding on a permanent name. Below are the most popular names for cats in 2005, culled from over 300,000 VPI policyholders.

MALE

1. Max	11. Charlie	21. Toby
2. Tigger	12. Simon	22. Milo
3. Tiger	13. Oscar	23. Buster
4. Smokey	14. Lucky	24. Leo
5. Oliver	15. Jake	25. Rusty
6. Simba	16. Sebastian	26. Oreo
7. Shadow	17. Jack	27. Gizmo
8. Buddy	18. George	28. Felix
9. Sam	19. Rocky	29. Chester
10. Sammy	20. Bailey	30. Harley

"Did you ever notice that there's a million cats named 'Mittens' but none named 'Scarf', 'Hat', or 'Snowsuit'?"

FEMALE

1. Chloe	6. Molly	11. Sophie	16. Jasmine	21. Daisy	26. Bella
2. Lucy	7. Kitty	12. Baby	17. Patches	22. Shadow	27. Abby
3. Cleo	8. Samantha	13. Maggie	18. Sasha	23. Ginger	28. Smokey
4. Princess	9. Misty	14. Zoe	19. Gracie	24. Sassy	29. Annie
5. Angel	10. Missy	15. Callie	20. Precious	25. Lily	30. Tigger

There's a better chance your cat will respond more readily to its name if it ends with an "ee" sound. So, the next time you're picking a name for your cat and feel inclined to name her Countess Olga von Ratzencatcher, consider naming her Kitty instead.

171 Cool Cat Names

1. Abracadabra
2. Absolut
3. Acapulco
4. Ajax
5. Aladdin
6. Alfresco
7. Ali McClaw
8. Anchovy
9. Aretha
10. Armani
11. Babar
12. Bagel
13. Ballofur
14. Ballou
15. Barkney Spears
16. Bashful
17. Beebop
18. Bilbo
19. Blessing
20. Boogoodoogada
21. Borat
22. Botox
23. Brillo
24. Bronx
25. Brooklyn
26. Brooooce
27. Bucephalus
28. Butthead
29. Calamity

30. Cashmere
31. Catpuccino
32. Chairman Meow
33. Charisma
34. Curiosity
35. Daiquiri
36. Dakota
37. Devo
38. Disco
39. Ditto
40. Dog
41. Dracula
42. Dr. Pepper
43. Dumbledore
44. Edward Scissorclaws
45. Eightball
46. Einstein
47. Ewok
48. Fajita
49. Fargo
50. Fatso
51. Felony
52. Fester
53. Fetch
54. Fonzie
55. Foobar
56. Frodo
57. Fungus
58. Furlicity

59. Furris Newler
60. Gandalf
61. Genghis
62. Geronimo
63. Gizmo
64. Godiva
65. Godzilla
66. Gulargambone
67. Habib
68. Hairy Potter
69. Hanukkah
70. Hitchcock
71. Honda
72. Hotdog
73. Inkling
74. Italics
75. Jalopy
76. Jaws
77. Jazz
78. Judge Judy
79. Julep
80. Junk
81. Kabuki
82. Kafka
83. Kahlua
84. Kaiten
85. Kamikaze
86. Karma
87. Kerouac

88. Kismet
89. Kleenex
90. Kramer
91. Laser
92. Latke
93. Laverne
94. Leonardo DiCatrio
95. Littlefeat
96. Lola
97. Luciano Catvarotti
98. Ludwig von Cathoven
99. Macintosh
100. Madmax
101. Magnifical
102. Mao
103. Martini
104. Meatloaf
105. Mingus
106. Moonshadow
107. Nappers
108. Neferkitty
109. Neo
110. Nijinsky
111. Ninja
112. Nosebud
113. Oprah
114. Oreo
115. Orwell
116. Ozone

117. Ozzy
118. Pablo Picatso
119. Pacino7
120. Peekaboo
121. Peezer
122. Phuket
123. Prunella
124. Quark
125. Quentin
126. Quincy
127. Radar
128. Rambo
129. Reebok
130. Repet
131. Ringo
132. Rocket
133. Romeo
134. Rover
135. Saki
136. Salsa
137. Sasquatch
138. Satchmo
139. Schnitzel
140. Shadow
141. Shazzam
142. Sherlock
143. Snowstorm
144. Sushi

145. Tabasco
146. Taboo
147. Tatters
148. Tonto
149. Tortellini
150. Tut
151. Tweaser
152. UFO
153. Uma
154. Valentino
155. Valium
156. Viagra
157. Voodoo
158. Whispurr
159. Wicket
160. Wonton
161. Wookie
162. Wuzzie
163. Xerox
164. Yenta
165. Yogi
166. Yoko
167. Yum Yum
168. Zero
169. Zippo
170. Zorro
171. ZZ

The Naming of Cats

by T. S. Eliot

The Naming of Cats is a difficult matter,
    It isn't just one of your holiday games;
You may think at first I'm as mad as a hatter
When I tell you, a cat must have THREE DIFFERENT NAMES.
First of all, there's the name that the family use daily,
    Such as Peter, Augustus, Alonzo or James,
Such as Victor, or Jonathan, George or Bill Bailey —
    All of them sensible everyday names.
There are fancier names if you think they sound sweeter,
    Some for the gentlemen, some for the dames;
Such as Plato, Admetus, Electra, Demeter —
    But all of them sensible everyday names.
But I tell you, a cat needs a name that's particular,
    A name that's peculiar, and more dignified,
Else how can he keep up his tail perpendicular,
    Or spread out his whiskers, or cherish his pride?
Of names of this kind, I can give you a quorum,
    Such as Munkustrap, Quaxo or Coricopat.
Such as Bombalurina, or else Jellylorum —
    Names that never belong to more than one cat.
But above and beyond there's still one name left over,
    And that is the name that you will never guess;
The name that no human research can discover —
    But THE CAT HIMSELF KNOWS, and will never confess.
When you notice a cat in profound meditation,
    The reason, I tell you, is always the same:
His mind is engaged in a rapt contemplation
    Of the thought, of the thought, of the thought of his name:
        His ineffable effable
        Effanineffable
Deep and inscrutable singular Name.

A vintage postcard from France.

43 Pairs of Names for 2 Cats

Abercrombie and Fitch

Adidas and Nike

Ali and Frazier

Alice and Trixie

Arm and Hammer

Batman and Robin

Beavis and Butthead

Ben and Jerry

Big Mac and Fries

Bill and Hillary

Bonnie and Clyde

Boris and Natasha

Brad and Angelina

Calvin and Hobbes

Carly and Sonny

Cheech and Chong

Coke and Pepsi

Dazed and Confused

Dorothy and Toto

Dr. Jekyll and Mr. Hyde

Felony and Miss Demeanor

Gin and Tonic

Houghton and Mifflin

Johnson and Johnson

Lennon and McCartney

Lewis and Clark

Lucy and Ethel

Macaroni and Cheese

Norton and Trixie

Pat and Vanna

Penn and Teller

Pride and Joy

Pride and Prejudice

Purrier and Ives

Regis and Kelly

Rhett and Scarlett

Sacco and Vanzetti

Search and Destroy

Simon and Garfunkel

Smith and Wesson

Starsky and Hutch

Thelma and Louise

Yin and Yang

8 Sets of Names for 4 Cats

Bart, Lisa, Homer, and Marge

Eeny, Meeny, Miny, and Moe

John, Paul, George, and Ringo

Kramer, Seinfeld, Elaine, Kostanza

Lucy, Ricky, Fred, and Ethel

Mick, Keith, Charlie, and Ron

North, South, East, and West

Simon, Paula, Randy, and Ryan

14 Sets of Names for 3 Cats

Harpo, Chico, and Groucho

Harry, Hermione, and Ron

Kukla, Fran, and Ollie

Larry, Curly, and Moe

Luciano, Placido, and Jose

Nina, Pinta, and Santa Maria

Oscar, Mayer, and Wiener

Shadrach, Meshach, and Abednego

Simon, Paula, and Randy

Snap, Crackle, and Pop

Tipsy, Topsy, and Turvy

Un, Deux, and Trois

Wynken, Blynken, and Nod

Veni, Vidi, and Vici

The Top Rasta Names for Cats

Irieness, dis list allows de fe get a real reggae name fe de cat, like so many reggae lovers appear fe give dem. Give de cat an irie name. After dat, all de has to do is start let the pet listening to reggae music night and day, and call it by its new name. Go deh!

Wailer	Rasta Lion	Bunny Demus
Tears	Bredda Scratch	Irie Lion
Bushdokta	Sista Africa	Deyazmach Ranks
Wailing Prophet	Junior Dread	Cool Fullpint
Don Ganja	Yabby Levi	Shabba
I Congo	Vibes Bongo	Mighty Satta

25 Reasons Why Cats Are Better Than Dogs

Cat people and dog people will be duking it out until the end of time. If you profess to love both cats and dogs equally, ask yourself this question: "If my house was burning down and I had only enough time to save one of my pets, would I save the cat or the dog?" Of course, we're biased, but here's why you might consider saving the cat.

1. Cats are cleaner, and their poops are neat and orderly.

2. You don't have to walk a cat.

3. Cats purr. Dogs drool.

4. Cats don't slobber.

5. Cats don't bark.

6. Cats rub your leg when they want affection, not when they're horny.

7. Why do you think they call it "dog breath"?

8. Cats eat less than dogs do.

9. Cats always land on their feet. Dogs don't let you throw them.

10. Cats require less care and attention.

11. Cats generally do better with apartments or close quarters.

12. Cats require far less exercise than dogs do.

13. Guys, take note: in a 2002 survey conducted by the charity Cats Protection in England, it was determined that 98 percent of all women would prefer to date a man who liked cats than someone who didn't.

14. Cats are less destructive.

15. Cats are better mousers than dogs are.

16. Cats are craftier and more cunning than dogs.

17. Cats are wise in that they don't trust anyone unfamiliar. Many dogs are friendly to almost anyone, burglars included.

18. Cats are more adept at climbing and negotiating intricate maneuvers than a dog is. (On the other hand, we don't recall ever hearing about firefighters trying to rescue a dog stuck in a tree.)

19. Some folks feel that a cat's love is conditional and that it will only love you once it has learned to trust you completely, whereas a dog's love is unconditional because it sees you as part of its pack.

20. Cats can make more than one hundred vocal sounds; dogs have only about ten. If you've ever heard two cats talking to each other, you know exactly what we mean. It can get pretty eerie.

21. Scientific studies reveal that cats have a better memory than dogs do. A dog's memory of an event lasts about 5 minutes, while a cat's is retained for as long as 16 hours.

22. Cats have a better sense of direction and are far more likely to return home than a lost dog is.

23. On the whole, cats live longer than dogs.

24. You can leave your home for a couple of days and know that your cat will manage. Dogs require supervision.

25. Garfield. Odie. 'Nuff said.

"Cats are smarter than dogs. You can't get eight cats to pull a sled through snow." — JEFF VALDEZ

Are You Sure You Want a Cat?

Cats are smart: they know if you're a first-time cat owner, and if they sense that this is so, they are bound to take advantage of you. To stay one step ahead, prepare yourself before Kitty arrives. Here are some tips that will catapult you straight to Planet Cat.

1. Take cold chicken-and-stars soup straight from the can, splash it across the carpet and the foot of the bed, and then walk in it in the dark with your socks on.

2. Set up a mousetrap at the foot of the bed each night, so that if you move a toe one inch while you are sleeping, you are sure to get snapped.

3. Cover all your best suits with cat hair. For dark suits, apply white hair; for light suits, only dark hair will do. Also, float some hair in your first cup of coffee in the morning.

4. Put everything cat-toy-sized into a water bowl to marinate.

5. Practice cutting your chicken into teeny-tiny pieces, so that later, when the cat steals from your plate, it won't take the whole breast.

"Let's try getting up every night at 2:00 AM to feed the cat. If we enjoy doing that, then we can talk about having a baby."

6. Tip over a basket of clean laundry, and scatter clothing all over the floor. Leave your underwear on the living room floor because that's where the cat will drag it (particularly when you have company).

7. Jump out of your chair shortly before the end of your favorite TV program, and run to the TV, shouting "No! No! Don't chew on the electric cord!" Miss the end of the program.

8. Put chocolate pudding on the carpet in the corner of the living room in the morning, and don't try to clean it up until you return from work that evening.

9. Chew the eraser off every pencil in the house.

10. Take a fork and shred the roll of toilet paper while it's still hanging up. Pull a few sheets off, and scatter them around the bathroom.

11. Use a staple remover to punch two holes in every scrap of paper around the house.

12. Buy a mixed bag of cat toys, and stuff them under the refrigerator. Practice getting up at 2 A.M. and fishing them out with a ruler or broomstick.

10 Reasons Why Cats Are Brought to Shelters

According to a survey conducted by the National Council on Pet Population Study and Policy, the reasons most frequently cited for leaving cats at a shelter are as follows:

1. Too many other cats in the house

2. Allergies

3. Moving

4. Cost of pet maintenance

5. Landlord issues

6. No homes for littermates

7. House soiling

8. Personal problems

9. Inadequate facilities

10. Doesn't get along with other pets

Cats and Courts: 4 Landmark Cases

1. In common law throughout the United States and elsewhere, cats are clearly considered to be property, and this has been true for centuries. The only disputes, as far as the courts were concerned, concern whether or not the cat constitutes property with intrinsic value. In *Smith v. Steineauf* (1934) the court declared that "the worth of the cat as a contributor to the felicity of the home is alone sufficient to require that it be regarded as property of the owner in the full sense of the term *property*." More recently, the court in *People v. Sadowski* (1984) affirmed a conviction of grand theft for the taking of a cat without the owner's permission. On the other hand, in *Commonwealth v. Massini* (1963) the court held that the cat does not fall within the state legislative definition of "domestic animal" and therefore cats have "no intrinsic value in the eyes of the law."

2. In the quintessential "cat and the canary" case of *McDonald v. Jodrey* (1890) the court stated that the owner of a cat is not responsible for the "predatory" habits of the species, only for the known "mischievous tendencies" of the animal.

3. In *Clark v. Brings* (1969) a babysitter injured by a cat sought to recover damages from the cat's owners. The court ruled that the injured person must prove that the particular animal was dangerous and posed a risk, and that the owners had prior knowledge of the animal's harmful propensities. In 1990 the court ruled in *Spradlin v. Williams* that homeowners were responsible for protecting guests (including housekeepers and other service workers) from the owner's "dangerous" cat. However, in *Burton v. Landry 602* (1992), the court determined that the homeowner was not responsible for injuries incurred by a worker in the house when the cat accidentally got "underfoot."

4. In a particularly famous cat case, *Miles v. City Council of Augusta, Georgia* (1982), or "The Blackie the Talking Cat Case," as it is commonly known, the plaintiffs, Mr. and Mrs. Miles, alleged that the Augusta police had wrongly insisted that the couple obtain a business license if they continued employing their talking cat (Blackie) to perform for a fee on the streets of the city. Mr. and Mrs. Miles believed this local ordinance infringed on Blackie's freedom of speech. The court, however, saw it differently and required that the license be purchased: "[T]hat a talking cat could generate interest and income is not surprising. Man's fascination with the domestic feline is perennial." The court declared the ordinance constitutionally valid, at least in relation to Blackie's business enterprise.

"I could have persuaded myself that the word **Felonious** is derived from the feline temper."
— ROBERT SOUTHEY

16 States That Have Cat Lemon Laws

Pet lemon laws, in effect in 16 states as of 2006, give pet store customers the right to return a sick or dead pet (most laws apply to dogs, sometimes cats) for a refund or replacement. Most also give customers the option of retaining the pet, having it treated, and getting some level of reimbursement for veterinary expenses (the amount is usually limited to the purchase price of the pet, plus sales tax).

In most states, the owner has one to two weeks to return the animal, with a certificate from a veterinarian stating that the animal has a serious disease or congenital defect that was present when it was sold. If the cat suffers from a congenital disorder, the owner may have up to a year to return it to the pet store and/or get a refund.

The following states have such a law:

Arizona	Nevada
California	New Hampshire
Connecticut	New Jersey
Delaware	New York
Florida	Pennsylvania
Maine	South Carolina
Massachusetts	Vermont
Minnesota	Virginia

5 Ways to Avoid Cat-Related Legal Problems

Cat owners should be aware of their local pet laws, which vary from state to state and even county to county. For more information about cat law, consult the Cat Fanciers' Association Legislative Committee, which works with communities to create and uphold responsible laws. Find out more at cfainc.org.

Here are some general guidelines for steering clear of legal trouble.

1. Know which vaccinations your cat requires, and make sure to keep records and receipts for these.

2. Be aware of nuisance laws. In most cases, the law recognizes the instincts of a cat and will not hold the owner responsible for damage caused to another's property unless the owner had prior knowledge of the cat's destructive propensities.

3. Cats are not generally required to be licensed, as dogs are, but for safety reasons, cats that are allowed to wander outside the home should have identification on them at all times. Some owners shave the fur off the cat's stomach and write their phone number with an indelible marker. The hair grows back, and the cat is permanently identified. (For another option, see page 292 for information about microchipping.)

4. Some cities impose restrictions on the number of cats that can be housed in a single residence.

5. Cruelty laws, held by all states, govern the treatment of animals by owners and non-owners alike. Minimally, these laws state that animals cannot be intentionally hurt or tortured, that they be provided with shelter and food, that they not be abandoned, and that they not be made to participate in animal-fighting sports of any kind.

12 Pioneers in Feline Medicine and Welfare

1. **Dr. Jane Bicks** has served as the president of the Veterinary Medical Association of New York City; served on the Advisory Board of the Cornell University Feline Health Center; helped set up the largest animal shelter in the world, the Center for Animal Care and Control; has authored three books on pet care; and has appeared as veterinary expert on CBS's *48 Hours,* ABC's *Good Morning America,* and many other national TV shows. At present she is veterinary expert for the Animal Planet series *Petsburgh.*

Dr. Bicks is one of the pioneers of veterinary nutritional/alternative medicine and is recognized nationally as an authority on the natural treatment of animals. Currently Dr. Bicks is the executive director of new-product development and education for HealthyPetNet, where she supervises a board of veterinarians and pet industry experts who ensure that HealthyPetNet's cutting-edge formulas meet the highest standards for quality and effectiveness.

2. As the pioneer of a feline-exclusive practice in Maryland, **Dr. Jane Brunt and the staff of CHAT** (the Cat Hospital at Towson) are dedicated to practicing the highest-quality medicine to care for their cat clients. Dr. Brunt founded Animal Relief, Inc., in 1996 to assist organizations in providing superlative health care to animals, felines in particular. Dr. Brunt is a fellow of the Academy of Feline Medicine, a board member of the American Association of Feline Practitioners (AAFP), and has held 13 different titles with the Maryland Veterinary Medical Association since becoming a member in 1980 (including president-elect in 1993–94, and president in 1994–95). Dr. Brunt is a national adviser on feline medicine, as well as the current representative of the AAFP to the American Veterinary Medical Association (AVMA). Dr. Brunt also chaired the Host Committee of the AVMA Annual Convention in Baltimore in July 2003 where she received many awards and accolades. Dr. Brunt has served on more than 15 advisory councils, has authored six publications, coauthored seven others, and is active in an extensive and diverse list of community activities.

3. Formed in 1927, **Cats Protection (CP)** has grown to become the United Kingdom's leading feline welfare charity. Its members now rescue and find new homes for around 60,000 cats and kittens every year, through their network of 29 adoption centers and 260 volunteer-run branches. Their work doesn't stop there, though: they also provide an array of cat-care information via a publication, a website, and the National Helpline. CP also promotes the benefits of neutering for a happier pet and distributes education packs to a third of schools in the United Kingdom. Today, the 5,500 volunteers and staff members of Cats Protection are busier than ever, working to meet the increasing demands of a growing domestic and feral feline population.

4. The **Cornell Feline Health Center** in Ithaca, New York, is a veterinary medical specialty center devoted to improving the health and well-being of cats throughout the world. The center, which was begun in 1974 as part of the Cornell School of Veterinary Medicine, has been responsible for breakthroughs in feline health care, such as the establishment of vaccine recommendations for feline panleukopenia (distemper) and respiratory viral diseases; the development of the ELISA test for detecting coronavirus antibodies (used as an aid in diagnosis of feline infectious peritonitis); the identification of feline immunodeficiency virus in nondomestic cats; the identification of panleukopenia as a cause of kitten loss in the endangered Florida panther; and the attenuation of feline infectious peritonitis virus

to establish an experimental vaccine. The center still strives to find ways of preventing and curing diseases of cats.

5. **Dr. Deborah Greco**, at the Animal Medical Center in New York City, is the leading researcher in the field of feline diabetes. She was the recipient of the Pfizer Award for research excellence at Colorado State University in 1996, and in 1998 she received the AAFP research award for her work on feline diabetes mellitus. Her research has shown that diet plays a significant role in the development of feline diabetes and that a cat's natural diet should guide cat owners as they select foods. She recommends plenty of protein and fat and very little carbohydrate, which cats find difficult to digest. The research also indicates that obese cats are much more likely to develop feline diseases other than diabetes. It is also her recommendation that cats be fed a wet diet since it supplies most of their natural dietary needs.

6. **Dr. Leslie Lyons**, at the University of California Davis School of Veterinary Medicine, along with breeders and researchers at other institutions, is collecting DNA samples from healthy purebred cats and those carrying hereditary disease, in order to map the feline genome. Purebreds have a higher risk for developing diseases of genetic origin. A better picture of a purebred's genetic makeup can help researchers better diagnose and treat feline diseases such as diabetes, asthma, heart disease, and a number of infectious disease as well. Her work will hopefully result in a genetic database that will help in identifying and addressing the problem of inherited diseases.

7. **Jia Meng**, founder of Catzone, has been the foremost proponent of animal welfare in mainland China. Catzone works in the Hangzhou and adjacent regions, but much of its work is done via the Internet. Catzone has about 1,000 members and 60 volunteers and is steadily growing. It set out to tackle two main issues — companion animal overpopulation and irresponsible pet ownership — and does this through public education, an animal-fostering plan, animal rescue, and an effort to introduce into China more professional, state-of-the-art animal welfare theory. Jia Meng cites government control of nongovernment organizations as the chief challenge; it is difficult for societies like Catzone to become officially registered. Chinese tradition is not entirely animal friendly, and therefore Meng is working to change certain attitudes through education. In a recent interview on Chinese television, Jia Meng was proclaimed "the pioneer for cat welfare."

8. The **Laboratory of Genomic Diversity**, led by Professor Steve O'Brien, has been performing pioneer studies in cat genetics for many years. Based in the United States, his group has now established many of the resources required to carry out high-quality genetic studies. O'Brien's group published a low-resolution genetic map for the cat, which covers approximately 90 percent of the cat genome. This map provides the vital information required to begin mapping inherited disease and phenotypic traits in the cat. The project's overall goal is to improve the health and welfare of cats through reducing the incidence of genetic diseases.

9. **Dr. Niels Pedersen** received his DVM in 1967 from the University of California, Davis; completed his internship in small animal medicine and surgery at Colorado State University in 1968; and in 1972 he earned his Ph.D. from the John Curtin School of Medical Research, Australian National University, Canberra. Dr. Pedersen and his team of researchers have furthered our knowledge of feline infectious peritonitis (FIP). In 1996, he was recognized for his contributions to feline retrovirus research and generosity in furthering the work of scientists worldwide.

10. **Richard Pitcairn, DVM, Ph.D.**, author of *Dr. Pitcairn's Complete Guide to Natural Health for Dogs and Cats*, is a pioneer in modern holistic care for cats and dogs.

Pitcairn's book started the trend in holistic methods of treating and feeding cats. He received his degree in veterinary medicine from the University of California, Davis, in 1965, and his Ph.D. in veterinary microbiology and immunology from Washington State University in 1972. He has presented his research findings in veterinary homeopathy to government and professional panels, such as the California Veterinary Medical Association and the U.S. Food and Drug Administration.

11. With the sponsorship of the **Winn Feline Foundation** (founded by the Cat Fanciers' Association [CFA] in 1968 to provide funds for medical studies to improve the health and welfare of cats), the School of Veterinary Medicine at the University of California, Davis, has been a leading center for feline nutrition research; its pioneers include Dr. James Morris and Dr. Quinton Rogers. Its discoveries have led to several changes in the formulation of commercial cat foods in order to combat disorders such as dilated cardiomyopathy and feline lower-urinary-tract disease. Since its beginnings, the Winn Feline Foundation has funded over $3 million in research. It is the only international foundation devoted solely to funding research in feline medicine.

12. **Dr. Janet Yamamoto**, a researcher at the University of Florida's College of Veterinary Medicine, discovered the link between the viruses that cause feline and human AIDS. This finding, which was unexpected, may mean that cats with feline immunodeficiency virus, also known as FIV or feline AIDS, could eventually be treated even more effectively by using some form of the experimental human vaccine. Dr. Yamamoto has theorized that the relationship of the two viruses could one day lead to a vaccine to prevent human AIDS.

"Most beds sleep up to six cats. Ten cats without the owner."
— STEPHEN BAKER

FRED FRANCIS

Welcome Home, Furry Baby!

So you've picked out your kitten (preferably two). Now what? Let the fun begin, but remember that it's not all fun and games. That fuzzy baby requires plenty of care and attention, all of which will pay off later. Even before you've brought it home, be sure you have consulted "19 Steps for Cat-Proofing Your Home" (page 256). Always treat your cat with kindness (the Golden Rule comes in handy here), and respect the creature for what it is, a glorious, mysterious, wondrous cat.

1. Soon after the kitten arrives, take it to the veterinarian for an exam, feeding recommendations, and the necessary vaccinations. Use a cat carrier for transporting the cat, both for its safety and sense of security. The carrier should become a "standard operating procedure" for any trips away from home.

2. Set up a nursery for the baby (or babies, if you have adopted two). This should ideally be a small room with an easily cleaned floor. Provide a bed, a litter box, food, and water (not near the litter box), items to scratch on, and safe toys. The bed may consist of anything from an expensive four-poster (Amazon carries one) to some old clothes (preferably yours, unwashed) placed in a basket. The kitten will appreciate a heated area; placing the bed near a radiator or other heat source will make up for the warmth of Mom, whom your kitty misses.

   If you can't manage a nursery, keep Kitty in a pet crate, which will feel like a safe haven. Monitor the kitten at all times when it's outside the crate.

3. Initiate a schedule of feeding, playing, and handling to provide the kitten with the structure of regular activities. Turning on a small nightlight will be its bedtime cue and will also help it navigate the room during the night. Be sensitive to the kitten's need for sleep, and watch that children leave the baby undisturbed while resting.

4. Handle your kitten gently and frequently for short periods of time. During these sessions slowly incorporate touching around the eyes, ears, paws, and so on, as if doing a veterinary exam. This will be good practice for the future.

5. Work with the kitten in its nursery until it is regularly using the litter box. Gradually expand this territory by letting it explore adjoining rooms under your watchful eye.

6. Direct the kitten to acceptable play and scratch items and away from unacceptable ones. When the youngster is under 3 months of age, supervised play is best in areas where it could get hurt or damage something valuable.

7. Introduce family members to the new kitten gradually. Young children should be supervised in their play, and the kitten should not be picked up more often than necessary. Ask your child to sit on the floor and simply wait for the kitten to approach. If the kitten does not want to play, the session should end.

8. In the beginning, provide food that the kitten has already gotten used to. If you want to change its diet, do so gradually by mixing in small amounts of the new food.

9. Even if you plan to allow your cat access to the outdoors, it should be kept inside for at least a week after completing the first course of vaccinations (usually at about 13 to 14 weeks). Until the kitten is 6 months old, you should be present for all its outdoor activity.

10. Cats are much more attention-needy than most people think. They can become bored and depressed if they are ignored, or they may misbehave just to get attention. When you get home from work each day, take the first ten minutes to visit with your cat. Your day may have been hectic and stressful, but Kitty has had no choice but to spend many long hours in a quiet house without any stimulation. You are, without a doubt, the most exciting part of its day. Talk to the cat, stroke it, and join in play. You both will be happier and healthier.

11. The more you involve your kitten in activities and interactions with others, the more likely it will respond without fear or defensiveness as it grows older.

19 Steps for Cat-Proofing Your Home

Holly D. Webber is the owner of HDW Enterprises and Foothill Felines Bengals and Savannahs. She is a longtime cat lover and breeder and has also written the Catty Cookbook (Culinary Catnip for People!) series. Holly writes, "It's finally time to bring your new kitten or cat home with you. While the event itself is very exciting, it is also a huge change and trauma for the feline, no matter how loving the new home and family. Being prepared ahead of time will greatly ensure that the actual transition for your new furry family member is as quiet, calm, and comfortable as possible." Here are some of her ideas.

1. Kittens and cats are by their nature *very* curious about their surroundings, so make sure there are no hidden "escape routes" that lead outdoors for your indoor-only kitty. If you have young children, or any concerns about the cat getting out, you can make and post KITTY KROSSING signs at each door, reminding the family to close it carefully and watch for kitties.

2. Install baby locks on cabinets where you keep medicines, household cleaners, and insect sprays to keep them out of paw's reach, just as you would for a toddler.

3. Inspect your window screens to make sure that they are sturdy. Better yet, treat your curious cat to a window enclosure so it can view what's going on in the neighborhood from a safe perch. Cats can easily slip through many types of childproof window guards.

4. Enclose electric cords in PVC covers made for the purpose of keeping chew-happy cats from harming themselves. These cord-cover kits have channels into which wires can be easily slipped. The covers feature adhesive backing that can be placed against baseboards or other flat surfaces.

5. Be tidy when you sew; keep needles, thread, and string off the ground, as they are tempting to kitties. Some cats are also attracted to the shimmer of earrings, rings, and shiny candy wrappers. A cat's barbed tongue can latch onto these items. If such an item is swallowed, the cat can choke or suffer internal injuries.

6. Always keep a collar with an identification tag on your cat, even when it is indoors. Also, microchip your cat in case it becomes lost and the collar is missing. (See page 292 for more about microchipping.)

7. Keep your curious feline out of the garage, to avoid contact with antifreeze or other toxic substances. (One teaspoon of ingested antifreeze can be fatal to cats.)

8. Keeping your toilet bowl closed after use is a must if you have small kittens or a breed of cat such as the Bengal, which seems naturally attracted to water. (But see page 312 for an alternative approach: kitty toilet training.)

9. Place glass or other breakable treasures inside a locked cabinet, or use special anchoring clay to keep them secure, so they won't be knocked over by an inquisitive paw.

10. Always keep your washing machine and dryer doors closed, and check carefully before and after each use to make sure your kitty hasn't somehow gotten inside.

11. For some reason, all kittens seem to love exploring underneath the refrigerator. Make sure that they cannot get

4 Questions to Ask Before You Get a Cat

1. Indoor cats live to be 15 to 20 years old; are you prepared to make a long-term commitment?

2. The average cost of caring for a cat is $500 a year. Can you afford it?

3. Are you prepared to cat-proof your home?

4. Do you have time, each day, to spend with your cat?

all the way under or behind the refrigerator or other large pieces of furniture by blocking those spaces with boards or other objects.

12. In the hope that curiosity won't kill your cat, move all toxic materials (household cleaners, paint, antifreeze) so that they are out of reach (or better yet, safely locked in a cabinet).

13. Be aware of lightweight table lamps that can fall over, heavy irons that can fall off ironing boards, and reclining chairs in which kittens can become trapped, injured, or even killed.

14. Look around before you sit in a recliner or a rocking chair. A cat may be napping under the legs or in a space inside the recliner.

15. It's best to keep real houseplants in a separate, closed area, away from any contact with your cats. Silk plants make an attractive, safe substitute. (See the list of potentially dangerous plants on page 296.)

16. Be aware that not all cat toys are safe: string, yarn, thread, needles, safety pins, rubber bands, and small parts of toys, such as eyes or bells, can easily be ingested. Cats seem to especially love twist ties, which can perforate the intestines if swallowed. Keep these out of reach.

17. To avoid the litter-box odor that causes guests to grimace, keep your home well ventilated. (And clean the litter box thoroughly before guests arrive.)

18. Keep all pets away from swimming pools unless you are closely supervising them.

19. Place a screen in front of the fireplace.

Warning: Potential hazards for kittens and cats include anything with loops, such as paper or plastic grocery bags with carry handles, a litter-box liner with a drawstring loop left where a kitten can get stuck in it, and even vertical pulls for window blinds. All of these can be deadly if the kitty gets its head caught in the loop. Keep **all** plastic bags safely away from kitties.

Kitty Accoutrements: What You'll Need

1. Food and water dishes. Stainless steel or ceramic dishes work best. Get the new kitty its own set, even if you already have a set for another feline.

2. Plenty of the food that the kitten is accustomed to. Note that cats love baby food, such as Gerber's lamb or chicken — it's a real treat.

3. A litter box.

4. Litter. The same litter the kitten is used to.

5. A perforated scooper for removing clumps of dried nasties.

6. A cat tree.

7. A scratching post. (Start them early; kittens love scratching posts.)

8. A bed. Just don't expect the cat to use it every night, no matter how many toys you use as a lure.

9. Enough safe toys to satisfy its curious mind.

10. A window-level perch from which the kitty can view the world outside.

11. A collar with identification, even for an indoor cat.

12. A walking harness and leash.

13. A cat carrier or crate.

14. A pair of nail clippers for those all-important pedicures.

15. A brush or comb for grooming.

How Much Will Kitty Cost?

It's difficult to put a price on your priceless, purring pal. But being a responsible cat owner comes with certain financial obligations. Even if you get a "free" kitten or cat, you need to include in your budget the cost of food, veterinary care, toys, litter, and other feline amenities.

Cats, especially indoor ones, can live well into their teens and even early twenties. If you merely multiplied $640 times 20, the lifetime cost would be a minimum of $12,800. That does not take into account inflation or unexpected injuries or illnesses — or your sudden desire to convert the spare bedroom into a room filled with feline amenities. *Kaching!*

According to the 2005–2006 National Pet Owners Survey conducted by the American Pet Product Manufacturers Association, Americans spend $38.4 billion on their pets annually.

According to the ASPCA, people spend approximately $640 during a kitten's first year. Here's how that breaks down:

Food: $120	Spay/neuter operation: $75
Medical: $150	Collar: $10
Litter: $150	Carrier: $30
Litter box: $25	Miscellaneous: $30
Toys: $50	

You can buy charming little ceramic feng shui cats to place in different areas of your house to attract good fortune. They are made in Japan and come in different colors that draw in various energies. The pink cat brings happiness and love when placed facing southeast; the red cat attracts good fortune in business when placed facing east; the white cat brings purity and good health when placed facing northeast; and the yellow one invites good fortune in finance when placed facing west. They stand two precious inches tall and are available at Exoticimports.com for $9 each.

Fang Shui

In Chinese mythology the cat symbolizes protection against evil spirits, as they are able to see in the dark and frighten away spirits that have bad intentions. A modern version of this idea is embodied by feng shui, the idea that cosmic breath, or ch'i energy, permeates the atmosphere, the earth, and all living things. Feng shui practitioners emphasize the importance of placing furniture and objects within our homes in order to channel various energies so as to attract wealth, health, and happiness. Animals, and cats in particular, are extremely sensitive to these energies. As the mystical scholar Andrew Harvey, author of many books, has said,

In the new world, if we get there, all homes will be temples. And the animal, your companion animal, should be worshipped as the representative of the creation and as the representative of the Divine Mother. So they are at the very center of the mandala of the home. And anything that you can do to make them happy, making special altars for them, finding out where they most like to rest and be, making that as comfortable and sacred an environment as possible, and playing the kind of music that they love is all to the good because it only increases their joy. And the deeper and the greater their joy, the happier the home . . . If your animal is happy, the house will smile. And if your house smiles, all your hopes will flourish.

The New Cat on the Block: And Then There Were Two

First impressions can last forever. In the wild, cats take great care, through scent-marking behaviors, to prevent chance encounters with other cats. By "reading" the marked areas, cats can tell who was there last and at what time the visit occurred. The territory can thus be used by different cats at different times of the day — the feline version of a time-share. In order to get your cat used to the idea of sharing the home turf with another feline, a gradual introduction is essential.

Time and patience are the keys to successfully introducing a new cat into the household, and the time you spend gradually habituating your cats will eventually be rewarded with years of harmonious feline companionship.

Here is the method recommended by Catsinternational.org.

1. The new cat should have a room of its own for a few days. Exchange the new cat's bedding with that of the resident cat so that they can become acquainted with each other through the all-important sense of smell before they have the opportunity to see each other.

2. Next, rotate rooms. Let the new cat explore the rest of the house while the resident cat spends some time in the new cat's room. When they are relaxed about this step, crack the door of the new cat's room so that they can see each other but can't push the door open. Give the cats treats on both sides of the door. Two small toys joined with several inches of string and slipped under the door will encourage parallel play.

3. When the cats are calm in each other's presence, it is time to let the new cat out for a few minutes. The length of the visits can be increased gradually each day. This process may take a few days or a few months, depending on the personalities of the cats. Usually it takes less time when one of the cats is under 4 months of age.

4. Throughout the introduction process, speak quietly and calmly to the cats. Praise them generously when they are tolerant of each other's presence. Never scold or speak in harsh tones when they are together, or they will associate unpleasantness with being near each other. Give special attention to the resident cat as it is this cat's territory that is being invaded, and this old friend is likely to need more reassurance. Until the two become friends, give the new cat loving attention only when the resident cat is not around.

5. If at any time the cats become fearful or hostile, return the newcomer to its room and close the door. A minor setback will not ruin the budding friendship, but a fiercely aggressive encounter will be remembered for a long time and should be avoided at all costs. Whenever you run into a problem, back up to a previous stage of the process and then move carefully forward again. Only you can determine the pace of the introduction process.

In Switzerland, an anti-cruelty law requires that anyone who adopts a cat must take in at least two.

12 Reasons Why Two Cats Are Better Than One

The old saying that "two heads are better than one" certainly applies to cats. There are several great reasons for having two cats. It is best, however, if they are similar in type, preferably from the same litter, and have ample room to live together comfortably. If you are going to adopt two adult cats, adopt them at the same time, so that neither has a territorial issue with the other.

1. Feline behaviorists generally agree that cats lead healthier and happier lives if there is another cat in the home.

2. They'll each have a buddy for life. Young males (3 to 24 months) have an especially strong need for a companion.

3. The work involved in housing two cats is as easy as having one, plus you double the fun.

4. If you're adopting, you'll be saving two lives instead of one.

5. A single kitten can become lonely.

6. Two cats that groom each other can reach spots on their bodies they can't on their own. Therefore they are often cleaner than "single" cats.

7. Two kittens tend to "self-train" each other.

8. A cat will remain more playful and youthful into its later years if it has a companion.

9. They'll provide each other with exercise and mental stimulation.

10. There will be fewer behavioral problems with two kittens since they will keep each other occupied and less likely to get into mischief. There will also be less hissing, biting, and shyness.

11. You'll get a better picture of the true feline nature by observing two cats as they interact.

12. They serve as warm little cushions for each other.

"I'm leaving early today to have my cat neutered. While I'm gone, select 9 people to be *Employee Of The Month* and award each of them with a kitten."

The Top 10 Essentials of Cat Care

Although your cat may act independent and be litter-trained, it still counts on you to provide food, water, shelter, regular veterinary care, companionship, and more. Heed these guidelines, provided by The Humane Society of the United States, for developing a rewarding relationship with your feline companion. You'll find information about all these subjects throughout this chapter.

1. Outfit your cat with a collar and ID tag that includes your name, address, and telephone number. No matter how careful you are, there's a chance your companion may slip out the door — an ID tag greatly increases the chance that your cat will be returned home safely.

2. Follow local cat registration laws. Licensing, a registration and identification system administered by some local governments, protects both cats and people in the community.

3. Keep your cat indoors. Keeping your cat safely confined at all times is best for you, your pet, and your community.

such as scratching furniture and jumping on countertops. Contrary to popular belief, cats can be trained with a bit of patience, effort, and understanding on your part.

8. Groom your cat often to keep her coat healthy, soft, and shiny. Although it is especially important to brush longhaired cats to prevent their hair from matting, even shorthaired felines need to be groomed, to remove as much loose hair as possible. When cats groom themselves, they ingest a great deal of hair, which often leads to hairballs.

9. Set aside time to play with your cat. While cats do not need the same level of exercise that dogs do, enjoying

An Easy Way to Tell If It's a Boy or a Girl Lift the tail and look for something that looks like a punctuation mark. If you see a colon, it's a boy; if you see an upside-down exclamation point, it's a girl.

4. Take your cat to the veterinarian for regular checkups. If you do not have a veterinarian, ask your local animal shelter or a pet-owning friend for a referral.

5. Spay or neuter your pet. This will keep her healthier and will reduce the problem of cat overpopulation.

6. Give your cat a nutritionally balanced diet, including constant access to fresh water. Ask your veterinarian for advice on what and how often to feed your pet.

7. Train your cat to refrain from undesirable behaviors

regular play sessions with your pet will provide it with the physical exercise and mental stimulation he needs, as well as strengthen the bond you share.

10. Be loyal to and patient with your cat. Make sure the expectations you have of your companion are reasonable and remember that the vast majority of behavior problems can be solved. If you are struggling with your pet's behavior, contact your veterinarian or local animal shelter for advice, and check out The HSUS's Pets for Life campaign information.

10 Things Humans Do That Drive Cats Crazy

Everything seems fine until you get that look — that steady stare, that glowering glare, that do-you-mind look of disbelief and disgust — from your cat.

Often without releasing a single meow, your cat conveys its displeasure in your lack of pet etiquette. Most times, feline housemates "tolerate" your follies and faux pas. But cats are candid creatures. They don't mask their feelings. They don't shrug off mistakes. From their vantage point, we often seem to try too hard — or not hard enough — to cater to their wants and needs. After all, we're only *human.*

Certain human habits can unleash frustration in felines. To help identify these irksome behaviors, we turned to two cat experts: Alice Moon-Fanelli, Ph.D., a certified applied animal behaviorist at Tufts University School of Veterinary Medicine, and John C. Wright, Ph.D., a certified applied animal behaviorist and professor of psychology at Mercer University in Macon, Georgia.

Our experts cite these top ten pet peeves:

1. Dirty litter boxes

Picture, for a moment, your home minus a clean bathroom. Your only option: a pungent port-a-potty in the backyard. You find yourself wishing for the lung capacity of an Olympic swimmer so that you can hold your breath and complete your deed before you need to inhale. Disgusting, right? Some cats belonging to delinquent litter-box-scooping owners feel the same way.

"Cats are fastidious by nature, so a dirty litter box is downright disgusting," says Dr. Moon-Fanelli. "They deserve a box that is scooped every day — and more than one box if there is more than one cat in the household."

Solution: Some feline-friendly gestures: skip the perfume-scented litter, lose the lid (for many cats, the hooded boxes trap odors inside the box, causing them to gasp or seek a new place to potty — such as behind your sofa). Win over your cat by actually cleaning the box and refilling it with clean litter once a week. Location is also key. Pick a private, quiet place in your home — not next to a noisy washing machine or deep in the darkest corner of your basement.

2. Blaring music

As your cat naps on the sofa, you rudely slip a Bruce Springsteen CD into your stereo and crank up the volume

"If you're leaving a message for Jerry, press 1.
If you're leaving a message for Carol, press 2.
If you're leaving a message for our cat,
get a life Mom!"

until your walls shake. *Yowl!* Your cat leaps skyward, lands hard, and then dashes to the opposite end of your home. Reason: feline ears are much more sensitive than human ears. They have more hair cell receptors, and their cone-shaped ears capture more sound.

"Playing loud music actually may be painful to them," says Dr. Moon-Fanelli. "I find that my cats are much more comfortable when I play classical or jazz music than when I play rock music on a high volume."

"Your owners pet you to relieve stress. If that fails, you could be sued for malpractice. That's why you need cat insurance."

Solution: Turn down the volume or wear headphones when you want to blare music. Or opt for classical music or jazz. Cats seem to like these musical styles best, perhaps because they are rhythmical and don't pack surprise beats.

3. Tossing and turning in bed

Cats, the Rip Van Winkles of the companion animal world, can sleep 15 hours or more a day. One of their true joys is to snooze uninterrupted through the night, curled up on your bedspread. That tranquility can be destroyed when you shift feet or flip from one body position to another under the sheets.

As a consequence, your cat is nudged, shoved, or even worse, tossed into the air. If would be as if someone woke you from a deep slumber by leaping up and down on your mattress. No wonder your cat reacts by pouncing on or biting your toes.

"Generally, cats that get upset by your movement in bed tend to be ones that startle easily," says Dr. Moon-Fanelli. "Also, cats instinctively want to attack things that move — such as feet under a bedspread."

Solution: Sleep on your back and don't move a muscle. Or, more realistically, provide a cat bed in your bedroom or leave your door open to allow the feline to exit. If necessary, protect your toes by wearing thick socks.

4. Shouting

The human equivalent of catfights — yelling and speaking in loud tones during a spat with your spouse or your strong-willed teenager — can cause cats to flee and seek quieter places, such as under your bed or deep in your closet.

"When you fight with a teenager or a spouse, cats typically are not sure what's going on," says Dr. Wright. "They go from first being alert, to being interested, and then to being terrified. Cats love ritualistic activities, set routines. They usually don't know how to deal with an upset in routine, such as their people's yelling. The loud voices often freak them out and cause them to dart out of the room."

Solution: Try to focus on solving problems in a civil tone, rather than yelling. Could your family benefit from an anger management class?

5. Super-stressed humans

A cat can tune in to you like a four-footed mood barometer. It knows when you're happy, sad, angry, and bummed.

"Cats read our body language so well," says Dr. Wright. "When we're stressed, our muscles tend to be tight, our posture rigid, and our pupils dilated — not inviting signs to a cat."

Solution: Recognize that you can't totally control your life and, more important, remember to savor positive moments and events. "When you come home from work, try to spend a few minutes with your cats," says Dr. Wright. "Spend quality time talking with your pets every night, and think of good things that happened that day that you can share with your animals. They may not understand your words, but they do understand your tone. This activity can help reduce your own stress."

6. Tardy feedings

Your alarm clock blares at 6 A.M. Five minutes tick off, then ten, and still you make no move to get out of bed. Impatience swells in your tail-thumping, hungry cat. More minutes pass and you still haven't approached the cat bowl.

"Cats are creatures of habit," says Dr. Moon-Fanelli. "They want to be fed at regular hours. If you get up and immediately feed your cat every morning, the pet gets into a routine and starts to expect to be fed within minutes of your waking up. When you miss the feeding schedule — or delay it — you can have one really upset cat."

Solution: Stick with a regular feeding schedule that you can realistically maintain. For those times when you can't be home to open and serve some canned food, consider getting a timer dish that keeps the canned food chilled and ready for on-time servings. Or enlist the help of a friend, relative, or pet-sitter to step in as surrogate chef for your hungry cat.

7. The carrier, the car, and the veterinary clinic

These "Three C's of Concern" can cause panic in some cats. Unlike dogs, cats prefer to be home-bodies.

"We don't travel with our cats as we do with our dogs, and usually the only time cats are in crates is when they must go someplace unpleasant — like the veterinary clinic," says Dr. Moon-Fanelli. "Also, many cats suffer from motion sickness."

Solution: Convert your carrier from a place to avoid to a place of comfort for your cat. Select a model that is truly the cat's meow — cushy and well ventilated, with a comfy towel or bedding inside. Leave it out and open in your house so your cat views it as no big deal. Improve the crate's appeal by placing treats and toys inside and putting it in one of your cat's favorite napping spots. Then get your cat accustomed to car rides gradually. During the ride, tune the car radio to a jazz or blues station at low volume. Try to avoid sudden, jarring stops.

8. Ill-mannered children

Youngsters, especially those under age 10, seem determined to lunge at, loom over, and force bear hugs on cats. When a cat approaches, they can't resist the desire to grab it, pat it, dress it up in doll's clothes, or, worse, chase it.

Solution: "Your cat needs an escape route and a safe zone

Children and Cats

Encourage youngsters to handle the kitten properly:

1. Provide support under the back legs and under the chest.
2. Avoid touching Kitty's sensitive tummy area.
3. Assign children kitten-related chores that are not essential to the cat's well-being. (For example, little ones can fill water bowls and gather scattered toys.)
4. Be alert to the "I'm About to Bite You" signs (see page 329). Have your kids disengage with the cat before the teeth are bared.

inaccessible to a young child," says Dr. Wright. "Once your child is old enough to learn and understand household rules, you need to teach the child how to behave around the family cat. Encourage youngsters to be patient and wait for the cat to approach them, and teach them not to disturb the cat when it is eating or sleeping. Demonstrate careful handling of the cat for your children, and monitor their interactions.

9. Adopting another cat or a dog

It's truly a cat's life — until the day you come home cradling another cat or kitten — or worse, a D-O-G. The notion of sharing its home with another pet can cause many a cat to spit up a hairball or rip up the arm of the sofa in protest.

Solution: "Introducing a new pet can really aggravate some cats," says Dr. Moon-Fanelli. "People tend to select cats primarily because they like the cat's looks and color instead of basing the choice on a cat's personality." Learn about breeds and what you can expect from each. Is harmony among these pets a realistic expectation? Make practical decisions about this type of pet adoption.

To introduce the new pet, Dr. Moon-Fanelli recommends that you let the two animals get to know each other initially by smell. Keep them in separate rooms, and run a shirt or towel over both coats to exchange scents. Then, let them view each other from a distance. Cats are territorial, so make sure that the new pet has its own possessions — do not force them to share a bowl, toys, or litter boxes.

10. Forced affection

It is easy to be guilty of this major cat sin. Many cat lovers return home after a business trip, vacation, or simply a long workday, burst through the door, chase down their cats, and engage in a big group hug. No surprise that your cats react by wiggling free and racing away. Once you calm down and sit on the sofa, magically, your cats will slowly approach and greet you on their own terms.

Solution: "The more you try to force affection on your cats, the less of it they want to give you," says Dr. Moon-Fanelli. "Not all cats are lap cats or want to be held tight and cuddled. Being overly affectionate can actually drive your cats from you. Play hard to get — in other words, act more like a cat, and pretend not to care — your cats will seek you out for attention and affection."

By heeding the advice offered here and practicing good manners, people can bond more closely with their cats. Happy, contented cats tend to exhibit fewer behavior problems. "Keep in mind that they are cats — not little adorable humans," says Dr. Moon-Fanelli. "By striving to learn animal behavior, you can better understand who they are, what their needs are, and really live harmoniously with them."

Basic Training — Before You Start

The following information is not intended for the cat owner who wants a cat to come, sit, shake hands, beg, or jump through hoops on command. Rather, it is aimed at encouraging the little guy not to wreak havoc around the house. For starters, bear in mind that a cat that has been spayed or neutered and is taken to the vet for regular checkups (to eliminate the possibility of hidden health problems) is more easily trained.

1. If Tiger is a pedigreed cat, research the breed's temperament and innate abilities.

2. Begin the training process early. Be consistent and patient; try not to become angry and frustrated with slow progress. Putting in the time and effort to educate Kitty will benefit you both.

3. Avoid all reprimands, regardless of what the cat is doing. They don't work. If you scold the cat for something it has done, it will continue the behavior when you are not around. If you scold the cat after the fact, it will have no idea what the scolding is for. Besides, scolding may frighten the cat and cause it to mistrust you. Instead, focus on having fun with the cat and rewarding *good* behavior. If you catch the cat in an illegal act, say no and clap your hands together sharply.

4. Cats can become hyperactive and destructive if bored. Play with Bongo daily, and give him the attention he needs.

5. Cats learn by experience. If something is pleasant, they will want to do it again. If it is unpleasant, they won't want to repeat it. Mephistopheles may derive a great deal of pleasure from scratching your favorite armchair, but it is up to you to train him not to do so and to make the scratching experience unpleasant.

6. The most valuable tool for training your cat is rewards. If Jojo is behaving appropriately (using a scratching post instead of your armchair), reward him with his favorite treats and plenty of affection and praise. (Note that culinary rewards won't work if his belly is full.) If he continues to scratch the chair, squirt the cat with a little water from a spray bottle.

19 Ways to Bond with the Fur Ball

According to catsandcritters.com, bonding is the first step toward successfully living with your cat. Bonding means creating a personal relationship. This includes mutual respect, trust, and love. You are a special person to your cat, and it should be special to you.

It's important that each member of the household develop a unique relationship with the family cat. The person who bathes, feeds, and trains the cat may bond as a substitute mother. A child who plays with the cat may relate to it as a brother or a sister, and the person who sits quietly with the cat on his or her lap and pets it may bond as a friend.

It's easiest to bond with a new kitten, but even if your cat is an adult and you've had it for several months or even years, it's still possible to strengthen the relationship if you are willing to work at it. Here are some suggestions for building a solid bond with your feline friend:

1. **Include your cat in your daily activities.** Invite your cat to be with you while you work around the house, watch television, sort the mail, work at the computer, or read the newspaper. The more activities your cat observes you doing, the more it will trust you in all situations.

2. **Let the kitty know it is a member of the family;** everyone should make the cat feel welcome.

3. **Talk to your cat often.** Verbal communication is one of the most important aspects of bonding. Don't feel silly about sitting down and talking to your cat. It may not understand the words you use, but it can understand a warm, friendly tone of voice.

4. **Use your cat's name often.** This will grab its attention and establish a personal relationship between the two of you.

5. **Get to know your cat's individual personality.** Every cat is different; some are shy and independent, while others are outgoing and crave attention. Adapt your lifestyle to the particular personality of your cat. Try different behaviors in relation to your cat and see what works. If you want your cat to be affectionate, you have to determine what you can do to make it act that way.

6. **Provide a consistent daily routine.** Cats don't like surprises. Establish an acceptable daily schedule in the relationship. Let the cat know how often and when to expect meals, walks on the leash, and play sessions. Don't spend two hours a day with your cat one week and only a few minutes a day with it the following week.

If Miss Kitty Hates Mister Right

If you're ready to take the plunge but there's just one small obstacle — your cat — try these measures:

1. Have Mister Right be the only one who feeds her.

2. Put a couple of his unwashed shirts in the cat's bed.

3. Ask Mister Right not to seek her out but rather patiently await her attention.

7. **You should be consistent about the behaviors** you allow and don't allow. Don't yell "no" when the cat jumps on the counter today and then let it slide tomorrow. If you are inconsistent in how you interact with your cat, you will confuse it, and the kitty won't trust you.

8. **Give a new cat plenty of privacy.** When you bring a new cat into your home, you should give it a room of its own for two to four weeks. Sit in the room for an hour a day, reading or just relaxing, but don't force the cat to interact with you. Make yourself available, but let your cat make the first move.

9. **If your cat starts walking toward you,** encourage its approach with a little catnip. Never reach out to grab a frightened cat or drag a cat out from under a chair.

10. **Respect your cat's fears and inhibitions.** Remind yourself that it is adapting to a new environment. Go especially slow with an older adopted cat that may have been a stray. Give your cat time to see you're not a threat, and eventually it will find its way in developing a relationship with you.

11. **Avoid harsh discipline.** If your cat misbehaves, do not hit it, holler at it, or punish it. You can tell the kitty "no," but do so only to stop unacceptable behavior. Don't yell or scream. Be forgiving.

12. **Play with your cat as often as you can.** This will get it to connect your presence with having fun. The possibility of play will motivate your kitty to seek you out. Do not, however, foster games that involve aggressive behavior, such as tug-of-war.

13. **Establish boundaries with a firm, fair hand.** You will gain the cat's respect and deepen your mutual bond. Get professional help with this if you're having trouble saying no to that sweet whiskery face.

14. **Housetraining should be done with a great deal of patience.** There should be no physical punishment for mistakes. That way, your cat will have an easier time learning what's expected.

15. **Always touch the cat with affection in your heart.** Cats crave physical contact, and a soft hand is a great way to show the kitty how much it is loved. Be sure to hold it with a firm but gentle grip. Dangling limbs can scare a cat and lead to aggressive behavior. Cats love being massaged. The more time you spend stroking it, the closer the kitty will feel to you. But be prepared to leave the cat alone if it gets irritable or fidgety. Grooming time is another opportunity to bond through touch.

16. **Let the cat sleep with you.** Once it's curled up in a little ball and snuggling close, it will truly begin to feel that you are Mommy.

17. **Make feeding time special.** Don't put food in the bowl and then walk away. Stroking the cat while it is eating is another way to reinforce your bond. Sit down beside your kitty and visit while it eats. Talk to it.

18. **Offer your cat some catnip.** Cats love this plant. And since it is a nonaddictive drug, it will not harm the cat. Keep in mind that kittens need some time to acquire a taste for this wonderful treat.

19. **Above all, be patient and understanding.** We all have our bad days, your cat included. Forgive mistakes and stay positive.

The 9 Most Common Mistakes Made by Cat Owners

Julia Wilson of Cat-World.com, an Australia-based website that caters to all cat lovers, from the novice to the expert, has this to say about the most common errors cat owners make. Many people have the notion that once they adopt a kitten or a cat, it will pretty much care for itself. But this is certainly not the case. So, before you decide to adopt a new feline friend, please do your homework to avoid the common mistakes listed below.

1. **Not desexing**: Many pet owners believe that it is okay to not desex their cat. Every year millions of cats are euthanized in shelters because of a chronic shortage of homes. As such, it is important for all cat owners to do their part and have their cat desexed to prevent the creation of more unwanted kittens. Not only is this the responsible thing to do, but also it is better for your cat to be desexed. Without this operation, females are at risk of developing the following conditions: breast cancer, pyometra, and tumors of the uterus and ovaries. Male cats risk developing testicular cancer.

> Behavior problems are the number-one killer of pets in this country.

2. **Obtaining a cat without considerable thought**: This is another common problem. People see a cute kitten and immediately decide to adopt it. Once home they realize they have made a mistake. They are not prepared for the responsibility of a cat, not all members of the family are happy to have a cat, resident pets don't adapt well to the new addition, or it just doesn't fit into the people's lifestyle. Buying a cat isn't the same as buying a new pair of shoes; time, thought, discussion with other family members, and research should all be done before making a decision to bring a cat into your home.

> Eight million pets are euthanized each year because of behavior problems.

3. **Obtaining a cat without thoroughly checking on its health and personality**: When a household decides to adopt a cat, be it from the shelter or a breeder, a great deal of time should go into selecting the right animal. Do you want a purebred or a mixed-breed cat? What kind of personality are you looking for? Is the animal in question in good health, friendly, and sociable? If you are buying from a breeder, ensure that they are registered with an appropriate cat council. Ask if the cat comes with a health guarantee. When visiting the cattery, note the overall health of the animals. If you decide to adopt a cat, have the details of your agreement put in writing, including the final cost of the cat, health guarantees, etc. If you have put down a deposit, make sure you obtain a receipt. For further information on buying a purebred cat, read on . . .

4. **Buying purebreds from pet shops or "backyard breeders"** (nonprofessionals who breed animals as a profitable hobby): Pet shops generally charge more for purebred kittens than a registered breeder will. In addition, the pet shop will not provide a history of a cat's parentage or registration papers. Some breeds of cats have genetic problems, which profes-

sional breeders can screen for. Pet shops and backyard breeders are less likely to provide this screening, however. As a result, without being aware of it, you may buy a cat that will run up substantial medical bills in the future or even pass away suddenly.

5. **Not seeking veterinary help:** Sometimes people don't realize the seriousness of a medical condition and fail to get the cat to a vet. Sometimes the owner doesn't have sufficient funds or the time to seek this care for a sick cat. It is advised that cat owners either purchase pet health insurance or set up a special "cat fund" in which they deposit $5 or $10 per week, to be used only in an emergency. Cat owners should be aware of their cat's physical and emotional state at all times. Look out for signs of illness such as loss of appetite, increase in appetite, coat condition, general appearance, changes in litter-box habits, and the presence of wounds or injuries. If problems appear, appropriate veterinary help should be sought in a timely manner. It is better to be safe than sorry, and delaying veterinary care may result in prolonged suffering for your cat and greater expense for you, since untreated medical conditions may become more difficult to treat or even result in death.

6. **Not vaccinating:** Failure to vaccinate can have dire consequences for your cat. Even if you have an indoor-only cat, it must still be vaccinated as recommended by your veterinarian. Vaccinating helps protect your cat from some serious and life-threatening diseases.

7. **Not cat-proofing the home:** This may result in injury or death to your cat. (For further information on how to cat-proof your home, see page 256.)

8. **Physically punishing a cat:** A cat should never be physically punished. Cats don't understand this type of discipline; rather, it induces stress and fear and doesn't teach your cat anything. If you struggle with how to address a specific behavioral problem, seek advice from a vet. Behavior modification done with kindness and respect will have a far greater success rate than smacking or hitting your cat.

> Between 50 and 70 percent of animals in shelters are there because their owners either couldn't or wouldn't deal with their behavior problems.

9. **Not feeding the cat an appropriate diet:** Cats have very specific dietary needs and as such need a balanced diet. There are many commercially available brands of cat food that will fulfill your cat's requirements. Don't attempt to feed your cat a homemade diet unless you have spent time researching the subject.

The Price of Pedigreed Kittens

The following are typical U.S. prices for pet-quality pedigreed kittens as of 2007.

Abyssinian: $650–$800

American Bobtail: $500–$1,000

American Curl: $600–$800

American Shorthair: $700–$900

Australian Mist: $550–$700

Australian Tiffanie: $600–$1,000

Balinese: $350–$400

Bengal: $350–$600

Birman: $400–$600

Bombay: $300–$600

British Longhair: $350–$450

British Shorthair: $1,000–$1,200

Burmese: $400–$600

Burmilla: $350–$500

Chartreux: $500–$700

Chausie: $500–$600

Colorpoint Shorthair: $300–$400

Cornish Rex: $300–$500

Devon Rex: $450–$700

Egyptian Mau: $600–$1,000

Exotic: $500–$700

Havana Brown: $800–$1,500

Himalayan: $350–$700

Japanese Bobtail: $225–$600

Javanese: $650–$800

Korat: $300–$500

LaPerm: $500–$600

Maine Coon: $350–$500

Manx: $400–$500

Munchkin: $500–$650

Nebelung: $300–$400

Norwegian Forest Cat: $400–$800

Ocicat: $300–$700

Oriental Longhair: $200–$300

Oriental Shorthair: $250–$600

Persian: $350–$500

Peterbald: $500–$800

Pixie-Bob: $300–$650

RagaMuffin: $500–$800

Ragdoll: $450–$950

Russian Blue: $525–$700

Savannah: $350–$700

Scottish Fold: $300–$700

The Norwegian Forest Cat takes a comic approach to life.

Selkirk Rex: $400–$600

Siamese: $325–$600

Siberian: $400–$800

Singapura: $600–$800

Snowshoe: $500–$600

Somali: $600–$800

Sphynx: $1,000–$1,500

Tonkinese: $500–$600

Turkish Angora: $700–$1,000

Turkish Van: $350–$600

Largest Breed

The largest cat breed is the Ragdoll, with a weight of 12 to 20 pounds for males and 10 to 15 pounds for females.

Smallest Breed

The Singapura males weigh about six pounds, while females weigh about four pounds.

8 Reasons Not to Buy a Kitten from a Pet Store

Face the feline facts. Pet store kittens come from kitten mills, and kitten mills are nothing but cruel, inhumane breeding factories. Yes, these felines merit our compassion — just as much as cats from a reputable breeder, rescue group, or animal shelter do. But buying kittens from a pet store simply allows kitten mills to stay in existence and churn out hundreds of thousands of kittens each year, thus adding to the number of felines that are destroyed each year.

Need more reasons? The Humane Society of the United States offers these:

1. Pet stores obtain their kittens and cats from brokers, kitten mills, and backyard, or "accidental," breeders. They are not carefully bred for health or temperament.

2. Cats in kitten mills are caged and continually bred for years, with little or no human companionship. They are then killed, abandoned, or sold to another "miller" after their fertility wanes.

3. Pet store clerks will never admit that their kittens and cats come from these mills. They focus on sales and making a profit, not the welfare of cats.

4. Pet store employees typically have only limited knowledge about cats and feline care.

5. Do not be fooled into thinking that a "USDA-inspected" breeder means a "good" breeder. The U.S. Department of Agriculture establishes only minimum care standards.

6. Kitten mill kittens often have medical problems that can lead to pricey veterinary bills.

7. Pet store kittens are not handled and socialized properly and are often separated from their mother and littermates too early.

8. One notable exception: Please consider giving a home to cats and kittens that are showcased by local animal shelters, breed rescue clubs, and other reputable groups at pet supply stores. Major chains such as PetsMart and Petco do not sell pets. Instead, they offer space in their stores for these groups, which seek to find loving homes for homeless cats and kittens.

How to Recognize Reputable Cat Breeders

Congratulations, you've done your homework. You've studied various cat breeds and narrowed your choice to a few. We salute you for putting in the time to candidly assess which breed best suits your lifestyle. You also plan to steer clear of pet stores. But how do you go about finding a reputable breeder?

Here's help: the Purebred Cat Breed Rescue is a nonprofit group whose mission is to provide a safety net for purebred cats. This organization is actively supported by the top feline registries — the Cat Fanciers' Association (CFA), The International Cat Association (TICA), and the American Cat Fanciers Association (ACFA). This breed rescue group provides pointers on its website, purebredcatbreedrescue.org, to assist you in finding a top-notch breeder who can unite you with the cat of your dreams.

A reputable breeder . . .

1. . . . is willing to talk to the prospective buyer and share information about the cat's history and, if available, about any personality quirks, special care needs of the breed, and cat care and maintenance, both before and after placement.

2. . . . will not sell kittens before they are 12 weeks of age and have been vaccinated.

3. . . . will place pet kittens after they have already been neutered or spayed. In some exceptional circumstances, reputable breeders may contractually require the kitten to be altered by a certain age, may charge a refundable fee to ensure this occurs, and will follow up to see that the contract is kept.

4. . . . makes every effort to be honest in evaluating the cat's soundness and will provide a veterinary health assessment. You can contact the veterinarian who did the assessment to confirm the findings.

5. . . . offers a health guarantee in writing and lists any health defects that may be present.

6. . . . provides references from people who have previously obtained kittens from the breeder and gives permission to discuss the breeder's cats with a veterinarian.

7. . . . will help in placing your cat if, in the future, circumstances arise that preclude you from keeping the cat.

8. . . . have the kitten microchipped or assist you in getting an identification chip.

9. . . . will often require a visit to inspect your home prior to placement to ensure the kitten will live in a healthy, safe, and caring environment.

10. . . . will ask you to sign a contract that spells out the terms of the adoption.

Just Exactly What Is a Cat Fancy?

Good question! **Cat Fancy** is the umbrella term that refers to the world of cat shows, breeders, and cat enthusiasts. They share a common goal of registering pedigreed cats and promoting the health and welfare of all cats. And, yes, there is even a major publication that sports this name.

If you want to learn more, visit www.fanciers.com/clubs.html for a listing of show schedules, information on shows, cat registering organizations, and cat clubs.

The Role of the CFA

Considered the granddaddy of all the breed registries, the Cat Fanciers' Association is a nonprofit organization founded in 1906. With headquarters in Manasquan, New Jersey, the CFA has grown from a one-person operation to occupying a 10,000-square-foot building that houses a staff of 21, who handle registrations, transfers of ownership, additions of cattery name suffixes, cattery name registrations, duplicated or corrected registration certificates, certified pedigrees, cattery offspring reports, reverse pedigree reports, and championship and premiership confirmations. Whew!

In addition, CFA shows are staged worldwide all year long. These shows are judged by individuals who meet high qualification criteria and have completed a rigorous training program that well qualifies them to evaluate the show cat based on CFA breed standards.

If you adore your purebred cat, prefer tabbies, or simply like cats, but are not able to have one in your home, you can still volunteer with the Cat Fanciers' Association in a variety of ways. You can assist at a cat show, work with purebred rescue groups, or participate in a fund-raiser. Or perhaps you have some ideas of your own. To learn more, visit www.cfa.org.

The CFA is committed to promoting and protecting all cats and has made contributions to feline health, feline health research, animal welfare, and disaster relief. The CFA is affiliated with the Winn Feline Foundation, a nonprofit organization that supports health-related studies of medical problems affecting cats. Read about some of the research funded by the Winn Feline Foundation by visiting its website: www.winnfelinehealth.org.

Cat Breeders to Avoid

1. One who isn't willing to take the time to meet with you in person and answer your questions.

2. One who overbreeds cats. (Females should never be bred more than once every two years.)

3. One who doesn't allow you to visit the kittens or cats in their own environment — who, instead, requests to meet you in a supermarket parking lot or other public place.

4. One who breeds cats for sentimental reasons alone — so that children can witness the "miracle of birth" or so the female "can have one litter" before she is spayed.

5. One who comments that she likes the extra spending money she makes from breeding cats on the side.

6. One who breeds more than two different cat breeds.

7. One who does not have a good working relationship with a reputable veterinarian.

8. One who does not belong to a professional breed registry group such as the Cat Fanciers' Association.

9. One who does not provide records of the kittens' vaccinations and medical tests.

10. One who claims to have created a new breed free of any hereditary diseases.

Catterysearch.com

This site enables you to find reputable breeders throughout the United States and abroad. Their online listing contains 3,220 cat breeders from 61 countries who specialize in 62 cat breeds. Click on the directory and get complete information, including location and contact information for the cat breeders.

The Socialized Kitty

Life for a new kitten is a cabaret, old chum. But it's not going to be that way forever. Introduce Fluffy into the human world with a plan in mind, and you'll all be happier for it.

Introduce Kitty to one person at a time, and then gradually to more people in noisier situations.

Invite friends, relatives, and their pets to meet your new addition, but when you see that Kitty is getting overwhelmed and crabby, take him to a neighbor's house for a well-earned rest.

When the veterinarian proclaims that she has been adequately vaccinated, take Kitty on an outing to the park or just around the neighborhood. Avoid unfamiliar animals, which may not have been vaccinated against disease.

Let Kitty visit all the rooms in the house, under strict supervision. Encourage him to explore but not exterminate family heirlooms.

Kitty should meet people of all ages and appearances so as to be familiar with them all—a man with a beard, an elderly person with a cane, a child on a bicycle, and so on. Give Kitty a treat whenever she makes a new friend.

All About Spaying and Neutering

Spaying is the medical term for the surgical removal of a female cat's ovaries and uterus via an abdominal incision. *Neutering* refers to castration, or the removal of a male cat's testicles. Both procedures have had their supporters and detractors. Those opposed to these procedures have claimed that it is an attempt to undermine the cat's true nature and that neutered cats are not as healthy as intact cats. What do you think?

Spaying

1. The most important reason for spaying a cat is to prevent unwanted litters and to eliminate sexual frustration and its discomfort. The best time to spay her is from 8 weeks to 6 months of age.

2. An unspayed female goes into heat three or four times a year. During these periods she may cry incessantly and become highly stressed. This behavior can persist for as long as a week at a time, and if the cat is never permitted to mate, she may behave like this all the time. It is best that she is spayed before she reaches this stage. Spaying also prevents her from spotting.

3. If an unspayed female is not allowed to mate after repeated heats, a condition known as pyometra can develop. This infection of the womb often results in depression, vomiting, loss of appetite, and increased urination.

4. A young cat who has been spayed is less likely to contract certain cancers, such as cervical cancer and highly malignant ovarian tumors.

5. Spaying eliminates the risk of cesarean section during delivery of kittens.

6. Spaying your little fur ball will help give her a longer and healthier life.

Neutering

1. A neutered male cat will be less likely to become amorous and stray away from home.

2. A neutered male cat will be far less aggressive and less likely to enter into combat.

3. If the cat is not castrated and one of its testicles has not descended into its scrotum, the remaining testicle could potentially grow into a tumor, a malignancy that can spread.

4. Neutering can reduce the possibility that the male will spray urine in the house, which can get pretty smelly.

5. Neutering your little guy will reduce his chances of getting testicular cancer and prostate tumors.

11 Myths About Spaying and Neutering

1. **Myth:** Preventing Petunia from being able to breed would be unnatural.
The truth: Destroying unwanted cats is unnatural.

2. **Myth:** Neutering will make my cat fat and change his personality.
The truth: If Abner is putting on some extra poundage, chances are you are overfeeding him or not providing him with enough exercise. If Abner does undergo a personality change, it will be for the better. He'll be happier, better adjusted, and more affectionate.

3. **Myth:** Princess is a pedigreed cat and should be bred.
The truth: One quarter of all cats brought to shelters are pedigreed.

4. **Myth:** It's better for Tinkerbell to have one litter before she's spayed.
The truth: Veterinarians have shown that Tink will be a lot healthier if she's spayed before her first heat.

5. **Myth:** Little Tiger will be a mere shadow of his former male self.

The truth: Tiger's brain doesn't work that way. He has no concept of being a male or what that's about.

6. **Myth:** It costs too much to have a cat spayed or neutered.
The truth: It's a one-time-only expense and is far cheaper than the cost of a litter. If finances are a problem, contact your local animal shelter or ask your vet if you can pay in installments.

7. **Myth:** I'll be able to find homes for all of Bernadette's kittens.
The truth: Maybe, maybe not! If you do you, you will have beaten the odds but nonetheless added to the overpopulation problem. Too many kittens wind up in shelters, where as many as 60 percent are euthanized. Will Bernadette's offspring be spayed? How many little Bernadettes and Bernies will she ultimately add to our cat population crisis?

8. **Myth:** Males don't have to be neutered because they can't give birth.

The truth: Come on — it takes two to tango.

9. **Myth:** I want my children to experience the miracle of birth.
The truth: Your kids can watch the miracle of birth on any of a number of nature programs, and observing an actual delivery can be traumatic for a child in the event that something goes wrong. They are better off learning about the tragedy of overpopulation.

10. **Myth:** The surgery is dangerous.
The truth: The chances of anything bad happening to General Tso while he's being neutered are minimal. Competent veterinarians are equipped to deal with any problem that might arise during the procedure.

11. **Myth:** Betsy will be a better pet if I let her have a litter.
The truth: Betsy might actually become more aggressive.

6 Reasons Not to Declaw Your Cat

The Humane Society of the United States has taken a firm stand on the issue of declawing. They write, "People choose to declaw their cats for a number of reasons: Some are frustrated with shredded drapes or furniture, some are worried about being scratched, and others simply feel that a declawed cat is easier to live with. In many cases, cats are declawed preemptively, as a part of a spay/neuter package offered by veterinarians, even before claw-related problems occur." Here are some important facts to think about before you even consider declawing as an option.

1. Too often people believe that declawing is a simple surgery that removes a cat's nails, the equivalent of a person having her fingernails trimmed. Sadly, this is far from the truth. Declawing traditionally involves the amputation of the last bone of each toe. If performed on a human being, it would be comparable to cutting off each finger at the last knuckle.

2. Declawing can leave cats with a painful healing process, long-term health issues, and numerous behavior problems. This is especially unfortunate because declawing is an owner-elected procedure and unnecessary for the vast majority of cats.

3. Laser surgery is one technique employed for declawing. During laser surgery, a small, intense beam of light cuts through tissue by heating and vaporizing it, meaning there's less bleeding and a shorter recovery time. But the surgical technique itself is similar to the traditional method (or "onychectomy"), with the laser simply replacing a steel scalpel. So while the use of a laser may slightly reduce the duration of the healing process, it does not change the nature of the procedure.

4. Tendonectomy, another procedure introduced more recently, effectively deactivates a cat's claws by severing the tendons that extend the toes. The surgery retains the claws in the paws and is often thought to be more humane because of its shorter recovery time. But the method has its own set of problems. Since cats who have undergone this procedure are unable to keep their claw length in check through vigorous scratching, owners must be extra careful to continually trim nails to prevent them from growing into the paw pads and causing infections. And though tendonectomies are generally considered less traumatic because of decreased post-operative pain, a 1998 study published in the *Journal of the American Veterinary Medical Association* found the incidence of bleeding, lameness, and infection was similar for both procedures. Furthermore, the American Veterinary Medical Association does not recommend tendonectomies.

5. While there have been changes in the way that cats are declawed, it's still true that for the majority of cats, these surgical procedures are unnecessary. Educated owners can easily train their cats to use their claws in a manner that allows animal and owner to happily coexist.

6. Declawing and tendonectomies should be reserved only for those rare cases in which a cat has a medical problem that would warrant such surgery — or after exhausting all other options, it becomes clear that the cat cannot be properly trained and, as a result, would be removed from the home. In these cases, a veterinarian should inform the cat's caretakers about complications associated with the surgical procedures (including the possibility of infection, pain, and lameness) so that owners have realistic expectations about the outcome. There is just as much evidence to support the case against declawing as there is research to support it, with some studies finding few or only short-term adverse reactions to the surgery and others finding medical complications and significant differences in behavior.

In Defense of Declawing

The Humane Society of the United States deems declawing an act of cruelty, and several countries have outlawed the practice as a viable procedure. But many veterinarians, including our own expert-in-residence, Dr. O'Reilly, have performed the procedure routinely and without any hesitation. Here are some of their thoughts on this subject:

1. The declawing procedure has often been described as the amputation of the phalanx bone, the last bone of the cat's paw. Many veterinarians maintain that this is not the case at all. They state that an onychectomy is merely the removal of the cat's retractable nail and that the phalanx is not removed or injured in any manner and that the removal of any toe bone should be performed only as a treatment for trauma or removal of a tumor.

2. The risk of infection, pain, or lameness is a complication of any surgery and is inherent in any surgical procedure involving an appendage. This is hardly the case in declawing. Few, if any, complications arise from the removal of a nail. In fact, in most cases the cat is able to walk comfortably on all toes and to jump off furniture within three days after the procedure.

3. Few veterinarians would knowingly perform any procedure on a cat that would result in pain and lameness, and to suggest otherwise is not acceptable.

3 Declawing Alternatives

Alternatives to declawing will not only help you resolve some of Kitty's destructive behavior but will eliminate the need for this often inhumane operation. Here are some alternatives to declawing.

1. Get Buzz a scratching post to redirect his scratching. (See page 324.)

2. Keep his nails trimmed. Do it carefully so as not to injure his paws. In any event, most cats don't enjoy this procedure; try to work carefully but quickly, and talk to your cat while you're working to keep him calm. Ask your vet to demonstrate the proper way of trimming claws.

3. Soft Paws are blunt acrylic nail caps that are glued onto the cat's claws. The idea is that the blunt nail will not be sharp enough to cause damage.

5 Reasons to Declaw a Cat

Dr. Ronald Hines, a veterinary practitioner for over 30 years and the owner of 2ndchance.com, writes, "Like the scales of justice, one must weigh all factors on the side of declawing the cat or leaving it intact before making a decision." Although Dr. Ronald Hines has declawed a number of cats, he has established strict guidelines that justify the procedure. Here are some instances that warrant the removal of a cat's claws.

1. Your cat is injuring another cat in the household.

2. The cat has developed an incurable disease, such as lupus-like conditions, and its claws may cause self-trauma and infection.

3. The cat has developed personality changes that make it a threat to owners and children.

4. A household member has lowered immune-system function due to chemotherapy, debilitating disease, heart-valve infection, or AIDS — situations in which a cat scratch could be life-threatening.

5. Blended households and new family members present an ultimatum to other family members, such as "either the cat is declawed or kept outside."

10 Basic Rules for Cats Who Rule the Roost

Learning to live with your new humans can be trying. They are slow on the uptake and often live in a state of denial, imagining that the home you inhabit somehow belongs to them. Nothing could be further from the truth, and it's going to be your job to educate them. Rule with benevolence — only when it's convenient, of course.

1. Those Dreaded Doors

Do not allow closed doors in any room. To get a door opened, stand on hind legs and hammer it with forepaws. Once the door is opened, it is not necessary to use it. After you have ordered an "outside" door opened, stand halfway in and out, and think about several things. This is particularly important during very cold weather, rain, snow, or mosquito season. Swinging doors are to be avoided at all costs.

2. Handling Visitors

Quickly determine which guest hates cats the most. Sit on that lap. For sitting on laps or rubbing against trouser legs, select fabric that contrasts well with your fur. Velvet takes precedence over all other cloth. For the guest who exclaims, "I love kitties!" be ready with aloof disdain, apply claws to stockings or arms, or apply a quick nip to the ankle. Always accompany guests to the bathroom. Just sit there and stare.

3. Around the House

If one of your humans is engaged in an activity and the other is idle, stay with the busy one. This is called "helping."

When supervising cooking, sit just behind the left heel of the cook. You cannot be seen and thereby stand a better chance of being stepped on and then picked up and comforted.

For book readers, get in close under the chin, between eyes and book, unless you can lie across the book itself.

For knitting projects or paperwork, lie on the work in a manner that obscures the maximum amount of the project. Pretend to doze, but every so often slap the pencil or knitting needles. Sit on the papers, and roll around on them, scattering them to the best of your ability. After you've been pushed away, knock pens, pencils, and erasers off the table, one at a time. Embroidery and needlepoint canvases make great hammocks, by the way.

When a human is holding the newspaper in front of his or her face, be sure to jump at the back of the paper. Humans love surprises.

Dart quickly in front of but as close as possible to the human, especially when your so-called owner is navigating stairs; carrying something large and unwieldy; moving from room to room in the dark; and getting up in the morning. This will help improve the human's co-ordination skills.

Laundry presents many opportunities for fun. Warm laundry fresh from the dryer makes a perfect bed. As soon as the laundry basket is put down for sorting, arrange yourself for a nap. If the human removes you, keep returning until the laundry isn't warm anymore. Now it's playtime. Pounce on anything the human tries to fold, especially underwear and nylons. For added fun, grab a sock and hide under the bed with it.

4. Playtime

This is an important part of life. Get enough sleep in the daytime so you are fresh for your nocturnal games. Here are some great choices:

Catch Mouse: The humans would have you believe that

those lumps under the covers are their feet and hands. They are actually Bed Mice, rumored to be the most delicious of all the rodents in the world, though no cat has ever been able to catch one. Maybe YOU can be the first.

King of the Hill: This game must be played with at least one other cat. Sleeping humans are the hill, which must be defended at all costs from the other cat(s). Anything goes. You'll need to develop unusual tactics to dominate on this unstable playing field. Warning: Playing this game to excess will result in expulsion from the bed. Should the humans

Hockey cats on a vintage German postcard.

grow restless, immediately begin purring and cuddle up to them. This should buy you some time until they fall asleep again.

Tube Mouse: This is a game played in the bathroom. Next to the Big White Drinking Bowl is a roll of soft white paper, which is artfully attached to the wall so that it can spin. Inside this roll is the Tube Mouse. When you grab the paper, the Tube Mouse will spin frantically as it tries to escape from you. When the Mouse is exposed, it dies of fright and stops spinning.

5. Toys

Any small item can be used as a toy. If a human tries to confiscate it, this means it is a Valuable Toy. Run with it under the bed. Look outraged when the human takes it away. Watch where it is put, so you can steal it later. Two reliable sources of toys are dresser tops and wastebaskets. Here are some more:

Bright, shiny things such as keys, brooches, or coins should be hidden so the other cat(s) and humans can't play with them. They work well as hockey pucks on uncarpeted floors.

Shoelaces can be a great source of fun, especially when your human is trying to tie them.

Within paper bags dwell the Bag Mice. They are small and the same color as the bag, so they are hard to see, but you can easily hear the crinkling noises they make as they scurry around the bag. Anything, including shredding the bag, can be done to kill them.

6. A Scratching Post by Any Other Name

If it feels good, go for it. Humans are often confused about what constitutes a scratching post and often become territorial about their belongings. Be persistent. If they purchase a special scratching post for you, ignore it completely.

7. Water, Water Everywhere

Dripping taps are the best sources of fresh water. Toilets are the next best. It is imperative that any sound of running water be investigated immediately for a possible drink.

8. The Vacuum Beast

This appalling appliance is known by many names, "Cat Eater" being the most prevalent. Humans will turn into raging monsters while under its influence, sucking up all the carefully shed cat hair and terrorizing the feline residents with evil glee. All you can do is run and hide. Occasionally, the humans are forced to open the vacuum cleaner and remove a swollen bag from within. This is its stomach, and must be destroyed. If the human starts to yell, ignore it; the person is just cheering you on.

9. How to Handle Illness

The vet is where your human takes you when you are sick. The place smells funny, and there are cats, dogs, and awful things like needles and pills. The following are some tips for dealing with vets and the inevitable aftermath.

When you see the carrier come out, hide. Once the human grabs you, struggle gamely. Splay your legs out so it is difficult to cram you into the carrier. If the human is trying to put you in with another pet, allow the other pet to bolt out the door. In the car, meow plaintively all the way to the vet's. Reach through the bars of the carrier and claw the human behind the steering wheel. At the vet's, once again splay your legs and brace yourself against the carrier's walls so they can't dump you out easily.

At home, resist attempts to feed you pills or liquid medicine. As soon as you hear the pill bottle rattle, hide. Whatever you do, do not open your mouth. Squirming is good. Shake your head vigorously to remove any medicine placed in your mouth. Refuse any food that smells as if medicine is sprinkled on it. Inspect your food carefully before you dig in, to make sure it's safe to eat. If you locate a pill (humans can be very sneaky!), eat around it carefully and make sure to leave it at the very center of the bowl when you're done.

If you have to throw up, get to a chair quickly. If you cannot manage in time, find an Oriental rug or a shag carpet. When throwing up, back up as you do it, so as to spread the vomit over the largest possible area.

10. About Sleeping Humans

Sleeping humans are boring. The "direct approach" is nearly always successful in rejuvenating a dormant human. Do one of the following: trample, purr, meow, or head-butt. If the human is stubborn, you may have to resort to more drastic tactics, such as clawing the bedclothes, rattling the blinds, or singing at the top of your voice. Remember that you are doing your human a great favor. After all, why sleep when the person could be spending quality time with you, the beloved cat?

"When you're done ruining the sofa, I want you to start clawing the new stereo speakers. After that, you need to leave your tongue prints in the butter, then take a nap on a pile of clean laundry."

The Best Cat Breeds for Allergy Sufferers

Achoo! We hate to break the news to you, but no cat breed can claim to be hypoallergenic. The reason? It's not the length or texture of hair that causes some folks to sneeze in the presence of a cat — it's an allergen found in a cat's saliva that dries on its fur and then becomes airborne.

So, the "bald and the beautiful" breeds like the Cornish Rex or the Sphynx can still trigger allergies because they shed skin cells. Among all recognized breeds, the Siberian seems to cause the least sneezing and the fewest itchy eyes, but the reason remains a mystery.

Sadly, about 10 million Americans are allergic to cats, according to the Asthma and Allergy Foundation of America. The cat allergen ranks as one of the top five most potent allergy-inducing compounds. Some of these people love their cats so much that they take anti-allergy pills and injections to minimize their symptoms.

But the future looks promising. According to reports published in *Catnip*, a national monthly publication affiliated with Tufts University, researchers at the University of California at Los Angeles (UCLA) are currently working on an experimental therapy that may, in essence, stop the molecular process that triggers a person's allergic reaction to cats.

In addition, in late 2006 a San Diego–based biotech company announced that through genetic engineering, scientists had bred the world's first naturally hypoallergenic cat, whose name is Joshua. Allerca officials report that their team searched for natural variations in the cat gene that controls allergy-producing properties and then bred cats with the desired trait. They are closely guarding the scientific details but submitted their findings to a peer-reviewed journal in 2007.

Scientists at Allerca began making Allerca Gene Divergence (GD) kittens available to allergy-prone customers in early 2007. The GDs go for about $4,000 each, plus $800 for shipping and another $2,000 if you don't want to spend the next two years on the waiting list. To find out more, visit Allerca.com.

FRED FRANCIS

A Feline Wellness Record

In addition to the following information, always keep a current photo of your cat with your pet records (helpful if the cat ever gets lost). The following data will come in handy when your cat is ill or lost.

Recent photograph

Vaccination history

Rabies certificates

Health certificates

Copies of medical records and payment receipts

Breeder's contact information, if applicable

Pedigree, if applicable

FeLV and FIV vaccination certificates

Normal body weight of the cat

A log of all vet and hospital visits

Names of all medications and the dates they were prescribed or administered

Names of doctors and others who have cared for your cat

10 Tips for Helping Your Cat and Dog Get Along

In most cases, dogs and cats sharing the same home will form a friendship — or at least a tame tolerance for each other. Pay heed to your cat's signals related to its sense of safety. When the feline starts to walk around your dog and sits with its back to the dog in a relaxed manner, these are good clues that a truce has been achieved between them. Here are some tips for getting to this point.

1. The best time to introduce cats and dogs is when they are young. The first two or three months of life are the prime socialization period, a key time for cats and dogs to cultivate friendships. But you can also successfully introduce adult cats to dogs.

2. Teach your dog to "sit" and "stay" on command, remaining in place even when your cat enters the room.

3. Bribe your dog with treats. Keep a bag of treats handy. When it starts to go after the cat, redirect the dogs' attention by showing it a treat. Calmly instruct the dog to sit or stay.

4. Keep your cat's claws trimmed to avoid injuries to your dog. All it takes is one sharp swat to a dog's nose to cause bleeding.

5. In the beginning, keep your dog on a leash at all times. When you are not home, keep your dog in a crate or in an area separated from your cat.

6. Yelling at Buck when he goes for Snowball won't work. It will only heighten his excitement and your cat's fearfulness.

7. Do not attempt to prevent your cat from fleeing to its safe spot when feeling threatened. Equally important: do not rush after the cat and shower it with kindness or sweet talk. These tactics only tell your cat that it has every reason to be worried about your dog. Instead, act calmly and speak in an upbeat tone.

8. Make sure your cat has escape routes and dog-free zones. Clear an area under your bed and provide a tall cat tree or wide, sturdy shelves for the cat to perch on, out of your dog's reach. If possible, install baby gates in doorways of rooms where you keep your cat's food, water bowl, and litter box.

9. Be patient. It takes some time for a dog to learn good manners around a new feline roommate. When your dog consistently demonstrates that it won't chase your cat, let the dog move around the house with his leash dragging behind. If the canine starts to chase your feline, step on the leash.

10. Never force a fur-against-fur introduction between your cat and dog. Cats feel most secure with "four on the floor." Control the contact between them and go slow. Always maintain control of your dog; let your cat enter and leave the room freely.

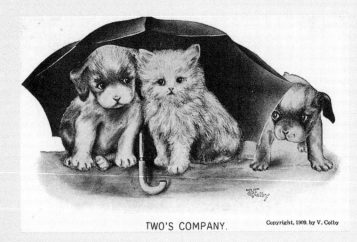

TWO'S COMPANY. Copyright, 1909, by V. Colby

13 Cats That Are Most Like Dogs

1. **American Bobtail** — Bobtails love to play games and often will initiate a game of hide-and-seek.

2. **American Curl** — This very attentive breed will follow its owner from room to room so as not to miss out on anything.

3. **Bombay** — This cat loves to play fetch and to greet visitors at the front door.

4. **Burmese** — Very eager to receive and give affection, a Burmese cat will be your shadow as you walk around your home.

5. **Chartreux** — This kitty loves to play fetch and come when you call it by name.

6. **Manx** — A Manx loves to retrieve items and will often bury its favorite toys.

7. **Ocicat** — This one plays fetch, walks on a leash, responds to voice commands, and obeys household rules.

8. **Oriental Shorthair** — These door greeters require a great deal of attention and affection, and they are extremely loyal.

9. **RagaMuffin** — Because of their sweetness, Raga-Muffins have been compared to endearing lap dogs. They thrive on affection and will follow you from room to room just to stay close.

10. **Ragdoll** — This loyal cat will greet you at your front door and follow you from room to room.

11. **Russian Blue** — It loves a good game of fetch and is extremely sensitive to its humans' feelings and moods. If you're feeling sad, the Russian Blue will pat your face to make you feel better.

12. **Siberian** — The Siberian is fiercely loyal, will greet you at the door when you come home, and will shadow you from room to room.

13. **Tonkinese** — Tonks love to play games and are great door greeters. They also love to be the center of attention and will perform for humans.

TOP: Like dogs, the Bombay loves to play fetch and greet visitors at the front door.
BOTTOM: The tailless Manx.

A CAT-tionary

Catacomb. Grooming device for Kitty. Good for removing cat-a-mats.

Catapult. What happens when the catacomb gets caught in the cat-a-mats.

Catnip. What Kitty will give you if you "pult" too hard with the catacomb.

Catcall. Signaling device used to open doors, fill food bowls, and receive undivided attention.

Catty-corner. A good place to keep the litter box.

Caterwaul. What sometimes gets hit instead of the litter.

Catkin. The results of an unaltered cat.

Cat's cradle. Where Kitty sleeps, that is, any bed, sofa, or other warm, comfy spot in the house.

Catwalk. Kitty's daily exercise routine, which consists of short trips to the food bowl (with occasional detours to the catty-corner).

Catalog. Useful outdoor scratching post.

Catalyst. Litter, cat food, treats, toys, etc. What humans use to shop for Kitty with.

Catgut. Essential internal part of the cat, which requires filling on an hourly basis.

29 Dogs Who Hate Cats

According to Dogbreedinfo.com, most dogs will get along with the family feline, providing that the socialization of the new puppy and the cat are done as carefully as possible. This process should occur when the puppy is around 3 months old. Since most reputable breeders don't let their puppies go to a new home before 12 weeks of age, this means that you will need to introduce puppy and kitty as soon as you walk in the door with your new bundle of fur. The kind folks at Dogbreedinfo.com also point out that it's easier to introduce a kitten into a household that already has dogs rather than the other way around. Still, there are dog breeds that generally don't like cats and shouldn't be left alone with them. They are as follows:

Afghan Hound	Basenji	Harrier	Rhodesian Ridgeback
Ainu Dog	Beagle	Ibizan Hound	Saluki
Alaskan Malamute	Border Collie	Jack Russell Terrier	Samoyed
American Blue Gascon Hound	Border Terrier	Norwegian Elkhound	Shiba Inu
American Foxhound	Bullmastiff	Otterhound	Vizsla
Australian Cattle Dog	Dandie Dinmont Terrier	Pharaoh Hound	Weimaraner
Australian Kelpie	English Foxhound	Plott Hound	
	Greyhound	Redbone Coonhound	

Catsup. Mealtime. It fills the catgut.

Catnap. What cats do when they're not catsupping.

Category. The icky stuff that Kitty leaves on the porch step after eating the outside of a mouse.

Catfish. What Kitty does in your aquarium.

Catbird. What Kitty's fur looks like after a walk in the woods.

Catamount. Any perch in the house that is higher than a human's head.

Caterpillar. The lady in the white coat who says, "Now swallow the medicine like a good kitty."

Catalyze it! What Kitty tells you when you find the broken vase ("Meow — it was the dog, I swear it!").

Cataract. What the house looks like if you leave Kitty alone for too long.

Catatonic. What humans drink after seeing the house.

Catastrophe. An award Kitty receives for having the most beautiful behind.

How Many Cats Does It Take to Screw in a Light Bulb?

Persian: "Light bulb? What light bulb?"

Somali: "The sun is shining, the day is young, we've got our whole lives ahead of us, and you're worrying about a burned-out light bulb?"

Norwegian Forest Cat: "Just one. And I'll replace any wiring that's not up to date, too."

Cornish Rex: "Hey, guys, I've found the switch."

Sphynx: "Turn it back on again, I'm cold."

Singapura: "I'll just blow in the AOV's ear and he'll do it." (AOV: Any Other Variety)

Siamese: "Make me!"

Birman: "Puh-leeez, dahling. I have servants for that kind of thing."

Maine Coon: "Oh, me, me! Pleeeeeeaze let me change the light bulb! Can I, huh? Can I? Huh? Huh? Can I?"

Exotic: "Let the AOV do it. You can feed me while he's busy."

Manx: "Why change it? I can still pee on the carpet in the dark."

Russian Blue: "While it's dark, I'm going to sleep on the couch."

Korat: "Korats are not afraid of the dark."

British Shorthair: "Light bulb? Light bulb? That thing I ate was a light bulb?"

Turkish Angora: "You need light to see?"

British Moggie: "None, catnap time is too precious to waste!"

The British Shorthair is one of the oldest of all cat breeds.

How to Choose Your Second Cat

If you already have a resident cat, it's important to take this cat's personality and activity level into consideration before selecting a companion, or your house may become a war zone. Keep the following guidelines in mind when selecting your next family member. Remember that they are only guidelines and that there are occasional exceptions to the rule. Whatever the combination, a slow, systematic introduction process will help ensure that the resident cat and the newcomer will eventually share the house amicably. Here are some more helpful tips from catsinternational.com.

If you have an adult female who has been an "only" cat for some time, it is best to get a younger female. Males, even friendly ones, can overpower and frighten females. Male kittens, while more easily dominated by the female, still grow up to be rambunctious teenagers that engage in a style of play that involves pouncing and wrestling (not a female's idea of fun).

If a young, active male is your family pet, he would really enjoy having a male buddy who shares his enthusiasm for vigorous play.

A laid-back, older (neutered) male cat may enjoy "mothering" a kitten — male or female. They usually make better mother substitutes than spayed females. Females, in general, are less accepting of newcomers.

Males tend to bond with each other unless both have dominant personalities. A dominant cat engages in a lot of rubbing — that is, scent-marking — behavior, likes to rest in high places (for surveillance purposes) and in doorways (to control the entrance to certain rooms), and shows little or no fear.

Have You Heard That One About the Vet . . .

A man runs into the vet's office, carrying his cat and screaming for help. The vet rushes him back to an examination room and puts the cat on the examination table. The vet examines the still, limp body and after a few moments tells the man that his cat, regrettably, is dead.

The man is agitated and demands a second opinion. The vet goes into the back room and brings out a cat. He places the cat down next to the other cat's body. The cat sniffs and pokes at the body, walks from head to tail to examine it, and finally looks at the vet and meows. The vet looks at the man and says, "I'm sorry, but the cat thinks that your cat is dead, too."

The man is still unwilling to accept reality. The vet brings in a Labrador Retriever. The Lab sniffs the body, walks from head to tail, and finally looks at the vet and barks. The vet looks at the man and says, "I'm sorry, but the Lab thinks your cat is dead, too."

The man, finally resigned to the diagnosis, thanks the vet and asks how much he owes. The vet answers, "$550."

"$550 to tell me my cat is dead?" exclaims the man.

"Well," the vet replies, "I would have charged you only $50 for my initial diagnosis. The additional $500 was for the cat scan and Lab tests."

How to Help Multiple Cats Get Along

When it comes to cats sharing the roost, the ideal of "the more the merrier" doesn't always work. As the number of cats increases, so does the risk for feline behavior problems. In fact, as the number of cats in a household climbs to ten, the chance that a problem will develop approaches, say, 100 percent.

So whether you are introducing a new kitten to your resident adult cat or bringing in a fourth adult to meet your tabby trio, here are some tips to create a harmonious — not chaotic — home:

Recognize that cats tend to be solitary creatures. Indoor cats have strong needs for personal space in order to remain calm and content. They are truly territorial animals.

Female cats and cats who are related to one another, in general, tend to form friendships more easily than unrelated males do (especially if they are not neutered).

A common cause of feline fights is a lack of highly valued resources — such as food bowls and litter boxes. Each cat in the household needs to have its own food and water bowls, litter box, bedding, and toys.

To intervene between feuding felines, first physically separate them into different areas of the home. A period of isolation behind closed doors can give each cat time to calm down and feel relief from the stress caused by a spat.

Once the cats have calmed down, gradually reintroduce them. Start by allowing one cat to have the run of the house while the other cat is confined in a room. Let them sniff and paw at each other from under the door.

After a few days, switch the roles, so the second cat now can walk around the house while the first cat is in the room by itself.

Take a cloth and rub the back of the first cat and then rub this cloth on the second cat and back to the first cat. What you are doing is sharing scents between the two cats so that they smell more familiar to each other.

Think like a cat. Cats are big into the concept known as "time sharing." Cat A may like to nap on the window perch in the mornings, while Cat B may prefer that spot during the afternoons. The goal is to get them used to the notion of living together and sharing objects and places in the house.

Never try to physically force the two together. Don't be dismayed if the two cats never become best buddies. If they can grow to tolerate and respect each other, consider this a victory.

In extreme cases, you may need to book an appointment with your veterinarian and consider using mood-altering medications to tone down aggressiveness and ease anxiety.

"You can visualize a hundred cats. Beyond that, you can't. Two hundred, five hundred, it all looks the same."
— JACK WRIGHT OF KINGSTON, ONTARIO, THE GUINNESS BOOK RECORD HOLDER FOR OWNING THE MOST CATS AT ONE TIME

17 Tips for Preparing Your Cat for the New Baby

Congratulations, you're expecting a baby! If your family already has a cat, you'll need to help that first "baby" adjust to the new one you'll soon bring home. You can help her cope with this big change in much the same way parents help children understand that a new brother or sister will be joining the family. By following the tips below, you can ease your pet's stress, help her welcome your new baby, and ensure that your pet stays where she belongs — with you and your growing family. Below are several suggestions from the HSUS for making that first introduction safer and smoother for all. Be sure to begin the process months before the baby's arrival to best prepare your pet. Note: If you are pregnant, be sure to consult "6 Things You Should Know About Pregnancy and Toxoplasmosis" on page 290.

1. Take her to the veterinarian for a routine health exam and necessary vaccinations.

2. Spay or neuter your pet. Not only do sterilized pets typically have fewer health problems associated with their reproductive systems, but they are also calmer and less likely to bite.

3. Consult with a veterinarian and pediatrician if the thought of your newborn interacting with Cleo makes you uncomfortable. By working with these experts before your baby is born, you can resolve problems early and put your mind at ease.

4. Address any pet-training and behavior problems. If Cleo exhibits fear and anxiety, now is the time to get help from an animal behavior specialist.

5. If his behavior includes gentle nibbling, pouncing, or swatting at you and others, redirect that behavior to appropriate objects.

6. Get her used to nail trims.

7. Train him to remain calmly on the floor beside you until you invite him on your lap, which will soon cradle a newborn.

8. Encourage friends with infants to visit your home to accustom her to babies. Supervise all pet and infant interactions.

9. Accustom him to baby-related noises months before the baby is expected. For example, play recordings of a baby crying, turn on the mechanical infant swing, and use the rocking chair. Make these positive experiences for him by offering a treat or playtime.

10. If the baby's room will be off limits to McGonigle, install a sturdy barrier such as a removable gate (available at pet or baby supply stores) or, for jumpers, even a screen door. Because these barriers still allow her to see and hear what's happening in the room, she'll feel less isolated from the family and more comfortable with the new baby noises.

11. Use a baby doll to help her get used to the real thing. Carry around a swaddled baby doll, and use the doll to get your pet used to routine baby activities, such as bathing and diaper changing.

12. Talk to her about the baby, using the baby's name if you've selected one.

13. Sprinkle baby powder or baby oil on your skin so she becomes familiar with the new smells.

14. Plan ahead to make sure she gets proper care while you're off having your baby.

15. When you return from the hospital, he may be eager to greet you and receive your attention. Have someone

else take the baby into another room while you give him a warm, but calm, welcome. Keep some treats handy.

16. After the initial greeting, you can bring Velvet with you to sit next to the baby; reward her with treats for appropriate behavior. You want her to view associating with the baby as a positive experience. To prevent anxiety or injury, never force her to get near the baby, and always supervise any interaction.

17. Life will no doubt be hectic caring for your new baby, but try to maintain regular routines as much as possible to help him adjust. And be sure to spend one-on-one quality time with your cat each day — it may help relax you, too. With proper training, supervision, and adjustments, you, your new baby, and Cleo should be able to live together safely and happily as one (now larger) family.

8 Tips for Avoiding Toxoplasmosis

If you are pregnant, avoid eating raw meat. Cook it thoroughly; avoid meat that is pink in color or bloody in texture. Avoid cured meats, such as Parma ham and salami.

Wash your hands, cooking utensils, and surfaces with an antibacterial soap after handling raw meat.

Wash all fruit and vegetables thoroughly to remove all traces of soil.

Avoid farms and farm animals. If you must visit farms, wash your hands thoroughly after any contact with sheep. Avoid handling newborn lambs.

Always wear gloves when gardening, and do not touch your mouth with soiled gloves.

If you are pregnant, have someone else clean the litter box. The person who cleans it should wear rubber gloves when handling dirty cat litter. Afterward, hands and gloves should be washed with antibacterial soap.

Avoid unpasteurized goat's milk and products made from it.

Cover children's sandboxes to prevent cats from using them as litter boxes.

6 Things You Should Know About Pregnancy and Toxoplasmosis

One of the first things your ob/gyn will ask you when you become pregnant is whether or not you have a cat. There is, after all, the risk of contracting the disease called toxoplasmosis. But though this possibility has in the past caused pregnant women to automatically give up their cats, the Centers for Disease Control recently concluded that relatively few cases of toxoplasmosis in pregnant women are caused by kittens or cats and that most people are infected through other avenues, such as eating undercooked meat. Simple, everyday habits of hygiene can reduce the risk of infection (from cats and elsewhere), making it safe to own and enjoy a cat. Here are some facts about this disease and its transmission, supplied by the ailurophiles at thecatgroup.org.uk.

1. *Toxoplasma gondii,* the small parasite that is responsible for toxoplasmosis, should be of concern to humans as well as cats, especially people with compromised immune systems. Cats become infested with this parasite through eating raw prey, but pass contagious feces for only about two weeks (and the feces themselves are infective only after one to three days have passed). It is believed that around 50 percent of all cats have been infected with this organism at some point in their lives, although the prevalence of infection varies according to the cat's lifestyle. Outdoor cats are more likely to become affected.

2. Recent research indicates that contact with cats does not increase the risk of *T. gondii* infection of people. Most cases of toxoplasmosis in humans occur after the ingestion of contaminated fruit or vegetables and meat, not from exposure to a cat. Veterinarians working with cats are no more likely to be infected with *T. gondii* than the general population.

3. A woman who was infected prior to a pregnancy cannot pass the disease on to her fetus, since she has already built up antibodies. However, women who are exposed to the disease during pregnancy have about a 40 percent chance of fetal infection, with the symptoms being most severe if the disease was contracted during the first trimester. A pregnant woman who has been infected runs the risk of miscarriage or stillbirth in the third trimester. The problems for a child born to an exposed mother are often not apparent at birth but may arise later.

4. Signs of toxoplasmosis include fever, loss of appetite, weight loss, lethargy, and flulike symptoms.

5. People in "high-risk" groups should not have contact with the cat's litter tray. Assign the responsibility for cleaning the litter box to someone else in your family. But have them wear rubber gloves and wash their hands thoroughly when done. It is also important that the trays be emptied daily so that oocysts don't have time to become infective while in the litter tray.

6. If you're pregnant and concerned about a possible exposure, ask your obstetrician to perform a simple blood test. If the result shows you were exposed to toxoplasmosis during pregnancy, you may be given medication and your baby may be tested and treated soon after birth. Keep in mind that the odds of contracting toxoplasmosis during pregnancy are extremely low, and even lower for your baby.

Simple, everyday habits of hygiene can reduce the risk of infection (from cats and elsewhere), making it safe to own and enjoy a cat.

15 Advantages of Keeping Your Cat Indoors

In 1992, The Humane Society of the United Stated approximated the average life span of an outdoor cat as 4 years, while indoor cats often reached 14 to 17 years, or even older. Of course, there are exceptions. One of our neighbors, who lives on a cul-de-sac, has an outdoor cat who is 12 years old and shows no signs of slowing down. But this is far from the norm, and most outdoor cats die young, nine lives notwithstanding.

Cats have been domesticated over the centuries and have therefore lost some of their natural survival instincts. Now they need responsible humans to care and make decisions for them. When you bring a new kitten into your home, be sure you understand the significance of the decision and the advantages of keeping the kitty indoors.

1. It won't be run over by a car.

2. It won't get lost.

3. It won't be frightened by loud blasts of traffic or construction noise.

4. It won't be susceptible to the whims of your neighbors. An unhappy neighbor might wish to do your cat harm.

5. It won't be attacked by a wild animal, dog, or even another cat.

6. It won't catch a disease from another animal, such as feline leukemia, rabies, or immunodeficiency viruses.

7. It is less likely to be infested with fleas, ticks, or worms.

8. It is less likely to ingest a deadly poison such as antifreeze or a pesticide.

9. It won't become ill from ingesting garbage or contaminated food left outside.

10. It won't run the risk of freezing in the winter and becoming dehydrated during the summer.

11. It won't wind up at the pound if lost.

12. It won't become trapped in a place from which it cannot escape, such as a neighbor's garage.

13. It won't be stolen.

14. It won't ingest poisonous plants.

15. It won't pose a danger to birds whose populations in some areas have been decimated by outdoor cats.

 **Outdoor Fun for the Indoor Cat**

Your indoor cat can enjoy the great outdoors too — safely.

1. Provide the kitty with a window seat or a perch, so it can enjoy watching the outside world and the little critters out there.

2. Build it a fenced-in backyard. (See "Please Fence Me In," page 292.)

3. If your apartment has a balcony, you can create a safe outdoor environment by providing some toys and kitty grass. Just make sure the cat can't climb onto the edge of the balcony or squeeze between slats.

4. Get a harness and leash; cats often enjoy being taken for a walk or, more accurately, taking you for a walk. Don't pull at the leash to control the cat, as you would for a dog. Let the cat roam, and just follow. If it gets into mischief, pull rank.

5. The kitty will be far happier as an indoor cat if you get a second cat and properly introduce the two. The cat's mind and body will be far more active with a pal in the same home.

Microchipping Your Cat

Having your cat microchipped is the best way to bring your cat home if it ever becomes lost.

These small computer chips are about the size of a rice grain. A veterinarian injects the chip under your cat's skin. Most cats tolerate this minor procedure with no problem.

The chip contains your cat's identifying information and can be read by a special scanner. If your cat gets lost and is taken to an animal shelter, most shelters can scan the information on the chip, identify your cat, and get it home to you.

The cost to microchip your cat at your local veterinarian is usually under $50. There is an additional minor fee to register your cat's microchip ID number to ensure that your cat's identification and your contact information are registered with as many shelters as possible, including those outside your area.

Some animal shelters automatically microchip their animals for adoption. If you adopt your cat from such a shelter, you usually have to pay only the small registration fee.

Local shelters often offer special rates to the community for microchipping. In my area, at certain times of the year cats and dogs can be microchipped for free. Call your local animal shelter to ask if this service is available.

Microchipping and microchip scanning are not available in all areas. It's especially important in these areas that your cat wear a safety collar with a pet ID tag. It provides the only chance that your cat, if lost and found, will make it back home.

Please Fence Me In

The Humane Society of the United States suggests that if you want to allow your cat outside in the privacy of your backyard, you can purchase or build a specially designed fence or enclosure that will prevent it from wandering off. But a fence may not prevent unfamiliar animals from entering your yard, so you should always supervise outdoor activity. Be sure to cat-proof the yard by checking that the fence has no escape routes and by making toxic plants, garden chemicals, and other dangerous objects inaccessible.

You can purchase a ready-made cat confinement system, or you can obtain plans designed for do-it-yourselfers. Here are leads for each type:

1. **The Underground Escape Proof Non-visible Cat Fence** is one of the most versatile cat-containment systems available anywhere today. It's very easy to use and install, and it works great in both small and larger areas. You can lay the boundary wire above ground in wooded areas or attach it to an existing fence. A harmless, noiseless radio signal lets you control your cats without raising your voice. Just place the transmitter in the area you want to protect, and create an instant non-visible barrier, which you can easily adjust. Visit Pet safe-warehouse.com.

2. **Cat Fence-In** stops cats from climbing over fences and up trees. It fits on fences of any height that are made of wood, vinyl, masonry, wire, or chain link. The system, which is easy to install, is mounted on top of an existing fence and prevents the cat from climbing above it. The fencing material is safe, narrow, strong, flexible, nonelectric, and almost invisible, and it has no gaps. A cat will climb only those structures that appear sturdy,

and although the Cat Fence-In is made of strong materials, it won't look that way to your cat. To find out more, visit Catfencein.com.

3. **The Purr . . . fect Cat Fence** is a complete free-standing backyard fence enclosure for cats. Your cat will enjoy exploring the great outdoors without any of the threats. The system can be self-installed in almost any configuration and does not require an existing fence. The enclosure material is flexible, so most cats won't try to climb it. For those dare-devil cats that do manage to get near the top, the "Houdini-Proof" arch along the top safely turns them back. Visit Purrfectfence.com for more information.

4. **Affordable Cat Fence** provides effective and humane cat containment by turning your yard into a secure enclosure. Rather than cause physical pain to your pets, as do electric fences or collars, this fence provides a barrier of netting supported by heavy-gauge steel stanchions that attach to your existing fence. The barrier angles into your yard, providing an overhang that cats won't climb. A vertical component inhibits the entry of feral cats and other animals. For more information consult Catfence.com.

5. **The Do-It-Yourself Cat Fence** is not for the faint-hearted or the unhandy. Be prepared to spend a considerable amount of time putting this one together. On the other hand, if you're an experienced builder, this fence will save you quite a bit of money. It's especially useful in keeping feral cats away from your little buddy. Visit Feralcat.com/fence.

6. **The Kittyview** is an indoor/outdoor cat enclosure that serves as a window perch. The Kittyview requires no assembly; it can be installed, using a few simple tools, in any window that is at least 20 inches wide. It takes about the same amount of work as setting up an air conditioner. Kittyview has walls of crystal-clear acrylic to give your cat a view of the great outdoors and a convenient opening into your living space, for safety. Its roof is bronze-tinted to reduce sunlight. Visit Kittyview.com.

7. Visit **just4cats.com** for instructions on how to build your own cat enclosure. You'll find over 65 detailed drawings with easy-to-understand instructions. This vast website covers all aspects of creating a safe outdoor haven for your cats.

---

5 Hotlines for Information About Cats

These are the numbers to call when you can't reach your vet or if there is an emergency. You can also consult these sources for general information about cat care. (See page 384 for numbers to dial for help with pet bereavement.)

1. **Animal Behavior Helpline:** (415) 554-3074. Dispenses general information.

2. **Dial-a-Vet:** (800) 719-8916. $19 for the first 10 minutes; $2 for each additional minute.

3. **Dr. Louis J. Camuti Memorial Feline Consultation and Diagnostic Service:** (800) 548-8937. Consultation fee by credit card.

4. **National Poison Control Center (ASPCA):** (800) 548-2423. Offers general and emergency advice twenty-four/seven. $55 per case.

5. **Tree House Animal Foundation:** (773) 506-3235. General information.

13 Ways to Protect Your Outdoor Cat

The ASPCA recommends keeping cats indoors in order to avoid the dangers of traffic, other animals, poisonous plants, and disease. People who want to give their cats the stimulation of being outdoors should consider full-screen enclosures for backyards and terraces. If you're set on allowing your cat to roam as it pleases, it's wise to take these precautions:

If you live near a road, it's safest to keep your cat on a harness and lead. A cat's lead can also be tied to a stationary object such as a post, but you'll need to keep an eye out to prevent accidents.

Consider converting a deck or porch into a screened-in cat playground, with climbing and scratching trees, ropes, and toys. You can get the job done cheaply with chicken wire.

Let your cat out during daylight hours only. At night, it is vulnerable to neighborhood predators and less visible to cars on the road.

Do not declaw an outdoor cat. It cannot effectively climb trees to escape trouble if it doesn't have claws on all four paws.

An ID tag will help identify your cat, and a reflective piece of tape around its collar will keep the cat visible after hours. Some people also tattoo their cats to help identify them if they get lost. You can also shave kitty's tummy and write your ID information in indelible ink. Of course, the fur grows back. (Also, see "Microchipping Your Cat," page 292.)

Teach your cat to come when you call. (See page 361.)

Place a bell on the cat's collar so you can hear your cat from a distance.

Be aware of other cats in the neighborhood, as territorial issues may exist all around you.

Spay female cats so they don't become impregnated.

Always pay attention when backing up your car. Make sure that a cat is not in your path.

Keep your cat up-to-date with vaccinations and other health precautions. Also protect your cat from parasites during spring, summer, and autumn. If your cat is bitten by a wild animal, call your local department of public health for advice.

Protect the cat from fleas with a flea collar.

Make sure that no one in your area is using rodenticide to kill mice and rats. Ingestion of this poison or a rodent that has consumed it can be fatal.

If you think your pet has chewed on or eaten a poisonous plant, contact your veterinarian, animal emergency clinic, or the poison control center for advice. Do not attempt to make the cat vomit. When you take the cat to a vet, try to bring a sample of the plant the cat has eaten. The ASPCA National Animal Poison Control Center hotline numbers are as follows:

(900) 443-0000 ($55.00 per case).
The charge is billed directly to the caller's phone.
(888) 426-HELP or (888)426-4435 ($55.00 per case).
The charge is billed to the caller's credit card.

Feline High-Rise Syndrome

When summer comes around, many pet parents eagerly open their windows to enjoy the weather. Unfortunately, they are also unknowingly putting their pets at risk. Unscreened windows pose a real danger to cats, who fall out of them so often that the veterinary profession has a name for the complaint — high-rise syndrome. During the warmer months, veterinarians at the ASPCA's Bergh Memorial Animal Hospital see approximately three to five cases a week. Falls can result in shattered jaws, punctured lungs, broken limbs and pelvises — and even death. Here's what you need to know:

Cats have excellent survival instincts, and they don't deliberately "jump" from dangerous high places. Instead, most cats fall accidentally from high-rise windows, terraces, or fire escapes.

Cats have an incredible ability to focus attention on whatever interests them. A bird or other animal can be distracting enough to cause a cat to lose balance and fall.

Because cats have little fear of heights and enjoy perching in high places, pet owners often assume that they can take care of themselves. But although cats can cling to the bark of a tree with their claws, other surfaces, such as window ledges and concrete or brick façades, aren't easy to grip.

When cats fall from high places, they don't land squarely on their feet. Instead, they land with their feet slightly splayed, which can cause severe head and pelvis injuries.

It is a misconception that cats won't be injured if they fall from one- or two-story buildings. They may actually be at greater risk for injury when falling shorter distances rather than from mid-range or higher altitudes. Shorter distances do not give them enough time to adjust body posture and fall safely.

When cats fall from high-rise buildings, they may land on sidewalks or streets that are dangerous and unfamiliar to them. Never assume that the animal has not survived the fall; immediately rush the animal to the nearest animal hospital or to your veterinarian.

There is a 90 percent survival rate for cats who are victims of high-rise syndrome if they receive immediate and proper medical attention.

To fully protect your pets, install snug and sturdy screens in all your windows.

If you have adjustable screens, make sure that they are tightly wedged into window frames.

Note that cats can slip through childproof window guards — these don't provide adequate protection!

Cat owners should also keep their cats indoors to protect them from additional dangers such as cars, other animals, and disease. People who want to give their cats outdoor stimulation can look into full-screen enclosures for backyards and terraces.

119 Plants That Are Potentially Poisonous to Cats

Pets, especially kittens and puppies, tend to explore their world by trying to eat it. This may help them learn about their environment, but it can also be harmful. Many plants are dangerous. Some may cause vomiting or diarrhea while others may cause organ failure and death. The pet-friendly house relies on silk and artificial plants for color.

The following are the more common poisonous plants, but this is not an all-inclusive list. Some of these plants may also have different common names, depending on the area of the country in which one resides. Every pet owner should know which plants grow in and around the home and their effect on animals.

1. Aloe
2. Amaryllis
3. Andromeda Japonica
4. Asparagus Fern
5. Autumn Crocus
6. Avocado

13. Carnation
14. Castor Bean
15. Cherry (seeds, wilting leaves, and pit)
16. Chinese Evergreen
17. Chives

24. Cyclamen
25. Daffodil
26. Delphinium
27. Devil's Ivy
28. Dicentra
29. Dieffenbachia
30. Donkey Tail

37. Fiddle-leaf Philodendron
38. Florida Beauty
39. Four O'Clock
40. Foxglove
41. Foxtail
42. German Ivy
43. Gladiolus
44. Hemlock
45. Holly
46. Honeysuckle
47. Hurricane Plant
48. Hyacinth
49. Hydrangea
50. Iris
51. Ivy
52. Jack-in-the-Pulpit
53. Japanese Yew
54. Jerusalem Cherry
55. Jimsonweed

56. Jonquil
57. Kalanchoe
58. Lace Fern
59. Lantana
60. Larkspur
61. Laurel
62. Lily
63. Lily of the Valley
64. Lobelia
65. Marigold (Marsh Marigold)
66. Marijuana
67. Mauna Loa Peace Lily
68. May Apple
69. Mexican Breadfruit
70. Milkweed
71. Mistletoe
72. Monkshood
73. Morning Glory
74. Mother-in-Law's Tongue

16 Plants Whose Scents Cats Love

Leeks	Papyrus	Catnip	Pinks
Eucalyptus	Silver Vine	Oleander	Mimosa
Lavender	Asparagus	Valerian	Catmint
Carnation	Mint	Tuberoses	Cat Thyme

7. Azalea
8. Begonia
9. Bird of Paradise
10. Boston Ivy
11. Caladium
12. California Poppy

18. Christmas Rose
19. Chrysanthemum
20. Clematis
21. Corn Plant
22. Crocus
23. Croton

31. Dumb Cane
32. Easter Lily
33. Elderberry
34. Elephant Ears
35. English Ivy
36. Eucalyptus

Deter cats from eliminating in your plants by putting stones on the soil's surface, so kitty can't dig.

75. Mountain Laurel
76. Mushrooms
77. Narcissus
78. Nephthytis
79. Nightshade
80. Oak Tree (buds and acorns)
81. Oleander
82. Onion
83. Orange Day Lily
84. Peace Lily
85. Peach (wilting leaves and pits)
86. Philodendron Pertusum
87. Poinsettia
88. Poison Hemlock
89. Poison Ivy
90. Poison Oak
91. Poison Sumac
92. Poppy
93. Potato (all green parts)
94. Pothos
95. Precatory Bean
96. Rhododendron
97. Rhubarb

98. Ribbon plant
99. Rubber Tree
100. Sago Palm
101. Schefflera
102. Shamrock Plant
103. Snake Plant
104. Sorghum
105. Star of Bethlehem
106. Stinging Nettle
107. Stinkweed
108. Sweetheart Ivy
109. Swiss Cheese Plant
110. Taro Vine
111. Tiger Lily
112. Toadstools
113. Tobacco
114. Tomato Plant (entire plant except ripe fruit)
115. Variegated Philodendron
116. Water Hemlock
117. Weeping Fig
118. Wisteria
119. Yew

67 Plants That Are Safe for Your Cat

1. Achillea
2. African Violet
3. Alyssum
4. Aster
5. Basil
6. Bean Sprouts
7. Begonia
8. Buddleia
9. Calendula
10. Catmint
11. Catnip
12. Celosia
13. Chamomile
14. Chervil
15. Chives
16. Cleome
17. Columbine
18. Coneflower
19. Coriander
20. Cosmos
21. Dahlia
22. Dianthus
23. Dill

24. Dorotheanthus
25. Forget-Me-Not
26. Heloptrope
27. Hollyhock
28. Hyssop
29. Impatiens
30. Japanese Matatabi
31. Lavender
32. Lemon Balm
33. Lemon Verbena
34. Lettuce
35. Lovage
36. Marum
37. Miniature Rose
38. Mint
39. Monarda
40. Nasturtium
41. Oats
42. Orchid
43. Oregano
44. Pansy
45. Parsley

46. Peppermint
47. Petunia
48. Phlox
49. Portulaca
50. Rose
51. Rosemary
52. Sage
53. Scabiosa
54. Shasta Daisy
55. Snapdragon
56. Spearmint
57. Spider Plant
58. Spinach
59. Strawflower
60. Sunflower
61. Tarragon
62. Thyme
63. Torenia
64. Verbascum
65. Violet
66. Wheat
67. Zinnia

A massive moggie who lost 11 kilograms in nine months was named Britain's "pet slimmer of the year" in 2005. Mischief, from Stevenage, lost 38 percent of his weight, slimming down to a svelte 14 pounds after his size had horrified vets. "Mischief couldn't fit through the cat flap or even wash himself," Sharon Harding said of her 6-year-old cat.

Mischief shared the award with a dog named Max, who went from 8 pounds, 9 ounces, to 5 pounds, 3 ounces, in less than six months. The winners accepted their awards at a ceremony in St. James Park, London, and each received a year's supply of pet food, £500 worth of pet accessories, and £2,000 worth of holiday vouchers.

The Well-Fed Cat

Proper nutrition and a balanced diet are essential to your cat's health. That's why it's important to make sure the feline is getting the right amount of vitamins and nutrients. Here are some tips to help your cat eat well and maintain a healthy body weight.

Feed him one ounce of canned food daily or ⅓ ounce of dry food per pound of body weight. You may also feed your cat a combination of dry and wet foods, a diet that most cats prefer.

Feed your cat either two meals a day or once a day, in which case you should leave food out for snacking.

Most cats at 1 to 4 years of age are very active and self-regulate their food intake in order to maintain a healthy body weight. If your cat is getting older, it might be less active and put on weight. If it's becoming too fat, consult your veterinarian.

Make sure cat food contains the right nutrients: niacin, vitamin A, taurine, and essential fatty acids.

The amount of nutrients for a cat depends on age and stage of life. For instance, kittens, adults, and seniors require different amounts of nutrients, as do pregnant and nursing cats. And just like people, active kitties need more calories while lazy ones need less. Work with your veterinarian in selecting the foods that meet your cat's needs.

A VET'S GUIDE TO CATS

"Must be an old book. The section on grooming says nothing at all about liposuction."

Don't expect to feed your cat just one type of food for its entire life. If it becomes overweight, the cat will need a food low in calories; if it develops frequent hairballs, the cat will need food that contains supplements to reduce those yucky upchucks; if the cat is at risk for diabetes, it will need food with a higher-than-average percentage of protein to stave off the need for daily insulin injections, and so on.

It's important to periodically review your cat's dietary needs with a veterinarian.

The ideal diet includes good-quality food and lots of fresh water. Since tap water is usually treated with chemicals and often chlorinated (cats are sensitive to these odors), you might opt for distilled water. It should be changed frequently to avoid bacteria buildup. Nonporous bowls such as ceramic ones are best. On warm days, drop a few ice cubes into the water bowl.

Curious About Catnip?

Gigi loved it, but her brother, Brandy, was indifferent. Crispy craved it, but Ethel was unmoved by it. There you have it: veterinarian Arnold Plotnick's quick inventory of his past and present cats' reactions to catnip. We're grateful to him for sharing these strange-but-true facts about this feline-fascinating herb:

The active ingredient in catnip that beckons felines is the oil called nepetalactone.

Big and little cats both get a kick out of catnip. In fact, hunters have used catnip to lure the bobcat and the lynx. Other big cats, such as lions and leopards and jaguars, also go ga-ga for catnip.

Domestic cats react in different ways to catnip. Some will first smell and then lick or chew the stuff for a few minutes. Others will rub their cheeks and chin into the catnip flakes and act a little dizzy. Still others will rub their body on the catnip, roll from side to side, purr, growl, and even leap into the air.

The response to catnip can last for 5 to 15 minutes. But get this — it takes at least another hour or two for a cat to display a second reaction.

Not every cat digs catnip. In fact, about 30 percent of adult cats show zero interest in this plant. The same goes for nearly all kittens under 2 months of age.

Genetics don't play a factor. Two cats from the same litter can have different responses to catnip.

The modern-day guru of catnip is a guy named Leon Seidman. About 25 years ago, he was a graduate student searching for the ultimate catnip for his cat, W.B. He discovered catnip growing wild on a friend's farm in Virginia, grabbed a bunch, and began growing an especially potent variety in his home in Maryland. Today, he and his wife, Pamela, operate Cosmic Pet Products, Inc., which packages and sells around 140,000 pounds of catnip a year — they are the world's largest commercial producers of the plant.

Feline Feasts

Grab an apron! If you enjoy cooking and occasionally want to treat your cat to some homemade meals, you're in luck: the cat café is open for business. Here are some recipes that are truly the cat's meow. They're all easy to prepare, and you can refrigerate leftovers in airtight containers for future meals.

Su-purr-b Scrambled Eggs

Makes 2 servings

- 1 tablespoon margarine
- 2 eggs, beaten
- ½ cup cottage cheese

Melt the margarine in a small frying pan over medium heat. Add the eggs and cottage cheese, and stir until the ingredients are well mixed — about two or three minutes. Pour half of the scrambled eggs into your cat's bowl, and allow it to cool before serving. Store the other half in the refrigerator and serve the next day.

Tuna-Rice Cats-erole

Makes 6 servings

- 1 cup low-sodium chicken broth
  Pinch of oregano
- ½ cup uncooked green beans, finely chopped
- ½ cup uncooked instant brown rice
- 1 hard-boiled egg, finely chopped
- 1 6-ounce can water-packed tuna, strained and flaked

In a medium saucepan, bring the chicken broth to a boil, then reduce heat and add the oregano, green beans, and rice. Cover and allow to simmer for 10 to 15 minutes or until the rice is cooked. Add the egg and tuna and stir well. Serve at room temperature.

Colossal Cat Chowder

Makes 6 servings

- ½ pound white fish, deboned and chopped fine
- 1 cup creamed corn
- 1 cup skim milk
- ¼ cup uncooked red potatoes, finely chopped
- 1 tablespoon chicken or beef liver, finely chopped
  Pinch of salt
- ¼ cup low-fat grated cheese

In a medium saucepan, combine all the ingredients except the cheese. Cover and simmer over low heat for 20 minutes, stirring occasionally. Remove from heat and sprinkle with cheese. Allow this dish to cool to room temperature before serving.

A vintage postcard from the Alfred Mainzer Company.

Sensational Kidney Stew

Makes 6 servings

- 1½ cups water
- 1 tablespoon corn oil
- ½ pound beef kidney, diced
- ½ cup uncooked brown rice
- 1 medium carrot, finely grated
- 4 mushrooms, finely chopped
- 2 tablespoons tomato paste
- 1 teaspoon bone meal

In a medium saucepan, combine the water, corn oil, and salt. Bring to a boil over medium heat. Stir in the beef kidney, rice, carrot, mushrooms, and tomato paste, and bring to a boil again. Cover the saucepan, reduce the heat to low, and simmer for 20 minutes, stirring occasionally. Remove from the heat and add the bone meal. Cool before serving.

Purr-fect Tuna Patties

Makes 5 servings

- 2 eggs
- 1 6½-ounce can of water-packed tuna, drained and flaked
- 1 cup bread crumbs
- 1 teaspoon brewer's yeast
- 1 teaspoon bone meal
  - Pinch salt
- 2 tablespoons margarine

In a medium-sized bowl, beat the eggs. Add the tuna, bread crumbs, brewer's yeast, bone meal, and salt. Thoroughly blend with a wooden spoon until moistened. In a skillet, melt the margarine over medium heat. Take small handfuls of the mixture and form five patties. Place the patties in the skillet. Cook each side for 3 to 5 minutes, or until golden brown. Place the patties on a plate. Once they are cooled, crumble them into small pieces to give as a meal or as treats.

Heavenly Kitty Hash

Makes 4 servings

- 1 cup water
- ⅓ cup uncooked brown rice
- 2 teaspoons corn oil
- ⅔ cup lean ground turkey
- 2 tablespoons chicken or beef liver, chopped
- 1 tablespoon bone meal
  - (available where garden supplies are sold)

In a medium saucepan, bring the water to a boil. Stir in the rice, corn oil, and salt, and reduce the heat to low. Allow the mixture to simmer for 20 minutes, covered. Then add the turkey, liver, and bone meal. Stir frequently and simmer for 20 minutes. Cool to room temperature before serving.

---

3 Reasons to Eat Grass

If your cat enjoys munching on grass, consider purchasing a kit of commercial cat grass or growing your own pot of wild oats or lawn grass (free of pesticides) inside your home, just for Cupid's delight. Although researchers have yet to pinpoint a precise explanation, there are three popular theories as to why cats eat grass:

1. Grass provides cats with an added source of dietary fiber.

2. Eating grass helps a cat to cough up a hairball. To use the scientific term, grass has emetic (vomit-inducing) properties.

3. Grass acts as a laxative, relieving constipation.

"Cat food looks better than it tastes."
— JUSTYN, AGE 3, MILLVILLE, NEW JERSEY

The New Cat Miracle Diet!

Most diets fail because we are still thinking and eating like people. For those who have never had any success with slimming down, behold the new Cat Miracle Diet!

Most cats are long and lean (or tiny and petite). The Cat Miracle Diet will help you achieve the same svelte figure. Just follow this diet for four days, and you'll find that you not only look and feel better, but you will also have a whole new outlook on what constitutes food. Good luck!

VIRGINIA CHANG

DAY ONE

Breakfast: Open a can of expensive gourmet cat food. Any flavor, as long as it cost more than 75¢ per can — and place ¼ cup on your plate. Eat 1 bite of food; look around room disdainfully. Knock the rest on the floor. Stare at the wall for a while before stalking off to the other room.

Lunch: Four blades of grass and one lizard tail. Throw it up on the cleanest carpet in your house.

Dinner: Catch a moth, and play with it until it is almost dead. Eat one wing. Leave the rest to die.

Bedtime snack: Steal one green bean from your spouse's or partner's plate. Bat it around the floor until it slides under the refrigerator. Steal one small piece of chicken, and eat half of it. Leave the other half on the sofa. Throw out the remaining gourmet cat food from the can you opened this morning.

DAY TWO

Breakfast: Pick up the remaining chicken bite from the sofa. Knock it onto the carpet and bat it under the television set. Chew on the corner of the newspaper as your spouse/partner tries to read it.

Lunch: Break into the fresh French bread that you bought as your contribution to the dinner party on Saturday. Lick the top of it all over. Take one bite out of the middle of the loaf.

Afternoon snack: Catch a large beetle and bring it into the house. Play toss-and-catch with it until it is mushy and half-dead. Allow it to escape under the bed.

Dinner: Open a fresh can of dark-colored gourmet cat food — tuna or beef works well. Eat it voraciously. Walk from your kitchen to the edge of the living room rug. Promptly throw up on the rug. Step into the mess as you leave. Track it across the entire room.

DAY THREE

Breakfast: Drink part of the milk from your spouse's or partner's cereal bowl when no one is looking. Splatter part of it on the closest polished aluminum appliance you can find.

Lunch: Catch a small bird and bring it into the house. Play with it on top of your down-filled comforter. Make sure the bird is seriously injured but not dead before you abandon it for someone else to deal with.

Dinner: Beg and cry until you are given some ice cream or milk in a bowl of your own. Take three licks, and then turn the bowl over on the floor.

FINAL DAY

Breakfast: Eat 6 bugs, any type, being sure to leave a collection of legs, wings, and antennae on the bathroom floor. Drink lots of water. Throw up the bugs and water on your spouse's or partner's pillow.

Lunch: Remove the chicken skin from last night's chicken-to-go leftovers that your spouse or partner placed in the trash can. Drag the skin across the floor several times. Chew on it in a corner and then abandon it.

Dinner: Open another can of expensive gourmet cat food. Select a flavor that has an especially runny consistency, such as chicken and giblets in gravy. Lick off all the gravy, and leave the actual meat to dry and harden.

How to Groom Your Cat

Cats, by nature, are meticulous about grooming themselves. Of course you've noticed how systematically they clean themselves and what a thorough job they seem to do. But very often our little fur balls need some extra attention. Grooming your cat is essential to its health and well-being. You'll help minimize hairballs with proper grooming, and you'll have an opportunity to notice any adverse changes to the skin or coat. The intimacy and contact during grooming also serves to strengthen the bond between you. Here are some helpful tips:

It is never too early to start grooming your cat. You can begin grooming it even as a kitten, provided it has been weaned from its mother.

Establish a grooming routine so the cat will anticipate and look forward to each session. Choose a time at which your feline is normally relaxed or even dozing. Don't attempt to groom it when it's in a playful mood. And be sure to choose a time — not the sort used on a dog. Brushing will prevent fur from becoming tangled and will keep the skin clean and free of irritants. If the cat's hair is short, you may need to groom it only once every few days. Use a natural-bristle brush and fine-tooth comb for this type of fur. If the coat is long, daily grooming with a wire brush and a wide-tooth comb is essential. Begin by brushing the

> "Cats are the ultimate narcissists. You can tell this because of the time they spend on personal grooming. Dogs aren't like this. A dog's idea of personal grooming is to roll in dead fish." —JAMES GORMAN

when *you* are relaxed. Any tension or stress you are feeling on a given day may affect your patience and upset your cat.

Try to keep your initial grooming sessions as brief as possible. Start with a five-minute session and gradually increase the time once the cat is accustomed to being handled. You might even start with a small petting session before you begin grooming.

You'll need a brush designed specifically for cats

cat's back a few times, then proceed to the sides of its body. Now gently brush the belly, going from chin to tail. Some cats are very sensitive to tummy brushing, so if your kitty starts to fidget, just get this part of the brushing done as quickly as possible. You can now go on to the legs and tail. Always brush in the direction of the hair growth.

A cat comb is an essential tool for removing matted hair. Be sure you are extremely gentle; this task can be painful to your kitty. Place a firm hand on the cat's skin below the mat, and make sure it is not being pulled while you remove the mat.

Have a small pair of scissors handy in case some matted fur can't be brushed free. Be careful not to cut skin when clipping off a mat. Cut skin can be very painful and might lead to an infection. If you are not confident about removing the mat, leave the job to a professional groomer.

Have a pair of tweezers on hand in case you come across a tick or a flea.

Claw clipping is an important part of the grooming process. It is best to clip the claws at least once a week, more frequently if the cat is ripping up your sofa. Use specially designed cat-claw clippers. You may need an assistant for this task.

Take time to examine the kitty's teeth and eyes. If you notice a broken tooth, bad breath, or inflamed or tearing eyes, it might be wise to take the cat to the vet. You can clean its ears with a Q-tip soaked in some hydrogen peroxide. If you notice excessive earwax, don't attempt to remove it yourself. Take the cat to the vet instead.

If the cat is shorthaired, chances are it won't need to be bathed unless it has a skin problem or has had a run-in with a skunk. If you have to bathe the cat (most felines hate this, but some don't seem to mind at all), choose a bowl just large enough for the cat to fit in and add a couple of inches of lukewarm water. Place a rubber mat on the bottom, to give the kitty a good foothold. This will make it feel a bit more secure and will also give you better control. Gently wrap your arm around the cat's back and stomach. Pour a little lukewarm water on its back, apply a little bit of shampoo to the fur, and gently work it into its coat. Never use a showerhead or other spraying device because it will frighten the cat. Towel-dry the kitty as best you can, or use a hair dryer — but keep it on a low, cool setting. And never bathe a sick cat.

Speak softly while you groom or bathe the cat, telling it how much you love your kitty. It will reward you with a nice long purr. (See page 306 for more bathing tips.)

Cat Bathing as a Martial Art

Bud Herron wrote this in 1984, when he was editor of the Indianapolis *Daily Journal*.

Some people say cats never have to be bathed. They say cats lick themselves clean. They say cats have a special enzyme of some sort in their saliva that works like new, improved Wisk — dislodging the dirt where it hides and whisking it away. I've spent most of my life believing this folklore. Like most blind believers, I've been able to discount all the facts to the contrary — the kitty odors that lurk in the corners of the garage and dirt smudges that cling to the throw rug by the fireplace.

The time comes, however, when a man must face reality; when he must look squarely in the face of massive public sentiment to the contrary and announce: "This cat smells like a port-a-potty on a hot day in Juarez."

When that day arrives at your house, as it has in mine, I have some advice you might consider as you place your feline friend under your arm and head for the bathtub:

Know that although the cat has the advantage of quickness and lack of concern for human life, you have the advantage of strength. Capitalize on that advantage by selecting the battlefield. Don't try to bathe him in an open area where he can force you to chase him. Pick a very small bathroom. If your bathroom is more than four feet square, I recommend that you get in the tub with the cat and close the sliding-glass doors as if you were about to take a shower. (A simple shower curtain will not do. A berserk cat can shred a three-ply rubber shower curtain quicker than a politician can shift positions.)

Know that a cat has claws and will not hesitate to remove all the skin from your body. Your advantage here is that you are smart and know how to dress to protect yourself. I recommend canvas overalls tucked into high-top construction boots, a pair of steel-mesh gloves, an army helmet, a hockey face-mask, and a long-sleeve flak jacket.

Prepare everything in advance. There is no time to go out for a towel when you have a cat digging a hole in your flak jacket. Draw the water. Make sure the bottle of kitty shampoo is inside the glass enclosure. Make sure the towel can be reached, even if you are lying on your back in the water.

Employ the element of surprise. Pick up your cat nonchalantly, as if to simply carry him to his supper dish. (Cats will not usually notice your strange attire. They have little or no interest in fashion as a rule. If he does notice your garb, calmly explain that you are taking part in a product-testing experiment for J. C. Penney.)

Once you are inside the bathroom, speed is essential to survival. In a single liquid motion, shut the bathroom door, step into the tub enclosure, slide the glass door shut, dip the cat in the water, and squirt him with shampoo. You have begun one of the wildest 45 seconds of your life.

Cats have no handles. Add the fact that he now has soapy fur, and the problem is radically compounded. Do not expect to hold on to him for more that two or three seconds at a time. When you have him, however, you must remember to give him another squirt of shampoo and rub like crazy. He'll then spring free and fall back into the water, thereby rinsing himself off. (The national record is — for cats — three latherings, so don't expect too much.)

Next, the cat must be dried. Novice cat bathers always assume this part will be the most difficult, for humans generally are worn out at this point and the cat is just getting really determined. In fact, the drying is simple compared to what you have just been through. That's because by now the cat is semi-permanently affixed to your right leg. You simply pop the drain plug with your foot, reach for your towel, and wait. (Occasionally, however, the cat will end up clinging to the top of your army helmet. If this happens, the best thing you can do is to shake him loose and to encourage him toward your leg.) After all the water is drained from the tub, it is a simple matter to just reach down and dry the cat.

In a few days the cat will relax enough to be removed from your leg. He will usually have nothing to say for about three weeks and will spend a lot of time sitting with his back to you. He might even become psychoceramic and develop the fixed stare of a plaster figurine. You will be tempted to assume he is angry. This isn't usually the case. As a rule he is simply plotting ways to get through your defenses and injure you for life the next time you decide to give him a bath. But, at least now he smells a lot better.

Bathing Your Cat: Survival Tips

Anne Moss is a cat behavior consultant and a member of the Cat Writers Association. She runs two of the largest cat-related websites on the Internet, TheCatSite.com, a large informational resource, and Meowhoo.com, an all-inclusive cat directory. Anne writes:

Many cat owners wince when faced with the prospect of bathing their cat. Past experience, or lurid secondhand tales from traumatized friends, often conjure up images of wet chaos, with the blurred shape of a soaked cat climbing the walls (or, worse, your arms) with claws fully extended. As a result, most owners avoid bathing their cat altogether.

In fact, cats can be accustomed to regular bathing. Professional cat breeders often bathe their cats as part of the grooming regimen. A continuous repetition of the procedure can accustom a cat to water.

Cats that are not used to being bathed will often panic, but most will happily go out and hunt in the pouring rain. The operative concept in bathing cats is to approach the event as calmly and in as relaxed a manner as possible. To help you do that, try the following suggestions. They won't work with every cat, but they will work with most.

Why Bathe Your Cat?

Cats spend hours a day washing themselves. In fact, most can do very well to keep themselves clean without additional help from us. However, there are times when your cat may need a bath:

When the cat is covered with a substance you don't want it to lick off and ingest, such as machine oil, pesticides, or cleaning powders and fluids.

When you need to bathe your cat with medicated shampoo to treat the skin for fleas or other disorders.

When you are showing your cats — a thorough bath a few days before the show is usually desirable.

It's a good idea to get your cat acquainted with bathing when it is still young. Small kittens rarely take violent exception to slightly warm water if you approach the job with confidence and soothing talk. Then when you have that emergency need to bathe your cat, the procedure will be familiar.

How Often Should a Cat Be Bathed?

Even if your cat is comfortable with baths, make sure you don't overdo a good thing. Washing the cat too often removes natural skin oils and may dry out the coat.

Tools and Equipment

You will need these basic items.

Shampoo — Choose a safe cat shampoo, especially if you use one that is medicated. If you must bathe the cat in a hurry and you don't have a cat shampoo, the only alternative is tearless baby shampoo. Regular shampoos for people are usually too harsh for feline skin and may cause irritation. If you need to use medicated shampoos, such as anti-flea solutions, make sure that they are cat-specific. Dog shampoos can be harmful and even deadly to cats!

Towel — It should be dry and fluffy. You can warm it slightly before bath time, but make sure it's not too hot!

A soft washcloth — You will need it for cleaning the cat's face.

A couple of cotton balls — These will protect the cat's ears.

Other Preparations

Unless you are very experienced and the cat is particularly calm, you should probably get a helper. Choose a patient, cat-oriented person, and let him or her know what bathing a cat is all about. Make sure it is someone your cat knows and likes.

Make all the preparations you need before you bring the cat into the bathroom. Get all the bathing equipment ready, and remove all breakable items in the bathroom. Cats don't like the slippery feel of the bathtub, so place a rubber mat on the bottom of the tub. Your cat will need it to grip onto.

Now for the guest of honor. A couple of hours before the bath, have a grooming session and brush the cat's coat. This is especially important for longhaired cats, since any mats and tangles are likely to shrink during the wash and become difficult to handle. Don't forget to trim your cat's claws sometime before the bath, to avoid injury.

After you have the room and props ready, gently pick up the cat and prepare it for the bath. Place half a cotton ball in each ear to prevent water from getting in.

The Bath

1. Get the cat into the bathroom and then close the door — you don't want a wet, soapy cat running around your home. Gently but firmly place the cat on the rubber mat. Use a gentle stream of warm water from a handheld nozzle or a pitcher. Make sure that the water is neither too cold nor too hot. It should be at about the cat's body temperature.

2. Thoroughly wet the cat's coat, avoiding the face area, and then lather some shampoo on the wet coat and gently rub it all over the cat's body. Finally, rinse off the shampoo, taking care not to leave any on the coat. As you wash, keep the nozzle close to the cat's body, to muffle the sound of running water.

3. Wet the washcloth with some warm water (but no soap) and gently wipe the cat's face. Never spray water directly at the cat's face, and definitely never dunk the cat's head in water!

4. Take the cat out of the tub, and wrap it in the towel. Keep the cat in a warm, draft-free room until it is completely dry. Some owners use blow dryers to dry the cat, but if the cat shows signs of alarm, just let its fur dry naturally. If you do use a blow dryer, use the lowest setting

and do not place it too close to the cat. Never blow air directly at the cat's face.

5. Above all, if you want to try to bathe your cat, remember that the key word here is *patience.* Be very gentle, and talk to the cat throughout the whole procedure in a soft and soothing voice. Never shout or lose your temper. Your cat is probably frightened enough as it is, so you don't want to upset it even more. If your cat is calm and you have a lot of patience, bathing the cat may not be such a nightmare after all.

The Flea-Free Home

There are many ways to keep fleas at bay. If you find fleas on a cat, you must treat both the cat and the environment it lives in, because most of the life of a flea is spent off its host. A flea needs a meal of blood in order to reproduce, but eggs generally are laid off the host. Practice these housekeeping habits to maintain a flea-free home:

1. Vacuum your home weekly. Don't forget the crevices inside sofas. A vacuum cleaner equipped with a "beater bar" that is powerful enough to suck up adult fleas, larvae, and eggs is your best bet. When you are done, seal the bag, toss it outside in a garbage bin, and cover it with a lid to keep the fleas from returning inside.

2. Run a flea comb through your cat's coat at least twice a week. With each stroke, dip the comb in a bowl of hot soapy water or diluted rubbing alcohol. Fleas can't swim.

3. Toss your cat's bedding in the washer on the hot-water cycle regularly — weekly during warm, moist weather. Also include your cat's favorite throw rugs, pillows, blankets, and toys, to kill fleas and their eggs.

4. Conduct flea patrol in your yard weekly. Remove sun-blocking vegetation near your home, rake up wet leaves and wet grass clippings, and never store garbage out in the open or under porches. All these conditions attract fleas.

5. Use a dehumidifier in your home to lower the humidity to below 50 percent.

Flea-Fighting Tactics

In your grandparents' day, flea-ridden cats were subject to flea dips and homes were bombarded with flea bombs. Both were dangerous to the cat — and the environment. Fortunately, veterinarians have discovered newer and safer ways to send fleas fleeing from your cat and your home. Let's look at the most effective options:

#1 Tactic: Chemical warfare.

A new type of flea-fighting weapon emerged in 1996, a topical treatment that is applied once a month and absorbed through a cat's skin. The potent ingredients include fipronil (which kills fleas and ticks) and imadacloprid, capable of killing adult fleas with 98 to 100 percent efficacy within one to two days. Just dab on once a month and no mess, no fuss — and goodbye, fleas!

#2 Tactic: The mighty flea comb.

Not high-tech, but certainly effective, these tiny-toothed combs can remove up to 90 percent of flea eggs and 50 percent of larvae through daily combings.

#3 Tactic: Borate and nematodes.

Fight fleas with their natural enemies. Borate, a form of the element boron, is a fine powder that appears to interrupt the life cycle of fleas. The product must be professionally applied to carpets, upholstery, and floor cracks. Borate is poisonous to fleas and can be effective for up to one year, unless you have your carpets cleaned. (Boric acid, however, can be toxic to infants if ingested.) Nematodes (roundworms) are itty-bitty yard and garden allies that feast on baby fleas nestling in the soil around your home. Like fleas, nematodes like to live in warm, moist, shady spots. Add nematodes to the soil monthly because they can't survive temperatures below 45 degrees or above 95 degrees Fahrenheit. These flea eaters are available from lawn and garden supply outlets. A third natural option is diatomaceous earth (DE), which works by drying out fleas; when applied to carpets it can be effective. These "natural" remedies oust fleas but don't touch ticks, by the way.

#4 Tactic: Flea collars.

Collars are convenient, but not all collars offer equal protection. Select collars that contain insecticides such as tetrachlorvinphos or propoxur. Also, choose breakaway flea collars for safety. These collars break away if they get caught or snagged on something to prevent a cat from choking.

What to skip: Flea sprays and bombs.

These products have been in existence for decades and usually contain an adulticide, such as natural pyrethrin, that quickly kills adult fleas on the pet. The problem is that pyrethrin doesn't last long on a cat, so it won't provide long-lasting flea protection. There is also a risk of using too much and causing your cat to become sick.

Always follow product directions carefully, and never use on cats a flea product designed for dogs. Certain chemicals that dogs can tolerate — such as permethrin — can be dangerous to a cat.

All About Flea Collars

There are many ways to repel or kill fleas, but a flea collar is one of the easiest. Collars aren't for everyone, though. Some cat owners fear that the toxins contained in certain kinds of collars are unsafe, while others are perfectly comfortable with them. Then again, some cats develop allergic reactions to flea collars, such as a rash or loss of fur on their necks. If you're trying to decide whether or not to use one for your cat, talk to your vet.

Flea collars work in one of two ways. One type of collar emits a gas that is toxic to fleas but not cats. This gas is absorbed into the cat's subcutaneous fat later and is usually effective against fleas near the cat's head and neck only. The second type is electronic and emits ultrasonic pulses to repel fleas and ticks. It is inaudible to humans and pets and contains no poisons or chemicals. Check with your vet about what type of collar best suits your cat.

Flea collars kill only adult fleas unless they have an IGR, or insect growth regulator, to prevent flea egg and larval development. Some collars also have an insecticide. If yours doesn't, use another product to control adult fleas if necessary. Collars with IGRs last up to one year.

Make sure you check your cat regularly, and don't leave the collar on long after the chemicals become ineffective.

Keep in mind that most flea collars aren't the breakaway type, meaning that they aren't stretchable and can choke your cat if they become tangled.

Check the quality of the collar. There should be no sharp edges, jagged buckles, or loose stitching.

Make sure that the collar is for cats and not dogs. Mixing them up can be dangerous.

Flea collars can be smelly, making hugging or carrying your cat rather unpleasant.

Flea collars are not suitable for cats that spend time around small children. Young children may grab the collar and then put their fingers in their mouth.

Be aware that some flea collars contain chemicals that may be harmful to sick cats.

You can put a flea collar in your vacuum bags to kill hoovered-up fleas and their eggs when you vacuum.

The Facts on Fleas

Itch, itch. Scratch, scratch. Chances are if your cat has fleas, everyone and everything else in your home does, too. Keep in mind that fleas are feisty and resourceful. Heck, they've been on this planet since the days of dinosaurs, so they know a thing or two about survival.

To fend off fleas, you need to first arm yourself with knowledge about these pesky parasites.

Flea Fact #1: Fleas do not stay on your cat all the time. They jump off and seek another blood source (like you or the dog) and take naps inside the fibers of your carpet.

Flea Fact #2: The life of a flea is fleeting. A flea's life usually averages seven days, but they can live up to 30 days.

Flea Fact #3: These parasites love to mate. Two dozen adult fleas can produce more than 250,000 offspring in one month!

Flea Fact #4: Fleas can jump the equivalent of 150 times their size. To put that into perspective, that's like a person leaping 1,000 feet in the air!

Flea Fact #5: Fleas love warm, moist climates. If given a choice, a flea will choose a climate with temperatures ranging between 65 to 80 degrees Fahrenheit and 75 to 80 percent humidity.

Caring for Kitty's Teeth

Just like humans, cats have two sets of teeth. However, unlike humans, who have 32 teeth, cats have only 30. Because cats are carnivores, all their teeth are designed for tearing into meat. Even their molar teeth, which are extremely narrow, lack the surface area for grinding. Twelve small teeth called incisors are located in the front of the mouth, six in the mandible or lower jaw, and six in the upper jaw. The eyeteeth, or what many people refer to as the "fangs," are directly behind the incisors. Ten sharp premolars and molars stand directly behind the eyeteeth and are also helpful in cutting food.

The cat's first set of teeth is called the milk teeth, or deciduous teeth, and they start to come in when the kitten is about 4 weeks old. They continue to develop until all 26 milk teeth have appeared, usually by 6 weeks. These begin to fall out from 11 weeks until 30 weeks. During the time when the milk teeth are falling out, new permanent teeth are coming in, until all 30 of them have developed and have replaced the milk teeth, usually by 6–8 months.

Dr. Ronald Hines, DVM, "the Pet Professor" and a popular writer, says that one of the biggest problems causing tooth and gum disease in cats is that their diets are formulated and textured to meet the desires of the pet's owners — not standards of good oral hygiene. The villain in tooth and gum disease in pets and people is plaque. Plaque is a mixture of remaining food and salivary mineral mixed with bacteria and fermentation acids, which slowly irritate the gums (a condition called periodontal disease), cause tooth decay, and result in bad breath. Particles tend to cling to the nooks and crannies that exist between the teeth. Tooth decay tends to be worse in the back of the mouth, where teeth are closer together. Some breeds of cats, such as the Siamese, are more prone to dental disease than others. Yet dental and gum disease can largely be prevented. There is no cure — once it has begun, we can only slow its progress. Here are some of Dr. Hines's recommendations that will help you properly care for Murray's teeth and gums.

A vintage German postcard from Raphael Tuck & Sons.

THAT'S A BRAVE LITTLE PUSSY!

Painless Extra

1. The most important thing you can do to preserve your pet's teeth is to **feed it a crunchy diet** exclusively and avoid table scraps. It's simply a matter of mechanics. A crunchy diet massages the gums and wears off plaque. Limiting the amount of canned and soft foods will help decrease the amount of plaque and tartar that can form.

2. Purchase an ultra-soft pediatric toothbrush, and **brush your pet's teeth once a week** with a poultry- or beef-flavored dentifrice (don't use human toothpaste; it may upset a cat's tummy if swallowed). Begin the brushing process slowly, and clean maybe just one or two teeth to start. Increase the number of teeth you brush according to the cat's reaction. Increasing the number of teeth you care for may take a few days. Be sure to reward Fluffy after a brushing session.

3. Take some extra time to **inspect your cat's teeth and gums,** but stop if it starts to growl or seems irritated. Look for fractures or discoloration on the surface of the teeth.

4. **Check for tooth mobility.** Press on the teeth gently and note if there is any movement. If teeth show any signs of mobility, the cat is probably having difficulty or pain while eating. Take it to the vet for treatment.

5. **Your cat's breath** should also be evaluated. If you detect a foul odor, chances are the kitty has an infected tooth or gums and should be taken to the vet.

6. **Examine the face for swelling,** especially below the eyes. Tooth infections can lead to abscess formation, which is often visible just below the eyes.

7. Two products have recently become available that are designed to **prevent and control tartar and gum disease** in pets. T/D is a dry food, produced by Hill's Company, that is engineered to reduce plaque and tartar accumulation, but if the teeth are already loose, this food may exacerbate the problem. C.E.T. Chews for cats, produced by Virbac Corporation, is a freeze-dried fish treat that provides abrasive cleansing action as well as antibacterial enzymes to combat gingivitis. Other treatments are also available.

8. If you are having difficulty dealing with any of your cat's dental needs, **take it to the vet,** who has special instruments designed to remove plaque and tartar.

7 Strange Questions Vets Have Dealt With

The following represent real questions pitched to veterinarians, who did their best to disguise their laughter:

1. "A husband called to say that his wife liked to clean the oven in the nude and that their cat liked to rub up against her while she was wearing only gloves. He asked if the fumes would harm their cat. At first, I thought it was a friend playing a prank, but when I realized it was a real question, I stifled my laughter and advised him to keep the cat away from the EZ Off."

2. "One cat owner asked me if it was possible for a cat to mate with a rabbit. He was convinced that his cat was a product of a cat-rabbit mating because his cat stood on his hind legs like a rabbit every now and then."

3. "I was recently asked if male cats had nipples."

4. "I was once asked to certify a cat dead that had been motionless and not breathing for three days. It was dead, okay."

5. "My wife and I (we are both veterinarians) were once asked why a cat sat on a tree branch for a day or so without changing position during a particularly cold winter. The cat had frozen to the branch and had to be peeled off, pads and all, unfortunately, due to frostbite."

6. "One person wanted to know what to do with the results of a visit to the pet psychic, who had mystically determined that the person's cat wanted him to go away."

7. "One client said she was having trouble sleeping. She then asked me why her cat was peeing on the pillow where she sleeps."

Potty Animals: How to Toilet-Train Your Cat in 8 Sometimes-Not-So-Easy Steps

Toilet-train a cat? It's easier than you may realize, says Eric Brotman, Ph.D., a clinical psychologist in Sherman Oaks, California, and the author of *How to Toilet-Train Your Cat* (Bird Brain Press). For owners who abhor litter-box duties, toilet training has great rewards. You can wow guests by showing off your cats' bathroom talents. Some cats can learn in as little as three weeks, but most may need a couple months. The keys: patience and persistence.

If your cat doesn't have a problem using a litter box and is at least 6 months old, there is no reason why it can't learn a new behavior and become trained to use the toilet.

But is your cat a toilet-training candidate? Confident and dominant cats make the best contenders because they tend to deliberately leave their urine and feces uncovered in their litter boxes. These cats are more outgoing and willing to learn. Toilet training may be more challenging for shy and submissive cats. In general, they prefer to cover their deposits to suppress their scent and do not embrace changes in the household routine.

Next, do *you* have what it takes to be a top-notch toilet-training teacher? The chances for success improve among people who are genuinely interested in their cat, who are sufficiently motivated, and who are very patient. People who don't like to clean the box and who want to save money on litter are the most motivated to learn.

Very important: You'll need two bathrooms. Training can be messy at first, and you will need to designate one bathroom for your cat and one for the rest of the household.

Step 1: Designate one bathroom in the house for the cat. Post a CAT IN TRAINING sign on the door and a KEEP THE LID UP AT ALL TIMES sign above the toilet.

Step 2: Gather the materials you will need: flushable litter, duct tape, plastic liner or kitchen plastic wrap, litter box, newspapers, and an aluminum roasting pan (best size: 12⅝ inches by 10⅛ inches by 3 inches deep).

Step 3: Place the litter box in the bathroom, perched on a sturdy stack of newspapers three inches high for five to seven days. Intermittently reward your cat with a food treat when it uses the litter box.

Step 4: Stack newspapers to raise the litter box about three to five inches until the height of the box is even with the toilet seat. Your cat may start to walk on the toilet seat. Praise it for doing this.

Step 5: Place the litter box on top of the closed toilet lid for a couple days to get your cat used to being on top of the toilet.

Step 6: Replace the litter box with the aluminum roasting pan filled with three inches of litter. Put the pan inside the toilet, securing it with duct tape on the sides. Close the toilet seat (not the lid) on top of the pan for a week.

Step 7: Use a screwdriver to cut a hole the size of a quarter into the bottom center of the aluminum pan. Each day make the hole bigger. After two weeks, cut the entire bottom out of the pan.

Step 8: Remove the pan and duct tape. Remember to keep the toilet lid up, so your cat can balance on it. Flush when the cat is not on the toilet.

Remember to expect some setbacks. If your cat makes a mistake, go back a step for a few days to reinforce the proper behavior. This is frustrating, but it's really the only way to overcome resistance to new learning.

If your cat has difficulty balancing on the toilet seat, replace it with a soft, padded type of seat or place no-slip bathtub strips on the seat. Also, keep a box of alcohol wet wipes in the bathroom to clean the toilet seat before using.

Toilet-Training Cautions

Be aware of the potential downsides to toilet training your cat, cautions Arnold Plotnick, DVM, a veterinarian with a feline-only practice, Manhattan Cat Specialists. He lists these cautions about toilet training:

Toilet seats can be slippery, causing a cat to lose its balance and fall into the toilet. (Use nonskid bathtub strips to provide a safe surface.)

Guests may forget to keep the lid up. In frustration, a cat may eliminate elsewhere in the house. (Make an attractive sign to hang in the bathtub asking visitors to cooperate, and make a point of alerting guests to Popeye's special talent.)

Owners cannot detect early signs of medical problems in urine or feces diluted by the toilet water as easily as they can with deposits in a litter box. (Take your cat to the vet for regular checkups.)

Jumping up on a toilet seat may be difficult for an injured, sick, or aging cat. (Okay, it's not for everyone.)

The Lowdown on Cat Litter

In 1947, Edward Lowe was toiling away at his job at his father's company in St. Paul, Minnesota. The business sold sawdust and absorbent clay called fuller's earth. When a customer complained that the ash she was using in her litter box led to her kitty's leaving ashy paw prints all over the house, Lowe got the bright idea of adding some of his company's absorbent material to the litter box. Soon, his trademark Kitty Litter became part of the American vocabulary. Today an entire industry is devoted to keeping feline bathrooms neat, tidy, and, ideally, free of unwanted odor. Here are the litter-box basics.

Today, choices abound in the world of litter. Clay ranks as the most popular choice because it forms clumps that are easy to scoop. However, clay dust can cause respiratory issues in people and cats.

The environmentally minded cat owner can consider litter made of pine or grain, which absorbs well and is biodegradable. Grain contains a natural enzyme that tones down the powerful ammonia odor in cat urine. Other litter choices include recycled newspaper, pine and cedar sawdust, flushable silica, silica gel, and plant-based litter (made of corn, wheat byproducts, beet pulp, or oat hulls).

The size of the litter granules ranges from itty-bitty to large-size pellets. Most cats favor fine-grained clumping clay because it is more comfortable on their feet. Of course, some cats prefer large-pellet-type litter.

Consider your cat's needs and preferences in shopping for litter. Test its preferences by buying small bags of a few different types. Put one in one litter box and the other in a second box. Pay heed to which litter box your cat frequents more. Perfumed litter may smell nice to your guests, but it doesn't do a thing for Allegra; in fact, perfume is actually a cat repellent. Cats who don't like a certain type of litter often boycott the box and eliminate right next to it. This is a cat's way of conveying to its owner that it wants to do the right thing but doesn't want to come in contact with that type of litter.

If you decide to change litter, put it in a new litter box but keep the old one handy until the kitty is ready to make the switch. You can put some soiled litter in the new box to give the cat the idea. Once you've both agreed on a brand, stick with it.

Top 6 Reasons Why Cats Don't Use the Litter Box

1. The litter box is too dirty.

2. There are not enough litter boxes for all the cats in a home.

3. Kitty doesn't like the litter's texture.

4. We're feeling stressed by household renovations or the arrival of a new pet.

5. A medical condition such as a urinary tract infection may be present.

6. The litter box has been placed in a busy or noisy area of the house.

Choosy About Cat Litter

Is it relatively free of odor?

Is it biodegradable?

Is it flushable?

Is it easy to maintain?

Is it free of perfumes, dyes, and chemicals?

Is it affordable?

Does it produce only a small amount of dust?

Does your cat seem to like the texture?

To Clump or Not to Clump

Clumping litter, first invented in 1984, is clearly the most convenient and most preferred by cats. But be aware that the cheaper clumping litter, which breaks up easily, has to be scooped daily and completely replaced twice a week. The better-clumping litters, such as Scoop Away, just need daily scooping.

12 Tips for Solving Litter-Box Problems

Hobbs writes a twice-a-year column for the PAWS Press, the newsletter of the PAWS Animal Shelter in Norwalk, Connecticut (Pawsct.org). Hobbs was rescued as a stray when he was a kitten and currently shares his home with five other rescued cats. He owns a human named Alexis Heydt-Long, who helps him edit his column and who is also president of the PAWS shelter.

According to Hobbs, nothing puts cats in the proverbial "doghouse" quicker than a urine stain on the carpet. Feline behaviorists, vets, and shelter workers report that litter-box issues are the number-one behavior problem they encounter with cats.

Fortunately, these problems are both preventable and correctable. You'll need to be something of a detective to identify the cause of Kitty's failure to use the litter box, and careful observation can provide clues. Does Patches get in and out of the box as quickly as possible? Maybe the sound of the furnace right next to the box is scaring him. Does the cat step in the box but still pee on the floor? Maybe the box is too small. It should be large enough so that your cat can get into it easily and turn around. The rule of thumb for the number of boxes is usually one per cat, plus one. If your home has multiple floors, there should be a box on each one.

Here are some of Hobbs's management tips.

1. Have your cat examined by a vet to rule out any health issues.

2. Evaluate the box itself, the litter, and the location of the box. Is the box clean? If we don't like the type of litter, if the box is covered or too small or in a location that makes us feel insecure, we won't use it. How would you like to be forced to use a tiny, smelly Port-a-Potty in the middle of a busy street? Litter boxes must be cleaned *daily*.

3. Stress can sometimes lead to box avoidance. Moving to a new home, the arrival of a new baby, and the presence of a work crew in the house can all cause anxiety. Identify and eliminate the stressor if possible, or be patient while the kitty becomes accustomed to the newcomer.

4. Problems can occur in multicat households. Minimize territorial issues by providing multiple feeding stations and more than one litter box; place these significant items in various locations. Be sure that each cat gets one-on-one time with the household's most valuable resource — you!

5. Make sure there's enough litter in the box. Cats prefer a depth of two to three inches, which allows them to dig. Remember to replenish the supply each time you scoop.

6. Thoroughly clean soiled areas with a strong enzyme cleaner to remove any lingering odor.

7. Place deterrents in the problem areas for at least one month to break the habit of resoiling the spots.

8. Provide a new box near the area where the inappropriate behavior is occurring. Make the new box more appealing than the corner of the living room. Gradually move the new box to the correct location.

9. Give a problem cat extra attention regularly by practicing play therapy with interactive toys.

10. Don't declaw your cat! Scratching litter can hurt the sensitive paws of declawed cats.

11. Don't punish your cat for accidents. Rubbing its nose in the mess or yelling will only make the cat nervous and fearful of you.

12. Don't give up! There is a humane solution for every behavior problem. If you still need help, contact Cats International for free advice. The organization can be reached at 262-375-8852 or on the Web at www.catsinternational.org.

If problems persist, consult **The Humane Society** animal behavior helpline at (408)727-3383, extension 753.

17 Cool Uses for Cat Litter

1. Cat litter provides great traction for vehicles stuck in snow. It can also be used in place of salt to improve safety on sidewalks, steps, and driveways.

2. To prevent a sleeping bag or tent from getting moldy while in storage, place half a cup of cat litter in a sock, tie it up, and place it inside the item.

3. Cat litter absorbs odors, so think of using it to deodorize trash cans. Just put a little at the bottom and change it when it becomes damp.

4. This also works for smelly shoes. Use the cat-litter-in-the-sock method here.

5. Litter can be used instead of baking soda as a refrigerator deodorant.

6. Moles hate the smell of soiled cat litter. Pour some into one of their tunnels and watch the exodus.

9. Create great dried flowers: place a layer of cat litter in an airtight container and lay a flower over it. Seal the container and set it aside for a week.

10. Got a grease spot in your driveway? Place some cat litter over it, wait a few minutes, and sweep or vacuum it away. Dispose of the residue in the same manner you would dispose of used oil. For old spills, add a little turpentine, but keep Fluffy away until you can clean the spot thoroughly once the grease spot is gone.

11. Refresh your musty old books by leaving them in a sealed container along with some cat litter overnight.

12. Place some litter in ashtrays to reduce odors.

13. Use cat box filler to anchor dried or silk flower stems.

14. Plant flowers, vegetables, and shrubs in equal parts soil and clean litter. The soil will remain moist, provid-

Create the sort of clay mask that spas use . . . It's great for detoxifying the skin!

7. You can use 100 percent clay cat litter to create the sort of clay mask that spas use to remove toxins from facial skin. Combine three tablespoons of cat litter with about three tablespoons of water, then mix with a mortar and pestle. It's great for detoxifying the skin.

8. Prevent grease fires by pouring a layer of cat litter into the bottom of your barbecue grill. This also provides a better draft for proper cooking, and it will direct heat upward because of the insulating nature of the cat litter.

9. Create great dried flowers: place a layer of cat litter

ing for better root development, and the litter will retain the humidity at root level. It can be used safely on any type of plant.

15. Use cat box filler to soak up pet accidents.

16. Cat box filler reduces musty, damp smells in the hold and cabins of boats.

17. Use cat litter to clean up oil or paint spills. A ten-pound sack of litter will absorb more than a gallon of liquid.

12 Things You Wanted to Know About Hairballs but Were Too Disgusted to Ask

1. When your cat grooms itself by licking its fur, it ingests its own hair in the process. Fur that gets caught on the barbs of the tongue is then swallowed. Much of this hair passes through the digestive system and is eventually expelled in the stool, but a significant amount accumulates as a solid ball in the cat's stomach or throat.

Putting a little Vaseline on a cat's front paws works as a hairball remedy.

2. A vomited hairball looks like a tubular brown mass accompanied by a small amount of foamy fluid.

3. There are two kinds of hairballs. One is formed in the back of the throat, the other in the stomach or small intestine.

4. Hairballs are the most common reason that cats vomit. Sixty to eighty percent of cats spit up a hairball once a month.

5. Although uncommon, hairballs the size of baseballs have been removed from the stomach of some cats.

6. Coughing up or vomiting a hairball, or "fur ball," as it is sometimes called, is Petunia's way of eliminating the accumulated fur from her digestive system and is actually a helpful process.

7. Other symptoms that Petunia might have while struggling with hairballs are gagging, loss of appetite, constipation, and sometimes a swollen tummy.

8. Large numbers of hairballs are dangerous because they can block the digestive tract, making it extremely difficult for a cat to vomit or move its bowels.

9. Hairballs do not cause respiratory symptoms.

10. Prevention is worth a pound of hairballs. Regular grooming can rid your kitty of excess fur and minimize the amount it swallows.

11. Adding aloe vera juice, small amounts of bran, psyllium seed, or even butter to a cat's diet will help prevent constipation and thus aid in hairball elimination.

12. Some cats will require a commercially available hairball prevention preparation such as Hairball Remedy or Hairball Relief, which can be purchased at a pet store or supermarket. The product you choose should contain at least 8 percent crude fiber.

How to Massage Your Cat

Face it: we don't speak fluent meow. So, one great way to communicate with our cats is through touch. And the best way to touch is through therapeutic massage. The fact is, your cat has a personal masseuse — you!

Animal behaviorists, veterinarians, breeders, and shelter workers agree that the power of touch, when properly performed, delivers many therapeutic benefits. Daily massage enables owners to spot fleas or ticks on their cats and then get early treatment. They can find cuts or suspicious lumps that may be the early signs of cancer. Early detection leads to a faster diagnosis and, hopefully, a better prognosis.

Massage plays a role in chronic conditions such as arthritis. Although not a cure, massage reduces joint stiffness and pain by delivering oxygen-rich blood to those trouble spots, says C. Sue Furman, Ph.D., an associate professor of anatomy and neurobiology at Colorado State University in Fort Collins and the owner of a canine and equine massage center. Massage also helps maintain muscle tone.

Emotionally, experts say massage strengthens the people-pet bond, helps curb aggression and other unwanted behaviors, and improves a cat's sociability with people and other animals. Massage improves the bond between you and your cat. Spend some time each morning massaging your cat, and you may discover that it is a stress reliever for both of you.

Regularly massaged cats become accustomed to being handled. They associate touch with positive experiences. That can take the stress out of combing and brushing, nail trimming, car trips, veterinarian visits, and cat breed shows for both the cat and the owner.

Many types of massages used for centuries on people, such as shiatsu, Swedish massage, and rolfing, can be customized for cats. But experts caution cat owners to learn the correct techniques before attempting to massage their cats. One needs to know a cat's anatomy and recognize that a technique that can be used on a person, a dog, or a bird may not be ideal for a cat. In your attempt to help, you could do more harm than good.

An important tip for newcomers: start with the basic massage stroke known as effleurage. It's a French word that means "to flow or glide" or "skim the surface."

Direction is vital, says Dr. Furman. Effleurage is always performed toward the heart in the direction of the venous blood flow. This direction helps remove wastes and toxins and refresh the tissues and muscles. On a cat's legs, for example, you would want to work from the toes toward the knees and hips.

To learn more, we recommend the book *Cat Massage* and the instructional video *Your Cat Wants a Massage*. Both are authored by Maryjean Ballner, a licensed massage therapist who tours the country to demonstrate 50 different whiskers-to-tail massage techniques on cats.

The Basics

All thumbs? When it comes to cat massage, you can use parts of your hand in several different combinations to work muscle-relaxing magic. Let's identify each one:

Finger pads: The cushiony, soft parts of your fingers.

Fingertips: The area located above the finger pads that ends at the fingernail.

Knuckles: Located by bending your fingers so that your hand is in a fist.

Knuckle nooks: The flat-surfaced short area on the top of your hand between the fingernail and the first knuckle.

Thumb: Use one or both.

Thumb pads: The soft, fleshy parts found on the palm side.

Open palm: The full hand, from fingertips to wrist, with fingers slightly splayed and the palm side touching the cat.

Closed palm: Same as open palm but with fingers together.

Thenar eminence: A fancy name for that fleshy part of your open palm that extends below the thumb.

The 6 Basic Cat-Massage Motions

Massage therapists say that these six basic massage motions work best on cats:

1. Go with the glide: This classic massage stroke is simply a straight, flowing, continuous motion. It usually moves from the top of the head, down the back, then to the tail.

2. Create circles: Move your fingertips in clockwise or counterclockwise motions that are the diameter of half-dollars.

3. Do the wave: Make side-to-side rocking strokes with open palm and flat fingers. Mimic the movements of a windshield wiper.

4. Focus on flicking: Pretend that you are lightly brushing imaginary crumbs off a table, and you've got the idea behind this motion. You can flick with one, two, or three fingers.

5. Here's the real rub: Move along your cat's body slowly, exerting feather-light, light, and mild pressures.

6. Heed the knead: This is a gentle caress using the flicking motion of your palm and all five fingers. An ideal motion for the spine area.

The Do's and Don'ts of Cat Massage

Performed properly, massage can trigger eye-winking, purr-pleasing pleasure in your cat. Holistic veterinarians and animal massage therapists offer these tips for newcomers to cat massage:

Do approach your cat slowly and speak in a soothing tone.

Do avoid lots of words with the s sound when you speak softly to your cat. Hissing sounds may seem threatening.

Don't force a massage on a cat.

Do let your cat pick the time and place.

Do bring your hand up toward your cat's chin and give it time to smell it and accept it.

Don't massage your cat when you feel stressed or hurried. It can read your body cues.

Do use clean hands — no need for oils, creams, or lotions.

Do massage with your hands and never your feet.

Do make slow motions.

Do pay attention to your cat's feedback signals. Friendly signs include purring, hanging around, kneading, eye blinking, and little cat kisses. Unhappy signs that tell you to stop include wiggling to leave, hissing, a low sinking back, loud meows, hard bites, or scratch attacks.

Don't press too deeply — you could harm your cat.

Do repeat a technique your cat likes.

Do look for any signs of ticks, fleas, cuts, scratches, swelling, or lumps, and alert your veterinarian if you find something.

Don't try to substitute massage for medical treatment for conditions like arthritis, but rather use it to complement the vet's care plan.

Scaredy-Cats: 4 Signs of Fear

When cats are afraid, they respond in one of four ways. Your cat may try various methods of coping, but generally, each cat has its preferred way of dealing with a crisis.

1. It loses control over bodily functions.

2. It spits, hisses, or growls, or its fur puffs out and thus makes the cat appear larger.

3. It hides.

4. It freezes in place until it believes it's safe.

7 Ways to Help the Fearful Cat

It's normal for a cat to feel insecure or frightened in a new environment, says the HSUS. Often, your new cat will hide for a day or two when you first bring it home. Sometimes a traumatic experience, such as a visit to the veterinarian or a new animal's arrival in the household, can disrupt its routine and send it under the bed for a few days. A stranger, a child, or a loud noise can all be perceived as a threat. Closely observe your cat to determine the trigger for its fearful behavior. Keep in mind that just because you know that your cat is safe doesn't mean the cat knows it, too. Take these steps to reduce your cat's anxiety and help it become more confident.

1. Schedule an appointment with your veterinarian for a thorough physical to rule out any medical reasons for your cat's fearful behavior. Cats don't always act sick, even when they are. Any sudden behavior change could mean that your cat is ill. (See "Poor Kitty: 20 Ways to Tell If Your Cat Is Sick," page 340.)

2. If your cat is healthy but hiding, leave her alone. She'll come out when she's ready. Forcing her out of her spot will only make her more fearful. Make sure she has easy access to food, water, and her litter box. Clean the litter box and change the food and water every day until she's ready to make her appearance.

3. Keep any contact with the fear stimulus to a minimum. If a particular person makes her fearful, put her in another room when that person visits.

3. Keep your cat's routine as regular as possible. He'll feel more confident if he knows when to expect daily feeding, playing, cuddling, and grooming.

A frightened cat can run at speeds of up to 31 miles per hour, slightly faster than a human sprinter.

4. Try to desensitize your cat to the fear stimulus. Determine what distance your cat can be from the fear stimulus without responding fearfully. Introduce the fear stimulus at this distance while you're feeding your cat tasty treats and praising her. Slowly move the fear stimulus closer as you continue to praise your cat and offer her treats. If at any time during this process your cat shows fearful behavior, you've proceeded too quickly and will need to start over from the beginning. This is the most common mistake people make when desensitizing an animal, and it can be avoided by working in short sessions, and by paying careful attention to your cat's progress. You may need help from a professional animal behavior specialist with the desensitization process.

5. If your cat is threatening you, another person, or an animal, you should seek help from a professional animal behavior specialist. To keep everyone safe in the meantime, confine your cat to an area of the house where all interactions with her are kept to a minimum and are supervised by a responsible person. Cat bites and scratches are serious and can easily become infected. Bites should be reported to your local animal control agency so that your cat can be quarantined and watched for signs of rabies. If you can't keep your cat isolated and you're unable to work with a professional animal behavior specialist, you might have to consider removing him from your home.

6. Never punish your cat for her fearful behavior. Animals associate punishment with what they're doing at the time they're punished, so your cat is likely to associate any punishment you give her with you. This will only cause her to become fearful of you, and she still won't understand why she's being punished.

7. Don't force her to confront the object of her fear. It will only make her more fearful.

My Cat Has Zits! All About Feline Acne

Yes, it's a feline fact. Teenagers aren't the only ones prone to acne. Some cats get it, too. Feline acne occurs when pores under a cat's chin become blocked with cellular debris, causing blackheads. Left untreated, these clogged pores can become swollen and infected. They eventually rupture and create bloodied scabs, raised lesions, and patches of baldness. Cats with white chins may look like they have goatees.

What triggers feline acne remains a medical mystery. Even more puzzling is the fact that feline acne can appear just once and disappear forever, or it can last for the cat's entire lifetime. There seems to be no rhyme or reason to this. Veterinary dermatologists theorize that the following factors may trigger this condition:

Heightened stress. The addition of a new pet or person — or the departure of a beloved pet or person — may elevate the stress level in a cat.

Use of plastic feed bowls. Some suggest that the material in these bowls (especially if the cat chews on them) may contribute to feline acne.

Genetic predisposition. Some cats may pass this condition on to future generations.

Allergies. Allergic reactions to certain foods or even household cleaning items may sprout acne in some cats.

5 Things You Can Do About Feline Acne

1. Work closely with your veterinarian and, possibly, a veterinary dermatologist. Common treatments include over-the-counter ointments and even prescription medications (oral antibiotics may be necessary if the area becomes infected). You need to find the medication that works best on your cat.

2. Keep your cat's chin area free of dried scabs and blackhead flecks by gently running a fine-tooth comb (such as a flea comb) under the chin daily.

3. Dab your cat's chin daily with a medicated acne pad to keep the blackheads from worsening. Let the area air-dry.

4. If there is swelling under the chin, hold a compress (using Epsom salts and warm water) on it for up to five minutes a day to reduce inflammation.

5. Do not squeeze a pimple — you risk causing an infection.

Living with a Cat Allergy: 16 Things You Can Do

It is estimated that 6 to 10 million people in the United States are allergic to cats. Many of them are cat lovers and owners who have learned to live alongside their cats successfully. Understanding the nature of the allergic process and how to minimize the degree of exposure is essential when learning how to live without irritating symptoms.

Cat allergies are caused by an allergen found in the cat's saliva, not by its dander, as is commonly believed. The transfer of saliva from the cat's mouth, which eventually dries on the fur and is sometimes referred to as dandruff, becomes airborne and spreads throughout your home. These tiny particles of dried allergen dust not only penetrate the sufferer's nasal passages but are also transmitted deep into the lungs, making symptoms quite severe. Red, itchy, or swollen eyes, nasal congestion, sneezing, itching, or coughing can be extremely distressing and are only some of the symptoms allergy sufferers have to bear. Here are some tips that can help.

1. Consult an allergist to determine whether you are *indeed* allergic to your cat. An allergy to any household substance or airborne particles can elicit the same symptoms. Once it has been determined that the allergy is to your cat, various therapies can be employed.

2. Immunotherapy, which involves a series of injections introducing the allergen in increasing dosages, is designed to produce a tolerance to the allergen. This type of therapy often takes time and can be expensive, though highly worth it.

3. Numerous over-the-counter med-

ications can be taken to relieve symptoms. These are the same drugs that one would normally take for any allergic reaction. They include bronchodilators; oral antihistamines such as Benadryl, Chlortrimeton, and Claritin; corticosteroids; and topical nasal steroids. Your allergist should be able to recommend one that will work best for you.

4. A number of natural supplements can alleviate allergy symptoms. They include vitamin C with quercetin, vitamin B_5, vitamin A, omega-3 fatty acids, vitamin E, selenium, grape-seed extract, and magnesium.

5. You can safely add these herbs to your allergy-relief treatment: marshmallow root, burdock, mullein, goldenseal root, and white pine. Check with your doctor to be sure that herbs won't interfere with other medications you may be taking.

6. Nambudripad's Allergy Elimination Techniques are alternative treatments that have been very successful in helping many allergy sufferers. NAET is a holistic, noninvasive way to treat food-related and environmental allergies. It uses a combination of kinesiology (muscle responsive testing), chiropractic, and Eastern medicine, including acupuncture.

7. Take your cat to a groomer or have a person without allergies bathe your cat every six weeks. This will remove any traces of allergen produced by your cat's saliva. A mild shampoo should be used and rinsed out thoroughly. Do not bathe your cat more often because it may dry its skin too much. Also, find someone else to brush your longhaired cat every day. Hint: If you get stuck with the grooming and bathing chores (try not to!), wear a pollen-filter mask.

8. Create cat-free zones in your home, and by all means keep the cat out of your bedroom. If you live in a warm climate, you may even consider setting up a safe and comfortable outdoor sleeping area for your cat.

9. Certain sprays can reduce or neutralize the allergens on your cat's fur. Anti-Allergen Solution, a clear, stain-free, nontoxic plant-based formulation proven to denature protein allergens on contact, is available at e-healthy-homes.com. Your vet can recommend other products.

10. To reduce the concentration of allergens in the air, improve the airflow and ventilation of your home by opening windows and letting in fresh air.

11. A commercial-size air purifier can significantly reduce the amount of allergens in your home. Avoid small room-size units; they don't seem to get the job done. Check out the Honeywell and Alpine Air systems. A new generation of air purifiers, called hydroxyl radical air purifiers, employ ultraviolet light and negative ions to eliminate all pollutants without the need for a filter.

12. You may want to consider getting rid of carpets, drapes or curtains, and synthetic fabrics in your home. Synthetics actually attract and retain dust and are difficult to clean. Use only washable fabrics.

13. Wash linens, bedspreads, curtains, sheets, and pillows as often as possible.

14. Vacuuming your home may actually spread allergens, unless you use a true hypoallergenic vacuum with a HEPA-celoc filter. After vacuuming, be sure to open windows to air out the room.

15. Litter that is formulated with chemicals to mask odor can in itself cause an allergy. Use low-dust litter. Get a member of the family without allergies to take on the litter-box chores.

16. If you are thinking about adopting a cat and you suspect that you may be allergic, spend some time around a friend's cats and see how you react. If you do decide to get a cat, think about shorthair breeds. Longhaired cats trap more allergen dust than shorthairs do. *Note:* Even furless cats such as the Sphynx can cause an allergic reaction. Their saliva is merely deposited on their skin instead of their fur.

Why Do They Fight Like Cats and Dogs?

Well, because they *are* cats and dogs. But with the right introductions, any feline can become buddies with a dog, especially one sharing the same home. As for specific breeds, in general, the American Curl, Bombay, Burmese, Ocicat, and Maine Coon breeds tend to get along well with canines.

For those who prefer to be "bi-petual" by welcoming both cats and dogs into their homes, please heed these tips to reduce the chance of any fur-flying incidents:

1. Introduce the resident cat to the new dog or puppy slowly. Crate the canine at first, and allow your cat to approach on its own.

2. Keep the dog on a long lead in the house so you can step on the lead to halt him from chasing after the cat.

3. Teach your dog important commands like "watch me," "wait," and "sit," which you can use to stop it from bugging your cat.

4. Reward your dog with high-quality treats whenever it behaves nicely around your cat. The dog will associate the presence of the cat with the presence of dog treats.

5. Provide escape routes for your cat, including space under the bed and tall cat trees that are out of paw's reach of dogs.

Scratching Post Basics

Scratching posts are great investments for your home. They will provide Cosmo a place to scratch and stretch to his heart's content instead of destroying your prized possessions. There are numerous scratching posts available on the market. They vary in size and shape; some are tall, some are cone-shaped, others lie flat on the ground, and some can be attached to a doorknob. Some posts are covered with carpet, some with rope, while some are just made of wood. Here are some things you should know about scratching posts.

Every cat should own several scratching posts, of varying sizes, angles, and scratching surfaces. Scratching posts are essential to cats for exercise, stress relief, and claw management, and they will prevent wear and tear to furniture and carpeting.

Getting Cujo to actually use the post may take a little work. At first, place the post in an area where your cat regularly goes to scratch, possibly near a piece of furniture he has been using. Don't make the mistake of placing his paws on the post to show him how to use it. He'll be highly annoyed. Instead, try feeding him and playing with him near the post.

You can also try rubbing some catnip on the post or tying one of his favorite toys to it. If you drag a toy or even a piece of string along the surface of the post, Cujo may sink his paws into it. Once he gets the feeling of the post and has marked it as his territory, he'll use it all the time. Start Cujo on the scratching post as early in his life as possible. Kittens love scratching posts.

Cats usually prefer a vertical post constructed with a large base, so they can get a great workout without making the post tip over.

A vertical post should be tall enough so that Audrey III can stretch her entire body. At first, you may want to place the post on its side and play with her until she starts investigating it. Once she's shown interest, you can reposition the post vertically.

Posts with round designs have more scratching surface and last longer than square posts.

Posts that lie flat on the ground may spare your carpet, but a tall post is preferable because it permits Audrey to stretch to her full length.

Don't make the mistake of getting a post that is pretty but too soft and therefore ineffective. Dino won't want to use it. The post should have rough surfaces that can be shredded by his claws.

Sisal posts made of sisal textile material are perfect for Suzie-Q's scratching delight. The material has the perfect texture and grain for her to rip and tear. No need to discard the post once it becomes worn; chances are, this is just how she likes it.

5 Reasons Why Cats Scratch

Scratching is a normal behavior for all cats, and there is nothing you can or should do to prevent it. If Little Steven is ripping up your furniture, it's not because he doesn't appreciate the decor. Here are some of the reasons he's compelled to scratch.

1. For the sheer joy of it. It feels good to scratch.

2. Scratching is a way for him to mark his territory. By scratching he is able to leave both a visual mark and a scent — there are scent glands on cat paws.

3. It's a great form of exercise. The act of scratching stretches and pulls the muscles. Think of it as a mini-workout.

4. He may scratch to relieve frustration when prevented from doing something else he wants to do.

5. Scratching helps remove the dead outer layer of the claws.

5 Things You Should Know About Cat Scratch Disease

The Centers for Disease Control provided the following information on the dangers and avoidance of cat scratch disease.

1. Cat scratch disease (CSD) is a disease caused by the bacterium *Bartonella henselae*. Most people with CSD have been bitten or scratched by a cat and developed a mild infection at the point of injury. Lymph nodes, especially those around the head, neck, and upper limbs, become swollen. Additionally, a person with CSD may experience fever, headache, fatigue, and a poor appetite. Rare complications of *B. henselae* infection are bacillary angiomatosis and Parinaud's oculoglandular syndrome.

2. Cats can spread *B. henselae* to people. Most people get CSD from cat bites and scratches. Kittens are more likely to be infected and to pass the bacterium to people. About 40 percent of cats carry *B. henselae* at some time in their lives. Cats that carry *B. henselae* do not show any signs of illness; therefore, you cannot tell which cats can spread the disease to you. People with compromised immune systems, such as those undergoing immunosuppressive treatments for cancer, organ transplant patients, and people with HIV/AIDS, are more likely than others to have complications of CSD. Although *B. henselae* has been found in fleas, so far there is no evidence that a bite from an infected flea can give you CSD. Cat scratch disease does not pose a serious health threat to people who are in good health.

3. You can reduce your risk of contracting cat scratch disease by avoiding "rough play" with cats, especially kittens (this includes any activity that may lead to cat scratches and bites); by washing cat bites and scratches immediately and thoroughly with running water and soap; by preventing cats from licking any open wounds that you may have; and by controlling fleas.

4. If you develop an infection (with pus and pronounced swelling) where you were scratched or bitten by a cat, or if you develop symptoms including fever, headache, swollen lymph nodes, and fatigue, contact your physician.

5. To find more information about cat scratch disease, contact the CDC at CDC.gov.

Cat Bite Bytes

When it comes to putting the bite on people, dogs draw more public attention than cats do. Yet cats can cause serious injury, too, with their needle-sharp teeth and razorlike claws. Do you think cats are mere pussycats? You might change your mind when you consider these details:

About 4.5 million animal bites occur each year in the United States, with 1 percent requiring hospitalization.

Cats represent about 10 percent of all reported animal bites.

Nearly 40 percent of cat bites become infected and require medical care. Only 20 percent of dog bites get infected and require medical care.

About 22,000 cases of cat scratch disease are reported annually in the United States. A cat's teeth cause puncture wounds, with the real risk of infection deep in the skin.

8 Reasons Why Your Cat Bites—and What You Can Do

Ron Hines, DVM, of 2ndchance.info and a veterinary practitioner for over 20 years, offers the following advice for dealing with a biting cat:

Cat owners report that biting is the second most common behavioral problem in cats — second only to inappropriate urination. This is because personality traits are as varied in cats as they are in people. Early experiences have considerable bearing on later aggressive behavior, but genetic diversity is a greater cause of problem aggression. Some cat owners just accept the unique temperaments of their pets, but others find aggressive behavior intolerable and search for a cure. Unlike other personality quirks, aggressiveness can be a real problem for owners and other pets alike. Cat bites hurt and can lead to infections. Here are various reasons cats bite and what you can do to prevent the problem.

1. The Problem: Aggression Toward Humans. Cats that threaten their owners usually have star-crossed beginnings. If they were not adequately handled, petted, and socialized at 5 to 12 weeks of age, they may grow up to be fearful, wary of people, or easily upset and angered. Cats that are frightened assume a characteristic position. They crouch with their ears back, their tails curled inward, and their bodies tilted away from the perceived threat. They will likely lash out and claw or bite anything that approaches them. This behavior often occurs when the cat is in new surroundings or being approached by a stranger. The cat's eyes dilate, and it hisses and shows its teeth. The hair may stand on end.

The Solution: Begin to correct the problem as soon as it first occurs. Do not wait until the behavior is ingrained in the cat's personality. The best time to get cats used to owners, strangers, and children is when they are still kittens. Take time to get kittens used to being touched everywhere, and introduce them to dogs and other cats while they are still young. To accustom a cat to being touched, begin when the cat is relaxed and content. Start off scratching and rubbing its head. Make no sudden moves. Progress to stroking its back and the base of the tail. Talk to the cat while you are doing this, and watch for any signs that the cat is becoming agitated. Finish this short lesson with a food treat. Eventually the cat will enjoy being touched and handled.

Fear-related aggressiveness in adult cats presents a much-harder-to-solve problem. When they feel threatened by strangers or a new owner, it takes much longer to overcome the problem. Let the cat get hungry, and then have the person hold the cat's favorite treat. Do not let the person approach the cat. Let the cat overcome its fear and approach on its own terms to develop confidence and trust. If the cat is too shy to approach, have a member of the family with whom the cat has a good relationship give the treat while the second person is in the house. Over a series of weeks the visitor can get closer and closer when the treat is offered.

2. The Problem: Redirected Aggression. Redirected aggression is a phenomenon seen frequently in cats. In this situation a strange person or animal upsets the cat. But instead of showing aggression toward this new individual, the cat turns its wrath on the pet owner or another pet. We see the same event occurring in marriages when an agitated wife or husband takes out frustration on the spouse.

Redirected aggression can destroy the bond between cat and cat or cat and owner, something that took years to establish. Sometimes nothing more than a stray cat passing by the window sets off such a confrontation. If a lower-ranking cat becomes the object of redirected aggression, it may defend itself, leading to a serious catfight.

The Solution: First, decide what stimulus caused the aggression, and remove it. Lower the blinds on the window if a stray cat has approached, and shoo it away. If the aggression is directed at you, leave the cat alone until it calms down. Do not punish or yell at the cat. If the cat is being aggressive with housemates, place each cat in a separate room with the door closed. Turn off the lights in the rooms. Interactions with a cat in this state are counterproductive. If the cat is highly agitated, it is best to wrap it in a beach towel when handling it. Calm your pet and praise it. Once the agitated cat has calmed down, reintroduce the other cats slowly. Place them far apart in a room, and stroke and praise each one. A food treat comes in handy in these situations. Remember, even faint smells of another cat can trigger redirected aggression. That is why cats returning from the animal hospital are sometimes attacked by their housemates.

3. The Problem: Aggression Due to Medical Problems. If it is unclear why your cat has suddenly become aggressive, the first thing to do is take it to a veterinarian whom you trust. Be very cautious when placing these cats in carriers, and under no circumstance bring the pet to the veterinarian without a carrier. If a thorough physical exam does not indicate a problem, an x-ray might. In some cats arthritis of the spine or limbs is the root problem. These cats will often growl and hiss when picked up or handled. Other cats develop neurological conditions that lead to sudden intense pain. I call these sudden twinges of pain "ghost pains." Often the spine and tail seem affected. The skin over the spine may ripple during an episode.

The Solution: When arthritis is the cause of aggressive behavior, you might try aspirin therapy; it's essential to get an appropriate dosage from a veterinarian. Unfortunately fewer than half of all cats can tolerate aspirin even when given every second or third day. Cats do handle chondroitin

Ouch! Treating Cat Bites

Any cat is capable of biting anyone at any time — and that includes your otherwise docile feline housemate. If you are bitten, follow these home-care steps, and always consult your physician for follow-up if needed. *Seek immediate care for major bites with profuse bleeding and gaping wounds.* Here are tips for caring for a minor cat bite at home:

Wash the wound promptly with soap and water. You can also use rubbing alcohol or hydrogen peroxide.

Apply pressure with a clean towel to stop any bleeding.

Elevate your arm above your heart if the bite is on your hand or arm to slow the bleeding, lessen the chance of infection, and reduce swelling.

Treat the wound with antibiotic ointment two times a day.

Place a sterile bandage or dressing over the wound, replacing the bandage each time you apply the antibiotic ointment.

Keep tabs on the condition of your wound, checking for unusual redness, swelling, red streaking, oozing pus, or tenderness. Immediately report these signs, as well as any indication of fever, to your physician.

You may need to get a tetanus shot if it has been at least five years since your last booster shot. Also, obtain proof that the cat who bit you has been vaccinated against rabies. It the feline culprit belongs to a friend or relative, ask for the cat's medical records. If the cat is a stray, contact the animal control agency or health department in your area to assist in finding the cat. If records of rabies shots cannot be produced, you will probably need to get a series of rabies shots (called post-exposure prophylaxis). Though extremely rare, the rabies virus can be fatal.

and glucosamine anti-arthritis supplements well, and in a few cases these drugs are effective. We do not know why cats develop ghost pains, but the pains often disappear when the cat is placed on birth control medications such as medroxyprogesterone acetate (Depo-Provera). Some of these

cases may involve a form of epilepsy. When I suspect this, I place them on a trial dosage of phenobarbital, a drug used to control epilepsy. Still other cases turn out to have the "dry" form of feline infectious peritonitis, a chronic and terminal disease caused by a coronavirus. I have heard that cats with severe dental disease can show personality changes, but I have never encountered this phenomenon.

When Purrs Become Bites

Your cat is sitting in your lap, purring contentedly as you stroke him, when he suddenly bites your hand and jumps down. What happened?

According to catsinternational.com, there are several possibilities agreed upon by behaviorists as to why a cat can turn hostile under such peaceful circumstances:

He has begun to doze in your lap, wakes suddenly, and is momentarily disoriented by his surroundings and by being "confined" by your hands. After he jumps down, he may look confused and begin to groom himself to calm down.

Sensitive or nervous cats can be overstimulated by prolonged petting. There are usually warning signs of the impending attack — restlessness, tail twitching, flattened ears, or head turned toward hand. It is important for the cat owner to be alert to these signals and to stop petting the cat *before* this point is reached. At this time a small food treat could be given, along with a few more strokes, to gradually increase the cat's tolerance. *Never physically punish the cat for biting, as it may cause it to become defensive and to seriously retaliate.*

Petting the cat's sensitive stomach area almost always elicits a natural defense reaction, which includes wrapping the paws around the person's wrist, holding on, and biting.

Cats vary in how much they like being petted or held. Cats that do not enjoy prolonged petting or holding may still play with their owners, follow them around the house, sleep on the bed with them, and even sit on their lap. All of these behaviors indicate attachment. Some cats are huggable and others are not, but both types of cats can be equally attached to their owners.

4. The Problem: Nonrecognition Aggression. Occasionally in multicat households, removing a cat for a period of time leads to aggression on the part of cats that remained in the household. The cat at issue is typically returning from the veterinarian, groomer, or boarding cattery, and strange odors are still lingering on it. Without the "right" odor, the other cats do not recognize the returning cat as the same animal that left. If the cats get into a fight, their relationship can take a long time to get back to normal.

The Solution: If you do take your cats to the groomer or veterinarian, take them all along for the ride, in separate carriers. Place the carriers side by side until late in the evening before releasing the cats, and try to release them in a neutral area that the cats rarely frequent. Feeding each cat a pungent canned treat before releasing it also helps. Some of my clients mist feline pheromone spray into the air in these situations.

5. The Problem: Your-Time-to-Pet-Me-Is-Up Biting. Cats that seem immensely pleased by your petting, only to suddenly whirl around and bite you, have always perplexed me. These cats purr up to the moment they attack. Some say that this is due to the cat's short attention span or that there is a fine line between what is pleasurable and what is annoying. Others think these displays occur when a sensitive area on the body has been touched. Some cats will beg for attention, only to sink their teeth into you a few minutes later.

The Solution: Release your cat at the first sign that it has had enough petting. Signals include restlessness, tail twitching, flattened ears, twitching ears, and a tendency to move the head toward your hand. One can attempt to deprogram these cats by feeding them a tasty treat just before you think they might attack. But no solution has been found for the Dr. Jekyll/Mr. Hyde cats, whose tempers turn on a dime. Just accept their idiosyncrasies, and sterilize any cuts and scratches with iodine and alcohol.

6. The Problem: Dominance-Based Aggression. A few cats treat owners like another cat in the household, and attempt to dominate them based on a pecking order, or hierarchy. These cats may growl or hiss when you join them on the bed or attempt to move them. Some will block doorways and show typical signs of aggression, such as tail switching, dilated pupils, flattened ears, and hissing and spitting. Signs of aggression between cats are often subtle. Some owners misread the maneuvers of these cats as simple play. Cats that are not dominant in these situations often lose their potty training and look unkempt. Generally, dominant cats are highly territorial as well. Cats do not reach social maturity until they are about 2 years old, so sometimes this problem can be late in onset.

The Solution: The best way to handle these cats is to withhold love, attention, and treats until the cat is mellow and relaxed. Relaxed cats carry their tails and head high. They stand high on their paws, with small eye pupils and a portion of the third eyelid showing. Punishment only makes the problem worse. The use of pheromone mist around the house can be very helpful, as are food treats given at just the right moment.

7. The Problem: Maternal Aggression. All mother cats are very protective of their kittens and may react violently if they perceive a threat to their young. Some queens react by moving their kittens around restlessly when they perceive a threat. Others may attack people, other cats, and dogs, even ones that they normally trust or ignore.

The Solution: Disturb cats with young kittens as little as possible. Aggressive behavior will subside as the kittens grow older. Let your cat give birth in a low-stress environment without foot traffic or the presence of other cats. If you must handle nursing mothers, put a little tuna juice on your hand first. Better yet, spay your cats.

8. The Problem: Instinctive Hunting Behavior. First, shame on you for letting your cat outdoors unsupervised! Cats have a normal urge to kill small prey, be it wild birds and rodents or the pet canary. It is unrealistic to expect them to change. A cat on the prowl looks like a miniature tiger stalking its prey.

The Solution: Keeping your cat indoors solves most of these problems. If you have indoor pocket pets, be sure they are out of reach of your cat. Never assume that because your cat usually shows fondness for a small animal or bird that it will not one day treat it like prey.

5 "I'm About to Bite You" Warning Signs

Samantha doesn't want to hurt you. In fact, she does everything she can to let you know when, for one reason or another, she is ready to strike. Heed these signals:

1. Hissing, spitting, or an open-mouth threat

2. Dilated pupils

3. Ears flattening sideways or flat against the head

4. Twitching of the tail

5. Pulling away or tensing muscles

Nice Kitty: How to Handle Behavior Problems

Even the sweetest cats do things that we don't quite appreciate. Whether it be failure to use the litter box when eliminating, scratching furniture, or any other inappropriate behavior, we often feel the need to chastise our cats in an attempt to correct their behavior. Punishment, however, is not the answer unless it is done correctly. Learning how to discipline your cat requires patience and an understanding of which techniques work and which don't.

The best way to prevent unwanted behavior is to eliminate the opportunity. You can place a blanket over your sofa to protect an area that Fuzzy likes to scratch; you can hike up your curtains if he likes to climb them. And if he's a real troublemaker, you can confine him to a single room in your house when you're out. Just leave him some food, water, a litter box, and a couple of toys to keep him occupied.

1. The most important thing to remember is that the *only* time punishment is effective is if you actually catch the kitty in the act. Punishing after the fact, even if you are a couple of seconds late, is never an option because the cat will not remember the act for which it is being punished.

2. Never hit your little animal. Cats do not respond well to hitting, and doing this can damage the bond between you. Hitting can injure a cat, and it may well bite you back in self-defense. Some people like to think that a gentle tap on the nose is an acceptable practice, but in fact, a cat's nose is very sensitive, and even a gentle tap can be painful. Remember that if you hit your cat, it may start viewing you as an enemy.

3. Rewards will help avoid problems. If the cat is about to pounce on the kitchen counter in search of food, for instance, say no in a calm but firm voice, and when the cat settles down, offer a treat and a couple of gentle strokes. Repeated rewards when used properly are highly effective. Fuzzy's life will be happier if you reward him for good behavior rather than punish him for being bad.

4. Getting Coco to associate a bad behavior with something unpleasant is a nonaggressive form of punishment. If you catch her scratching your favorite sofa, squirt her with a little stream of water from a water gun, and watch her fly away. Coco will now associate scratching the sofa with getting wet. It's important, however, that the cat doesn't see you with the gun, or it will just continue this behavior when you are out of the room. The cat needs to respond to a mysterious force.

5. If Fuzzy tends to play too rough, get him some toys that will redirect this predatory behavior. Choose toys that he can chase and hunt. (See "4 Cat Toys You Can Make," page 360.)

6. Certain odors are quite unpleasant and will keep a cat away from areas where it does not belong. You can use commercial cat repellants, or you can rub orange peels or orange solvent (cats hate the odor) on objects you wish to protect.

7. Vinnie hates having sticky paws. Place some double-sided tape on a spot you want him to avoid.

8. Harsh noises are upsetting to cats. Use any sort of noisemaker as you observe an unwanted behavior. Try some coins in a can, pebbles in a small cardboard box, or a party noisemaker.

9. If the misbehaviors persist, it might be a good idea to have the cat checked by the vet to make sure there are no underlying problems.

Bad Kitty: How to Prevent Your Cat from . . .

. . . Chewing on Electric Cords

Most cats find electric cords fascinating. If your cat begins chewing on a cord, not only is its safety at risk, but also you are facing a possible fire hazard in your home. Here are some tips to keep Ginger and your home safe:

1. Dispose of any cords whose insulation has been compromised, exposing electrical wires. If the cat has already gone to town on a particular cord, get rid of it.

2. There should be no dangling cords in your home; they are especially enticing to cats, who consider them toys just waiting to be played with.

3. Discourage the cat from chewing on cords by saying a firm "no" as a verbal cue. If that doesn't work, clap your hands together while saying no. This will reinforce the command.

6. Spray cords with an unpleasant-tasting substance. Cats hate the taste of bitter apple spray, toothpaste, and hot pepper sauce, such as Tabasco and lemon juice.

7. Tape loose cords to the wall with electric tape.

8. Hide excess lengths of cord behind furniture or appliances.

9. Shorten the distance between the outlet and an appliance as much as possible, and tuck the extra cord length behind the appliance.

10. A "wire loom jacket" is available at automotive suppliers and can be used to cover exposed cords and wires. This durable plastic material has a slit in its side; you can place cords within it. PVC pipe can serve the same purpose but won't look as attractive.

11. CritterCord, a clear, flexible protective

"Dogs have owners; cats have staff."
— SNEAKY PIE BROWN, AUTHOR OF RITA MAE BROWN'S CAT

4. If the cat doesn't respond to a verbal command, try spraying it with some water. Kitty will get the message.

5. Put contact paper, sticky side up, near electric cords that your cat wants to chew. Cats hate sticky stuff on their paws.

cover, has a long-lasting citrus odor that cats hate. Electric cords can be easily slipped into this product.

12. Don't overload outlets. Too great a load on the circuits can cause shorts in the system or

even electrical fires. And that's not even taking account of the temptation that overloaded outlets present to cats.

13. Cats much prefer thin cords, so use heavy-duty cords wherever possible.

14. Unplug appliances you don't use much, and put them away in a safe, cat-free space until needed. When appliances are in use, do not leave them unattended.

. . . Climbing Curtains

Cats love to climb curtains, and they enjoy the sensation of shredding them to bits. Protect your lovely window treatments by following these tips:

1. Use tension rods. If your curtain is suspended with a tension rod, the curtain will come crashing down and frighten your cat if it tries to climb up the fabric. The cat will soon learn that climbing the curtain will bring it down.

2. Use the squirt gun or hand-clap methods to teach your cat to avoid this behavior, but be sure that your cat doesn't associate you primarily with deterrents, or it may become frightened of you. Don't make eye contact with your cat while using these methods of behavior modification.

3. Purchase a motion detector, such as The CatScram Cat repeller, which is an infrared motion detector with

an ultrasonic speaker that emits a tone inaudible to humans. It will sound a disturbing alarm whenever your cat gets near your valuable curtains.

4. If none of these methods work, you can always switch to blinds! Just be aware that Rosie will love the sound these make as she rattles them.

. . . Eating Houseplants

Many houseplants are poisonous and therefore lethal to your cat if ingested. This hazard requires your immediate attention. It takes only one snack on a Dieffenbachia to seriously harm your cat. On the other hand, having a cat doesn't mean you can't enjoy greenery all year long. (See "67 Plants That Are Safe for Your Cat," page 297.) These tips will keep Beyoncé out of harm's way.

1. Move any harmful plant out of the cat's sight.

2. Supply the cat with its own kitty garden. A number of plants are harmless to cats, and your kitty will enjoy sampling them. You may have to lure the cat to the garden with its favorite treat until it gets the idea. A number of kitty herb gardens are commercially available.

3. You can discourage the cat from eating a particular plant by spraying the underside of the leaves with bitter apple spray or by coating them with hot sauce. The presence of ammonia or mothballs

will also keep your cat away from a houseplant.

4. Stay Away Automatic Pet Deterrent is one of the commercially available products that can be sprayed on leaves without harming the plant or your cat.

. . . Unrolling Toilet Paper

This is certainly not one of Kitty's worst habits, but if you find it annoying and you don't want your bathroom to have that "distressed" look, here are some simple things you can do:

1. Install the toilet roll so that it unrolls from the bottom and not the top. When the cat figures out that it can no longer unroll the paper, it will probably stop trying, and you can then install subsequent rolls so it rolls off to the front, if that is your preference.

2. You can cat-proof your toilet paper by buying toilet paper roll protectors sold in the baby section of Target, K-Mart, or Wal-Mart.

3. Put the roll in a nearby cabinet.

4. Keep bathroom doors closed.

12 Ways to Prevent Your Cat from Disappearing

1. Even indoor cats need to be protected from suddenly opened doors and insecurely latched windows.

2. Make sure your backyard is fenced in and that no gaps in it tempt your kitty to take off. Keep gates locked, not only to keep the cat in but also to keep other animals out.

3. Your cat should be equipped with two forms of identification in case a tag, for instance, falls off. Microchipping has become popular (see page 292), or you can ask your vet about pet tattoos. Keep a pet license tag on the collar.

4. It's a good idea to keep a rabies tag on the cat's collar. If a rabies alert takes place in your area, all pets picked up without rabies tags will be automatically euthanized.

5. Always transport the cat in a carrier, and be careful about opening it in strange places. Bobo can easily become frightened in a strange environment and bolt into a crowd.

6. Take photos of your cat now and then, in case you need them for identification purposes later.

7. Teach your cat to come when you call or to respond to another signal, such as the sound of a bell or a whistle.

8. Spay or neuter your cats; they'll be less likely to roam.

9. Keep cats inside at night.

10. Don't leave a cat unattended at home for days at a time, even with sufficient food and water. The cat might go off in search of its favorite thing — you. If you must leave for an entire day, place something with your scent on it — unlaundered socks, for instance — in the cat's bed to let it know you'll be back.

11. If construction work is being done in your house, consider finding a temporary home for Tippy until the dust has literally settled. If that's not possible, make sure the workers are aware of the cat and that it is kept in a closed-off area as doors are being opened and closed.

12. Introduce your cat to the neighbors, and let them know whether it is an indoor or outdoor cat. Then they'll know they should alert you if indoor-only Zorro happens to be spotted near the hedge.

17 Steps You Can Take If Your Cat Is Missing

If you've ever experienced the disappearance of a cat, you know how stressful it can be, especially if it is an indoor cat unaccustomed to the outside world. Outdoor cats, of course, disappear more frequently, and their owners tend to assume they will come home when they are ready. But if your cat is missing for an inordinate amount of time, try to find it as quickly as possible. The sooner you start, the better your chance of finding the cat. If you've had the foresight to provide an ID tag and collar or even a microchip, you've improved your chance of retrieving your pet. Here are some steps you can take.

1. Search every inch of your house, calling the cat's name. Check all rooms, tight spaces, closets, boxes, cabinets, the basement, the freezer, spaces under furniture, your washer and dryer, the garage — anywhere the cat might be accidentally trapped. If it doesn't respond to its name, the cat might be extremely frightened or ill. If Pumpkin is sick, she is not likely to respond. The wish to stay hidden is a self-defense mechanism. When your cat is sick, it might even look upon you as a threat.

2. Walk around your neighborhood, talk to anyone you meet, and leave your phone number.

3. Some cats respond to dog whistles. You might want to try that.

4. Put some of the cat's toys, its favorite food, and its litter box outside. This might get the cat's attention and lure it back.

5. Let neighbors know that your cat is missing, and ask them to kindly check their homes and garages. A wandering kitty can wind up in the strangest places.

6. Check outside and call the cat's name. It may have been frightened by something and is merely hiding. If the missing pet is an indoor cat, chances are it hasn't strayed too far from home.

7. Post as many photos of the cat as you can throughout your neighborhood — in shops, schools, the library, and the post office. Alert the school crossing guard and others who work in the neighborhood. You may get better results if you offer a reward, although this may bring a host of strangers to your door with cats that don't remotely resemble yours. Include only your phone number, and no other personal information.

8. Get some of the neighborhood kids to help you search. Most youngsters will love the challenge, but make sure they have their parents' permission to join the search party.

9. Report your baby's disappearance to your local police. Be sure to let them know if the cat shows up.

10. Report the cat's disappearance to all the veterinarians in your area.

11. If your home is being remodeled, make sure that all contractors are aware that the kitty is missing. Have them check behind new walls, in basement crawlspaces, and in their trucks and equipment. If a neighbor is having construction work done, ask the person to search for your cat, or get permission to search the premises yourself.

12. It is essential that you contact the local animal shelter immediately. Most shelters are online, and you can e-mail a picture of Pumpkin directly to them. Visit the shelter every day or so to look for your cat.

13. Speak to anyone who frequently comes to your home, such as your letter carrier, FedEx driver, milkman, and so on. These people probably are familiar with your cat and may have seen it somewhere. There's also a chance that the cat may have climbed into the rear of a delivery vehicle.

14. Place an ad in the lost-and-found section of local newspapers. Read the paper each day to find out if someone has reported finding your cat.

15. When you finally locate your cat, be very cautious as you approach. Buffy may be extremely frightened and may disappear again. If she avoids you, create a friendly trap. Lure her in by leaving a bit of food, water, and one of her blankets inside the trap.

16. Check with your local department of public works or animal control crew that may have found your pet either dead or injured on the road.

17. Don't give up your search. Check out our list of inspiring stories of cats who have made "15 Incredible Journeys," on page 132.

Removing Cat Stains and Odors

The folks at cozycatfurniture.com care about your furniture. That's why they offer Kitty an array of alternatives: a comprehensive line of furniture just for cats, including scratching posts, cat trees, houses, gyms, condos, stairs, and beds. Our favorites are the Catnap Vertigo Bed, the hot-pink plush Catnap Beetle, and the Catnap Loveseat in a feral cheetah print. They also know that even under the best circumstances, Sparkle can have an accident. So they offer a detailed guide to getting rid of cat stains, and they've graciously allowed us to share this information with our readers.

Anyone who owns a cat knows that stains and odors from cat urine can be a problem. Cat urine that seeps through carpet, into padding, and down to the floor beneath can give your home an unpleasant aroma and bad look. In almost all cases, cat urine is the worst perpetrator of pet stains and odors. And because cat diets are richer in protein than dog diets are, feline urine produces a harsher odor and is more likely to cause stains.

You must be extra vigilant about cat odor and attack problems as soon as they occur. Be careful to remove all traces of the odor, for if the scent remains, the cat will likely soil the same spot again.

Urine can saturate absorbent materials such as carpet and padding, upholstery, and mattresses, penetrating well below the surface. It is extremely difficult to remove all the urine that has soaked in. Even after a thorough cleaning, stains and odors often remain. Here are some guidelines that will help you eliminate them.

How to Clean Cat Urine from Carpet

First, blot up as much of the urine as possible with a soft, clean white cloth or absorbent paper towel. Press down firmly (do not rub) for 30 seconds. The more fresh urine you can remove before it dries, the simpler it will be to remove the odor. Remove the towel and repeat the process until the area is fully dried. Rinse the accident zone thoroughly with clean, cool water. After rinsing, remove as much water as possible by blotting it up.

Next, you have some options:

1. Baking soda works well to eliminate surface (but not deeply penetrated) odors. Dampen the area with clean water and then sprinkle baking soda over it. Rub the baking soda into the soiled area and let dry. Brush or vacuum to remove the dry powder.

2. Another option is white vinegar. Mix a quart warm water with ½ cup white vinegar, and dribble the mixture onto the stain. Place dry towels over the stained area, and put something heavy over the towels to increase the pressure. After a few hours remove the towels, and raise the nap of the carpet with a soft-bristled hairbrush. *Note:* Before you begin, test the vinegar solution on a piece of fabric that is hidden from view.

3. To clean old or heavy stains in carpeting, consider renting an extractor or wet vac from a local hardware store. This machine looks like a vacuum cleaner; it forces clean water through carpet and then pushes the dirty water back out again. When using this machine, make sure to follow the instructions carefully.

4. You can also make your own cleaning solution that is 30 percent peroxide and 70 percent water. Add ½ teaspoon baking soda and a few drops of Listerine mouthwash (it helps eliminate odor). The fizzing action of the mixture will help remove stains. Apply it to the soiled area, and leave it for about five minutes. Then blot up as much as you can with absorbent paper towels. Rinse

the area, using a solution made of ⅓ cup white vinegar and a quart of water. Allow to dry. *Note:* Peroxide can bleach some fabrics; test the mixture on a hidden area of the carpet before treatment.

5. One of the newest technologies for cleaning cat urine involves penetrating the soiled area and deactivating the odor with peroxide or detergents. Simply spray on any commercial cleaning product that contains at least 3 percent peroxide. Wait five minutes, then use a clean white absorbent cloth to blot the area, pressing down firmly (do not rub) for 30 seconds. Repeat this blotting process until the area is dry. If the stain or odor persists, repeat the process. You can also add a few drops of Listerine mouthwash to the peroxide/water mixture, to help eliminate the odor.

Once the soiled area is really clean, use a high-quality pet odor neutralizer available at pet supply stores. Test the affected surface for staining first, and follow all instructions.

When the treated area is completely dry, check the results. If it still looks stained, purchase and apply a special stain-and-odor-removing bacteria or enzyme cleaner, such as Outright Pet Stain Eliminator, Pet "Oops" Remover, or Stain Gobbler.

How to Clean Cat Urine from Upholstery

When it's impossible to remove the cover of your upholstered couch or chair for laundering, try this cleaning procedure to get the cat urine out:

Dab the stain with a soft, clean white cloth or absorbent paper towel. For stubborn stains, a commercial cleaning solvent may be needed, but don't apply it directly on the stain; instead, pour it onto a clean cloth. Clean the stain in a circular motion, rubbing gently and working from the outside in. After removing the stain, dry the area immediately with a handheld hairdryer, using a cool setting. Direct the air first toward the outer area,

Shannon Garrahan to the Rescue . . .

This dog-and-cat lady par excellence should know what she's talking about. When the territorial wars rage between Trafalgar, a spirited Jack Russell Terrier, and Marty, a cat who simply refuses to say uncle, it's not just the fur that flies. Shannon recommends a product called Nature's Miracle for the removal of urine, stool, blood, or any organic material. It's nontoxic, so you can use it around kids and pets. You can find it online or at most pet supply stores.

then work toward the center. Use a brush with soft bristles to remove residue.

How to Clean Cat Urine from Hardwood Floors

Cat urine can cause a hardwood floor to rot. If you catch the problem while it's still "fresh," you'll be better off.

Blot the entire wet area immediately and firmly with paper towels. Wash the affected area several times with white vinegar. Rinse thoroughly with warm water. Blot the area dry with paper towels. Apply a special stain-and-odor-removing bacteria or enzyme cleaner (see above for suggested brands). If you can't remove old stains, try sanding them away with fine sandpaper. Then you can revarnish the wood.

The 9 Best Things About Older Cats

Most veterinarians consider a cat to be a "senior" at the age of 12, and since the average life span of a cat is about 15 years or older, adopting an older cat can provide you with years of wonderful companionship. Yes, kittens *are* cuter, and you probably won't be able to resist one, but are they right for your home? Here are some considerations that may influence your decision.

1. Although kittens are adorable, they are also very energetic and inquisitive, so the potential for destructive mishaps around the house is far greater than it would be with an older cat. Older cats can be trusted. They prefer naps to priceless figurines.

2. Older cats are less likely to be injured by an overzealous child.

3. Older cats are far more manageable for the elderly, since these felines are less rambunctious.

4. Older cats have already been socialized and are quieter.

5. Older cats need less one-on-one time with their humans.

6. Older cats are already familiar with the litter box and people, and they won't require training.

7. If you rescue an older cat from a shelter, chances are she's already had her shots and has been neutered.

8. If you adopt an older cat, you'll immediately know its full-grown size and disposition.

9. An older cat is usually a more affectionate cat. It would rather cuddle than play.

Choosing a Veterinarian

Choosing a good veterinarian for Zaza is an important task that might require a bit of legwork. The vet you choose should have both the medical knowledge and the skill to communicate with you in an effective and sensitive manner. Here are some criteria.

The best way to begin this process is to simply ask some of your pet-loving friends which veterinarians they recommend.

Call a few local kennels and catteries for recommendations. You may also consider contacting groomers, shelters, or emergency clinics. If you are planning on moving to a new area, ask your current vet to recommend someone.

Do some comparison shopping. Some vets charge more than others. Find out why one vet charges more for a particular procedure. If there is a good reason, you might want to consider choosing this vet.

The best way to evaluate a veterinary practice is to pay a visit. Call ahead, asking to see the facility, but don't bring your cat. The condition of the office will give you a good idea of your vet's priorities. The waiting room should be calm and clean, and the examination rooms should be clean and free from odor. Check the cleanliness of the cat quarters also. Instruments should be arranged in an organized manner. Ask the vet about new developments in cat care and whether the office has the latest equipment.

Prepare a list of questions in advance:

🐾 How long has the vet has been in practice?

🐾 What methods of payment are accepted?

🐾 What are the charges for emergency and after-hours visits?

🐾 Does the vet make house calls?

🐾 Is the staff helpful and friendly?

Some folks seek out "cats only" veterinarians. This may or may not be a wise decision. Although the cats-only vet will have a more detailed understanding of feline medicine, a vet with a general practice and a larger staff may provide better care.

The vet you choose should be outgoing and sympathetic. He or she should call both you and your pet by name and never rush the visit or speed up an exam. Find a vet who has enough time for you and Clarence.

If the practice is an animal hospital, it should be certified by the American Animal Hospital Association (AAHA).

If Your Cat Has to Be Hospitalized

Get a written estimate of charges upon admission.

If your cat will be hospitalized for a few days, ask about visitation.

Leave an old shirt or something that bears your scent in the cat's cage.

Keep records of all hospital visits and notes on the illness, the prognosis, follow-up procedures, and recommended medications.

Give copies of the discharge instructions to everyone in the household.

Toxic Hotline

If you suspect that your cat may have accidentally swallowed human prescription drugs or over-the-counter medications, immediately alert your veterinarian or call the ASPCA Animal Poison Control hotline number: (888) 426-4435. This national center operates 24 hours a day and is staffed by veterinarians knowledgeable in the field of toxicology. Please note that a minor charge will be assessed on your credit card for this service.

Veterinarians who choose to have a certification must undergo regular inspections and maintain certain standards. This does not mean, however, that a clinic that is not AAHA-certified is not good.

Find out if the vet is active in social or community organizations. If she is involved in community events or participates in animal rescue, you know her heart is in the right place. If she is a member of a professional veterinary association or taking continuing education courses, all the better. What sorts of pets does *she* have?

The veterinarian you choose should have a good bedside manner, take a complete medical history of your cat, handle your cat gently, encourage you to ask questions, and provide you with literature on health care. It is up to you and your vet to work as a team to provide the best possible care for your cat.

Be patient in establishing a good working relationship with your vet. You must earn your vet's respect in the same way he or she earns yours. If, over time, your first choice just doesn't measure up, seek out a different vet.

Poor Kitty: 20 Ways to Tell If Your Cat Is Sick

Cats are proud creatures, and they are experts at hiding the fact that they are ill. Their innate programming tells them that being sick may make them vulnerable to a predator. Unless you are very observant, it may take days to find out that anything is wrong. It's important to have a working knowledge of how your cat behaves when well so that you will be able to identify signs of illness. If any normal behaviors change dramatically, it might be cause for concern. Give the cat a periodic examination or at least be in tune to its body during grooming sessions. And please, don't try to treat the illness yourself. If your cat is sick, get it to the vet as soon as possible. Be sure to report any major changes in your household or in your cat's normal routine; these may shed light on its condition. Here are some telltale signs that Kitty is ailing:

1. If Gabriella has **stopped eating or drinking**, it might be a sign that she is getting sick. It is extremely important that she not become dehydrated. If she refuses water, get her to the vet immediately.

2. The cat **suddenly turned glutton** may have developed a thyroid disorder.

3. If Wilbur seems to be **sleeping more** than usual, there very well may be a problem.

4. Watch the watering hole. Replenish your cat's water bowls each morning with fresh water. Take note of how much water your cat consumes each day. Cats developing diabetes, liver disease, hyperthyroidism, cancer, and renal failure often start **drinking more water** than normal.

5. If Kitty's **personality** or the way she relates to the family has changed, she may either be in pain or feeling stress and anxiety. She may even attack you if you approach her in a way that makes her feel threatened.

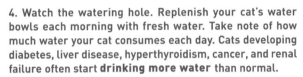

6. **Changes in litter-box use** may also indicate illness. Practice consistent poop patrol. Early signs of disease often show up as changes in your cat's bathroom routine. Smaller clumps of urine in scoopable litter may indicate the start of liver disease or a urinary blockage. Conversely, larger-than-normal urine clumps could be signs of the early stages of diabetes.

7. If Virgil has **difficulty urinating**, or perhaps can't urinate at all, there is probably something serious going on. Get him to a vet as soon as possible.

8. If you see Theodora **limping**, she may have been injured or is experiencing the onset of a more serious problem.

9. If you find the cat **breathing rapidly or panting** while resting, there may be cause for concern.

10. Don't brush off **grooming habits**. Most cats devote about 30 percent of their day keeping their coats looking their best. Sick cats tend to groom much less, and their coats become greasy and matted. Stressed cats will groom excessively and even resort to hair pulling in a condition known as psychogenic alopecia.

11. If Petunia's **nose is running** or you hear her sneeze, she may have caught a cold. Her nose should be cool, moist, and clean, not dry or scabby. If sticky or brownish discharge runs from her nose, or if she has watery eyes, have the cat treated. Pneumonia may result if the problem is left to "run its course."

12. A cat's **eyes should be bright, moist, and clear**. If they appear dull or sunken, the cat is probably sick.

13. The **ears should be clean and odor free**. Any discharge or strong odor could indicate a serious condition and requires immediate medical attention.

14. A hairball might set Kitty off on a coughing jag, but it might also mean something more serious is going on. **Coughing** is sometimes an indication of heart disease or asthma. If your cat coughs without producing any evidence of hairballs, consult your vet.

15. **Vomiting** may be a sign of illness unless the cat is coughing up a hairball. Any traces of blood in the vomit may indicate a serious problem.

16. You may notice **skin abnormalities** or ticks or fleas while you are grooming your cat. If its coat appears thinner or drier, have the vet investigate.

17. If the cat acts **sluggish**, or if its ribs begin to show, the animal might be in physical decline. To stay informed about your cat's typical size, weigh it from time to time. You can do this by weighing yourself while holding the cat and then subtracting your weight from the total. If the cat's weight has changed significantly over a brief period of time, get it to the vet right away. If, on the other hand, Kitty has gained weight, put it on a diet right away. Do this by cutting back 10 percent on daily food portions for a month. Weigh the

Kitty 911: First-Aid Kits for Cats

Be prepared. That's a motto embraced by Boy Scouts and Girl Scouts. It should also be embraced by all pet owners.

Cats may wow us with their agile, athletic antics, but even the most coordinated of cats can take a spill from a high shelf and injure a leg. Or accidentally step on broken glass and cut a paw. Or need to be ushered quickly out of a house due to a pending hurricane.

Short of keeping our cats inside protective bubbles (and who wants that?), we cannot always prevent accidents or illnesses from happening to our cats, but we can be prepared in case they do.

Every feline household should contain an emergency pet kit, and these are readily available in pet supply stores. Each comes with a booklet and instructions for using its contents.

cat again, and see if you might need to reduce the food by another 10 percent.

18. Feline **teeth should be clean and white**. Gums should be pink. Any sign of loosening teeth, foul mouth odor, excessive tartar, and red or bleeding gums should be noted and treated. A foul odor might be an indication of a digestive illness.

19. If a cat's belly has any **lumps or bumps**, have them checked. Familiarity with the cat's physique will help you discern any changes; after all, some internal organs may feel like a lump and don't need to be examined by a vet. Learn what's normal, so you'll know what isn't.

20. Note any **vocalization changes**. If your cat is normally quiet as a mouse and suddenly starts yowling, it could have throat problems, a respiratory ailment, tumors, or even "kitty Alzheimer's."

How to "Summerize" Your Cat

Summer is a time for both you and your pet to enjoy the sunshine, but along with the fun, the season also presents situations that can endanger your pet. By taking precautions, you can decrease the chance of disaster. According to the HSUS:

In nice weather you may be tempted to take your pet with you in the car while you travel or do errands. *Don't.* During warm weather, the inside of your car can reach 120 degrees Fahrenheit in a matter of minutes, even if you're parked in the shade. This can mean real trouble for your companion animals left in the car. Dogs and cats can't perspire and can dispel heat only by panting and through the pads of their feet. Pets who are left in hot cars even briefly can suffer from heat exhaustion, heat stroke, brain damage, and can even die. Don't think that just because you'll be gone "just a minute" that your pet will be safe while you're gone; even an air-conditioned car with the motor off isn't healthy for your pet. To avoid any chance that your pet will succumb to the heat of a car this summer, be sure to play it safe by leaving your pet cool and refreshed at home while you're on the road. And if you do happen to see a pet in a car alone during the hot summer months, try to locate the owner. If that's not possible, call local animal control or the police department immediately.

Want to help educate others about the dangers of leaving pets in hot cars? During the summer months (May through September) the HSUS has educational posters available for purchase ($3 for 10, $5 for 25) that store managers can post in their windows to remind shoppers that Leaving Your Pet in a Parked Car Can Be a Deadly Mistake. Flyers are also available (50 for $3). To order, please send a check, your mailing address, and the number of posters or flyers that you would like to receive to the following address: HSUS/Hot Cars, 2100 L Street NW, Washington, DC 20037. You can also receive a free sample flyer by sending a self-addressed, stamped envelope to the above address.

Summer is often a time when people fertilize their lawns and work in their gardens. But beware: plant food, fertilizer, and insecticides can be fatal if your pet ingests them. In addition, more than 700 plants can produce physiologically active or toxic substances in sufficient amounts to cause harmful effects in animals. (See "119 Plants That Are Potentially Poisonous to Cats," page 296.)

Check with your veterinarian to see if your pets should be taking heartworm prevention medication. Heartworm disease, which is transmitted by mosquitoes, can be fatal to both dogs and cats.

Pets plus pools can equal disaster. Prevent free access to pools and always supervise a pet in a pool.

Provide plenty of water and shade for your pets while they're enjoying the great outdoors so they can stay cool.

If you plan on traveling with your pet during the summer, take the time to prepare for your furry

KATHERINE FLETCHER

7 Winter Cat-Care Tips

Dan Christian, a veterinarian and the manager of veterinary services for Friskies PetCare Company, explains how to properly care for cats when the colder months arrive.

1. Dry heat can give even healthy cats dry skin and dull fur during winter. Use a humidifier if the air in your home tends to be dry then.

2. Check for dry, flaking skin by rubbing fur the wrong way on the cat's back, especially near the tail. This is where loose hair starts. Also check its cheeks and ears for dry skin.

3. Diet can be a good combatant for dry skin and dull fur. Add a serving of canned food to a dry food regimen during the winter, or replace dry food completely with canned food, since it contains complete nutrition.

4. If your cat really prefers dry food, snip open a cap-sule of vitamin oil, fish-oil concentrate, wheat-germ oil, or cod-liver oil, and sprinkle it over dry food. Cats will like the taste. Do so every other day.

5. Oil-packed tuna is another good source of omega-3 fatty acids, which are good for the cat's joints and coat. Drain the oil from the can, and store it in the refrigerator. It should last up to a week. Pour a little over the food each day.

6. To remove excess hair, wipe down your cat with a Baby Wipe, rubbing fur in both directions with the wipe.

7. Extra brushing and combing help maintain fur during the winter.

---

friends in advance. Many airlines have summer pet embargoes, and most trains and ships do not allow pets other than service animals. The HSUS has information on traveling with your pet that may make the difference between a pleasant trip and a vacation nightmare. (See also "Cats on the Go," page 367.)

Pets need exercise even when it is hot, but extra care should be taken, especially with older animals. On very hot days, limit exercise to early morning or evening hours. Remember that asphalt gets very hot and can burn your pet's paws.

Another summertime threat is fleas and ticks. Use only flea and tick treatments recommended by your veterinarian. Some over-the-counter flea and tick products can be toxic, even when used according to instructions. (See "Flea-Fighting Tactics," page 308.)

Pets can get sunburned too, and your pet may require sunscreen on his or her nose and ear tips. Pets with light-colored noses or light-colored fur on their ears are particularly vulnerable to sunburn and skin cancer.

Don't take your pets to crowded summer events such as concerts or fairs. The loud noises and crowds, combined with the heat, can be stressful and dangerous for pets. For your pet's well-being, leave it at home. Be especially aware of these threats during holidays, such as the Fourth of July.

In summer heat your pet can suffer from heat exhaustion and heat stroke. These conditions are very serious and could cause your pet to die. You should be aware of the signs of heat stress:

    Heavy panting
    Glazed eyes
    A rapid pulse
    Unsteadiness
    A staggering gait
    Vomiting
    A deep red or purple tongue

If your pet does become overheated, you need to immediately lower its body temperature. Move your pet into the shade, and apply cool (not cold) water over its body to gradually lower the core body temperature. Apply cold towels or ice packs to your pet's head, neck, and chest only. Let your pet drink small amounts of water or lick ice cubes. Most important, get the animal to a veterinarian immediately.

How to Give Your Cat a Pill in 20 Easy Steps

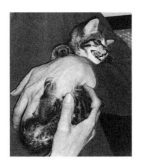

1. Sit on sofa. Pick up cat, and cradle it in the crook of your elbow as though you were going to give a bottle to a baby. Talk softly to cat.

2. With right hand, position right forefinger and thumb on either side of cat's mouth and gently apply pressure to cheeks while holding pill in right hand. (Be patient.) As cat opens mouth, pop pill into mouth. Allow cat to close mouth and swallow. Let go of cat, noticing the direction in which it runs.

3. Pick the pill up off the floor, and get the cat from behind sofa. Cradle cat in left arm and repeat process. Sit on floor in kitchen, wrap arm around cat as before, drop pill in mouth. Let go of cat, noticing the direction in which it runs.

4. Retrieve cat from bedroom, and throw soggy pill away. Bring cat back into the kitchen. Take new pill from foil wrap, and cradle cat in left arm, holding rear paws tightly with left hand. Force jaws open, and push pill to back of mouth with right forefinger. Hold mouth shut for a count of ten.

5. Pry back-leg claws out of your arm. Release cat.

6. Retrieve pill from goldfish bowl and cat from top of closet. Call spouse from backyard. Kneel on floor with cat wedged firmly between knees. Hold front and rear paws. Ignore low growls emitted by cat. Get spouse to hold cat's head firmly with one hand while forcing wooden ruler into its mouth. Drop pill down ruler and rub cat's throat vigorously.

7. Retrieve cat from curtain rod, and get another pill from foil wrap. Make note to buy new ruler and repair curtains. Carefully sweep shattered Royal Doulton figurines from hearth and set to one side for gluing repairs.

8. Get spouse to lie on cat, with cat's head just visible from below spouse's armpit. Put pill in end of drinking straw, force feline mouth open with pencil, and blow down drinking straw into cat's mouth.

9. Check package label to make sure pill is not harmful to humans, and drink glass of water to take taste away. Apply Band-Aid to spouse's forearm and remove blood from carpet with cold water and soap.

10. Retrieve cat from neighbor's shed. Get another pill. Place cat in cupboard, and close door onto neck to leave head showing. Force mouth open with dessert spoon. Flick pill down throat with rubber band.

11. Fetch screwdriver from garage, and put cupboard door back on hinges. Apply cold compress to cheek, and check records for date of last tetanus shot. Discard soiled clothing.

12. Call fire department to retrieve cat from tree across the road. Apologize to neighbor whose car crashed into fence while swerving to avoid cat. Take another pill from foil wrap.

13. Tie cat's front paws to rear paws with garden twine, and bind cat tightly to leg of dining table. Find heavy-duty pruning gloves from shed, and force cat's mouth open with small spanner. Push pill into mouth, followed by large piece of steak. Hold head vertically, and pour one cup of water down throat to wash pill down.

14. Get spouse to drive you to emergency room, and sit quietly while doctor stitches lacerations to fingers and forearm and removes pill remnants from right eye. Call at furniture shop on way home to order new dining table.

15. Get last pill from foil wrap. Go into bathroom and get a fluffy towel. Stay in the bathroom with cat, and close the door.

16. Sit on bathroom floor, and wrap towel around Kitty, leaving only its head exposed. Cradle Kitty in the crook of your arm, and pick up pill from counter.

17. Retrieve cat from top of shower door (you didn't know that cats can jump 5 feet straight up in the air, did you?), and wrap towel around it a little tighter, making sure its paws can't come out this time. With fingers at either side of its jaw, pry it open and pop pill into mouth. Quickly close mouth (the cat's, not yours).

18. Sit on floor with cat in your lap, stroking it under the chin and talking gently to it for at least a half-hour, while the pill dissolves.

19. Unwrap towel, open bathroom door. Wash scratches with warm soapy water.

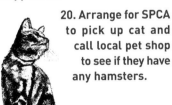

20. Arrange for SPCA to pick up cat and call local pet shop to see if they have any hamsters.

How to Give Your Cat Medications

Next to litter-box cleaning, one of the most dreaded tasks facing cat owners involves giving pills, injections, or other types of medicine to a cat. Some cats seemed tuned in to the sound of a pill bottle being opened and scramble under the bed — just out of arm's reach. Other felines perform contortionist-like moves and wiggle free before the medicine reaches their mouth.

We know that veterinarian-recommended medicines can often restore a cat's health. Still, pill time is no fun for owners or their cats. We solicited the advice of Debra Eldredge, DVM, a veterinarian in New Hartford, New York, and the author of *Pills for Pets: The A to Z Guide to Drugs and Medications for Your Animal Companion* (Citadel Press, 2003). Dr. Eldredge shares these ways to make the medicine go down easily without a feline fuss:

Find the right drug in the right form for your cat. Be honest with your veterinarian about your skills as an at-home nurse.

Consider going the "medicated" food route if your cat is a real food fan. Open a capsule and stir in the powder, or crush a pill or pour the correct amount of liquid medicine into canned food.

Mask the smell of medicine by using the juice from a can of tuna or chicken broth.

Some compounding pharmacies specialize in tasty versions of medications for cats — especially medications that cats might be on for a long time. Consult your veterinary clinic for compounding pharmacies in your area that might offer tuna- or liver-flavored versions of medicines in pill and liquid forms. Some pain medications are available in patches that dispense the medication through the skin pores, though cats often chew them off.

Opt to give liquid medicine in a plastic syringe. Hold your cat, and slowly drizzle the liquid into its cheek pouches by prying open the jaws.

To pill your cat, set your cat calmly in your lap, facing away from you. Reach down over your cat's head and squeeze it gently behind the whiskers. This makes the mouth open slightly. Then pull down carefully on the bottom jaw, deposit the pill toward the back of the tongue, close the mouth, and blow air softly into your cat's nose. Coat hard-to-swallow pills with a little margarine to make them go down easier.

9 Vaccinations and Preventive Treatments for Cats

Keep records and receipts for all vaccinations.

1. FVRCP Combination Vaccine

Given at 9 weeks and again at 12 weeks. Repeat annually.

The FVRCP is the basic combination shot given to cats. *FVR* stands for *feline viral rhinotracheitis,* an upper-respiratory infection resulting in conjunctivitis, sneezing, nasal discharge, eye lesions, and occasional coughing. The *C* stands for *calicivirus,* a virus that can cause similar respiratory conditions. These diseases account for 95 percent of upper-respiratory infections in cats. Many adult cats are carriers, even though they may have no symptoms of the disease. The *P* is for *panleukemia,* which is known as feline distemper virus. This disease causes vomiting, diarrhea, loss of appetite, fever, and sudden death in cats.

2. Rabies Vaccine

Given at 3 months of age. Repeat annually.

The most commonly used vaccine is a three-year vaccine. It can be administered at 3 months of age or older and initially protects the cat for one year. Subsequent vaccinations are given after 6 months of age and protect the cat for three years each time it is administered. The initial vaccination protects the cat for one year no matter when it is given.

3. Feline Leukemia Vaccine

Given at 9 weeks, then again in 2–4 weeks. Repeat annually.

Feline leukemia is a salivary contact and intrauterine infection. Today the general recommendation is not to vaccinate strictly indoor cats that do not live in multiple-cat households. Also, no benefit is derived from vaccinating a cat that tests positive for feline leukemia yet is symptom-free. Outdoors cats absolutely should get this vaccination.

4. Feline Infectious Peritonitis (FIP) Vaccine

Given at 4 months, then again in 2–4 weeks. Repeat annually.

Feline infectious peritonitis is another virus that can cause vomiting, diarrhea, eye infections, fluid in the abdomen, and death to a cat. FIP is a very serious disease that is almost always fatal. The virus that causes FIP is difficult to test for, and the symptoms in cats are so varied that the diagnosis is mostly an educated guess. Even so, vaccinations are controversial, as many veterinarians feel there is not enough infection in the cat population to warrant it. This disease has a tendency to affect cats under 2 years of age and cats over 9 years of age.

5. Intestinal Worm Checks

Given at 9 weeks old, then again at 16 weeks. Repeat twice yearly.

Kittens and cats can be at risk for a host of worms, particularly heartworms and tapeworms. Here is the recommended veterinary schedule for each.

Heartworms: A medication is given monthly to outdoor cats, especially those who live indoors but spend part of their time outdoors. Do not miss a treatment. Heartworm disease is spread by mosquito bites and is on the rise among cats. As long as the cat takes the medication regularly, it will be protected. If a dose is missed, the cat may contract the disease.

Tapeworms: These worms are a common intestinal parasite of dogs and cats. The most common tapeworm is transmitted by fleas. Cats eat infected fleas, and the tapeworm attaches to the intestine. Over time, worms grow up to 12 inches in length and shed portions of their body, called proglottids, through the host animal's feces. These small pieces of tapeworm actually move and look like grains of rice. They are actually egg packets, which are later eaten by fleas — hence, the next generation of tapeworms is launched. Research has shown that cats groom up to 75 percent of the fleas off their body in 24 hours, so many cat owners may not be aware that their cat has any; they also may not notice the tapeworm segments in the litter box. Thus the problem can go undetected, though symptoms do exist and include vomiting, diarrhea, an unkempt coat, and itchiness around the rectum.

6. Fecal Exam

Given annually.

The microscopic examination of the stool determines if your cat is harboring internal parasites. Symptoms are not always evident, but they can include general poor condition, vomiting, and diarrhea. Living with parasites can result in malnutrition and even death.

7. General Checkup

Given annually.

A general checkup ensures that your cat remains healthy and includes a dental exam. Often signs not visible to cat owners may be discovered by a well-trained vet, leading to proper treatment in the early stages of any problem. It's also a great time to ask questions and stay up-to-date on the latest medical news about cats. Annual exams also provide the vet with a chance to get to know your cat, its habits, and its character.

8. Neutering or Spaying

Performed at 5 to 6 months of age.

See page 274 for information about these procedures.

9. Feline Immunodeficiency Virus (FIV) Vaccine

FIV attacks the cat's body much as HIV (AIDS) affects humans. The symptoms vary depending on the cat, but the immune system is always compromised. Cats that test positive never get rid of the virus and are susceptible to other illnesses. The virus is spread through the bite of another cat. Fortunately, the incidence of FIV is not high for indoor cats.

FIV-positive cats may live for many months or years. With good health care aimed at recognizing and treating FIV-associated problems early, these patients can enjoy good quality of life. Effort should be taken to preserve the health of these cats by protecting them against other diseases and injury. This is best accomplished by requiring FIV-positive cats to live indoors; this choice also helps prevent the spread of the disease.

In 2002, the first vaccine against FIV (Fel-O-Vax FIV, Fort Dodge) became available in the United States. This vaccine may help protect high-risk groups of cats. However, the vaccine introduces a testing dilemma. Current FIV antibody tests cannot distinguish between antibodies from vaccination and antibodies from disease. Newer testing methodologies are in development to devise tests based on the virus itself, so eventually it may be possible to tell a vaccinated cat from an infected cat.

More information on feline immunodeficiency virus can be found at http://www.winnfelinehealth.org/health/FIV.html.

How to Trap a Feral Cat

The following instructions on how to humanely trap a feral cat and have it neutered was provided to us by the Feral Cat Coalition of San Diego, California. To trap a feral cat, you'll need a trap. Havahart.com has designed stray-cat trap rescue kits for people who want to help control the feral cat population. Follow Havahart.com's easy instructions for setting and opening the trap rescue kit.

1. Before you attempt to trap a feral cat, get the cat used to being fed at the same place and time of day. You might try leaving the trap unset and covered with a large towel during routine feeding so that the animal will get used to seeing and smelling it. Don't feed the cat the day or night before you are going to trap it, so the cat will be hungry. Be sure to notify others not to leave food out then, either.

2. Plan to trap the cat at a time when it won't have to wait in the trap too long before surgery. Trapping the night before the operation is usually the best approach. Cats should not eat for 12 hours prior to surgery.

3. Prepare the area where you will be keeping the cat before and after the visit to the clinic. A garage or other sheltered, warm, protected area is best. Lay down newspapers to catch the inevitable stool, urine, and food residue. You may want to use pieces of wood to elevate the trap above the newspapers so that the mess will fall through the wires, away from the cat. Spraying the area ahead of time with a cat-safe flea spray (such as Adams or Ovitrol) will keep ants away.

4. Prepare the vehicle you will use to transport the cat. Plastic will protect upholstery, but you'll need to put something absorbent over it.

5. Plan your target day carefully. Remember that if you trap an animal and release it for some reason, it is unlikely that you will be able to catch it again; it will learn very quickly to avoid you.

6. If there are young kittens involved, remember that they should not be weaned before 4 to 6 weeks of age. If you are trapping a lactating female, you may want to wait until you have located the kittens and they are old enough to wean. If you wish to tame and foster the kittens so they can be adopted, they should be taken from the mother at 4 to 6 week of age. If you wait until the kittens are older before trying to tame them, you will find the job more difficult.

7. Plan to set the trap just before or at the cat's normal feeding time. This is often at night. Dusk is usually the best time to set traps.

8. Don't attempt to trap a cat in the rain or the heat of day without providing adequate protection from the elements. Cats are vulnerable in the traps and could drown during storms or suffer from heat stroke in the sun. Use common sense!

9. If trapping a cat in a public area, place the trap where it will not be noticed by passersby (who may not understand that you are not trying to harm the cat). Bushes provide good camouflage for the trap, and cats tend to hide among them.

10. Use food with a strong odor to bait the trap. Canned mackerel is very effective and relatively inexpensive. It is best not to put any bowls inside the trap to hold food, since the animal can easily hurt itself on it in a panic or while recovering from the anesthetic.

11. After setting the trap, cover it with a large towel, and fold the material at the front end of the trap to expose the opening. This will help to camouflage the

trap and also calm the cat after it is caught.

12. Once you have trapped the cat, take the trap to a quiet area and make sure you've caught the right cat and not someone's pet. If you have captured a lactating female, check the area for kittens, and remember that this female must be released 10 to 12 hours after surgery so she can care for and nurse her kittens.

13. After you have finished trapping, you will probably have to hold the cat overnight until you can take it to the vet, unless you have made previous arrangements to bring it to the clinic directly.

14. Place the cat in the protected area that you have prepared. Don't feed it. You can place a small bowl of water in the trap by opening the door just a couple of inches and placing the bowl inside. Use a bowl that won't be tipped over easily; an empty cat-food can works fairly well. Remove the bowl before transporting the cat to the vet.

15. Wash and change clothes before having contact with your own pets as a precaution against spreading any contagious diseases the feral cat might carry.

16. Always get feral kittens checked by a vet, and isolate them from your pets. Some deadly diseases can in-

About Feral Cats

Cats roaming outside come in two main types: feral and stray. It is easy to understand why some people mistakenly refer to all independent outdoor cats as stray or feral. So, how can you distinguish between the two?

Stray cats are felines who have been previously owned and now find themselves abandoned or lost. Strays tend to be vocal, sport dirty or disheveled coats, and will immediately gobble down bowls of food offered them. Some will slowly approach people and accept being petted.

Ferals are felines rarely spotted during daylight hours. They move silently and sport well-groomed coats because they have adapted to living outside. They are more likely to approach a bowl of food only well after you have left the scene or after you have moved far away from the bowl. They have no desire to be petted or picked up by people. In fact, they survive by hunting and scavenging for food.

At best guess, the United States is home to more than 10 million feral cats. Many live in small groups, called colonies, around businesses and homes of caring people who leave out food for them.

Feral cats fare best outside and living independently of people. However, to reduce the risk of spreading feline disease, animal humane groups (formal and informal) strive to protect these cats through a worldwide campaign known as TNR (trap, neuter, and return). Feral cats are trapped humanely, given medical exams and vaccinations, and are spayed or neutered. Before they are returned to their colonies, a tip of one ear is notched — usually the left — as a universal sign that this feral cat has already received veterinary care.

cubate without symptoms. Consult your veterinarian and use caution.

17. When the cat is ready for release, return to the area in which it was captured and release it there. Do not relocate the animal, or it will be disoriented and most likely will die. It's probable that cats in the new area will drive it away.

18. Make sure the spot you pick for release does not encourage the cat to run into danger (such as a busy street) to get away from you. Keep the trap covered until you are ready to release the cat. When ready, simply hold the trap with the door facing away from you, and open the door. The cat will probably bolt immediately. If it is confused, just tilt the trap so the back is slightly up, and tap on the back of the trap to encourage the cat to leave. Never put your hand in the trap.

19. After releasing the cat, hose off the trap and disinfect it with bleach. Never store traps in the "set" position (door open); animals may wander into even unbaited traps and starve to death.

Handling an Injured Cat

Moving an injured cat must be done with the utmost care. Unless you handle it properly, you risk injuring it even further, and if its injury is internal, serious complications can arise. Needless to say, get your cat to a vet or animal hospital as soon as possible. Here are some do's and don'ts for moving an injured cat.

1. Keep yourself safe first. Be sure to watch for oncoming traffic or other dangers before you attend to an injured cat that is in the road.

2. Proceed with caution when approaching the cat. Keep in mind that even if the injured cat is yours, it may panic, not recognize you, and even try to scratch or bite you. Wrap the cat up in a thick blanket to protect yourself.

3. Attempt first aid if the cat is cooperative. If the cat is unconscious, try mouth-to-nose resuscitation by sealing the cat's lips shut and blowing air into its nostrils.

4. If the cat is bleeding, apply a pressure bandage to the area until you have reached your vet.

5. If you suspect that the injury is to the back or spine, place the cat on a hard surface to prevent further injury.

6. When you pick the cat up, do so by grasping it by the nape of its neck. Most cats, when grasped in this manner, immediately relax. This is the way Mommy carried them around.

7. As you carry the cat, hold it close to your body for extra support, and hold the front and back legs firmly to prevent movement. Keep its head and neck uncovered.

8. Place the cat in a well-ventilated cardboard box or a carrier. Try to keep the cat in a prone position. Make the bed as comfortable as possible.

9. If you haven't done so by now, wrap the cat in a blanket to keep it warm.

10. Try to position its head in alignment with its spine.

11. If you can't transport the cat, contact a local shelter, the animal hospital, or the police for help.

28 Strict, Unbending Rules for Dealing with Stray Cats

1. Stray cats will not be fed.

2. Stray cats will not be fed anything except dry cat food.

3. Stray cats will not be fed anything except dry cat food moistened with a little milk.

4. Stray cats will not be fed anything except dry cat food moistened with warm milk, yummy treats, and leftover fish scraps.

5. Stray cats will not be encouraged to make this house their permanent residence.

6. Stray cats will not be petted, played with, picked up, or cuddled.

7. Stray cats that are petted, played with, picked up, and cuddled will absolutely not be given a name.

8. Stray cats with or without a name will not be allowed inside the house at any time.

9. Stray cats will not be allowed inside the house except at certain times.

10. Stray cats will not be allowed inside the house except on days ending in *y*.

11. Stray cats allowed inside will not be permitted to jump up on or sharpen their claws on the furniture.

12. Stray cats will not be permitted to jump up on or sharpen their claws on the really good furniture.

13. Stray cats will be permitted on all furniture but must sharpen claws on the new $114.99 sisal-rope cat-scratching post with three perches.

14. Stray cats will answer the call of nature outdoors in the sand.

15. Stray cats will answer the call of nature in the three-piece, high-impact plastic tray filled with Fresh 'n' Sweet cat litter.

"We've got a faster computer, a faster modem, and a bigger screen, but we forgot to upgrade the cat."

16. Stray cats will answer the call of nature in the hooded litter pan with a three-panel privacy screen and plenty of headroom.

17. Stray cats will sleep outside.

18. Stray cats will sleep in the garage.

19. Stray cats will sleep in the house.

20. Stray cats will sleep in a cardboard box lined with an old blanket.

21. Stray cats will sleep in the special Kitty-Komfort-Bed with non-allergenic lambs' wool pillow.

22. Stray cats will not be allowed to sleep in our bed.

23. Stray cats will not be allowed to sleep in our bed, except at the foot.

24. Stray cats will not be allowed to sleep in our bed under the covers.

25. Stray cats will not be allowed to sleep in our bed under the covers except at the foot.

26. Stray cats will not play on the desk.

27. Stray cats will not play on the desk near the computer.

28. Stray cats are forbidden to walk on the computer keyboard on the desk when the human is asdfjjhhkl;ljfd.;oier puuykmm4hbdm9lo9jmdskdm USING IT.

11 Things You Should Know About Kitty Acupuncture

When cat owners think of alternative medical treatments for their cats, acupuncture is usually the first solution that comes to mind. Acupuncture involves the placement of tiny needles into various parts your cat's body. These needles stimulate acupuncture points, which in turn stimulate your kitty's natural healing processes. Traditional Chinese medicine has used acupuncture to treat a wide variety of conditions for about 3,500 years, but the treatment wasn't really applied to small animals until the 1950s. Acupuncture, as an alternative therapy, is now widely accepted in the United States and abroad. Here are some facts you should know about acupuncture before considering it for your sick cat.

1. Having a cooperative patient is essential. Although many dogs will sit still for an acupuncture treatment, many cats can't stay still long enough.

2. Acupuncture is given in sessions, with each session lasting about 15–20 minutes. Most acupuncturists will require two to four sessions per week in order to evaluate the treatment's effectiveness. Many owners, though, simply can't make it to the vet that often, making the evaluation of this treatment very difficult. To these owners, other holistic treatments, such as herbal or nutritional therapy, may be more practical.

3. Therapy sessions may involve either the basic needle-alone technique, needles used in conjunction with electrical stimulation, or laser stimulation. Sometimes, in order to effect a permanent change, objects such as gold beads, magnets, or surgical staples are placed into an acupuncture point so that constant stimulation is possible.

4. Cost is definitely an issue, with each session costing from $25 to $40. For a minimum of eight sessions, this can get pricey.

5. Acupuncture compares quite favorably with traditional medical treatments, but effectiveness varies depending on the nature of the disease. In some cases, acupuncture may be preferred when conventional techniques, such as long-term steroid use, are ineffective or possibly harmful.

6. Acupuncture is often used as a last resort when the owner simply can't afford more expensive treatments, such as surgery.

7. There are generally no side effects with acupuncture, but occasionally an accident, such as the puncture of a vital organ, can occur. Infection at the site of needle placement is another possible problem. And, although quite rare, the needle can break, and surgery may be needed to remove it.

8. Keep in mind that you may not see a visible improvement in Potsy until days after the treatment, when the acupuncture has had some time to stimulate her body to heal itself. This won't happen overnight.

9. Acupuncture, in itself, is usually not painful, but Kitty will have some sensation as the needle enters the skin. However, once the needles are in place, most cats will relax, and some may become drowsy. Overly anxious or testy cats may require sedation.

10. Acupuncture can be used for a variety of pet problems, but is most often thought of as a treatment for problems involving pain and inflammation. Other conditions, such as arthritis, spinal disease, chronic gastrointestinal disease, and skin problems such as allergies, may be helped by acupuncture. Some vets use acupuncture to boost the pet's immune system.

11. In order to find a qualified and licensed veterinary practitioner who offers acupuncture therapy, it's best to contact the American Academy of Veterinary Acupuncture at aava.org. Outside the United States please contact the International Academy of Veterinary Acupuncture at Ivas.org.

Cats and Disaster: Be Prepared

Our pets enrich our lives in more ways than we can count. In turn, they depend on us for their safety and well-being. The Humane Society of the United States, in cooperation with the American Red Cross, suggests these guidelines for protecting your pets when disaster strikes.

Create a Disaster Plan
The best way to protect your family — all of them — from the effects of a disaster is to have a plan in place before disaster strikes. Being prepared can save lives.

Different disasters require different responses. But whether the disaster is a hurricane or a hazardous spill, you may have to evacuate your home.

In the event of a disaster, if you must evacuate, the most important thing you can do to protect your pets is to evacuate them, too. Leaving pets behind, even if you try to create a safe place for them, is likely to result in their being injured, lost, or worse. So prepare now for the day when you and your pets may have to leave your home.

Have a Safe Place to Take Your Pets
Red Cross disaster shelters cannot accept pets because of states' health and safety regulations and other considerations. Service animals who assist people with disabilities are the only animals allowed in Red Cross shelters. It may be difficult, if not impossible, to find shelter for your animals in the midst of a disaster, so plan ahead. Do not wait until disaster strikes to do your research.

Contact hotels and motels outside your immediate area to check policies on accepting pets and restrictions on number, size, and species. Ask if "no pet" policies could be waived in an emergency. Keep a list of "pet friendly" places, including phone numbers, with other disaster information and supplies. If you have notice of an impending disaster, call ahead for reservations.

Ask friends, relatives, or others outside the affected area whether they could shelter your animals. If you have more than one pet, they may be more comfortable if kept together, but be prepared to house them separately.

Prepare a list of boarding facilities and veterinarians who could shelter animals in an emergency; include 24-hour phone numbers.

Ask local animal shelters if they provide emergency shelter or foster care for pets in a disaster. Animal shelters may be overburdened caring for the animals they already have as well as those displaced by a disaster, so this should be your last resort.

Assemble a Portable Disaster Supplies Kit

Whether you are away from home for a day or a week, you'll need essential supplies. Keep items in an accessible place, and store them in sturdy containers that can be carried easily (duffel bags, covered trash containers, etc.). Your kit should include the following items:

🐾 Medications and medical records (stored in a waterproof container) and a first-aid kit (see page 341).

🐾 Sturdy leashes, harnesses, and/or carriers to transport pets safely and ensure that your animals can't escape. With a permanent marker, write your contact information and the name of

5 Insurance Policies for Your Cat

If you never want to have to decide between your cat's well-being and your wallet, you should consider pet insurance. Policies range from minimal coverage (for accidents only, for instance), at a cost of around $75 a year, all the way up to VIC plans that can cost up to $1,000 annually.

1. **Veterinary Pet Insurance**, the nation's oldest and largest provider of health insurance for pets, offers a number of policies that include coverage for accidental injuries, emergencies and illnesses, routine office visits, prescriptions, diagnostic tests, x-rays, and lab fees. See petinsurance.com.

2. **ASPCA Pet Health Insurance** offers a comprehensive policy that covers accidents and illnesses as well as routine wellness care, such as annual checkups, vaccines, dental cleaning, and other preventive treatment. A portion of first-year premiums goes directly to support the organization's mission. See aspcapetinsurance.com.

3. **PetCare Pet Insurance Programs** cover everything from falling accidents to treatments for allergies and cancer. Various plans are offered, so you can find one to fit your needs and budget. See petcareinsurance.com.

4. **Animal Friends** is an ethical insurance business located in the United Kingdom. It dedicates its net profits to the care of animals and their environment. They offer two basic plans to help protect your cat. See animalfriends.org.uk.

5. **Petshealth Care Plan** offers five health-care plans for your cat, from accident-only coverage all the way up to its Best Pet Plan. See petshealthplan.com.

your pet on each of these. A carrier should be large enough to accommodate your cat, a small litter pan, and a water bowl.

🐾 A two-week supply of any of your cat's medications.

🐾 Current photos of your pets in case they get lost.

🐾 Food, potable water, bowls, cat litter pan, and can opener.

🐾 Information on feeding schedules, medical conditions, behavior problems, and the name and number of your veterinarian in case you have to foster or board your pets.

🐾 Pet beds and toys, if easily transportable.

Know What to Do As a Disaster Approaches

Often, warnings are issued hours, even days, in advance. At the first hint of disaster, act to protect your pet.

🐾 Call ahead to confirm emergency shelter arrangements for you and your pets.

🐾 Check to be sure your pet disaster supplies are ready to take at a moment's notice.

🐾 Bring all pets into the house so that you won't have to search for them if you have to leave in a hurry.

🐾 Make sure all dogs and cats are wearing collars and securely fastened, up-to-date identification. Attach the phone number and address of your temporary shelter, if you know it, or of a friend or relative outside the disaster area. You can buy temporary tags or put adhesive tape on the back of your pet's ID tag, adding information with an indelible pen.

🐾 You may not be home when the evacuation order comes. Find out if a trusted neighbor would be willing to take your pets and meet you at a prearranged location. This person should be comfortable with your pets, know where your animals are likely to be, know where your disaster supplies kit is kept, and have a key to your home. If you use a pet-sitting service, its staff may be available to help, but discuss the possibility well in advance.

🐾 Planning and preparation will enable you to evacuate with your pets quickly and safely, but bear in mind that animals may display unusual behavior under stress.

🐾 Transport cats in carriers.

🐾 Don't leave animals unattended anywhere they can run off. The most trustworthy pets may panic, hide, try to escape, or even bite or scratch.

🐾 When you return home, give your pets time to settle back into their routines. Consult your veterinarian if any behavior problems persist.

"Howliday" Hazards: How to Keep Your Cat Safe During Holidays

Holidays find many cat owners breaking away from the daily routine, which can be upsetting to cats. Homes become filled with houseguests, strange new foods and drink, and decorations — all of which can pose potential health threats for cats. Here are some factors to consider when you prepare to celebrate.

Valentine's Day

There are many ways to say "I love you" to a cat; feeding it chocolate is not one of them. Here's what you need to know:

Chocolate contains the compound theobromine, which is a diuretic as well as a cardiac stimulant. It's harmless to humans but potentially lethal for cats and dogs. Dark chocolate contains higher levels than milk chocolate and poses a greater risk to your pet. (We don't encourage you to feed *any* type of chocolate to your cat.)

Cats like the taste of chocolate, so if they come upon it, they will attempt to ingest it.

Chocolate is high in calories and can contribute to obesity, especially if a cat consumes it often and thereby loses its taste for nutritious food.

Sadly, some cat owners assume that the worst consequence for this kitty treat will be an upset stomach; this is far from the truth. Chocolate poisoning can occur, potentially causing diarrhea, lethargy, vomiting, depression, and muscle tremors.

If you suspect that your cat has ingested chocolate, consult your vet — pronto. Treatment for chocolate poisoning in its advanced stage can be very unpleasant for your cat.

> Never allow your guests to tempt your cat with even small amounts of beer or other alcoholic beverages.

Fourth of July

Cats generally don't savor the American celebration of independence from Great Britain — especially when loud fireworks are involved. Keep your cat inside your home on this holiday so it won't be exposed to loud noises that will upset those sensitive feline ears.

Usher your cat into a comfortable room detached from the noisy celebrations outside. Play some soft music, and place feline amenities — food and water bowls, bedding, and toys — inside. Keep the door closed until the celebration has ended.

Halloween

The black cat's association with Halloween can be unfortunate because some people use the occasion to harm these innocent beasts. In fact, most shelters will not give up black cats during Halloween season as a protective measure. Take precautions:

1. Make sure the cat can't run out the front door when you open it for trick-or-treaters. Keep it in another room.

2. If you have an outdoor cat, keep it indoors on Halloween. If the cat does wander out, make sure it's wearing proper identification and a reflective collar.

3. Keep Kitty away from Halloween candy and the plastic bags it comes in. Chocolate, especially, can be very toxic to cats.

4. Keep Jackpot away from jack-o'-lanterns and candles.

5. If you insist on dressing your kitty in a costume, be sure that no tight elastic bands cause discomfort. Avoid loose parts, which might cause choking or get caught or stuck somewhere, trapping your kitty. Be sure that the cat doesn't eat any portion of the costume.

6. If your cat has a litter of black kittens, do not offer any for adoption until well after the holiday is over.

Thanksgiving

Never feed your cat turkey bones. They pose a choking hazard. Small bones or bone splinters can lodge in a cat's throat, stomach, or intestines.

Resist the temptation to provide your cat with a treat of poultry skin or gravy. Both are laden with fat and can cause gastrointestinal upset or even pancreatitis.

Make sure your cat is not begging houseguests for table scraps or getting into the kitchen trash can.

Christmas

Keep poinsettias, holly, and mistletoe out of paw's reach. These plants are poisonous to cats — and dogs. If possible, opt for silk varieties rather than the real plants.

Block the cat's access to the water in your Christmas tree stand. This water may contain fertilizers, which, if ingested, can cause stomach upset. Stagnant tree water can be a breeding ground for bacteria, which can also lead to vomiting, nausea, and diarrhea, if ingested by a cat.

Decorate your tree with cat safety in mind. Avoid using tinsel, which can be swallowed and cause intestinal obstruction. Also, do not place breakable ornaments on the tree. A tree-climbing cat can swat them, knock them off, step on the broken pieces, and cut its paws.

Avoid using edible ornaments, or cranberry or popcorn strings. Your hungry cat can get sick from or choke on these items.

Cover or hide electric cords to prevent your cat from chewing on them and being shocked or even electrocuted.

Don't leave holiday food items on the counters when you step away: alcoholic beverages, chocolate, onions, and yeast dough can cause problems for a counter-surfing cat.

Keep lit candles out of your cat's reach. Its tail or paw can tip over a candle and cause a fire — or burn the cat.

Avoid placing catnip-filled gifts under the tree. That is a tempting scent that most cats can't resist.

Keep your cats away from liquid potpourri. Light it only when you can be in the room to supervise — or your cat is in another room with the door closed. If any of the liquid lands on a cat who then grooms itself, the potpourri could cause damage to the skin, mouth, or eyes.

Facts About Cats in Trees

This feline behavior is only too familiar. Animal control officer Debbie Dawson, of Edmonds, Washington, assembled these facts about tree-climbing cats:

🐾 Most cats will come down on their own in three to five days. They either choose to come down, or they become weak and fall.

🐾 Most tree-climbing cats are between 6 months old and 1½ years old.

🐾 Most cats will come down in the dark (they're naturally nocturnal).

🐾 They must descend backward, not head first.

🐾 Declawed cats absolutely cannot find their way down and should not be left outside unattended.

11 Tips for Getting a Cat out of a Tree

If you need help, call the animal control hotline in your area first. Most fire departments will help you if they are not otherwise engaged, but call the police in advance of the fire department; the police need to give the order to dispatch a fire truck. Of course, you should try to get Pooky down on your own before you call for assistance. Note that most landscape companies will refuse to help; those that do respond are likely to charge plenty.

Of course, you should try to get Pooky down on your own before you call for assistance. Here are some suggestions.

1. Place food (tuna or something else the cat likes) as high up in the tree as you can reach with a ladder.

2. Make your best efforts in talking the cat down and placing food in the tree just before going to bed.

3. Do not let the cat see you in the house or on a deck; do all your coaxing from the base of the tree.

4. If possible, provide a ramp that will give the cat a way down.

5. Be patient. Nature is on our side — birds, windstorms, and the need to relieve itself will eventually take their toll on the cat's hesitation to descend.

6. Put all dogs in the house or the garage until the cat comes down, especially at nighttime.

7. Make sure the treetop feline is really your cat.

8. If the tree is not on your property, you will need permission from the property owner to climb the tree.

9. If the cat is declawed, ill, or on medication, it should be rescued at once.

10. If the cat is only 8 weeks to 4 months old, it should probably be rescued right away. These kittens tend to go to the very top.

11. If your cat is stuck on a power pole, you'll need to contact the utility company for assistance. It is illegal for an unauthorized person to climb a power or other utility pole.

An I.Q. Test for Cats

This is a simple intelligence test for cats to find out just how smart and clever your furry feline really is. Spread the test sessions over a period of several days, allowing a rest day between the practices. Do them right before your cat's mealtime, and try to keep the sessions brief and fun.

To start the testing, you will need an 18- to 24-inch hoop and a container of your cat's favorite treats. The object of the test is to see how quickly your cat can learn to jump through the hoop. You will record the number of times you must repeat the training command before your cat masters the skill.

With your cat standing beside you, hold the hoop about a foot above the floor. Use your other hand to show your cat the kitty treat within the middle of the hoop. Use a command such as "Come on" or "Jump" to call your cat

Eine kleine Unterbrechung.

through. It might help if you wiggle the treat to entice the cat. If your cat gets up on its hind feet and grabs the treat from your hand on the first try, don't worry. This is an acceptable response.

The next step is to pull the treat back through the hoop, speaking your command, as you encourage your cat to follow. Don't let your cat cheat by going around the hoop. It must jump through it before you give the treat as a reward.

When your cat performs willingly, stop holding the treat in your hand but continue holding your hand as though there is still a treat in it. Keep the treats somewhere else (maybe a pocket) and reward your cat ONLY when it jumps through the hoop for you.

The test is finished when your cat jumps through the hoop on command at least two out of three times.

Scoring

60 or more commands = Sorry, your cat is below average.

50–59 commands = Your cat is slightly below average.

40–49 commands = Just your average cat.

30–39 commands = Your cat is above average.

29 or fewer commands = Change its name to Einstein!

4 Cat Toys You Can Make

It's easy to unleash your credit card at a pet supply store. You want to spoil your cat with the best food and the coolest toys. Here's a reality check: cats don't give a paw about designer labels. They don't have the desire to "keep up with the Siameses" down the block, either.

Here is a rundown of some easy-to-make toys for your favorite feline:

1. **Cat swat toy.** Take an old shoelace from a pair of sneakers. Tie one of your cat's favorite small toys on one end, and wrap the other end around an interior doorknob so that the toy dangles about four or five inches off the floor. Most cats can't walk past this toy without giving it a good swat.

2. **Nothing to sneeze at.** Think of this homemade toy as the Rubik's cube for cats. Take an empty tissue box and insert a Ping-Pong ball inside. Place it on the floor in front of your cat. Shake the box a bit to garner the cat's attention. It will spend hours trying to fish out the mysterious toy inside. A real cat teaser.

3. **Cat's in the bag.** Place a brown paper shopping bag on its side on the floor. Be sure to cut off the handles so your cat won't accidentally choke. Sprinkle a teaspoon of fresh or dried catnip far inside the bag. Your cat's super scenting ability will drive it right into the bag.

4. **The catnip sock.** This is the easiest homemade cat toy ever. Fill an old cotton sock with tissue paper and a pinch of catnip. Tie the open end of the sock into a knot. Give it to your cat to bat around the house.

The 5 Top-Selling Cat Toys

Anne Moss is a cat behaviorist and the founder of TheCatSite.com. Thanks, Anne, for this list.

Cat toys provide your cat with proper stimulation. They encourage your cat to perform much-needed exercise, both physical and mental. And hey, it's sheer fun for us humans to watch Kitty go crazy over that cute little squeaky rubber mouse. But if Milo has grown tired of the same old "cat and mouse," here are some interesting alternatives. They are the top-selling cat toys on Amazon.com.

1. Da Bird Interactive Feather Cat Toy
This is the best-selling cat toy on Amazon.com and for good reason! Set on a swivel, its feathers look, sound, and feel like real bird wings. Most cats find this action irresistible and jump after the feathers in a frenzy — great for exercise and fun. Go Cat makes 2 types of Da Bird. The ORIGINAL Da Bird is a single pole that is 36 inches long. They also make a version that has a pull-apart pole (it's actually two 18-inch poles that connect on the ends, so it can be easily stored and/or mailed). Both offer your cat great fun! The single-pole version has its own advantage — if your cat jumps high enough and forcefully grabs the feathers, it won't pull the poles apart.

2. Mews Ments 5-in-1 Laser Pet Toy and Exerciser
Most cats, though not all, go bonkers over a small laser image running across floors and walls. Mews Ments brings you a compact yet very effective laser pen, equipped with five different images for your pet to chase, including a smiley face, star, mouse, dot, and butterfly. It provides great exercise for your pet and comes on a handy key ring, so you can rest in your armchair while Kitty does all the "work."

3. Fur Mice — 12 pack

The good old fur mice keep their place as one of the all-time favorite cat toys. This pack of a dozen white-and-gray furry mice makes for an inexpensive toy — a good thing, considering your cat is likely to destroy them with use. This brand is reported to be more durable than similar toys, but even then, it is not likely that one of these furry mice will last for more than a couple of weeks. To keep Kitty excited about her fur mouse, just take it away at the end of every play session, preferably tucking it away in a toy box sprinkled with some catnip. Next time the mouse comes out, it will be as appealing as a brand-new cat toy.

4. Blitz 70128 Turbo Scratcher Cat Toy

Happy customers are ecstatic about this toy, which doubles as a scratching post. Its corrugated cardboard scratching surface is extremely appealing to cats, and as they move over it, in an effort to catch the ball, they are likely to get the urge to do some scratching. Catnip is included, and for some felines, it can make the scratching surface irresistible. As a cat toy, this one deserves a medal. The ball is always within reach (no need for you to send out search-and-rescue missions behind the TV cabinet anymore!) and always there to get Kitty chasing happily. The Turbo Scratcher measures approximately 15 by 15 by 3 inches, and replacement scratch pads are available separately.

5. Peek-A-Prize

Cats, and kittens in particular, just love this "hunting ground." It consists of a smooth-surfaced box with holes in it, in which you can hide a selection of balls and furry mice. Kitty has fun "fishing" them out. This ingenious invention even looks good in the living room.

How to Teach Your Cat to Come When You Call

Most folks assume that because cats are independent and aloof, they are therefore untrainable. Well, cats are neither *that* independent nor *that* aloof. They are highly intelligent animals, and with time, patience, and the proper techniques, they can easily be trained to learn any number of tricks, including coming when called. This learned behavior can be very useful in emergencies and may even save the cat's life. Follow these suggestions:

1. Convincing Petunia that it is a good idea to come to you when called is the name of the game. She won't come just because you want her to; she'll come to you if there is something in it *for her.* So forget about issuing a command; the best you can do is to make the proper request.

2. Chances are you've already partially won the battle. If Petunia comes running into the kitchen every time she hears the can opener, she has already made the "come to you" connection. It's now time to create a signal you can use regardless of where in your home you are.

3. Once your cat associates the sound of the can opener with coming to you, combine that sound with the sound of your voice as you call her name. You can use a different cue such as "come" or "here, girl," if you wish. A bell, whistle, or clicker can also be used to get her attention.

4. Begin by signaling her when she is nearby, and then increase the distance each time you try to get her to come. Eventually, extend the distance so that you can get her attention wherever she may be; signal her at random times as well. Always reward her with her favorite treat and a couple of strokes when she comes to you. Be patient; this training might take a few days.

5. Use your special signal or word every day. Be sure to have her treats on hand regardless of which room of the house you are in.

3 More Tricks You Can Teach Your Cat

Move over, little doggies, felines can perform some fascinating feats, too. Cats can be trained by reinforcing a pattern of behavior with rewards. The psychological term for this is *conditioned response,* the very same principle Ivan Pavlov used to elicit responses from hungry dogs by using the sound of a bell.

It is important to reinforce a desired behavior with a special signal and reward. Always be consistent. In most cases, cats are motivated by food. Other popular motivators are verbal praise, friendly petting strokes, behind-the-ear scratches, and toys (especially cat wands or toy mice).

Timing is critical in successful training. Pick a time to teach a new trick when your cat appears to be a willing student — just before mealtime or when your cat is in a spirited, frisky, playful mood. Each cat will react differently when a training session commences. Some may ignore you at first, while others may be very curious and eager to learn from the very start.

Cat Trick #1:
Sit Pretty, Kitty

Once a cat can sit on command, it will be more receptive to learning other tricks and behaviors. You may want to use a clicker to give the "sit" command an associated sound.

1. Select a quiet place where your cat feels comfortable and safe. Place it on a table, and give it some friendly petting to make the cat feel at ease.

"You missed 247 calls. Your cat has learned how to use the speed-dial button and she sounds hungry!"

2. Take a single food treat in your hand, and hold it in front of your cat. Slowly bring the treat up over your cat's head, giving the "sit" command, accompanied by the cat's name, such as "Callie, sit."

3. When your cat tips back its head to follow the treat, it will need to sit down to keep its balance. It's a law of physics. When your cat sits, say, "Sit, good sit," use the clicker, and hand over a treat.

4. Repeat steps 1 to 3 until your cat obeys the "sit" command without your holding a treat over its head.

5. Once your cat has perfected the "sit" command from a tabletop, practice it when the cat is walking on the floor.

Quick Tip: If your cat does not sit when you ask it to, gently press down its hindquarters. Be gentle and patient, so you do not frustrate or frighten your cat.

Cat Trick #2:
Silent Hello

This is a great trick to teach cats who are slightly skittish — making the initial contact on their terms helps them feel more at ease when they are then petted or picked up. For the first few training sessions, be sure that your cat is in a calm, contented mood before approaching.

1. Kneel down within an arm's length of your cat. Curl the fingers of one of your hands into a soft fist. Slowly raise your arm until it is extended in front of you and your fist is at your cat's eye level.

2. Be patient while waiting for your cat to approach you. If and when it gives your fist a rub or head-butt, give the cat a scratch behind the ears and then get up.

3. Repeat steps 1 and 2 several times a day as a form of greeting your cat. It will soon learn to come quickly to your hand.

Cat Trick #3: Shake Hands

Some cats are natural paw shakers. Others need much training and patience before they'll get the hang of it.

1. With your cat positioned in front of you, touch its front paw with a small treat and say, "Shake."

2. The moment the cat lifts its paw, gently take it in your hand and shake it. Heap on the praise and give the kitty a small treat to eat.

3. Repeat these steps in sequence four or five times. Discontinue training once your cat delivers a couple of paw shakes or becomes bored and departs for a much-preferred catnap.

 ## 9 Cat Toys You Can Find Around the House

Your cat could not care less about how much money you spend on toys. In fact, some of the most common household objects make wonderful inexpensive alternatives with no effort on your part.

1. **String.** Place a long piece of string on the floor in front of your cat. Then pull the string slowly toward you. Wiggle it to produce some fast action. You can even tie something to it. Try tying a feather or even a small piece of white cloth at the end of the string, and dangle it in front of your cat. If you attach the string to a stick or pole, you can play "fisherman" with your cat. Never let your cat play with string unless you are there to supervise; pieces of string can be a health hazard if swallowed.

2. **Paper.** Take a large sheet of white paper or a paper shopping bag, roll it into a ball, throw it across the room, and watch the fun.

3. **Toilet paper rolls.** Cardboard paper rolls are great cat toys. Cats can swat them around and pounce on them. When the cardboard tears, replace it with another. In a house full of kids, there's always an endless supply.

4. **Stuffed animals.** Cats love these, but make sure there are no loose pieces that Kitty can swallow. A plain rag doll works very well — the softer, the better. Kitties like to knock them around and may even form a personal attachment to the "woobie."

5. **Ping-Pong balls.** Your cat will swat the ball around with accuracy and precision. (Throw a couple in the bathtub and be prepared to videotape the fun!) Rubber balls are fine also, provided they don't have a bitter-tasting surface. (Yes, you have to lick a clean ball to determine its safety.) Whichever sort of ball you choose for your cat, make sure that it doesn't have any glitter on the surface or liquid inside.

6. **Flashlight.** Cats often enjoy chasing a beam of light. Any small flashlight with a focused beam works well, as does a laser pointer. Kitty will enjoy this even more if the room is darkened.

7. **Homemade scratching post.** Cats use a scratching post not only to strengthen their muscles and their grip, but also because it is highly enjoyable. You can make such a post by attaching a piece of carpet to a wall. Be sure it's tall enough so that Kitty will be able to stretch her body to the max.

8. **Plastic canister.** Place a marble or small pebble inside a plastic or metal container, and roll it across the floor. It will certainly get Kitty's attention, and it will love chasing the toy.

9. **Blanket.** Put Kitty on top of a blanket. Run your finger along the underside of the blanket, and watch Kitty attack. This was our cat Ethel's favorite game.

Note: It's not a good idea to use balled-up aluminum foil as a cat toy. Kitty can choke on the small bits she many bite off. Likewise, ribbons should be avoided: They shred, and the dye can give her a tummy ache.

Are You Talking to Me?

You and your cat may speak different languages, but that doesn't mean that you can't communicate. While every cat is different, there is a common code of expression — a set of signals — that you can learn to read easily. Indicators such as the look in your cat's eyes, the tone of its voice, the position of its ears, and the motion of its tail can provide important clues regarding your companion's feelings and intentions. See the next list for a dictionary of your cat's body language. The Humane Society of the United States has provided us with a set of guidelines that will help you better understand and communicate with your precious kitty.

1. For starters, you *can* talk to your cat. Some people feel silly speaking to cats because they think animals can't understand them. Yet these same people may feel comfortable carrying on long one-sided conversations with infants. Cats do receive information from your conversation: praise, comfort, and a sense of security.

2. You can get information, too. The more cats are spoken to, the more they will speak back. You will learn a lot from your cat's wide vocabulary of chirps and meows.

20 Household Objects That Are Unsafe for Your Cat

When choosing playthings for Shadow, keep her safety in mind. An unsafe "toy" is one that can be ingested. Remember that because her tongue has backward-pointing barbs, it is difficult for her to remove an item once it is in her mouth. Here's a list of objects that she might be attracted to but that can be dangerous to her health.

1. Paper clips

2. String, twine, and yarn

3. Thread (especially with a needle attached)

4. Rubber bands

5. Balloons

6. Q-tips or cotton balls

7. Shoelaces

8. Bells

9. Plastic bags, and the twist ties that come with them

10. Baby bottle nipples

11. Any toy that has a glued-on decoration that can be detached

12. Any toy that is filled with things like polystyrene beads or nutshells

13. Any toy made with tinsel-like materials

14. Toys stuffed with cotton

15. Feather toys

16. Soft foam balls that shred easily

17. Toys with itty-bitty parts or glued-on pieces that can be swallowed

18. Discarded cellophane wrappers, which can cause choking

19. Coins

20. Dental floss

You will know when it is time to get up (at least in your cat's opinion), when your cat is feeling affectionate, or when your cat is feeling threatened or is in pain. Your cat doesn't necessarily have something urgent to tell you; a passing meow in the hallway may be a simple hello.

3. You can tell a great deal about what cats want or how they are feeling simply by the look in their eyes or their reaction to things. Are your cat's ears twitching in your direction like satellite dishes when you are speaking? It is absorbing everything you are saying. Does your cat's back rise up to meet your hand when you pet it? This means your cat is enjoying this contact with you. Does its back seem to collapse away under your slightest touch? Your cat is on its way somewhere and doesn't want to be held up, even by a favorite person.

4. Most kittens are eager to learn how to please you. You can easily correct behavior in a young cat with a gentle but firm tone and a demonstration of the proper way to do things. Praise your kitten when you point out the litter box and scratching post.

10 Truly Amazing Cat Products —NOT!

Ray Strobel wasn't satisfied with ordinary cat accessories, so he wrote *The Ultimate Cats' Catalog* — a collection of off-the-wall products that we only wish were real. After all, who can do without cat litter made with genuine Egyptian sand or a scratching post that looks exactly like a Labrador Retriever? Here are a few of our favorite entries, perfect for the cat lover who has everything. Don't miss this wonderfully imaginative book. The photos are realistic enough to fool even your cat!

1. A software program that analyzes key-press timings and combinations to distinguish cat typing from human typing and emits a shrill sound at the former.

2. Whisker extensions for a more glamorous look.

3. Fur-to-Dye-4, which comes in a variety of colors.

4. For a really happy cat, a patch that releases catnip into its system all day long.

5. A petting machine that comes with a snap-on tongue.

6. A fur-ball sculpture kit. "Bend it, shape it, any way you want it."

7. A tabletop crawfish factory, a must-have for Louisiana cool cats.

8. Henna cattoos.

9. Breakfast Vita-Juicer. Mice — you gotta love 'em. You like them fried and roasted. Now enjoy them in liquid form.

10. The TurboNail Sharpener for keeping those weapons in tip-top shape.

How to Talk Cat

Jean Craighead George is the award-winning author of over 80 books about nature and animals, including the now-classic novels *Julie of the Wolves* and *My Side of the Mountain*. She is also the author of the now (sadly) out-of-print book *How to Talk to Your Cat*, illustrated by the clever Paul Meisel. You can still find used copies online.

"The cat uses the sound meow to speak of its needs to humans," says Jean. "Individual cats have worked out as many as 19 different meows to get their points across. Your part in the meow conversation is to do what is being asked of you." The following is Jean's guide to interpreting "Catalian."

66 MEOW This is the command sound. The cat wants attention or a deed performed. If given near the door, your cat wants to go outside. The tail will often sport a crick. If given near the food bowl while weaving around your feet and with the pupils of the eyes small, the cat is asking you for food.

Listen to your cat's meows. You'll hear the difference between "Let me outside" and "Feed me, I'm starved."**99**

66 MEE-O-OW (starting high and dropping) This is a protest. Your cat has not gotten what it wanted. It is whining. Your response: He wants more food or attention; try both.**99**

66 MEE-O-OW (same sound, only much louder) This is a strong protest. You haven't yet figured out what is wrong. You are stupid.**99**

66 MYUP (given sharply) It's the "meow" contracted into one note. You have stepped on her tail, removed her favorite pillow, not understood what she was saying, and she is myuping in righteous indignation.**99**

66 MERRRROW This is the car's swear word. It is given quickly and loudly, the "row" cut short. Better get out of the way.**99**

66 MIER-R-R-R-OW (chirped and with a cadence) This is a loving expression of intimacy. You are being told that you are the most beloved piece of property in your cat's domain. Enjoy your status while you have it.**99**

66 RR-YOWWW-EEOW-RR-YOWOW This blood-curdling sound is the caterwaul given by the tomcat calling to a mate at night. Love is a wonderful thing.**99**

"'Meow' is like 'aloha.' It can mean anything."
— DENNIS THE MENACE

Cats on the Go: 31 Travel Tips

Cats like being homebodies, but in this highly mobile world, even they must deal with road trips, air flights, and occasional relocations. For owners, these trips can be filled with howls, yowls, and other unpleasant sounds — and odors. Quite frankly, some cats freak out when placed inside a carrier and shuttled inside a car or plane.

Make the trip far less frustrating — for both of you — by employing these tactics:

1. Introduce your cat to a carrier at least a few days before a big road trip or flight. Place the carrier inside your home near a location your cat likes to spend time in, and leave the door open for the cat's own sniffing and exploration. (If there's a chance the cat might eliminate in the carrier, buy some absorbent "puppy pads" and use them to line the bottom of the carrier.)

2. Place a favorite catnip-filled toy or a blanket inside the carrier to make it more inviting. Once your cat is going in and out of the carrier freely, toss a few of its favorite treats inside, wait for the cat to enter, and gently close the door. Praise the kitty, and speak in a happy tone for a few moments before opening the door and letting the cat exit on its own. Build up the time your cat spends inside the crate, using treats as a lure.

3. Place the cat inside the carrier inside your car, and take a short trip around the block. Gradually build up the distances.

4. Be sure to attach identification information to your cat carrier. Especially when flying, put large strips of fluorescent tape all over the crate, so you can spot it a mile away.

Mark the crate LIVE ANIMAL and THIS SIDE UP.

5. Be aware that some cats vomit, urinate, or defecate not due to stress, but motion sickness. If your cat does get motion sick, consult your veterinarian about prescribing one of these two effective medications: Acepromazine (a sedative drip that aids in motion sickness by inhibiting vomiting) or Buspar (an anti-anxiety drug that helps stabilize moods).

6. Consider using a few drops of Rescue Remedy (Bach Flower Remedies) if you prefer holistic treatments. This bottle contains flower essences that naturally help to diminish stress and instill a feeling of calm. It's inexpensive, nontoxic, and available at pet supply stores and drug stores. It is safe for use with people, too. In fact, holistic veterinarians often recommend that you add a few drops of this remedy to your glass of water to help you de-stress about a big trip or house move.

7. Another product designed for pet travel is called Pet-Alive EasyTravel Solution. It contains a combination of herbs and homeopathic ingredients known to address motion sickness.

8. Avoid using tranquilizers, as they may heighten stress for some cats. Tranquilizers inhibit a cat's ability to regulate body temperature and can cause most to lose motor control. Consult your veterinarian about safer alternatives.

9. If you're traveling to a foreign country, be sure you know what vaccinations are required or what quarantine restrictions might exist. At the very least, rabies vaccinations are a must for all travel abroad. Petswelcome.com offers a country-by-country list of regulations.

10. While some local transportation companies allow pets, most do not, Amtrak and Greyhound among them.

A mother mouse and a baby mouse are walking along, when all of a sudden, a cat attacks them.

The mother mouse yells, "BARK!" and the cat runs away.

"See?" says the mother mouse to her baby. "Now do you see why it's important to learn a foreign language?"

Kitty's Travel Bag

Bring these items on all extended trips:

- A portable litter box
- Some disposable "scoop 'n' toss bags"
- Food and water bowls
- Copies of prescriptions
- A copy of your cat's medical history
- A recent (obtained within the past 7 to 10 days) health certificate from your veterinarian
- Paper towels or cleanup rags
- Your cat's own food from home
- A collar and leash
- Favorite toys from home

11. Plan ahead — make sure that your cat will be welcomed at your destination, whether you're staying at a hotel or with friends. Today, hotel chains from Holiday Inn to Ritz-Carlton accommodate pets in various ways. Call in advance to make sure that your pet's needs will be met.

12. Maintain a low profile, even when fellow passengers stop to admire Minerva. Do not allow the people around you to be disturbed by your cat's presence.

13. If your cat is especially hyperactive, or if the travel experience is its first, talk to your veterinarian about using a tranquilizer just this once, as well as anti-motion-sickness medication — for everyone's sake.

14. Don't allow your cat to eat or drink for three hours before you set off on a trip. Introduce food and water again when you can, but don't be surprised if Kitty needs time to "wind down" before he partakes.

15. Never open your cat's crate unless you are prepared for it to come bounding out, snakes-in-a-can style. Unless you are in a quiet, private place, you can't predict how your cat might respond to crowds and bustling activity.

16. Make sure that your cat and your cat's carrier are clearly identified.

17. Never leave your cat loose and alone in a hotel room.

Its cries may annoy other guests, and even the most well behaved cat might cause some damage in an unfamiliar environment. Leave the cat in its carrier while you're out, and put a towel over it if it helps the cat settle down.

18. To keep Kitty quiet at night while you sleep, schedule some energetic play or exercise just before bedtime.

19. Hang the Do Not Disturb sign on the door, or keep the dead bolt locked while Kitty is loose in the hotel room. The sudden appearance of a housekeeper might mean the permanent disappearance of Elvis.

20. In hotels, be respectful of the housekeeping staff, who should not have to clean up after your pet, no matter how pet-friendly the place might be. Put a towel under your cat's water and food bowls, and pour used kitty litter into a sealed plastic bag. Don't forget to leave a generous tip before you check out.

In the Car

21. Many veterinarians recommend buckling up all pets in cars just as you would a child. That works for most medium- and large-sized animals, but it's difficult to find restraining devices for cats. Instead, use a cat carrier that is anchored into the vehicle in some way.

22. Kitty might ride more quietly if you cover its crate with a blanket.

23. If yours is an especially cooperative cat who enjoys quietly curling up on the seat beside you during car trips, at least keep it in the backseat, away from the dashboard and the area where the brake and gas pedal are located.

24. Like humans, cats get carsick. If you have a long trip planned, take the cat on some short "dry runs." Start by letting your cat sit in the car without the engine running. Then take the cat on short trips in the weeks leading up to your departure. Even if your vet provides anti-motion-sickness medications, bring a bag and some paper towels just in case.

25. Be aware of the effects of heat buildup in a parked car. It takes only a few minutes for the temperature inside a car to build up to 40 degrees above the outside temperature, especially if the car is in direct sunlight. Even in the shade, with a window slightly open, your cat can easily suffer heat stroke. Generally, avoid leaving pets in an unattended parked car.

For Flying Cats

26. Small pets can fly in the cabins of many airlines, including American, Continental, United, and US Airways, in addition to others. Although they are allowed to fly for a reduced fare (usually around $50), only a few animals are allowed on any single flight, so it's wise to call ahead and make a reservation for your cat. As each airline has its own policies concerning pets, phone in advance to find out if Maury must fly as baggage, specifications for carriers, and other requirements. If he must fly as baggage, try to schedule a nonstop flight, and ask that your cat be hand-carried to and from the plane.

27. Airlines require that your pet carrier fits under the seat (you must keep it there at all times) and that it has an absorbent liner.

28. It's not a good idea to tranquilize your cat before a flight. The combination of high altitude and limited oxygen could challenge its body functions.

29. At the security gate, have your pet's ticket handy, and politely request that the cat not be exposed to x-ray. The agent can use a handheld metal detector to examine your pet.

30. Do not offer food or water to your cat while you are in the air. Cats have been known to live for days without food and water. Remove food and water three hours before flight time. As soon as you land, offer Kitty some food, but don't be surprised when she refuses.

31. A free booklet, *Air Travel for Your Dog or Cat,* is available from the Air Transport Association. Send a self-addressed stamped envelope to ATA, 1301 Pennsylvania Boulevard NW, Suite 1100, Washington, D.C. 20004.

If You Have to Leave Home Without It

The fact that Marty prefers to sit out your next vacation doesn't mean you have to go catless. Check into the Anderson House hotel in Wabasha, Minnesota, where they gently turn back the hands of time to surround you with the same furnishings and food they've been offering since 1920. (The noodles in the chicken soup are homemade, and each night they deliver a hot brick in a quilted envelope to keep your feet warm.) But their most unique feature is their cats. Guests are invited to adopt one for the duration of their stay. The owners, Teresa and Mike Smith, help you choose from among their brood: Morris doesn't like to be picked up; Ginger can get active at night; Goblin is a purrer; Arnold likes kids; and Aloysius is shy. All care accoutrements are provided, and guests are free to choose cat-free rooms if they so desire. (Why in the world would they?)

26 Cat Spas for the Pampered Cat

When you hit the road, there's no reason for your Lulu or Elvis to settle for a mere kennel. Fabulous feline resorts can run from the merely splendid to the sublime. A kennel does provide basic boarding amenities, but perhaps you want to treat Lulu to something special. Here is a sample of the plush catteries around the world that will see to puss's every need.

1. A Country Cat House

12006 SW 64 Street
Miami, FL 33183
(305) 279-9770

Even the most finicky feline will love the ambience. Choose a large, custom-designed one-, two-, or three-level condo with a full view of beautiful tropical gardens, a fishpond, a cascading fountain, birdbaths, bird feeders, and thousands of garden creatures, including lizards, birds, butterflies, moths, and frogs, all for Kitty's entertainment.

This family-owned, accredited cat-care facility has served South Florida for more than 20 years. A professional and experienced staff offers 24/7 attention, so your cat is never alone in this quiet, peaceful, stress-free environment. Your cat never has contact with any other cats, and you can count on strict adherence to dietary needs, plus gourmet-quality, healthful foods and treats, an immaculate and odor-free environment, and individual playtime, pampering, and cuddling several times per day. There's a veterinarian on call in case of emergency, and a loving and patient professional feline groomer works on the premises (pet-icure, anyone?).

2. Applewood Pet Resort

6909 East Lincoln Drive
Paradise Valley, AZ 85253
(480) 596-1190

Is the hardest part of your trip saying goodbye to Kitty? Applewood Pet Resort can offer a relaxing stay for your pet while you're away for a week, a weekend, or even just a day. Here, love and attention come standard.

Owned and operated by a local Paradise Valley resident with more than 30 years of professional pet service experience, Applewood draws its clientele from miles around. Luxurious accommodations come with spacious indoor, climate-controlled rooms with skylight views. A state-of-the-art salon offers a simple bath and brush that always includes a pedicure, as well as top-of-the-line professional grooming.

3. Barkington Inn and Pet Resort

Barkington I
203 Blossom
Webster, TX 77598
(281) 338-PAWS (7297)
ServicesBark1@barkington.com

Barkington II
12105 Highway 6
Fresno, TX 77545
(281) 431-WOOF (9663)
ServicesBark2@barkington.com

Standard services include luxury resort, dog-free accommodations (including luxury townhouses), cat condos, monitoring via closed-circuit TV, flea-free environment, and a vet on call 24 hours a day. With outdoor exercise yards, this spa also provides optional services and accommodations such as personal playtime in an indoor playroom, a separate geriatric area, gourmet treats, massage, and more. We only hope you're treated as well wherever *you're* going.

4. Broadlands Cattery

Broadlands Cattery
Searby Top
Barnetby, Lincolnshire, DN38
6BL United Kingdom
Phone: 01652 629029
www.Broadlands-cattery.co.uk

Traveling abroad? This resort, located on five acres of beautiful property in the Lincolnshire Wolds, treats cats like the kings and queens they are. There are large, spacious, fully insulated chalets, and all diets and special requirements are catered to, including injections. Cats will enjoy optional grooming and training sessions in a setting with plenty of wildlife to enjoy. Constructed by the Feline Advisory Board and run by a fully trained staff, the Broadlands Cattery offers relaxing accommodations for cats of all ages.

5. Cambridge Cat Boarding

Cambridge Cat Boarding
74 Ainslie Street South
Cambridge (Galt), Ontario, Canada
(519) 623-2711
icats.ca/cat_boarding/

Housed in a converted apartment above a veterinary clinic, this full-range feline facility is climate-controlled and offers peace and quiet for a change of pace from Kitty's workaday world. Large windows invite the sunshine in, and allow Coffee to view the world from a safe perch. Choose a comfortable condo or a cozy cage. Multiple-cat discounts and grooming are available.

6. Cat Hotel

1807 Magnolia Boulevard
Burbank, CA 91506
(818) 845-0222
www.home.earthlink.net/~cathotel
cathotel@earthlink.net

Plush private condos, in-room cable television, and 24-hour room service make this the perfect getaway for your stressed-out, overworked cat. Check out the 240-square-foot Enchanted Forest, featuring five natural cedar tree trunks recycled from a Utah forest fire and specially treated for cats. The humans have thought of every convenience and luxurious appeal: panoramic views, sofas to hide under or lounge on, privacy, safety, and cleanliness. After enjoying the padded perches, subtle lighting, and exotic atmosphere, your cat may never want to go home again.

7. Cat's Paradise Spa and Boarding Retreat

659 John Kennedy Way RR4
Almonte, Ontario, K0A 1A0
Canada
(613) 256-8833
info@catsparadise.ca

This cat-exclusive facility for pampered cats offers clean and roomy lodgings with private gardens. Nestled in the woods and located just off a quiet gravel road, this spa offers clean air and a peaceful environment for cats to enjoy. They can spend their time by the cozy woodstove or outside, watching the birds or the horses just beyond their

---

I'll Take Manhattan: A Pet-Sitters Network

Katie's Kitty is a pet-sitting service in New York City that offers something few others can boast – a loving family. Katie Lindenbaum and her dad, Peter, have a network of 47 host families who will care for cats while their owners are away. They even arrange an advance "play date" to ensure a harmonious transition. All homes are screened, and in most cases, your animal will be the only one in the household. Find out more at KatiesKitty.com.

contained garden. They will especially enjoy the cedar playgrounds in each cat's individual garden terrace.

For their dining pleasure, a variety of the finest natural cat foods are served. And to ensure no detail is overlooked, this paradise also offers all-natural, biodegradable litter, without harmful silica gel or dust. And let's not forget to mention cat massage therapy, reiki, grooming, and cat photography.

8. Cat Chalet

551 Route 10 East
Randolph, NJ 07869
(973) 989-6160
Catchalet.com

Why leave your cat in a small cage when you can have a Cat Chalet condo? All accommodations are condos, with enough room for a human to go in, close the full-size door, and sit down. Each condo has a clean litter box, food and water, and two shelves with curtains for privacy. Litter boxes are cleaned once a day or more, and the Cat Chalet is equipped with a special ventilation system to provide fresh, clean air. Food and water are provided and changed twice daily.

9. Cats in the Cradle

131 Historic Town Square
Lancaster, TX 75146
(972) 218-CATS
Bonnie_Arnold@msn.com

This full-service facility offers boarding, grooming, a boutique, kittens, and Toyland Miniature Persians. Accommodations include two- and three-level suites and lots of homey touches to make Kitty's stay purr-fectly comfortable, healthy, and safe. Facilities were designed solely for cats, with suites in three sizes ranging from a deluxe multi-level single to a two-story vacation suite.

10. Chestnut Boarding Centre for Cats and Kittens

2 Esgors Cottages
Thornwood Common
Epping, Essex, CM16 6LY
United Kingdom
01992.573.842
info@catboarding.co.uk

While traveling in England, check out the brand-new, separate luxury annex to the renowned Chestnut Cat Sanctuary, with its long-established facilities and care. With an excellent reputation, this place is recommended and used by rescue organizations and vets throughout Essex, Hertfordshire, and East London. The luxurious heated boarding facilities are the result of requests from thousands of clients who have adopted cats and kittens here.

There is a separate large family unit for three to six cats. Buildings are heated, illuminated, and insulated, with an outside main building if your cats prefer to see the garden. It's a completely safe and warm environment in a quiet country setting far from the road. Catnip tea, anyone?

11. City Cat Boarding

(212) 679-0991
meow@citycatboarding.com

Is your cat a hip and happening city cat? City Cat Boarding is an affordable service for boarding cats in the New York City area. It's a very friendly, in-home environment, where Kitty can relax and feel special and pampered while you are away. The staff gives personalized attention to your cat 24 hours a day and boasts that every need will be addressed, including individualized service for cats that have special medical requirements.

The Cats Are Not Pampered!

One Cat Lady's Answers to Questions That Family and Friends Have Asked
by Glenda W. Moore

I did NOT add rooms to the house just for the cats. The 18-by-14-foot fully screened porch enclosure with fully weatherized cedar posts COULD be used by people if we could fit through the cat door. And yes, I know I spent $90 on the "playground" out there, but each cat NEEDS its own perch: ask anybody!

And the $100+ "cat's bathroom" is just a big custom-made box that holds three litter boxes side by side so the litter doesn't get pushed out onto the floor. The wood panels with melamine on both sides weren't even a special order. And it only takes up one-fourth of the laundry room. And I only had to go to four stores, not every store in town, to find that looped-pile entry-way rug for their bathroom. (Note: Here are the instructions for building your own cats' bathroom.)

The cats DON'T get special food. Buster only gets that special brand of food five days out of seven. And Libby, the poor little baby, will only eat her food if it's mashed up well with a fork and is fully covered by all the liquid from the can.

I haven't had curtains on the windows for ten years now; buying the vertical blinds (textured PVC vinyl) wasn't just so the cats would be able to get to the window; vertical blinds are very contemporary.

I don't ALWAYS microwave the cats' food . . . only if it is still cold from the refrigerator. And they DON'T get fed immediately after they meow; they have to wait sometimes as long as five minutes.

No, the cats DON'T have special food dishes — those are "ordinary" crystal bowls; and they like the place-mats.

I did NOT order special sofa pillows just for Galahad. The fact that people haven't been able to get near them is simply coincidence.

I did NOT buy special area rugs for the cats. They just ended up in places where people don't have an opportunity to step on them.

The same is true for those three blankets; I just forgot that I hate wool, but the cats love it.

Yes, I know that we could have gotten a regular screen door — but it was only $50 more (each) so the cats could look out without having to stand on their back legs. And I wanted that extra-wide shelf under the window in the den, the one that Stanley keeps pushing everything off from so he can sleep on it.

Note: I did NOT insist that we had to have a special $400 "greenhouse" window in the kitchen just for the cats. But all the plants ended up in the sink, so the cats may as well get some sun in it. And I didn't buy the extra-plush towel just for that window. Really.

12. Club Pet

4 Stor Mor Drive, East Pea Ridge
Huntington, WV 25705
(304) 733-1963
ClubPet.com

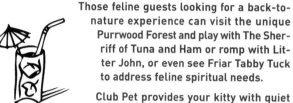

Those feline guests looking for a back-to-nature experience can visit the unique Purrwood Forest and play with The Sherriff of Tuna and Ham or romp with Litter John, or even see Friar Tabby Tuck to address feline spiritual needs.

Club Pet provides your kitty with quiet lodging in a wing separate from canine visitors. Each Purrwood Forest guest is provided with private time in a large indoor play area that is artistically designed to resemble an outdoor getaway. An optional gourmet menu completes the picture.

13. Man's Best Friend Pet Resort

8100 Augusta Road
Piedmont, SC 29673
(864) 299-0540
(888) 252-3451
mansbestfriendresort.com

Yes, they also take cats. This is a true vacation paradise for cats and dogs (housed separately), with no shortage of green grass, fresh air, sunshine, and tail-swishing fun. The concept is simple: provide beautiful accommodations at affordable prices, make the resort colorful and attractive, keep it immaculately clean, and ensure that the guests have fun.

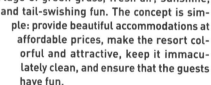

All rooms are private inside and out, so everyone is able to relax and enjoy themselves. But guests are never lonely . . . each one hears its name at least 25 times a day and gets lots of hugs from a cat-caring staff.

The decor features a travel theme: travel posters, international flags, plastic tropical fish, birds and palm trees, and music from abroad played 24 hours a day. Kitties enjoy the same amenities you do, with private rooms, daily room service, fresh linens, catered meals, covered private patios, and a very attentive staff. The food is Nutro's Max, Nutro's Lamb/Rice, Frozen Bil-Jac, or your own, and feedings adhere to your at-home routine. A certified master groomer is on staff.

14. Mazzu's Canine and Feline Luxury Hotel

334 North Water Street
Philadelphia, PA 19106
(215) 923-8326

This luxury hotel and spa for cats and dogs provides walks, TVs and DVDs inside suites, bottled water, and maid service. With spa treatments that include baths, ear cleanings, and manicures, the only thing missing are the mud packs.

15. Olde Towne Pet Resort

8101 Alban Road
Springfield, VA 22150
(703) 455-9000
www.oldtownepetresort.com

This is a one-of-a-kind cat spa where your cat can expect unique spa treatments, salon services, snacks, daily housekeeping, and lots of love. It's a state-of-the-art, 27,000-square-foot resort featuring hotel suites with scenic views and play facilities. When they're not watching birds from strategically placed bird feeders, your cats can watch television programs preselected for feline fascination. Featured in *Newsweek* and *National Geographic* magazines, this resort is a haven for only the finest of felines.

16. Paradise Ranch's Cat Nap Inn

P.O. Box 36
Boyd's Turn Road
Owings, MD 20736
(301) 855-8308
(410) 741-5011
countrysidekennels@starpower.net

Being away from home can be a very frightening experience to many cats, and that's why this private, low-stress, homelike cat-boarding environment is superb. Staff bring a wealth of experience as caring pet lovers to create a unique atmosphere that is more "cat vacationing" than "cat boarding." Each cat or family of cats takes up residence in a private suite with full maid service, calming music, cable TV, and lots of love and attention from the 24-hour kitty-loving staff. During the day cats can lounge on the comfy full-sized beds or on windowsills and purr along to the light tunes playing in the background. Frisky cats can explore their rooms, which are appointed with scratching posts, hanging toys, and jingle mice, or they can chase the laser light beamed by one of the playful staff. For the cats that absolutely adore human attention, there's always someone to cuddle. If Kitty is accustomed to sleeping with you, a bed buddy service provides a staff member to sleep with your cat and ease any insecurities.

17. Purr'n Pooch

80 Gilbert Street West
Tinton Falls, NJ 07701
(732) 842-4949

State Highway 35
Wall Township, NJ 08736
(732) 528-8100
info@purr-n-pooch.com

This full-service pet-care and boarding/grooming facility has two locations in central New Jersey. Designed by a veterinarian to provide optimum levels of comfort, safety, and care to a wide variety of pets, Purr'n Pooch has a professional staff that is fully trained to make sure your pets receive the very best in daily care and services. They proudly boast that some employees have worked there for more than 25 years.

Over the past 30 years, more than one million pets have stayed at these facilities to enjoy top-quality care, exercise, proper nutrition, and socialization with other animals. They are the recommended pet-care facility for more than 100 veterinarians.

18. Rover Oaks Pet Resort

2550 West Bellfort
Houston, TX 77054
(713) 662-2119

1011 South Katy-Fort Bend Road
Katy, TX 77494
(281) 693-7687
katyinfo@rovroaks.com

The Southwest's premier destination for boarding and grooming has locations in Houston and Katy — two beautiful and spacious facilities, acres of play area, and a wonderful and talented staff. Count on unparalleled care for your pet.

Kittens and cats love to stay in their own private condos in Meow Manor, a separate air-conditioned and ventilated cattery at Rover Oaks. Your cat will enjoy daily housekeeping service, nutritious meals, and playtime with the staff. Meow Manor also features a 150-gallon aquarium designed specifically for the constant enjoyment and entertainment of guests.

19. Sleepy Hollow Feline Bed and Breakfast

171 Lowell Road
Groton, MA 01450
(978) 448-2722
rsgvh@earthlink.net

Feline guests stay in two air-conditioned rooms adjacent to an animal hospital, but this is no clinical environment. It's a clean, quiet environment (no dogs) where guests are tended to day and night (despite the name) in comfortable, stress-free, healthy, safe surroundings, with the full-facility Groton Veterinary Hospital just next door.

Accommodations feature self-contained, two-level units that measure a comfy three feet high by three feet wide, allowing space for cats to move up and down (and a place to sleep above the litter pan and food area). Units can be set up to group family cats together or isolate shy cats. Special-needs (single-level) units, with oversized litter pans and greater floor space, are also available for cats requiring special care.

20. The Canine Country Club and Feline Inn

4201 Marna Lynn NW
Albuquerque, NM 87114
(505) 890-8900

7327 4th Street NW
Los Ranchos de Albuquerque, NM 87107
(505) 898-0725
caninecountryclub.com

With state-of-the-art facilities and highly trained staff, the Canine Country Club and Feline Inn will be your pet's favorite home away from home. Punkin will enjoy spacious, comfortable living areas, a country club atmosphere (jacket and tie at dinner?), large and luxurious accommodations, and a secure enclosed environment. The professional staff insists on a safe, sanitary, and impeccably clean resort, just as you would at home. Lots of love and petting are standard.

21. The Cat Connection

14233 Inwood Road
Dallas, TX 75244
(972) 386-6369
(866) 386-MEOW

At the Cat Connection, your cat is among a staff of avid cat lovers, so you can count on lots of loving human interaction. Cat condos are constructed seamlessly and come in sizes to fit from one to four cats. If you have more than one cat, you can order adjoining suites, so they won't get lonely. The large, brightly colored playroom is furnished with catwalks, toys, and cat furniture, as well as videos, caged birds, and mice for visual entertainment.

22. The CatSpa

170 East Madison Street
East Islip, NY 11730
(631) 277-3675
catspa@optonline.net

This spa offers long-term boarding, geriatric care, and special care for cats on medication or special diets. Your cat will always be pampered by very experienced and competent cat lovers, who are on site at all times.

Excellent accommodations feature climate-controlled suites with a window for bird and squirrel watching. Services and facilities include lots of petting and playing, and an exercise program; brushing, combing, and claw cutting are available with the owner's approval. For the ultimate pampered pet, there's a chauffeur service available, a private dining area, and a custom menu. They encourage frequent visits from owners and offer multicat discounts.

23. The Country Kitty B and B

1159 Ridge Road
Queensbury, NY 12804
(518) 792-MEOW
Countrykitty.com

Spacious five-foot-by-nine-foot guest rooms feature a large window, with a seat for hours of bird watching, as well as cubbies for playing hide-and-seek, plush beds, cat chairs, and toys to please even the finicky feline. Kitty will appreciate private litter boxes, temperature and air-quality control, and relaxing background music.

Arrangements are cheerfully made for special diet and health concerns. Fully monitored 24-hour fire detection and security systems are provided, and emergency veterinary service is also available. For the ultimate in hands-on care, the owners reside on the premises.

24. The Pet Resort

2040 South 142nd Street
Seatac, WA 98168-3712
(206) 241-0880
info@hillrosepetresort.com

The mission here is to provide loving care for pets at a level commensurate with their position of honor as valued members of your family. The staff take great pride in treating your friends as their friends. With luxury amenities such as a gift boutique, planned playtime activities, and a pet taxi service, your cat can be living in style. Services also include a worldwide pet travel agency.

25. Toothacres

1639 Parker Road
Carrollton, TX 75010
(972) 492-3711
toothacres.com

This newly remodeled cattery features nine square feet of personal accommodations for each feline guest. Decorated in bright colors, the room is for cats only; no dogs allowed. Spacious and exclusive kitty cottages allow Puss plenty of room to stretch out and relax or curl up and watch the world go by. There's an elevated bench in each cottage, a large bay window with a view of the courtyard and bird feeders, 24-hour climate control for comfort, and classical background music for the cultured cat. There's also jungle-style play for frolicking on an individual basis.

26. Wag Hotels

1759 Enterprise Boulevard
West Sacramento, CA 95691
(916) 373-0300
(888) WAG-LINE
info@waghotels.com

This sounds like a canine accommodation, but au contraire. Even the fussiest feline will be treated like royalty from check-in to departure at this five-paw resort. Here you'll find unsurpassed convenience and excellent service along with personalized, affordable care. There's a welcome basket upon check-in, and feline guests stay in two-story cat condominiums that surround a pristine tropical fish tank — perfect for both stimulating play and tranquil catnaps. Here every guest enjoys a room with a view, a private bath, and individual attention from trained staff. Of course, there's plenty of catnip to go around!

23 Cat-Friendly Hotel Chains

PetsWelcome.com makes it easy to find cat-friendly hotels by offering specific listings and recommendations all over the United States and in numerous other countries. The national hotel chains listed here not only welcome pets but in some cases even provide complimentary food and water dishes, and their staff will direct you to cat-friendly attractions. Visit their websites for a list of their pet-perks.

Candlewood Suites

Clarion Hotels

Comfort Inn

Crowne Plaza

Econo Lodge

Holiday Inn

Howard Johnson

InterContinental Hotels and Resorts

Kimpton Hotels

La Quinta Inns and Suites

MainStay Suites

Motel 6

Novotel

Quality Inn

Red Roof Inn

Ritz-Carlton

Rodeway Inn

Sheraton

Sleep Inn

Staybridge Suites

Studio 6

Suburban Extended Stay Hotels

Vagabond Hotels

PetsHotel provides a safe, clean, loving environment with the 24-Hour PetCare Promise that safety-certified caregivers will be on site 24/7. Veterinarians are always on call. Pets-Hotels are located right inside selected PetSmart stores. Find locations at petsmart.com.

Bob Walker photographs surprisingly cooperative subjects.

11 Helpful Hints for Photographing Your Cat

Your cat just struck a darling pose (again). Where's the camera? To help capture your cat's amazing antics and oh-so-cute looks, we turned to Bob Walker, photographer extraordinaire from San Diego. His best-selling book, *The Cats' House* (1996; see page 167), sets the standard in feline photography. He and his wife, Frances Mooney, happily share their home with a dozen or so camera-ready cats. Walker offers these 11 timely tips to achieve picture-frame-worthy photographs:

1. Take lots of pictures and experiment. The most interesting pictures are often unplanned or unexpected. Especially with a digital camera, which allows you to delete images before they are printed, it costs nothing to take extra shots. And, of course, no one will see the pictures that you trash.

2. Your cat is in charge. Photograph what your cat wants to do, not what you want it to do. You'll be less likely to get a picture of your cat running away.

3. Trick with treats. The first ques-

frontal position. Light from a flash travels in a straight line, bouncing the red from the retina's blood vessels back to the camera.

8. Eyes represent the window to a cat's mood. Watch for an interesting expression and start snapping.

9. Acknowledge that fur is beautiful. To preserve light-colored fur detail, set your camera exposure compensation at -0.3 (minus ⅓ EV).

10. Anticipate action. By the time you "see" the picture in your camera viewfinder/screen, the moment has already passed. Cats are fast, and most cameras are slow. Press the shutter release when the action is beginning to happen. Cross your paws, and hope that you get a good shot of what you are about to see.

11. Consider a photography course. Study photo how-to and art books. Train your eye and instincts. When image making becomes effortless, your photos will have the grace of a cat.

tion your cat will ask is, "What's my motivation?" Mutual respect and love can elicit cooperation, but its favorite treat will usually work much faster.

4. Get close. Your cat is large in your life, so make it large in your photos. Plus, you'll be able to make more detailed enlargements.

5. Always keep your camera handy. Cats sleep 16 to 17 hours daily. Additional hours are spent eating and washing, leaving little time for action. If you have to run off to find your camera, the cat will likely be catnapping by the time you return.

6. Consider setting your camera on a tripod in a feline-favorite area of your house to instantly snap your cat napping, grooming, or delivering oh-so-cute poses.

7. To avoid red eye, photograph your cat from an angle rather than a

In order to create great photos, you need to heed backgrounds. The rule is to keep the background as simple as possible. Muslin backdrops or seamless paper is recommended by experts at the New York Institute of Photography. We invite you to visit their website, www.nyip.com, where you'll find more tips on photographing cats and other popular subjects.

17 Gifts for the Cat Who Has Everything

If extra cash is burning a whole in your pocket, treat Tinkerbell to something really special — and pricey. Here, to satisfy your extravagant shopping needs, are some very expensive gifts you can buy for your furry baby.

1. Welcome Home! Cat Gift Basket. Catniptoys.com sells a gift basket stuffed to the gills with a huge variety of unique natural wool toys and tasty all-natural treats, including organic catnip, valerian-spiced catnip, and honeysuckle. And if that's not enough, just consider your kitty's reaction to these products: Wildside Salmon for Cats, IcelandPet Trout Paté by Ifex, a PetGuard Purrlicious Organic Tartar Control Crunchy Chicken Kitty Cat Snack, a Kitty Hoots Butterfly Crackler, some Yeowww! Pollack Fish, a Tabby Tuffet, SmartyKat Flutterballs, a Tossabout Cat Toy, a Honeysuckle Rat, and other goodies. The price is only $84.75, shipping not included.

2. KatKabin Outdoor Cat House. This feline equivalent of a kennel is an innovative and exciting new product that has already proved a big hit with cats. The KatKabin is a light, tubular outdoor shelter that will appeal to both the independent tabby or the aristocratic pedigree. The Kabin can be placed in the garden or on the patio or balcony, ensuring that pets do not have to wander far from home to find comfort and security. Guaranteed for five years, the KatKabin is finished with a special nonchemical material that will not fade in sunlight. It will stand securely on any surface and is supplied with a front-door flap. Developed to withstand extremes of temperature, the KatKabin comes in a variety of colors and has a special polystyrene floor that adds extra insulation, keeping Kitty warm in cold weather. Available at catsplay.com, for about $150.

3. Luxury 5-Strand Pet Necklace. This unusual piece of cat bling will surely turn heads! Tink will look like a real princess in this gorgeous piece, made of Austrian Swarovski crystal and designed by renowned artisan Dorothy Bauer. Each piece is handmade. The necklace offered by catsplay.com lists for $80. Be sure and measure your pet's neck carefully to ensure proper fit.

4. Cradle in the Sky 6-Level Rustic Cat Tree. This cat tree is an incredible, one-of-a-kind creation that will create a true paradise for Muffin. Easy to climb, it's the perfect perch for nature watching or afternoon catnaps. Crafted with attention to detail, with heavy-duty construction and quality carpet, this piece is safe for climbing, with staggered stairs between levels. It's sturdy enough for Maine Coons and active kittens. Features of this rustic tree include five levels, three sleep cradles, a pagoda, a tunnel, two round platforms, and a flat platform. Each Rustic Cat Tree is handmade by a skilled craftsman. It's priced from $755, plus $175 for shipping, at catsplay.com.

5. The Cat Hotel, offered by pawshop.com, is the *pièce de résistance* for a home with multiple cats. Your cats will think they are staying at the Ritz in this unique cat activity center. A Cozy Fur Condo serves as the "penthouse suite" and a cozy shelter. Five Plush Fur Hammocks plus the roof of the condo provide a choice of areas for resting, sleeping, and playing with friends. Each Plush (faux) Fur Hammock provides a tender cradle into which your cat can sink to rest or sleep. The carpeted legs are perfect for climbing and scratching. The horizontal carpeted beams provide a sturdy framework for walking and jumping. The Spring Action Toy is set in one of the end caps. A circular opening in front serves as a door and window, so you can peek in and enjoy the fun. Priced at $219.95, shipping not included.

6. Outdoor Pet Gazebo Tent. If Tinkerbell is an indoor cat but yearns for the great outdoors, this gazebo might be just what you are looking for. The tent helps protect cats from excessive sun, heat, insects, and moisture. It's constructed of lightweight aluminum, with a polyester fabric shell. The gazebo can be zipped shut for maximum protection, offering your pets a great way to enjoy the outdoors safely. Available at pawshop.com for $125.99.

7. Pet Murphy Bed. Available at pawshop.com, this product provides a comfy fold-down-bed alternative to traditional pet beds. It's stylish and compact and a smart space-saver. Thoughtfully made from tree-farmed rubber wood, it's lighter than other woods and helps save our forests. The bed comes in three finishes and is priced at $249.99.

8. AT3 All-Terrain Pet Stroller. You can take Baby out in style with a stroller that features various baskets and trays. Rear-wheel shock absorbers make for a smooth ride, mesh windows keep out bugs, and safety reflectors ensure nighttime safety. It costs about $170 at just-petstrollers.com.

9. Classic Wedding Dress for Cats. Don't let Miss Katz get married in just any old dress. PamperedPetsCatalog .com carries an absolutely exquisite creation with flowered ribbon, satin buttons, and lovely attention to detail. The price of the dress is $149.99. The veil is sold separately.

10. Tuxedo Sweater. Will Marmaduke be best cat at the wedding? Why not get him a tuxedo sweater? This very special shimmer-chenille tuxedo sweater for cats is perfect for those elegant evenings or wedding nuptials. PamperedPetsCatalog.com offers the sweater for $79.

11. Kittywalk Grand Prix for Cats. Your indoor cat can play outside in this safe contained environment. The circular system allows Kitty to safely navigate the great outdoors — up, down, in, and around — without having to stop at the end of the enclosure. The penthouse allows cats to climb or lounge on three levels of comfy hammocks. It can accommodate as many as three cats. PamperedPetsCatalog.com offers this product for about $350.

12. Wrought-Iron Feather-Canopy Bed. Princess will know she is adored as she lazes in her wrought-iron bed, complete with a plush pink faux-fur cushion and a frilly, feathery canopy. The price is $339 at DrPasten.com.

13. Mahogany Sleigh Bed. This beautifully handcrafted sleigh bed has a rich mahogany finish and comes with a fitted pillow and head roll in elegant ebony toile. Concealed zippers make for easy removal of covers, which are machine washable. The covers are also available in Trouville red and a leopard pattern. The price is $389 at PamperedPetCatalog.com.

14. The Leopard's Lair Cat. It has seven large levels, a detachable climbing ladder, seven large lounging pedestals, hanging kitty toys, five scratching posts, and a spacious playhouse. The gym is carpeted in rich faux leopard and is supported by a solid wood frame. Available at PamperedPetsCatalog.com for $420.

15. Tunnel of Fun. Cosmo will be feelin' groovy all day long in this retro-1960s flower-power plush tunnel. He'll have a cozy place to chill or play, and three large openings allow easy access. The crackle material inside creates an enticing sound to pique Cosmo's curiosity. It's priced at $49.95 at PamperedPetsCatalog.com.

16. Thing in a Bag. How can Tessie possibly resist what appears to be an ordinary paper bag, but one that wriggles and rustles, just to drive her nuts? It's battery powered so you can control it as you watch the fun, and the "paper" bag is actually claw-resistant.

17. Royal Catnip Spray. This gift is hardly expensive at all, but Kitty will be thrilled and will probably appreciate it more than anything. The spray is a combination of pure catnip oil and spring water. Spraying will give old cat toys new life and will keep Kitty interested in her scratching posts and play areas. Cattoys.com carries this product for just $5.49 for a one-ounce bottle.

Special Care for Your Aging Cat

Observe your aging cat carefully, and you will easily find ways to help it. Does it have trouble getting up on the bed? Some "doggie stairs" or even a simple wooden platform might help. Is it sleeping more? Maybe a second bed in the cat's favorite spot will make it more comfortable. The golden rule applies here more than ever; how would you like to be treated in your old age?

Here are some of Dr. Ronald Hines's tips on things you can do to make life easier for your senior cat.

1. **Groom your cat more often.** Older cats often do not groom themselves as well as they did when they were young. This is due to arthritis, dental problems, and general debility. They need your help with a weekly bath and daily combing with a soft slicker brush. Brushing removes the loose hair that gets swallowed and causes hairballs and constipation. It also stimulates circulation and oil secretion, leading to a healthier coat. Clipping the hair that surrounds the rear helps keep longhaired cats sanitary. As you brush your cat, look for any new growths on the body. Growths on cats are more serious than those on dogs because they are more commonly malignant. Your veterinarian should promptly remove them all. Make extra visits to a professional groomer as needed.

2. **Buy your elderly cat a larger bed.** Older cats are not as supple as they used to be and are less able to curl up in small beds. Elderly cats seem to love beanbag beds because the beans help keep Kitty warm and help support its old body and stiff limbs. Keep the bed away from drafts. If the cat gets lonely at night, move its bed close to yours.

3. **Keep your outdoor cat safe.** If its vision or hearing is failing, make sure it is protected from harmful situations. The cat may not be able to hear the lawn mower, for instance. If it naps in the sun, put some sun block on its fur; older cats are more susceptible to skin cancer.

4. **Replace the cat flap.** If you've been using a cat flap but the kitty no longer has the strength to push it open, replace it with a piece of cloth, or remove the flap altogether during the hours the cat uses it.

5. Because older cats tend to be bonier, they might find sitting in your lap uncomfortable. **Put a pillow, blanket, or cushion on your lap** so the cat can still enjoy the experience of getting close and cuddling.

6. **Trim its nails more often.** The claws of older cats are often brittle and overgrown due to lack of scratching activity. Its nails can overgrow to the extent that they penetrate the footpad, causing a painful ulcer.

7. **Encourage your cat to play.** Older cats are less agile than they once were due to muscle atrophy and arthritis. Regular play with your cat helps it retain muscle mass and increases tone and circulation.

8. **Listen.** Older cats tend to be more talkative. Be patient.

9. **Keep things quiet.** Older cats don't appreciate the stress caused by loud noises.

10. **You can't teach an old cat new tricks:** This is not the time to start leaving the kitty at boarding facilities for the first time, nor will it appreciate a new face at the feeding bowl at this stage. Sudden changes late in life appear to precipitate latent disease. **No surprises, please.**

11. **Take the cat to the vet more often.** Many veterinarians are geriatric specialists and can help maintain its health and increase longevity. Elderly cats are at greater risk of kidney disease, tumors, and others illnesses. Make sure your cat is getting all its booster vaccinations.

12. **Keep the cat's weight down.** Feed it a diet designed for older cats.

13. **Provide extra water.** Older cats are more susceptible to dehydration related to stress, hot weather, or the fatigue associated with common diseases of older cats, such as failing kidneys and thyroid disease. Elderly felines are also often poor drinkers even when water is available. Place several bowls of water in different areas of the house.

Marcellus Bear Heart Williams is a multitribal spiritual leader of the Muskogee Nation–Creek Tribe and one of the last traditionally trained "medicine persons." His book, **The Wind Is My Mother**, has been published in 13 native languages. He offers this prayer of hope for our departed friends.

O Great Spirit, we come to you with love and gratitude for all living things. We now pray especially for our relatives of the wilderness — the four-legged, the winged, those that live in the waters, and those that crawl upon the land. Bless them, that they might continue to live in freedom and enjoy the right to be wild. Fill our hearts with tolerance, appreciation, and respect for all living things so that we all might live together in harmony and peace.

When It's Time to Let Go: 12 Questions to Ask Yourself

Some vets view disease as a challenge and death as an insult to their competence, regardless of the animal's condition. Others believe that prolonging an animal's life through treatment is inhumane. Most fall somewhere between these extremes and recommend that life be prolonged only for as long as the cat has a reasonable quality of life. While a second opinion may be helpful to you, don't prolong a cat's existence in the hope that the fourteenth, or fifteenth, or twentieth vet consulted knows of a treatment. Don't prolong its life purely in the hope that a treatment will be available before the illness or condition reaches its inevitable conclusion. Sarah Hartwell suggests asking your vet the following questions. The answers will help you make the right choice.

1. Is my cat in pain, distress, or mild discomfort?

2. How feasible is it to alleviate this pain and give the cat a reasonable quality of life for a period of time?

3. Are any new treatments available for this condition?

4. Are there any surgical advances for this condition?

5. Would a second opinion be beneficial to the cat?

6. Can I afford the treatment?

7. Can I administer treatment at home, such as daily tablets, daily injections, a prescription diet, manually expressing cat's bladder and/or bowel, or syringe feeding through a tube into the stomach?

8. Will the cat physically resist treatment?

9. How fast will my cat deteriorate without treatment? How fast will it deteriorate with treatment? How fast does the illness progress, and what are the signs of its progression?

10. Will treatment prolong life or merely prolong suffering?

11. Will the treatment or its side effects cause distress for either of us?

12. Do my other cats risk being infected, or can they be inoculated?

8 Pet Bereavement Hotlines

1. **Chicago Veterinary Medical Association**
(708) 603-3994
Leave a message on voice mail; calls will be returned 7 P.M.– 9 P.M., Central Time.

2. **Cornell University Pet Loss Support Hotline**
(607) 253-3932,
Tuesday–Thursday: 6 P.M.–9 P.M., Eastern Standard Time.

3. **University of California, Davis**
(916) 752-4200, Monday–Friday, 6:30 P.M.–9:30 P.M., Pacific Time.

4. **University of Florida**
(904) 392-4700, then dial 1 and 4080, Monday–Friday, 7 P.M.– 9 P.M., Eastern Standard Time.

5. **Michigan State University**
(517) 432-2696,
Tuesday–Thursday, 6:30 P.M.– 9:30 P.M., Eastern Standard Time.

6. **Virginia-Maryland Regional College of Veterinary Medicine**
(540) 231-8038, Tuesday and Thursday, 6 P.M.–9 P.M., Eastern Standard Time.

7. **The Ohio State University**
(614) 292-1823, Monday, Wednesday, and Friday, 6:30 P.M.–9:30 P.M., Eastern Standard Time.

8. **Tufts University**
(508) 839-7966, Tuesday and Thursday, 6 P.M.–9 P.M., Eastern Standard Time.

7 Good Reasons to Euthanize

A responsible owner has the power of life and death over his or her pets, says Sarah Hartwell, a volunteer for Cats Protection in the United Kingdom, and this power must be used wisely. An owner can choose between a quick and humane release from a poor-quality existence or a lingering, suffering end.

It is easy to become emotionally caught up in keeping a pet alive when common sense tells you there is no hope that it will regain its health. Sometimes it seems that your own life can't go on when you have to make the decision to euthanize a long-term feline companion. It is hard enough to end the life of an old and frail cat; perhaps if you give it another day, or another week, the cat might die naturally in its sleep, even if you know that it will linger uncomfortably until it succumbs to dehydration, starvation, or the gradual poisoning of its blood by liver or kidney failure. If the cat appears outwardly healthy but has an untreatable medical condition, the decision is made yet harder.

A good vet will help you to weigh the pros and cons of further treatment versus euthanasia, but ultimately it is your decision. It is never easy, but it helps if you are prepared. The following situations often tip the pet owner's judgment in favor of euthanasia:

🐾 A cat is in incurable pain that cannot be alleviated by drugs.

🐾 A cat has severe injuries from which it will never recover or which severely compromise its quality of life.

🐾 A kitten is born with serious defects (for example, progressive hydrocephalus) that cannot be surgically corrected and cannot be endured by the cat; it may not survive weaning or reach maturity.

🐾 A cat has unresolvable behavior problems, such as aggression toward humans or other animals, that prevent you — or anyone else — from keeping it at home. If these problem behaviors have not responded to therapy or drugs, euthanasia may be the only option.

🐾 A cat has an age-related condition, such as advanced senility or incontinence, that cannot be alleviated and causes misery.

🐾 A cat is terminally ill and will naturally deteriorate. Euthanasia may not be an immediate concern, but it will be later on. Euthanasia may be chosen immediately to prevent future suffering.

🐾 Cost of treatment may be the deciding factor at a very early stage. Sometimes, sadly, available treatment may simply be too expensive. If this is the case, ask the vet if he or she would agree to payment in installments.

8 Signs That Your Cat Is in Mourning

Your aloof feline is just as susceptible to feelings of mourning as are people, dogs, or any other species. If Lucy can't seem to manage now that Ethel's gone, take her to the vet. Keep your eyes peeled for these signs:

1. The cat may become even more aloof or lethargic.

2. It might eat less. The ASPCA states that 11 percent of cats in mourning stop eating completely.

3. The cat becomes needy and craves company.

4. It may sleep more than usual.

5. The cat may become restless or develop insomnia.

6. It may become confused or disoriented.

7. It may meow or howl incessantly.

8. It may stop playing with favorite toys or people.

If I Should Grow Frail

If it should be that I grow frail and
    weak
And pain does keep me from my sleep,
Then will you do what must be done
For this — the last battle — can't be
    won.
You will be sad I understand
But don't let grief then stay your hand.
For on this day, more than the rest
Your love and friendship must stand the
    test.
We have had so many happy years,
You wouldn't want me to suffer so.
When the time comes, please, let me go.
Take me to where my needs they'll tend,
Only, stay with me till the end.
And hold me firm and speak to me
Until my eyes no longer see.
I know in time you will agree
It is a kindness you do to me.
Although my tail its last has waved,
From pain and suffering I have been
    saved.
Don't grieve that it must now be you
Who has to decide this thing to do.
We've been so close — we two — these
    years,
Don't let your heart hold any tears.

                — Author Unknown

8 Unusual Cat Memorials

Cat people can be an eccentric lot, and it sometimes shows in the ways they choose to memorialize their beloved pets. While some visit gravestones and others scatter ashes, there are those who require something just a little more original. Here are a few out-of-the-ordinary ways to pay tribute to your cherished companion that you might not have considered — or want to consider.

1. **Life-size figurine urns:** This life-size, hollow figurine urn with glass eyes comes in 11 different cat breeds. There is a plug on the bottom of the urn for easy insertion of your cat's ashes. As a personal touch, many customers attach their companion's collar or nametag to the figurine. Available at foreverpets.com.

2. **Teddy bear urns:** This urn is designed for parents struggling to comfort their children's pain from losing a pet. Shaped like a soft, furry teddy bear, this unusual urn has a Velcro opening in the bottom for easy installation of your pet's ashes. This way, people can hug the bear as they mourn for their animal friend. You can also purchase a set of bears and divide the ashes among family members. Available at foreverpets.com.

3. **Freeze-drying:** This method of preservation eliminates the decaying process of living tissues. The animal is prepared and posed, then placed in a sealed vacuum chamber at an extremely low temperature. It preserves your animal's body in a natural state, without any alterations, as opposed to taxidermy, which retains only the hide of the animal. This process allows owners to touch and hold their pets without ever

really having to "let go." Check out petpreservations.com for more information.

4. **Virtual memorials:** Countless websites allow you to set up a page for your deceased cat. But at rainbowsbridge.com, you can register your cat in their virtual memorial home and become the "guardian" of the residency that you create. Each time you visit, you may leave toys or treats or change the flowers and shrubbery. There are many services provided once you join, such as an online Pet Loss Grief Support Center, a boutique with gifts of sympathy, and a Monday evening candle service where you and other mourners light virtual memorial candles.

5. **Cremation jewelry:** If you thought urns were only made for shelves, check out evrmemories.com, where you can have your cat's ashes incorporated into a fashionable pendant.

6. **Memory pillows:** Preserve the memory of your cat with a memory pillow that has a picture of your cat printed on its surface. You and Tidbit can still take naps together. Available at petangelmemorialcenter.com.

7. **Walking sticks or canes:** Hand-carved in cherry wood and painted to the likeness of your cat, these canes are hand-stained to match the photo that you supply. The head of your cat will be featured on the handle of your walking stick. Available at wilsonwalkingsticks.com.

8. **Ashes to ashes:** For about $20 a year, Jikeiin, a Buddhist foundation in Tokyo, will cremate your cat's or dog's ashes and preserve them until your own death and cremation, upon which you and your cat can be interred forever in the Tama Dog and Cat Memorial Park.

No. Heaven will not ever Heaven be
Unless my cats are there to welcome me.

Housemate, I can think you still
Bounding to the window-sill,
Over which I vaguely see
Your small mound beneath a tree,
Showing in the Autumn shade
That you moulder where you played.
— THOMAS HARDY

No worthier cat
Ever sat on a mat
Or caught a rat
Requies-cat.
— JOHN GREENLEAF WHITTIER

To mark a friend's remains
These stones arise;
I never knew but one,
And here he lies.
— LORD BYRON

Cat Epitaphs

Not the first, not the last,
but always remembered.

You were not our whole life, but you
made our lives whole.

To my beloved friend. You taught me
love, laughter, patience, and nobility.
You are missed every single day.

She was not the sunrise
She was not the sunset
She was the sun

An Old Russian Prayer

Hear our prayer, Lord, for all animals,
May they be well-fed and well-trained and
happy;
Protect them from hunger and fear and
suffering;
And, we pray, protect specially, dear Lord,
The little cat who is the companion of our
home,
Keep her safe as she goes abroad,
And bring her back to comfort us . . .

— Anonymous

Grieve not
nor speak of me with tears
but laugh and talk of me
as if I were beside you
I loved you so
'twas Heaven here with you.
I am at peace, my soul's at rest,
There is no need for tears.
For with your love I was so blessed
For all those many years.
A cat on earth
An angel in Heaven . . .
If tears could build a stairway,
And memories a lane,
I'd walk right
Up to heaven and bring you
Home again.
Do not mourn my passing for if you could
only see
by slipping all my earthly bonds, I'm young
again and free.
By day I run the Heavenly Fields, my body
healthy and strong.
At night I sleep at Angels' Feet, lulled by
Celestial Song.
So do not mourn my passing, just close
your eyes — you'll see
I'm once again that playful cat, just as you
remember me.

— Author Unknown

Rainbow Bridge

This anonymous essay is commonly shared among bereaved pet owners, and it is has brought comfort to many. These wise and well-loved sentiments have been adapted in many other forms.

Just this side of Heaven is a place called the Rainbow Bridge. When an animal who has been especially close to someone here dies, that pet goes to the Rainbow Bridge. Here there are meadows and hills for all our special friends so that they can run and play together. There is plenty of food, water, and sunshine so our furry friends are always warm and comfortable.

All the animals who have been ill or old are restored to health and vigor; those who were hurt or maimed are made whole and strong again, just as we remember them in dreams of days gone by. The animals are happy and content, except for one small thing; they each miss someone very special who had to be left behind. They all run and play together, but the day comes when one animal will suddenly stop and look into the distance. His bright eyes are intent; his eager body quivers. Suddenly he is flying over the green grass, his legs carrying him faster and faster.

You have been spotted, and when you and your special friend finally meet, you cling to each other in joyous reunion, never to be parted again. The happy kisses rain upon your face; your hands again caress that beloved head and you once more look into the trusting eyes of your pet, gone so long from your life but never absent from your heart.

Then you cross Rainbow Bridge together.

Tombstone of Tiddles, the church cat, St. Mary the Virgin Church, Gloucestershire, England.

Index

Cat Fanciers' Association (CFA)
    breeds recognized by, *190*
    contact information/overview,
        171, 172, 236
    role/functions, 236, 272, 273
Cat Fanciers Federation (CFF), 237
"cat fancy" definition/description,
    272
Cat Fancy magazine, 15, 40, 238
cat flaps, 8, 382
catgut, *58*
"cat" in different languages, 77
Cat in the Hat, The, 39, 91, 92, *92,* 93,
    100, 150
"Cat Lady" warning signs, *69*
cat litter
    allergies to cats and, 322
    invention of, 14, 313
    "other" uses for, 316
    See also litter box
catnip, 222, 267, 296, 299, 357, 360,
    381
Catnip newsletter, 239, 281
Cat of the Year, 144, 189
cat ownership
    aging cats, 382–83, *382*
    arrival of human baby, 288–89
    care essentials, 261
    cat-proofing your home, 256–57,
        269, 331–33, 364
    costs, 258
    forced affection and, 265
    introducing new pet to resident
        cat, 255, 259, 264–65, 282,
        286, 287, 323
    items needed, 257

mistakes (common), 268–69
multiple cats, 194, 259, 260, 287,
    315
older cat adoption benefits, 338
preparation, 256, 257
selecting second cat, 286
selecting/websites, 233, 240,
    241, 268
See also caring for cats
cat people movies, 91
cat-proofing your home, 256–57,
    269, 331–33, 364
cat racing, 9
cats
    benefits to people, 235, *235*
    concepts cats symbolize, 15, *15*
    dominant cats, 278–80, *280,* 329
    of famous people, 63–66, 108–11,
        112–15
    feline companionship, 194, 259,
        260
    feline-feminine connection, 30,
        30
    human habits irritating to,
        262–65
    learning from, 116
    pampered cats, 373
    reasons to love, 239
    unusual friends/adoptions by,
        131, *131,* 135, 140
    wealthy cats, 134–35
    See also kittens
"cat's cradle," 34, *34*
cat scratch disease (CSD), 325
cat shows
    children and, 173

description, 172
disqualifying traits, 183, 184,
    190, 196
divisions, 172–73
documentary on show cats, 228
history, 9–10, 11, 15, 54, 55
judging of, 173
major shows, 171
Cats (musical), 106–7
Cats Protection (CP), 252
catterysearch.com, 273
CAT-tionary, 284–85
CatWatch newsletter, 239
Catwoman, 14, 98
cat words, 79
    "CAT-tionary," 284–85
Cat World magazine, 238
Charles, Ray, 59
Chaucer, Geoffrey, 43, *43*
Cheshire cat, 37, *49,* 159, *159,* 169
Chessie the cat, 13, 145–46, *145*
children and cats
    basic advice, 264, *264*
    cat shows and, 172
    human baby, 288–89
    literature (overview), 169–70, *1
    69*
    myths, 196
China and cats, 4, 18–19, 208, 258
Chinese Year of the "Cat"/symbol,
    67, *67*
chocolate, 356
Christmas and cats, 357, *357*
Church of England, 21
cigar brands named after cats, *147*
circus cats, 142, *142*

claws of cats
    clipping, 304
    description, 180, 192, 199
    See also declawing
Cleopatra/makeup and cats, 118
Clinton, Bill, *122*
cloned cats, 17, 118–19
coat color
    of original domestic cat, 180
    overview, 211–13, *211*
    solids, 211–12, *211*
    tabby cats, 212
Cocteau, Jean, 13
Colette, Sidonie-Gabrielle, 30, 115, 138, 153, 190
collection of cat memorabilia, 117
color of cats. *See* coat color
colorpoint, 181, 184, 212–13
commandments for cats, 177
communicating with your cat
    description, 364–65
    talking "cat"/"meow" meanings, 366, *366*
    See also body language/ meanings
Co-ordinating Cat Council of Australia (CCC of A), 236
Cornell Feline Health Center, 252–53
Cornish Rex cat (breed), 281
Coronation Cat Show, 15, 54
costs
    of cat ownership, 258
    most expensive cat, 117, *117*
    of pedigreed kittens, 270–71
creation of cats/theories, 28–29

cremation/burial with owner, 65, 386, 387
cures from cats, 31, *31*
"curiosity killed the cat," 27
curtain climbing/prevention, 332

D

Dangerfield, Rodney, 4
Darwin, Charles, 10
Darwin, Erasmus, 219
deafness, 179, 209
Dean, James, 63
declawing
    alternatives to, 277
    harm from, 195, 276, 358
    reasons against, 276, 277, 358
    reasons for/defense of, 277
definitions of cats, 71, 191
deification/idolization of cats, 3–4, 5, 6, 8, 12, 18–19, 30
demonization of cats, 7, 8, 18, 19, 22–24, *23*, 26–27
    See also witchcraft
Dennis the Menace, 366
dental care. *See* teeth care
development stages of kittens, 206
Dewey the cat, 155–56, *156*
diet. *See* food for cats
disaster preparation/handling, 353–55
distemper, 205
documentaries, 154, 155, 228
dogs and cats
    cat breeds that get along with dogs, 323

    cats most like dogs, 283, *283*
    dog breeds that hate cats, 284
    introducing/socializing, 282, 323
dogs vs. cats
    in behavior, 192, 218
    diets, 192
    hearing, 62, 176
    human relationships, 176–77, 192, 218, 223
    hunting techniques, 192
    Mark Twain on, 45
    owner's death and, 193
    reasons "why cats are better," 248
    summary list, 192
domestication of cats, 3
dreaming
    of cats, 78–79
    by cats, 213
Dupuis, Madame, 134

E

ears
    functions, 210, 216
    reading emotions by, 198, 210, 220, 328, 329
    See also hearing of cats
earthquake sensitivity, 124, 143
Egypt and cats
    ancient art, 6, *6*, 150
    historical treatment of cats, 3–6, *6*, 9, 10–11, 18, 26, 44, 116, 150
electric cord chewing/prevention, 331–32

About the Authors

Sandra Choron is a writer, editor, literary agent, book packager, and designer. She and her husband, **Harry Choron**, a graphic designer, are the authors of *Planet Dog, College in a Can, The Book of Lists for Teens,* and *The All New Book of Lists for Kids,* among other works.

Arden Moore is a best-selling author, editor, and professional speaker. The editor of *Catnip* magazine, published monthly in affiliation with Tufts University School of Veterinary Medicine, she is the author of 17 pet books, including *The Cat Behavior Answer Book* and *The Kitten Owner's Manual.* Visit her website: www.ardenmoore.com.

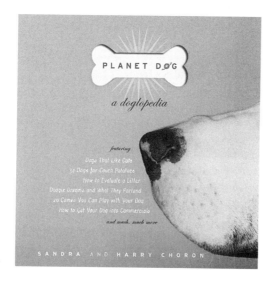